Nagas

The Ancient Rulers of India

Their Origin and History

The History of the Indigenous People of India
Vol. 2

Dr. Naval Viyogi

Originals
(an imprint of Low Price Publications)
Delhi-110052

First Published 2002
Second Impression 2020

ISBN 13: 978-81-7536-287-1
ISBN 10: 81-7536-287-1

Published by
Originals
(An Imprint of Low Price Publications)
A-6, 2nd Floor, Nimri Commercial Centre,
Ashok Vihar Phase IV, Delhi 110052 (INDIA)
Tel.: +91-11-47061936
website: www.LPPindia.com
e-mail: info@LPPindia.com

Printed at
Anvi Composers
Delhi

PRINTED IN INDIA

Dedicated

To

His Excellency

Shri Babu Parmanand Ji

Governor of Haryana.

PREFACE

Before I begin to write a preface to the second volume of multi-volumed 'Research-Project', I wish to quote a most interesting , legendary event as cited by learned British scholar J. P. H. Vogel in his famous work titled 'Indian Serpent Lore' —"King Nagpal, when ruling chief of Kashmir, betook himself to Delhi, in the days of Akbar, the great Mughal. There, as a result of a quarrel arosen at the well in between the water carriers of king Nagpal and Akbar, he was summoned in the royal court, to explain why his servant had humiliated the royal Maski and thrown him in to the well. King defended his servant's behaviour by saying that, 'the water, he wanted, was intended for the worship of Basuki Nag and that it would have been polluted if the royal Maski had been allowed to draw first.' .... Emperor asked,who this Basuki Nag Was ? And was he mightier than himself ? One next day when king appeared again before the emperor, a five headed snake, issued from his turban and threatened to ascend the throne. Then Akbar became very much afraid and promised him a boon if he would take the snake back. So the king did and obtained the privilege of the royal-drum (Naubat), which is still present and beaten in the temple of Basuki Nag at Bhadarvah."

In fact[2], according to a tradition, the king Nagpal of Kashmir, after whom the royal family took its name,was born from Basuki Nag and the princess of Kistavār, who had become widow six months after her marriage with prince Bisambar Pal.

Although, the above legend does not seem to reveal realistic history, we can reasonably conclude from this event that Naga kings were existing and were in power in the age of emperor Akbar (1556-1605AD)

But aforesaid event gives rise to many questions of immense interest such as : who were these Naga kings ? where have now they and their progeny gone ? Were they ethnically related to the Naga tribes of North-East of modern age ? The present research work is an answer to any of such like questions.

If we cast a glance at the historical scenario, we will be astonished to know that most of the Indian scholars are in a habit to see Central Asia as the centre of most of the human activities, giving rise to his progress and prosperity in historic and prehistoric age. But, quite contrary, this has been the centre of producer of savage tribes like Aryans, Scythians, Kushanas, Huns, Mongols etc, who, destroyed most of their contemporary human civilizations of Eurasia, which were raised after thousand years of hard labour of mankind. But, quite inversally, Western Asia can be given the credit of being the cradle of the blooming of many great cultures, in a time, while other races of

---

1. Vogel J.PH, "Indian Serpent Lore" P-251
2. Vogel J.PH. P-250

the world were still in their early stage of civilization, as far ascredit of producing first human civilization of the world at Catal Huyuk and Jericho[1], ten thousand years before present, goes to this land. Not only this, the technique of potting, weaving[2], producing copper and iron[3], art of house-building and writing system[4], (pictograph and phonetic both) republic system of rule, guild like system of trade and industry, great religions like Christianity and Muslim (Buddha and Jain religions also got inspiration from Meg religion of Sumer[5]), which have been the basis of great push to the human progress and prosperity, also took their birth in Western Asia.

Although, infilteration of human population from Western Asia to India has been a general practice due to trade activities or any other reason, yet their three mass movements took place in the main : The first one (of Mediterranean people) in Neolithic Age[6], these were the people who founded Indus Valley civilization in the north-western region of India. Another wave[7] of Mediterraneans and Alpines came through the passes of north-west, from the same region. They reached Indus Valley at about 2000 BC, the mature Harappan Age and added much to the culture of Indus Valley. Owing to capture of western Asia and overwhelming raids of Assyrians, another third migration took place through land and sea routes both in about 1000-800 BC. They brought with them Iron and the Megalithic Culture and Phonetic type of writing system. As a result of these three mass movements, the tradition of serpent worship, cult of mother goddess, Megalithic system of disposal of dead bodies also reached India, which made their roots in Indian soil and later spread in every nook and corner and initiated a new shraman religion based social, political and economic revolution during the post Mahabharat age, which was native and non-Vedic

About one and a half century back, it was not possible for anyone to think of any sort of rich civilization or heritage among the ancient native non-Aryan population, but T. W. Rhys Davids, a British officer, was the first

---

1. Bottero, Cassin and Vercoutter, "The Near East, The Early Civilization" PP 16-17
2. Hawkes Jacquetta, "The First Great Civilization" P-115
3. Hawkes Jacquetta P-113
4. (a) Buhler G., "Indian Paleography" PP 31-32

   (b) Rapson E. J. C. H I I P-55
5. (a) Chapelkar M. Nalinee,"Ancient India and Iran" P-33

   (b) Fergusson James, "Tree and Serpent Worship" P-78
6. Swell and Guha, "Memoirs Anthropological Survey of India No. 35" (1932) PP 56-81
7. Wheeler R. E. M. "A I" Vol III (1947) BASI PP 83-85
8. MB Adi Parva-67

scholar, who, in the middle of nineteenth century, after an in depth study of Buddhist Pali literature, concluded and unveiled the secret that in ancient time the native republicans were most civilized. What was the reason of putting the facts behind the curtain is expressed by Rhy Davids T. W. He, passed a remark to this effect in the introductory part of his most valuable venture titled "Buddhist India" which, being most important, is being reproduced below in full- "It is significant that this important factor in the social condition of India in the sixth and seventh century B. C. has remained hitherto un-noticed by scholars either in Europe or in India. They have relied for their information about the Indian peoples too exclusively on the Brahmin books. And these partly because of the natural antipathy felt by the priests towards the free republics."

Thus the republic or Sangha system was a creation of non-Aryan non-Vedic native peoples, which was basis of their economic, political and religious life.

James Fergusson was the first scholar, who wrote an important book on the origin of Naga-worship and Naga people titled "Tree and Serpent Worship" which was published in 1868 A. D. Fergusson has put in a very hard labour in writing this book. He has collected most valuable, yet unnoticed information, from myths, hearsays, inscriptions, ancient art and literary records of very high value, archaeological rare findings from different Eurasian countries, for compilation of his valuable venture. Humankind will remain indebted to him for this imparallel contribution to his knowledgé.He scientifically examined human figures, formed, in the statues and bas-reliefs of Buddhist stupas of Sanchi and Amaravati and expressed his opinion on the ethnical identity of people represented in them and concluded that people, bearing cobra-hoods on their heads, are alike Meenas, Gonds of central Province[2] and some of them resembled those sculptures, found by him at Taki-Bahai North of Peshawar or of present Pakhtoons.[3] It means, according to Fergusson, they were native Dravidians and Alpine type or their blended race.

Further ahead, J. P. H. Vogel, compiled his book on this subject titled "Indian Serpent lore" in about 1901, which throws light on the distribution of serpent worship and worshippers in India. He has given detailed information of Naga temples and shrines and hearsays, myths attached to each one of them, where, periodically, fairs are held even in modern age.

Later on, Colonel Oldham, a medical officer of British Army, took this task in his hand and wrote a famous book titled "The Sun and the Serpent", adding fresh knowledge on the origin of Naga race & Naga worship and revealed that, origin of serpent worship took place in Western Asia, which was later transferred to Indian soil by the Dravidian people, alongwith their migration, thus disclosing the secret that Dravidians were also racially Naga people.

---

1. Davids Rhys T. W. "Buddhist India" P-1
2. Fergusson James PP 224-25
3. Fergusson James P-122

Prof D. R. Bhandarkar, of Calcutta University and a renowned scholar of early twentieth century, has contributed one of his important works to the knowledge of humankind titled "Lecture on the Ancient History of India" in 1919 AD and opening the secret, of origin of Sangha or republican system in Ancient India. Although, Sangha or republican system was originally introduced by native people, but on account of his feeling of antipathy against them, he could not do justice to them. As far as, he has tried to prove origin of some of the well known Naga royal families of South like Chera, Chola and Pandya from Aryan race. This is the secret of his higher scholarship and fame.

In 1933 AD, renowned and one of the most sincere scholars K. P. Jayaswal, broughtout one of his famous unique work titled "History of India" which is the first of its kind and provides real historical account of different Naga dynasties viz Nagas of Vidisa, Bharsivas of Padmavati and Kantipuri, Yadavas of Mathura, Vakatakas of Purika and Ikshwakus of Sriparavata etc. He has made use of Puranic accounts, inscriptions, coins and other archaeological evidences of historical importance to establish his theories and facts of history. But he also could not do justice to the Vakatakas owing to his inherent feelings of antipathy and has tried to prove them (Aryan) Brahman. But on the basis of solid evidences I have disproved his theory on chapter XII of this book.

After a very long gap of period Prof V. V. Mirashi of Nagpur University compiled his work on the origin of Vakataka royal family in 1964 titled "Vakataka Rajbansha Ka Itihas Tatha Shila-lekh" His work is also highly commendable but he also has followed the foot-steps of Jayaswal and taken a stand that Vakatakas were Brahman (Aryan). But I have proved that they were of Naga origin follower of institution of Rajrishi or God kind or non-Aryan priest or Brahman.

In fact Brahmanical historians are committed to ignore or minimise the role of Native Indians in making the Indian history, that is why they are inclined to distort historical fact deliberately, where fact goes against their proud or proud system (Varna) or political motive in modern age. For achieving their goal, they have been using every possible tact. If the native kings were most important and it was not possible to wipe them out from the pages of history, then their origin was made controversial or shown from some demigod like sun, moon, serpent and Vayu etc. Similar was the attitude of native non-Aryan kings, either they refrained to expose their origin or caste likewise Guptas, Satavahanas or they claimed their origin from Aryan race, although, there was not even a single drop of Aryan blood in their veins.[1] In modern age the situation has become more pitiable. The modern scholar, either try to make the origin of native kings controversial or does not touch their history at all. Exactly this has happened to the history of Naga race. Although thousands of books are being written every year yet not a single on Naga History. In fact, after K. P. Jayaswal, no scholar has come forward to work on their history, that is why, I have been pressed to pickup my pen to work on this subject.

In modern age, however, on getting inspiration from Dr. Ambedkar's book titled "The untouchables", H. L. Kosare of Nagpur has brought out a unique book under title, "Prachin Bharatatil Nag" in Marathi–language, which was published in 1989. While his work was still in progress, he came in my contact and became active member of Indian National Historical Research Council. Although his work is a landmark on the history of Nagas, yet the field of his work remained confined to the Maharashtra state only. While propounding the theory of origin of Nagas, he has followed in the foot-steps of Dr. Ambedkar viz from the Aryan Kshatriyas, which is an outdated theory in modern age. On the other hand, he remained in confusion about their ethnical identity. But the historical data collected and reproduced to explain the complicacy of origin and history of natives, is in fact a great endeavour which has helped me a great deal in compiling this research work, in the absence of which, it would not have been possible for me to create such an authentic piece of work, as it is now in our hand.

In conducting this research work, Dr Pradeep Kumar Meshram, Prof and Reader, Department of Ancient History and Archaeology, University of Nagpur, has been kind enough to forward his all sort of help and co-operation without which, perhaps, it would have not been possible for me to complete this work. Dr. Meshram from the very beginning, remained attached to the Indian National Historical Research Council, and provided research paper and books related to the subject, of immense value and help, from his own resources, as far as, he provided me a copy of Hindi translation of research work of Sh. H.L. Kosare, which became a basic help to complete this work. I am sure, if Dr Meshram had not come forward with his helping hands and co-operation, it would have not been possible for me to give this shape to this research work. I am gratefully indebted to Dr. Meshram as well as to late Shri H. L. Kosare.

Prof R. D. Tiwari of D. A. V. College Jalandhar,Prof Iqbal Singh, Head of the Deptt of English at Lyallpur Khalsa College Jalandhar, Dr. R. S. Tank former Professor, Deptt of Sociology. Guru Nanakdev-University Amritsar, have been kind enough to read my script and improve its language. Similarly, Dr. L. R. Parwana, Chairman, Indian National Historical Research council, S. Rajendra Singh former DySecretary ministry of Communication govt of India, Major J. S. Rishi advocate Jalandhar, D. S. Jassal Senior vice President Panjabi S. A. Ludhiana, Dr Darshan Singh Kaul D. M. F. C Lundhiana and Usha my wife have always been at forefront to guide, help, and inspire me to complete this tough and arduous job. Ashok kumar, my son helped me in preparing index of this work. I am indebted and thankful to all of them.

Babu Parmanand Ji, His Excellency Governor of Haryana, has been taking keen interest in the research project of our council, while deeply understanding the importance of this work for the upliftment of indigenous people of India. He was kind enough to forward a grant for publication of this work. I am much thankful for this help, encouragement and act of kindness.

Dr. Naval Viyogi

Indian National Historical Research Council,

518-Sit a Nagar Ludhiana (PB) **25-4-2002**

ACKNOWLEDGEMENT

I am sincerely thankful to the authors and publishers of the following works from which I have frequently quoted matter and put maps and figures in my humble venture :

Ashthana Shashi, History and Archaeology of India's contact with other countries, B. R. Publication (1976) Delhi; Banerjee N. R., Iron Age In India, (1965) New Delhi; Bhandarkar D. R., Lecture on the Ancient history of India, University of Calcutta (1919); Bhandarkar R. G., Early History of Deccan, Chakravorty Chaterjee and Co (1928) Calcutta; Bottero, Cassin and Vercoutter, The near East; The Early Civilization, Weiden field and Nicolson (1967) London; Chanda. R. P., The Indo-Aryan Races, Indian Studies, Past & Present (1969) Calcutta; Chapelkar M. Nalinee, Ancient India and Iran, Ajanta Publication (1982) Delhi; Chopra P. N. and others, History of South India "Vol-I S. Chand and Co. (1979) Delhi; Cunningham A., Ancient Geography of India, Indological Book House (1932) Varanasi; Davids Rhys T. W., Buddhist India, Sushil Gupta Calcutta; Deo S. B. Mahurjhari Excavation, Nagpur; Dixon B. Roland, The Racial History of man, Swat Publication (1989) Delhi; Fergusson James, Tree and Serpent Worship, Indological Book House Delhi; Gokhle B. G. Buddhism in Maharashtra, Popular Prakashan (1971) Bombay; Gopalachari K., Early History of the Andhra Country, Madras University Historical series No. 16 Madras'; Grierson G. A. Linguistic Survey of India, Vishveshwaranand Institute (1973) Hoshiarpur; Gupta S. P., disposal of the Dead and Physical type in Ancient India, Orient Publication (1972) Delhi; Gurdon PRT, The Khasi, Low Price Publication (1990) Delhi; Gustab oppert, The Original Inhabitant of India, Oriental Publication (1972) Delhi ; Hawkes Jacquetta, The First Great Civilization, Hutchinson (1973) London; Hodson T. C., The Naga Tribes of Manipur, Low price Publication (1990) Delhi, Jayaswal K. P., Hindu Polity, Butterworth and co- India Ltd (1924); Jayaswal K. P., History of India, Moti Lal Banarsi Dass (1932) Lahore; Kosare H.L.; Prachin Bharatatil Nag, Gian Pradip Prakashan (1989) Nagpur; law B. C., Some Kshatriya tribes of Ancient India, Bhartiya Publishing house (1975) Varanasi; Madan Mohan Singh, Puratattva ki Ruprekha, Janaki Prakashan Patna; Mahajan V. D., Ancient India, (1981) Delhi; Mirashi V. V., Vakataka Rajbansh Ka Itihas tatha Silalekh, Tara Publication (1964) Varanasi; Mishra S. N. Ancient Indian Republics, (1975) Delhi; Pandeya Chandrabhan, Andhra Satavahan

Samrajya ka Itihas, National Publishing house (1961) Delhi; Rao K. P., Deccan Megaliths, Sandeep Prakashan Delhi; Robert Briefoult, The Mothers, George Allan and Union London; Sastri Nilkant K. A., Age of Nanda and Maurya, Motilal Banarsidass (1967) Delhi; Saxena K. S., Political History of Kashmir, (1974) Lucknow; Tod James, Annals and Antiquities of Rajasthan, Low Price publications (1995) Delhi, Vaidya C. V., History of Mediaeval Hindu India, The Oriental Book Supply Agency (1920) Poona; Vogel JPH, Indian Serpent Lore, Indological Book House (1972) Delhi; Roman Ghirshman, Persia from the Origin to Alexander the Great, Thomson and Hudson France; Sastri K. N. Newlight on the indus civilization Vol I Delhi; Wheeler M., The Indus civilization III Cambridge University press,

I feel highly indebted to all the authorities on the subject mentioned above upon whom I have heavily drawn. I shall fail in my duty if I donot place on record my gratitude to them.

Ludhiana

Dr. Naval Viyogi

25 April 2002

CONTENTS **Page No.**

ABBREVEATION

'A'

AI.	Ancient India
AN	Angutara Nikaya
ABNUHS	Annual Bulletin of the Nagpur University Historical Society
AAR	Annals and Antiquity of Rajasthan
ABORI	Annals of the Bhandarkar Oriental Research Institute
ACI	Ancient Civilization of Indus
Ait Bra	Aitreya Brahman
ARASI	Annual Report Archaeological Survey of India.
ASIC	Anthropological Survey of India Calcutta
ASR	Archaeological Survey Reporter
ASWI	Archaeological Survey West India.
A.V.	Atharva-Veda

'B'

BDCRI	Bulletin of the Deccan College Research Institute
B. G.	Bombay Gazetteer
BP	Bhagwat Purana

'C' 'D' 'E' 'F' 'G' 'H'

CHI	Cambridge History of India.
EI	Epigraphia Indika

'I'

IA	Indian Antiquary
IAR	Indian Archaeological Review
ICPB	Inscriptions in Central Provinces and Berar
IHQ	Indian Historical Quarterly
IHR	Indian Historical Review
I. O	Inscriptions of Orissa

'J' 'K'

JAOS	Journal of the American Oriental Society.
JBBRAS	Journal of the Bombay Branch of the Royal Asiatic Society.
JBRAS	Journal of the Bengal Royal Asiatic Society

JBORS	Journal of the Bihar and Orissa Research Society.
JKRCOI	Journal of the KR Coma Oriental Institute.
JNSI	Journal of the Numismatic Society of India.
JOI	Journal of Oriental Institute.
JRAS	Journal of the Royal Asiatee society.
	'L'
LSI	Linguistic Survey of India.
	'M' 'N' 'O' 'P' 'Q'
MASI	Memoirs of the Archaeological Survey of India.
MB	Mahabharat
MP	Markandeya Purana
MRE	Madras report on Epigraphia.
MR	Modern Review
	'R'
RT	Rajtarangini
RV	Rigveda
	'S'
SBE	Sacred Books of East
SP	Skand Purana
Sat Bra	Satpath Brahman
	'T'
Tait Sam	Taitreya Samhita
	'U' 'V' 'W' 'X' 'Y' 'Z'
VIJ	Vishveshwaranand Indological Journal
V. P.	Vishnu Purana
VSMV	Vidarbha Sansodhan Mandal Varshiki.

LIST OF ILLUSTRATIONS

A TABLE OF NAGA TRIBES & ROYAL FAMILIES

Yadava Or Yadu race (Iranian)

(Four Bramches)

- Vrasti
- Kukkar
- Andhra (Andhaka) Tribe
  - Takshaka or Taka (Vahika) Karpati Gotra
    - Madra (Vahika) or Taka
      - Salva
      - Karaskar (Aratta)
    - Taka (Karpati)
      - Satavahan (Maha Ratta + Maha Bhoja)
        - Paithan (Capital)
        - Dhannakatka (Capital)
      - Karkota
      - Sesh Naga or Bharsiva
        - Eran + Vidisa
          - Vakataka
            - Purika
            - Vatsgulma
        - Padmavati
        - Mathura
        - Kantipuri
    - Malava (Karpati)
- Bhoja (Associate of Satavahana)

Chapter 1

The Mythical Origin of the Naga Race

The Mahabharata

In the Mahabharata[1] we come across a myth of the origin of serpents as narrated by Vogel J. Ph : During the age of Devayuga there were two sisters named Kadrū and Vinatā. They were fair and beautiful daughters of Prajapati. Their husband was Rishi Kashyapa, who by grace granted a boon to each of them. Kadrū expressed her desire to become a mother of one thousand serpents of splendour. Vinatā wanted only two sons but more powerful than the sons of her sister. In the course of time, Kadrū brought forth a thousand eggs and Vinatā two. These eggs were carefully nourished in vessels of liquid, and when five hundred years had elapsed, the thousand Nāgas, or serpent-sons of Kadrū came forth. Then the other sister, not yet seeing her issue appear, grew sore, ashamed and, in her longing for offspring, she broke one of the two. But the time, not being full, the son, who was thus born, was possessed with only the upper half of his body and the lower part being unformed. (It was Aruna who became the charioteer of the sun–god). In his wrath, he cursed his mother and spoke, "As, owing to thy greed, thou hast made me deformed of body, therefore, O, mother for five hundred years thou shalt become the slave of her with whom thou hast contended". He added "that her other son would free her from his curse, if only she would patiently await the time of his birth for another five hundred years." At last her second son was born the giant-bird Garuda, who preys on snakes. As soon as he was born, leaving his mother, he flew up in the sky in order to seize the food which had been ordained for him by the Creator.

On learning this, Kadrū spoke to her sister Vinatā, " Of what colour is the horse Uchchaihsravas ? good lady, say it quickly." Quoth Vinatā, "white is that king of steeds or what deemest thou, fair sister ? Say thou too his colour and let us lay a wager". Answered Kadrū, "Black-tailed I deem the horse, O sweetly smiling one come and bet with me, may she that loses be the slave of her that wins."

Thus, having made this pact, both went home saying, "we shall see tomorrow." But Kadrū who wished to play false, gave order to her thousand sons " Append ye yourselves quickly to that steed in the semblance of tail hairs black as antimony, so that I may not be a slave," Those who refused the snake-mother cursed, "when the serpent, sacrifice of king Janmejaya, the wise son of Pāndu, taketh place, the pure god of fire will consume you."Brahma, the Creator, hearing the curse pronounced by Kadrū, rejoiced together with the hosts of gods. For he saw that the snakes were great in number and that owing to their deadly poison, they caused great danger and dismay to other creatures.

In the meanwhile, those among the Nagas who were obedient to their mother, did as she had bidden them. When at daybreak Kadrū and Vinatā flew over ocean, they beheld on the further shore the horse Uchchaihsravas white coloured like the rays of the moon, but blacktailed. Thus Kadru made Vinatā her slave, and the latter, being vanquished by her sister, was sorrow-striken at her pitiable plight.

Once upon a time, Kadrū[2], the mother of the snakes, ordered her sister to carry her to the abode of the Nagas, situated in the womb of the sea. Vinatā was obliged to obey the command, and Garuda, at his mother's bidding, carried the Nāgas thither. But as in his flight he came too close to the sun, the snakes were scorched by the heat and fainted. The snake-mother Kadru then took refuge with Indra and lauded him as the god of rain, thunder and lightning and as the chief among gods. And the lord of the fallow steeds, moved by her prayer, overcast the whole sky with masses of dark-coloured thunder clouds and gave order to the clouds, "Cause ye nectar-like rain to flow."

The clouds, flaming with lightning and incessantly roaring in the sky, let loose abundant water. The Nagas felt the utmost joy while Indra rained, and with their mother they reached the island of Rāmaniyaka.

This island, fashioned by Visvakarman himself and surrounded by the waters of the ocean, is covered with forests abounding in sundry flowers and fruits. It is adorned with charming abodes, with lotus–ponds and heavenly lakes of limpid water. Fanned by pure winds carrying celestial perfumes, it is bedecked with lofty sandal trees which are haunted by birds and bees and pour down a shower of blossoms. The Nagas, refreshed by the showers of rain and by the dew trickling down from the flowers, rejoiced in this place of delights, but after some time they spoke to Garuda, " Carry us to some other island exceedingly lovely and of pure water, for thou in thy flight seest many lovely lands, O Bird." Garuda wondered why he should have to do the bidding of the snakes, and his mother told him how she had been deceived by her sister. Then Garuda asked the Nagas, "what am I to bring or to know or what deed of valour am I to accomplish whereby I may be freed from slavery ? Speak the truth, ye serpents (lit lickers,)". The Nagas answered, "Do thou seize the nectar, then thou shalt be freed from slave, O Bird ".

The story thus narrated in the Mahabharata, (Adi XXIII) and quoted by vogel is very lengthy and it tells us that Garuda was very hungry, hence, he flew in the sky in search of his food. He ate up thousands of Nishadas, living in the land amidst the water. Later on he devoured one elephant and a tortoise also which were fighting with each other in a lake.

The story further proceeds to relate at great length in what manner Garuda succeeded in winning the Soma after having vanquished the gods, extinguished the fire which surrounded it, and overcome the two poisonous snakes which guarded it. Even Indra, the chief of gods, was not able to withstand him, for when he hurled his terrible weapon, the thunderbolt-(vajra), at the king of birds, the latter only dropped one of his feathers. Moved by his opponent's valour, Indra offered him boon and Garuda chose that henceforth the Nagas might become his food. Indra now concluded friendship with Garuda and the latter invoked the god's help in order to deceive the Nagas in his turn. He told the Nagas that he had brought them the nectar, but that they should bathe and prepare themselves before partaking of the heavenly food This they did but as soon as Garuda had placed the nectar on a litter of Kusa or darbha halms, it was seized by Indra, who carried it away to heaven. Thus, Garuda had fulfilled his task and obtained the freedom of his mother and himself. But the snakes, on returning from their bath, found the nectar gone. All they could do was to lick the sharp kusa blades to which some of the precious substance still adhered. The result was that from that day the snakes became double tongued, and the kusa grass obtained its purifying virtue by its contact with the nectar.

In this myth of origin of the serpents and Garuda, it is to be noted that at one place (M. B. Adi XXIII)[3] Vinatā states that she has been made slave by her non-Aryan sister by foul means. It means the family of Kadru was from a non-Aryan race. The whole myth is also not beyond doubt. But above concept gives us a hint to believe that origin of serpent race was not Aryan but non-Aryan. It seems that Kasyapa, the primogenitor of Nagas, was also a non-Aryan Rishi who was in origin a worshipper of serpents or serpent being his totem.

In the Rigveda the Vasistas are described as svetyam or white, kanvas as svavo or Krishna dark (VII-33-1 and X-31-11). The appcarance of black Rishi in the nordic Aryan society is indeed a land mark. R. P. Chanda[4] thinks that there were two sacerdotal of the sacredotal class, Brahmans by descent, Brahmans by adoption and they were of different physical type.

Brahmanical Rishis, authors of Mahabharta and later authors have taken the serpent worshippers to be real serpents or Nagas and likewise, concocted myths have been added to them and their origin. Dr. C. F. Oldham Brigadier and surgeon of Indian-Army supports this view. He writes, ''Originally the Nagas were not demons, but they were men who claim their origin from sun, whose totem was cobra with a hood. Takshila was their main centre in northern India and Takshak was their chief. Janmejaya, the Bharata king of Indraprastha, after a successful attack on Takshila, performed a serpent sacrifice (Nag-yajña) at the instigation of the Brahmana Uttānkā. On this occasion, Nagas, who were made captive in the battle of Takshila, were made prey. They were thrown alive into the fire, according to the Brahmanical customs as described in the Mahabharata."[5]

Colonel James Tod[6] has gone in the depth of this complication. He gives details of his observation, "The international wars of the Surya and the Yadu race, as described in the Ramayan and Mahabharata, are lost between allegory and literal interpretation. The Suryas or Saivas were depressed; and the Indus, who counted fifty six grand tribes under the appellation of Takshak (serpent), Aswa (horse) Sasa (hare) etc, had paramount sway. Krishna's schism produced a new type that of the eagle (Garuda), and the wars of schismatics were depicted under their respective emblems, the eagle and the serpent, of which latter were the Kauravas and Takshaks, the political adversaries of the Pandus, the relative of Krishna,'' Further Tod[7] throws light on the history of conflict between Surya and Takshak race-" The Mahabharata records constant wars from ancient times amongst the children of Surya (the sun) and the Tak or Takshak (serpent race). The horse of the sun, liberated preparatory to sacrifice, by the father of Rama, was seized by the Takshak Ananta; and Parikshata, king of Delhi, grandson of Pandu, was killed by one of the same race. In both instances the Takshaka is literally rendered the snake. The successor of Janamejaya carried war into the seats of this Tak or serpent race, and it is said to have sacrificed 20,000 of them in revenge; but although it is specifically stated that he subsequently compelled them to sign tributary, engagements, the Brahmans have nevertheless distorted a plain historical fact by a literal and puerile interpretation."

It is crystal clear that Brahmanical authors have concocted the events of history, and allegorize the meaning of real names. This Tak or Takshak indigenous Naga royal family seems progenitor of most of the later Naga families of ancient historical age.

Takshila, the original seat of Nagas

Now question arises whether these Nagas originated in India or they came from outside. Most of the historians first trace them in Takshila, from where they spread up in other parts of India.

They were essentially serpent worshippers, Naga and Takshak being synonymous appellation in Sanskrit for the snake and Takshak is the celebrated Naga bansha of the early heroic history of India.' They were also essentially the artificers and architects of India and lastly they are known to have possessed Asarur in Panjab in ancient and middle ages and may have settled there from time immemorial. Their original seat was Takshila which was also the metropolis of serpent worship and the spot whence it spread all over India[8]. In the myths of Nagas, generally their origin, is the land of North West frontier of India.

Famous Chinese traveller Hieuntsang[9] in the description of his journey, gives a myth of Udyān, which now-a-days is known as Swat valley on the North West frontier of India. One prince of Sakya tribe, who escaped from the holocaust of his blood relatives by the fierce Virudhaka king of Kausala, mounted on the back of a wild goose, which flew away and took him to the side of lake in the north-west region. As a result of an unavoidable incidence, then he met a Naga maiden. After his marriage with the maiden, his father-in-law presented him a beautiful sword, which might help him to kill the king of Udyān and seize his kingdom.

Further Vogel Writes-"But the former demerits of the Naga girl were not yet effaced and their consequences still remained. Every time he went to rest by her side from her head came forth the ninefold crest of the Naga. The Sakya prince, filled with fright and disgust, finding no other plan, waited till she slept, and then cut off the dragon's crest with his sword. As a result of which progeny of the royal pair always suffered from pains in the head. After the death of the Sakya youth, his son succeeded him under the name of Uttarasena[10]." According to the account of Hieuntsang (SI-YU-KI (Beal) vol I PP 126 FF) this king Uttarasena obtained a share of the relics of Buddha.

Similarly, Sir Alexander Cunningham[11] has recognized the sacred tank of Elapatra in a small square tank of clear water from Hasan-Abdal situated about 10 miles to the north-west of Shah-Dheri, the site of the ancient city of Takshila. This place was also visited by Chinese traveller Hieuntsang[12]. This Naga was a Bhikshu who, in the time of Kasyapā Buddha, destroyed an Elapatra tree. Hence in the present times, when the people of that country ask for rain or fine weather, they must go with the Shamanas to the side of the tank and then cracking their fingers after praying for the desired object, obtain it.[13]

The residence of Basuki Nag was also in Kashmir on the mount Kamalas. The lake near the top (Kundkaplas) is one of the great Tirthas of Bhadarvāh. It is believed that Basuki Nāg, who originally resided in Kashmir, found here a refuge from the attack of Garuda[14].

Takshila is very close to the Kashmir valley which was the residence of Karkota Naga. Loharas (who claim their origin from Sātavāhanas) Karkota, Gonanda, Nagpal (Bhadravaha) Naga Royal families have been ruling in Kashmir during historical period. Still today, there are countless temples of Nagas in Kashmir, such as temple of Basuki Nag, in the little town of Bhadarvah and in two villages. Bheja-uparla (i e. upper Bheja, the lower village is called Bhejā-Jaklā) and Nalti.[15] At the village of Satingal, there is a shrine of Sāntan Nag. The temple of Svār Nag is near Chintā in the forest of Deodar[16] (See Illustration No. II)

Serpent Worship in Iran

It has been stated on foregone pages that the largest centre of serpent worship and serpent race was Takshila. It is certain that tradition of Naga or serpent worship did not originate in Takshila, rather it would have been taken from north-west. When we look into the history of Iran, with great surprise, we find there evidence of serpent worship and existence of Naga race in abundance. James Fergusson[17] gives detail of these evidences as under–

"By far the most important and interesting person in the ancient Persian history, for our present purpose at least, is Zohak. According to all accounts, he came from Arabia and took his title Bivar-asp from his bodyguard of 10,000 horsemen by whom he was always accompanied (Glossary S. V. Dahaka). His genealogy from Tazi or Taj, the eponymous of the Arabs, is given both in the Bundehesch and the Mojmil. His father is represented as a simple possessor of flocks and herds, but he is said to have conquered central Asia and to have fixed his residence at Babul. His reign, or rather that of his dynasty, is said to have lasted 1000 years, when he was overthrown by Feridun, with the assistance of Gavah, the black smith, by whom the original line of Jemshid was then restored.

Feridun has been identified almost without doubt with Thraetaona of the Zend-Avesta, celebrated as the slayer of the three headed serpent Dahaka, who was the creation of the evil power Angra-Mainyus (Weber's Indische studien Vol III P-416) or more popularly Ahriman.

Zohak is represented by all the Mohomedan historians as having two snakes growing at his back, one from each shoulder, and they add that it was necessary to appease these monsters by sacrificing daily two young men in order that their cravings might be satisfied with their brain. All this has hitherto been mysterious enough, but as we shall presently see, all women of the Naga race had one serpent between their shoulders, and all men-in India one with three,five or seven heads; the two of Zohak seem an earlier form, being the exact duplication of those of the females, and it is also probable that the three heads of Zend-Avestā (Tribus oribus prae-ditum tribus capitibus, Masaudi, III P-252 and the Mohomedans, on the contrary, always speak of two serpents borne on the shoulders of Dahak) include the human head between the two snakes. We shall be in a better position to judge of this presently, but whatever explanation we adopt, it seems only to be an earlier form of a myth with which we are now becoming familiar in India. The human sacrifices are only what we find so universally accompanying serpent worship all over the world..... The last material trace of serpent worship that is found in Persia occurs in a bas-relief at Nakshi-Rustem, near Persepolis. It represents Ormuzd bestowing the circlet of royalty on Ardishir Babegan, the first king of the Sassanian line (AD. 226). Beneath the feet of the horse on which the god (?) is seated, lies Ardevan, the last of the Parthians, and round his head are twisted two writhing snakes not such as probably adorned the shoulders of Zohak, but still, sufficiently important to mark that the sculptor intended to represent the Parthian as of the hated race of Zohak, the follower of the accursed Ahriman, whom Ormuzd tramples under foot while bestowing the emblem of royalty on the Zoroastrian Fire-Worshipping Sassanian."

In above bas-relief, there is a representation of victory of Sassanian Aryan on the non-Aryan serpent race. It is also clear from the myth, that before coming of Aryan, the original inhabitants of Iran were serpent worshipper Nagas, and Aryan people snatched power from them. Another important secret also comes to light : Feridun has been identified almost without doubt with Thraetaona of the Zend-Avestā, celebrated as the slayer of the three-headed serpent Dahaka, who was the creation of the evil power, Angra Mainyus or more popularly Ahirman. This Angra Mainyus can be identified with the Manavah or Manavya of India tradition who is stated to be the most celebrated ancestor of the Naga race (see chapter XI P 316-17.)

Further, Fergusson[18] quotes another interesting myth according to which Nagas came from Iran and made their permanent settlement in Kabul (Afghanistan). He writes, "One remnant of the race of Zohak seems to have survived in Kabul and it would be especially interesting to us, if we knew more about it, as it seems the connecting link between Persian and Indian serpent worship. According to the Mojmil, "when Taj, the primogenitor of the Arabas, was settled in Babel, one of his sons married a daughter of Feridun and settled in Kabul, and his son was Rustem's maternal grandfather (Windischmann, 37). We find further particulars of the family in the Shah Nameh. When Zāl the son of Sām went to Kabul, he found Mihrab, a descendant of Zohak, on the throne, and having fallen in love with his daughter, Rudabeh, he was forbidden by the Mubids to marry her, because the chief of Kabul was of the family of Zohak, the serpent king. The father too from this circumstance dreaded the resentment of Manuchehr if he allowed the union, and not without reason, for the king ordered Sam to destroy Kabul by fire and sword and especially the house of Mihrab, then ruler of the serpent race, and all his adherents, were to be put to death. Fortunately for the lovers, the difficulty was got over, and the result was the birth of Rustem, the most wonderful hero of Eastern Romance."

It seems clear from the above myths that before the advent of Aryans, the Naga tribe, the original habitant of Babul and Iran, first of all reached Afghanistan, and from there, later entered the North-West region of India. Archaeological evidences of this entry are clearly traceable from Takshila or Swat Valley.

Famous anthropologist Dixon B. Roland, with the help of skeletal remains and other material goods of archaeological value, found from excavation of old cemeteries of the world, has compiled a most valuable book on, 'Racial History of man'. He[19], on the basis of his venture, gives an account of racial elements of Iran and their movement towards India as a result of sudden invasion of Aryan race from the North, "We may probably assume that the earliest traceable population of the region was of brachycephalic type, probably in the main Alpine and comparable to that which we are also obliged to assume for the Anatolia plateau further west. In speech these early people were probably non-Indo-European. In the south, along the shores of the Persian gulf, there was a narrow fringe of dark skinned, frizzly- haired folk of simple culture .... The results from the racial point of view of these (Aryan) invasions were; I belive, in the main two : First as a consequence of the pressure of the invading people,some of the older, brachy-cephalic folk were forced out south-east-ward, the region of the Indus delta and soon, down the western coast of the Indian peninsula; others perhaps across to Oman, in-southern Arabia, where they contributed a strong brachycephalic factor to the population."

Above view gets the support of Vibha Tripathi[20]and B. S Guha.[21] R. P. Chanda[22] stating that these round headed Alpine Iranians were Yadu, Turvasa, Anu, Druhyu and Puru tribes, whose detailed description is given on chapter IX. P -235 Skeletal remains of these Alpine people have been found out from the excavation of H and G cemeteries of Harappa.[23]

Origin of Naga Worship in Western Asia

It has been stated earlier that according to ancient myths of Iran, the tradition of Naga worship was taken to India from Iran. Now let us see where this tradition took its birth.

Scholars[24] are of the view that Australoid and Mediterranean (Dravidian) tribes originally took their birth in the coastal land of Mediterranean sea. It is also an open secret that first civilization of mankind also came into existence in the aforesaid land.

The earliest civilization of the globe was Catal Huyuk[25]. In pursuance of some local folk tales, Mr. James Mellart, a French archaeologist, unearthed an impressive city site in front of the full view of modern scholars in 1965, the age of the earliest human civilization had to be recalculated. Surprisingly, history of human civilization on both the east and west banks of Charshomba river of Anatolia province in Turkey was brought to light. The Radio Carbon dating of this culture is calculated to be 7200-7100 BC and 6700-6300 BC. Similarly Jericho is another site of the same age (7000 BC-Bottero, Cassin and Vercouter) which supports the above fact.

Thus it is clear, that human civilization came into existence in the aforesaid region in about 2500 years earlier than the great civilization of the Egypt and Sumer. Thus the culture of Catal Huyuk is earliest in the world traced out so far. The people of this culture did not construct road system in the town. They felt no necessity of roads because they never constructed any door on the ground floor of their houses. They used to travel from one end to the other end of the town over the roofs.

Similarly, whenever, we conduct a search for a place where the first seed of human upliftment of any kind, was sown in the past, we find in amazement that it was no where else but in Western Asia that the beginning of the techinques of making of pots, weaving of cloths, use of metal including steel[26] and invention of writing system[27] and so on took place. Similarly whenever we look for the earliest centre of origin of serpent or Naga worship it is also found in the same land. Although James Fergusson informs us that it was Turan or Turkistan, but when we conduct a search for its evidences, immediately the pointer turns towards the Western Asia. The tradition of Naga worship first originated in Palestine and Assyria. We further take up this subject for discussion in detail.

Famous historian and Sanskrit scholar, Dr. Bhagwat Saran Upadhyaya,[28] has taken a note of certain verses from the Atharv-Veda which contain some non-Aryan elements in them, and can be unerstood only with the help of non-Aryan language and history. These verses are as under : Atharv-Veda (V-13-6 to 10)

ASITASYA TĒMĀTASYA BABHRAPOD KASYA CHA ।

SĀTRĀ SĀNASYĀHAN MANYO KHĀJYOMIV DHANVNO VIMUNCHĀTI RATHOIVA ॥ (6)

ALIGĪ CHA VILIGĪ VA PITĀ CHA MĀTĀ CHA. ।
VIDMA VAH: SARVTO BANDHVA RAṢĀH: KIM̃ KARIṆYATHA. ॥ (7)

URUGULĀYĀDUHITĀJĀTĀ DĀSYA SIKANYĀ ।

PRATAṄ KE VATRUŚO ṈĀM̃ SARVĀSĀMARAM̃ VIŚAMA ॥ (8)

TĀBU VAM̃ NATĀBUV̄AM̃ VETVA MASI TĀBU VAM̃ TĀBUVENARAŚAM̃ VIŚAṂ. ॥ (10)

These verses are translated by an Indian scholar B.G. Tilak on the basis of research work of Bloomfield. This is as under :

You are released from the most powerful upodak poison and black brown coloured snake Taimāt, like wise a chariot is released from the horse and bow–string from the bow. (6)

I know Aligi and Viligi (Alai and Valai) who are your father and mother and all your relatives. You are poisonless and you can not put to harm. (7)

This daughter of Urugulā is born from karet (black). The poison of them all has become devoid of power, and they have run away to their shelters. (8)

Tābubam (or) and no Tābubam (O, serpent!) you are not Tābubam. Your poison has been made devoid of power with the help of Tābubam. (10)

B. G. Tilak has thrown light on the origin of the words like Taimāta, Aligi, Viligi, Urugulā and Tābubam and informs us, "These words are non-Vedic and Akkadian (Khandi)". He has again tried to compare the word 'Taimāt' with the Timāyat and 'Tābubam' with the Tobā. But he could not trace the meaning of the words Aligi, Viligi and Urugulā in Sanskrit language. He thinks these words are not Indian. But English scholars like Macdonell, Keith and Grifth are also connecting the words Taimāta, Upodak, Aligi, Viligi and Urugula with some unknown species of snakes[29] . Viligi is a deity of Assyrian myths.[30]

But endeavour of Dr. Upadhyaya to trace out the origin of these words is highly appreciable. He has traced out the names of Aligi (Alalu) and Viligi (Balalu) in the genealogical table of Assyrian kings, belonging to the period of 3000 B. C. in the guide book composed by Dr. Burnette, department of Assyria and Sumeria. Alalu and Balalu are shown to be the names of father and son[31]. This genealogy is also given in the Cambridge Ancient History-Vol-I.

The study of above verses of Atharv-Veda and veiw-points of different scholars on them, brings out the following conclusions :

(1) The ojhas (priests) of Atharv-Veda age had knowledge of above serpent kings.

(2) According to Yaska these are the words with no meaning.

(3) Macdonell, Keith and Grifth connect them with some unknown species of snakes.

(4) Aligi and Viligi were father and son who were Assysian kings of 3000 BC

(5) Above genealogical table has been traced out from excavation of Ur an ancient city of Sumer.

(6) These names are non-Indian and "Akkadian" or semitics.

We can draw a final conclusion from the above study that certain serpent worshipper tribes of Assyria or Sumer came to India along with the above names of their kings in a period after 3000 B. C. or roughly Indus Valley period (2700-1600 B C). Either the knowledge of above names and words was transferred to ojhas or priests or they were themselves among the immigrants Although it is a farfetched idea, yet I think this will be the most acceptable view-point, because verses were composed at a very later period, the composer would have belonged to the instituition of immigrant priest class. It is equally possible that Atharv-Veda would have been related to the black section of Rishi of Assyrian immigrants like wise black section of Yajurveda or Kanva as suggested by some scholars[32]. There are clear evidences of Indus seals or seal impressions with figures of Nagas or serpents depicted on them. Similarly there is another supporting evidence of Rigvedic description (IV-28-1) of Nagas also. We will discuss this issue on next pages.

To understand this important secret we have to study the available evidences of Naga worship in Babylonia, Sumer and Assyria. (see Illustration V-D) James Fergusson[33] produces detail of such evidences as under, "In addition to the Tyrian coins and other monuments which in themselves would suffice to prove the prevalence of serpent worship on the seaboard of syria, we have a direct testimony in a quotation from Sanchoniathon, an author who is supposed to have lived before the Trojan War. This passage is in itself sufficient to throw light on the feelings of the ancients on this subject. It may be worthwhile to quote it fully. Taautus attributed a certain divine nature to dragons and serpents, an opinion which was afterwards adopted both by the phoenicians and Egyptians. He teaches that this genus of animals abounds in force and spirit more than any other reptiles; that there is something fiery in their nature, and though possessing neither feet nor any external members for motion common to other animals, they are yet more rapid in their motion than any other. Not only has it the power of renewing its youth, but in doing so receives an increase of size and strength, so that after having run through a certain term of years it is again absorbed within itself. For these reasons this class of animals was admitted into temples, and used in sacred mysteries. By the Phoenicians they were called the good demon, which was the term also applied by the Egyptians to Cneph. who added to him the head of a hawk to symbolize the vivacity of that bird.

After this, Eusebius or Philo goes on to quote several other authors to the same effect, among others the Magian Zoroasters, who describes the hawk-headed deity as "the chief, the best, and the most learned of the gods;" but from the context it appears that there is here some confusion between the serpent god and the eagle- headed deity of the Assyrians, who is generally supposed to represent Nisroch (Layard, Nineveh and its remains, abridged edition P-46) and whose image so frequently occurs in the sculptures. It scarcely admits of a doubt but that this eagle-headed deity of the Assyrians became the Garuda of the Hindu mythology, who before the time when Eusebius wrote, had taken so important a position in the serpent worship of the Hindus, but it is still not clear how the confusion between the two objects, crept into the passage as we now find it. Eusebius certainly understood the quotations as applying to the serpent ....The coins of Tyre represent in some instances a tree with a serpent coiled round its trunk, and on either hand two rude stone pillars (Petrae Ambrosiae... ?) or an altar with two serpents rising from the angles of its base. Others represent the serpent coiled around a rude stone obelisk, with Tyrian Hercules contending with serpent. Taken in conjunction with the above quotation, these, with others that might be quoted, suffice to show that the serpent was honoured, perhaps worshipped in Tyre from an early period down to the time of Alexander."

It is crystal clear from the description of Sanchoniathon that, as a result of above thoughts of Taautus, the tradition of serpent worship came into being in Western Asia and Egypt, which caused origin of a serpent worshipper Naga race. Not only it did become popular among the masses even the Assyrian Kings like Aligi (Alalu), Viligi (Balalu) adopted it as a part of their religion. This tradition was not only in practice in Babylonia, Sumer, Akkad and Assyria but also in Egypt, Crete and Greece. We give their detailed description in the following lines.

The Serpent Worship in Babylon, Sumer and Akkad

Although James Fergusson could not trace out exact country of origin of tradition of serpent worship but whatever information he has contributed to the knowledge of mankind, it is most valuable, and mankind will remain indebted to him for ever. He[34] gives detail of tradition of serpent worship Prevailed in Mesopotamia—

"The earliest native historian (Berosus) lived after the time of Alexander (270 B.C.), so that he too was likely to pass over what had been so long forgotten The one chance that now remains to us for recovering it is from the cuneiform inscriptions. Serpent worship, so far as I know, has not yet been looked for among them, and till they are examined with special reference to the inquiry, it is impossible to say where it may or may not be found. In the meanwhile, Sir Henry Rawlinson informs us, that Hea or Hoa, the third person in the Babylonian trinity of great gods, may be considered the serpent deity, "since there are very strong grounds for connecting him with the serpent of scripture, and the paradisiacal tradition of the tree of knowledge and the tree of life.

The only direct testimony we have of serpent worship in Babylon is in that part of the book of Daniel which is now printed separately in the Apocrypha (story of Bel and the Dragon V-23 et seq) though it is difficult to understand why this should be so. The story told there of the fraud of the priests and the indignation of the people at the destruction of their god all bear so strong an impress of probability that it is difficult to doubt their truth.

The story as it stands except in its catastrophe, is not unlike one related by Elian (Elian, de Animal XVI-39) as occurring in Egypt, in the days of Ptolemy Euergetes. The description of the serpents of Metele is nearly identical with this of Babylon, but there the only result was that the prying priest went mad and for all we know, the serpent continued to receive his daily dole for long afterwards. Herodotus, strange to say, deserts us in this difficulty, and the only indication in Diodorus is in his description of the three statues that adorned the great Temple of Belus; that of Rhea being accompanied by two very large silver images of serpents each weighing 30 talents; and that of Juno, standing with her right hand resting on a serpent's head (Diodorus, II. 9. 5.)"

We have already told in the context of Iran, that Zohak who had two serpents on his shoulders, had his capital at Babylona and it was necessary to appease these monsters by sacrificing daily two youngmen. It is quite clear that serpent worship was practised in Babylon and Sumer.

The Serpent Worship in Egypt

Egypt, being a neighbouring country of Western Asia, also had tradition of serpent worship from remote past.

There are very clear evidence of prevalence of this tradition in Egypt. The serpent was worshipped on the banks of the Nile[35] among other animals, perhaps in some instances with a certain degree of pre-eminence, but on the whole the accounts are hardly sufficient to enable us to say that the serpent was more honoured than his associated animal gods. At the same time it must be admitted that the serpent very frequently appears in the sculptures of the temple walls, and frequently in a place of honour, as on the brow of the king, or as a prominent ornament of his dress, but hardly ever there with that pre-eminence he attained in other countries.

The great[36] test of such a subject in Egypt are the sculptures which cover the walls of the temples. These are the Bible of the Egyptians in so far at least as we know it. Any one studying these with that object might easily pick out fifty or hundred examples which would tend to show that the Egyptians were both tree and serpent worshippers.

The Serpent Worship in Greece

Greece, although situated at a distance and neighbourhood of the place of origin of the tradition of serpent worship, yet it was one of the greatest serpent worshipping country of ancient, as far as the greatest hero of the nation, Alexander the great is said to have born of a serpent (deity). In Greece the study of serpent worship, from the testimony and archaeological evidences, is very interesting. James Fergusson [37] gives detail of such like description, "Such an hypothesis is still more indispensable when we refer to the tree and serpent worship that certainly prevailed to a greater or less extent during the whole period of Grecian history, though of course more prominently during the earlier part. Here it is again necessary to make a further distinction. All the earlier myths refer to the destruction of serpents or of serpent races. This continues down to the return of the Heraclidae; after that time, when Hellenic supremacy was assured, we meet with a kindlier feeling. The serpent then became the oracle, the guardian of the city, or the healing god, the Agathodaeman in short .... one of the oldest and most celebrated myths of Greece relates the destruction of the dragon Python by Apollo, and his taking possession of the oracle which the serpent guarded. Cadmus fought and killed the dragon that devoured his man and sowing its teeth raised soldiers for his own purposes. In Indian language, he killed the Naga Raja of Thebes and made sepoys of his subjects. The tradition of the close of the career of Cadmus and his wife is even more suggestive of serpent worship than the events of their life. Their conversion into serpents as a cure for ills that had become unbearable, and the respect with which it is represented they were afterwards regarded, point to a form of faith that must have been at that time familiar to the inhabitants of Greece.

The Argonautic expedition was undertaken to recover a fleece that hung on a sacked tree, guarded by a dragon that Jason and his companions would have been unable to cope with, unless they had been aided by the enchantments of Medea. But the great destroyer of serpents in those days was Hercules. Most appropriately was he represented as strangling two serpents sent by Juno to destroy him while he was yet in his cradle. .... His fight with the many–headed Lernean Hydra, on the other hand, suggests the origin in the west of many-headed serpents with which we are becoming so familiar in the East. In the earlier representations, apparently, he had only seven heads, but afterwards, as was also the case in India, they were indefinitely multiplied. A still earlier, perhaps the earliest, mention of this mythological animal is in Homer, who speaks of a three-headed snake as adorning the baldrick of the buckler of Agamemnon. (Iliad,XI 38) .... Though generally represented as the destroyer of serpents, Hercules, on the other hand is said to have been the progenitor of the whole race of serpent-worshipping scythians, through his intercourse with serpent Echidna (Herodotus IV-9) .... After the return of the Heraclidae, serpents as hinted above seem to have been kept at Delphi and in the caves of Trophonius. In both instances, apparently, for oracular purposes, but the great centre of serpent worship was Epidaurus, where stood the famous temple of Aesculapius and the grove attached to it, in which serpents were kept and fed down to the time of Pausanias. Some of these, according to him, were of great size, measuring, he says, 30 cubits in length. It is not, however, clear whence the myth of Esculapius came, and when it was introduced into Greece. There was a temple dedicated to this god in Alexandria in which a huge serpent was kept; but this worship is as likely to have been taken there by the Greeks as brought thence though the name and many features may be thought to betray an Egyptian origin.

Perhaps, the most remarkable event connected with the Epidaurian serpent was the embassy sent from Rome in the year 462 A. U. C. under Quintus ogulinus. The description of the advent of the divine serpent is one of the most animated passages in Ovid's Metamorphoses (Metamorph XV-5) and which, so far as the main facts go, is confirmed by livy (X-47), Valcrius maximus- (Val Max 1, 8, 2) and Aurelius Victor. (Au victor, XXII-1). That such an embassy was sent, and brought back a serpent, seems undoubted, as also that it was received with divine honours by the populace of Rome, and it may also be admitted that the plague was stayed after its arrival, but whether in consequence of it or not, is another question. The Romans thought it was, and serpent worship was established in Rome from that time forward. On the other hand, we learn from Pausanias mention of it, that the Aesculapian serpent continued to be venerated in Greece till after the Christian era. .... Nothing, for example, can well be more curious than the story of Alexander's birth, as told by Plutarch. That Olympias his mother should have kept tame snakes in the house is scarcely to be wondered at, as Illyria is a country where they abound, and where also their worship was prevalent. It is curious, however, that it should be thought worthy of record that one was found in her bed, and that Philip should have believed in the possibility of the serpent being the real father of Alexander the Great. The same view is taken by Lucian, who seems to adopt without hesitation the idea that Alexander was born of serpent. Even Cicero (de Divinat II.66) does not discountenance the story when he tells us that on the occasion of the illness of Ptolemy, one of Alexander's generals, from a poisoned wound, the serpent of Olympias appeared to him in a dream, having a root in his mouth. This serpent, who, from the context we are led to infer, was the father of Alexander, then pointed out the place where the herb grew, and the wound cured by its application."

It is clear that serpent worship was practised in Greece likewise Assyria and other countries of Western Asia. We can suppose, being in neighbourhood of Palestine and Assyria, this tradition must have been transferred from there. We can sum up above details as under :

Summary and Conclusion

(1) According to a myth of Mahabharata, Nagas are offshoot of Kadru (the earth mother goddess, daughter of Prajapati) from Rishi Kasyapa.

(2) Takshila was original seat of Takshakas or Nagas, from where, they onward moved south and eastward and spread up throughout the country, such as the myth of Kausal's prince, marrying a Naga maiden of Udyān (Swat valley), myth of tank, residence of Naga king Elapatta near Shah dheri (ancient site of Takshila), movement of Prince Salivahana from Salivahanpur and Takshila was capital of Takshak Nag.

3. The tradition of Naga worship did not originate at Takshila but came from Iran. The Avestan myth, of Naga king Zohak, brings him from Babylonia. It means this tradition originally took its birth in Western Asia, which is duly confirmed from the Atharva-Vedic account of Naga King Aligi, Viligi, who were Assyrians in origin.

4. This tradition took birth on the seaboard of Syria. Taautus teaches that this genus of animal abounds in force and spirit etc more

than any other reptiles hence was admitted into temples and used in sacred mysteries This information is quoted by Sanchoniathon, an author, who lived before Trojan War. From Syria this tradition was later adopted both by the phoenicians and Egyptians. It can be imagined that from Syria and Phoenicia this tradition was further transferred to Babylonia and in the East upto Iran and ultimately reached Kabul through Naga King Zohak and his offshoot, where Mihrab, a descendant of Zohak royal family, has been noticed ruling the country of Afghanistan in Kabul Takshila and Swat valley is situated in the south of aforesaid land.

5. From earliest known period the tradition of snake worship is noted all over the Western Asia, Egypt and Greece. The earliest Greek-historian Berosus (270.B.C.) has mentioned in his description that Alexander and his father Philip were also snake worshippers, as according to a story told by Plutarch, Alexander was born of a serpent It is curious, however that, it should be thought worthy of record that one (snake) was found in her (Olympias, the mother of Alexander) bed and that Philip should have believed in the possibility of the serpent being the real father of Alexander the Great. It is conclusive that cult of snake worship and Naga race took its birth in Western Asia and was transferred to India in due course. Thus, the cult of serpent worship took its birth in Western Asia.

References

1. (a) M. B. Adiparva XIV to XX and XXVI.
   (b) Vogel J. Ph. "Indian Serppent Lore" PP 49-53
2. MB Adiparva XXV and XXXIV.
3. MB Adi XXIII.
   DĀSĪ BHŪTĀ SMYANĀRYĀYĀ BHAGINYĀ PATGUTTAM, PANAM̃ VITATH MĀSTĀYA SARPERŪPDHINĀ KRITAM̃,,9,,
4. Chanda R. P., "The Indo Aryan Races" I C - 25.
5. Oldham C. F. "The Sun and Serpent" PP 30 F and 59 F.
6. Tod James : AAR Vol II P-625.
7. Tod II P-626 see note below.
8. Fergusson James, "Tree and Serpent Worship" P-95.
9. (a) SI-YU-KI (Trans Beal) vol I PP-128 FF.
   (b) Vogel J. Ph., "Indian Serpent Lore" P-123.
10. Vogel J PH-P-124.
11. ASR Vol II PP 135 FF.
12. SI-YU- KI (Beal) Vol I P -137.
13. Vogel J PH PP-208-09.
14. Vogel J PH P-251 foot note No. 2.

15. Vogel, J PH PP 248 and 50.
16. Vogel, J PH P-250 foot note no.4.
17. Fergusson James PP 41-42.
18. Fergusson James. Ibid P-42.
19. Roland B. Dixon, "The Racial History of man" pp 307-08 .
20. Tripathi Vibha, "The Painted Grey ware; An iron age culture of Northern India" P-56.
21. Guha B. S., "An outline of the Racial Ethnology of India" (Calcutta) 1937 P-134.
22. Chanda R. P. "Ibid" IC 33and76.
23. Sarkar S. S., "Aboriginal Races of India" PP 143-45.
24. Hutton J. H., "Caste in India" P-3.
25. (a) Biswas S. K.; "Autochthon of India and the Aryan Invasion P–19.
    (b) Bottero Jeans, Cassin, Vercoutter "The near east; The Early Civilization." P-17.
26. Fry Somerset P, "History of the World" P-48.
27. (a) Rapson E. J., "CHI" Vol-I P-55.
    (b) Buhler G., "Indian paleography" PP-31-32.
28. (a) Bhartiyā samāj kā Etihāsik vishleshan P-44.
    (b) According to Ṇ K. Dutt (Aryanisation of India P-55) the period of composition of Atharva-veda is-1100-600 B. C. Which is the same period when the Megaliths tradition and Iron reached India.
29. (a) Dr. Bhagwat Saran Upādhyaya "Bhartiyā Samāj Kā Etihasik Vishleshan" P-46.
    (b) Upadhyaya, "Bhartiya Kalā Tatha Sanskrit Ki Bhumika" P-176.
30. Aggarawal VS. "Some foreign words in Ancient Sanskrit Literature" IHQ Vol 27 (1951) P-2.
31. (a) Carleton R., "Buried Empires" P-90.
    (b) Asthana Shashi "History of Archaeology of India's contact with other countries" P-130.
32. Chanda R P. "Ibid" I C 25.
33. Fergusson James "Ibid" P-10.
34. Fergusson James. "Ibid" P-11.
35. Fergusson James "Ibid" PP-5-6.
36. Ibid.
37. Fergusson James "Ibid" PP 12-15.

Chapter 2

The Expansion of Serpent Worship and Nāga Race in India

Places of serpent worship are probably spread all over India but their highest number is found in hilly area of north.[1] But as a result of repeated invasion of foreigners, changes in sovereignties, on plains, their number have reduced to a great extent. However, on the occasion of Nāgpanchami festival, serpent worship is practised all over India.[2] Important places of serpent worship in different states of India are given below.

Kashmir

In Kashmir different[3] temples, lakes and springs are attached to the names of different serpents. Serpent or Naga temples, which are generally outside, but not far away from the habitation area, are constructed in forests. Each of the temples has one priest and two chelas or disciples. In these temples, generally, there are statues of serpents or Naga-men, one is Nagraj and other his minister. Horns of those animals are also fastened to the door which, some times ago, were sacrificed.

Basuki Nag, who is regarded as the presiding deity of the village, has temples in the little town of Bhadarvāha and in two villages, Bhejā-uprālā (ie upper Bheja, the lower village being called Bheja Jaklā) and Nālti.[4]

More details of snake worship in Kashmir has already been given in chapter-I on Pages 5 and 6.

There are several towns in Kashmir having their name after some Naga, such as Veri Nag, Anant Nag, Shesh Nag etc.

Neela[5], the lord paramount of the Nagas or serpents of Kashmir, was believed from early times, to dwell in the main source of the vitastā (River). Hence this fine spring was known as Neela-Naga or Neela-kunda, "The deep blue colour of the water", as Sir A. Stein observes, "which collects in the spring–basin, may possibly account for the location of the Neel Nāga in this particular fountain". It goes by the name of VerNaga and is surrounded by a stone embankment and to its east are temples of stone. Neelānaga is still worshipped in Kashmir and fairs related to him are also held even today.[6]

In the district of Nāgām (Ancient Nāgrām) which is watered by the Dūdhgangā (Milkgangā) a small stream which joins the Vitasta at Srinagar, there is a small lake, likewise, known by the name of Neelā Nāg.

Himachal Pradesh

Most probably Nagas moved from Kashmir valley and settled in different valleys of Himachal Pradesh. Still today these Nagas can be seen in numerous temples and heard in legends throughout the modern province of Himachal Pradesh.

Basuki Naga is worshipped in the ex-hill state of Chamba,[7] which comprises the Ravi valley and a portion of the valley of the upper Chināb. It is said that the cult of Basuki was introduced from Bhadarvāh in the beginning of the nineteenth century because a disease had spread among the cattle of the state. For some time, the Naga had a temple at the capital likewise, named Chambā, but unfortunately it was burnt down. Evidently the means of his devotees were insufficient to have it rebuilt; the Naga with his Vāzeir found refuge in a small shrine of the goddess Hirmā or Hidimba, which belongs to the ancient temple of Champāvati Devi, the family goddess of the king of Chamba. In the temple, the statue of Basuki Nag, the smaller one of the two, wears a royal crown surmounted by an eleven fold hood. In his right hand he holds a sword marked with a snake, and in his left hand a Damaru or hand-drum on each side of his feet is a cobra in an erect attitude. Basuki Naga also has a temple of Himgiri[8].

There is also another Naga in Chamba state called Indru Naga. This is the same as Nahusha whose story is told in the Mahabharata. Indru Naga is worshipped at several places : at Kuārsi on the road leading to Dharmasala, at Sāmrā in Ranhun kothi, at Chinota and Trehta. There is also another temple of Indru Naga at Kanhiarā in Kangra.[9]

Among the numerous other serpent deities found in Chamba we wish to mention only Mul Naga and Stūhr Naga. The shrine of Mul Naga is immediately above a very fine fountain at the village of Brehi. The Stūhr or Satūhr Naga is worshipped at the village of Tur on the road to the Baleni pass by which the Dhaolā Dhār is crossed[10].

This is to be noted[11] that Pujari and Chela attached to the Naga temples of Chamba commonly belong to the agricultural caste of the Rāthī, but in good many cases only the Pujari is a Rāthī and the Chela is a Hāli. Naga temples are also found in the valley of the Chinab. At Kilār in Pāngi, there is a shrine of Det Nāga. It is said that he was originally located in Lahul and human sacrifices were offered to him. There is also a temple of Kalihar Naga (Kelang Naga) at Dughi, it is famous about this Naga that he also hailed from Lahul[12]. Similarly Eighteen Nagas or serpents are also worshipped in Kulu[13] valley.

In the local language of this area of Himalayas, 'Kir' or 'Kiri' means serpent, and the people of above area are called 'Kirata', a word used for the people of internal part of Kashmir in Rajtarangini. Hence 'Kirāt' is another form of 'kir'[14]. Varamihir also has cited this word 'Kir'. Similarly, in the copper plate, published by Prof Kilhorn, this word also occurs[15].

There is mention of the word 'Kirgrama' in the inscription of Baijnath temple of Kangra valley. This shows that Kirgram would have been local name of this place.[16] In the local language, the meaning of 'Kirgram' is "The village of serpent or Naga race". Till today serpent is the most loving deity of Baijnath. Not only this, the venerable deity of people of surrounding area of Baijnath is also serpent. It means that in ancient time this town was inhabited by the Naga people. Kir is synonymous of Nag or serpent and it is apparent these Naga worshipping Kir people of Himalaya are near relatives of Dravidian Cher, Ker or Keral of South.

According to Vogel–

"The hilly area of Uttarpatha and Nepal is also a homeland of numerous snake shrines and temples and snake worship is a basis of religious life of people."

The North–Eastern region

Serpent origin is also afforded by the ruling house of Manipur[17]. The peculiar god of the royal family is a species of snake called Pā-kung-ba, from which ex-Raja claims descent. When it appears, it is coaxed on to a cushion by the priestess in attendance, who then performs certain ceremonies to please it. This snake appears some-times, they say, of great size. His appearance[18] is indicative of his being displeased. So long as he remains of a diminutive form, it is a sign of his being in good humour.

Similarly all the eastern region which includes, Assam, Arunachalam, Nagaland, Mizoram, Manipur, Tripura is inhabited by ophiolatery tribes like, Bodonaga, Kukinaga, Khasi, Mao, Tangkhul, Koliya, Kabui etc.

The Naga tribes of Manipur

T. C. Hodson[19] in his work titled 'The Naga tribes of Manipur', has given description of mainly four Naga Tribes in Manipur (1) The Tangkhul, who inhabits the hill immediately to the east and north-east of the valley of Manipur (2) The Mao and Marām Nāgas or Angames who inhabit the hills north of valley; (3) the Koliyā, Khoirao or Māyang Khong group in the hills south of Mao and Karām; (4) The Kabuis who inhabit the hills to the north-west of the valley. Most of these tribes came from west. In support of this view, here we give the origin of Tangkhul[20] and Koliya Nagā. Hodson informs us, "That from the records of Manipur, we gather some important information regarding the origin and antiquity of the Tangkhuls. One of the earliest raids mentioned in the chronicles of Manipur is dated 1435 and is said to have been the work of Tangkhuls who then, on subsequent occasions availed themselves of the opportunity offered to them by the temporary absence of the forces of Manipur, on what the local historian calls a march of conquest in the direction of Thaungdut to make a raid on the valley." It means Tangkul tribe reached there in 1435 AD as an invader. This shows this Naga tribe is a migrant to this land during Muslim period. Perhaps they were pushed eastward by the Muslim invaders from eastern part of Bengal or Nepal since one branch of them was settled there from the time of Buddha, known as Moriya. Another branch of them along with their Taka coins appears in Chhota Nagpur during Kushana period, who gave their name to Dhaka (see chapt VI P-156)at some later period.

A tradition is prevalent among the Tangkhuls that their fore-fathers were born in a local village named Hungdung.[21] But above event of invasion seems to be more reliable and historical, and hearsay cannot be the sole basis of history.

Ethnically, they are a hybrid race of Mediterranean and Mongoloid. Their eyes are brown and black, hair curly and wavy, beards very uncommon and hair on face is very rare.[22] It shows the invaders were of Dravidian race who came from west where as earlier native population was Mongolian. Weaving is a speciality of every housewife. Although some villages are specialist in the art of weaving and rest of the male members generally are farmers and some others fishermen. [23] It is compulsory for every male member to be a skilful warrior and without head-hunting no young lady comes forward to marry them.[24] This reminds us of prevalence of traditions of citizens' army among the Nagas of West, where learning art of use of arms was compulsory for each member. (See Chapt V P-112 and VI PP 133-34)

Against matriarchy of Khasi tribe, the Tangkhul Naga families are patriarchal. Hence inheritance goes to sons and not to daughters.[25] In case of any epidemic or social troubles they worship Naga Monster Python.[26]

Head of the village clan is known as Khullapha or Luptakpa, who also acts as priest for any religious rite. Hence he is a clan or village administrator as well as priest[27](priest-king).

The custom[28] of disposal of their dead bodies is of similar type as found in the graves of Swat valley which were used by the Asuras, it means they used to bury their dead bodies in a grave having stone walls to prevent any earth from touching it. (See chapter IV P-67)

These institutions prove their close association with the ancient Nagas of North, West and South India. Although they differ in the form of their families from their ancestors, perhaps that would have been due to their association with the Aryan tribe of patriarchal tradition for a very long period, now not known to us.

The Koliya Nagas are said to be the descendants of Marām Nagas[29], who came from west. It is apparent that Tangkhul and Koliya Nagas both came from west and settled here. The Koliya Nagas were living in Nepal (Ramagrama) during the life time of Buddha (567-487 BC) who were a branch of Sakyas tribe of Buddha (See Chapt VI PP-164 & 67) later known as Kulinda (Madra).

The Khasi Nagas

Major P.R.T. Gurdon, in his book 'The Khasis', has given description of an event of 1835 AD. This event is related to Assam state where he was posted. He writes[30] —

"In 1821, an attempt was made to kidnap a native of Sylhet proper and while the agent employed were punished, the Raja was warned not to allow such an atrocity to occur again. Eleven years later, however, four British subjects were kidnapped in the Nowgong district and taken to Jaintia. Three of them were actually sacrificed (to the Thlen serpent monster), but the fourth escaped and reported the matter to the authorities. The Raja (Siem) of Jaintia was called upon to deliver up the culprits, but he failed to do so and his dominions were in consequence annexed in 1835 A. D."

We have described in chapter V that Aryans had patriarchal family and heredity tradition, but on the other hand matriarchal tradition was prevalent among the Naga people. This tradition sometimes ago was prevalent among the Khasi tribes, the resident of Khasi and Jaintia hills of eastern India. Khasi is a Naga Tribe in origin. Matriarchal tradition is prevalent among them, and ownership of the land goes either to the clan or tribe or the village[31] and not to the individual. As they are great traders, they pay toll tax to their king (Ahom), which is the only source of revenue of state.[32]

Similarly they build up megaliths on the graves of their dead still today likewise ancient Nagas of south and central India, which may be seen everywhere on hills or land, in which Menhirs Dolmens and Cairns are most important. Taking the different megaliths in order the Menhirs are larger, their height varying from 2 or 3 feet to 12 or 14 feet, but in exceptional instances rising to a more considerable elevation.[33]

Khasis speak a language which is akin to Mon-khmer group of languages now spoken in Chutia Nagpur and a part of Satpura hills in central provinces. These languages are closely related to the Kolarian group of languages and now also known as Munda language spoken by Munda and Ho tribes.[34] skill in the art of war is also a part of the characteristics of the tribe. The Khasiś tradition of human sacrifice for Nag demon Thlen can be equated with the ancient tradition of Naga worship. Such a tradition was prevalent in Kambodia and Western Asia (See chaptet I PP 6-7; Legend of Naga king Zohak). The tradition of Naga worship was in vogue in India from the time of Indus Valley Civilization.

Thus in modern age, social, religious and cultural traditions prevalent among them are strikingly the same as were in practice among ancient Naga tribe of Central and South India and middle-east countries, such as burial system of their dead bodies and raising of megaliths on graves, matriarchal family and heredity system, Naga worship, human sacrifice, guild based like economic system. According to AB Keith, Khasi is an Alpine race of Dinaric origin[35]. It is well known that Khasis are still inhabitant of Kishan Ganga Valley of Kashmir known as Bomba clan[36]. They[37] are a branch of Kanets, inhabitant of Himachal Pradesh, who are at par with the Rathis of Kangra. Khasi Rajput of Uttaranchal and Nepal still claim their origin from the Khasa tribe. They are, according to Manu (X-22) Vratya, like Jhalla, Malla, Nichchhavis, Nat, Karan and Dravids. It shows Khasi moved from west to east.

But according to Gurdon there are evidences of their migration from east to west[38]. He produces following evidences in support of his theory:

(1) There is general belief among the Khasis that they originally came from east.

(2) Khasi grammar states that tradition connects the Khasis with the Burmese to whose king they were upto a comparatively recent date, rendering homage by sending him an annual tribute in the shape of an axe, as an emblem merely of submission.

(3) According to Shadwell, the oldest living authority, they originally came from Burma via the Patkoi range having followed the route of one of the Burmese invasions.

(4) Gurdon himself opines that the tendency for outside people to move into Assam from the east still continues. Hence they came from the East.

But there are solid evidences to prove that this movement was from West to East in general. These are being enumerated below. In origin, following traditions, which are a part of characteristics of their society, took their birth in Western Asia :

(1) Cult of mother goddess and Naga Worship.

(2) Megalithic tradition of disposal of dead.

(3) Matriarchal form of family and inheritance.

(4) Priest-king and Nation- in-Arms tradition.

(5) Khasis[39] and most of the other Naga tribes speak a language akin to Kolarian or Mon-Khmer group of languages now known as Munda also spoken in the region of Chutia Nagpur by the tribes like Santhal, Munda and the Koruks.

These traditions (1 to 5) took their birth in Neolithic-Chalcolithic age (4000-1000 B. C.) in Western Asia (see chapter V for detail) and reached Indus Valley and North and South India in about 3000-800 BC and further reached Vindhyanchal region in the same period. Khasis, Koliya Nag[40] and Tank or Tangkhul (Moriya) were present in the region of Nepal and North Bihar during the life-time of Buddha (567-487 BC). In a period of third century AD many hoards of Taka coins have been recovered from Chutia Nagpur region[41] which were introduced by the Taka Nagas of North-West. Linguists have informed that these Taka people reached and ruled in the region of Dhaka of Bangla Desh, since the word 'Dhaka' is a linguistic (Pali) variation of Taka[42]. This well known "Taka' coin is still in prevalent in Bangla Desh. But according to a historical record of Manipur, Tangkhul invaded Manipur in 1435[43] AD. Perhaps they were pushed eastward from East Bengal by the Muslim invaders who had reached as far as Assam in this period. This invasion of Tangkhul Naga, who were in origin ethnically of Dravidian race, was laid on the native people of Mongol race. Perhaps most of the males were killed and women were made inmates which caused to create a blend of complicated race now known as (Indo-China) Mongolo-Dravidian race whose language is an admixture of language of both the races but more akin to Kolarian group of languages. Khasi Nagas ruled in Kashmir and Himachal Pradesh in historical age and their off shoot kanet are still residing there. Koliya Nagas were a branch of Sakyas, ruling at Ramagama during life time of Buddha.

Traditions that they came from east now prevalent among these tribes, are of quite a modern period and the evidences I have produced, are of remote past. Since the Naga rulers of South India made their colonies in Indonesia and Burma, who reached there by sea as early as 137 AD and used power of their navy to launch incursion as far as South Indo-China or Champa.[44] They carried aforesaid tradition along with them in that region particularly Megalithic tradition went from South India (see map no. II). Under these circumstances tradition of coming of some tribes from the east has no meaning.

However variation in physical type or tradition in individual tribe may be due to some particular reasons in historical age which should be investigated and found out for the satisfaction of all. But evidences of their movement from west are more realiable and based on historical fact and well proved.

The ex-Raja of Chutia or Chhota Nagpur derives their origin from Naga Pundarika. How it happened is most interesting : Pundarika[45], as the story says, once assumed the form of a Brahman and repaired to the house of a certain Guru at Banaras to acquaint himself with the sacred scriptures. The learned instructor was so pleased with his pupil that he gave him to wife his only daughter, the beautiful Parvati. Unfortunately the Naga even in his human form could not rid himself of his double tongue and his foul breath. He begged his wife not to question him about the secret of these unpleasant peculiarities, but once while they were making a pilgrimage of Puri, she insisted on knowing the truth. He had to gratify her curiosity, but having done so, he plunged into a pool and vanished from her sight. In the midst of her grief and remorse, she gave birth to a child. When the child grew up he became king of Chhota Nagpur. The royal family is progeny of the same Naga King.[46]

Famous ancient Buddhist university of Nalanda also had relation with the Nagas. J. Ph Vogel[47], to show above relations, produces archaeological evidences-" A very fine specimen of a seated Naga (See title page) was found on the site of Nalanda in the course of excavations carried out in the cold season of 1920. This Naga holding a rosary in his right hand and a vase in his left hand is shown sitting in easy posture on the coils of a snake, whose windings are also visible on both sides of the figure,whilst a grand hood of seven cobra-heads forms a canopy overshadowing him. This image has been tentatively indentified with the Buddhist saint Nagarjuna, master of the Mahāyānā. The sculpture, however, presents a type of Nāga images peculiar to the mediaeval art of India. (A. S. R. for 1912-13 Part I Pl IX 6), although it would be difficult to point out another specimen of equal artistic merit. In this connection, it is interesting to note that according to the Chinese pilgrims Nālandā was named after a Naga (Hieuntsang, si-yu-ki. (Beal) Vol ii P-167). Other instances may be quoted of Buddhist sanctuaries such as those of Sārnāth and Sankisa, which were at the same time dedicated to serpent worship. ...... In Amaravati also we find a likewise image of Naga king with snake hood surrounding the head in nimbus like manner. The Naga-maiden grouped in varying attitudes around the throne on which the precious casket is placed are distinguished by a single snake issuing from behind their heads."

Takshila and Panjab :

Takshila was the largest centre of Nagas, which was named after the name of Takshak Naga. In ancient time it was the largest centre, from where most of the Naga chiefs are stated to have moved southward i.e. towards the Punjab plains. Some times back North-West Punjab was known as Taksha, or Takkha or Takka country after the Takka tribe of Punjab.[48]

According to Greek historians, in the days of Alexander's invasion, serpent worship was practised in Punjab.[49] According to writings of Strabo, the king of Abhisara kept two serpents, one of which was 80 and the other 140 cubits in length. As described by JWM Crindle[50] of Greece, Indians used to capture animals and besides them snakes, which the Indians, regarding as sacred, kept in caves and worshipped with much devotion.

Rajasthan

In addition to Eastern Punjab, Naga Guga Pir is worshipped in Rajasthan[51] also. Guga, the ruler of the land of Bāgar, as the great prairies of Rajputana are called, is said to have been a valiant Rajput of Chauhan clan, contemporary of Prithvi Raj. According to Sir Denzil Ibbetson, he is supposed to be the greatest of the snake deities.

Rajasthan was sometimes the greatest Centre of Naga Rulers. Present Tonk town was a centre of Naga rulers and is called in the Chauhan Chronicles Takatpur after the name of Takshak Naga (Tod IP-110 Foot note No.3).

Our account of Takshaka[52] would be incomplete without noting the curious fact that, down to the present day, the serpent-king of the Paushya-Parvan possesses a shrine in central India, where he is worshipped under the name of Takshakeswara or Tākhāji; and curiously enough, he shares the worship of the country folk with Dhanvantri, the Indian Aesculapius.[53] The shrine in question stands on a most romantic spot far from the village of Navali or Naoli which is situated on the table land at the foot of which Bhanpura lies. It now forms a part of the territory of Indore and in ancient times must have belonged to the Malava country.

Kathiavar or Sourashtra

Kathiavar[54], the peninsula or western portion of the province of Gujrat, is great centre of Naga worship. There are temples of Basuki and his brother Vanduk locally called Vāsang ji and Bandia Beli respectively, at Thān and Mandhogarh. The two[55] Nāg brothers are said to have settled here after having rid the country of a dangerous demon, Bhimāsur, at the request of five famous Rishis. To the present day no one is allowed to cut a tree in the grove that surrounds Bandia Beli's shrine, and it is said that, should any one ignorantly cut a stick in this grove, the snake appears to such a person in his dreams and orders him to return the stick and should he fail therein, some great calamity shortly befalls him; and in fact, in or near the grove may be seen many logs or sticks accidently cut and subsequently returned.

The Vāsuki[56] temple at Thāna contains the image of a three-headed cobra with two smaller monocephalous ones, one on each side-carved on the same slab. Besides which there is a figure of the four armed Vishnu, while on and in front of the altar on which the images are placed are Sāligrām stones and sankh shells. A common votive offering at this shrine seems to be a representative of the three snakes in alto-rilievo on a flat earthen ware tile.

Other shrines in Kathiavār are that of Pratika at Talsānā in Jhālavār, and that of Devānik Charmālia in the village of Chokri under Chudā. But the most famous snake temple of Gujarāt is that of the celebrated Dharanidhara or 'Earthholder' situated at the village of Dhemi, a few miles to the North-West of Tharād, in North Gujarat. This shrine is visited by pilgrims from all parts of India. There is a well executed image of a cobra in the temple of the Dhem-Nāga, as the Dharanidhara is locally called. There are many other local temples in Gujrat and Kathiavar where cobra is worshipped.[57]

It is quite clear that Kathiavar is an important centre of Naga worship, which simultaneously is also a big centre of Megaliths. The round headed Alpine race is also settled, here in a very high number.

Bastar, the ex-feudatory state in the south-east corner of the central province, was ruled by a Naga-dynasty, whilst most Gond chiefs in the same province likewise pretend to have descended from the Nagvansa.[58]

Maharashtra and Vidarbha

Ancient Naga[59] culture has very deep roots in the cultural and religious life of the people of Maharashtra, which can be seen even today, from the intensive study of their traditional gods and goddesses. The original symbol of Mātangi is Vālmiki (whiteant-hill). Renukā, Enammnā and Mātangi, are worshipped in the form of Vālmiki at different places in south. Santeri is worshipped in the form of Bambi or serpent dwelling. This Valmiki is Yoni or vulva of earth and the serpent, who lives in, is representative of manhood or Linga. The meaning of the word Renukā, in origin, is earth (Renu+ka = like Renu) that is why she is called "of Kori Bhumi" or "Kumari Bhumi". Santeri is also known by the synonymous name of "Bhūmi-kā" in Gomāntaka. Similarly local gods like Marugan, Subrahmani, Khandova, Jyotivā, Khalnāth and Bheron, which are worshipped in the form of Vālmiki, are considered to be Kshetra-pati or Kshetra-pāla (protector or keeper) Nagas. Subrahmanyā still to-day is worshipped by the name and form of Vālmiki. Particularly, Manmēlār (Manumilār = Melar of earth) in Bellari and Ādimelār in Jejuri, situated at the bank of river Kānhā, are also Vālmiki-Nāga. Why does the sculpture of Santeri of Gomantakā, have a serpent in its hand ? or why does the worshipper of Mātangi have a Nag-garland (Nāgkanth) in her hand ? It can be understood from its protectorship form of Naga.[60]

Vālmiki is worshipped as an important deity in the temple of Adi-Subrahmanyā. Similarly an image of Naga or serpent was also worshipped along with the Vālmiki. There is one image of Kārtikeya on upper portion of altar, another of serpent king Bāsuki in centre and third one Sesha Nāga below the above in the temple of Subrahmanya.[61] It means Bambi or dwelling of snake and snakes are important objects of worship in this temple. These objects are worshipped here, in the form of Subrahmanya, and it is considered to be another name for Kārtikeyā. But Subrahmanyā is worshipped in the form of serpent. The word Subrahmanyā has come into existence from Skand-Nag and Subbarmani Tamil word owing to similarity of sound or fictitious Sanskritization. The original meaning of this word is Nāg mani or Nāgrāj or Nāgshresthi (superior[62] Nag). In South India this name is meant for skand and its meaning is serpent and if at any place, any deity is being worshipped by this name, that is also serpent.

At many places, in the South, where Subrahmanya is worshipped as serpent, along with Vālmiki, is recognized as 'skand-kartikeya'. It is also originally a serpent deity. Hence, Subrahmanyā does mean a serpent.

Therefore in South Gurgan, another form of Subrahmanyā and a well known serpent protector deity, is also considered to be a serpent by the local people. Murug Subrahmanya, a serpent protector, invites special attention among all the deities.[63]

Jyotiva of Maharashtra and Khalnāth of Konkan Gomantak, both are recognized as serpent protector god. There is mutual intercourse between the protector deities and the serpents. The reason of this secret is that serpent is protector as well as lord of lands. Vālmiki is a form of vulva of earth and serpent is a form of man-hood or Linga. It is being worshipped particularly in the form of giver of issue.[64]

The Bherava form of Jageshwari and protector of Mhāskovā are famous in Maharashtra likewise Jyotivā of Thamāi and Khalnāth of santeri, Mhāskovā is particularly a deity of Dhangars. It appears to devotees in the form of serpent with five hoods and take shelter in Vālmiki. It seems that there is similarity in between Jyotiva of Mhāskovā, Khalnāth, Murug Subrahmanyā etc famous protector deities.[65]

It is clear that Jyotiva serpent deity is recognized and worshipped in the form of protector. This serpent is also Kshetra-pati or lord of land. Vālmiki is a form of vulva of earth and serpent is a form of manhood or Linga. It is particularly worshipped in the form of deity of issue giver. Most of the protector deities of south are maintaining their form as serpent. Their most favourite and influencing protector deity, Murug, appears to his devotee in the form of serpent. Kartikeya who is identified with Subrahmanya is worshipped in the form of Valmiki and serpent both and he represents serpent king.

South India

In whole of the southern India, serpent worship is more popular. It is specially the cobra which is held sacred. The higher castes consider it a sin to kill it, and believe that the man who does so will be striken with all kinds of misfortunes.[66]

The great popularity of this cult, in the south, is testified by the snake slabs or Nagakal, which are usually found, sometimes, in great numbers, at the entrance of a town or village. Groups of such stones may be seen in a corner of the coutryard of a temple, either Hindu or Jain, near a tank or under a sacred tree. They are mostly due to childless wives who make a vow to install a snake-stone if they are blessed with an off spring.[67]

The Naga-Kals show a considerable variety of pattern. The simplest and perhaps commonest type of these snake-slabs exhibit a single cobra–, standing as it were on the tip of his tail and curling upwards with expanded hood. The number of the heads varies between three, five and seven, but apparently there exists a certain preference for the figure five. The number of heads, it will be noticed, is always uneven.[68]

Usually the cobra is carved in relief on a stone slab some four feet in height. But at Adichanallur[69] (a well known large centre of Magaliths) in the Tinnevelly district, there is a large group of Nāgākals which shows the peculiarity that they are carved in the round. The snakes are either single-hooded or many-hooded and several of the later have a little human figure seated on the coils and overshaded by the serpents' hood.

Finally we would notice a type of snake-stones in which the serpent deity appears as a hybrid being, its upper half being human and the lower half serpentine. This hybrid is a female and in all probability represents the serpent-goddess who in Southern India is known by the name of Mudam[70]. Over her head, she wears the usual hood combined of three,five or seven snakes' heads. She holds both hands, joined in front of her breast and in each arm she has a baby snake.

In the South Kanara [71] district' on one of the highest mountains of the Western Ghat named, Subrahmanya, there is one of the most famous serpent-temples of India. Here the locality is extremely wild and full of fever excessively, so during the cold and dry seasons; nevertheless, great numbers of pilgrims resort thither especially during the December festival.

Other famous serpent temples are reported to exist at Nagapatnam (or Nega Patam) the well-known ancient seaport on the coast of Coromandel and at Bhomaparanden in the Hyderabad state. The shrine at the former place is dedicated to the serpent deity under the name of Nāganātha. Inside the temple near the image there is a white-ant hill to which large offerings are made in honour of the serpent[72] god.

The Malabar[73] coast according to Vogel is a great seat of the serpent cult. Usually a clump of wild jungle trees luxuriantly festooned with graceful creepers is to be found in the south-west corner of the gardens of all respectable Malayali Hindus. The spot is free to nature to deal with it as she likes. Every tree and bush, every branch and twig is sacred. This is the Nāgakotta (Snake Shrine). There is mostly a granite stone carved after the fashion of a cobra's hood set up and consecrated in this waste spot. If the shrines are not respected, it is supposed to have a bad influence on human beings. Leprosy, itch, barrenness in women, deaths of children, the frequent appearance of snakes in the garden and other diseases and calamities supposed to be brought about by poison, are all set down to the anger of the cobras. In this[74] district the Naga is the tutelar deity of the house and god and shrine are conveyed with the property and frequently specified in deeds of transfer. Puja is offered at least once a year, often by a Brahman; and the serpents are periodically propitiated by songs and dances, called 'Nagam-Pattu'. The high[75] priest of the serpent cult in Malabar is the Pāmbanmākkād Nambudri who lives in the town of Ponnāni in a house full of cobras which are said to be harmless to his family.

In South Kānara[76] two curious rites are known to exist in connection with serpent worship; they have been described as follows : Three afflictions are looked upon as due to the wrath of serpents for having killed a snake in a former life, namely leprosy, childlessness and sore eyes. People so afflicted often perform costly ceremonies to remove the curse which are superintended by the Mādhava Brahmans, originally fishermen, and not acknowledged as Brahmans out of Kānara.

The great festival[77] in honour of the serpents in the Nagpanchami, which, as the name indicates, is celebrated on the fifth day of the bright fortnight of the month of savan, the first month of the rainy season. Ananta, Basuki, Sesha, Padma, Kambala and even so Nagas Karkotaka and the serpent Asvatara, Dhritrashtra, Sankhapala, Kaliya and like wise Takshaka and great Naga Pingla are lauded month by month.

The Expansion of Chera (Sera), Nevar, Kirita Nagas In India

Kashmir to Assam, Himalyan ranges have been the largest centre of the abode of Naga race since dark age of prehistoric time. But their traces are still visible in the form of ethnic groups, social and religious traditions, old architectural remains, inscriptions, coins, name of cities and places all over India.

In some parts of Ceylon and in ancient Malabar country, ancient Nagas established their rule. The Tamil literature of first century A. D. has repeated description of 'Naga-Nadu' or the 'Country of Nagas'. Still today Malabar coast is one of the largest centres of Naga worship. In South, Travancore temple of Nagercoil[78] is famous.

CF. Oldham has thrown much light on this subject. He writes[79]- "The Dravidians were divided into Chera, Choru and Pandyas in ancient time. Chera or Sera (in ancient Tamil Sarai) is synonym of serpent in Dravidian language. It is clear from the words like Chera-Mandel(Coro-Mandal) Naga-Dipa (serpent Island), and Naga-Nadu' (Naga country) that Dravidians of South were of Asura or Naga family. In addition to the above, the Cheru or Sirai had also spread in all the Gangatic valley, which are in existence still to-day. They maintain their origin from some Naga deity or Devta. (Elliot, sup Glossary Ṇ W. F PP 135-36) Cherus are most ancient people. They possessed a large part of Gangatic valley and lived there from time immemorial. During the incendiary, time of the Muslim invaders, Cherus were forced to draw hands from their lands and now they are landless people. They are undoubtedly blood relatives of Dravidian Cheras.''

From the various traditions of Chera people, it seems that they were closely related to Lichchhavis and Nevaras of Nepal such as election of king of five or six families, ceremonial royal functions and coronation and wearing of royal insignia.[80] Various customs of both the Nevars and Lichchhavis and Dravidian people of South are quite similar. All are snake worshippers. As Neel Nag is venerable in Kashmir, similarly Karkotak Nag is venerable in Nepal. The venerable deity of Vaisali at the capital of Lichchhavis, was serpent or Nag. The marriage customs of Nevars and Lichchhavis are similar to those of Tamil of South On the basis of these evidences, it can be concluded that these people would have been of one race or tribe in origin.[81]

Among the Nevars, heredity is decided after the matriarchal tradition. Such a tradition of heredity was sometime prevalent among the Arattas, Andhakas Vahikas and also Takkas or Takhya people of Punjab. It means heredity right was transferred to sister's son instead of once own son[82]. Hence Nevars are blood relatives of Dravidians.

Similarly people of Naga race residing in Himalaya region of Himachal Pradesh were known Kirtas. The word 'Kir' means serpent or Nag. Chera people living in the Khasi hills of Assam are also of Naga race. Their chiefs or kings are known as 'siem' whose deadbody is buried in a hallowed out trunk of a large[83] tree.

The town of Cherapunji (Means, estate of Cheras) is also named after the name of this tribe. Col James Tod[84] informs that, ''This ancient relation between the Suryabanshi chiefs and the Chawaras or Sauras of Saurashtra (Saura + Rashtra) is still maintained after a lapse of more than one thousand years...... the present heir apparent of a line of one hundred kings, the prince Jawan Singh (1828-38) is the off spring of Chawara mother, the daughter of a petty chieftain of Gujrat.'' It is clear from this description that Chawara Rajputs were born from the Sauras or Chauras after whom Saurashtra took its name. Saura is Gujrati form of Chaura or Chera.

In short, we can say that the Kir or Kirit of Himalaya region, Saraj or Sevraj of Satluj Beas valley, Saura or Chawara of Saurashtra, Sevari or Cheru of Gangtic valley, Saurya of central province, Chera or Sera of Khasi hills and Kera, Chera, Sera or Serai of South India all are worshippers of serpents and they are all different branches of Naga race.[85] Chera branch of Khasi has been stated to be of Dinaric Alpine race by

Sudhakar Chattopadhyaya[86] and A.B. Keith. It means some of them were ethnically of Alpine race, some others were Dravidians and others blended race of both of them.

Summary and Conclusion

From Takshila, the people, who worshipped serpent and practised the tradition of Naga totemism, spread all over India up to Assam in the east, up to Ceylon in the South. It is clear from the evidences of spreading up of snake worship and snake worshipper tribes throughout the nation.

Temples of Naga deities are still existing in a very high number in Kashmir valley and are worshipped by the local people. Among them temples of Naga Basuki, Sāntan Naga, Shesh Naga and Neel Naga are most famous.

Hilly area of Himachal Pradesh also has been one of the largest centre of Naga worship. The temples of Basuki Nag, Indru Nag (Nahusha), Mul-Nag, Stūhr Nag, Det Nag, Kelang Nag, are famous and are spreading all over the Himachal region. It is said that there are 18 Naga deities which are worshipped in Kulu Valley alone.

Neel Naga and Karpati Nag are worshipped in Nepal. The royal famlies of Manipur and Chhota Nagpur are said to have descended from the Nagas called Pa-Kung-ba and Pundrika respectively. In Assam Naga tribes like Naga-Bodo, Kukki-Naga, Mao, Tangkhul, Khasi, Koliya are still existing.

Takshila has been the most ancient and the largest seat of Takshak Nag. The ancient name of Punjab, Taka-Desha, was named after Takshak or Taka royal family. Gugga pir is still worshipped in the plateau of Punjab and Rajasthan. Tonk town of Rajasthan once was centre of Naga rulers. A shrine of Takshakeswara or Tākhā ji in central India exists still to-day. Kathiavar or Saurashtra has been the home of Naga-worshipping people from time immemorial. There are famous centres of worship of Naga deities like Vasuki, Vanduk, Pratika, Devānikcharmalia, Dharnidhar etc in Gujrat state.

Maharashtra is also one of the well known centres of Naga-worship Mātangi, Renuka, Santeri, Marugan, Subrahmani, Khandowa, Jyotiva Khalnath and Bheron are deities related to Naga-worship. Similarly images of serpent or Nagas like Kārtikeya, Basuki, Skand Nag, Murug Subrahmanya, are also worshipped in every corner of Maharashtra.

South India has been the home of Naga-worship since prehistoric period, where every house and village worships cobra. The great popularity of this cult in South is testified by snake slabs or Nagakals,which are usually found some times in great number at the entrance of town or village. Some famous serpent temples are reported to exist at Nagpatnam, Nagercoil, etc. So it is clear that Naga-worshipping people or Naga race had their sway throughout India in remote past. In short we can say that Kir or Kirit in Himalayan region, Saraja or Sevaraj in Satluj and Beas valley, Soura or Chawara in Saurashtra, Sevari or Cheru in Gangatic valley, Saurya in central province, Chera or Sera in Khasi hills and Kera, Chera, Sera or Serai in south India all are Naga–worshipping tribes who were putting up and are still putting up in different parts of India. It means they were in power in the whole nation in pre-historic and historic times. Thus the tradition of Nag-worship and Naga race had spread up in the whole nation in ancient time.

References

1. Vogel J. PH. "Indian Serpent lore" P-250
2. Vogel J. PH, "Ibid". P-225

   In Neelmata 1051-1113 (M. S. 901-65) list of names of prominent Nagas, whom to be worshipped, is given, their number is 561
3. Vogel J PH,–PP 248-49
4. Vogel J. PH. P-250
5. Vogel J PH. P-227
6. Vogel J. PH. "Ibid" P-228
7. Vogel P-252
8. Ibid
9. (a) Oldham "Sun and Serpent Worship" P-73

   (b) Rose H. A., "Glossary of the tribes and caste of Punjab" Vol IP-154
10. Vogel P-253
11. Ibid
12. Ibid
13. Vogel P-255
14. Stein, A. "Rajtarangini" Part VII P-27-67
15. Rapson E. J."JRAS" (July 1900) P-533
16. Jane "JRAS" (1903) P-37
17. (a) Vogel J PH P-35

    (b) Fergusson, James "Tree and Serpent Worship" P-64
18. Vogel J. PH P-36
19. Hodson T. C. "The Naga tribes of Manipur" P-2
20. Hodson TC P-11

21. Hodson T. C., P-8
22. Hodson T. C. P-5
23. Hodson T. C. PP 39, 45 and 47
24. Hodson T. C. P-81
25. Hodson T. C. PP-70-71
26. Hodson TC P-137
27. Hodson T C PP 79-80
28. Hodson T C P-150
29. Hodson T C PP- 4 and 14
30. Gurdon P.R.T. "The Khasis" P-103
31. Gurdon P.R.T. P P-69-70 and Intro XXIII
32. Gurdon P.R.T. PP-67
33. Gurdon P.R.T. P-145
34. Gurdon P.R.T. P XXII Intro
35. Chattopadhyaya S. "Racial Affinities of Early N. I. Tribes" P-71
36. Saxena K. S. "Political History of Kashmir" P-12
37. Ibbetson Denzil "Panjab Caste" P-198
38. Gurdon P.R.T. PP10-11 and Intro XXII
39. Gurdon P. Intro XXII
40. Davids Rhys T. W. "Buddhist India" P-9
41. Gupta Chandra Shekhar "Foreign Denomination of early Indian Coins" VIJ (1978) Vol 16 Part 1-2 PP 92-93.
42. B. D. C. R. I Vol I (1939-40) P-192
43. Hodson T.C. P-11
44. Mahajan V. D. "Prachin Bharat Ka Itihas" P-779
45. Vogel J PH P-35
46. Ibid
47. Vogel J. PH P-43
48. (a) H. L. Kosare, "Prachin Bharatatil Nag" P-179
    (b) Tod James- "AAR" Vol I P-43 F/Note no.3
    (c) Cunningham. A "Ancient geography of India" P-48
49. Crindle JWMC "Ancient India as Described in Classical Literature" P-34
50. Crindle JWMC P-145
51. (a) Cunningham A, "ASR" Vol XIX P-79 FF vol XVII P-15.
    (b) Vogel J. PH PP-263-64
52. Vogel J. PH P-206
53. Ibid
54. Vogel J. P.H. P-268

55. Vogel J. P.H. P-269
56. Ibid
57. Ibid
58. Vogel J. P.H. P-36
59. Dr. Dhere R. C. "Lajjagauri" P-65 cited by Kosare H. L. P-215
60. Dr. Dhere R. C. "Lajjagauri" P-65 cited by kosare HL. PP-215-216
61. Kalyān Tirthak year 31 no 3 January 1957 P-324 Mentioned by H. L. Kosare P-216
62. N. V. Mandlik, "Writing and speeches of late Vishvanath Narayan Mandlik," Bombay 1896 P-245 Mentioned by H. L. Kosare P-216
63. Mandlik N. V. PP 159-61 Mentioned by H L Kosare P- 216
64. Mandlik N. V. P-162 Mentioned by Kosare H L P-217
65. Mandlik N. V. PP-188-89 Mentioned by Kosare P-218
66. Vogel JPH p-270
67. Ibid
68. Vogel JPH P-271
69. Ibid
70. Vogel JPH P-272
71. -Ibid
72. Vogel JPH P-273
73. Vogel JPH PP-273-74
74. Vogel JPH P-274
75. Ibid
76. Ibid
77. (a) Vogel JPH P-274-75
    (b) Rao Gopalachari TA, "Element of Hindu econography" vol-II Nagpur university
78. Proceedings of the 7th All India Oriental conference PP 248-49
79. Oldham CF.; "The Sun and the Serpent" PP157 and 191
80. Sherring M.A., "Races of N. W. Province" PP376-77
81. Sherring M. A. P-376
82. M. B. Karan Chpt. 15
83. Gurdon PRt PP 138-39
84. Tod James I P-123
85. Beal Semul, "Si-yu-ki" I P-195
86. Chattopadhyaya Sudhakar, P-71

Chapter 3

The Megalithic Culture-its Origin and Expansion in India

Burial of their dead bodies under Megaliths was one of the chief characteristics of Naga Culture. Henceforth we will throw light on its origin and expansion in Indian subcontinent.

The Megaliths:

The kings and nobles of Egypt were buried in pyramids and Mastabs. The relics of Buddha and the distinguished Buddhist monks were buried under imposed stupas. Over the remains of the Scythian warriors were raised huge mounds. The Wanchos of NEFA bury their chiefs in a wooden coffin and the Khasiś Cherra of Assam make a mummy of their dead chief or Siem and bury the body in a hollowed out trunk of tree, Ka-Shynagoid.[1] These are fabulous in contract with those afforded to the commoners i.e. in Egypt and Mesopotamia the commoners were simply wrapped in mats and buried in trenches or simple pits. Similarly in ancient time, in South and Central India, the dead bodies or their remains, single or collectively, were buried under erected large and crude heaps of stones, known as megaliths or megalithic burials.[2]

As a matter of fact, Megaliths are the pyramids of commoners and memorials of large stones, where bones of so many dead persons were collectively buried. These are generally placed collectively on the slope of hills and high grounds away from fields, in valleys or at the bank of irrigation tanks. These are spread up in all the peninsular South India.[3]

The Origin

Now the question arises, whence came the urge of erecting Megaliths in India ? (See Map No.II) Gordon has placed the original home of the Indian Megaliths in South Arabia[4]; Leshnik and Heine Geldern in Central Asia;[5] Walter Ruben in Palestine. Whereas Banerjee has placed it in Baluchistan[6], scholars donot give any importance to the theory of Baluchistan.

The Theory of Central Asian Origin

(a) Allchin's Theory :

Allchin[7] thinks that some types of graves are reminiscent of those of Central Asia, Iran and the Caucasus and could well represent traits, brought from these areas by Indo-European speaking immigrants. He produces a detailed description of aforesaid parallels as such, "One pair of dates from Hallur suggests that the introduction of iron followed between 1050 and 950 B. C., a date which corresponds surprisingly with that obtained for the beginning of the Iron Age in the North. Archaeology can supply some cross-datings to support this date. Aiyappan excavated two graves in the Perumal hills far to the South in the Madura district which produced jugs with long raised channel spouts, channel spouted bowls and a small bowl-on-stand with vertical cuts in the stand. These forms have analogies in Sialk Necropolis B and more locally the bowl-on-stand occurs in one of the earliest Iron Age graves at Maski. The horse-bits and bells in the graves suggest that at least one part of the cultural equipment of the makers is derived from outside India, and one is forcibly reminded of the Late Bronze and Early Iron Age graves of the Caucasus and Sialk Necropolis B. The discovery of horse-bones in the transitional Chalcolithic Iron Age levels of Hallur is suggestive."

This viewpoint produced by Allchin B & R has been supported by Leshnik.

(b) Leshnik's theory :

Leshnik produces his own theory of Central Asian origin on the basis of following parallels of evidences of artefacts found from Central Asia belonging to a period between 3rd century B C and 2nd century A. D. as enumerated by Gupta[8] :

(1) Decorated Bronze lids and ladles found from South have been compared with certain items found in Parthian Takshila.

(2) Small bronze iron jingles, found from South, have been taken to belong to Central Asia.

(3) Copper bangles with incised decoration on the two ends have been compared with similar bangles found from Caucasian region of an earlier date.

(4) A buckle from Junapani has been compared with few moveable tongues of 3rd Century B. C.

The Revocation of Central Asian Theory By Gupta

But S. P. Gupta[9] does not accept above theory of Central Asian origin and revokes with strong evidences and forceful argrument as such :

(1) Scholars have overlooked time and space factors at all, the period of beginning of Indian Megaliths in the South is 1000 B. C. (Hallur and Dharwar) and in the North 900 B. C. (Gandhara graves, Swat valley) whereas parallels produced by scholar belong to a period between 3rd century B. C. and 2nd century A. D. According to Ghirshman (Fouilles de sealk "Vol II, Gupta P-186)" there is a big gap in space between the Western and Indian Megaliths strictly speaking, there is hardly any typical Megalith between Georgia on the Black Sea and peninsular India. Some of the cists reported at Sialk in Iran and near Karachi in Pakistan fall slightly short of known typology of Indian Megaliths.

(2) Theories of movement of Megalithic people from North to South and vice versa, are also not acceptable. He (Gupta) feels that the Megalithic folks once arrived in the zone of first arrival along with the Western Coast they diffused rapidly throughout the Peninsula within a few centuries i.e. 8th to 6th century BC .

(3) Scholars argue of homogeneity in the material equipment from Indian Megaliths but that has been due to some other reasons also : Before arrival of the Megalithic builders in South India there was a post Neolithic-Chalcolithic culture called the Hallur culture which was characterised by the presence of the Black and Red Ware, both plain and painted and iron implements. The immigrant Megalith builders, where ever and whenever entered South India, found only this complex which they readily adopted and then later on, while colonizing the country, they themselves became the medium of diffusion to this complex. Leshniks' theory is therefore pretty interesting but hardly convincing.

The Theory of Persian Gulf, Yemen and Arab

We now take up the theory of Persian Gulf, Yeman and Arab. Allchin B and R has produced some evidences from the aforesaid region as under[10] :

(a) Stone-cist graves, with or without port-holes, are found in the Levent and on the coasts of Arabia.

(b) Pottery Sarcophagis occur in Mesopotamia and the Persian gulf region during the late centuries. These were in practice in Baghdad, Beth-shan and at several places in Palestine earlier than 1200 B. C. and in Mesopotamia since 3000 B. C. (Dikshit K.N; "The Origin and Distribution of Megaliths in India (SPPM) memoir No. 3 of ancient History, Culture and Archaeology, Banaras Hindu University Ed A. K. Narain P-5)

(c) Legged urns identical to Indian types are reported from the Yemen.

Such stone cists have been traced out in Brahmagiri[11], in South India

According to S. P. Gupta Cairns were in use in the islands of Persian Gulf and South Arabia during Chalcolhic and Iron Age. This tradition most probably reached India from the same region by land and sea routes. He gives a detailed description of such evidences as under "Agreeing that some of the Cairns could be of the middle of the first millennium B.C., one would like to know if this tradition did not come from outside. As the evidence exists to date, it is possible that their origin lies in the practice of erecting Cairns in Southern Arabia and the Persian Gulf islands. There, they belong to two different periods (i) Bronze Age (later part of the 3rd and 2nd millennia BC) and (ii) Iron Age (from 1000 to 600 BC). The sites with Cairn Burials cover practically all the South Arabian States of Aden, Yemen, Oman and East Arabian states of Katar, Abudhabi, Behrain etc. We are here concerned with the Cairns of the later period (1000-600 BC) ie, the Iron Age. The date has been fixed on the basis of Himyaritic inscriptions on some of the Cairns, e.g. those near Jejran. In this connection, Bowen has quoted the observations of a number of explorers. Thus, Philby found them in thousands and called them 'Pill Boxes.' They were circular, usually built of flat limestone slabs. Many of them, however, were 'just heaps of stone' no more than a metre high. Miss Meulen also reported these circular Cairns in Northern Jal, H. J Carter found them on the Southern shores of Arabia."[12]

The Theory of Mediterranean Sea Board

Above region includes modern countries like Syria, Israel, Palestine, and Cyprus etc. Primarily, because of the known chronological data, the mediterranean region has been accepted as the original home of Megaliths.[13] It has some times been presumed that ancient traders took the tradition both to the West European countries and the Middle East. Similarly traders of Middle East[14] had trade contacts with Indian peninsula also.

Megalithic culture reached India through the sea route from the aforesaid regions ie Levent, Yemen at the coast of Arabia, Mesopotamia and the Persian Gulf, which provide evidence of rock cut graves with shaft like entrances in forms strikingly reminiscent of those of the Malabar Coast.[15]

Dr. Thompson[16] has found out evidence to fix the period of Megalithic culture of Arbian sites, "In Hadhramaut, Aden protectorate, on Wadi- Amd opposite town Hureidha. They are round chambers with rock-cut benches along the cave walls, Grave no A6 yielded the bones of three persons, beads, earthen pots, a pair of seals etc. According to the excavator following the opinion of Beck, the beads are of Eastern Mediterranean type of the sixth century BC and the seals are of the Achaemenian type. Harding, on the other hand, dated the pottery to the 9th century BC...... It appears, therefore, that the graves belong to the 1st half of the 1st millennium B.C.

Such type of graves were being built from ancient time in Palestine and Cyprus and it seems that this tradition reached aforesaid region from there. As cited by S. P. Gupta[17], K. S. Rama Chandran has collected a large number of references of the shaft graves occurring in Palestine and Cyprus, "In Palestine these graves range in date from the end of the 4th millennium B. C. to the 5th century B. C., well into the Iron Age. In Cyprus also they belong both to the Bronze Age and the Iron Age. In both the countries along with complete inhumation, fractional burials are found. Although in Palestine and Cyprus the graves are circular, trapezoidal and rectangular, in Kerala they are near rectangular only. Kerala type steps are found both in Cyprus and Palestine (at Tell Fara) during the Iron Age. Megiddo in Palestine is a site where the grave was as multi-chambered as it was in Kerala. Benches of the Kerala graves type are also found both in Palestine and Cyprus"

Walter Ruben has placed origin of Megaliths in Palestine,[18] Haimen dorf[19] has accepted this view point but has called this region Mediterranian Coastal land.

The Causative Factors of Increase of Trade Activities

Megalithic culture was transferred from its place of origin i.e. Mediterranean coastal land to India through land and sea routes for the following main reasons (1) Coming into overwhelming power by the Assyrians in Western Asia who created a terror, which caused fleeing of the people from Western Asia to India between 1200-600 BC (II) and sudden increase in trade activities. This increase occurred due to two reasons :

(1) Deporting of Israelite to Mesopotamia and Babylonia (2) Discovery of iron in Asia minor

1. Deporting of the Israelite to Mesopotamia

The kingdom of Israel began to decline as the old habit of tribal-quarrelling continued. In 721 B. C., Sargon[20] II, king of Assyria, invaded Israel, captured Samaria, and deported the Israelites' leaders and most of the people to Mesopotamia, from which they did not return. In their place the Assyrians made their own people settle, and everything was done to obliterate the traces of Hebrews. As such the tradition of Megaliths was also transferred to Eastern region of Mesopotamia and presumably further in the East in Western and Central Iran.

Similarly, in 586 B. C. the Babylonian king Nebuchadrezzar II, invaded the country and captured Jerusalem. He destroyed much of Solomon's great temple and many other public buildings. The leaders and part of the population were transported to Babylon.[21]

It is apparent from the above events that the Megalithic user people of Palestine and Israel who were great traders were transported to the area of Babylonia, Persian Gulf and Arab, who established there, their trade centres too, who further made trade contacts with India by sea routes and took Megalithic tradition with them.

2. The Discovery of Iron in Asia-Minor

The Indo-Europeans who invaded the civilized people of Western Asia were themselves very backward. In about 1900 B.C. the Hittites[22] came from Armenia over the Caucasus mountain and settled in Asia Minor, South of the black sea. They were as barbarous as any of the other Indo- Europeans, but they had one advantage, not shared by other civilized races of Western Asia. They or their subjects had mastered the use of Iron[23], which is harder than bronze and melts at a much higher temperature. They discovered and held the secret of producing this higher temprature for centuries together. When their greatness came to an end in about 1200 B.C., the Assyrians became master of Iron which helped them to build the most powerful empire in the Western Asia, which includes Syria, Palestine, Asia Minor and Mesopotamia and some parts of Iran, Arbia and Egypt. Even they held a sway over the Northern region of Persian Gulf.[23A] It means they also had their control over the gateway of trade of East, which helped to promote trade relation with Indian peninsula to a great extent. In addition to Jews, Assyrians were themselves great traders. Assyrians ruled over all the Western Asia for a period of 600 years (1200-612 BC).This was the period, when, owing to the new circumstances which were created by the history, the Megalithic culture was transferred from Western Asia to Indian peninsula through land and sea routes. We produce an account of trade relations of two lands in following lines.

Trade relations of India with Assyria and other Countries of Western Asia

Trade between the Indus Valley and Mesopotamia is, no doubt, very ancient. (See Map No.1) The earliest trace of this intercourse is probably to be found in the cuneiform inscriptions of the Hittite kings in Kappadokia, belonging to the fourteenth or fifteenth century B.C.[24], On the stone built stupa of Assyrian king Shalmaneser[25] III (860 BC), figures of elephant, ape and Bacterian camel may be seen even today. Most probably these animals would have been brought from India through the land route of Makran.[26] This archaeological evidence supports exporting of these animals, particularly elephant and ape from India to Assyria. In addition to above animals, some birds were also exported to Assyria. There are clear evidences to the fact that peacock was a strange bird, a gift of which was received by Tiglath Pileser[27] III (749-727 BC). Some other Indian articles were also exported to Assyria during the reign of above king. Most of the articles, which were presented to this king by Vitaykien of Cheldia, were Indians, such as precious stones and timber, pearls, cloth and spices of various kind. The ports of Persian Gulf, were very big centre of maritime trade during this period.[28]

Indian cotton was also very famous in foreign countries. Sennacherib (704-681 BC) was the first Assyrian king responsible for sowing cotton seed in his country.[29] He had a big fleet in Persian Gulf, which was constructed by Phoenician carpenters. He sent this fleet against Meroduck Balden, the king of Babylonia, who fled away to Maguttu at the frontier of Elam. The cause of this dispute seems command of maritime trade with India. The articles of demand from India were mainly cotton, rice and peacocks.[30] They used to call cotton 'Sindhu'. This secret has come to hand from the cuneiform writings on clay tablets found from the library of Assyrian king Assurbanipal[31] (668-627 BC), who went to ascertain arrival of cotton from India. These trade contacts caused to develop relation in other fields also. According to some scholars, Brahmi script, which was related to phoenician alphabet, was taken from Mesopotamia to India by the traders.[32]

It is obvious that during this period (1200-600 BC) the trade relations of India with Assyria were at its top. Evidences of such relations with South India are also clear during this period.

Evidences of trade relations with the South India

After the decline of Indus Valley civilization, the native Dravidians and round headed Alpines escaped towards South India and established their Centres of culture there in places like Maski and Brahmagiri, which also became main centres of trade and industry. As such, the trade and industry of North were transferred to South India.

S.V. Vishwa Nathan[33] brings to light some more evidences of trade activities between South India and West "The traditional fame of South

India, as the seat of the precious metals and gems, seems to have been carried down to the time of the Arthshastra where we read that-with the exception of blankets, skins and horses, other articles of merchandise such as counch-shells, diamonds, precious stones, pearls and gold are available in plenty in the South.

The South Indian Dravidians were a great maritime people in antiquity. It is no wonder, being surrounded by the sea on three sides, that they should have developed the arts of ship-building and sea-borne commerce. In the Manimekalai, one of the most ancient pieces of literature of the Tamils, there are a good number of original words denoting the sea : Kadal, Paravai, Punari, Arkali, and Munnir. The waves of the sea were known to the Tamils as ola. The only word in the Rigveda which has been interpreted to contain a reference to the sea is Samudra."

It is clear from the above evidences that Dravidian speaking people of South were themselves a great maritime people who were engaged in this task from the Age of Indus Valley Civilization. These traders were exporting these goods not only to Assyria but also to Babylonia, Israel and Palestine. Dr Sayce[34] has mentioned in his Hibbert Lectures (1887 PP-136-38), the fact of taking sandal wood, ivory, apes and peacocks from India in his boats by Jewish king Soloman (974-937 BC). The Jewish 'Tukian' a synonym of pea-cock resembles the Tamil word 'Tokai' which is also a synonym of peacock. The use of the word 'Indus' for Muslin in their language reveals that this cloth was imported from the Indus land.

In 606 B. C. Assyrian empire was over thrown by Nabuchadrezzar and Babylonia became an important city of Western Asia. The traders of different countries, particularly from Egypt, Palestine, Phoenicia and India used to assemble there to hold a meeting in the market of the city.[35] There was also a colony of Indian traders which survived to a very later period. Here, the most striking evidence of presence of Indian traders are those clay tablets of trade account, which were related to the Nippur's famous company named 'Murashu and Sons.[36]' Some Greek terms came into being from the Tamil words as a result of these trade relations, such as Arsi (Rice) Orija; Karur (Cinnamon), Corprain; Injiwar (dried ginger) Triniveses and Pippi (Pipal) Pepeti.[37]

Quite inversely, some merchants of West reached India and established their colonies in south as well as Western Coast. Evidences of Roman merchants are very clear. KN Sastri[38] produces some evidences of them—

"Of the active part played by Roman merchants in the maritime trade with India, in the early centuries A. D., we have ample evidence. Large ships from Egypt are said by the author of the Periplus and by

Strabo to have visited India in their times. The Tamil works of the Sangam Age mention colonies of Yavana merchants in the coastal cities. Recent excavations at Arikamedu, (near Pandicherry) have revealed the remains of a Roman trading station (the first of its kind discovered in India) with numerous fragments of Roman pottery of the first two centuries A. D. Hoards of Roman imperial coins have been found on other Indian sites, especially in the South. In the first century A. D., moreover, Arab merchants are directly mentioned in the Periplus as making voyages in their own ships to Indian ports.''

It is quite clear that Indian goods were exported not only to the West Asian countries but also to Greek and the traders of both the lands were usually going and coming to each other's countries and established colonies at both the ends in a period under discussion (1000 BC-100AD). It can be surmised from this activity that while traders of Western Asia came to South India, they would have not only brought with them the knowledge of iron but also tradition of Megalithic graves which is confirmed from the evidences of archaeology.

The Theory of Diffusion of Megaliths in India

According to Allchin,[39] an examination of South Indian Megalithic graves shows that the graves of Neolithic and Metallic Age were the result of development of indigenous tradition. Generally the beginning period of Megaliths and iron in India is accepted to be 1000 BC, but G. R. Sharma[40] has created a fresh difficulty by announcing his hypothesis, according to which some of the Mirzapur Megaliths went back to the Chalcolithic time, (1500 B. C.) thereby making them the oldest of the lot we have in India. It is the direct blow on all the theories of Western origin of Indian Megaliths.

Above evidence shows that Megalithic culture was a local innovation, from where perhaps it diffused in different direction. But S. P. Gupta[41] does not accept this theory on the grounds detailed below—

"The Megaliths in India are largely concentrated in regions South of the Vindhyas, rather South of the Godavari . They are generally marked by a basic uniformity in culture-complex, observed particularly in Black and Red ware pots and Iron tools and weapons of characteristic shapes. Unfortunately, it is often termed as the 'Megalithic culture'. However, since no culture expresses its ethos only in graves and also because this complex has been first located in a habitational context of the highest antiquity at Hallur (1000 B. C.), we have termed it as the 'Hallur culture'. We strongly feel that Hallur culture was of pre-Megalithic origin and that it was adopted by the Megalith builders on their arrival in South India. It may, however, be pointed out that within the overall uniformity of the cultural traits, there are strong and significant regional variations which are often overlooked. The Megalithic monuments in India contain fractional bones of post exposure nature collectively of more than one person...... . In the Indian context collective burials are predominant although single and double extended burials have been sometimes found, not only that false extended burial, cist with urns and sarcophagi etc are also not wanting. Most of these features are frankly non-Megalithic. This leads us to the principle of hybridization the Megalithic types crossing or fusing with the non-Megalithic types of an earlier origin. This incidentally determines the relative chronology of the monuments as also their directional changes which passed through three distinct stages viz. (1) the stage of Struggle, (2) The stage of Adoption and (3) stage of Nativization. This has been worked out on the presumption that the real Megalithic inspiration came from the West. On the present showing it appears that it came both through the Western coast and the North-Western passes. It has been suggested that the Rock cut caves, dolmens and cists came primarily through the sea route while cairn-circles and menhirs came through the land route."

It is evidently clear that the theory of diffusion has no legs to stand on and Megalithic culture reached India through sea route as well as passes of North West. Because this culture was existing already in West Asia with effect from a date about 4000 B.C.,hence it can not be a local innovation as suggested by G. R. Sharma. His date 1500 BC, however, suggests a pre-Aryan entry of Megalithic people in Indian soil. Presence of B and R ware pottery in Kakoria site of Vindhya region (See chap IV) shows that Megalithic builders were Harappans consisting of Mediterranean and Alpine race. These people also had some hand in establishment of Hullur culture also, as shown in concluding part of this chapter.

The Chronology

It is most interesting that date of origin of Megaliths in North and South is not dissimilar. S. P Gupta[42], taking the chronology of Megaliths in to consideration, puts forth his conclusive remarks, "Their initial date of entry into India was for long a matter of speculation on the basis of archaeological evidences. Wheeler took it to 300 B. C. and Banarjee 700 B.C. . However, recent C-14 dates of the Hallur culture at Hallur and Dharwar, places the Black and Red ware complex, with Iron artefacts, within a narrow limit of 1000-900 B.C. This, incidentally, leads to another very important question regarding the introduction of iron in India. Although, Wheeler took it to 500 B. C., the C-14 dates of the Swat valley Iron age graves (900 BC) and of the Painted Grey ware levels at Atranjikhera, U. P (1025 BC) and Noh, Rajasthan (800 B.C.)

conclusively place it in 1000-800 B.C. bracket. Thus, the earliest date of the introduction of iron, in the North and the South both, comes to circa 1000-800 B.C. . One is, therefore, forced to conclude that the iron metallurgy came to South India independent of the source which introduced it in Northern India. It is not impossible because tool typology of the two repertoires are astonishingly different.'' Thus, the final date of introduction of iron and Megaliths, falls in a period between 1000-800 B.C. . This is the same period while Western Asia had been captured by the Assyrians and the people of Eastern region were fleeing further Eastward owing to overwhelming attacks being conducted by them on one hand and on the other Israelite and Assyrian traders have reached in Persian Gulf region, the gateway of Eastern trade, to begin with their maritime trade activities with Indian peninsula.

The Expansion of Iron and Megaliths in India

Further, S. P. Gupta[43], while answering the question who introduced iron and Megaliths in South India, gives details of his conclusion in consideration to different causative factors,"It may be recalled that we have already taken the stand that on the present evidence it can safely be said that the metallurgy of Iron existed at places like Hallur in the pre-Megalithic context. Obviously, even though the Megalith builders might have augmented the tool types and perfected the process of smelting and forging the metal, they can not exclusively be given the credit of bringing in the technical knowhow of iron metallurgy in South India. If so, was it the local innovation ? That does not seem possible, because of two reasons : firstly, if that were so, we would have got the iron implements at some stage within the Neolithic-Chalcolithic pottery complex (with the coming of iron pottery also changes, even at Hallur) and secondly, the overall evidence in favour of iron in the Ancient World is against several independent centres of origin. It is significant to remember that with the coming of iron, entirely new culture-complexes appear on the scene, both in the North and the South. Obviously, some new impetus is behind it, although we may not be able to specify it at the moment. It is possible that the iron-smelters were the fore-runners of the Megalith builders : they might have been even related to them but they themselves did not start building Megaliths. But all this; for the present, is only a hypothesis and may be discarded if on the basis of some intrinsic evidence, the Megalithic graves are themselves dated to 1000 B. C. Fortunatelly, the tentative chronology of the Indian Megaliths (800 BC-100 AD) appears to overlap partly with the well documented period of the history of South India. The Sangam literature, according to Srinivasan, contains traditions going back to 3rd century B.C. He has quoted a number of references from anthologies and epics, like

Manimekalai and silpadikaram, which were actually composed during the middle of the first millennium A. D. but which testify to the existence of the Megalithic monuments in a much earlier context. It is an important chapter in which the archaeological and literary traditions seem to corroborate each other admirably well.

It is also a chapter in which the archaeological evidence is corroborated by the anthropological data. Archaeologically, there seems to exist a number of cultural traits which came to India during this period and intermingled with the Indian elements, some of which have been recorded by Allchin. They are supposed to have come both from Central Asia and the Mediterranean, the latter movement took place through the gulf of Amman. The studies made on the human bones from Megaliths also show that besides the proto-Aurtraloids the Megalith builders consisted of, according to the term used by S. Sarkar, the Indo-Europeans coming from Northern Iran and central Asia, and the Mediterraneans (the Dravidians) from Western regions."

Above discussion can be summed up as follows : Inspite of the fact, that there are some cultural variations also, there is overall uniformity of the cultural traits i.e. :

(1) Presence of B and R wares on all sites is one of the most significant characteristic of this culture.

(2) Collective burial was one of the well known general trait of Megaliths. In the Indian context collective burial was also predominant, but single double and extended burials have been sometimes found. Similarly false, extended burials, Cists with urns and sacrophagi are also unwanting. This leads us to the principle of hybridization of the Megalithic and non-Megalithic type or of earlier origin. This hybridization of two races consisted of two people : first earlier the founders of Indus valley civilization, the Dravidians and Australoids; second the latter settler in mature Harappan age, the Alpine Yadavas. This gets the support of later royal families of historical period who ruled South, who originated from the Yadavas or Naga race, This is further corroborated by the Sangam literature too. Since the tentative chronology of the Indian Megaliths [800 B. C.-100 AD] seems to overlap partly with the well documented period of the history of South India. The epics like Manimekalai and Silpadikaram have chapter in which the archaeological and literary traditions seem to corroborate each other admirably well. This gets the support of B. B. Lal also who says that B and R ware is connected with Harappan culture on one hand and with the Megalithic culture on the other.[44] It means Megalithic builders were successor of Harappans, who were Australoids, Mediterraneans and Alpines or their admixture race.

We know, the rulers of South India in ancient period were either Dravidians or predominantly Yadavas (Alpines). But Gupta thinks that (1) the builders of Megalithics came both from Central Asia and Western Asia, both and (2) after S.S. Sarkar, he thinks that in addition to Dravidians they were indo-Europeans of Central Asia and not Yadava Alpine.

Here one point is notable that on one hand S. P. Gupta earlier (PP 39-40) has himself refuted the theory of Central Asian origin of Megaliths, propounded by Leshnik and Allchin Band R. but here he is accepting quite a divergent theory of S. S. Sarkar (see chapter VIII P-208-09). This is apparently an unscholarly attitude of a prominent scholar, thereby disproving the theory of Central Asian origin of Megaliths.

Hence it is obvious that no human element came from Central Asia to contribute Megalithic culture in India.

Summary and Conclusion

We can conclude the above detail of the whole chapter as follows : Four theories have been put forward on the origin of Megaliths and their transfer to India ie (1) Benerjee's Theory of Baluchistan, Heine Geldern and Allchin's Theory of Central Asia, Gordan's Theory of South Arabia and Walter Rubenś theory of Palestine. (A) No one gives importance to the theory of Baluchistan (B) Theory of Central Asia has been propounded by Heine Geldern and acceded to by Allchin B and R, its greatest pleader is Leshnik. But this theory has been refuted by S. P. Gupta on the basis of solid evidences. (C) Similarly third theory of Arabia and Persian Gulf's origin, has been put forward by Gordan. He has found out some stone cist graves with port-hole from Levent on the Arbian sea coast, which can be compared with such graves of South India. (D) Fourth theory belongs to Walter Ruben who claims that original home of Megaliths was Palestine. K.S. Rama Chandran has collected a large number of references of the shaft graves occurring in Palestine and Cyprus. In Palestine they range in date from the end of the 4th millennium B.C. to the 5th century B. C. well in to Iron and historical Age. From this area, on account of political and commercial activities, these graves reached Mesopotamia, Iran, Gulf region, Yemen and South Arabia. Onward from this land, during the period of Assyrian empire (1200-600 BC), the Assyrian and the Phoenician traders took this tradition to Malabar coast by sea route, from where such type of few graves have been discovered. According to S.P. Gupta, Levent, Yemen in Arabia, Persian Gulf and Mesopotamia provide evidences of rock cut graves with shaft like entrance strikingly reminiscent of those of the Malabar coast. Hence, this is evident that Megalithic tradition came from Western Asia by sea route. Similarly, in addition to Megalithic tradition iron also came from the Gulf Region by the same route. Not only traders, but also Assyrian kings took active part in trade activities with South India. On the stone built stupa of Assyrian king shalmaneser III (860 BC) figure of elephant, ape and Bacterian camel may be noted still to-day. This proves trade relation of West-Asia and India and strengthens the theory of Western Asian origin of Megaliths and its transfer to India.

(2) After the break-up of Hittite power, as soon as, the secret of smelting of iron spread up in all directions, it reached India earlier than Megaliths that is why iron appears in Hallur in Pre-Megalithic context.

(3) The Megalith builders reached India, while gateway of eastern maritime trade, the Gulf Region,was captured by the Assyrian rulers (1000-800 BC) and trade activities extended to its maximum extent, as much as, the traders established their colonies on the Western Coast of India.

(4) Perhaps owing to furious attacks and capture of most of the Western Asia by Assyrian kings like Assur Nasirpal III (885-860 BC) some of Assyrians and Iranians began to flee towards India through North West passes, who appears in Swat Valley at about 900 BC. They joined their descendants of early Harappans of Naga race or Takshaka of North-West, who were already at war with the Aryan Pandavas, who added their strength with their strong war weapons manufactured from Iron and established Megalithic culture whereever they went.

(5) This discussion and conclusion will remain incomplete until and unless the following questions are answered : (a) who were Neolithic Chalcolithic people ? (b) who were fore-runners of Megalithic people who established Hallur culture ? (c) who were Megalithic people?

There were three notable mass movements of people from North India to South India, in the main, in prehistoric age: (a) While Alpine people reached Indus Valley from North as an invader (Cemetery H and G) in mature Harappan Age.; some of the early Harappans of Australoid and Dravidian type would have moved southward to save their life, which is evident from the beginning of Neolithic-Chalcolthic Age in Gujrat, Madhya Pradesh and Maharashtra at about 2000 B.C. . These were the people of Neolithic-Chalcolithic Age (Harappans)[45] who reached South India in between 2300-1000 BC and established there their culture. Carbon-14 date of this culture is 2300-1000 BC at Brahmagiri, Takalghat, Pikalihal and Ootnoor (See chapter IV PP-72- 73) This culture appears as pre-Hallur culture at Hallur.

(b) At about 1600 B. C., while Aryans invaded Harappan cities another second large wave of early Harappans, consisted of Australoid, Dravidians and Alpine (Yadavas) out of fear moved South ward. These people while reached Gujrat (at Lothal and Prabhasa) adopted B and R.

Ware pottery.[46] While, at the Western Coast of Arbian sea, owing to their maritime trade, contact with Western Asia (Dravidians were great traders) they learnt use of iron, since iron had come into common use between 1200-1000 BC in Western Asia.[47] These people reached Hallur at about 1000 BC as fore-runners of Megalithic people. That is why they appeared to have knowledge of B and R Ware pottery and iron both, who established themselves there in Pre-Megalithic context. This culture is known as Hallur culture.

(c) At about 1000 BC. Assyrians had captured Persian Gulf, known as gateway of eastern trade, henceforth trade activities of Assyrians and Jews extended to a great extent as far as they established their centres at Western coast of Central and South India (i) These people were, culturally and racially not much different from those of second earlier wave (b) i.e. Alpine and Dravidian. They brought tradition of Megalithic with them and adopted Hallur culture. Since they were advanced culturally, hence their tradition of Megalith was also adopted by Hallur people. They reached Hallur at about 1000 BC (ii) Due to heavy blow of raids conducted by Assyrian rulers on almost whole of Iran, some of the Iranians ran away and passed on to India through North-West passes, who built Megaliths in Swat Valley at about 900 B.C., who have left there evidences of Visage Urn with human face[48], who joined there Takshakas to strangthen their power.

Since, tentative date of Megalithic Culture in India is 800 B.C.-100 A. D., it seems Andhras[49] who were earlier in Afghanistan (Swat valley) reached Maharashtra in this period but before Mauryan Age. Hence it can be concluded that tradition of Megalithic took its birth in Western Asia and reashed India by sea and land routes.

References

1. (a) Gurdon P.R.T. "The Khasis" PP 138-39.
   (b) Piggott Stuart, "The Dawn of the Civilization" p-320.
2. Gupta S.P., "Disposal of the Dead and Physical types in Ancient India" P-11.
3. Ibid.
4. Gordon D. H., "The Prehistoric Back Ground of Indian Culture" PP 153-188.
5. Banerjee N. R., " Iron Age in India" PP Foreward IX and X.
6. Banerjee NR : PP-64.
7. Allchin B and R "The Birth of Indian Civilization" P. P. 229-30.
8. Gupta S P P-230.

9. Gupta S. P. PP-230-32.

10. Allchin B and R, "The Birth of Indian Civilization" PP-229-30.

11. Gupta S. P. PP-200-201.

12. Gupta S. P. P-144.

13. Childe V. G., "Megaliths" Ancient India No.4 (1947-48) P-12.

14. Childe V. G. P-12.

15. Gupta S. P. P-226.

16. Canton Thompson G., "The Tombs and Moon Temples of Huriedha (Hadhramaut) South Arabia" PP65 and 103 Mentioned by S. P. Gupta P-326.

17. Gupta S. P. P-226 footnote no 128 below.

18. Ruben Walter, "Eisenschmiede and Damonen in India ," International, Archiv Fuerethnographie Band XXXVII supplement, Leiden (1939) PP 154-58 Mentioned by Gupta S P P-225.

19. Haimendorf C. Von fuerer, "New Aspects of the Dravidian Problem" Tamil Culture Vol-II.

20. Fry P. Somerset, "History of the World" P-79.

21. Fry P. Somerset P-79.

22. Fry P. Somerset P-48.

23. According to Jacquetta Hawkes, Iron was discovered in 14 th and 15th century B. C. in Asia Minor. "The First Great civilization" P-113.

23. A Fry P. Somerset P-81.

24. Rawlison H. G., "Intercourse between India and the Western World" P-2.

25. Iyengar, P. T. S. "The trade of India"IIIQ II P-42.

26. Majumdar R. C., "The Age of Imperial unity" P-612.

27. Meissner, "Babylonian and Assyrian" I PP223-53.

28. Wilfred H. Schott, "The periplus of the Erythaeon sea" PP 123-60.

29. King, In Proceedings of the society of Biblical Archaeology (1909) PP-339-43.

30. Thomson "A Dictionary of Assyrian Botony" (1949) PP-106-07.

31. Rawlison H G. PP 2-3.

32. (a) Zimmer, "The Art of Indian, Asian" P-49.

(b) Turner R "The Great cultural tradition" Vol-I P-39.

(c) Buhler G, "Indian Palaeography" PP 31-32.

33. Vishwanath S. V. "Racial Synthesis in Hindu culture" P-62.

34. Reo Vishweshar Nath, "Rigved Par EK Itihasik Drishti" P-236.

35. Kennedy, "The gospels of Infancy, the Lalit vistara and Vishnu Purana or the transmission of Religious legends between India and West." Journal of Royal Asiatic society (1917) P-237.
36. Iyengar P.T.S., I.H.O. Vol-II P-42.
37. Iyengar PP-42-43.
38. Sastri KN Nilkant "Age of the Nanda and Mauryas" P-440.
39. Allchin B and R P-230.
40. Gupta S. P. P-228.
41. Gupta S P. PP 236-37.
42. Gupta S. P. PP-237-38.
43. Gupta S. P.- PP238-39.
44. Lal B. B.. "From Megalithic to the Harappa; Tracing back the Graffito on the pottery" AI. XVI (1960) PP 4-24.
45. Madan Mohan Singh, "Puratatva Ki Ruprekha" P-183.
46. Rao S. R., "Lothal and the Indus Civilization" P-54.
47. Hawkes Jacquetta P-113.
48. Gupta SP PP 263-64.
49. Jayaswal KP "Hindu polity" P-130.

Chapter 4

The Civilizations of the Dark Age and Megalithic Culture; An Archaeological Review

The period from the downfall of Indus-Valley Civilization up to the pre-Buddhist age ie between 1700 B.C. and 600 B.C., has been called the dark-age by some historians. But archaeological researches of modern age have enlightened this period to a great extent, we find rise and fall of many cultures of India in this age. During the Harappan period, there was existence of culture of Neolithic-Chalcolithic Age in North-West India. Similarly in Maharashtra and Southern India, the form of this culture was also Neolithic-Chalcolithic Age, which was inter-related with the Harappan culture and belonging to the Dravidian people. The period of this culture is up to 1000 B.C. in general. Later begins the Iron (Megalithic) Age. The beginning period of the Megalithic-Iron Age is accepted to be 1000 B. C. and development period up to the pre-Buddhist Age. During this period (1700-600 B.C.) archaeologists have traced out so many other cultures also such as ochre-coloured pottery (OCP), Black and Red Wares, (B and R Wares) Grey ware (G W) and Painted Grey ware (PGW) and North Black polished ware (NBPW). The Neolithic-Chalcolithic culture was developed by the Dravidian speaking people. In this way, all these cultures of dark age, closely follow one after the other.

The Sequence of the Cultures in India

The Indus Valley :

The ancient history of India, was all of a sudden pushed back by a period of about two and a half thousand years from the life time of Buddha, while the department of archaeological survey of India explored the great culture of Indus valley lying underneath the remains of Mohenjodaro and Harappa. This was the culture of aborginal Dravidians of this land. These aboriginals were using the Burnished Red wares and living in beautiful multi-storyed Pucca houses. The scholars have fixed the life time of this culture between 2700-1700 B. C.. We have given detailed description of this culture in the first volume of this series or earlier volume.

Sequence of Cultures in Northern India

Name Of The Culture	The Period of existence	The Important sites
1. Indus Valley	2700-1700 BC	Mohenjodaro, Harappa, Kalibanga, Lothal, Chanhudaro
2. Ochre Coloured Pottery (OCP)	1700-1500 BC	Nagar, Dhaderi, Katpalon, Sanghol, Bara, Rupar
3. Black and Red Ware Culture (B and R ware)	2400-100 BC	About at all sites in Gujrat, Maharashtra and all South, South-East of Uttar Pradesh and Rajasthan
4. Grey Ware Culture (G W)	1600-1500 BC	Manda, Nagar, Dhaderi, Katpalon, Bhagwanpur
(5) Painted Grey Ware (PGW)	1500-800 BC	Bhagwanpur, Rupar, Alamgir, Hastinapur, Ahichhatra, Atranjikhera Jodhpura, Nuh, Allahpur
6. North Black Polished Ware (NBPW)	550-50 BC	Takshila, Tamarluk, Amaravati, Pauni Atranjikhera, Vaisali Malhar,

In this way, from the aforesaid archaeological study of cultural stratification, we can derive a cultural sequence of different civilizations, belonging to the period. It begins with the Indus Valley Civilization and ends with the historical period (2700 BC-50 BC) as follows : Harappan Culture, Ochre Coloured Pottery, Black and Red Ware Culture, Grey Ware, Painted Grey Ware and North Black Polished Ware.[1]

It is to be noted that Black and Red wares have been found out among the cultures which developed in Gangetic Velley and in Megalithic culture, which developed in Vidarbha region of Maharashtra and South. Black and Red wares of Megalithic age developed in Gangetic Valley later than the Ochre coloured pottery and earlier to PGW.

The South and the Central Indian Cultures of Chalcolithic Age : (Ahar, Kayatha, and Malava)

The remains of Chalcolithic culture have been recovered from the excavation of Ahar and Gelund sites of Bana valley in Rajasthan.[2] The date of this culture is 2000 BC-500 BC. Later it was occupied by the 'Iron Age People'. The latest Carbon date of Kalibanga has been calculated to be 1500 B.C. It means Harappan culture survived there later, for a period of about 300 years. In this way Harappan culture of Kalibanga and Chalcolithic culture of Ahar lived contemporarily for a long period of about 700 years (2000 BC-1300 BC). The date 1725 BC, derived by the Tata Institute of Technology Bombay, is also not less contemporary. Since the carbon dates of Eran (Distt Sagar in Madhya Pradesh), Navadatoli (Distt Nimad in Madhya Pradesh), Nevasa (Distt Ahmad Nagar), Songaon, Inamgaon Chandoli (Distt Pune M.R.) etc have been fixed within the second millenium B.C. From this it has become clear that Chalcolithic culture developed in the South and the Central India[3] during the last period of Harappan culture or last phase of some sites or just after.

In this age, the successive development of three cultures of Kayatha, Malava and Jorve is also evident. The Sāvalda culture of Tāpti valley is of some specific type, but it is similar to Kayathā culture. Remains of whatever Chalcolithic culture have come to hands from Maheshwara and Navadatoli (9 km South of Indore) lying in between Ujjain and Indore, has been named as Mālava culture. On a later date, from excavation of Kāyathā (on the bank of Kali Sindh) we have come to know about a rich Chalcolithic culture, which developed a few centuries (about 2000 BC) earlier than the Mālava culture. Ahār, Kāyathā and Mālavā cultures are so similar that it will be justified to call them fundamentally one culture. The Ahar and the Kāyathā cultures should be taken as parent cultures of Malava.[4]

Owing to fixation of carbon-14 date[5] of Malva culture between 1660 $\pm$ 130 and 1445 $\pm$ 130 BC, period of its origin has been decided 1500 BC. (Aggarwal-1971). Evidences of extension of this culture from the region of Ujjain and Navadatoli up to the Tapti and onward up to the Bhima valley, has been noted from the excavation of Chandoli, Songaon and Inamgaon[6]

The Jorve Culture

The Jorve culture, found from the district of Ahmadnagar, is Chalcolithic in character. Evidences have been noted that this culture had extended from Pune in the West, up to Amaravati in the east, and in the North from Khandesh, up to the upper valley of the Krishna river in South. The main centres of Jorve Culture Prakasha in the Tapti valley Dāyamabad in the Pravar–Godavari valley, and Ināmagaon in the Bheema valley, are most notable. Its carbon-14 date has been fixed between 1500-700 B. C. This culture suppressed Andhra and Karnataka Cultures in south (Krishna Godavari valley) and the Malava culture in north in about 1200 B. C.[7]

The Neolithic-Chalcolithic Culture in Eastern India

In archaeological excavations, conducted in the Eastern zone of India, evidences of Chalcolithic culture have been recovered from the remains of earlier layer of North Black polished wares. Evidences of Neolithic culture have also been found out from Kuchāi in Orissa. From carbon-14 dating process, the beginning period of Neolithic culture of Chirand has been brought out 2400-2300 B.C. and the ending period 1700 B.C. Later on, Chalcolithic Age begins. Afterwards, the people of this culture in particular began the use of B and R wares (Polished and Unpolished both). The remains of Chalcolithic Age culture have been recovered in Bihar from Oriyapa and Sonpur and in Western Bengal from Pandu-Rajar-Dhibi, Mahish-Dal and Haraipur. From carbon-14 dating technique, the Chalcolithic age of Chirand has been fixed at 1700-1000 B. C. Later appears the phase of Iron Age (II B)[8]. In the third phase appears the Black polished wares.

In this way the sequence of evolution of cultures in Eastern India can be ascertained like this :

Neolithic culture contemporary to Harappan culture, Chalcolithic culture, pre-Iron Age NBPW and later NBPW.[9]

In South, Neolithic age continued up to 1000 B.C. Last form of this Culture was Neolithic-Chalcolithic, then begins the age of Megalithic culture. There are very clear evidences of use of iron among the remains of Megalithic culture in South India at Maski, NagarjunKonda, Amaravati and Yelleswaram etc. and in Vidarbha region of Maharashtra at Mahurjhari; Junapani; Khapa, Takalghat etc. From this, it is evidently proved that the people of Megalithic culture and Iron Age culture were one. The beginning period of Iron Age-Megalithic culture has been fixed at 1000 BC[10].

In this way, ancient human culture by and by remained developed from the Harappan Age upto the Pre-Buddhist Age. As a result of coming of Aryans in Northern India, the indigenous Pre-Aryan culture and Aryan culture were affected and mixed up with each other to some extent. Similarly, progressive local indigenous cultures developed all over India and from them Iron Age culture came into being.

The Megalithic Culture

The Mode of Disposal of Dead, Aryan and Non-Aryan

As a matter of principle, Aryans used to cremate their dead bodies, whereas native non-Aryans used to bury them. But Vedas contain description of both types of funeral rites i.e. burial and cremation. Later Sanskrit scriptures also have description of both of them. Scholars are of the view that there was tradition of both types of funeral rites among ancient Aryan society, but in later period the burial system came to an end.

But in the beginning, among the ancestors of Aryans, burial system was only in vogue. Graves of the original inhabitants of India were of different type than the Aryan's. According to Satpath Brahmana (XIII-8-1), there were two types of burials viz Vedic and non-Vedic, designated as Daivya and Asura. A burial should not be built too soon after the death, but when people forget the year of the death. Clearly it shows secondary burial viz the memorial and not the primary inhumation. According to this practice, no memorial is erected on the grave of complete inhumation. The verse further tells the burial monument of Aryans (gods) should be of four corner and those of Asuras round shaped. Another verse (VIII-8)[11] of Brahmna gives outline of clear distinguishable difference between the two types : the Vedic people make their sepulchral monuments so as not to be separate from the earth while Asuras make them so as to be separate from the earth either on a stone basis or a similar thing. Hence the pit burials are classified as Aryan and cist burials as Asura or non-Aryan. On this classification, S. P. Gupta puts forth his own comments,[12] "Now, how to reconcile with the situation in which both the urn burials and pit burials appear as Aryan customs. Probably, the Vedic practice often involved reburial, i.e. the primary burial was of the ashes in urns and secondary burial involved emptying the ashes from the urns into pits or over the ground. It is further stated that a cairn of stones was raised over the bones thus taken out of the urns and that its height differed according to the caste and sex of the deceased but higher than the height of the dead." Although above interpretation creates confusion yet one indication is quite clear that non-Aryan Asuras practised urn or cist burial and Aryan pit burial. Later Aryans discontinued the practice of burial at all, and instead adopted cremation.

It can be further clarified that since Aryans believed in the theory of immortality of soul, hence they were not builders. That is why they did not raise any Megaliths etc on their graves in the memory of their deceased persons. That is why all the (memorial) buildings of note belong to non-Aryans and literature to Aryans.

The Aryans not Builders

As highlighted above, this is very interesting to note that the Aryans were not builders. Up to the Gupta age they did not build even their religious buildings or temples since temple of Bhitari near Kanpur, which is said to be their earliest work, was built during Gupta period. What was the reason behind it ? James Fergusson answers this question[13] in a most admirable manner :

"As I have frequently had the occasion to point out in another work (History of Architecture, Introduction, et pussim) the Aryan races are not builders. They always had too firm a conviction of the immortality of the soul, and consequently of the existence of a future state, ever to care much for a brick or stone immortality in this world; and no material art satisfied the cravings of their higher intellectual powers. The Turanians (He had a misleading veiw, that non-Aryan Nagas were Turanians which has been discarded by the modern researchers) on the contrary, never rose to a distinct idea of an external god, nor of a future state, but supplied the place of the latter by metempsychosis and final annihilation, while their intellectual status never enabled them to create such a literature as would satisfy that hankering after immortality which is inherent in the human breast. It consequently happens that all the literature of India belongs to the Aryan or Sanskrit speaking races, and all the buildings to the Turanians or those speaking Dravidian or Cognate tongues. The result of this distinction, in so far as the present subject is concerned, is this; so long as the Aryans retained their purity of blood and supremacy of power, no permanent buildings were erected in India. On the other hand, if there is one fact with reference to Buddhism more clear than another, it is that it is the religion of a Turanian (Dravidian) race. It was not a reform on the Vedic religion of the Aryans, but simply that when they had lost their purity. .... It was when these Turanians (Dravidians) first came in to power that permanent architecture was thought of in India". The above viewpoint of Fergusson is most convincing, rather perfect. Hence, it is clear that Aryans were not builders; then how they can be held responsible for raising of Megaliths, on the contrary Dravidian speaking people were great builders.

There are still today numerous magnificent temples in South India standing as evidence. They adopted Buddhism and built Buddhist stupas at places like Amaravati, Sanchi, Pauni and Bharhut etc, we will throw light on this subject in following lines.

In Rigveda, we find description of cremation only, on the other hand among ancient Iranians, (Harappan cemeterries H and G) there was a different tradition of disposal of their dead bodies. They[14] first used to expose their dead bodies to be devoured by the birds and animals, later only the skulls and few long bones were selected and were placed in a funeral jar for deposition in the cemeteries. But the Dravidian people, as is evident from the cemetery R-37, had the tradition of burying their dead bodies in which for heavenly life of dead, personal ornaments and a large property of pots, eatables like flesh of fouls and animals were also buried with them.[15] The early Harappan related to the cemetery R-37 and Alpine related to cemetery H-I and G. Both adopted the pottery of B and R wares in Gujrat and mixed up with each other.[16]

After their decisive defeat and having been chased out by the Nordic Aryan invaders, they moved Southward , a large group of them followed the Coastal route and reached as far as far South to settle there, where they founded civilization similar to that of Harappan in Maski and Brahmagiri, where they carried B and R wares with them. There in about 1000 BC, they manufactured goods like beads and chank articles and some terracotta figurines and buried their dead bodies following the tradition of cemeteries R37 and H-II[17] i.e. they buried remains of their dead bodies in urns after they had been devoured by the birds and animals.[18]

It has been stated earlier that the period of reaching of B and R ware in the South, is about 1200-1000 B. C.[19] This is also the period of beginning of 'Megalithic and Iron Age culture' in India. It is indicative from this, that they were the people, who gave birth to "Megalithic Iron Age culture" though impetus was derived from other sources which have been explained in earlier chapter III.

In Central and Southern India, the people of aforesaid culture, began to raise large stones on the graves of their dead simply to make their memory immortal or to give them honour,which is known as Megaliths or Megalithic culture. This is to be noted that the people who used Black and Red ware, were also using Megalithic graves for burying their dead bodies We will give detailed description of Black and Red ware culture in Chapter IX. Here we take only Megaliths for consideration.

Etymology

The Megalithic cemeteries are most important remains of dead bodies of that period. The meaning of the word, "Megalith" in English language is 'big stone'.[20] This word has constituted from the Greek word 'Megas' and 'liths'. 'Megas' means big and 'liths' means stone. It means cemeteries which consisted of big stone slabsare known as 'Megaliths'.

Famous archaeologist, Wheeler,[21] has given another interpretation of the word Megaliths- "Memorials constructed of rough, unhewn big stone pieces raised for burying the dead bodies or for their memory or both." Such memorials can be accepted to be related to cremation or burial of any religious tradition. It is possible that in the beginning these megaliths were built for burial of dead bodies and later in the form of memorial. This tradition of Megaliths later developed into stupas the effect of which is visible in Buddhist age and in later period also. Along with the remains of dead bodies have been found the remains of poultry and other animals, in the Megalithic burials of Junapani, similar to that of Harappan cemetery R-37 and H-II which are related to Dravidian people.[22] This evidence strengthens the viewpoint that Megalithic tradition was definitely affected by the Indus Valley people. This viewpoint has been accepted by B.B. Lal also.[23]

Type of Megaliths

S. P. Gupta and K. P. Rao[24] have divided the Megaliths into six categories :

(1) Pit burial

(2) Cist burial

(3) Dolmenoid cists,

(4) Rock-cut chambers,

(5) Sarcophagus, and

(6) Urn burials.

(1) Pit burials

Pit burial is the simplest mode of disposing the dead. The skeletal remains and other funerary assemblage are kept in a pit specially dug out for this purpose which is then filled with earth and cairn packing. Sometimes the pits are found sealed by huge cap-stones. The pit may be of varying dimensions and depth.

(2) Cist burials

These are box-like constructions made of stone slabs, essentially under the surface of the earth. The slabs of the cist are arranged in such a manner that the slabs support each other from internal collapse. Various sub-types occur depending on the constructional pattern, and these can be discussed under various heads as given below.

(i) Square and rectangualr cists without slab projections :

Cists with slabs arranged perfectly square or rectangular without any projecting orthostats come under this category.

(ii) Oblong cists :

These are cists with projecting orthostats on either side, between which the smaller orthostats are fixed. This type of cist has its orthostats on longer axis projecting beyond the smaller orthostats which are fixed between these two projecting parallel orthostats.

(iii) Svastika-Patterned cists :

In this type are included cists with their orthostats arranged in svastika pattern, either clockwise or anti-clockwise. Four orthostats are used with each slab projecting on one side beyond the next slab which is arranged in a right angle to it. The covering slab is provided above these orthostats.

(iv) Transepted cists :

The cist divided into two or more chambers by insertion of dividing slabs in the cist is known as transepted cist. As these sub-chambers are separated from the chamber with port-hole, access is usually provided through port-holes to the dividing slabs also.

(3) Dolmenoid cists

Dolmenoid cists are chambers built of stone slabs resembling cists which are partially buried and partially exposed above the ground, capped by a stone slab. They resemble in every sense the cists except that some portion of their chamber is intentionally built above the ground level. Constructional method may vary leading to their classification under two main types.

(i) Dolmenoid cists without projecting orthostats

(ii) Dolmenoid cists in svastika pattern.

Dolmenoid cists are sometimes provided with a port- hole to one of the orthostats and there may also be found a passage adjoining the chamber in some cases. These are found at Kemjhar Distt Chandrapur, at Chāmirshi Distt Garh-Chirouli and Kheri, Nipani, Pipalgaon etc.

(4) Rock-Cut chambers

Under this category come the underground chambers excavated in rock to house the skeletal remains of the dead and other assemblage. Access to these chambers is provided generally through a circular aperture at the top, which is sealed by a cap-stone. Skeletal remains are placed directly on the floor or in a sacophagus. such a chamber has been found out at Kondanisseri at Cochiṇ

(5) Sarcophagus burials

Sarcophagus is a coffin for placement of skeletal remains and other funerary assemblage. These coffins are made of different materials and can accordingly be divided into three sub-types.

(i) Terracotta sarcophagus with/without legs

(ii) Stone sarcophagus

(iii) Wooden sarcophagus.

(6) Urn burials

Earthen pots used for the deposition of skeletal remains and other assemblage found buried below the ground are called urn burials. These urns are generally sealed by a lid and protected by cap-stone and cairn packing. In later Magalithic age, instead of dead body only bones were buried. In historical age, this tradition had a great effect on Buddhist culture as the valuable ashes of Buddhist monks kept in pots were placed in Stupas.

Protective and memorial markings

The various types of Megalithic burials discussed above are protected from all sorts of danger, whether natural, human or due to animals, by providing lithic appendages. In providing such appendages the main aim was not only to protect the burial but also to demarcate and erect a memorial to mark the place. For this purpose the Megalithic people devised various methods of erecting such monuments as can be discussed under following heads :[25]

(1) Stone circles

Huge dressed or undressed boulders arranged on ground forming a circle enclosing a burial constitute this class. The number of boulders used and the diameter vary from circle to circle. Inside this circle is often filled with cairn packing and such circles are known as cairn circles.

(2) Slab circles

Slabs planted in concentric circle around a burial come under this category. These slabs usually have trimmed edges on sides as well as tops.

(3) Cairn burials

A heap of rubble, quarried or in natural form, over a burial is known as barrow or cairn burial. Here, the main reason for providing the cairn packing appears to be the protection of the burial lying below. Below these cairns are usually found urns, sarcophagi or simple pit burials. Such burials are found at Raipur, Hingan in the West of Nagpur.

(4) Dolmens

Stone slabs or boulders arranged in a square or rectangular plan supporting a cap-stone, the whole construction being above the ground known as dolmen. Below these dolmens are found other types of burials like cists, sarcophagi or urn burials. As these dolmens are above the ground and do not contain any funerary material, these can be included in the group of memorial markings.

(5) Menhirs and anthropomorphlic representations

A huge dressed or undressed stone erected vertically over or near a burial is known as Menhir. These menhirs may be very rude in their form without any shape or may be dressed to represent some anthropomorphic form. These menhirs neither enclose a burial nor protect it and hence can be considered as memorial monuments. Such examples are visible at Pānchgaon in district Nagpur on Umred road and also near Panchkheri on Kuhi Mandal Road.

The Evolution and the Distribution of Main centres of Megaliths in India

There are six main centres of Megaliths in India viz (1) Swat valley and Kashmir (2) Baluchistan and Sindh (3) Kathiavar (4) S. E. region of Uttarapradesh or Vindhya (5) Vidarbha region of Maharashtra (6) South India. (See Map No. II and VI)

From the situation of aforesaid centres of Megaliths, we can very easily calculate the route of their movement from the West i.e. from the Megalithic Centre of Iran through the route of passes of North West, they reached Swat Valley near Takshila, than Baluchistan and Sindh, which was ancient centre of Vahika or Taka Naga race known as Pātālpuri. They onward moved from Sindh and reached Kathiavar, which has been the centre of Saura Nagas whose name still exists in Saurashtra. From there onward, one of their offshoot branch reached south-east region of Uttarpradesh or Vindhya, where their fourth main centre of Megaliths was established. This branch reached as far as Bengal. Magadha, later became their main centre, where Buddha and Jain religions took their birth.

A part of their main branch, on the other hand, moved Southward from Kathiavar and reached Vidarbha region of Maharashtra and established there another largest fifth centre of Megaliths, which was in ancient time known as Naga-Bhumi (See chapter XIV P 393-94) or land of Nagas. A very high number of Megalithic sites have been traced out in the Nagpur region. A part of this branch, came in contact with the other second branch, in coastal land which had directly come by sea route for trading purpose. They further, perhaps jointly, moved Southward following the route of Malabar coast. In South, these people met with their another third most advanced branch, which had directly reached earlier by sea route on account of trade activities. Here they established southernmost sixth centre of Megaliths and adopted Hallur culture, which was readily available there and added much to the tool technology of Hallur culture. We know Hallur people reached here with iron and B and R wares both. People, who came by sea racially and culturally, were not much different from the later Harappans. Although this movement account is based on speculation but fits admirably well with the archaeology, particularly accounted for at Hallur site proper. (See P- 72 and chapter III PP 51-52). However, the race which reached by sea route from the Persian Gulf,was long headed (brachy cephalic) in the main and which came through the North-West passes, was round headed Alpine and long headed (dolicho-cephalic) Dravidian and their admixture race.

Kashmir and Swat Valley

Burzahom was the main centre of Megaliths in Kashmir valley from where skeletal remains of a dead body have been recovered from a Megalithic grave. According to excavator T. N. Khajanchi, it is clear that relation of dead body could not be established with the Menhirs. Menhirs have been recovered from one place of District Anantnag in Kistwar Valley also.[26]

The Swat Valley Graves have been excavated by several Italian (stacul) missions and Pakistani expeditions (Dani). By now more than a dozen cemeteries have come to light. Some of the important cemeteries explored so far are located near Timargarha, Thana, Butkara Loebanr and Katelae.[27]

The following chronological chart and periodization of the graves, based mainly upon C-14 dates are self explanatory :

Iron Age	Period III 900-600 BC	It is characterized by post exposure burials and post cremation burials, Iron implements were found

× × ×	× × ×	(Break (?)
Copper Age	Period II (1200-1000 BC)	It is characterized by post cremation burials in urn. Copper objects were found
	Period-I (1600-1300 BC)	It is characterized by complete inhumations, copper objects found.

It is clear from the period III that these newcomer people were Iranians since post exposure burial is an Iranian characteristic, post cremation may have been tradition of later population. These Iranians were the first to introduce Iron. This was the centre of Takshak Naga people, their capital was Takshila.

Were the Cemeteries of Swat Valley Aryans ?

Now the question arises whether the cemeteries of Swat Valley belong to Vedic period or of later Sanskrit literature period ? Historians have decided the period of these cemeteries between 1500-400 B.C. In this way they show their relation with the whole of the time while Sanskrit scriptures were composed. S. P. Gupta[28] gives detailed description of cemeteries of Aryan and non-Aryan type—

"The cemetery of Timargarha, which is partly the oldest in the series, is supposed to reflect the burial customs of the Rigveda. Unfortunately it has primarily yielded pit circles erected over rectangular pits lined with stones. Clearly, in spite of the fact that there were no cists or urns for the bones, the pit was lined with stones and the bones were protected from getting in touch with the earth. The Rigveda does not support this evidence. In the light of the references in the Satapatha Brahmana, the position becomes more strange. The Swat Valley sepulchral monuments are, therefore, both Aryan and non-Aryan at one and the same time. It is impossible. As far as the actual disposal of the dead body is concerned, according to Stacul, the excavator, burial and cremation both were known and practised. However according to Dani (Timargarha and Gandhara Grave- Culture "Ancient Pak Vol-III-P-47) cremation appeared later in period II."

It is crystal clear from the evidences found from the exploration of cemeteries that they were not completely Aryans. It means there was a non-Aryan element too, which used stone slabs for lining the pit, in round shaped cemeteries, just to avoid the touch of dead bodies with the earth. I am of this view that non-Aryan element consisted of long headed Mediterranean and round headed Alpine or their admixture, who before coming of Aryans were spread up in a large area from the eastern coast of the Mediterranean sea up to the East and Northern part of Iran,[29] who built Megaliths in a large part of Iran, likewise Palestinian and Israelites did in their own land. But owing to Aryan threat from North, they moved east and southward and settled in Swat valley in the afore-said land[30]. There are strong evidences in support. S.P. Gupta[31] puts forth a clear account of their presence, "During this unusually long period, (1600-400 BC) the people practised cremation, complete Inhumation and Fractional Burial. Their sepulchral monuments included, stone circles, pits lined with stones, and urns. Interestingly enough, some of the graves, called "Mixed Burials" contained the skeletal remains and offerings of two different periods. In the Indian context, these are unique. Similarly, some of the burial urns with human facial features, called 'Visage Urns'are rare in India. They are reported either from a few Palestinian caves of the 4th millennium B. C. (Anati E., "Palestine Before the Hebrews) or from Khurab, Bampur and Katukan in the Persian Makran of the 2nd 1st millennia BC.''

It is evidently clear that graves and mode of disposal of dead of Assyrian Nagas were quite different from those of Aryans and were close to Iranian and Palestinian type called 'Visage Urns.'

Megalithic centre of Sindh is known as Pātālpuri which was centre of Vahika or Takshak Nagas as noted by the historians[32] of Alexander while going back or retreating by sea route. This Pātālpuri has been referred in the Mahabharata accounts too as centre of Nagas.

The third centre of Megaliths in Kathiavar was the well known centre of Yadavas of Mahabharata fame, where Krishna, the black hero of Yadavas lived in Dwarika. These Yadavas were round headed Iranian belonging to Naga race. (see chapter IX PP 237-39 for detail). Saurastra is named after Saura or Chera Naga race of this land.

South-Eastern Region of Uttar Pradesh (Vindhya)

In the, South-Eastern region of present Uttar-Pradesh or Vindhya Megalithic sites have been excavated by G. R. Sharama and A. K. Narayan. Sharma has excavated site of Kakoria situated in district Banaras. He has mentioned the period of these sites between 1700 –1500[33] B. C. and placed them in Neolithic Chalcolithic Age, other well known sites are Banimilia, Bahera, Chunar, Kotia, Khera, Satmas, Dausa etc.

Kakoria

The importance of this site lies in the fact that it has both cemetery and habitational area. According to excavater G. R. Sharma,[34] "The habitational deposit at this site is about 1.40 metre thick. The entire accumulation is of a single cultural complex, however it has been divided into three phases (A) The earliest phase is characterized by Microliths, such as blades, lunates and points, ill fired red wares and mud-houses, out of which only two were excavated. (B) The second middle phase yielded in addition to the above material excepting the rooms a copper ring, sling stones, pestles, beads of stone and terracotta and crested-ridge blades (c) The last third uppermost phase is marked by the continuance of phase B material, but of an inferior workmanship. This level, although yielded four copper pieces and some beads including etched carnelian ones. Iron has not been encountered in any of the trenches.''

The pottery, on whose basis this site has been dated, belongs to the Chalcolithie period,which includes Red ware, Black ware and Black and Red ware, which resembles that at Sonpur and Chirand in Bihar and Chalcolithic sites of Malava, Rajputana and the Deccan. According to Sharma, some of the types survived in the modified forms are in the Painted Grey and NBP wares (IAR 1962-63 P-41).

Of the twelve graves opened, there were eight Pit Cairns and four Cist cairns; the stone-circles round the cairns were not very well marked. In one instance, a pit was found with in pit which resembles those found from Brahmagiri[35]

From another site, named Banimilia-Bahera Tehsil Chunar, have been found out similar type of pottery, other goods and life of people which is not much different from that of Kakoria[36].

Kotia

This site is situated in district Allahabad, at the bank of river Belan. Only five graves have been dug out, out of about 300 graves in the cemetery. Of these four are Cist-Cairns and one is Pit-Cairn. From aforesaid grave remains of human dead bodies have been recovered in a very limited number but bones of domesticated animals like pigs, sheep and cattle have been recovered in a very large number[37].

The pottery they yielded includes Black and Red ware and coarse Grey ware. They include types like hollow and solid pedestal, sharply carinated cooking vessels, knobbed lids, large elliptical Jars, bowls with ledged shoulder etc. Some of these types particularly the cooking vessels have no parallels at Kakoria or Banimilia-Bahera. The graves at Kotia have yielded a number of Iron implements which include types like adzes, spearheads, sickles and arrow–heads.[38]

These sites of cairns in the Vindhya region of Uttarpradesh and Rajasthan are at present difficult to date. They, however, seem to be nearer to the Kotia cairns of the Iron Age than the Kakoria graves of the

Chalcolithic period.[39] However, it is quite clear that inhabitants of these sites were successors of late Harappans who used B and R wares as they used in Vidarbha region and in South India.

In this region, Megalithic culture flourished in Neolithic Age between 1500-700 BC. This period is earlier than North and South Indian Megalithic Culture which begins in 1000 BC. Naga Culture of later period also flourished in this region.

The Megalithic sites of Southern India

Some of the important sites of Southern India are as under : Brahmagiri, Jadganhalli, Maski Halingali, Hanur Hallur, Sanur, Kannathur, Yelleswaram, Nagarjun Konda, Kesarpalli etc.

Brahmagiri

In 1946, Wheeler[40] excavated the site of Brahmagiri in South India, from where remains of Neolithic-Chalcolithic culture has been recovered. Brahmagiri is in the region of Molakalmaru in district Durg of Mysore state. Inscription No-1 of Ashoka emperor has been recovered from the village of Sidhapur of this region.

In excavation of Brahmagiri have been recovered three cultures which developed here. They are as under[41]:

(1) Neolithic Culture

(2) Megalithic Culture

(3) Andhra-Satavāhana culture

No gap could be traced out in between these cultures. Hence, it can be surmised that these cultures developed one after the other without any break.

After the Neolithic age, while Megalithic age began, earlier culture was not destroyed but both ran parallel for some time. In the long run later culture became prominent leaving the earlier behind. Similarly while Andhra Satavahana culture came into existence, this culture developed parallel with the Megalithic for some time. Neolithic-Chalcolithic culture also has been traced out at Pikalihal, Utnoor, Tekkalkota etc. Their carbon-14 date has been determined 2300-1000 B. C. Therefore date of Brahmagiri-I will also be the same.[42]

In the later period, there is deposit of Megalithic culture, which is absolutely an Iron Age culture. It is spreading, in the south of Vindhya region, generally from the Nagpur region of Vidarbha upto far South and there are evidences of uniformity of this culture, on all the sites, since there is Black and Red ware culture along with remains of Iron Age culture i.e. availability of different iron weapons and appliances, which is one of the peculiarity of this culture. S. P. Gupta produces detail of grave goods recovered in excavation,[43] "There are 300 graves in the cemetery of Brahmagiri and two types of Megalithic graves i.e. stone cist circle and pit circles have been recovered. Cist circles are stone circles bounding in each case a fully under ground cist. These cists were made of granite slabs 1.60 to 2.20 metres long, 2 metres broad and 5 to 10 cm thick. They were always arranged in the Swastika pattern clockwise or anti clockwise, the device made them self-supporting. The floor was paved with one or more slabs and the top was covered with another slab, which is called capstone, generally 30 c.m. thick and 5 metres across. In addition to these big cists, the cemetery consisted of a large number of small cists erected almost on the surface of ground. It seems that big cists belonged to rich or important families of the village, while the smaller one belonged to the masses. This shows a social gradation in the society. But this gradation does not mean social segregation because large and small cists are found existing side by side. One such cist was containing offering pots anywhere between 6 and 62 in number. The iron objects, stone-beads and terracotta spindle whorls etc found with them were generally not more than half a dozen. The bones were of post exposure nature. Since these Megaliths were collective burials, the skulls and long bones often account for four to six person."

Such type of burial system has been traced out in Harappan cemeteries H and G which were pre-Aryan and Iranian, introduced by Alpine race, where remains of dead bodies were buried after their exposure and placing the skulls and long bones in a urn.

The Rouletted wares (Andhra-Satavahana Age Wares)

The third period of Brahmagiri is related to Andhra-Satavahana Culture. The important aspect of this culture is its well developed pottery known as Rouletted wares, such type of wares have been found out from Arikamedu also. From this pottery not only dates of Brahmagiri but of all sites of South India, have been fixed. Generally pots of such type were being made in all the countries of Mediterranean sea during the first and second century AD. Therefore the date of Andhra culture has been fixed from 1st century to 3rd century A.D.[44]

Halingali

This site is located near the town Halingali, District Bijapur in Mysore. It was excavated by A. Sundra (IAR 1965-66). This place is known for Greek-cross Megaliths or the plan of a house with a long entrance or passage. Some of these houses are constructed with sand stone slabs. They have multiple chambers with a primary axial corridor or alley and coursed dry bond construction of the enclosure. Of the four Megaliths Sundra dug, two are most[45] important.

The pillared cairn (Meg IV) monument is simple but it is important for the potteries it has yielded. They included both the Neolithic Chalcolithic Gray Ware sherds and the pots of Hallur (Megaliths) red ware[46].

The Hallur Culture

This was excavated by Nag Rajan Rao. In South India, this culture was found at Payampalli, Tekkalkota and Hallur. Because complex of this culture was first located in a habitational context of the highest antiquity at Hallur (1000 BC), we have called it the Hallur[47] culture. Homogeneity in the material culture from Indian Megaliths has however been due to some other reason also; before the arrival of the Megalithic builders in South India throughout the Western peninsula there was a post Neolithic-Chalcolithic culture called the Hallur Culture; which was Characterized by the presence of the B and R ware both plain and painted and iron implements. The immigrant, Megalith builders, wherever and whenever, went to South India, found only this complex which they readily adopted. The date of Hallur culture is 1000 BC[48]. The Megalithic culture of South India seems similar to Hallur culture in character.

(1) The Environment :

The environment of the cemeteries in which the graves were laid, is generally marked by an ancient irrigation tank, cultivated paddy fields and high barren rocky ground over which the Megaliths were raised. It seems that the people in the past might also have been engaged in rice cultivation and tank irrigation. This is proved by the types of iron implements found in the graves which include a number of hoes, sickles, billhooks, plough shares[49] etc.

The Megalithic structures were often imposing heavy and well chiselled stones, such construction required a large number of hands skilled and unskilled. They were, therefore, founded either by a professional class of people round the year and this was a flourishing trade or collectively by all the able-bodied persons of the village only in certain seasons of the year when they had practically no work in the fields[50] or workshops. However structural peculiarities do imply the existence of a cadre of skilled persons more closely concerned with the structures than the common man. This was, of course, over and above their usual agricultural or other pursuits of everyday life.[51]

S. P.Gupta gives detailed account of grave goods findings[52], "The graves goods, apart from pottery, included about forty types of iron tools, weapons, house hold goods, ornamental pieces etc. The objects of bronze with incised and moulded decorations, and gold beads diadems are also of more than a dozen types. Conch shells and shell beads and discs with incised decorations, some terracotta bulls (/) etc, have also been reported from them. These objects show on the one hand a well developed metallurgy of iron, copper and bronze and on the other hand the agro–nomadic pattern of the life of the people, because the iron artefacts include not only agricultural implements but also weapons of war and chase e. g. lances, dirks, sword, spearheads, arrowheads. The bones of the horse, iron stirrups, horse-bits and ornamental copper-iron face covers, found in the graves, strengthen the evidence in favour of the nomadic nature of the people. We can visualize that the people moved far and wide on horse back with weapons of war and chase. That they subdued the pre- existing Neolithic-Chalcolithic folk, who not only accepted the superiority of the Megalithic builders in material culture but also in spiritual culture."

Such a characteristic of Megalithic builders i.e. the fine workmanship in metallurgy of iron,copper, bronze and stone, horse riding, warrior ship, reminds us of indigenous Sangha people or republicans like Malava, Kshudraka, Vahika, Nagas, Bhar-siva, Sakya, Koliya, Moriya, Lichcchavis etc. (See chapter VI for detail), who had tradition of Nation-in-Arms

Payampalli

This site is situated in the North Arcot district of Tamil-Nadu, which was recently excavated by S. R. Rao.[53] This is perhaps the only site excavated so far which has yielded three successive floors with regular post-holes arranged in circular and oblong manner, clearly indicating circular and oblong huts, whose (circular) diameter is ranging from 1.5 to 3 metres and longer axis of the oblong huts varied between 1.7 and 4 metres.[54] Although most of the houses were of single huts but in one example the house was double-roomed. It is important to note that the floors of these huts were paved with stone-chips covered with Murrom and plastered with lime, that these huts were provided with movable doors which is evident from the findings of a perforated stone base found from the site.

This site is equally important for the enormous quantity of iron slag and ore found all over the mound since it proves that the people smelted iron and made tools locally. The tools found in the habitation layers include sickles, spears, chisels, nailes etc.[55]

Nagarjun Konda

The site, situated opposite Yelleswaram on the right bank of the river Krishna in . Guntur district, has been excavated by the Archaeological Survey of India. Although 15 burials have been excavated out of which 13 were pit burials and the remaining two oblong cists without port-hole. Skeletal remains and associated objects were placed usually on ash or lime bed. Pottery and iron objects were found in abundance.[56] Animal bones were also found frequently in these burials, which indicate burial type which was prevalent in cemetery R-37 (Dravidian).

Adichanallur

This site is situated at a distance of about 20 km south-east of the Tirunvelli town in Tamilnadu. It covers about 114 acres of waste land concealing hundreds of urn burials. Black and Red wares have been recovered from this site. Generally urn burials containing fractional bones have come to hands. A few examples of complete skeletons have also been reported.[57]

Sites in Maharashtra (Vidarbha)

Kaundinyapur

This habitational site,[58A] situated on the west bank of the river Wardha in Chandur Taluk of Amaravati district, has yielded four successive layers of occupation[58B]. Period I showed distinctly Megalithic affiliation by the presence of B and R ware, etched carnelian beads, graffiti marks on pottery and occurrence of iron. The succeeding period II (800-600 BC) showed continuation of B and R ware, while period III (Mauryan 300-100 BC) yielded punch marked coins and Northern Black polished ware. Period IV is assigned to the Satavahana period (150 BC to 200 AD).[59]

Mahurjhari :

Mahurjhari is an important site of Megalithic culture from where evidences of cult of mothergodess have been found out. Rao[60] gives a detailed excavation report of site, "Mahurjhari situated about 15 km west of Nagpur, contains one of the largest concentrations of Megalithic monuments in Central India. The cairn circles, which are visible on the surface, have been noticed at four localities numbered serially I, II, III and IV. Localities I and III are rich in having 40 and 70 circles respectively, whereas the localities II and IV contain 15 and 16 circles each. A total of fifteen burials have been excavated, out of which locality III account for nine burials. All are pit burials having very shallow pits. It seems some burials do not have any pit at all. Most of the burials contained fractional human bones, except four burials from locality III and one from locality IV. Out of these two are double burials. Megalith from locality III is remarkable as it revealed two skeletons, one above the other. Most of the full skeletons were found to have their lower parts missing. (this shows an Iranian tradition of burial). Full skeletons are usually associated with gold ornaments and sometimes also with horse bones. Apart from human skeletal remains, the Mahurjhari burials also yielded horse bones and teeth along with copper sheet ornaments for horses. A rich variety of iron tools and weapons were found and these included axes with cross ring fasteners, daggers, spear-heads, javelins, arrowheads, chisels hoes, adzes, nailparers, ladles etc. Copper ornaments found were bowl-lids, sheet ornaments for horses, bells and bangles. Ornaments made of gold included spiral ear rings, cabled gold strips, ring made of sheet, necklaces etc. Micaceous red pottery is more profuse though B and R ware, black burnished and coarse red wares were also encountered."

From a Megalith Hunter has recovered a carnelian ring which bears the name of Appāmād. There is one independent chapter of this name in Boddha pali Dhammapad. It means Mahurjhari was related to Buddhist religion.[61] A statue of naked mother goddess has been found out from this site, proving thereby that residents were worshippers of mother goddess.

Khapa

The site[62] situated on the left bank of the river Krishna, near Takalghat, has a fairly large concentration of stone circles. Although nine Megalithic burials have been opened at this site, the graves are pit burials which are shallow. The stone circle was arranged round the cairn packing. Skeletal remains are very few, represented by fragmentary bone pieces. One burial yielded an incomplete horse skeleton. Micaceous red ware occurred in profusion while other wares like B and R ware were scanty. A variety of iron objects were recovered and they included ladles, daggers, chisels, a sword, fragmentary blade pieces, adzes, nailparers, an axe with cross ring fastener and couldron. Copper objects found were bangles, bells, a dish with lid and horse ornaments made of copper sheet. Beads, both plain and etched were found in very high numbers and they showed variety of material used for bead makers.[63] This shows that Megalithic people were bead makers, warriors as well as prosperous people, which very closely resembles indigenous people who organized themselves in to craftsmenś guilds and were great warriors skilled in the art of use of arms.

Takalghat

Takalghat is one of the few Megalithic sites which revealed co-relation between the Megalithic burials and habitation. The site situated on the right bank of the river Krishna (Tributary of the Godavari) in Nagpur District is just on the opposite bank of the burial site Khapa and at a distance of one and a half miles from Gangapur, another Megalithic burial site. A total of 6.60 metres of habitational deposit was noticed, which was divided into three phases called A, B and C in successive order[64] The earliest occupation (Phase 1 A) revealed evidence of houses with rammed brown clay floorings. Post-holes suggested wooden posts supporting the wooden roof above. Pottery included painted black on red, finer B and R Ware and micaceous Red Wares. Iron is scarce and only shapeless and highly rusted pieces were found[65] Agate and carnelian beads were also found. Phase IB revealed construction of mud walls lime and brown clay floorings, pottery of 1st phase remained unchanged in second phase. Phase IC showed continuation of same material culture but it was without evidence of structures. The date of phase has been fixed at 700-400 BC. The material culture of the site resembles not only that of Khapa and Gangapur but also with that from South India[66].

Paunar

Paunar, situated[67] on the right bank of the river Dham in Wardha district, is one of the habitational sites going back to the Megalithic period in the Vidarbha region. Though the lowest stratum of this site goes back to Megalithic period, so far no Megalithic burial have been noticed in the close vicinity. Four periods of occupation were noticed at this site, which ranges from 1000 BC to 16th century[68] AD. Period I and II A can be assigned to Megalithic period on the grounds of associated objects. Period I is related to 1000-800 BC. This layer did not yield any metal objects but painted pottery, which can be compared with that from other Megalithic sites of this region suggests that the habitation of this layer belongs to Megalithic period, period II A is assigned to the period circa 4th-3rd century B. C. to first centary B. C. . Iron was first noticed in this period and the objects found were included nails, chisels, sickles etc. Copper bangles, antimony rods and stone ear ornaments were also found in this period.[69]

The end of Megalithic tradition signifies Aryanization of the inbabitants who began to cremate their dead bodies.

The Cultural unity of Eran and Malhar from early Megalithic-Period to Historical Period

The Black and Red ware pottery, Megalithic tradition of burial and emerging of Iron Age are the three characteristics of a single culture. H. L. Kosare[70] endeavours to show homogeneity of " Megalithic Iron Age culture" and early historical age culture as such, "In the process of development of Indian culture, the culture, which developed between the Chalcolithic culture and the North Black Polished ware culture of historical Age, is called Megalithic culture. It is quite clear from the evidences, recovered from archaeological excavations of many sites that there is no gap between the Megalithic culture of Iron Age and the culture of ancient historical Age. There are evidences of inter-locking of Megalithic culture of Iron Age and ancient culture of Historical Age at the same sites. From this, one point is quite clear, that the relation of beginning of Iron Smelting technology undoubtedly, is with the Megalithic culture. The people of Megalithic culture used artefacts of copper besides those of iron. Hence it can be said that the evolution of Megalithic culture took place later than the Chalcolithic culture which is a natural characteristic of evolution of cultures. But some scholars are of the opinion that the Megalithic culture was brought from outside India, because there are no evidences of its evolution and it appeared all of a sudden in North and South India, (Burzahom and Adichanallur, Hallur) in about 1000 B C and it was definitely brought by traders in South by sea-route. (This subject has been discussed on chapter III at length) Here one point is notable that there are no evidences of invasion of any other culture after the megalithic culture of Iron Age. Whatever cultural changes, have been noted after this culture, they are indicative of change due to transfer of sovereignty."

It seems from the above evidences that the edifice of Historical-Age was raised on the foundation of 'Megalithic- Iron Age Culture'. This view gets the support of evidences found from the excavation of Megalithic site of Malhār in Bilāspur district of Madhya-Pradesh. Prof K.D. Bajpai, Head of the deptt of Ancient History and Archaeology, University of Sāgar, excavated above site of ancient historical significance in 1975-77. From this site, he has found out evidences of regular habitation since 1000 B. C. upto the mediaeval period. From the first stratum or the earliest period, which belongs to the 1000-350 B. C., evidences of remains of Chalcolithic-Megalithic culture have been unearthed. From the second period evidences of remains of Maurya, Sunga and Sātavāhana Age, have been explored. From this period findings of sherds of Black and Red Ware and North Black Polished ware have been noted.[71]

The second interesting evidence of this culture is worth mentioning: The excavation work of ancient site of Eran[72] situated in Sagar district of Madhya Pradesh, was also taken up into hands by Prof K. D. Bajpai, in between 1960-65. This exploration has thrown light on the history of Malava, beginning from the early period of second millennium B. C. The evidences of regular habitation, since Chalcolithic-Age upto 18th century A. D. have been unearthed from this site. The first habitation stratum belongs to Chalcolithic Age, whose carbon dating is between 2000-700 B.C. From this phase, in addition to remains of Chalcolithic-Age, some iron artefacts also have been recovered. Similarly sherds of Black and Red ware have been achieved in abundance. The pottery found from there, generally belongs to Chalcolithic Age. These people were ancient Iranian, this view has been expressed by Prof Bajpai[73], on the basis of findings of a spouted pot from this assemblage. The date of second period (II A) is 700 -200 B. C. The maximum use of B and R ware and Iron, was made in this period. Some NBP wares also have been recovered.

The date of second period. (II B) is between second century B. C. and beginning of Christian era. The date of third period is between beginning of Christian era and 600 A. D. There is fall in the examples of B and R ware pottery in II B stratum, which is totally found missing in stratum third.[74]

It seems from the excavation of Eran, that beginning of Iron Age, is, between 1000 B.C and 700 B. C. The specific pottery of Iron-Age, the B and R. ware was also specific pottery of Eran of this period. We can derive two results from this evidence : (1) both the habitations of Malhar and Eran were parallel to each other and both with the other sites of Megalithic culture. (2) There is no evidence of coming of any other foreign culture in this age. (3) Presence of N. B. P. Wares in Eran Period II shows that Buddhism was religion of Naga people and their society.

It is obvious, the site of Eran was situated in the vicinity of place which was a well known "Megalithic Centre'' of Vindhya-region on one hand, on the other, it was a centre of earlier Naga rulers of Malava. Black and Red ware culture flourished in Eran from 2000 B.C (Indus Valley Age) up to the beginning of Christian era. We know the Sesha Naga republic people ruled this region (Capital at Vidisa) from 110 BC to 31 BC. It shows that Naga rulers of this republic ruled here in the period covered by B and R ware pottery, thus B and R ware culture was related to them. Black and Red ware culture has been found out from the lowest stratum of Paithan (known as Nag-ghat, this Author personally visited excavation operation at Paithan site and collected B and R ware pottery) which was capital of Satavahanas. This proves homogeneity of cultures of two sites. It means Satavahanas were also of Naga origin like wise Seshnagas. This conclusion is most important in historical prospectus. Bajpai KD on the basis of findings of spouted pot from Eran period II, has concluded that users of B and R ware were ancient Iranians or round headed Alpine Yadavas. It is supported by another solid evidence produced by K. P. Jayaswal[75], "The malava republics seems to have been formed by peoples and clans akin to the Nagas. Those around vidisa were worshippers of Nagas from early times as the republican coins of Eran prove. Eran, the Airikina town, is itself after the name Airikina a Naga and the Eran Coins bear a Naga (a serpent) figure." It shows Nagas were ruling here from remote past perhaps from the time of earlier phase of B and R ware culture. It seems, from this, the period of arrival of seshas and Sātavahanas in central India was one. This is a direct and solid evidence to prove that B and R ware culture was related to Naga race. This gets support of another evidence. According to B B Lal.[76] "This (B and R ware) culture remained attached to Harappan Culture on one hand and with the Megalithic on the other." Hence Harappans and Megalithic builders were ethnically related to Naga race. The continuity of B & R Ware culture from the Indus Valley period (2000 BC) up to the early period of Naga rulers of Vidisa and Paithan is meaningful.

The Cultural Unity in Vidarbha from Megalithic to the Satavahana Age

The Dravido-Iranian, after their settlement in Madhya desha, established their own social, political, religious and economic tradition i.e. tribal republic confederacies, guild based trade and industry system and in place of Vedic Religion they adopted non-Vedic Jain and Buddhist religions and developed their own independent culture. Their culture developed uninterrupted with effect from 1000 BC up to the Sātavahana Age (215 AD). This is confirmed by the evidences found from the exploration of different sites of Megalithic culture and Buddhist stupas. Dr S. B. Deo produces details of archaeological evidences proving the similarity of culture of different sites.[77] "The pottery used by the people of first stratum of Paunar was similar to those of Junapani and Kaundinyapur. Megaliths have not been traced out in Paunar but mutual relation of Junapani, Kaundinyapur and Paunar were of a similar culture ... The assemblage of pottery recovered from Takalghat was consisted of B and R. Wares, Red wares, Red wares with mica and ornamental painting in black on red slip. These potteries are similar to those of Paunar. From the above evidences, the mutual relations of Kaundinyapur Paunar, Takalghāt are well established. In addition to the above, in excavations of Tākalghāt the remains of numerous settlements have been unearthed, but all these settlements were related to the people of one culture .... In the Megaliths of Khapa in addition to skeletal remains, pottery of B and R ware, Red ware with mica also have been recovered. Such type of pottery has been found out from the residential area of Tākalghāt. Hence there was similarity in the culture of residential area of Tākalghāt and Megaliths of Khāpā.... . It is proved from the excavation of Paunar, Kaundinyapur, Tākalghat, Khapa, Mahurjhari and Junapani that in ancient time the culture of people of first stratum of Nagpur or

Vidarbha region was one. In addition to this it is also proved that there was similarity in the pottery of Pauni, Paunar, and Tākalghāt. Therefore in pre-Mauryan period, the people of Pauni, Paunar, Kaundinyapur, Tākalghāt, Khapa and Mahurjhari were of Megalithic culture." It is obvious that area around Nagpur was first settlement of Megalithic people. Since this area is covered by the sites as cited above. From there they moved onward.

Dr. S.P. Gupta[78] informs us that 'The culture of Tākalghāt existed between 700 B C and 400 B. C. From this similarity of culture and period it can be surmised that people of 1st period began to settle in the seventh century B. C. in Pauni.'

It is also clear from the evidences produced above that the people of Megalithic Iron Age culture of Vidarbha, who at about 1000 BC-800 BC established their culture in Madhya-Desha, were related to one and the same culture.[79] This culture flourished in Vidarbha up to the Maurya and Satavahana age ie up to 3rd century A. D. After, the people of this culture had established themselves permanantly,in this duration, there are no archaeological evidences of entry of people of any other culture. Therefore, the culture, which was developed and established by the Nagas of Megalithic culture during the life time of Buddha or earlier, can be identified admirably well with the culture of Nagas of Nagbhumi in Vidarbha. What happened to this culture in later period is a most important question ? Its answer is very simple. This was the period of Aryanization of this ruling race. As soon as they were Aryanized, they changed, their tradition of disposal of dead to Vedic. It means they stopped to bury them and began to cremate. Thus Megaliths came into disuse for ever.

The Economic life and Agro-Industrial Set up

We have seen earlier that the movement of Megalithic people was very fast. It is crystal clear that they were valiant warriors and fast horse riders that is why local earlier residents could not checkup their movement. But there must have been some other sound reason of their fast life and economy, proving their superiority on local population. This was their innovation in the field of economic life and Agro-Industrial set up which is proved well from the archaeological findings.

(a) A detailed description of economic life and agro-industrial set up of this culture is given by Gupa[80] S. P., "The Megalithic builders got full credit from late V. D. Krishnaswami for bringing about a green revolution in South India. According to him these people built hundreds of tanks near the catchment areas and established a chain of villages around them. That is borne out from the location of the cemeteries and also the impression of husk and rice on all types of earthen pots recovered from the graves. In this connection a 'Roman coulter' (?) from Brahmagiri, plough-shares from Nagpur and Hyderabad sites and a large number of small iron hoes from Adichanallur, Junapani and other sites may be significantly mentioned. Although, by and large, the excavated evidence is in favour of huts and mud brick houses in the villages, at Peddabankur District Karim Nagar Andhra Pradesh, Abdul Wheed Khan found the remains of a baked-brick structure in association with Black and Red ware and iron sickles, arrowheads, a dagger,etc. ..... That the people quickly diffused far and wide with their superior tool technology and fast running horses, is equally an important aspect of the life of the megalith builders. The amount and the variety of iron tools and weapons that one encounters in the megalithic graves is extremely impressive. Similarly, different types of horse bits and horse, face-covers coupled with the skeletal remains of domesticated horse recovered from graves are also significant.

In the process of diffusion, they are, at times, likely to have come into conflict with native people. That is made out from a large number of swords, lances and spear-heads recovered from the excavated graves. Although it is difficult to comprehend the nature of resistance that the autochthonous folks would have offered with their far less effective weapons yet some resistance, however weak, was certainly met with by the Megalith builders is more than clear .... They also show that it was transitional phase between a limited agricultural economy and an intensive agro-industrial set up by the people of two strains : one which consisted of men who were essentially sea-faring and adventurous and the second, which had men who were war like and nomadic. It was certainly a turning point in the socio- economic set up of the people."

(b) These people were also efficient craftsmen which is proved from the evidences of their fine workmanship in metallurgy of iron, copper, bronze, gold, silver and stone, yielded from different sites. The site of Payampalli is important for the enormous quantity of iron slag and ore found all over the mound, it proves that the peoples melted iron and made tools locally[81] Similarly beads both plain and etched were found from khapa in a very high number and they showed variety of material used for bead makings, apparently khapa[82] was a centre of bead-makers, where as payampalli was a centre of black-smiths. The builders of megaliths were a great stone worker which is proved from their efficient workmanship, visible in different type size and shapes of Megaliths. Megaliths of Hallur are very heavy and large in size and definitely would have needed high efficiency and workmanship of skilled and non skilled workers in a very high number.

Similarly, enormous beautiful gold and silver ornaments, of use by men and women both, have been discovered from sites like Hallur,

Adichanallur, Nagarjunkonda, Mahurjhari, Kaundanyapur,Nekund, Junapani and Khapa etc, which throws light on their workmanship on one hand and their immeasurable wealth on the other. Roman coins and ceramic have been discovered from South India. This proves that their trade and trade relations were not only with whole of India but also with the Western Asian and European countries. This picture is not different from that of craftsmen and trade guild system of indigenous non-Aryan people of India. (See chapter VI PP-124-25) According to Bhandarkar,[83] "From about 500 BC to 600 AD India was studded with guilds of various type showing how well Industry and trade were specialized and developed." Perhaps the beginning period of Megaliths was development period of craftsmen and trade guilds in India.

(c) It is also evident from the findings of war weapons like lances, dirks, swords, spear-heads, arrow-heads, javelin and tonged daggers in a very high number from megalithic sites of Hallur, Yelleswaram, Adichanallur, Mahurjhari, Nekund, Junapani, Khapa and Paunar etc, that these people were originally great warriors. This view gets the support of presence of horse in most of the sites, from where not only, horse bones and skeletal remains have been discovered in a very high number (sometimes along with human skeletal remains,) but also their ornaments and equipments of use for horse riding like copper and iron face covers, bells and bits, iron stirrups have come to hand in abundance. It means Megalithic builders were not only great warriors but also great horse lover and efficient horse riders too. This reminds us of tradition of Nation-in-arms prevalent among the Sangha or republican peoples. (see chapter VI PP 133-34)

The Evolution of Megalithic tradition into the Buddhist Stupa Tradition

As the burial system of Indus-Valley in any form affected the megalithic burial system similarly the Megalithic architecture tradition affected the Buddhist Stupa tradition. This is clear from the following examples :

(1) In the architectural structure of stupa, whatever is known oval, the same form is known as cairn circle in the culture of Megaliths. In stupa under the oval were placed urn-cineraries and under the cairn circle were placed remains of dead bodies. In stupa tradition, an outer wall at a distance of 6 feet encircling the circumambulation is raised on the pattern of outskirt of cairn circle built of round shaped large stone. Its object was to save the oval from any outward damages, because oval was considered to be most sacred[84].

(2) The use of "Stone umbrella" tradition is also made in the stupa tradition, which is always seen in the construction of stupa on the

top. An umbrella is raised on the cinerary urn placed on the head of statue of an elephant standing on the arch of gate way of stupa of Sanchi. Keeping an umbrella above the head of Buddha who is alive in this world (under oval) seems to be most appropriate. In ancient age this umbrella must have possessed some definite object the philosophy of which is available in the cultural heritage of age of Buddha.[85]

(3) The rock-cut grave chambers were later developed into Chetya, which first of all were used for residence purposes by the Buddhist monks.

(4) Menhir tradition developed in the form of stone pillars of Ashoka, which was used as a symbol of memorial.

(5) Similarly 'urn burial' tradition, which was a tradition of Indus Valley, developed into urn cinerary of stupas, which was thought to be most sacred and according to Buddhist tradition still they are worshipped in Modern age.

This is the main reason that in the form of aforesaid chain of evolution we find existence of these stupas even before Bhagwan Buddha. We find description of a stone pillar of sixth or seventh century B.C. in Dipanikaya which was constructed in Vaisali. Bhagwan Buddha himself has made mention of such a pillar of Lichcchavis. There is a description in Mahaparinirvan Sutta, that out side or inside of Vajji Sangha, Chetyas were highly respected and they were also being worshipped.[86]

VAJJI CHETYĀNI AVYATRANI CHAV ।

Bhagwan Buddha himself has praised Vajji Sangha. He has stated that sepulchre should be raised on the ashes of great persons (Chakravartin). Most probably such a stupa has also already been constructed in Vaisali. It is very clear from the conversation of Ananda and Bhagwan Buddha (Mahapari-Nirvan Sutta)[87]

Megalithic, a Naga Culture

The Megalithic-Iron Age- Culture was related to Naga race. Its direct evidences have come to hands from an archaeological excavations very recently. Department of Ancient History, culture and Archaeology of Nagpur University has excavated the remains of a culture of Chalcolithic and Iron Age from the site of Tārsā (Tehsil Maudo, Distt Nagpur). The people of this culture, during Chalcolithic and Iron Age, used to live in houses, which were made of wooden poles, round shaped and small in size. They used granaries made of clay for storing grains. They used to build platform with river sand and applying plaster of marl, on which granaries were raised. These people, worshipped serpents. A copper serpent has been recovered from there, which is seated on its coiled body. Similarly a serpent of gold, has been recovered from Bhokardhan in 1973 whose hood is fitted with a gem. Still in modern age gold–smiths, fashion copper serpents of small and large size, for sale in the region of Nagpur and they are being worshipped in the Deva-temples or Naga temples or at the occasion of Naga Panchami. The serpent recovered from the excavation of Tārasā belongs to 1000 B. C. Similary, a Naga-ring has been found out from excavation of Mahurjhari.[88] This Naga ring definitely might have been of Satavāhana Age. From this, the relation of Satavahanas is established with Naga culture, from the prehistoric period up to the Megalithic Age. On the basis of archaeological findings from Eran and Paithan we have established earlier that B and R ware culture which is connected with Indus-Valley culture on one hand and with Megalithic on the other, was related to Naga race who ruled there from the time of beginning of B and R ware culture.

Summary and Conclusion

The period between Indus-Valley culture and the beginning of historical age has been called 'Dark Age of Indian History' by some historians. But archaeological excavations, have discovered many cultures in this age. (1) The sequence of these cultures in North is as under : Ochre coloured pottery (1700-1500 B.C.), Black and Red ware (2400-100 BC), Grey ware culture (1600-1500 BC), Painted Grey ware culture (1500-800 BC), North Black Polished ware (NBPW 550-50 BC).

(2) Neolithic culture flourished in South-Eastern region of Uttar Pradesh or Vindhya Pradesh, in between 2400-1700 BC. This is most interesting that these people used B and R wares which was also used by later Harappans in Gujrat and further in South. It means these people also had some relation with the Harappans.

(3) In Central India Chalcolithic culture of Ahar, Kayatha, Malava and Jorve flourished between 2000-400 BC. The Iron Age culture begins at about 1000-800 B. C. which covered most of the earlier cultures of India.

(4) Rigvedic account clearly mentions that Aryan after their arrival in India generally used to cremate their dead bodies.[89] Although their ancestors practised burial system. It shows that megaliths were related to non-Aryan indigenous population. The tradition of burying their dead bodies in megaliths was alike those of Harappans (Cemetery R̄37 and H and G) ie pit burials and urn burials. From this similarity of mode of disposal of dead bodies, it can be concluded that Megalithic

builders were successor of Harappans. This is evident from the B and R wares which on one hand remained adherent to Megaliths from beginning to end and on the other it had its root in Indus valley culture. This is confirmed by B. B. Lal on the basis of archaeological evidences.[90]

(5) Main centres of Megaliths were six : Swat and Kashmir Valley, Sindh, Kathiavar, Vindhya region, Vidarbha and South India. The beginning period of Megalithic culture at Swat-valley and Southern India is between 1000-800 B.C. . Although according to Sharma this period is much earlier in Vindhya region ie 1500-700 B.C., but the megalithic centre of Vidarbha and South India are largest and most important for study purposes, which shows that this culture was brought from West Asia through land and sea routes both, which was existing there from a period of about 4000 B.C.

(a) It is indicative from the study of stratification of sites like Payampalli, Brahmagiri and Hallur that Megalithic culture first appeared in Hallur culture which was post Neolithic-Chalcolithic culture. Hallur Culture was characterized with B and R ware and iron. It proves iron reached some time earlier than the Megalithis at Hallur.

(b) A study of archaeological evidences, found from sites of Eran, Malhar and many others from Vidarbha, reveals that there was a cultural unity from the beginning period of Megaliths, up to the Satavahana Age. It means Satavahanas had definitely some relations with the builders of Megaliths of Vidarbha, which is further confirmed from the findings of B and R wares from early phases of Paithan site.

(6) The economic basis of this culture was well developed Agro-Industrial set up.

(a) The environment[91] of the cemeteries, in which the graves were laid, is generally marked by an ancient irrigation tank, cultivated paddy fields and high barren rocky ground over which the Megaliths were raised. It seems that the people in the past also might have been engaged in rice cultivation and tank irrigation, this is proved by the types of iron implements, used in farming like hoes, sickles, axes with cross rings fasteners, adzes, plough–shares, Roman coulter etc which were discovered from the archaeological excavations of Megalithic sites like. Hallur, Payampalli, Mahurjhari, Nekund, Junapani, Khapa and Paunar etc. This can be pronounced with certainly that it was beginning of a green revolution in South India.

(b) From findings of enormous quantity of iron slag and ore from the mound of Payampalli and beads both plain and etched and bead material from Khapa in great quantity proves that there were workshops of Black-smiths at Payampalli and Bead-makers at Khapa. Similarly discovery of enormous beautiful gold and silver-ornaments of use by men and women both from different sites shows workmanship of people on one hand and their immeasurable wealth on the other. Such like activities of Megalithic builders reminds us of great tradition of craft and trade guilds of Buddhist age.

(c) Similarly, recovery of iron weapons of different shape and size in a very high number and findings of horse bones and ornaments of their use from different sites, force one to think of glorious tradition of Nation-in-arms among the Sangha people.

(7) It has been proved well that the architectural tradition of megaliths, developed into Buddhist stupas, hence, builders of later were successors of earlier. In other words the offshoot of megalithic builders were great pioneers of Buddhist religion. Many more evidences can be produced in support of this view point : carnelian ring has been discovered from Mahurjhari[92] which bears the name of appādmād. There is an independent chapter of this name in Buddhist Pali Dhammapada. The evidence of excavation of Buddhist stupas at Amaravati and Pauni also stands is support of this view.

(8) From the archaeological excavation of site of Tārsā (1000 BC), a copper serpent, a serpent ring from Mahurjhari and a serpent of gold from the site of Bhokardhan have been traced out. This clearly proves that builders of megaliths were serpent worshippers or people of Naga race.

Excavation of Eran site confirms that B and R ware using Megalithic people were of Naga race, who were ancient Iranians in origin known as Alpine Yadava people, some of them were long headed Dravidian or Mediterranian type.. These Naga or Sesha were ruling eastern Malava from Vidisa and Eran from a very early time. This is a direct evidence to show that Indus Valley culture, B and R. ware and Megalithic culture were related to Naga race.

References

1. Dr. Madan Mohan Singh "Puratatva Ki Ruprekha" (1989) P-54.
2. Dr. Madan Mohan Singh, 'Ibid' P-55.
3. Dr. Madan Mohan Singh 'Ibid' P-56.
4. Ibid.
5. Dr. Madan Mohan Singh P-57.
6. Ibid.
7. Ibid.
8. Dr. Madan Mohan Singh P-58.
9. Ibid.

10. Dr. Madan Mohan Singh P-59.
11. Sat Brah XIII-8 DEVAŚCHĀ SURĀŚ CHO BHAYE PRĀJĀPATYA TE CHAMBAṄ TVADYA SINSYASTVAṬ. ॥
12. Gupta S. P., "Disposal of the dead and Physical type in ancient India." PP-163-64.
13. Fergusson James, "Tree and Serpent Worship" P-78.
14. Piggott stuart, "Prehistoric India" P-232.
15. Wheelers R.E.M. "A. I" Vol-III PP 83-85 Bulletin of A.S.I. Jan 1947 and Bose N. K. and others, "Human skeleton from Harappa" Bulletin of ASI (1963) PP 58-59.
16. Dr. Jani, "Chronology of Gujrat" P-24 mentioned by Nanavati J.M. "Somnath" PP-88-89.
17. 'Majumdar D. N., "Races and Culture of India" P-29.
18. Piggott stuart PP 231-32.
19. Gupta S. P PP 182-83.
20. Gupta S. P. P-184.
21. Ibid.
22. (a) Wheeler REM PP 83-85.
    (b) Bose N.K and others PP-58-59.
23. Lal BB, "From Megalithic to Harappans; Tracing back the graffito to the pottery" "AI." No. XVI (1960) PP 4-24.
24. (a) Gupta SP PP-194-202.
    (b) Rao K. P. "Deccan Megaliths" PP 9-14.
25. Rao KP PP-13-14.
26. IAR (1961-62) PP 109-110.
27. Gupta SP P-147.
28. Gupta S P. P-165.
29. Dixon B. Roland, "The Racial History of Man" PP 307 and 314.
30. Dixon B. Roland P-307.
31. Gupta S. P. P-168.
32. Crindle MC, "Alexander" P-356.
33. Gupta S. P. P-170.
34. Gupta S. P. P-171.
35. (a) Gupta S P.P-172.
    (b) A I No 4 (1947) P-196.
36. Gupta SP P-173.
37. Gupta SP. P-175.
38. Ibid.

Chapter 5

The Origin of the Naga Culture in the Western Asia, and its Transfer to Indus Valley

Arrival of Sumerians and Semites in Mesopotamia

We have already shown in chapter I that the earliest civilization of globe took its birth at Catal Hayuk and Jericho in Western Asia, ten thousand years before present. Western Asia has generally been a cradle of human civilization in ancient time.

Western Asia includes present countries like Iraq, Iran, Syria, Israel, Palestine and Arabia etc., but owing to nearness the other countries like Egypt, Greece, Cyprus and island of Crete also had immense effect of civilization and political activities of these countries, but the main centre of civilization in the past was generally Mesopotamia.

The large plain[1] between the lower ends of the two rivers is known as Mesopotamia (The Greek meaning is between the rivers) and the area is very fertile. Here a dark-skinned race came from north-west India and settled. They called themselves the 'black headed people' or the 'people of summer' and we call them the 'Sumerians'. They were the first people in the world to become civilized, who have left some form of written record. The Sumerians probably began to move into Mesopotamian plains before 5000 B.C. from north-east direction.

This view gets the support of Jacquetta Hawkes. She[2] writes - ''It is reasonably certain that most of these pioneers irrigator came from the hills to the north and east from Elam and the fringes of the Iranian plateau. It might be thought that this would mean a change of environment of intolerable violence, but at that date the southern Iran was less arid than it has since become, and some of its valley had marshy conditions........ However, modest, the first attempts at irrigation may have been, it is very probable that exodus from Persia was to some extent planned and carried out by groups of settler under their own leaders. Many settlements were made on sites so well chosen that they remained to grow in the cities of historical times.''

In my opinion this migration took place either from north-east Iran or possibly from north-west India or present Afghanistan, since only one skull of Alpine race from old cemetery R-37 of Harappa and two from the streets of Mohenjodaro have been recovered.[3] It seems these round headed Alpine, were settled in north eastern part of Iran and whole of hilly track of Afghanistan and north-western area of Indian territory before advent of Aryan races in this region.[4] According to Dixon[5] Pathans, who with the Afghans proper of Kabul and vicinity now speak an Indo-European language, are predominantly Alpine in type. But they claim their origin from Jewish or Semitic race or a long headed race. Sankalia[6] also thinks that cemetery 'H' people (Alpine) of Harappa came from a nearby place within Panjab.

It seems clear that these Sumerians were originally round headed Alpines. Dixon, an eminent anthropologist, throws light on the racial affinities of these people[7]- "Hamy has endeavoured to show that on the basis of sculptured heads and bas-reliefs the ancient non-semitic Sumerians were brachycephalic, whereas the semitic speaking peoples, who already at the earliest known historical period were acquiring dominance in Babylonia, were on the contrary dolichocephalic."

This second race to enter in Mesopotamia was Semites, which was a majority in the population, and played a vital role in the progress of physical and political life during historical period. This entry of people took place from the western desert of Mesopotamia. Now another question arises whether these Semites were original inhabitant of plain or not ? Some[8] of them were definitely in the beginning of historical Age. Because there were Semitic names and words present even in most ancient writings. These semites were called Akkadians by now. Indeed, as has been said, some scholars have identified their arrival with the devastating flood of the kings list (i.e. 3300 B.C.). There[9] must have been a continuous shift of Semites southward down the Eupharates. They came to dominate the land, that was to be Akkad, and in the Diyala region developed Sumerian cultural traditions in ways of their own. The city of kish, whose, according to the kings' list, most of the rulers before Mebaragesi had Semitic names, must have become a power centre for their thrust into ancient summer itself.

It is difficult[10] to judge, how in political terms, the Akkadians and Sumerians conducted their affairs as they met and mingled on the plain. There is no evidence either in archaeology or epic tradition that they clashed on racial lines. In petty wars between states, they must some times, have fought one another, but on terms of neighbourly enmity, not as semites against Sumerians. It is clear they had good relations and there was no difference on the issue of race.

It is conclusive that Semites came from the western deserts in about 3500 B.C. They were long headed Mediterranean or Dravidian. We can draw another clear conclusion from the above facts that in Mesopotamia the distribution position of both the races was likewise that of India. In Gujrat and Maharashtra they were living in mixed-up condition. In south, Dravidians were predominant. It is to be noted that Alpine people reached Indus valley in about 2100 B.C., who were original inhabitant of Afghanistan and north-west region.

Invasion of the Semites or Hyksos on Egypt

In between 1730-1750 B.C. Semites or Hyksos invaded Egypt from east. Josephus[11], Jewish historian of first century of our era in his "Contra opionem" quotes this passage from Monetho, describing the Hyksos invasion, "Unexpectedly, men of an unknown race from the east were emboldened to invade the country (Egypt) and without a battle easily seized it by force......Their whole nation was "Hyksos" that is "Shepherd kings" for "hyk" in the sacred language signified "king" and "sos" is "shepherd" or "shepherds", in the common speech "Hyksos" comes from joining these together. This etymology has long since been shown to be only partially correct. Hyk comes, indeed, from Heka "chief" "Prince" etc. but sos can not be a transcription of Shashu, "nomad" ; it is rather an abbreviation of Khasut, "Foreigners"; the expression Heka khasut is known in Egypt as early as the twelth dynasty, when it was used to designate the chiefs of nomad tribe, who wondered the deserts of Syria-Palestine, under the old kingdom, it had been used for the skeikhs of the Nubian deserts. Both the Turin Papyrus and contemporary scarabs apply the term to known "Hyksos" kings."

These people were mostly Semites and bore names already familiar among Egyptians, Asiatic neighbours from middle and even old kingdom times. The name Hyksos which should be translated as "Chieftain of foreign hill country" applied only to the rulers and was indeed a term which had long been used for Bedouin Sheikh.[12] It is evident that these people were of Dravidian race in origin belonging to Arabian Seikh or Jews stock.

The Hyksos, invasion was certainly not a sudden as Manetho[13] implies. Now-a-days it is agreed that we ought to speak rather of a progressive infiltration than of an invasion in the strict sense. In addition, the invaders were not a single people, this was a heterogeneous concert of various inhabitants of western Asia (semites for a most part, but not entirely) who had been thrust out of their home pastures by Indo-European invasions of Anatolia and upper Mesopotamia either directly or indirectly. The Egyptians[14] themselves call them various things; sometimes Amu, some times Setetiu or Mentiu of Setet, or "man of Retenu" ; i.e. all the old names used under the old and middle kingdom for the Asiatic peoples who were Egypt's neighbour ; which means they did not like, Manetho, consider them a hitherto unknown peoples a new invading race.

Dates of Invasion of Hyksos and Their Sun Deity Baal

As regards the date of invasion of Hyksos, it is generally stated that they began their slow entry into Egypt in the period of beginning of 12th dynasty (2000 BC). Jean Vercoutter[15] gives exact date on the basis of sound evidences, "We have been able to fix the date of this event by a monument known as the, "stele of the year 400" for it commemorates the four hundredth anniversary of the reconstruction of the temple of the god Seth at Avaris. Now we know that the cult of Seth at Avaris was fostered by the Hyksos, who saw in this very old Egyptian god (he is attested under the first Dynasty) a local version of one of their own semitic divinities, Baal or Resheph. There can be no doubt whatever that the reconstruction and enlargement of his temple were the work of his invading votaries. The fourth centennial of that work was celebrated about 1320 B.C., in the reign of the Eighteenth Dynasty Pharaoh Horemheb, as the stele erected by Ramesses II at Avaris states. This means that the temple was originally rebuilt in about 1720 BC ; in other words, by this date the Hyksos had laid hands on the far eastern parts of the Delta, quite close to the frontier, which is the region of Avaris."

From the above description and evidences, we can draw following conclusions :

(1) That the Hyksos were semites or long headed Mediterraneans or Dravidians who originally lived in the north-west desert of Arabia. who were known as "Foreign chiefs" or "Hyksos" from very ancient times. (about 2700 BC). They were thrusting Egypt since 2400 B.C. and were defeated severally by East Bedouins in Veni.[16]

(2) These Semites were also called Akkad or Akkadian in Mesopotamia. They founded a city in their dominion under similar name ie Akshak.[17]

(3) Baal was their prominent deity, who was representative of sun god.

It is very clear that the words Hyksos, Akkad, and Akshak were related to one and the some race. According to Dr. Buddha Prakash.[18] "Among these peoples (who took part in Rigvedic 10 kings war), the

Yakshus may be equated with the Akkaeoi known to the great poet Homer or the Akavasa, who invaded Egypt. Later on they seem to have known as Okkaka (Pali language) and Ikshwaku (Sanskrit).''

Perhaps these people accompanied those immigrants (meso-cephal or round headed Alpines), who reached India in mature Harappan Age (about 2100 BC), who, later on, had a collision with Aryan king Sudas in ten kings war from east direction under Sanskritized name Yakshu.[19]

It shows that these Hyksos were Ikshwakus of India to which famous king of Ayodhya Rama belonged. Although this seems to be a farfetched idea that two peoples, living at such a long distance from each other with no definite dates, have been equated merely on the basis of similarty of their names. But we have strong evidences in support of this view point : Baal, the prominent deity of Hyksos, most probably, reached, Indus valley along with them, which appears in Rigvedic account attached to panis (later Banik) as their religious deity. (See chapter XIII P P 376-77) Lichchhavis of Vaisali are said to be Vaishya or Banik on one hand and Ikshwaku on the[20] other (I.A. IX-178) that is why they were allied to the Sakya-Ikshwakus. Baal deity who is a sun god, at a later date appears attached to Ikshwakus of South India. (Siriparvata)

According to Rigvedic account these were the first aboriginals who had collision with Indra,[21] the Aryan militant leader. Above deity is still a part of religion of Jain Banik under a bit addition in Name 'Bahubal' in south India, which is still being worshipped there.

According to H.D. Sankalia[22] the original source of Ramayana was Ur Ramayan which was composed earlier than any earliest addition. He writes- ''Thus I have tried to show that the original Ramayan was quite different from the Ramayana we have at present. The origins or sources of the Ur might go back to a period between 1500 and 1000 BC, whereas the present Ramayan could be as late as the 11th century A.D. for the earliest manuscript we have today is of A.D 1020.'' It is very strikingly true that Ikshwaku family of Ramayana took birth in western Asia before 1500 B.C.

The word Hyksos was in use for Semites before 2400 B.C. These people were of Brown colour and have been called 'Manavah' in Puranic literature. Sufficient light is thrown on this topic at some proper place of this chapter. Perhaps due to pressure from barbarian race (Hittite) of North some of them moved towards Egypt and perhaps a part of them towards India, for which we have no direct evidences at present. It is also possible they reached in about 2100 B.C. along with the Alpine people. But no one can deny from this probability owing to strong circumstantial evidences.

The Origin of the Cult of Mother goddess and Matriarchal Form of Family

It is most interesting to note that in ancient society of Middle East, against patriarchal system of Aryan society, matriarchal system of family was prevalent even up to the historical age. Robert Briffoult gives a detail of this system in practice in Crete as follows,[23] "Female figures are equally predominant in the Neolithic art of the whole Mediterranean region ; there is not a single male idol to be found before the Bronze Age. Dr. Rodenwalt says that the prominence of women is even more pronounced in continental Greece than in Crete and points out that, whereas in Cretan frescoes women are assisted by men, in the Mykenan palaces of the Peloponnesus. 'we see, everywhere women and women only taking part in religious cult. At the opposite end of the mediterranean the evidence of matriarchy is even more emphatic. 'Among the Cantaberians' says Strabo, "The men bring dowries to the women. With them the daughters alone inherit property. Brothers are given away in marriage by their sisters. In all their usages, their social condition is one of gynaecocracy."

The later Sumerian[24] tradition knows several deities who are mentioned with the epithet "old" this may preserve some fragments of ancient religion "old" occurs with these names : Gatumdu, "the mother of Lagash"; Nisiba of Eresh ; Nunbarshegunu of Nippur ; Belili, the sister of Dumuzi, and Bilulu. All are goddesses. The[25] names that have any meaning we can understand are sumerian : Nisaba is a word for grain, Nunbarshegunu contains the Sumerian word for a kind of barley (hordeum rectum nigrum). Whether these goddesses were worshipped in Protoliterate times is uncertain. It is worth noting, however, that the pantheons of a number of the oldest cities were headed by a goddess. They had consorts, but of clearly lower rank : in Lagash, Gatumdu Baba with her consort. Ningirsu : in Nina, Nanshe with Nindara; in Kesh, Nintu with Shulpa-ea. Inanna and Dumuzi (the Semitic Ishtar and Tammuz) probably also belong in this category, although the goddess husband in this case was a mortal.[26]

It would be altogether understandable if, when the idea of anthropomorphic deities first develoved, a civilization based on agriculture and stock-breeding were first to ascribe divinity to goddesses who, like Nisaba represented grain, or like Turdur the ewe or who simply were able to guarantee fertility, in the fields, in the herds, in the homes of men.[27] It means the relation of above mother goddess was with the deities of creator of world or fertility, which we may call 'Earth mother' or 'Bhumata'.

There is the purely historical element for example the fact that in the formative period of the fourth and third millennia B.C. the prehistoric cult of the earth mother or mother goddess was still powerful, but was being overtaken by other cults more appropriate to an urban civilization.[28]

We can imagine from the above details that the cult of Bhūmatā or the mother goddess is the oldest, the worship of other gods began at a later date. Bhūmatā or mother goddess was purely worshipped in the form of mother creator of world. It perhaps began while man was still in the stage of hunter. Jacquetta Hawkes[29] throws light on the issue how the system developed in ancient time "The same drives, to some extent even the same symbolic forms, can be seen already in the first ascendancy of Homosapiens in late palaeolithic times. We can see that the same excitement and concern roused by birth and fertility which found expression in the female figurines of the hunters was also celebrated in the great temple and cult figures of Ninhursanga, Inanna and other versions of the Mother Goddess of ancient civilization we can see how the emotion roused by death and the desire to defeat its sting which caused the palaeolithic peoples to bury their dead with care and give them valuable tools and food wares, when social wealth permitted it to swell to such extravagances as the royal graves of Ur and the pyramids."

It is obvious that root cause of above cult was not only birth but also death.

Matriarchal Families Among the Semites

Semitic[30] kinship terms refer, as among most peoples, to maternal rather than to paternal descent, and the clan or tribe to which a man belongs is frequently spoken of as his 'mother'. The Arab genealogists of the time of the rise of Islam, when Patriachy was strongly established, were at pains to exhibit Semitic descent as patriarchal, but they were often compelled to recognize that older clans were metronymic.[31]

Among the Hebrews, who had left the Peninsula many centuries before the Arabs, the same situation had arisen long before, and they endeavoured also to interpret their genealogies in terms of a male descent. Yet the Jewish rabbis themselves, at a comparatively late date, acknowledged that the 'four matriarchs,' Sarah, Rebecca, Rachel and Leah, had occupied a more important position than the 'three patriarchs,' Abraham, Issac and Jacob.[32]

According to Robertson smith, the tribe of Levi was originally metronymous being the tribe of Leah for whom the husband Levi had to be invented.

Israel itself, the tribe which gave its name to the whole nation, was originally the tribe of Sarah, Israel being her son. With the early Hebrews the regular practice was for the man to leave his father and mother and cleave to his wife; that is ; to take up his abode with his wife's clan.[33]

It is a tradition among Jews even today, that they can marry daughter of his father or his own real sister.

Matrilocal marriage passed on when the Jews settled in Cannon, but survives to this day among the Bedawi of Arabia. To the true Bedawi, marriage is almost always Matrilocal. The wild men, says Burton, do not refuge their daughters to a stranger but the son-in-law would be forced to settle amongst them.[34]

Further Robert Briffoult[35] throws light on the status of women in all the countries of Western Asia, in ancient society, "As we should expect from the former existence of materilocy, there are indications that formerly the position of women, both among the Jews and Arabia, was high. The oldest existing fragment of Hebrew literature represents the Hebrew tribes as led by a woman (Judges IV-V). Among the Arabs likewise many of the judges were chieftainesses. Queens, from the queen of Sheba to Zenobia, occupy a prominent place in Arab history. In every one of the references to Arabia kingdoms in the historical inscriptions of Assyria, it is with a queen that we have to do. The position of those queens appears to have been exalted. Their husbands were merely their consorts. 'The female sex rules among the Sabians.' says 'Claudian', and a large proportion of the barbarians is under the armed domination of queens."

This shows the cruelty of behaviour of woman towards man, while she was in power. Robert Briffoult further produces details of this cruelty-"women in ancient Arabia were commonly the owners of wealth, possessing large flocks and herds ; their husband commonly acted as herdsman. Mohammed himself was able to carry out his mission, thanks only to the wealth which he acquired from his first wife. In early and pre-Islamic literature we come upon women like Mawia bint Afzar, who changed her husband whenever she pleased.[36]"

Matriarchal society in Egypt

The society of Egypt was also matriarchal from the time immemorial and continued till the first half of the first century A.D. Perhaps this change took place owing to their contact with the Aryan society of patriarchal tradition. The conservative[37] society of Egypt never lost its essential matriarchal character, though continuous progress towards patriarchal institutions is clearly traceable through the various phases of Egypt's four thousand years career. We shall have to ignore here the rules of succession to the throne of the Pharaohs, and we shall see that functions of royalty were transmitted in the female line. While every Egyptian princess was born a queen and bore the titles of the office from the day of her birth, a man only acquired them at his coronation, and could do so only by becoming the consort of a royal princess. It was in the queen that mystic or divine virtue resided.[38]

Nevertheless, scanty as our information is we have enough to see that Egyptian social life generally was in the highest degree matriarchal. Dr. Hall says[39] that the constitution of Egyptian society was characterized by a distinct preservation of matriarchy, the prominent position of women and a comparative promiscuity in sexual relations.

Professor Mitteis confirms that Egypt was immemorially a land of matrilinear descent, a usage which continued in Christian times until the seventh century. There[40] the maternal uncle is often named as important. The father of the mother was more important than the man's own father. In consequence, there were no illegitimate children in Egypt, a child born out of wed lock enjoying the same rights as one born in marriage.[41] All children belonged to the mother. The Nomes, or primitive totem clans, of which the nation was formed, were maternal clans or mother hoods, and their headship was transmitted through women.[42]

On the other hand, Flinder Petrie observes, "The family in Egypt was based on a matriarchal system. The house and property went with the women and daughters". Sir Gaston Maspero[43] says, "The Egptian women of the lower and middle class were more respected, more independent, than any other women in the world." The husband had no power as head of the household, and the word 'husband' is only found in marriage contracts after the reign of Philopator. Marriage was matrilocal, and where there were two wives each remained in her own house, the husband visiting them in turn. As late as the XIXth Dynasty, there was still surviving the idea that a man was only a boarder in a woman's home. All landed and house property was in the hands of the women, and, if a man built a house, it passed immediately to his wife. .....The eagerness which Egyptian husbands seem to have shown in making over their property to their wives was probably due in part to the fact that, according to matriarchal usage, it would otherwise have passed not to their own but to their sister's children. Thus, by a curious paradox, the anxiety to secure patriarchal succession contributed to accentuate the economic power of women. To the same desire to combine inheritance in the male line with the matriarchal organization of the family was also doubtless due to the practice of marrying sisters, which appears to have been more prevalent in Egypt than among any other people of which we know. The majority of marriages were between brothers and sisters as late as the second century AD in some districts.''

Crete Island and the Cult of Mother Goddess

The society of Crete island was also matriarchal likewise neighbouring countries of Egypt and Israel. Archaeological evidences in a very high number have been discovered in support of above view. Briffoult Robert produces a vivid account of them,[44] ''The marvellous remains of Crete provide eloquent testimony to the matriarchal character of Cretan society. The enormous predominance of female over male figures is without parallel. Cretan divinities are almost exclusively feminine as are the innumerable votive figures. Women alone figure as priestesses in religious ceremonies. These characteristics are equally marked from ancient Neolithic times to the height of Minoan culture. 'It may be admitted without reserve'. Remarks Dr. Mosso, 'That at this epoch, that is to say, about 1500 BC, Minoan religion had preserved its matriarchal character. The supremacy of women in religion was thus maintained until Mykenean times.' Secular art also speaks for the predominance of women. There are numerous representations of men in Minoan art, but they are all engaged in subordinate occupations, cup-bearers, pages, musicians, harvesters, soldiers and sailors. Not once does it depict a king, prince or hero, or show a man in a position of domination. The female figures, on the other hand, invariably exhibit an attitude of self-possessed independence. Minoan women are seen mixing freely with men at festivals, riding in chariots driven by female charioteers. 'It is certain', remarks Dr Hall, 'that they must have lived on a footing of greater equality with the men than in any other ancient civilization.' That the state was governed by women is suggested by Klidemos, who tells us that after the death of Deukalion the throne passed to Ariadne, who concluded a treaty of peace with Athens. Marriage in Crete was matrilocal, as appears from Strabo, and from the laws inscribed on the walls of the temple of Gortyna, which contain many traces of older matriarchal usages. Thus the mother's brother occupies an important position and is responsible for the bringing up of the children. A woman, on marriage, retained full control of her property, and like the husband, had the right of divorce at pleasure. A man's property passed to his children, but in the absence of children his sister's children might be heirs.''

It shows not only Israel, but all the countries and islands around it, had the tradition of matriarchy from the remote past.

Mother Goddess ; The Real Lord of Royal Wealth and Revenue

In the administrative documents, there is constant reference to temples. A very large number of persons is mentioned in their service cult personnel, artisians, labourers, as well as large numbers of men liable for the performance of compulsory public duties. For this reason the social and political system of a sumerian city such as Lagash has been called the "temple state".[45]

They (temple states) deal with temple cult (sacrifices, festivals) management of the temple lands (grain cultivation, vegetable gardening, temple herds, provision of sacrificial animals, sheep shearing,) fisheries in fresh water and at sea, crafts and commerce (acquisition of foreign goods by merchants acting for the state), and accounts of wages paid to personnel. The head of the whole machine, often mentioned as receiving revenue, is the ensi or, in the temple of the city goddess, the Ensis wife.[46]

Jacquetta Hawkes[47] upholds the above view point like this, "The head of this whole organization, often mentioned in the Lagash tablets as receiving revenue from the god Ningirsu's estate, was the Ensi, the ruler who was seen as- Ningirsu's human steward. In the temple of the city goddess, Ningirsuś wife Baba, the Ensi's wife played the corresponding role."

It is obvious that in the beginning the basis of origin of state was temple of mother goddess or the worship of an ancient mother goddess. And upto that age all the powers of kingship or sovereignty were vesting in her. That is why all the expenses and collection of revenue were assigned to her.

No texts so far known give us direct information on the private sphere of the economy. Archives on the management of large estates in private hands do not occur until the old Babylonian period (1995 B.C.)[48]

Our oldest class of documents from Sumer, some of which go back to Early Dynastic II, are land-sale contracts. Interestingly[49] enough, these are written not on clay tablets but on stone, for the sake of preservation. We may suppose, a sign of the importance attached to the transaction. The great majority of them come from the area of Akkadian settlement.Akkadian personal names occur often, and we get the first attempts at writing down the Akkadian language. Sales are made, for the most part, not by individuals but by families or clans. These documents on stone are found individually and not in archives, as they are private and not public records.[50] It is evident, that the system, which was in vogue in Sumer, was likewise that of guild system in India in ancient period.

The Cult of Mother Goddess in Indus Valley and Matriarchal System

We know that the cult of mother goddess was in prevalence not only in the countries of middle-east but also in Egypt and Crete island. It is now a proved theory that the founders of Indus-Valley Civilization, in Neolithic Chalcolithic age, came from the same region of middle-east and Mediterranean sea from where the figurines and cult of mother goddess have been discovered. Hence it will be reasonable to say that they brought cult of mother goddess along with them. Figurines of mother goddess have been unearthed most probably from every site of Indus Valley towns (Plate no. VI). These figurines are of terracotta. The commonest type is a standing figure adorned with a wide girdle, often with a loin-cloth and almost always with a necklace and an emphatic head dress, which is generally fan-shaped above, sometimes with a shell like cup or pannier.[51] These female figurines are generally found in broken fragments are very strong evidences to show that these are the figures of the great mother goddess, which was worshipped in the vast area of middle-east and Indus Valley in ancient times.

Martimer Wheeler throws light on the outward shape of the figure and writes,[52] "The feature and general modelling are of the crudest ; the eyes and breast are circular pellets, the nose beak like, and the mouth on applied strip of clay with a horizontal gash. No special artistry went to the making of these figures. Occasionally a lump of clay is added to represent an infant at the breast or on the hip ; and the general notion of fertility ; whether in thanksgiving or in anticipation is further indicated by representation of pregnancy although there in no emphasis of the generative organs such as is normal to mother goddess cultures."

A plant is seen issuing from the generative organ of a figure of a mother goddess depicted on a Harappan seal.[53] She is mother goddess of fertility (see Illustration VI-5) In India even today she is the guardian of the house and village, presides over child birth and taking a more human interest in their needs is altogether closer to her worshippers than any of the recognised Hindu gods. It seems likely that she was honoured by the ancient inhabitants of the Indus valley, but whether she was ?[54] For in no[55] country in the world has the worship of the Divine Mother been from time immemorial so deep-rooted and ubiquitous as in India. Her shrines are found in every town and hamlet throughout the length and breadth of the land. She is the mother or 'Great Mother' and prototype of the power (Prakriti) which developed into that of Shakti.[56]

In Vedas, this goddess is known as Aditi, Viraj, Vasupatni, Visvarūpā, Vaisvadhāyā, Kevali, etc. She is the great principle of motherhood identified with universal nature or infinity. She is described as intact (anarvo), widely expanded and extensive belonging to all men and producing heaven and earth, the mistress of the cosmic order (rta)[57]

The Patriarchal form of Families among the Aryans

As a matter of fact, originally neither mother goddess worship was prevalent among the Aryan, nor matriarchal family system was part of their life. Jacquetta Hawkes[58] puts forth her viewpoint on this aspect of Aryan culture, "There is no question of any pure or coherent Indo-European race. But still it seem's to be true that originally they were a nomadic cowherders who had a strong patriarchal social system and definitely their all deities were masculine."

The position of woman among the Hindus was more pitiable than the patriarchal society of Rome. According to the code of Manu in her childhood she should live under the command of her father, in her youth under her husband, while widow she should live under the will of her sons. A woman should never be allowed to enjoy her own will. She should worship her husband like a god.[59]

But in Vedic age, position of woman was better, there were learned women like Gargi. Robert Briffoult comments upon the position of woman of Vedic age,[60] "But the oldest Indian records reveal a very different position. "Let a wife" a Vedic hymn declares, "be absolute mistress over her father-in-law, absolute mistress over her mother-in-law ; let her be mistress over her husband's brother." Writers of the epic period were aware of the change. Thus Pandya in the Mahabharata says, "Women were not formerly immured in houses and dependent upon husbands and relatives. They used to go about freely enjoying themselves as best they pleased. They did not then adhere to their husbands faithfully ; and yet, O beauteous one, they were not regarded as sinful, for that was the sanctioned usage of the times. The present practice of women being confined to one husband for life hath been established but lately."

It shows that in early Vedic age Aryans' woman enjoyed freedom to some extent but soon after their settlement in India she was put down. But, on the other hand, indigenous peoples worshipped their woman.

The Matriarchal Inheritance among the Nagas and non-Aryan Tribes.

While, in the second stage of evolution of human civilization, land was naturally distributed among the tribes or families for the purpose of hunting and collecting roots and fruits, but the families or tribes were still matriarchal. But owing to increase in conflicts among different tribes, for the purpose of possession of land, importance of man grew and the men showing topmost courage and bravery were slowly emerging into tribal heads or chiefs. As woman was a traditional chief of family or tribe, she was still a real lord of land or dominion. But if such a brave person was chosen by woman to be her husband he immediately after marriage, became tribal chief or king. In other words husband used to get power of sovereignty from his wife, who was a born queen. Vedic and Puranic period was a like wise age of non-Aryan dominions. In different parts of India[61] there were matriarchal kingdoms of Naga tribes. There are numerous examples of them in history. It is apparent from the description of the Ramayan (vii- 87 – 89), the Mahabharata (I-75-18, 25) and Bhagwat Purana (IX - 1 - 13, 42) that Vahlika had a matriarchal kingdom. Bhagwat (IX - 1 - 41) again informs that at, some times, there was a sovereignty of woman in south India. According to description of Magasthenes (322 BC), Pandya kingdom of south was ruled by a woman.[62] According to Atharvaveda (v-22-7, 8, 14) there was sovereignty of woman in Mujwant, Vahlika, Mahabrab, Anga and Magadha kingdoms. As stated in Mahabharata (VIII-44, 45) Vahlika, Āratta, Kāraskar, Mahinsak, Kalinga, Kerala, Karkotaka (kingdom of Malva) were kingdoms of women's sovereignty. (Gauri Shankar Ojha, Rajputane Ka Itihas Part I P-34). According[63] to the Ramayana (I-24-26), there was reign of a Yakshi, named Tātak in Kurush and Malad countries, situated in the south of junction of Saryu and Ganga. According to description of the Mahabharata (I-156, 163) there was reign of demon woman Hidimba in a country in the neighbourhood of south Panchala, in the south of Ganga. There was also rule of Bākāsura in the capital of Ek-Chakra of another country (I-156-163). According to a description in Haribamsa (II-6), there was a kingdom of Sakat (Dev-Kshettra) under dominion of demon woman Putana (son giver, Pali-Bahuputtaka) near Mathura at the bank of Yamuna.Again, according to description of the Mahabharata (II-31-21, 59), in Mahishmati, which was capital of country at the bank of Narmada and at one time 'Capital of Sahasrarjuna of Hehaya, there was rule of woman. (Sharad Patil PP-143-44)[64]

The Ikshwakus of Kausal and Kashi, a Matriarchal Family

We have earlier shown that Ikshwakus originally came from western Asia. In ancient times, the tribes, which most probably can be called as Manvya or Naga, all had matriarchal heritage and family system. It means inheritance right of sovereignty was adherent to the eldest daughter of the royal family. According to the Ramayana, the consort virgin queen of Dashratha was Kausalya ; the word 'Kausalya' means 'princess of Kausal'. Lakshman reminded Rama, that their mother Kausalya was real lord of 1000 villages. She could, very easily, feed all the persons who depend upon her.[65] From this, we can conclude that Kausalya was Rashtri (real lord of lands See Chapter VI P-140) of Kausal, that is why she married her brother Dasratha. Similarly Sita, being the legal heiress of that matriarchal family, was married by Rama and would have become king of Kausal.[66] According to Dasharath Jatak story no 461, which is a work of earlier time than Ramayana, in Banaras, the capital of Kashi-Kausal kingdom, Rama Pandit, the son of Rajrishi Dasratha, married his sister Sita and came to throne after his father.[67]

A similar example is in Udaya Jataka story no 458 : The Prince of Kashi, Udayabhaddā, could only come to throne, after marrying his own younger sister, whose name was also Udaya-bhadda.[68]

The Adi-Tirthankar of Jain- tradition. Rishabhadeva also married his own sisters Sumangal and Sunanda.[69]

Before the marriage of Rishabhadeva,[70] boy and girl, the twin child used to be born at the same time from the womb of the same mother and by the passage of time, while youth, the couple used to turn into wife and husband. It means in those days the marriages of brothers and sisters were in vogue. Rishabhadeva was first Rajrishi (King-priest) of Kausal and his father was Nabhi and name of his mother was Marudevi. His Gotra was Kashyapa and family (racial) or tribal name Ikshwaku.[71] Father Nabhi, in the pedigree of Ikshwaku family was seventh Kulkar (family heir). It means Mārudevi was still legal Rashtri (Real lord of lands) of Kausal. And for the purpose of coronation, it was compulsory for Rishabha to marry his sister, the legal heiress of Kausal.[72]

Here, the king Dashratha and Rishabha have been called Rajrishi. Such a system was in vogue in Sumer and Indus Valley as will be described on some latter pages. As such all these traditions of Kausal and Kashi indicate that their origin was western Asia. Similarly Sakya family of Buddha was also matriarchal; (see detail in chapter VI PP-164-65)

Satavahana-a Matriarchal Family

There was also a tradition of matriachal form of family among the Satavahanas. In the Karle cave inscription[73] of Vasishthi Putra Sri Pulmavi, there is mention of : RANNO. VĀSITHI PUTS SIRI PUL MĀVIS. Similarly there is also mention of name of Siri Yagya Satkarni, in the Nasik cave inscription[74] RANNO GAUTAMĪ PUTS SAMI SIRI YAGYA SĀTAKĀRISA.

This proves that there was a tradition of maternal names among the Satvahanas. In ancient times, there is no trace of use of maternal names among the Aryan Rishis and Kshatriyas of Vedic Age. But, during Brahmana age, we find traces of use of maternal names in Particular. Its main reason was that in Gangetic Valley Aryans were much impressed by the tradition of use of maternal names by Dravidian[75] people. Hence, it is clear that tradition of use of maternal names was prevalent among the Naga race and Satavahanas and continued in their family. As we notice the effect of tradition of maternal names among the Aryans of North India. Similarly, we notice the effect of paternal name among the Nagas of South India.

The Ikshwakus of Sri Parvata, Matriarchal family.

According to some scholars, the Ikshwakus of Sriparvata were-good or Aryan Kshatriya. Prominent advocate of this theory is Dr. K.P. Jayaswal.[76] He puts forth his remarks- "The family was of a good Kshatriya stock from the North. They married cousins like the ancient Ikshwakus. They very likely had migrated to the South in the imperial days of Satavahanas when the latter reached the United Province and Bihar."

Later, they established themselves in the eastern zone of Satavahanaś empire to share the responsibility of security.

This family was matriarchal in character similar to Ikshwakus of ancient age i.e., the families of Rishabhadev, Parashwa Nath, Rama and Buddha. We have following evidences in support of this view. (A) The names of kings of this family were matriarchal in forms such as Maharaja Vasisthiputra, Ikshwakusiri Chatmul I and Raja Mathhariput siri vir Purisa Data.

(B) Vira Purisa Data[77] married his three maternal and cousin sisters, likewise ancient Ikshwakus.

(C) Most important evidences are 18 inscriptions[78] traced out from Sri-Parvata. All these inscriptions are grants issued by ladies of this royal family and none by king or male member. Because among matriarchal families ladies are real heiress and lord of estate and progeny etc, even revenue collection and expenses of kingdom were dealt with and account for in the name of queen that is why all above grants were issued by ladies only. Such a tradition was in prevalence among the Satavahanas, their ancient overlords.

The Khasi Naga of Assam, a Matriarchal tribe.

Similar to Naga Kukki, Bodo, Tangkhul, Koliya, Mao, Angamis, Ringma etc., Khasi is also a Naga tribe in origin. According to A.B. Keith,[79] Khasi is a Alpine race of Dinaric origin. Khasi mother is not only head and source but also bond of union of the family. In the most primitive part of the hills, the Synteng country, she is the only owner of real property and through her alone is inheritance transmitted. The father has no kinship with his children, who belong to their mother's clan, whatever he earns goes to his own matriarchal stock, and at his death his bones are deposited in the cromlech of his mother's kin.[80]

In the Khyrim or Nongkrem[81] state, there is a spiritual head i.e., a High Priestess, Kasiem Sad, who is responsible for the due performance of the state religious ceremonies, although as already stated, the Siem also performs some of these duties. The temporal power here is delegated by High Priestess to a Siem, who is her son or her nephew or occasionally some more distant male descendant.

She[82] is succeeded by her eldest surviving daughter, failing daughters, by the eldest daughter of her eldest daughter, failing daughters of her eldest daughter, by the eldest daughter of her second daughter, and so on.

The Siem is appointed from the Siem family, there being such family in each of the fifteen Khasi states.

Causes of Rise and Fall of Matriachal Tradition.

A most genuine account of cause of rise and fall of the tradition is given by Frezer.[83] He writes-

"In those countries where women were considered to heiress of kinship and kingship, the kings used to get the power of sovereignty from the hereditary princesses of royal families, the real rulers of government, which was solely depending on marriage relation. In several examples, the princes with the object of possessing royal crown married their real sisters, the royal princesses. This happened repeatedly otherwise there was risk of going of possession of royal crown into the hands of other tribes or Ganas. After the death of wife or royal queen, it was compulsory for the king to vacate the royal throne because his possession of royal throne was solely depending on marriage alliance. If he wished to continue his office after the death of his wife, it was necessary to marry his eldest daughter, than the real heiress of Royalty or royal power."

We have shown earlier that such like custom was in vogue in Egypt. This custom was not limited to royal families only but was prevalent among general public also. Either this system went from India to Egypt or Egyptian system came to India. Since, it is well known that civilization of Egypt was older than India, one can very easily conclude that this system reached India from Egypt like wise Indus. Valley civilization came from Sumer. We have also shown that this custom was in vogue in all the other countries of western Asia i.e., Israel, Syria, Babylonia, Mesopotamia etc., so it is clear that this migration took place through these countries. According to Mikawaltari (the Egyptian) in ancient time, this tradition was in prevalence from India up to Egypt and particularly in Naga tribes. Its main reason was woman who being the representative of Bhumata (Earth mother), was considered to be real owner or lord of land (earth) or Rashtri or Ratt, that is why right of sovereignty went to woman.[84]

We have also shown on earlier pages that Aryans had patriarchal tradition. So, it is clear that there were two different cultures in India: first ancient matriarchal culture of Dravidian Nagas and other patriarchal of new immigrant Aryans. But owing to expansion of Aryan tribe towards east and south, both the cultures came in contact with each other and later due to Aryanization of indigenous royal families, this system faded to some extent. But main reason of its rapid fading was another as and when the royal queen daughter of matriarchal side went to patriarchal family, the tribal or family royal throne was also transferred to the other side. Owing to this difficulty the tradition faded very rapidly. Such examples of transferring of sovereignty from one family to the other can be quoted from the history. Bharsiva Nagas were ruling in central province, but their right of inheritance was transferred to the Vakataka family, because their royal daughter married to Gautami putra of Vakataka. That is why the Rudarsena I, who was born from the Bharsiva Royal daughter, became legal heir of Naga throne.

It means Naga kingdom of Bharshiva was annexed in the Vakataka empire.[85]

According to Haribamsa,[86] four kingdoms of south India, were estabilished by the four sons of Yadu, born from four Naga Royal maidens. But historical fact behind this event is that the original founder of Pallava Kingdom, Virakurcha, married a Naga Royal maiden of Bharsiva and became legal heir and king of Naga country of Bharsiva.

God-King or Raj-Rishi Tradition in Sumer.

Originally there were city-states in Sumer which had their control over city and its surrounding area. But this is most interesting to note that development of the cult of mother goddess gave birth to political and religious custom of Raj-Rishi (godking) also. It means one man was head priest of city temple, either he was himself national god or representative of god. Equally significant was the emergence of the concept of kingship and all the complex forms of ritual and of art that went with it. Sometimes, as with the Pharaoh, king and high priest were united in the same person who acquired godlike attributes and godlike power.[87] The rulers of Sumer and Akkad were seen as stewards of the gods, their title of 'lugal' means 'great man'. Pharaoh was above humanity, he was Horus himself, universally portrayed on equal terms with the greatest divinities.[88] It means kings of Egypt and Sumer had god like powers and were head priest as well. In equal term duties of non-Vedic Indian Brahman (Priest) and non-Vedic Kshatriya (warrior) were assigned to one man or he was a Raj-Rishi of later Indian tradition.

Development of the System

Robert Adams[89] throws light on the development of system of god king in Mesopotamia-"Apparently the first specialized administrative group or ruling stratum, was composed of hierarchies of priests. These priests were associated with monumental temples and were in the service of gods who were regarded as resident in the individual community."

There is, however[90], no evidance in the Early Dynastic period for the divinization of kings during life, such as we get in that of Agade. There are cases of posthumous deification (Lugalbanda and Gilgamesh of uruk), but these are early and are not repeated in Early Dynastic III. But, with Mesalim, and with Eanatum of Lagash, we have the earliest known cases of divine filiation. Mesalim in one inscription calls himself "Beloved son of Ninhursanga" (the Sumerian mother-goddess) Eanatum claims to "drink the good milk of Ninhursanga". None of this means that the ruler regards himself divine.[91]

We can conclude from the above evidences that the system of God-king (Raj-Rishi) developed as a result of reaction from both directions that the kings became priests, seems to be an ambiguous viewpoint. But on the other hand, it is evidently clear that priesthood developed in the kingship due to enhancement of too much responsibilities of the former.

It has already[92] been seen that Sumerian titles En, Ensi and lugal were current by Protoliterate times. As they emerge into the light of history, their (no doubt changing and evolving) meanings can be translated respectively as priestly-lord, governor, and king, the literal meaning of lugal being "great man". It may be, however, that originally these titles did not imply distinct functions but were simply terms selected by different city-states for their rulers-such as in England, through various historical chances Oxford colleges are headed by rectors, presidents, masters and deans, although their duties are now all very much the same.[93]

Certainly the title En had a special meaning for the city-state of Uruk. During most of the Early Dynastic period there, and there along, it was used for the ruler in his secular, including military function. Else-where it was applied to high priests, and it was in this sense that it survived into later times that En was a holy and ancient title is shown by the fact that it was incorporated in the names of two of the oldest and greatest of the gods Enlil and Enki.[94]

The National Kingdom or Republic Confederacy in Sumer.

The National kingship[95] had a special relationship with the cosmic states of the gods, quite distinct from that of the city state-which a god simply held for his own livelihood, like a lord of the manor. The national kingship was determined by Anu and the assembly of gods, and the great god concerned, the owner of the dominant city state, was an official of the cosmic state charged to exercise the Enlil function.

This meant that the human king of the state was also acting for the cosmic state. Nippur, which belonged to Enlil, was a holy city that never became a city-state. Presumably, the god was regarded as residing there for the purpose of exercising his Enlil function over the National state, and that was why all aspiring National kings needed to claim possession of Nippur.[96] Moreover, when a city first won the hegemony, its presiding duty had to go to Nippur to seek Enlil's acceptance of his or her human deputy in his office as supreme king. Evidently, this would have been impossible if Enlil's city had been in unfriendly hands.[97]

City-States and God-kings in Indus Valley

Famous archaeologist E.Mackay has pointed to the obvious importance of the great central building or buildings, now capped by the ruined stupa and itself set high upon an artificial platform of mud brick, some twenty feet thick. Dr. wheeler has recently investigated just such a central mass of buildings among the ruins of Harappa, which he regards as a citadel and the stronghold of a bureaucratic or priest-king regime. At Mohenjo-daro there is some evidence that the regime was a theocracy very similar in type to the contemporary theocracies of Sumer.[98]

Similarly, findings of a line of quarters of brass-workers and granary in fort area of Mohen-jodaro and another granary attached to fort at Harappa, proves control of priest-kings on craft and farm product both like those of Sumer.[99] It shows that in Indus valley, theocracy like those of Sumer and control on craft and farm product, was in prevalence.

God-Kings Tradition in Later Indus Valley Period.

It can be proved from the Rigvedic account (IV-19-8; II-11-5 and II-20-7) that regime of- Sapta-Sindhu was under control of Vritra. He has been stated to be a Ahi or serpent(II - 12-3). As such Ahi-Vritra was chief of those people of Sapta-Sindhu who have been called Dasas.[100]

Thus, Dasas also would have been Ahi or serpents. Their chief, Vritra, called Ahi, himself was a Naga king. Hence, Dasas were Nagas.

Tvashtā asked Indra to shape vajjra, to kill Ahi-Vritra (R.V. I-32-2). In response to the above, Indra appointed Trisirā (three-headed), the son of Tvashtā, as his priest. But, later for fear of rise in revolt he beheaded him. (R.V. X-8-8, 9). This Trisirā is also known as Vishvarupa.[101]

Why, Indra suspected Trisirā, to rise in revolt, we get the answer of this question from Taitreya Samhita, where it is mentioned that Indra, for fear of rise in revolt, broke heads of Vishvarupa son of Tvashtā, nephew of Asuras and priest of gods.[102] Trisirā son of Tvashtā, whose name has been mentioned in Rigveda and Ajhi-Dāhak of Avesta, is one and the same. In Yāsht-9, Dāhak has been described as Trimukhā and Trisirā (threeheaded). The Sanskrit form of Dahāk would be Dāsa. The, Trisirā, the priest of Indra described in Rigveda, was a Asura is clear from the Taitireya Samhita. Therefore it is proved that Asura and Dasas were one and the same and these Dasas were Ahi or serpent also.[103] Hence Asura were also Nagas.

There is a reference of Vritrajita in the Mahabharata (Adi-281-1). In this myth, Bheeshma, admires Virtra of his great virtues of high glory, religiousness and limitless sciences. As soon as Indra killed Vritra, Brahma-hatyā came out of his body and encircled Indra. (Tatireya Samhita Kand 2/5/1). In Aitireya-Brahman (Chapt 35 Part 2) There is a myth in which Indra has been blamed for five sins i.e. killing of Vishva (Tirisirā), killing of Vritrā, feeding of Yatis to dogs, killing of Asurmadhana and attacking of Brahaspati. From these events Dharmanand Kosambi[104] has concluded that Vritrā was a Brāhman. He has also further put forth his view that there are evidences of Brahmana (priests) of Sumers, who became kings as well. Kings were also sometimes priests of some gods, or some times duties of Brahmanas and Kshatriyas invest in one man. Here Kosambi is indicating towards the system of Raj-Rishi or god-king about which we have given a detailed description on foregone pages.

The Mahabharata refers to the powerful Gramas on the banks of the Indus, it seems a probable reference to the city states on the banks of that river.

In the Sabhaparva[105] of Mahabharata (II-29-8) the northern campaign of Arjuna is described. There in are obvious references to the city states. He subjugated the city of Abhisari, than the city of Urga along with its president Rochamāna, and the city of Simhapura protected by Chitrāyudha (MB 2-24, 18-19) since Rochamāna and Chitrāyudha are not mentioned expressly as kings with their honorifics.

Here the ''president of city state'' means these were small republics, existing in the north-west region of India. These presidents were kings as well as priests of their states. Since presidents or kings of republics were originally sacred persons, K.P. Jayaswal[106] produces evidence in support of this view, "We gather from Panini that there were two Rajanyas amongst the Andhaka-Vrishni (VI-2-34), The Kasika commenting on that says that the rule does not apply to the members of the Andhakas and Vrishnis as such but to their Rajanyas only the Rajanyas being the leader of the families consecrated to rulership. The names of several of these 'dual' groups of rulers of the Sini and Vasudeva, Svaphalaka and Chaitraka are cited in the Kasika".

Legend of Visvamitra is found in the Aitreya Brahmana (VII-13-18). According to account of legend, although, Visvamitra was a Black non-Aryan Brahmana of Ahivritra linage, adopted Sunassepa son of Ajigartta descendant of famous Aryan Angirisa Rishi, to legalize his Brahmanhood. He has been called by Sunassepa as Rajaputra. His progeny is said to be Andhra, Pundra, Sabra, Pulinda all Dasyus. (See Chapter X P-p 265-67 for detail). This shows Visvamitra was non-Aryan Raj-rishi.

Rajrishi tradition was followed by Buddha and Mahavira both, they were princes of Sakya and Lichchhavi Kshatriya royal families respectively on one hand and founder and promoter of Buddhist and Jain religion on the other or Raj-rishi. According to famous historian K. P. Jayaswal such a system was prevailing in the republican society of ancient period also where king was a sacred person in origin. Even in modern age, the Pujari or priest of Naga temples in Himachal Pradesh is a Rathi, who is a Rajput farmer (Chapter II P-20-21). Perhaps, these Rathis are Ratte or Rashtra of Satavahanas who gave birth to Radde or Reddi Rajputs of South. But on the other hand, owing to rigidity of Varna system among the Aryans such a system was impossible. If somewhere it happened so, that would have been owing to effect of long term mutual relation with non-Aryans.[107]

Social System in Sumer; Three Classes

Basis of Aryan social system is four varnas and caste, but there was no such system in Sumerian society, there were three classes only. It will be seen that, Sumerian society was made of nobles, commoners-(presumably including most merchants) clients and slaves. If the "clients" are looked at more closely, they appear to be divided into dependants of the temple, including administrators and superior craftsmen; the mass of the temple personnel; and thirdly, the dependants of nobility.[108]

But Dr. Fry has divided the society of Sumer more clearly[109] "There were three main classes of people in Sumer. The highest contained the priests, the government officials and the army officers. The middle class included the traders, farmers and craftsmen, and last were the slaves (war captives)." Perhaps a similar system was in vogue in native Naga society, who knew no caste system.

Common Man, Warrior

Similar to Sparta common man of Sumeria was a Warrior. It is interesting to note that in Sumerian society, common man was a warrior. It seems that the arrangements for calling up were the same for both. The officials, incharge of civilian and military service, had similar titles. As we have seen, the term Eren was probably applied to men who were liable either for carvee labour or for army.[110] In theory at least it probably comprised all free citizens. Hawkes explains it through an account of an event. "In Mari men called to the army in times of crises included tribesmen as well as settled citizens. The documents for the first time give us an idea of the troops as human beings. It will surprise no one to learn that men were often reluctant to be called to the standards, and the kings' officers were prepared to use tough methods to bring them in. On one occasion, when conscripts from a particular area failed to report, an officer wrote, "If the king approves, let them kill one of the guilty men, cut off his head, and let them take it around among these towns...so that people may be afraid and will quickly assemble.''[111] It is apparent from this event that common man was kshatriya or warrior. Similar system was prevalent among the Naga tribes of India, who were organized into guilds or republican states (see chapter VI PP124-34 for detail).

Kings Public Assemblies.

A single textual reference dating from the Akkadian age suggests that at that time the assembly was on occasion empowered to choose a king. In the common of Ereth, a field belonging to Esabad, the temple of Gula, Kish assembled and Iphurkish, a man of Kish, they raised to kingship. Before that there are no historical records, but evidence of a kind comes first from epic and then from the myths of the gods.[112]

The epic source[113] is the poem known as Gilgamesh and Agga, a story unique among Sumerian epics in being entirely concerned with human being and free from any divine interventions. Gilgamesh in fact appears in it, however unreliably, as the historical king of Uruk of Early Dynastic time. The relevance of the story here is that when Agga, king of kish, sends envoys demanding the submission of Uruk, Gilgamesh first appeals to the convened assembly of the elders of his city to be allowed 'to smite Kish with weapons'. When[114] the elders are cautious and rule in favour of surrender, Gilgamesh turns 'the man of his city'- taken as the assembly (in Sumerian Unken) of the fighting males. The elder's decision is reversed, the men advising,. 'Do not submit to the house of kish, let us smite it with weapons'. From above event, we arrive at a conclusion that upto the beginning of the Early Dynastic age Unken used to take important decision of peace and war. It is also clear that there were two public assemblies to control the vagary of king.

Buddhist and Jain Religions; Indigenous and Asur.

Sham Sastri believes that not only the Buddhist but along with it Jain, the Sankhya and the Zoroastrian systems all deserve the name of Asura religion. He produces evidences in support of his view. "The Mahabharta (Adiparva 67) describes the Buddhists and Jains as descendants of the old Asuras.[115] Again Kapila's Sankhya philosophy is said to be Avaidika opposed to the religion of the Veda". It was, therefore considered to be the religion of Asuras. Shamsastri suggests that Asuri, the disciple of Kapila might have been an Asura. He also refers to the Satpath Brahmana. (X-5-2-20), where Asuras are said to serve the divine person under the name Maya. The same fact is revealed in the Atharvaveda.

Here the name Maya (Mother Goddess) is the mysterious wisdom of Asura.[116] In the Bhagvata-gita also Maya worship is said to have formed part of the Asura religion vide.

NA MĀM DUSKRITINE MŪDHĀḤ PRAPADYANTE NARĀDHAMĀH ।

MĀYAYĀPA HRTAJNĀNĀH ĀSURAM BHĀVAMĀSRITĀH ॥ (VII-15)

Sham Sastri explains the purport of this verse as, "The Asuras as expounded in the Sankhya system or in the Zend Avesta are entirely devoted to the worship of Māyā alone and they do not worship God at all as one supreme being, worthy of worship'. 'Shamsastri'[117] further adds, "According to the Sankhya philosophy it is Māyā termed Prakriti that is productive of the whole world consisting of good and bad."

According to L.H. Mills, "Magism makes the world to consist of two principles, the good principles Ahura Mazda and Angara Mainu the bad principles". Further he asserts, "that the Sankhya is an Asura-religion. Now these Asuras are the Mlechchhas, referred to in the ancient Sanskriti literature and according to him, the original settlers in India before Aryans and they were progenitors of the later Jains, the Buddhists and the Sankhyas" (Journal of K.R. coma oriental institute vol 1-5 Bombay 1922-26).

All scholars can not agree with this odd view point of Sham Sastri, but when a critrical study of, social, religious, political and economical traditions of semitic culture is conducted, we come to the conclusion that it was very close to the Indus Valley as well as with the later Asura and Naga culture. The cult of mother goddess of Sumer and Maya worship of Asurs were not different from each other. Here the Maya means Māttra-Shakti, which was the basis of human religion from mediterranean sea up to India in ancient time. They recognized mother goddess as supreme being and creator of universe, instead of God or Ishwara. Devas or Aryans worshipped God and Asuras worshipped Mother goddess or

Maya, who in later period, is known as Yakshi Matridevi, Bhumata and Haritimata etc.

The Ikshwakus, Dravidians of Naga Race.

Scholars are of the view that Adi Jain-tirthankar, Rishabhadeva[118], whose emblem was a bull, would have been in either way a spiritual guide to the peoples of Indus-Valley Civilization. It is now an open secret that figure of Bull was a well known emblem of Harappan seals or seal impressions, whose evidences have been unearthed in abundance from the excavation of ancient cities of Indus. It is interesting to note that Bansha of Rishabhadeva and Parswanath was Ikshwaku and according to Jain traditions, Parashwanath was prince of Kashi and Kausal with his Gotra Kashyapa and Manavya. It seems that he maintained the Sumerian matriarchal tradition and married his real sisters, named Sumangal and Sunanda. It is also to be noted that all the Jain Tirthankars were god-kings or Raj-Rishi and 22 of them were Kashyapa and Ikshwaku.[119] (See chapter. X P 256-FF for detail).

Similarly Mahavir was also a Raj-Rishi of Kashyap Gotra and a Lichchhavi princes. (See Chapter-X P-260 for detail).

Bhagwan Buddha,[120] the founder of Buddhism was also an Ikshwaku prince. The tradition of marriage with real sister was also prevalent in his family. Sakya Gana of his father was an associate of Vajji tribal confederacy. Thus he was also a Raj-Rishi. Buddha, with great pride, used to call himself a Kshatriya of Ikshwaku family. Obviously here Kshatriya means a non-Arya Vratya Kshatriya. In Many of statues Buddha is seen sheltered by Naga Muchilinda with a canopy of his many fold hoods (See Illustration no. IV) thereby proving his relation with the Naga race. Similarly in the myth of a Sakya youth of Kausal (See P-16) he married a Naga maiden of Udyān. This strengthens the relations of Sakya family with the Naga race.

This is important[121] to note that Parashwanātha, the twenty third Jain Tirthankar, in addition to being an Ikshwaku, was also an Urga Banshi Naga. It means Ikshwaku family was non-Aryan Naga, to which famous king Ram Chandra belonged, since similarity of family or Bansha denotes similar ethnical identity. Family of Ram Chandra was also matriarchal. Hence this family seems to be non-Aryan belonging to the native Naga tribes of Dravidian race. This view gets the support of F. E. Pargitor also. (See Dynastic list chapter IX P 243). The soldiers of his army, according to Ramayan were, totemistic tribal people, like Banaras (monkeys), Richchhas (Bears) instead of Aryan Kshatriyas, adhered to varna system. In the first volume,[122] of this series, a different view point has been expressed that the relation of Ikshwaku family of

Rama was with the first wave of Aryan invaders, which used Gray ware (G.W.) pottery, whose evidences have been found out from Vaisali, Kosambi, Rajghat, Gulrihvaghat and Prahladpur.[123] But above noted social, religious and political evidences are very strong and clear and we are forced to believe that Rama was definitely of non-Aryan origin. An advance and more deep study is necessary to reach any final conclusion. Rama with his family was the resident of Ayodhya but on the other hand extensive excavation work conducted by B.B. Lal, exposed not a single example of G.W. and PGW pottery from the ancient site of Ayodhya. This corroborates our viewpoint as stated above. However we can put another evidence in support of our viewpoint. In Sumangal Vilasini, the birth of Sakya or Ikshwaku family of Buddha and Lichchhavi of Mahavira has been described to be from real brother and sister (see chapter VI PP 161& 164 for detail). Quite similar is the myth of birth of Sakyas or Ikswakus[124] as stated easlier, Lichchhavis were also Ikshwaku (I. A. IX P-178)

The law of Manu (X-22) describes the Lichchhavi as Vratya which clearly implies thereby that they were of outside the pale of Vedic Brahmanical civilization (Manava Dharma shastra X-20-22). It is true that like the Sakyas, the Lichchhavis are also described as Kshatriya but the term Kshatriya in this context may be taken to mean representative of political power rather than a specific caste in the Brahmanical heirarchy. (Rechard Fick'' social organization in north-east India in Buddha's time'' translated by Maitra P-81).

It means both the families ie Lichchhavi and Sakya (Ikshwakus) were also non-Aryan tribes of Matriarchal tradition. Rama was also of black complexion like wise Krishna Yadava. In Balmiki-Ramayan he has nowhere called Arya-Putra or Arya like Pandavas of the Mahabharata.

Homogeneity in Iranian and Indian Cultures.

We have earlier discussed at length that before the appearance of Aryan race in the vast piece of land extending from India upto the Israel, there was culturally, socially, racially and linguistically oneness in the society. The cult of mother goddess and serpent worship was prevalent in western Asia as well as in Indus Valley. Similarly matriarchal form of family and heredity was peculiarity of their societies at both the places.

Ancient language of Iran was very close to Pishacha or Prakrit-Pali of India (see chapter VII P-188). Of some importance in this regard is David MC Alpin's recent work which gives some evidence for us to believe that in antiquity there was a proto-Elamo-Dravidian language family which covered all southern Iran and extended into the western portion of South Asia (MC Alpin 1975). The cultural historical importance of such a linguistic tie would seem to be important and far reaching.[125] It is also corroborated from this that Brahui (Dravidian of Bluchistan) is a remnant of the same linguistic belt, which was in use in Indus Valley.

Mr. Tarapad Bhattacharya throws light on the similarity of cultural and religious tradition of ancient India and Iran.[126] "Even before the Vedic age, the religions of both the countries (India and Iran) were alike. The excavations in Luristan and other places of Iran and Indus valley sites of India reveal that cult of mother goddess was prevalent in both the countries. The inhabitants of these countries were followers of matriarchal culture and they also used to worship serpent deity from very beginning of their civilization."

Similarly, if a map of habitation of different races is prepared for both the lands, you will be astonished to see that there is a remarkable similarity in their situations also.

Dixon[127] informs us that the people of Alpine race used to live in the northern region of vast piece of land spreading from Iran to Asia-Minor and in the region south and west of Mesopotamia, were the dolicho-cephalic, Semitic Mediterraneans or Dravidians,[128] and in between above mentioned two races were living their blended groups or races who gave birth to the great sumerian culture. A slim fringe of sea shore of south Arbia[129] and Iran is covered by the population of Negroid and a blended race of Negroid and Alpine in South Arabian population like wise those of southern India. It seem that Luristan was also inhabited by the blended races of mediterranian and Alpines, which have been called Meso-cephalic by the anthropologists and perhaps this habitation area was stretched out up to Tepe-Sialk and Tepe Hissar of Central Iran.

Dr. Fry P. Somerset[130] tells us 'that round headed, (Alpine) Sumerian race went to sumer from North Frontier region of India and Afghanistan.' It means this race was original inhabitant of this land from where they moved north and Westward into Western Asia. It proves that north-west region of India (upper valley of Indus) was inhabited by round headed Alpine race and South region by long headed Mediterranean and in between them their blended races alike Western Asia. There is also a belt of round headed Alpine in South West India, alike one in Southern Arbia. It means these vast pieces of land i.e., Western Asia and India both were alike culturally, linguistically, socially and ethnically. In addition to passes of north-west the southern desert of Iran and Baluchistan was easy to pass in ancient time. According to Jacquetta Hawkes[131] "At that time southern Iran was less arid than it has since become and some of its valley had marshy conditions."

Hence it is crystal clear that transmigration of people of both the lands was through Makran desert. Since people of both the lands were great-producer and traders, which is also proved from the similarity of name of many goods (rice, peacocks, cotton[132], etc.) and seals[133] and seal impressions of both the lands that this transmigration of people of both the countries was a usual practice. It seems from this long account of evidences that this transmigration was in practice from the time while Sumerians reached India and founded Indus Valley Culture. Hence this oneness of peoples and cultures of two countries was as old as Indus Valley Culture. It seems that Indus Valley Culture was an extension of Sumerian culture.

Summary and Conclusion

The ancient society of Sumer, in general constituted of two races, first round headed Alpines or Sumerians, second long headed mediterraneans or Dravidians also known as Semites, Akkadians and Hyksos. Sumerians came from north-west India (Afghanistan and North east Iran) and Semites from nearby desert west of Mesopotamia.

These Semites or Hyksos invaded Egypt in 1750 BC and ruled there for quite sometime. Names of their princes were Dushratha and Ramesses and their deity was Baal or Resheph representing sun god or Surya. Dr. Buddha Prakash has identified them as Akkakus, Yakshus or Ikshwakus of Puranic tradition, who first of all appeared as a participant in 10 kings war of Rigvedic fame. They were also known as eastern Manavah and Kashyapas. As such these people, perhaps, as a result of threat from Hittite invasion from north moved towards India and settled in Indus valley, perhaps during mature Harappan Age.

The earliest civilization of mankind took its birth in Western Asia about ten thousand years back from present. Henceforth earliest social, religious, political and economic traditions also took their birth and developed there. The earliest example of cult of mother goddess has been traced out from Crete island and countries of eastern coast like Israel, Palestine, Syria and Mesopotamia. In this way the cult of mother goddess (Earth mother) or mother creator of universe took its birth in this land. Similarly form of matriarchal family also developed from aforesaid cult, which made the woman all powerful in every sphere of life. Her husband was simply a life companion and boarder, who practically had no right, whereas woman possessed them all, such as heiress of royal throne, hereditary property, house, flocks, progeny etc. Her husband used to take authority of kingship from her and was ruler only upto the time he was husband of real lord of the sovereignty.

This tradition was also transferred to Indus Valley along with their migration, that is why evidences of cult of mother goddess are found in

Indus Valley towns, Similarly tradition of matriarchal form of family is noted among the non-Aryan families of Rishabhadeva, Parashwanath, Ikshwakus of Kausal, Sakyas of Buddha, Satavahans, Ikshwakus of Sriparvata and also Nagas of east and south India in modern age.

According to Frezer, matriarchal tradition developed and reached its top heights while marriages of real brothers and sisters began, which helped in avoiding transfer of royal throne to other families or tribes in Egypt and Western Asia during Chalcolithic Age. This tradition began to exinguish in historical age, in efforts to avoid transfer of inheritance as cited above, transfer of royal inheritance of Bharsiva Naga family to Vakataka family is a very clear example, while royal daughter of Bharsivas was married to Gautamiputtra of Vakataka family that is why Rudra sena I, who was born from this royal daughter, became legal heir of Naga throne. Owing to this difficulty, this system faded very rapidly.

At the same time, the institution of god-king also took its birth in western Asia. According to Robert Adams, the first specialized administrative group or ruling stratum was composed of hierarchies of priests. These priests were associated with the monumental temples and were in service of gods who were regarded as residents in the individual communities. Later, that priesthood developed in to kingship due to enhancenment of too much responsibilities of the former. We note at Uruk that the En is not merely a priest, he also became ruler of the city and leader of its troops in war. This led to existence of institution of priest king in Sumer. In later period, developed the institution of National kingdom or empire at Nippur which belonged to Enlil. It was a holy city that never became a city state. Presumably the god was regarded as residing there for the purpose of exercising his Enlil function over the National states. He was just like chief of confederacies of Indian clans or republicans in ancient time like Vajji, Trigarta-Shashtha and Andhraka-Vrishini, Videha-Lichchhavi, Malava Kshudraka etc.

Similarly, there were two assemblies of kings-one consisted of elders of city and other of youths of the city i.e., the fighting males known as Unken. These assemblies can be equated with two assemblies of republics in India.

Since the institution of state took its birth from the cult of mother goddess in remote past, hence the head of this whole organization, often mentioned in the Lagash tablets as receiving revenue from the god Ningirsuś estate, was the Ensi, the ruler, who was seen as Ningirsuś human steward. In the temple of the city goddess, Ningirsuś wife Baba, the Ensi's wife played the corresponding role. Thus the real royal power vested in the Ningirsuś wife Baba. This was similar to Rastri or Ragyi (Queen) of Indian pantheon.

No text, so far knowns gives us direct information on the private sphere of the economy and we get the first attempts at writing down the Akkadian language, sales are made for the most part not by individuals but by families or clans. As such the system of ownership of property in Sumer was similar to that of guild system in India. Common man of Sumer, like wise in sangha system of India, was warrior and every one was suppose to learn art of use of arms compulsorily and was suppose to attend war as and when necessary or ordered by the king.

According to Dr. Fry, the social system of Sumer consisted of three classes, the first contained the priest, the government officials and army officers, the second middle class including the traders, farmers and craftmen and last were the slaves who were war captive in general and there was no caste system in their society. There was one class of priest-king against Vedic two Brahmana and kshatriya. Such a system was in existence in Indus Valley and Rigvedic period, among the non-Aryan society. Ahi-Vritra of Rigvedic fame was a Raj-Rishi of Indus Valley society. His towns and citadels were destroyed and he was killed by Indra. He was Asura, Dasa as well as Naga king. In early histroic age we come to face with Jain Tirthankars, Mahavira, and Buddha who were princes and religious persons at the some time at the pattern of sumer.

According to scholars like Sham Sastri, the root of Buddhist, Jain religions, Kapila's sankhya philosophy, was in the religion of Assyrians. These were considered to be the religion of Asuras.

Cult of mother goddess, matriarchal form of family and inheritance, Raj-Rishi system were prevalent among the Ikshwakus of Kausal-Kashi, Brahmadattas of Kashi, or royal family of Parashwanath, Sakyas of Kapilvastu, Ikshwakus of Sriparvata. Since above traditions and Ikshwaku family itself took birth among the Dravidian society of western Asia, hence this family was of non-Aryan Dravidion race in origin.

Before the coming of Aryans from central Asia, there was cultural, social, religious, political, linguistic, social, homogeneity in western Asia and India. Hence people and culture of both the land were one and both of them were different from Aryan society who came from central Asia.

References

1. Fry P. Somerset, "History of the world" P - 16.
2. (a) Hawkes Jacqetta, "The First Great Civilization." PP32-33.
   (b) Dixon B. Roland, "The Racial History of man." P-252.
3. Wheeler REM, "A I Vol. III PP 83-85 (Jan 1947) and Bose N.K. and others, "Human Skeleton from Harappa" ASIC (1963) PP 58-59.
4. Dixon B. Roland P-307.

5. (a) Dixon B. Roland P-311.
   (b) Ibbetson Denzil. "Panjab Castes" PP59-60.
6. Sankalia H.D. "Cemetery H Culture" ACI PP 324-27edited by Passel L. Gregory.
7. Dixon B.Roland PP 252-53.
8. Hawkes Jacquetta PP 66.
9. Ibid.
10. Hawkes Jacquetta P - 67.
11. Bottero Jean, Cassin Elena and Vercoutter jean, "The near East ; The early civilization." PP 391-92.
12. Hawkes Jacquetta. "Ibid" P-305.
13. Bottero, Cassin and Vercoutter P - 392.
14. Ibid.
15. Bottero, Cassin and Vercoutter PP - 392-93.
16. Hawkes Jacquetta P-305.
17. Bottero, Cassin and Vercoutter PP-43-81.
18. Dr. Buddha Prakash, "Rigveda and the Indus Valley Civilization." PP 101-102.
19. R.V. VII-83-7 and VII-18-19.
20. Jayaswal K. P., "Hindu Polity" P-184.
21. See chapter XIII PP 374-75 for detail.
22. Sankalia H.D. "Ramayana Myth or Reality" P-57 peoples Publishing house. New Delhi (1991).
23. Robert Briffoult, "The Mothers" P-86.
24. Bottero, Cassin, and Vercoutter, P-47.
25. Ibid.
26. Bottero, Cassin and Vercoutter P-48.
27. Ibid
28. Hawkes Jacquetta P -187.
29. Hawkes Jacquetta PP 8-9.
30. Robert Briffoult P-80.
31. Ibid.
32. Robert Briffoult, P-80.
33. Robert Briffoult P-80.
34. Robert Briffoult P-81.
35. Ibid.
36. Robert Briffoult PP 81-82.
37. Robert Briffoult P-82.
38. Ibid.

39. Ibid.
40. Ibid.
41. Robert Briffoult PP 82-83.
42. Ibid.
43. Robert Briffoult P-83.
44. Robert Briffoult P-84.
45. Bottero, Cassin and Vercoutter P-76.
46. Bottero, Cassin and Vercoutter PP75-76.
47. Hawkes Jacquetta P-149.
48. Bottero, Cassin and Vercoutter P-76.
49. Bottero, Cassin and Vercoutter P-75.
50. Ibid.
51. Marshall John,"The thousand syllabled speech." Vol I P-49.
52. Wheeler M. "The Indus civilization" III P-91.
53. Shastri K. N. "New light on the Indus Civilization" Volt I P-45 Fig. VIII-5.
54. Mackay E, "Early Indus civilization" PP 53-54.
55. Marshall Sir John, "Mohenjodaro and the Indus Civilization" I P-51.
56. Ibid
57 Aggarwal VS. "Vision in long Darkness" (1963) P-95.
58. Hawkes Jacquetta P-80.
59. Manu V-147, 148, 149.
60. Robert Briffoult P-76.
61. Kosare H.L. "Prachin Bhartatil Nag" P-134.
62. (a) Menon P. "History of Kerala" Vol I PP 65-66.
    (b) Sastri Nilkant KA, "History of South India" PP 81-82.
63. Kosare H.L. 'Ibid' P-134.
64. Kosare H.L. Ibid P-135.
65. Ramayan II-31-22, 23.
66. Patil Sharad "Das Shudrachi Gulamgiri" P-322.
67. Cowell E.W., The Jataka no 461.
68. Cowell E.W. "The Jataka no 458".
69. Acharya Hastimal, "Jain Dharm Ka- Maulik Itihas" Vol. I. PP-24-25.
70. Mullar F. Max, "The Sacred Books of the East".
    Vol. 22 , PP 281-82.
71. Acharya Hastimal Vol I P-23.

72. Patial Sharad P-328.
73. E.I. Vol. VII P-71.
74. E.I. Vol. VIII P-94.
75. Dutta N.K. "The Aryanization of India" P-81.
76. Jayaswal K.P. "History of India" PP 175-76.
77. Jayaswal K.P. P-174.
78. Jayaswal K.P. P-172.
79. Chattopadhyaya S. "Racial Affinities of Early North Indian Tribes" P-71.
80. Gurdon P.R.T. "The Khasis" P-XXIII, XXIV.
81. Gurdon P.R.T. P-68.
82. Ibid.
83. Frezer J.G., "Adonis Attis Ogirish" Part I PP-41-42 mentioned by H.L. Koshare P-136.
84. (a) Kosare H.L. P-137.
    (b) Patil Sharad Vol. I. P-106.
85. Jayaswal K.P., "History of India" PP 16-17.
86. Jayaswal K.P., PP-179-80.
87. Hawkes Jacquetta. Intro P. XXV.
88. Hawkes Jacquetta P-13.
89. Hawkes Jacquetta P-8.
90. Bottero, Cassin and Vercoutter P-73.
91. Ibid.
92. Hawkes Jacquetta P-155.
93. Ibid.
94. Hawkes Jacquetta P-155.
95. Hawkes Jacquetta P-160.
96. Hawkes Jacquetta P-161.
97. Ibid
98. Mackay E. "Early Indus civilization" Intr P XII and XIII.
99. Mackay E. P-45.
100. Kosambi Dharma Nand. "Hindi Sanskriti. Ani Ahimsa" P-14.
101. Ibid.
102. Ambedkar B.R. "Who were the Sudras ?" P-109.
103. Ibid.
104 (a) Kosambi Dharmanand PP 15-16.
105. Mishra S.N. "Ancient Indian Republics" P-5.
106. Jayaswal K.P., "Hindu Polity" PP37-38.
107. (a) ParpolaAshko "The Indus Script Decipherament" (1976).
    (b) Jayaswal K.P. "Hindu Polity" PP 37-38.

108 Hawkes Jacquetta PP-150-51.

109. Fry. P. Somerset, "P-19.

110. Hawkes Jacquetta P-165.

111. Hawkes Jacquetta P-167.

112. Hawkes Jacquetta P-152.

113. Ibid.

114. (a) Hawkes Jacquetta P-153.

115. (a) Chapelkar M.Nalinee, "Ancient India and Iran" P-33.

(b) Fergusson also accepts this view, "Tree and Serpent worship" P-78.

116. Chapelkar M. Nalinee P-33.

117. Chapelkar M. Nalinee P-34.

118. Jyoti-Prasad Jain "Bhartiya Itihas, EK Drishti" P-27.

119. Oldham C.F. "The Sun and Serpent" P-177.

120. Oldham C.F. P-178.

121. Jyoti Prasad Jains PP-36-38 and 45.

122. The Founders of Indus Valley Civilization Vol I P-94.

123. Tripathi Vibha, "The Painted Grey ware: An Iron Age Culture of North India" P-81.

124. (a) Law B.C. "Tribes in Ancient India" P-299.

(b) Gokhale B.G. "Samudra Gupta" PP-25-32.

125. Passehl L. Gregory A.C.I. (1979) P-255.

126. (a) Chapelkar M. Nalinee P-18.

(b) Bhattachārya Tarāpad. "ABOR" Vol. 51 (1970) P-36.

127. Dixon B. Roland P-314.

128. Dixon B. Roland PP-252-53.

129. Dixon B. Roland P-255.

130. Fry P. Somerset P-16.

131. Hawkes Jacquetta, P-32.

132. (a) Iyengar, "The trade of India" I H Q II P-42.

(b) Meissner, "Babylonian and Assyrian" I PP 223-53.

133. "Wheeler REM, " PP 117-18.

Chapter-6

THE SANGHAS OR REPUBLICS IN INDIA

It is most interesting to note that at the day-break of Indian History we found a glorious system of Native Indian Culture known as Sangha or republican, which controlled social, economic, political, religious and military life of people at the same time which took India to its glorious heights.

Etymology : The brightest aspect of the indigenous Naga culture was tradition of guild or Sangha system. This was the best system so far invented by humankind to derive definite object. According to Bhandarkar- "The Word Sangha comes from the root san+han" "to collect together." The regular noun formed from it is Sanghāt, which means merely a "collection" or "assemblage". But there is another noun derived from it, though it is irregularly formed viz 'Sangha'[1]

Sangha or Gana is, therefore not a disorderly composition conglomeration, but a combination of individuals for a definite object, in other words a corporate body. It will be seen that there can be as many kinds of Sanghas as there are different purposes with which they can be constituted.[2]

During the Vedic age, the term Gana signified the tribe but according to renowned historian K.P. Jayaswal[3], "later this term signified 'the form of government,' on the other hand Sangha, signified 'the state'. As Patanjali says Sangha is so called because it is one body, a unity (Sanhanana Panini V-1-59). As we shall see presently, the Sangha, as a unit, a bodypolitic had its arms like a king or a corporation aggregate."

Types of Sangha

There were three kinds of Sanghas, prevalent among the ancient society of India : (1) political (2) religious (3) trade and crafts. Indian History begins with the advent of Buddha and his religion. At the day, break of our history, we find enormous political republics in Northern and Central India. Even the organizations of Buddhist and Jain religions were formed on the basis of Sangha. S.N. Misra[4] gives details of organization of Jain religion. "Jain religion was split up into a number of Ganas, the Ganas into Kulas, Kulas into Sakhas and Sakhas into Sambhagas. According to Jacobi Gana designates the school, which is derived from one teacher (There Were nine Gandhras in the Jain Sangha during the time of Mahavira) kula, the succession of teachers in one line and Sakha the line which branched off from one teacher (Datta S. 'Early Buddhist monarchism' P-114)." Similarly we may also have a Sangha for the purpose of trade and industry i.e. for commercial activities known as guilds. They were usually called Srenis or Sanghas. These guilds or Srenis were of potters, carpenters, basket-makers, leather-workers, copper-smiths, weavers, dyers, black-smiths, corn-grinders, oil-crushers, farmers, herdsmen, stone-workers, bamboo-workers, fisher-men, Perfumers, Jwellers, flower-gardeners, physicians etc. Chief of guilds were known as Jetthaka or Pamukha.[5]

Tribal Origin

We know in different times and stages of human civilization, evolution has played a vital role. All the scholars unanimously agree on the point that in ancient time, origin of institution of Sangha or Sreni, what soever may have been the time and stage of civilization, would have been tribal. Famous scholar Bhandarkar forwards his opinion on this issue,[6] "The best known form of political Sangha is Gana. What I have said so far, to prove the existence of the political Sangha applies really to Gana. This, Gana as Kātyāyan and Kautilya give us to understand, was tribal in character and was confined to the Kshatriya (meant warrior) order." This view is corroborated by Jayaswal also stating that[7] "Basis of every state has been in all ages and in all time to a great degree ethnic tribal or National." The phrase 'tribal origin' can be explained like this: suppose in remote past, one family of basket-maker or potter settled at a place, suitable to his workmanship, began to flourish in number and craft, say after a ten generations the family became a village of 500 basket-makers or potters of a single ethnical group, with its chief the elderman known as Gramani or Jethhaka, where no one individual was owner of the estate and whole body was functioning as a corporate body. We have sufficient examples of such village in our history. According to Jataka stories (500-600 B. C:), there were numerous such villages flourishing around Banaras. We read[8] of such villages settled around Banaras, we read about whole village (especially near Banaras) settled by basket-makers, potters, smiths, weavers and the like. These artisans, though kinship group, generally formed guilds (Sreni) naturally with a tribe like organization inherited from their own past. This process is still visible in semi tribal areas e.g. Asam. The guild as a unit had considerable wealth at its disposal which was not the private property of any member, but might be disbursed at need by the head man of guild council either to any member of the guild or to some external individual or organization. This happens to be the present day custom in the poorer Indian professional castes.

These villages had their own village administration functioning under the supervision of 'Gramani' (Headman) and each member of the village was a warrior, providing security to whole of the village.

Transfer of the Guild System from Western Asia

Now it is a well established theory that the founders of 'Indus Valley Civilization' were Dravidians, who came from Mesopotamia in Neolithic-Chalcolithic Age. Their second migration took place in mature Harappan Age (2100 B.C.), from North West. They, in addition to culture, came alongwith their craft and trade system also. There are evidences to show that such a system was prevailing in Western Asia even before the end of third millennium B.C. Jacquetta Hawkes produces an account of such evidences,[9] "The guildlike companies (Ugula, Akkadian Aklu) of skilled craftsmen such as weavers, smiths, brewers and carpenters had official palace or temple overseers." Further author informs,[10] "Yet in Sumeria already before the end of the third millennium B. C., it was a highly organized industry, ... Weaving was a hereditary profession and there was much specification, not only were there spinners, weavers, dyers and fullers, each organized into a guild like group, with an organization man at its head, but even the weavers seem sometimes to have been specialists as for example in coloured cloths."

Crafts and Trade Establishments in Indus Valley

It has been shown in the first volume of this research series that the basis of economy of Indus Valley Civilization was trade and industry. A very high number of workshops of crafts-men like bead-maker, brass-worker, shell workers, copper-smiths, ivory-workers etc have been discovered from Lothal, Chanhudaro, Mohenjodaro and other sites of Indus-Valley Civilization[11]. Findings of Lothal dock[12] has shown that Indus-Valley people were great maritime people, who exported their goods as far as Mesopotamia, Babylonia, Greece and Egypt in ancient time, that is why goods imported from India had their Tamil names in the ancient languages of these countries as shown in earlier chapters. These were guild like establishments which were great producers and traders both. This is not merely an imagination of a poet but a reality. We have evidences in support of it. D.R. Bhandarkar[13] produces an account of such evidences- "I may also mention that Gana, (Vrāt or S̄ardha), in the sense of guild, appears to have had Vedic precedent as was first pointed out by Roth in the ST Petersburg Dictionary. They are referred to in the Panchvimsa Brahman (VI-9-25; XVII-1-5-12) Vājay Saneyi Samhita (XVI-25) and Taittreya Samhita I-8-10-2, (all are works of dates-1000-600 BC). And as the passage from the Upnishadas speaks of Gana only in the case of Vaishya and not Brahmana, Kshatriya or Sudras, it appears that there were commercial Gana i.e. Sreni, first among the Vaishyas before there were political Gana among the Kshatiriyas. If the former is the proto type of the latter, the former must have been divided into Kulas as the latter were. .... There were definitely Kulikas even among merchants belonging to a guild. This evidence is furnished by the seals found in the excavation at Bhīta and at Basarh (ASIAR 1903-04 P-107 FF, 1911-12 P-563, 1913-14 P-138 FF) or ancient Vaisali, capital of the Lichchhavis. We have here seals not only of Kulikas, but also Prathama-Kulikas, meaning Kulikas who apparently were chiefs of Ganas.'' Some of these seals have on them the legends Sreshthi-Sarthavaha, Kulika- Nigama, Sreshthi- Kulika Nigama, Sreshthi-Nigama and Kulika Nigama, Nigama means corporation).

Here the Vedic precedent means pre-Vedic period i.e. Indus Valley period. It means the system was in prevalence during the Indus Valley period. The last point raised by scholar is Kula origin or origin from one ethnical group, it means tribal origin, but the quotation of Upnishadas, that the system of Sreni first appears in the Vaishya and later in the political Gana of Kshatriya, seems to be wrong since according to later law books, like Gautam Dharm Sutra (X-62), Markandeya Purana (15-7,8) and Vishnu Purana (III-8-32), most of the commercial occupations were jointly assigned to both, the Vaishya and the Sudras i.e. the occupations of Vaishyas and Sudras were sometimes common. Hence this interpretation of Bhandarkar seems misleading that guilds were originally related to Vaishyas alone and not Sudra. This view point gets the support of Rhys Davids T. W. also. According to him[14] – "These men of commercial activities were of Dravidian race. South Indian names of the goods imported, as were adopted in the West (Soloman's ivory, apes, and peacocks for instance and the words rice and cotton) were adaptation not of Sanskrit or Pali but of Tamil words." We know these Dravidian people were definitely part of Sudra community or of Indigenous origin who were founders of Indus-Valley Civilization.[15] In this way it is proved that these guilds were originally formed by Indigenous non-Aryan people i.e. Sudras and Baniks.

We have earlier shown that a culture and life system, likewise that of Sumer was in prevalence in Indus Valley, while this culture was put to an end by the semi-civilized Aryans, the aforesaid system also faded to a great extent. But after the Mahabharata war, the Vedic culture and power began to decline and indigenous culture revived, the evidences of existence of such like guilds of craftsmen and republican began to re-appear in Brahmanas, Samhitas as stated earlier.

It becomes very clear that this system was indigenous and its origin was tribal. But such a view point has been discarded by K.P. Jayaswal[16], He says- "Gana or clan means 'tribal' seems wrong because at that time (600-500 BC) Indian Society had long passed the tribal stage of society."

I think learned scholar has passed such a remark without going into the details of facts. There are clear examples of villages of craftsmen, which were guilds and settled around Banaras as described in Jatakas (600-500 B.C.). These villages were of basket-makers, potters, weavers and carpenters[17], all being just or outset result of tribal evolution, according to Kosambi, "The Mote halls of clans were simply thatched with grass and branches without any wall[18] where Kulikas or said kings used to sit together and take decision of political importance." This is further corroborated by another evidence being produced by Nilkant Sastri[19] "Alexander, while retreating from his campaign, met with Sibis, Agrasenis and Malavas. These sibis were a wild people clad in skin and armed with clubs, who claimed descent from the soldiers of Hercules." This is confirmed by an account of Apastamba Dharma Suttra (Ī-1-2-39, 40), a work of 800-300 BC, according to N.K. Dutta, while Aryan students used to wear dresses made of skin of panther, deer and hide of cow.

We know this was the period of village life in India as supported by extensive excavation work of archaeology.[20] Urbanisation began in the period of Ashoka the great (269-232 BC). Aryans were a semi-civilized people and their capital Hastinapur was not more than a large village (B.B. Lal Ancient India No. 10 and 11; Taylor Isaac, The origin of the Aryans P-77). Hence society in the early stage of this period would have been tribal while this tradition was just in its outset stage.

Evolution From Family to Clan

We have earlier shown that guild system grew from a single family expert in any particular primitive craft with father of the family as its chief. Later, after a big gap of time, that family grew into a whole village of craftsmen with its head the Jetthaka or Gramani. These villages were known as craft guilds in origin which were sometimes large enough. According to Alinachitta Jataka (No. 156), there was a village of 500 carpenters near Banaras and according to Jataka No 456, there was another village of 1000 carpenters. In Gagga Jataka (No. 155) there is description of a village corporation i.e. large guild.

This was the Jataka Age or a period earlier than 500 B.C., while first of all such villages appear around Banaras or Kashi as informed by D.D. Kosambi.[21] It means the above development took place after the Mahabharta war between 950-600 B.C. . Likewise guilds were flourishing not only around Banaras but also in whole of the country. According to Bhandarkar,[22] "From about 500 BC to 600 AD India was studded with guilds of various type showing how well Industry and trade were specialized and developed."

After a big gap of time, when these villages of a single craft became overpopulated, some other villages of the same craft or one clan grew around the earlier. As such, a group of villages of one craft or one ethnical group or clan came into existence in a particular area or land with its chief Kulika or Gana-Pungavas or king. In this way, many such groups of villages of different crafts or clans came into being. This was an initial unit of local government of a single clan or Kinsmen. This was life time of Buddha (567-487 BC) while enormous Republican States of different clans were flourishing in Nepal and South of Nepal and Bihar such as the Sakyas of Kapilvastu, Bhaggas of Sumsumara, Bullis of Allakappa, Kalamas of Kasaputta, Koliyas of Ramagama, Mallas of Kusinara, Mallas of Pava, Moriyas of Pippalivana, Videha of Mithila, Lichchhavis of Vaisali and Kshudrakas, Mallavas, Ambasthas, Kathamias, Andhrakas, Vrishni, Madrakas, Yaudheyas, Agrasenis, Arjuneyas, Kambojas, Khatriyas, Saurashtras, Kukuras, in North Central India.

The Republican Confederacy

But in case of any foreign attack, these clans used to form a corporate body, who used to elect their kings or chiefs by turn[23] from the Kulikas of the corporate body. This would have been a real birth of large political paramount unit, most powerful and invincible, known as Mahasangha or republican confederacy. We have enormous evidences in support of aforesaid evolution and existence of such like large political units. We have reliable details of Vājji Gana of Vaisali which was a Sangha of herds-men. This great clan gave birth to Mahavira, the 24th Tirthankar of Jain religion, who himself was a prince of Vaisali Gana. This Vajji Gana was a chief[24] of confederacy of 10 clans. These confederacies were most powerful and invincible and also prosperous as stated by Buddha and Kautilya. Buddha, while on his visit to Pataliputra, on being questioned by king's minister answered[25]-"It is not possible for the king of Magadha, Ajatsatru to win over the Vaisali Gana since each one of their citizen is a warrior and they are invincible." It means Vājji Gana had its inner constitution likewise that of Sumer and a strong army of citizens. These Sanghas were not only invincible but also most prosperous, being productive commercially as well, as informed by Kautilya. Some[26] of the famous Maha-Sangha or republic confederacies were Vaisali-Videha, Videha-Lichchhavi, Lichchhavi-Malla, Vajji, Malawa-Kshudraka, Andhraka-Vrishini, Trigartta-Shashtha, Ambastha-Agraseni etc.

Vajji Gana was constituted of tribe of herds-men. Similarly the Sakya Gana of Kapil-Vastu, which gave birth to the great Buddha, the founder of Buddhist religion, was a Sangha of cultivators[27]. Suddhodana, the father of Buddha, king of Sakya clan himself used to plough his own fields. Similarly, Koliya Gana of Rama Gama, belonging to the maternal grand-father of Buddha, was a Gana of weavers, who generally used to forward gifts of garments to Buddha, specially made for him with their own hands. These Koliya Nagas were a sort of subordinate sub-division of the Sakya clan.[28] Videha were Carvaneers (Vedehika[29]). According to Kautilya (XI-1-5 KAMBOJA-SURĀSHTRA, -KSATTRIA SRENYĀDAYA VĀRTĀ-SASTR-OPAJIVINĀH) Kamboja, Surāstra, Khatriya Srenis (fighting guilds) and so forth are Sanghas which subsist on industry (crafts) and arms. This is apparent from this fact that their training genius were not one sided. They were not solely political animals. They were economic animals equally. Kautilya characterises them as martial and industrial in the same breath; they were forced to be industrial and martial by their laws, attention paid to trade and agriculture kept their treasury and themselves rich.[30]

Type of Republics in Sanskrit Scripture

Jayaswal informs us of two types of republics : (1) Vārtashastropajivins[31] (2) Rajasabdopajivins. Vārtashastropajivins means those which were dealing with and earning their livelihood by rearing of herds, ploughing of fields, running of industrial and trade establishments and use of arms. The chiefs of such Ganas were not using the title of kings. But to be a warrior was compulsory for each of male member or citizen. It means the art of use of arms was compulsory for each member from childhood. In addition to this, they were doing occupations of their choice for their livelihood. But in case of emergency everyone was supposed to attend War. Rajasubdopajivin[32] Sangha means, according to Kautilya, the Sangha whose rulers assume the 'title' of Rajan. The Artha-Sastra contrasts of the Sastropajivin Sanghas with Rājasabdopajivin Sanghas which means, according to Kautilya, the Sanghas whose ruler assume the 'title' of Rājan. Upajivin can not mean 'living by' as a republic cannot live by the title rāja. Upajivin in that sense would mean that the Sangha called Sastropajivin observed the practice of arms or military art and that the Sanghas called 'Rajasabdopajivin, observed the practice of assuming the title Rajan[33] in other words, their respective constitutions enjoyed on the members to be skilled in military art in the former and on the rulers or every privileged member to bear the title in the latter.

According to Jayaswal, the theory of mercenary life by certain republics called Ayudhajivin or S̄astropajivin is not acceptable. He quotes the description of Macedonian writers to refute above theory,[34] "The Macedonion writers describe many of those republics two of which are the grammarianś, military (Ayudhajivin-or Sastropajivin) Sanghas ; the Kshudrakas and the Malavas. Their territories and population were large. Their state comprised several cities. They were very rich. Any idea of mercenary life is excluded by the Greek description. They were large sovereign states with noted wealth, prosperity and civil organization..... They say that these free communities were the most famous for their military skill ..... The Āyudhajivins of Panini are to be taken as denoting those republics which considered military art as the vital principle of their constitution. That was the chief feature of their constitution in the eyes of their contemporaries, as the chief feature in the other class of republics was the law which allowed the elected president to be called Raja or King .... Although the citizens in general are alluded to as Rājans in the sense that they composed the sovereign body and also that every one had the possibility of being elected Rajan (See note No 15 below)." B.C. Law[35] produces a perfect explanation of the tradition of Rajasabdopajivinah —"According to Kautilya the Sanghas of the peoples like the Lichchhavis, the Vajji, the Mallas, the Madras, the Kukuras, the Kurus, the Panchalas and others were Rājsabdopajivinah. This apparently means that among these people, each citizen had the right to call himself a Raja i.e. dignitary who did not owe allegiance or pay revenuves to anyone else; but each of whom held up his head high and not merely looked upon himself as a Raja, but considered that the word Raja was his usual designation recognised not only by his fellow clansmen but also by the other peoples of India. This is corroborated by the account of Lalitavistara (Chapter-III-P 23) which preserves that there was no respect for age, nor for position, whether high or middle or law, each one there thought that he was a Raja. According to Kautilya's account, this designation of each individual clanś men was not confined to Lichchhavis alone but was shared by them along with many other warrior peoples of Northern India." In development of such a character of Sangha or republican people, I see a developing seed of future Rajput clan.

Kulikas or Kings as the Members of Assemblies or Republican confederacies.

We have earlier shown that although Gana or Sangha of Vajji of Vaisali belonged to herdsmen yet they were chief of federation of clans. These clans were constituted of the tribes working in different crafts. These clans were basis of the republic system or confederacy. Their heads or chiefs were known as Kulikas or Kings. These rulers have been divided into two parts by D. R. Bhandarkar. He putsforth its detail,[36] "Our account of political Sangha will not be complete unless I say a few words about Kulas, its corporate unit. Kula, you are aware, denotes a clan or group of families. In the Anguttara Nikaya (III-76) we have a passage in which Buddha distinguishes between the different kinds of rulers. We are told that one class of rulers was Pūga-gāmanikas or, as commentator explains it, Gana-jetthakas, i.e. 'Elders of Ganas' and that another class of ruler was Yevāpana Kulesu Pachchek-Ādhipachchaṁ Kārenti i.e. those who severally exercise autonomy (Ādhipatyam) over the Kulas or clans. Perhaps a most typical example of this kind of rule is furnished by the Sākya clan to which Buddha himself belonged. This clan had spread itself over a number of towns like Chātuma, Sāmgāma, Khomadussa, Devadahe with its chief town Kapilvastu."

As in Sumer[37] there was one body of elders and another perhaps of youths (See Chapter V.P-112 for detail) who were conducting rule over the Kulas or clans or Ganaraja.

A Similar type of system was prevalent among the Sanghas of those days.[38]

This can be understood well by the following event, which occurred in Vaisali : Chetaka[39] puts the problem before these Ganrajas and they decide in favour of war. Here neither 7707 nor 500 members are consulted, only the president takes the decision in consultation with a small body of 36 Ganarājaya. Obviously matters of vital importance were only discussed in this small body and not in the general assembly. It seems that this was done in order to guard the secrecy of counsel.

It is very clear that council of Ganaraja was perhaps more important and powerful.

How the Chiefs were Elected ?

Usually, the oldest member of the family represented his Kula. According to Mahabamso, the ten sons of Sishunaga ruled jointly, while according to Puranas, the nine Nandas consisted of a father and eight sons who ruled collectively.[40] Even in royal families, father or eldest member was important who was basis of politics of those days. Similarly, basis of republican system was Kula or head of the Kula. How the supreme ruler was elected from them is informed by Jayaswal[41], "It is with regard to Kula-state, that supreme rulership (over the chiefs of Kulas) was by turns (Anguttara Nikaya Vol III P-76) Kātyāyan the law giver says that Gana is the assembly of Kulas (KULANĀNHI SAMUHASTU GANAH SAMPARI KĪRTITAH-vir mitrodaya P-426)". Thus Kula or family was, basis of political right and power.

For how much period above kings or chiefs were elected is also uncertain. According to Davids Rhys T.W.[42] – "A single chief, how and for what period chosen, we do not know, was elected as office holder presiding over the sessions and if no sessions were sitting over the state, he bore the title of Raja which must have meant something like the Roman Consul or the Greek archon. We hear nowhere of such a triumvirate as bore corresponding office among the Lichchhavis nor of such acts of kingly sovereignty as are ascribed to the real kings mentioned above. But we hear at one time that Bhaddiya, a young cousin of Buddha, was the Raja." But famous scholar B.G. Gokhle produces a definite view point[43] - "The Sakyan chief was elected by rotation which led to the later fable of the Buddha being born a prince, actually the title Rajanya denoted Kshatriya eligible for election to chieftainship. In another passage Suddhodana, the Buddha's father (who is else where spoken of a simple citizen, Suddhodana the Sakyan) is called the Raja."

Now the question arises how these corporate bodies of councils or guilds were functioning ? Mahabharata (Shanti 107-23-25) throws sufficient light on this subject. What these verses tell us is that two, three or five members of a corporate body should be appointed Mahattmas or chiefs and their counsel should be carried out by a Gana craftguild or village community.

Characteristics of Sangha or Republic System

The Citizens' Army or Nation-in-Arms

The other chief feature of their constitution was that they enjoined on their citizens the duty to acquire military skill. In other words, they had a citizen Army.[44] Each state was a Nation-in-arms. Conversely, the other class, where the 'king' consul constitution obtained, probably had, like monarchs, a regular or hired (standing) army. The Nation-in-arms class, however, did not become purely military, for their constitution also required their citizens to devote attention to industry and agriculture (VĀRTASASTROPAJIVINAH). Hence they were most prosperous as well as powerful.[45] But in case of arising of emergency, soldiers in desired number could be called immediately. In this way a large army could be built in no time. Dr. Jayaswal has called such a system Nation-in-Arms, but some scholars have named it citizens' army. The[46] occupation of soldier, according to Vedic Varna system, was strictly assigned to Kshatriyas only. According[47] to Jayaswal, 'Katyāyan while commenting on Panini (IV-1-166-68) that the rule in making a derivation from the national designation of Kshatriya will hold good only if the Kshatriya is, not a member of Sangha for the rule is limited to the case of a monarchy.' It means only a monarch was a valid or Aryan Kshatriya and not a member of Sangha, because Kshatriyas of Sangha were non-Aryan. We find enormous evidences of their warriorship from excavation of Megalithic sites, from where high number of arms and remains of horse and their face covers etc have been discovered (See Chapter-IV P-82). On the other hand each member of the guild on the pattern of Sumerian city states[48] was compulsorily supposed to learn the art of use of arms. It means this system was brought to India from Sumer (See Chapter V P 112). When[49] they formed an offensive and defensive league, they were regarded according to Buddha as well as Kautilya invincible. Once while venerable Buddha was in Pataliputra, on being asked by the chancellor of the Magadha, answered, "It would not be possible for the emperor of Magadha to win the Vaisali Gana since their every citizen is a great warrior and hence they are invincible."[50] These famous confederacies were Trigartas, Vajji, Andhaka-Vrishini, Malava Kshudrakas etc.

The Wealthy Guilds

Because every Sangha was originally a commercial guild, they were most prosperous. Greek historians, while accompanying Alexander in his campaign of North West India, noted enormous wealth of these republics, whose each member or king, while met Alexander for compromise, were in richly clothes embroidered with gold and silver threads. Macedonian[51] writers describe, "Many of these republics, two of which are grammarianś 'military' Sangha : the Kshudrakas and the Malavas, they were very rich . They were large sovereign states with noted wealth prosperity and civil organisation."

These free communities were most famous for their military skill. They were also famous, according to the Mahabharta, in their financial administration. Their treasury remained always full[52]. According to numerous inscriptions and copper plates of grants they donated caves, Chetiyas and temples of very high value. Their evidences are testified in the Gupta period in the main : The Indore copper-plate inscription of 465 A. D. mentions a Tailika-Sreni guild of oilmen of which the president (Pravara) is named Jivanta. This oilmen's guild was trusted even by a Brahman with the custody of his donation to be held by it in perpetuity under a contract which was registered. The Mandsor inscription of the reign of Kumar Gupta II mentions a guild of silk-weavers and its prosperous finances as shown by its construction of an unequalled-temple of sun.[53] Similarly there is a big list of such prosperous guilds in Mahavastu.[54] Hence it is obvious that these guilds were most wealthy. (See chapter XV PP 407-08 list of Naga donors)

Moral Assets

The laws and administration of law in the republican state of India are unanimously praised by the Greek observers and their praise is confirmed by the Mahabharata. Even their sworn enemy Kautilya[55] says that a republican chief in his state has the beneficial propensity of justice. A high sence of justice was maintained. Without it no republic can last very long. Kautilya notices as a feature that republic chief was a man accustomed to discipline. (DĀNTO YUKTA JANASTI STET). The Mahabharta points out, as we have seen, that discipline was maintained amongst members both junior and senior by responsible leaders (MB-Shanti 107-18). The leaders further made themselves and their action popular (SARVA CHITTĀNOVARTTAKAḤ) Krishna, in the Mahabharata, is reported as mentioning to his friend Nārada his difficulties in conducting his federal council.[56]

Principle of Equality and Casteless Society

Referring to Panini V-3-114 to 117 Dr. Jayaswal thinks that there were castes in the Sanghas of Vahika country like Brahman and Kshatriya. Here Brahman, Kshatriya means priest and warriors class who were, artisians also at the same time, which cannot be possible in Vedic Varna system. Hence view point of Jayaswal is not liable to be accepted.[57]

As the Mahābharata records that equality prevailed in the Ganas or Sanghas. This was naturally necessary being the basis of republic character. The more democratic an institution, the greater must have been the emphasis laid on the principle of equality. This[58] is implied by the Mahabharata (Shanti Parva Chapt-107 JATYĀCHA SADRISAH SARVE KULENĀ SADRISASTATH) when it says that there is equality among the Ganas by families (Kula) and by birth. Equality by birth and family made up the constitutional equality inside the republic. Every freeman in a Sangha was equal by birth and every family was equal for political purpose.[58] But such a system is against the Vedic Brahmanical Varna system whose fundamental basis is gradation in the society, hence it was a non-Vedic non-Aryan system. Here the word 'political equality, is misleading since in such a system everyone was a Kshatriya or a warrior. This is the main reason, Kautilya was sworn enemy of Sanghas or republicans.

But the most valid evidence is again produced by K.P. Jayaswal himself. He writes, "Kātyāyanā while commenting on Pānini (IV-1-168) that the rule (of the aňpratyaya) in making a derivation from the national designation of Kshatriya will hold good only if the Kshatriya is not a member of Sangha for the rule is limited to the case of a monarchy.[60]

[JANAPAD SHABDĀT KSHATRIYĀDAṆ (4-1-166 Pānini) Kātyāyan KSHATRIYAD EK RĀJĀ TSANGHA PRATIŚEDHĀR-THAM- Ek Raja Means sole sovereign]"

It means only a monarch was a valid or Aryan Kshatriya and not a member of Sangha because Kshatriyas of Sangha were non-Aryan. (Nation-in-Arms system was prevailing among them). Thus there was no caste system among the Sanghas. In corroboration of this conclusion the most striking evidence is produced by T.W. Rhys Davids[61] based on his study of Jatakas "They (Sakya mass) held it degradation, to which only dire misfortune would drive them, to work for hire. They were proud of their standing, their family and their village. And they were governed by headman of their own class and village very probably selected by themselves in accordance with their own customs and ideals." Further Rhys Davids writes,[62] "Among the first we are told of workers in rushes, bird-catchers and cart-makers-aboriginal tribesmen who were hereditary craftsmen in these three ways. Among the latter mat-makers, barbers, potters, weavers and leather workers. It is implied that there was no hard and fast line determined by birth, people could and did change their vocation by adopting one or the other of those 'low trades'. (1) Thus at Jataka V-290 fall a love born Kshatriya, works successively (without any dis-honour or penalty) as a potter, basket-maker, reed-worker, garland-maker and as a cook and still remains respect of his high born relations." As such Sakyas knew no caste and they were one people.

(2) Another prince[63] resigns his share in the kingdom in the favour of his sister and turns trader (Jataka 4- 84)

(3) A third prince goes to live with a merchant and earns his living (by his hands) Jatak 4-169.

(4) A noble takes service for a salary as an archer Jatak 2-87

(5) A Brahman takes service to make money to give away Jatak 4-15.

(6) Two other Brahmans live by trade without any such excuse Jataka 5-22; 471.

(7) A Brahman takes the post of an assistant to an archer who had himself been previously a weaver Jatak 5-127.

(8) Brahmans live as hunters and trappers Jatak 2-200; 6-170

This shows, in pre-Buddhist period, the republican society was casteless and caste was not known to them. Since most of the republican tribes became followers of Buddhist order, they became perfect casteless society. Buddha declared that just as the great rivers Ganga, Yamuna, Achiravati, Sarabhu, and the Mahi on reaching the great ocean lose their separate identities, likewise the four order Brahmana, Kshatriya, Vessa and Sudda on joining the order lose their separate names and Gotra and are known only as the ascetics of the order of the Sakka puttiyas.[64] It is crystal clear that society of these Sanghas was casteless[65] although Vedic Aryans believed in Varna and caste system very strictly, this proves Sangha or republican society was non-Aryan in origin.

The Non-Aryan Origin of Republicans

About one and a half century back, it was not possible for any one to think of any sort of rich civilization or heritage among the ancient indigenous non-Aryan population. But T.W. Rhys Davids was the first scholar who after an indepth study of Buddhist literature concluded and unveiled the secret that in ancient time the indigenous republican people were most civilized.[66] He passes remark to this effect in the introductory part of his valuable book which is being produced below,[67] "It is significant that this important factor in the social condition of India in the sixth and seventh century B.C. has remained hitherto unnoticed by the scholars either in Europe or in India they have relied for their information about the Indian peoples too exclusively on the Brahmin books. And these partly because of the natural antipathy felt by the priest towards the free republic."

Later, this subject was taken into their hands by scholars like D.R. Bhandarkar and K.P. Jayaswal. Works of both the scholars are commendable, but they too could not do justice with the subject because of their feeling of antipathy as high-lighted by the learned scholar Davids Rhys T.W. as above. But in third decade of twentieth century, while ancient towns of Indus-Valley Civilization were explored by the British archaeologist like, Marshall, Mackey and wheeler, the picture emerged in full and it was fully proved that civilization of indigenous peoples was very high in remote past.

We have earlier proved in reference to origin and evolution of guild system, that this system was taken from Sumeria, it took its roots in Indus Valley and flourished in pre-Buddhist and Buddhist period and it was non-Aryan. However it can also be proved that each one of these republicans was non-Aryan : Sakya and Lichchhavi both pioneers of republican tribes, had matriarchal family system against Patriarchal of Aryan. And they used to marry their own or real sisters and according to Buddhaghosa and Sumangalbilāsini both of the families were born from real brothers and sisters.[68] According to Manu (X-22) Lichchhavis were Vrātya Kshatriya, who were out of Hindu Pantheon and non-Vedic. Sakyas are said to be descendant of Āditya or Surya and Ikshwaku family (Mahāvastu III-246). These Ikshwakus were original inhabitant of eastern coast of Mediterranean sea, known as Hyksos or Akkaku (Sanskrit Ikshwaku[69]), who used to worship sun god Baal[70] (see chapter V PP-93-94) which appears as a deity of Pani or Banik in Rigveda. (See Chapter-XIII P-376 for detail) These Hyksos perhaps migrated to India in about 2100 B.C. in mature Harappan Age. Sakyas and Lichchhavis used to worship non-Vedic Shrines, which were situated quite close and outside their towns just before they adopted Buddhism and Jainism. Learning of Silpa and use of arms, was compulsory for Sakya princes, (See P-165 for detail) in absence of which marriage of princess Yasodhara with Buddha was once refused.[71] It means Sakyas and Lichchhavis were non-Aryan Kshatriya, silpa cannot be profession of Aryan Kshatriya. Similarly Moriyas, Mallas of Pawa and Kusinara and Koliyas of Ramagama were also part of the same society, who, each one, on this very ground (that they were also Kshatriya) preferred claim in relics of blessed one.[72] Similarly it also can be proved that other clans were also part of non-Aryan indigenous society.

According to Gokhale[73] B.G. the Sakyas called themselves Khathiya and were an oligarchy. As Kosambi points out, "There were no Brahmins or caste-classes within the tribes, nor have high Vedic observances ever been reported of the Sakyas. Inspite of being Kshatriyas who wielded arms at need, the Sakyas also worked the land. All Sakyas, including Buddhaś father put their hand to plough."

It is crystal clear that there was no caste system among the Sanghas or republicans. It means they were indigenous non-Aryan population opposed to the Vedic Varna and caste system. What happened at a later stage, while these people were Hindusized, the royal families turned into Rajputs or Brahmanas and others who still remained traders or artisan became petty traders or artisan Sudra. According to Bhandarkar[74] "modern representative of Ganas like Yaudheya or Malava are Ranas of the Panjab hills or Ranas of the Goa territory (JRAS 1408 PP 540-41)" The modern[75] representative of the Malla of eastern Uttar-Pradesh or the Malla caste of district of Gorakhpur and Azamgarh generally given to trade (H. Pandeya JBORS 1920 PP 262-65).

Similarly Sudras or Suds of Panjab are modern representative of Kshudrakas[76]. Modern representative of Sakyas are Sakka or Kackhi, the vegetable growers and hawkers.

We have earlier shown that the base of economy of Indus Valley Civilization was trade and industry. A very high number of workshops of crafts-men like, bead-maker, brass-workers, shell-workers, copper-smiths, ivory-workers etc have been discovered from Lothal, Chanhudaro, Mohenjodaro and other sites of Indus Valley Civilization.[77] Finding of Lothal dock[78] has shown that Indus Valley people were great maritime people, who exported their goods as far as Mesopotamia, Babyloina, Egypt and Greece in ancient time. That is why goods imported from India had their Tamil names in the ancient languages of aforesaid countries[79] (See Chapter III PP 43-45) It means commercial guilds of India were related to non-Aryan Dravidian peoples, who were pushed to fourth varna during later Rigvedic period. It has also been proved earlier that political Sangha or republican states also grew from commercial guilds, existing in India from pre-Vedic period. It means these republican states were also related to indigenous non-Aryan Sudra population. We are producing here some more evidences in support of this view : According to Bhandarkar[80] –"Panini mentions several of them, some situated in Vahika and some in Trigrate, both parts of Panjab. But perhaps the most interesting referred to by him are the Yaudheya, Parsu, Asura and Rakshasas. Of the Yaudheyas I shall speak later on, Parsus are certainly the Parsis or old Persians and Asuras the Assyrians, Rakshasas must be the same as Rākshasas, an original race referred to in early Sanskrit works, and in particular the Ramayana. This indicates that some of the mercenary bands at any rate were foreigners."

Now it is an open secret that Indus Valley people were in origin long-headed Dravidians who came from Sumer and round-headed Assyrian-Iranian Alpines and their admixture race,which have been called Dasyus, Dasas, Asura and Rakshasas in Rigveda[81]. They were evidently indigenous people, the Dravidians who were founders of Indus Valley Civilization, settled in India before the invasion of Aryan race of Central Asia. I could not understand how Bhandarkar used the word "foreigners" for them. Either he did so in absence of knowledge of Indus Valley Civilization which was discovered in later period or this is simply a case of misinterpretation or distortion of historical facts. But aforesaid evidences produced by Bhandarkar are most striking to prove my theory that Sangha people were native people.

Much light has been thrown in Chapter V P-108 on origin of God-king or Raja-Rishi tradition in Sumer. Development of tradition of city states and God-King in Indus Valley and post Indus Valley period and Western Asian origin of matriarchal family tradition which was an important characteristic of non-Aryan Naga society.

This is to be noted that chief of the guild or republican was also formerly a religious person.[82] or a God-King.

Fundamental Principle of Equal Distribution of Rashtri or Gana-Bhumi

One of the peculiarities of Gana system was 'Joint or common estate of Gana' and its equal distribution among the subjects. H.L. Kosare gives a detailed description of this system.[83]—

"In Pali language of Buddhist literature the word 'Damil-Ratha' has been used (Bhikshu Darma-Rakshita, "Buddha Kālīn Bharata Ka Bhaugolik Parichaya" Sarnath. Banaras P-15). Damil-Rattha means "Dravida Rāshtra." "Rattha" is synonymic form of "Rāt". Hence Rāt of Mahar-Gana means "land" or "Rattha of Mahārs" and Mahārt Rattha = Maha-Ratha or Maha-Rashtra, means "joint or common estate of Mahar Gana." The real lord of this Rashtra was Matra-Devi or Mother-Goddess of Gana (on the pattern of Sumer See chapter V PP 95-96) According to laid down principles of Gana, Rāt or land, being the joint estate of Gana, was distributed among the tribal associates of Ganas, on the principles of equality under the set rules. The Mahar Gana also had to follow these set principles. If an in depth and thorough study of history and basic principles of form of administration and function of Gana, is conducted, we will come to the conclusion that different tribes of Maharashtra known by different names, were different components of large family of Mahārashtra. As the Ganas were known as Nation or Rashtra, hence the Ganasangha of Vajji was also a Rashtra, or Nation. Similarly the republic of Mahar-Gana was also Rashtra of Mahar-Nagas. Henceforth Rāt of Mahar-Nag (Mahar+Rattha = Maharattha) became Maharashtra. An example, regarding the system of equal distribution of land can be noted from the Gana system of ancient India : King Asur Bali, after gaining victory over whole of the Triloka of Devas (Gods or Aryans), acquired the seat of Indra. In Maharashtra, at the occasion of celebration of Bali-Prati-Pada-day, in the month of Kartika, there is a tradition of a pronouncement : "ĪDĀ PĪDĀ TALE, BALI RĀJĀ YEO" (all the misfortunes will disappear on coming of the king Bali). The subjects of the king Asur Bali, were very happy, because, he used to distribute lands equally among them. After a fixed period, the equal distribution of land of Nation among the members of Gana, was the topmost and the fundamental duty of seat of kings. (Sharad Patil, Das Shudrachi Gulamgiri Part 1 Sub-Part-1 PP-86-88)

The first distribution of Gan-Bhumi used to take place among the associate tribes, and than these tribes used to distribute amongst their families (Sharad Pawar P-92). During the time of king Asur Bali, there was a perfect system of equal distribution of 'land of nation' or 'Rashtra-

Bhumi' among the members of Gana. Such a tradition was in prevalence among the Mahar Gana also. The 'land of Nation', which was of joint ownership of Mahar-Gana-Sangha, was known as 'Mahar-Gana' that is why, owing to being a 'Gana Rashtra,' the national land of Mahar Gana was named Maharashtra.''

Smilarly, Buddha's Sakya tribe was also Sakya-Gana of the people of Sakya families. Whatever land or estate was the property of Sakyas, that was "the land of Gana" or "the Nation of Sakya Ganas". The land of the Sakya Nation was also known as the joint estate of Sakya-Gana, that is why all the families of Sakya Ganas and father of Buddha, though a king, had to take joint active part in the work of cultivation.[84]

It is clear from the above detail of information that as the land of Sakya Gana was Sakya Rashtri or Nation, similarly the land of Mahar Gana was also Maharashtra.

Here the land of Nation or Rashtri represents the Matra-Bhumi (Bhumata or Mother goddess of land) or Matradevi who was the real lord of the land, hence Rashtri or Ragyi or Rani words came into existence. This Bhumata (Maya) was the creator of every thing. The source of origin of such a tradition was Western Asia, where mother goddess Baba was real owner of Rashtri or Bhumi.[85] Hence this cult or tradition was non-Aryan. It means Mahars and Sakyas both were non-Aryans and Asurs like Asur Bali. Whatever perfect and the best system, they developed in such a remote past is really most wonderful.

Dr Jayaswal[86] on the basis of study of the Mahabharata (12/107), Arthshastra, Buddhist literature and Coins, has drawn following important conclusions of the characteristics of republic system :

(1) Generally all the associated members of Sanghas were recognized as rulers, as they used to call themselves king. Their constitution was based on solid principles.[87]

(2) Ganas were the symbol of political unity, it is apparent from their available coins that they were using their political designations for the public work like other confederacies of the same age.

(3) There were public assemblies of chiefs or heads, and eldermen to conduct administrative work of sangha. They had the right to rule and used the title of King. They were also known as Gan-Kula or families of Ganas.

(4) The duties were assigned to all, under set rules. Similiary, power to each one was also fixed, to establish balance among the ruling associates, and it was the sole object behind it.

(5) The store-house and treasury of Gana was always full with limitless valuables and they were always ready to move for fatal wars.

(6) There was always question of heroism, high desires, high respect and social limitations.

(7) According to Mahabharata, all the associated members of Gana were dealt with at the level of equality. (SADRASHAḤ SARVE)

(8) There was exchange of thoughts on the different problems of state in the assemblies. Tathāgatā Buddha had himself seen many such assemblies and he advised them for some more improvements.

(9) Justice and judiciary system was viewed more seriously.

(10) With the object of enhancement of their powers, the Ganas, at many instances used to organize themselves into a large confederacy known as Mahasangha. Such a Mahasanga was considered to be invincible.

(11) The land of Nation was distributed equally among the subjects. Taking into consideration the aforesaid conclusive points we come to the final conclusion that mutual unity was one of the peculiarities and objects of Gan-Sangha (GANĀH SANGHĀT VRATTAYAḤ— Mahabharata 12/107/13).

But the most important characteristic was a system of equal distribution of land among the associates of Gana-Sangha and the families of tribes. It is claimed by the modern Western scholars that a best political system suitable to the needs of mankind like democracy or republic is a contribution of Western civilization, but the above historical fact bluntly condemns any such claim.

The Origin and History of Some Important Republics or Sanghas

It seems that earliest Sanghas came into being in North West region of India or the Indus Valley. This system moved toward east and south, with the coming of invaders from the West and movement of Harappans owing to new threat. Vahika or Takshak or Taka seems to be one of the oldest families, about whom we have sufficient evidences to make out a complete History.

Sangha or Republics in North East of Gangetic Valley

The name of the clans, which were united in the confederacy of Vajji, after Davids Rhys T.W., are as under :

(1) The Sakyas of Kapilvastu.
(2) The Bhaggas of Sumsumara Hill.
(3) The Bulis of Allakappa
(4) The Kalamas of Kesaputta
(5) The Koliyas of Ramagama
(6) The Mallas of Kusinara
(7) The Mallas of Pava
(8) The Moriyas of Pippalivana.
(9) The Videha of Mithila } The Vajjis
(10) The Lichchhavis of Vaisali. }

Sanghas or Republics of North and West Region

(1) The Kshudrakas
(2) The Malavas
(3) The Ambasthas
(4) The Kathamias
(5) The Andhrakas
(6) The Vrishnis
(7) The Madrakas
(8) The Yaudheyas
(9) The Agrasrenis
(10) The Arjuneyas
(11) The Kambojas
(12) The Khatriyas
(13) The Saurashtras
(14) The Pātālas
(15) The Kukuras
(16) The Sibis

The Takshak or Taka (Vahika) of Panjab

There is a description of seven Mahanagas in Mayashilpa. They are : Basuki, Takshak, Karkotak, Padam, Mahapadam, Sankhpaul and Kulika.[88] In Skand Purana, Takshak Nag has also been called Mahanāg (77/17,18;106/5, 6, 7). These Takshak, or Takkas were of Taka family, since the words Takkhas or Takka or Taka are corrupt forms of Takshaka and in Sanskrit language, Takshak means Nag or serpent, hence they were Nagas. As a matter of fact, totem tradition was a peculiarity of indigenous people of ancient India. As such these Takshakas or Nagas used to worship serpents and at certain occasions wore artificial hoods of cobra (See Plate No.–III) on their heads, hence were called serpents or Nagas. These people, in origin were inhabitants of Panjab or Indus Valley.[89] Still three parts of this land are known as Taka, Majha (Madra) and Malava, which were ruled by three royal families or blood relatives of the same names. Malava is Southern part of Satluj river, land between Beas and Jhelam in general, is known as Mājhā and whole North-Western part beyond Jhelam or present Pakistan is known as Taka. This Taka is named after the name of royal family of Taka. One province of Afghanistan is still called Takhar. Name of their tribe was Andhra.

The History

The name of Takshak Nag first appears in the Mahabharata as opponent of Pandavas. Hence, this seems to be one of the most ancient royal families of Naga race, who gave birth to the most of the Naga royal families of ancient India. Their capital was Taka-shar (Taki or Takka-war) near Sialkot. Cunningham mentions other names of this city as Taki and Asurar[90] (of Assyrians). Their ancient traditional capital was Takshila. H. L. Kosare after Mahabharata informs that Arattas had their three branches Takka, Vahika and Jertika (Kosare P-253)

In Mahabharata, the family Gotra of Takas has been given Karpati[91] and among them, alongwith the Malavas of Rajputana and Panjab, Panch-karpatis also have been included. These were people of republic society. It seems that they were relatives of their nearest neighbourers, the Malavas. Because these Malavas used to worship Karkota Nag, hence Takas were also worshippers of above deity. They later shifted from Panjab to Rajputana and settled there in the east.[92] It is clear that Takas were republicans or guild or Sangha people. They had their two other families or blood relatives Malavas and Madras and their Gotra was Karpati. (See chapter XII PP 349-50 far detail)

Madras were called Vahika and Jertika.[93] Hemchandra, in his Abhidhan-Chintamani (IV-25) has equated Vahikas[94] with Takas. These Takas were Vahika Nagas, therefore Vahikas, Jertikas and Madras were also Nagas and all the four Naga tribes were blood relatives of Arattas . There was a tribal confederacy of TakaNagas in Panjab that is why the Panjab was known as Taka–Mulka or Taka-country[95] as mentioned by Hieuntsang. It is obvious that Vahikas were from Taka family.

Some scholars think these Jertikas were Jats. But it is not acceptable since Taka or Takshakas and Vahika appears in the Mahabharat period (950 B.C.) where as Kushanas, the progenitors of Jats appears on the horizon of history about 1000 years later, as invaders from North. On the other hand, Jat is the name of a Gotra of Taka Kshatriyas. Hence above Jat is not related to Jat caste or Kushanas but Takas.

It has been already[96] observed, that ancient inscriptions in the Pali or Buddhist character have been discovered in various parts of Rajasthan of the race called Tastas , Takshak and Tak relating to the tribes, the mori (or Maurya) Parmar their descendants. Nagas and Takshakas are synonymous appellation in Sanskrit for the snake, and the Takshak is the celebrated Nagabansha of the early heroic history of India. The Mahabharata describes in its usual allegorial style the war between the Pandavas of Indraprastha and the Takshaka[97] of the North. The assassination of Parikshata by the Takshaka and the exterminating warfare carried on against them by his son and successor, Janmejaya, who at last compelled them to sign tributary engagements, divested of its allegory, is plain historical fact[98]. Their warfare lasted for a longer period, ultimately progeny of Pandavas had to leave Hastinapur, while the city was washed away in a terrible flood of the river Ganga at about 800 B.C. Later on it was taken over by the Nagas (See Chapter-X PP 260-63 for detail).

"In the Bhavishya Purana." According to James Tod[99-A] "Prince Sahasra-Arjuna is termed as Chakravartin or paramount sovereign. It is said that he conquered Karkotaka of the Takshak, Turushka or snake race and brought with him the population of Mahishmati and founded HemNagara in the North of India, on his expulsion from his dominions on the Narbuda. Traditional legends of this prince yet remain on the Narbuda, where he is styled "Sahasrabahu or with a thousand arms," figurative of his numerous progeny. The Takshak or snake race, here alluded to, will engage our attention. The name of animals in early time, planets and things inanimate, all furnished symbolic appellations for various races."

It is evident that race of Takshak, being at the entry gate of India in North West not only suffered at the hand of invaders from North and West but also those from South.

From the Mahabharat account, Son of Takshak was Ashwasena who was saved by Indra, while Khandava-van was put into flame by Pandava Arjuna (1000 BC-950 BC).

It seems that there was also possession of Nagas over Gandhara country in the time of Parshwanath (887-787 BC), because Nagjit or Naget, the king of Gandhara[99B], has been said to be the follower of Parashwanath. Perhaps this Naga king Nagjit would have been related to Takshaka since country of Gandhra or Takshila was their main centre of rule from remote past. We know that the primogenitor of Naga, according to Mahabharata was Rajrishi Kashyapa, who was national guru of Parshwanath also.

During the life time of Buddha (567-487 BC), Takshila was the capital of Gandhar country or the modern Kandhar. Then, the king of Gandhar was Pukkusati, who is said to have sent an embassy and a letter to king Bimbisara of Magadha.[100] He was a follower of Buddha. He died in his old age on his first and last trip to Magadha, a week after his meeting with Buddha.[101]

Like Nanda dynasty, Taka family also suffered at the hands of Puranic Chronicles. Contemporary Puranas have ignored pedigree and chronology of this family in general. However we have traced out a very handful names from different sources; when Alexander invaded India (325 BC) he found the Paraitakai, the mountain (Pahar) Tak, inhabiting the Paropamisos range; nor is it by any means unlikely that Taxiles [Arrian says that his name was Omphis (Ambhi)]. Hence, perhaps (from Tak), the name of Indus Attok, not Atak or forbidden according to modern signification the ally of the Macedonian king, was the chief of the Takas; and in the early history of the Bhatti prince of Jaisalmer, when driven from Zabulistan, they dispossessed the Takas on the Indus, and established themselves in their land the capital of which was called Salivahanpura. It is by no means unlikely that Salivahana or Salbhan (who was a Takshaka) the conqueror of the Tuar Vikrama, was of the very family dispossessed by the Bhattis who compelled them to migrate to the South.[102]

These Takas or Takshakas, whose chief was Omphis or Ambhi, was a snake worshipper Tribe as noted by the Greek historian M.C. Crindle.[103] He reproduces as such, "They found in many of them besides other animals, a snake, which the Indians regarding as sacred, kept in a cave and worshipped with much devotion. The Indians accordingly with every kind of entreaty implored Alexander to let no one molest the animal, and he consented to this (Strabo XV-1-28). Now when the army was marching past the cave the snake heard the sound that arose (that kind of animal being very sharp both of hearing and sight) and hissed so loud and emitted such gusts of rage that every one was terrified and quite confounded. It was said to be seventy cubits long, and yet the whole of it was not seen, except its head that projected from the cave. Its eyes, moreover are reported to have equalled the size of the large round Mecedonian shield." It shows these Naga worshippers were of Naga race whose chief Ambhi was of Takshak race.

The Bharsiva Naga Royal family of Padmavati : A Taka family

The description of this name (Taka) is found in Bhavasataka,[104] which is dedicated to Ganpati Naga. We have come to know, the history of the family of Ganpati, from the copy of such a manuscript of Mithila, which was composed during the ruling period of Ganpati Ṇaga and was dedicated to him. The poet writes, "The Naga king possesses both Vāk (learning) and Padamalaya (Padmavati).'' In poem his name is said to be Gajavaktrasri Nag (The Naga king with the face of an elephant). In another poem he says- "That all the Naga kings on seeing Ganpati king are terrified." (Jayaswal, The catalogue of Mithila MSS Part-II P-105).

In the Eastern[105] Panjab there was the feudatory dynasty of Singhpur[106] who were the 'Kings' of Jalandhara. This receives corroboration from the history of the migration of Yadavas from Mathura as recorded in the Sabha Parvan Chapter-XIV Verse 25 FF. The Sālvas and Kunindas had migrated along with and at the same time as the Yādavas from Mathura (Sūrasena) and its neighbourhood and settled in Panjab. The Takas who later migrated to Malava from the Salva country, the Singhapura Yadavas and the Mathura Yadava-Nagas thus seem to have all belonged to the great Yadava stock, which explains their special patriotism for Mathura. The Singhpur family was thus a family allied to the Bharsiva.[107]

It is obvious that Taka family was a part of great Yadava race. These Yadavas were round-headed Alpine Iranian race in origin. Bharshiva of Padmavati was also related to Taka family of Panjab.

While great Chinese traveller Hieuntsang came to India in 630-44 AD, he visited Takashahar the capital of Takas, which was situated at the bank of river Apaga near Sialkot in the north west of Lahore. This was in the north west of Kingdom of Jalandhar.[108] The historians and bards of Rajputs have included Tank-Kshatriya among 36 royal families of Rajputs. The reference of Taka royal family has come in the Chachanama and Rajtarangini of Kalhan where mention has been made that while the king Bhoja of Kanauj invaded the capital of Takas then they were helped by Shankar Varman, the Naga king of Kashmir. When Hieuntsang came back from Sindh, Multan was under sway of Taka Royal family. When Kasim invaded Multan in 712 AD, then Taka ruler named Bajhra Taki[109] was in power. They were once indisputed lords of Panjab and they still exist as a numerous agriculture race in lower hills between the Jhelam and the Ravi.[110] This view gets the support of Cunningham[111] that there were centres of abode of Nagas around Jammu and plains of Panjab. It is crystal clear that the hilly track, south of Jammu was the largest centre of Takshak Nagas, where their population is still in existence in abundance in modern age. A coin[112] bears the sun god head on the abverse, and there is a legend with the words. "King of Multan" at the end and on the reverse the rayed head of the sun with the name in the Nagari of 'Shri Vasudeva' and "Panchan Zabulistan." According to Cunningham, a king by name Vasudeva ruled in Multan some time very near the days of Chacha. He was probably same as Taki.

The Hun kingdom[113] of Sialkot (of Mihar Kula 515-540 A.D.), destroyed by Yasodharman, was subsequently seized by a new dynasty of kshatriyas called Tak or Takshaka. This name is mentioned in the Chachanama. The kingdom lay between the Ravi and the Chinab rivers. But, according to Cunningham, it was extended up to the Sindh.[114]

In mediaeval period there was Bhatt village named Takkarika in the central province.[115] Chandarvardai poet and bard of Rajputana and Muslim historians have given description of their royal family.

We[116] have already mentioned the Takshak Mori (or Maurya) as being lords of Chittor from a very early period and a few generations after the Guhilots supplanted the moris, this palladium of Hindu liberty was assailed by the arms of Islam. (725-35AD) We find amongst the numerous defenders who appear to have considered the cause of Chittor their own "the Tak from Asirgarh" (in Khandesh). This race appears to have retained possession of Asir for at least two centuries after this event as its chieftain was one of the most conspicuous leaders in the array of Prithviraja. In the poems of Chandar he is called the 'Standard, bearer, Tak[117] of Asir. '

The earliest Muhammadan[118] author, who mentions Taki, is the merchant Suleman, who visited the east before A.D. 851. He mentions tafak, as not of great extent and its king as weak and subject to the neighbouring princes but he adds that he possessed "the finest white women in all the Indians. (Henry Elliot P-49)."

The Inscriptions

In the Rewa[119] stone inscription of MalayaSimha dated in Kalachuri era 944 (1193 AD), it is stated that he expended 1500 Tankkas stamped with the figure of Bhagwati, for constructing a tank near Rewa. It means these Takas were worshippers of Mother goddess or their family was matriarchal in form.[120] This view is stengthened by Sherringś viewpoint. We have come to know from the inscription discovered by Col Tod (I.A. XIX P-55) from the Kanaswa, which is situated at the bank of river Chambal, South of Kotah, that the king Salindra (409 AD capital Salpoor) of Sarya family, was a king of Takkas (Takhyas). These people of Sarya family were famous among other tribes too.[121]

It is obvious that these were the same Takkh or Taka of Panjab who met Hieuntsang. They were lord of Malava and were known as 'Sarya' also. The land of Valley of Satluj and Beas, in the neighourhood of Himalayas is also known as 'Suraj' or 'Sewaraj'. This word is a local linguistic variation of Saura, Chera, Kera, words. These Souraj were Surya Banshi[122] Naga. (See Chapter XII PP 348-49 Vakataka for detail).

The chief diety of this land is serpent or Naga and all of them Worship their deity. The people known as Sewaraj, living in the upper Chenab valley also worship this Naga deity.

This view gets the support of Cunninghan, who draws our attention towards thick population of this race in lower hills south of Jammu between Ravi and Jhelam. This ancient race, the foe of Janamejaya and the friend of Alexander, closed its career in a blaze of splendour. The celebrity of the kings of Gujrat will make amends for the obscurity of the Taks of modern time, of whom a dynasty of fourteen kings followed each other in succession commencing and ending with the proud title of Muzaffar.[123]Saharan the Tak was the first apostate of his line who under the name of Wajihu-I-Mulk concealed both his origin and tribe. His son Zafar Khan, was raised by his patron Firoz to the government of Gujrat, (1391 AD) who later became independent and mounted the thrown of Gujrat[124] (1401 AD) under the name of Sultan Mujaffar Shah. He was succeeded by his grandson Ahmad Shah (1411-1441 AD) who changed the ancient capital Anhilwara for Ahmadabad. Later this name Tak seems to have been obliterated from the tribes of Rajasthan. Mahmood Bigarh ruled between 1458-1511 AD. His daily diet was equavalent of one Gujrati maund. In 1572, Gujrat was subjugated in the Mughal empire by emperor Akbar.[125] Afterwards we don't find any trace of their successors. This is a notable point here that Takas before their conversion to Muslim were known as Rajputs. It means indigenous Naga royal families turned into Rajputs. This event defies the Aryan origin theory of Rajput families.

Although they were residents of Uttarpatha but carried their trade with the Dakshinapatha in precious goods like gold and ivory and it shows that they were great traders.[126]

The Expansion of the Taka Naga rulers and Their Different Branches

Although main branch of family of Takka ruled in north west Panjab with capital at Takshila from the time of Mahabharata upto the mediaeval period while their kingdom was annexed into Muslim rule, but owing to furious invasion in past from North West, their branches ruling in the plains of Panjab were forced from time to time to make room for the powerful invaders and migrated towards East or South, where they established their new powers. K.P. Jayaswal[127] gives an account of their expansion as such-"The Nagas performers of the ten Ashvamedha, to put it in modern phraseology, the Naga emperors, fostered the republic which covered the whole of Eastern and Western Malava and probably also Gujrat the whole of Rajputana (Yaudheya and Malavas) and probably also a portion of the Eastern Panjab (Madras) all connected territories, to the West of the Valley of the Ganges. These were certainly free in the next, the Vakataka period, when Samudra Gupta emerges on the stage. The Malava republic seems to have been formed by peoples and clans akin to the Nagas. Those around Vidisa were worshippers of Nagas from early times, as the republican coins of Eran prove. Eran the Airkina town, is itself after the name Airaka, a Naga and the Eran coins bear a Naga (Serpent) figure. The Malavas near Jaipar had founded their capital KarkotaNagara naming it after the Naga Karkota, which now lies within the territory of the Raja of Uniyar at about 25 miles southeast from Tonk. The word Nāgara itself in the capital KarkotaNagara is connected with the word Naga. It is important to recognize this fact that the Naga monarchs and the republican Malavas were, by their civilization and also probably ethnically, connected. Raja Sekhara says that the Takkas and the people of mark used apabhransa idioms. As we have already seen the family of Ganapati Naga of Padmavati was a Taka-Bamsa, which means that the family migrated from the Takka-desa. Thus we see that the Malavas and the Nagas spoke the same dialect. It seems that with the original migration of the republican Malavas from Panjab, the Taka Nagas had also migrated and that the Nagas themselves originally belonged to a republican community (the five Karpati) and they were a Panjab people settled in Malava."

We will show in different chapters that the Mauryas, the Satavahanas, the Vakatavas, the Guptas and the Karkotas were offshoot branches of this great Taka family.

The Modern Offshoot of Takshakas

In the Modern age, when we conduct a search for the offshoot of Taka race in Panjab, with most surprise we find a class which is known as Taka Kshatriya and whose description is given by Sir Denzil Ibbetson in his popular work titled "Panjab caste." This caste is traditionally known as Chimba or Chhimba derived from Chhipa or its Sanskrit form

Shilpa (art, craft or technology) engaged in the occupation of fuller, dyer, printer (shilpa) and Tailor i.e. decorator or outfitter of clothing. This technology is known in modern market as "production of ready made garments" one of the five Panch-Piaras of Great Sikh Guru Sh. Govind Singh, Mohkam Singh was from this class. Denzil[128] Ibbetson, informs us about this class- "The chief or head of this class in Western Panjab (Now Pakistan) is known as Bareta and Khalifah. Khalifah was originally a title of chief or head of Guilds (Sanskrit form sreshthi or Sethi) in ancient time. In west it is known as Charhoa, engaged in the profession of washing, dyeing, printing and sewing of clothes. These professions are not separate castes but subdivisions of one class, known as Charhoa or Chhimba, functioning still as remains of ancient guilds." It means this class is the descendant of guilds of ancient tradition which was existing amongst the indigenous people of India on the pattern of ancient Sumer.[129]

History of Weaving, Dyeing and Printing Technology

We have to trace out ancient history of guilds working in weaving and dyeing and printing technology. We will remain indebted to Hawkes for providing desired information from ancient Sumer[130] on the subject thus "One important craft was that of the spinners and the weavers of textiles. In social psychology it was at the apposite extreme from smithing for it gives gradually art of a simple prehistoric craft practized by the women of the house by the fire side or outside the door. Yet in Sumeria already before the end of third millennium B.C. it was a highly organized industry, much of it carried on in near factory conditions. As has so often happened when a skill or craft passes beyond the domestic scale, men began to take part in what had been women's work, though women were still employed in larger numbers. Weaving was a hereditary profession and there was much specialization. Not only were there spinners, weavers, dyers and fullers, each organized in to a guild like group with an organization man at its head, but even the weavers seem sometimes to have been specialists as for example in coloured cloths. It is not surprising to learn that there were also linen weavers and for this involved distinct technique."

It is clear from this description that textile and its related industry of fullers and dyeing was most important because in the absence of modern like machinery, a very high number of skilled and non-skilled workers were kept engaged to meet with the demand of large population of those days since the process was too slow. Prof Kramer has calculated that it took a team of three women eight days to spin and weave a piece measuring 3½ by 4 meters. When it is remembered that every year many thousands of tons of wool were worked up at Ur alone. It is evident how very many hands must have been employed.[131]

We have earlier shown that Indus Valley Culture was founded by Sumerian immigrants and Sumerian culture and their traditions also, reached India along with them. Their three main migrations are noted by historians. That is why, we find aforesaid craft or craft-guilds at work in Indus Valley also. (see PP 126-27)

Weaving and Dyeing Industry in Indus Valley

The head and shoulders of a bearded man,[132] the whole fragment 7 inches high carved in steatite was found at Mohenjodaro in the D.K. area at a depth of only 4.5 feet and may therefore be late Harappan date, the head is bearded with the upper lip shaved, the eyes are narrowed to an extent which has been thought to indicate a state of Yogi. Across the left shoulder is a clock carved in relief with trefoils which were originally filled with red paste. This human statue bears the sign of being rapped in fine cloth. The ancient Sumerians and Babylonian priests wore such dress. This shawl is painted or embroidered since idea of printing would be too early.[133]

Mr. wheeler,[134] who traced out a shop of dyers in Mohenjodaro, observes, "Of another kind is a building fronting upon one of the main streets, first street in Mohenjodaro. Its outside dimensions are 87 × 64.5 feet but within that considerable framework are included not only residential quarters round the courtyard but also towards the street industrial or commercial premises of some note in particular, three rooms neatly paved with brick on edge, one room with five conical pits or holes sunk in the floor and lined with wedge shaped bricks apparently to hold pointed basis of large jars. In corner of room is a well, near by is the usual brick stair-case. ....it seems that jars were rather dyeing vats."

It seems that it was a workshop of weaver, fuller and dyers, since earlier it was a joint set process of work as noted by Jacquetta[135] Hawkes in Sumer, "When the weaving was done the lengths of cloth went to the fuller to be steeped in his alkaline vats and afterwards trampled under foot.'' Perhaps dyeing process was followed up afterwards. Presence of well in the premises, in addition to space for dyeing Vats, seems to confirm the viewpoint of Jacquetta Hawkes. It seems that art of printing came into existence in a much later period but embroidery was in practice.

Enhancement in General Demand of Clothings and Flourishing of Guilds

Perhaps this was the time, while tradition of general use of cloth among the masses began. It is apparent from the use of garbs of ochre or orange brown colour by the Buddhist monks[136] which infact began in this age. Hindu Sadhus or ascetics of Vedic Pantheon used simply a small piece of clothe to cover up their private parts of body. Perhaps, in addition to general enhancement in population, this was the main cause a very high demand of cloth began in this age. Hence guilds of weavers, fullers and dyers flourished to a great extent. These guilds perhaps later divided into two parts : first weavers and second dyers, fullers and decorators. We know that during the life time of Buddha (567-487 BC) in addition to Madras there was a Sangha of Koliyas of Ramagama who were weavers of Naga race. As proved on following pages, second parts of guilds would have been related to the tribe of Takshak Nagas. Since only one word Rajak has been used in sanskrit for both the occupations i.e. 'Rajak' means dyers and fullers, perhaps technology of printing was not yet invented. Since they were themselves, decorators, producers and traders (See page 149) hence wealthy too. There are evidences of copper plate inscription of charities of high value issued by Rajak-lady discovered from Mathura (See P-159). Here one point is notable as already stated these Sangha people knew no caste system, hence they were not caste groups but producer and traders of a single ethnical group. This gets the support of Davids Rhys TW[137] who informs : "They held it degradation to which only dire misfortune would drive to work for hire. They were proud of their standing, their family and village they were governed by headman of their own class and village selected by them." It means they were workers and lords both at the same time. Being warrior they were lords of land covered by the groups of their villages or clan. It means they were themselves sovereign rulers or kings also, that is why original meaning of the word "Rajak" is "body of rulers" or "chief of kulas" of confederacy or body of kings[138] (Amar Kosha II-8-4). According to B.C. Law, among the Sanghas of Rajsabdopajivinah each citizen had the right to call himself a Raja or Rajan. It means a person who did not pay revenue to anyone else, each one of whom held up his head high and not merely looked upon himself as Raja. Thus Raja was his usual designation (See P-131) a body of Rajas was Rajak. We know in later history of Western Asia, chief of guild or Khalifah became sacred Rulers. This happened in Sanghas of India also.

It seems that this process of division into weavers and dyers-fullers took place in upper Panjab and in pre-Buddhist Age. This is the reason why Takas[139] (fullers and dyers) and Meghs or Koliyas[140] (weavers, who were Kolinda or Madras) both have high population in the area South of Jammu between Ravi and Jhelam and both are land-owners and cultivators, although earlier class is predominant. Both the peoples have been rulers in ancient period.[141] Both are living together in Manipur state in present time known as Tangkhul (Tank Kul) and Koliya or Khoeroo

Nagas[142] and during the life time of Buddha, Mori (a branch of Taka or Vahika) and Koliya Naga lived in present Nepal. This unity confirms their division from a single productive unit. The occupation of Takshakas as above is well confirmed since their blood relatives Koliya (Kulindas or Madras) were weavers, as per Buddhist record in Pali.

We know Takas were rulers in North West of India from the remote past. They had a confederacy in Panjab that is why the Panjab was known as Taka-Mulk (Taka country).[143]

It is obvious that in ancient period (third millennium BC) there were guilds of fullers and dyers in Sumer which had organizational man at their heads, whose migration during Indus Valley Age has already been proved. Their heads, were called Khalifahas in Western Asia as well as among the Takas or Chhimbas of Panjab.[144] Further migration of these people took place to Maharashtra and Vindhyachal region during Megalithic Age, and later to Bihar, Bengal and Orissa. Chief of guild in Sanskrit is known as Sreshthi. Famous and venerable saint of this community Shri Namdev, who was born in Maharashtra was of Seth or Sreshthi gotra. Similarly some families of Bihar and Orissa also bear this family or Gotra name Sethi Arjuncharan, Minister for water resources and supply from orissa, in the government of Shri Bajpai, who belongs to this community, is one of the clear examples. Hence it is confirmed that this community was related to ancient craftsmen's guild (Shilpa Sangha) in origin that is why it is known as Shilpi Samaj in Gujrat, Maharashtra, Harayana and Panjab and Rajak in eastern states. Thus this group of community had a complete hold on the occupations which now whole of the textile and readymade garments industry has, hence would have been very wealthy. This conclusion is significant in historical prospectives, Visible in their history.

Etymology

According to Dr. Bharat Singh[145] there is a peculiar tendency in certain alphabets while changing them from Sanskrit to Pali or Prakrit language. Few examples are as under :

R becomes L	T becoms Th or DH
P — B	Ch — J
K — H	SH — CHH

As explained, while changing from Sanskrit to Pali P→B and SH→CHH, the word Shilpa or Shilpi becomes Chhipa or Chhipi, L being silent. These titles are used in Haryana and Panjab for this caste. Similarly Chhipa becomes Chhiba or Chhimba in Panjab. Before invention of modern machinery the work of printing of cloth was done by hands with hand made wooden blocks, which was the most important occupation of this community. Hence this community was named as Shilpa or Chhipa or Chhimba. This title Chhimba is indicative of the beginning of printing technology, tracing of whose definite date seems impossible at this juncture of our research.

Further, we take up the second title 'Bareta' : According to Kautilya[146]- this community or Sangha was sworn enemy of Vedic Aryans, hence in contemporary Puranic literature they have been completely ignored. In, Hindi dictionary of Nalanda, the meaning of this word is given "washerman" and "Taka-Desh" means Taka country situated between Chenab and Beas rivers of Panjab. We have traced out different forms of this word in different states : In Panjab and Pakistan this form is Bareta, in Maharashtra and part of Gujrat is Baratakke.[147] We take Baratakke first :

Baratakke = Bara (Barha, means big or senior) + Takke (Plural form of Takka) it means big or senior Takkas. Bareta is a corrupt form of Baratakke, where consonant K' is silent owing to difficulty of speech, which is a tendency of Pali language where consonants, more often are preserved and at a time lost, due to difficulty of speech.[148] Infact this later word is a corrupt form of Bartakke. Hence this word 'Bareta' or 'Baratakke' is a title of chief of the tribe of Takka, which later became family or Bansha name in Maharashtra, which signifies a definite ethnical affinity of this class with the Taka tribe or community of ancient Panjab. This derivation of Banshaname Baratakke from Taka royal family confirms our theory, unquestionably well.

We have shown in Chapter V (PP-109-10) that a tradition of Raj-Rishi was prevalent among the Nagas, from the age of Indus Valley and Rigveda, where we note the names of Ahivritra and Trisira the son of Tvasta and Visvamitra, among them Visvamitra was most important to which Andhra Satavahanas (Takas) belonged. (see chapter. 11 P-283) An important Gotra, Rajrishi still exists in the Tank Kshtriyas of Panjab. This is most striking evidence to prove their relation with the ancient Rajrishi tradition of Andhra-Satavahanas or Takas. There are many other Banshas or Gotras of this class which strengthen our theory such as Andoria or Andhra, Bhatti (Yadava), Kanait or a branch of Madra, Koli, Malwan, Tak or Tank, Mahar and Rati or Rathi etc. (See P-160)

As referred earlier one of the title, according to Sanskrit scripture was 'Rajak' which means dyer and washerman both. But in ancient time its meaning was different. According to Jayaswal,[149] "The member of the federal council (Mahasangha) were designated Gana Rajak. Probably it was to a federal council of this class that the technical term Rajak of Amar Singh (Kosha II-8-3,) originally applied." But due to antipathy felt by Brahmanical priest class its meaning changed to dyer or washer-man like ancient meaning of the word 'Dasa'[150] 'great donor' later changed to 'slave'; Buddha means person believing in application of brain but later changed to foolish person (Buddhu). Similarly the word 'Ther' means a 'Buddhist monk' but now this word is used in the sense of "a man of low dignity," for the same reason.

Capital of Taka Satavahanas was Paithan hence some families of Taka tribe which would have lived in this city are called Paithan. As Sanskrit 'P' becomes Pali 'B' hence some of their familes are called Batham, Bath or Baitha in Bihar and Madhya Pradesh and Uttar Pradesh. Baithon is one of the well known Gotra of Tak. Kshatriyas. President of India Shri K. R. Narain is of Paithan Gotra and Taka.

The Language (Taka or Takshali)

In the second act of Sanskrit play Mrcchakatika,[151] (work of Shudrak) a dialect has been used by the author, known as Takki. Taki, Takka or Dhakka is the Prakrit dialect which has been called by Pischal language of East Bengal being spoken around Dhaka, but there is another interpretation too, since word 'Ta' has been changed to 'Dha' due to the tendency of change from Sanskrit to Pali or Prakrit[152] as cited above, hence the original word is Taka.

Rajtarangini names this dialect Takki. This was spoken in the Taka country of North Panjab. Scholars consider the genesis of this dialect to be in the mixture of Sanskrit and Sourseni. It was the language of Takki or Tak royal family and their subjects or tribe. This language had relation with the Dardric or Pishacha group of language in origin.[153] This is most surprising that edition of Tripitaka of Pali Prakrit of Buddhist religion was prepared in a language which was spoken in Takshila University. This language was infact Takshali (See Chapter VII P-201 for detail). This conclusion is far reaching and meaningful in historical prospective.

The Script, Takari (Munde or Lande)

The foremost importance[154] of this tribe (Takka) is perhaps best shown by the fact that the old Nagari character, which is still in use through out the whole country from Bamiyan to the banks of the Yamuna, is called Takari, most probably because this particular form was brought in to use by the Taka or Takkas. I have found these characters in common use under the same name amongst the grain dealers (traders) to the West of the Indus and to the East of Satluj. It is used in the inscriptions as well as upon the coins of Kashmir and Kangra. The only copy of the Rajtarangini of Kashmir was preserved in the Takari characters. In many of these places, the Takari is also called Munde and Lande (means with out head). This script is still used by some traders to maintain their account or Wahikhata.

The Coins

Regular coinage[155] had come into use before the end of the seventh century to judge by the coins found. Originally the coins were issued as silver blanks by the traders (guilds) themselves and the weights checked regularly by their guilds during the period of circulation. The Takshilan currency belonged to a foreign weight standard just 11 grams which would approximate to the Indian rupee in historical time. Tanka was a very popular denomination during mediaeval period. The silver coins of the Muslim rulers are called the Tankas. The famous bilingual Tanka of Mahmood Gajanavi bears legend AYAM TANK MAHMŪDPURE GHATE, Tankas were issued by Allauddin Khilji and Akbar and later by British rulers also.[156]

Tanka coins were issued by Malaya simha from Rewa in 1193 AD as cited above,which bears the stamp of Bhagwati.

Cunningham has referred to the coins of Raja Ananta of Kashmir who according to Rajatarangini issued Takkas. He identified these coins with the copper Panchis (CMI P-34) .The mention of Tanka occurs also in South.[157]

Dr. Chandra Shekhar Gupta[158] gives description of the spreading of these coins further in Bihar and Orissa, which is indicative of movement of Taka race in that region– "The so called Puri Kushana coins exhibit the crude imitation of the Kushana coins. The issuers of these coins were named by R. D. Benerji the 'Puri Kushana' or 'Oriya Kushana' by V. A. smith as the rulers or kings of Kalinga in the 4th or 5th century AD, while Allan called them 'Puri-tribal coins, Belonging to the end of the third or early fourth century AD. No further information about these people could be gained from the numismatic data.

A reference may be made here to the coin denomination Tanga muli (or atgamuli) found in the Kharoshthi documents from central Asia (JNSI, 16 (1954) 220 Fn 4). In the present state of our knowledge, it is not improper to assume that probably these people migrated from the North West region of India to the Eastern coastal area for some unknown reasons. Probably this was due to some political pressure or economic causes. In the vast region comprising-Orissa, Mayurbhanj, Singhbhumi, Ganjam and Balasore districts, they established their colonies. This is supported by the findings of the so called 'Puri Kushan' copper coins from this area. The legend Tankas discussed above, has no other satisfactory explanation than this, that these coins were struck by the tribe of the Tankana (Takka) in the name of their community like those of the Yaudheya and Malava.

It appears that the name inscribed by these peoples on their coins gradually came to denote the name of the coin. In the Amarkosha we find the word Tanka (Chisel) and Rupyadhyaksha, who is referred to as a Tankapati (mint master) by the commentator Ksirasvāmin (Bhandarkar P-133). Allan had rightly observed that when the supply of Kushan Copper Coins, to which they were used, began to fall then, the people of Kalinga or Orissa, took to copying them, as there was enough copper in the mines of Kalinga. A commentary on Mrcchakatika gives the term Sivonka Tanka for Nōnaka which is definitely used for the Kushana copper coins."

It seems from the aforesaid evidence of coins that some branch of Taka Royal family owing to severe attack of Kushanas up to Magadha, reached Mayurbhunj, Singhbhumi, Ganjam and Balasore and established colonies there, where remains of their offshoot, the Royal family of Dhavaldev is still existing at Dalbhumigarh near kharagpur. (as per report of Shri Vijay Kishore now Dy Commissioner, Dhanbad)

According to BHAGWAT (IX-1-13,42) and MAHABHARATA (I-75-18, 25) and RAMAYAN (VII–87-89) Vahlika (TAKA) had a matriarchal kingdom[159]. They also had a confederacy in Panjab.

The vernacular name Takashāl for mint very clearly proves that first mint of any kind was first of all introduced by the royal family of Taka. Similarly, it seems likely that script of Takari is earliest form of Devanagari. Hence it seems that they had some hand in its initiation.

The first appearance of Takshakas or Takas is noted in the Mahabharata Age (950 BC), where they came in conflict with the Pandavas for power. Being rulers of mountainous region they were invincible, but it seems that in case of severe attack from West, some of their branches, from time to time moved Eastward or Southward and established their rule at Singhpur, Mathura Tonk, Padmavati, Paithan Kantipuri, NandiVardhan, Vidisa, Eran, Singhbhumi in Bihar and in Kashmir in later period. But in fact they have left their traces throughout India, in the form of names of places like Takshila, Attok, Rohtak in the North West, Takalghat, Takal Kota, Bhejtek, Vena Katak, Narang-Katak Nandikatak, etc. in the Centre and South and their off shoot branches like Mauryas Satavahanas, Bharsivas and Guptas and so many others which remained untraced so far. They ruled upto the Mediaeval period (1572 AD). It means they remained in power from time to time for about a period of 2500 years or more (950 BC-1570

AD). That is why they left their name in the names of country (Taka desa), capital, (Taki shahar), languages (Takki, Takshali or Dhakki) script (Tākari or Munde or Lunde), inscription (from Rewa and Chambal valley) and coins (Tankas). I think there is no any other royal family in Indian history to stand by them. They seem to be the Central hub of Naga power and politics in ancient India, who gave birth to Most of the Naga royal families covering the longest period and the largest area of rule. Their relation with the Chhimba or Tak Kshatriya caste and its branched off castes, is most striking and beyond doubt. We know they were, in origin a tribe, working in weaving fulling and dyeing of cloth, belonging to a single ethnical group, organized into guild to manage their productive, religious, political and militia activities whose chiefs (khalifahs) though elected, in the long run became hereditary rulers. They left behind their tribe as common man, while Aryanized Kings being all powerful (priest and ruler) either became Brahmans or later Rajputs. Since their tribesmen were non-Aryan crafstmen hence were pushed to fourth varna and their Nation-in-arms tradition was banned forcibly for the same reason.

But, before their Aryanization, they were persons of high respect and riches. There are evidences in support of it: their common man issued big donation whose copper plate inscription has been discovered from Mathura. This donation was issued by women of Rajak, perfumer and carpenter.[160] Since these charities were issued by women members of the donor families and not man thereby proving matriarchal society. This is further confirmed from Puranic literature that Vahika or Taka royal family had matriarchal form of family and heredity also (see chapter V PP 104-05 for detail). These Vahikas or Takas had republican or sangha system of rule hence their kings or rulers were priests also in origin or they were priest-kings.[161]

In addition to royal families like Mauryas (progenitors of Parmar Rajputs), Bharsivas, Satavahanas, Vakatakas, Guptas, Karkotakas, this family (Taka Tribe) gave birth to many castes of later Hindu society such as Meghas (Koliya Nag or weaver) dyers (Rangrej), fuller or washerman, shilpas, Lilaris, Tailors (Darji), Bhars, Rajbhars (Rajputs), Marathas, Kurmis, Mahars and so many others yet to be traced out. In addition to famous Rajput family of Parmar, famous Rana family of Chittor also took birth from aforesaid tribe. According to Bhandarkar[162] –"Modern representative of Ganas like Yaudheya or Malava are Ranas of the Panjab hills or Ranas of the Goa territory (JRAS 1908 PP 540-41)"

This view gets the support of coins of Salivahana king (who was a Taka) the founder of Satavahana dynasty. These coins[163] bear the legend of Rāmno (or Rānno) Siri Sadavahana. It means Satavahanas were Progenitor of Rana royal family. This view is strengthened by another evidence: In the Nasik cave inscription (E. I. VIII P-94) Satavahana king

Siriyagya Satkarni: bears the title of Ranno (Gautami puts Sami Siri Yagya Sātakāsiri). In the Karle cave inscription of Vasisthiputtra Pulamavi, there is mention of-RannaVasithiputs Siri Pulumavi (E. I. Vol VII-P-71) Malavas[164] were also a branch of Taka family. It is very strange why Dr Bhandarkar relates Malavas with the Ranas of Panjab and Ranes of Goa territory only and why not Rana Rajputs of Chittor. Bappa Rawal claimed his birth from Suryabansha, where as Takas were also Suryabanshi.[165] Hence my claim is more justified (see Chapter. XII PP-348-49 for detail)

List of some important Gotras of Tak kshatriyas which explains some of the historical facts as cited earlier :

Andoria (Andhra)
Bath
Bathon (Paithan or Paitan)
Bhat
Bhatti (Yadavas)
Chohan (Rajput)
Chema or chima (Shilpa)
Darji
Dogra (Rajput)
Gawhar (Gowharwal Rajput)
Jassall
Jat
Kakar
Kalal
Kandhari
Kanait (a branch of Kulindas)
Kori (Koliya Nag)
Kanaujia
Kanpuri
Khas (Khasa Nag)

Taka (Takshat)
Khakhar
Lodhi
Lata or Lahota (Nag)
Mahar, Mahra, Mahtar
(Branch of Satavahanas)
Mair
Madar (Madra)
Malwan (Malava)
Mor (Morya)
Nagara (Nag)
Nila (Nag)
Pal
Panwar or Pawar (Parmar)
Raj-Rishi
Rangrai (Rajput)
Rathor (Rajput)
Rati (Ratti or Rastri)
Salotri (Salvagotri)
Tank
Wattu

It is most interesting that some of the Gotras of Tank Kshatriyas and Naga tribes of Assam have similar names Viz Lhota , Tangkhul, Khasa, Kori or Koliya etc. thereby proving them of Naga Race.

The Lichchhavis of Vaisali

The clan of the Lichchhavis figures very prominently in the annals of early Buddhism. They are invariably described as Kshatriyas. Buddhaghosa, the celebrated Pali commentator has the following story to tell about the origin of the tribe of the Lichchhavis,[166] "It come to pass that the chief queen of the king of Banaras was with child. When her time came, she was delivered, not of a child but a lump of flesh, of the colour of Lac and Bandhu and Jivaka flowers. Fearing the displeasure of the king if he should hear of this, the queen put the lump of flesh into a basket marked with the royal seal and placed it in the flowing waters of the Ganges. However a god, wishing to provide for its safety wrote with a piece of cinnabar on a slip of gold the words,"the child of the chief queen of the king of Banaras" tied it to the casket and replaced it in the river. The casket was discovered by an ascetic and taken by him to his hermitage, where he cared for the lump of flesh. After the lapse of some time, the lump broke up into two pieces of flesh, which gradually assumed shape, till finally one of them became a boy resplendent like gold and the other a girl. Whatever entered the stomach of these two infants looked as if put into a vessel of precious transparent stones (Mani) so that they seemed to have no skin (Nichchhavis) others said that the two were attached to each other by their skin (Linachchhavi) as if they had been sewn together, so these infants came to be designated as Lichchhavi (BC. law "Tribes in Ancient India'' P-299. This is obviously a fanciful interpretation of the two variant forms of the name Nichchhavi and Lichchhavi whose precise meaning Buddhaghosa does not seem to know but the significant point in the narrative comes further on when we are told that on coming of age the boy and the girl were married to each other and from this brother and sister union sprang the race of the Lichchhavis. In this connection, we may refer to the remarkable similarity in the stories connected with the origin of the Sakyas and the Lichchhavis since both these groups are described as progenies of brother and sister unions (Sumangalavilasini I P-258). The laws of Manu (X-22) describes the Lichchhavis as Vratya, clearly implying thereby that they were out of the pale of the Brahmanical civilization (Manava Dharmashastra X-20-22). It is true that like the Sakyas, the Lichchhavis are also described as Kshatriyas but the term Kshatriya in this context may be taken to mean representative of political power rather than a specific caste in the Brahmanical hierarchy (Richard Fick "Social Organization in North East India in Buddhaś time'' translated by Maitra P-81). The Lichchhavis were one of the most prominent of the republican tribes of ancient India."

Famous historian Bimala Charan Law does not accept the above origin of Lichchhavis and he puts forth his indifferent remarks as follows, "Although Pujavaliya, a Ceylonese Buddhist work, also gives a similar account though with some slight variations, these stories, of course, are entirely mythical and must have grown up in very recent times, there being no evidence in the sacred canon itself to corroborate any part of the narrative. It shows at least that Lichchhavis were regarded as Kshatriyas."

It seems true while most of the indigenous royal families established themselves well and came into heights of their fame, on one hand, but were surrounded by the caste ridden society of Hindus on the other, such like stories were concocted to maintain their prestigeous position and pride. We have example of Chandela[167] Rajputs and Karkota Nag family of Kashmir (See chapter XII P-350) But there is something in this story which can help us in deciding the origin of the royal family and its clan. The story further tells us- "On the request of cow-herders, the ascetic handed over the children to them. The cow-herders securing the goodwill and permission of the king obtained that country and measuring out a town there, thus anointed the boy as king. After giving marriage of the boy, who was then sixteen years of age, with the girl, the king made it a rule. "No bride is to be brought in from the outside nor any girl from here be given away to anyone" The first time they had two children, a boy and a girl and thus a couple of children was born to them for sixteen times .... as the city was thus again and again made larger and still larger (Visalikata) it came to be called Vaisali."[168]

It shows that these Lichchhavis were herdsmen and there was a tradition of real sister's and brother's marriage among them. It means they had matriarchal tradition. Such a system was not possible in the Vedic Aryan social system. It proves this family was non-Aryan or indigenous. We have proved earlier (See chapter V PP 102-05) that matriarchal system was prevailed among the indigenous people and even real brothers and sisters marriages were also in practice similar to Pharaoh of Egypt and Semites of Western Asia. There are some more evidences too in support of this view. They had religious traditions quite similar to those prevailed in Western Asia. B.C. Law[169] produces some examples of them, "Kandara-Masuka, a naked ascetic of Vaisali sought to please the Lichchhavis by professing a great attachment to their city, he says, So long as I live, I will never go beyond the Udena shrine on the east of Vaisali; the Gotamaka shrine on the south, the Sattamba shrine on the west and the Bahuputta shrine on the north (Dialogue of the Buddha Part-III P-14). From this boasting of Kandara-masuka, it is evident that these shrines were situated in the outskirts of Vaisali, making its boundaries as it were." Although, there is description in Satpathbrahmna that a cairn should be raised on pit burial (of god) but it is not clear. However this book is a work of much earlier period, but we know these shrines or stupas were evolution of Megaliths, which were brought to India by the Naga tribes from Western Asia, who made South eastern region of Uttar Pradesh second centre of their abode i.e. centre of Megaliths. (See chapter IV PP 68-69) Because Aryan races believe in immortality of soul hence they never raised any monument in the memory of their dead ancestors.[170] Hence they were non-Aryan native people.

This view gets the support of Dr. Satish Chandar Vidya Bhushan[170] also. He holds that they (Lichchhavis) were of Persian origin. His strongest argument is the verbal coincidence between Nasibis in the Persian Empire and the word Nicchivi which occurs in Manu (X-22). Dr. Bhusan[171] writes, "It appears to me very probable that while about 515 BC. Darius, king of Persia, sent an expedition to India or rather caused the Indus to be explored from the land of the Pakhtu (Afghanistan) to its mouth, some of his Persian subjects in Nisibi (of Herat) immigrated to India and having found Panjab over-populated by the orthodox Brahmans, came down as far as Magadha which was at that time largely inhabited by Vratya or outcaste people."

Here venerable author is connecting Nisibi of Persia with the Lichchhavi although this time of their migration is too late. At about 500 B.C. they were well settled persons in the Vaisali but it proves to be an event of migration. However, this evidence helps us much in establishing the theory. But there are many more evidences also in support. One of the traits of indigenous society was a casteless society whose every member was a warrior as already stated. Anjana, a resident of Vaisali, was a trader or Baniya who was Raja of Vajji clan i.e. a warrior also.[172] Hence their society was casteless. According to Kautilya,[173] the Sanghas or corporation of the people like Lichchhavis, the Vajjis, the Mallas the Madras, the Kukuras, the Kurus, the Panchalas and others were Rajasabdopajivinah. This apparently means that among these people, each citizen had the right to call himself a Raja dignitary, who did not owe allegiance or pay reverence to any one else, but each of whom held up his head high and not merely looked upon himself as a Raja, but considered that the word Raja was his usual designation recognized not only by his fellow clansmen but also by the other peoples of India. This is corroborated by the account of Lalitvistara (Chapter III-23) which preserves that there was no respect for age nor for position, whether high or middle or low, each one there thought that he was a Raja. According to Kautilya's account, this designation of each individual clansman was not confined to the Lichchhavis alone but was shared by them along with many other warrior peoples of northern India from the land of the Madras upto the North eastern part i.e. the land of Vajji. In the dynastic inscriptions of Nepal these Lichchhavis are said to have branched off from the Ikshwakus (IA IX P. 178) that is why they were allied to the Sakyas.[174]

The Sakyas

The origin of the Sakyas is traced back to king Okkaka i.e. Ikshwaku. It is stated in the Sumangalavilasini that king okkaka had five queens. By the chief queen he had four sons and five daughters. After the death of chief queen, the king married another young lady who extorted from him the promise to place her son upon the throne. The king there upon requested his sons to leave the kingdom who left with their sisters for the hermitage of sage Kapil, where they built Kapilvastu. In due course of the time the four brothers married their four sisters excepting the eldest one and they came to be known as the Sakyas.[175]

This fact, of tradition of sister's and brother's marriage among the Sakyas, is confirmed by another event quoted by B.C. Law who writes:[176] "While, there a dispute arose on the issue of watering of fields among the people of Koliyas and Sakyas, the Koliya labourers abused thus- : "Be off, with you people of Kapilvatthu, men who like dogs, Jackals and such like beasts cohabit with their own sisters, what will their elephants and horses, their shields and spears avail against us?''

We have earlier told in connection with the origin of Lichchhavis that such a system prevailed among the indigenous people of India which is a symbol of prevailing of matriarchal system among them against partriarchal among the Aryans. According to BC Law :[177] "These Sakyas have been called in the Mahavastu (II P-303) Adityavandhu or people a kin to the sun. This refers to their descent from the solar dynasty to which the Ikshwaku belonged. This book, also speaks of king Suddhodana as born in the Ikshwaku family (Mahavastu III P-247). Another passage in the same work speaks of the Buddha as a Kshatriya of the Aditya Gotra and of the Ikshwaku kula, that is born in the family of the Ikshwakus; who derived their descent from the sun (III-246). The Lalitavistara (P-112) also speaks of the Buddha as born in the royal family of Ikshwaku."

We have already described[178] in Chapter V (PP 92-94) that these Ikshwakus migrated from the Western Asia during mature Harappan Age (2100 BC) where their sun deity was known as Baal who appears in the Rigveda (IV-33-34-35) in the account of Pani[179] (See Chapter XIII PP

375-76). These people had matriarchal form of family, marrying their real sisters. Hence they were indigenous non-Aryans Dravidian people.

The Art of Silpa and the Use of Arms Compulsory For Sakya Youths

Siddharta had only one wife, even hand of this girl was not granted untill he satisfied his knowledge of Silpa.

B.C. Law describes this event thus, "The Lalitavistara (PP 243 FF) thus makes Dandapani, the father of Gopa, reply to the Purohita sent by king Suddhodana. The honourable prince has been reared at home among luxuries. This, however is our family custom that a girl is to be made over to one proficient in the arts or Silpas and not to one ignorant of them. The prince has no knowledge of the Silpa, nor is he acquainted with the methods of fighting with the sword, the bow or other weapons. How can I then make over the girl to the prince.[180]" Whereas knowledge of Silpa was not compulsory for Aryan kshatriya (Manu I-89).

The same reply is given in the Mahavastu (II-73) by Mahanāma, the father of Yasodharā, when Suddhodana demands his girl as a bride for the young prince. Then the work goes on to narrate how he stood easily first in a tournament in which five hundred Sākya youngmen took part. The wife of Siddhartha is named Yasodhara in the Mahavastu and her father is called Mahānama.[181]

There was a technical college of the Sakyas in the Mango grove. The translator on the authority of the Sumangalvilasani, the commentary on the Dighanikaya by Buddhaghosa is as under[182]–"It was long terraced mansion made for the learning of the crafts. The learning of one or the other of the arts was incumbent upon every Sakya youth." We know main occupation of Sakya clan was ploughing of land which was compulsory for each member of the clan that is why although Suddhodana was a king but he also had to put hands to the handle of plough. But here learning of the one or the other "Silpa incumbent upon every youth" does mean, Sakyas, in addition to ploughing of land, were also engaged in other occupation or Silpa like, weaver, carpenter, smith etc. It means weavers of Khomadusa village were also ethnically of Sakya clan. This is most significant conclusion yet remained un-noticed by the historians.

The village of Khomadusa of Sakyas was solely inhabited by weavers producing linen cloth.[183] Similarly, Koliyas of Ramagama, who were a branch of Sakyas, were also weavers.[184]

We know the basis of indigenous culture of Indus Valley was trade and industry or silpa, the basis of indigenous Sangha or republic culture was also trade and industry, similarly the use of arms or art of war was also essential part of the life of people of aforesaid culture.

Supremacy or Rule of Head of the Clan

Dr D.R. Bhandarkar thinks that Kula or clan sovereignty was prominent among the Sakyas. Kula, which was more extensive than the family, was the lowest political unit amongst the political Sanghas. To quote his words, 'Kula, denotes not simply the domination of a chief over his clan but also and principally his supremacy over the territory occupied by the clan. That is why, in the time of Chinese[185] travellers Fa-hian, Sung-yun and Hieuntsang, there was no central government at Kapilvastu. There existed a congregation of priests and about ten families of laymen. Each town appointed its own ruler and there was no supreme ruler.[186] Such a system is quite compatible with that prevailed in Indus Valley[187] and Sumer, where city-state ruling system was in vogue from the very beginning, these city states were headed by a city ruler cum head priest of the city temple who was helped by citizenś two bodies of elders and youth. Chief profession of Sakyas was cultivation, mainly growing rice. The land was owned by the clan and further distributed among the villages and the families. Still in modern age as noted by me in district Farrukhabad, (U.P.) Kācchi, who are vegetable growers are known as Sakkas or Sakyas.

It seems, the Moriyas, the Mallas of Pawa and Kusinara and the Koliyas of Ramagama were also parts of the same society. The message sent by each of these clans to the Mallas of Kusinaras is as follows : "The Blessed one belongs to the soldier caste, we too are of the same soldier caste, we are worthy to receive a portion of the relics of the blessed one"[188]

Before the advent of Jainism and Buddhism, the Mallas also seem to have been Chaitya Worshippers like their neighbours, the Lichchhavis, one of their shrines called Makuta Bandhana, to the east of Kusinara is mentioned, where dead body of Buddha was cremated.[189] Chaitya or shrine worshipping is definitely non-Aryan tradition.

It is stated in the Mahāparinirbana Suttanta of the Digha-Nikāya that the inhabitants of Ramagama (Koliya) belonged to the serpent race[190] or Nagas. They were a subdivision of Sakyas and maternal grandfather of venerable Buddha, professing weaving of clothes hence close relative of Sakya, Ikshwakus or Suryabanshi.

Similarly, Videhas, who later emerged into Lichchhavis of Vaisali, were also Suryabanshi- a subdivision of Ikshwakus family to which Buddha himself belonged. It is most interesting that in Samyutta Nikaya Ajätsatru has been called Videhiputta[191] as such- "Samyutta Nikaya preserves a saying of the exalted one-Look Ye Bhikkus here, how these Lichchhavis live sleeping with logs of wood as pillows, strenuous and diligent, zealous and active in archery. Ajatasattu, Videhaputta, the

Magdhan king, confined no defeat in them, nor can be discovered any cause of action (against them)." It means Videha or Ikshwakus and Sakya were also of Naga race since Ajatsattru was of Sishu-Naga family.

The Madras

The Madras according to the Arthsastra of Kautilya were a corporation of warriors and lived by the title of a Raja (Rajasabdopajivinah). The Mahabharata tells us that it was a custom of the Madras to give their daughters in marriage on taking a fee (Sulka). This was their family custom (MB Adi chapter 113 P-119).

B.C. Law[192] quotes a legend which illustrates ethnical origin of Madras with the Yadavas, "At Banaras there was a king named Kusa, who belonged to the Ikshwaku family. One day he approached his mother Alindādevi and asked her to bring for him the most beautiful bride. The minister in quest of a beautiful girl, reached the city of Kanyakubja in the kingdom of Sursena, where the Madra king Mahendra ruled. They saw one day his beautiful daughter and thinking her to be the best possible selection they approached her father who readily consented to give her in marriage to king Kusa of Banaras."

It is obvious that Madras were originally Sursena or Yadavas by birth, which was a well known indigenous race and part and parcel of Indus Valley Culture as proved in chapter IX. B.C. Law[193] also informs us on the basis of Mahabharata account that Madra king Sālya was from Valhika dynasty, these Valhikas were Taka Nagas (See P-144) but according to the writing work of classical authors, the relation of Madras is proved with Pauravas also as such- "In the city of Sakala, Alexander found the second Paurava king, whose dominions he annexed to the Satrapy of his relation and rival, the great Paurava, who ruled over the adjacent territory between the Jhelum and Chenab. We may conclude that the kings of the Madras claimed to be Purus."[194]

It appears that the Madras were ancient rulers of Vedic age, who have been mentioned Bansha Brahmana of the Sāmveda. They continued their power till ninth century A.D. when we find the Madras as the allies of Dharmpala, the monarch of Bengal who with the assent of the Madras and other northern powers dethroned Indraraja, the King of Panchala. According to Jayaswal Madrakas are also known as Kunindas.[195(A)] These Kunindas or Koliyas still function as priests in non-Vedic religious rites. General Cunningham[195(B)] believes that, 'The hills of the Panjab were once occupied by a true Kolian race belonging to the same race or group as the Kols of central India and Bihar and that the present Kolis are very probably their representatives. He points out that dā the Kolian, for water is still used for many of the smaller streams of the Simla-hills. The name of Kūlu (a lingiustic corrupt variation of Koli or Kolia), however, he identifies with Kulinda. As above, K.P. Jayaswal indentifies these Kulindas or Kunindas with the Madrakas or Madras who ruled in Panjab for quite some time. It means these Kulinda or Koli were also of Yadava race and as well as of Naga race. Cunningham identifies Kanets (of Kulu and Kangra) with the Kunindas or Kulindas of the Sanskrit classics and of Ptolemy, and is of the opinion that they belong to the great khasa race (Denzil Ibbetson P-198) who before Aryan invasion, occupied the whole sub-Himalyan tract upto Brahmputra.

The Kambojas

Sir George Grierson holds that without discussing the correctness of the statement that Sava has a connection with Savathi, we can gather from this that Yāska thinks that the Kamboja were not Aryans and that they spoke Sanskrit but with dialectic variations of vocabulary. Savathi does not occur in Sanskriti at all but it is an Iranian word.[196] It means Kamboja were a non-Aryan ancient race of Iran like Yadavas. If we read the verses 43 and 44 of Chapter X of Manu, we find that the following tribes of Kshatriyas, namely the Kamboja, the Sakas, the Yadavas and so forth, have been gradually degraded to the condition of Sudras on account of their omission of the sacred rites and of their not consulting the Brahmanas[197] i.e., they were not followers of Brahmanical religion.

The Arthshastra of Kautilya states that the corporations of warriors of Kamboja and some other countries lived by agriculture, trade and wielding weapons (Vārtasastropajivin). From this statement also it is clear that Kamboja were Kshatriyas. Here Kshatriya means a non-Aryan warrior and not Aryan.[198] Some scholars, think that Kam-boja or (Kambhoja) means inferior Bhoja. Bhoja were a branch of Yadavas[199] race and component of the great Satavahana power.

The Kshudrakas and the Malavas

During his retreat, Alexander[200] came across a number of republics. In fact, all the states he met on his way back, down the Indus and up to the Indian frontier in Baluchistan were republican. The most powerful amongst them were the Kshudrakas and the Mālavas. They are spelt by the Greeks as Oxydrakai and Malloi respectively. They are on the Hydaspes, by which the Greeks apparently mean the passage of the Jhelum after its union with the Chenab. The two states formed one league. Arrian[201] (VI-4) says that they were the most numerous and war like of the Indian 'nations' in those parts.. "Alexander first reached the nation called the Malloi. The Mallois are called a race of independent

Indians (republic); their cities were along the Chenab and their capital was near the Ravi. It was in the siege of the capital or one of the cities of the Malloi that Alexander nearby lost his life. Owing to the unity of the league, the Greek writers could not decide whether Alexander's narrow escape relates to the city of the Malloi or to that of the Oxydrakai. The strength of the army as given by Curtius was 1,00,000. These Indians were regarded by the soldiers as "fierce nation" who would not let them proceed without drawing their blood.''

They were occupying southern part of Panjab, where their language-Malavi is noted in Patiala and Bhatinda districts.

These war like people were republics and of Naga race. They, in later period, moved toward south i.e. in modern Malava or Southern Panjab, Rajasthan and later settled in Western Madhya Pradesh still known as Malava after their name. Other Shudrakas were Sudra, who were ruling in Sind some times before the invasion of Kasim. In a later period, these Malavas migrated to South Eastern Rajputana and ruled quite some time. The Malavas[202], the Yaudheyas and the Kunindas (Madrakas) all re-strike their coins in the Naga period. It may be possible to discern on a minute study their connection with the Naga coinage disclosing the symbols of hegemony or suzerainty of the Nagas. The connection of the Malava republican coins with those of Padmavati has been already realized and noticed. Dr. V.A.[203]Smith says, "They (Naga coins) are closely related to some of the later Malava coins. The Malava coins re-appear after a break about the same time as the Naga coins of Padmāvati about the second century A.D. The Yaudheya coinage revives about the second century A.D. and the Kuninda coinage in the third century who are evidently the last to be liberated. In other words, the re-rise of the Yaudheyas and the Malavas is contemporaneous with the Nagas."

The first[204] state of later Nagas is Malava. Nagara or Karkota Nagara, was the capital of the Malavas, whose thousands of republican coins as thick as shells on the sea-shore, have been found there. The Bhāgavata calls them the Arbuda-Malavas and the Vishnu locates them in Rajputana. They were, thus decidedly in Rajputana from mount Abu upto Jaipur. The territorial designation Mālavar seems to be based on their names. They are noticed at their new home in 150-100 B. C. as evident from coins found at Karkot Nagar.

The Ambasthas and the Agrasenis

Alexander[205] met in the neighbourhood of the last two republics the Agsinaes, who had mustered an army, if we believe Diodorus, of 40,000 foot and 3000 horses. They barricaded their narrow streets, fought with great vigour, so that Alexander in pressing the attack lost few Macedonians (Mc Crindle, Alexander P-285). The next republic mentioned by the Greeks was that of the Ambashthas, spelt as Sambastai and Abastanoi. They[206] were a people inferior to none in India, either in numbers or in bravery. Their form of government was democratic (Mc Crindle, Alexander P-252). Their army consisted of 60,000 foot, 6000 cavalry and 500 chariots. They had elected three generals renowned for their valour and military skill (Mc Crindle P-252).

Here Agrasrenis or Agrasini can be Agrasena kings of Agroha who is said to be a progenitor of Aggarwal who has been proved to be a non-Aryan Sudra tribe in Chapter XIII of this book. These ambasthas were kayasthas since one of their branch is still known as Ambasthas (H.H. Rishy, ''Tribes and Castes of Bengal'' vol I P-443). As such it is clear that all these republics were non-Aryan indigenous people, where every citizen was equal by birth and family which can not be a part of Brahmanical Vedic Varna based social system. K. P. Jayaswal[207] gives description of some minor Sanghas of North West India as such-"They, in the Puranas are identical with the Sātvats. The Sātvats, according to Aitreya Brāhmana, had the Bhaujya constitution, and their rulers were called Bhojas (AB-Book VIII-14). In the Mahabharata, the Andhaka rulers are called Bhojas and a sub-division of the Yādavas itself is laterly called Bhoja (Sabha-Chapter XIV; Shanti Chapter LXXXI). The fact that the Vrishnis had no Rajan in their constitution, is expressed in folklore and legend in that they had been cursed not to be crowned kings."

The Surashtras were in Kathiavar. Their name still live in modern Soratha. They seem to have survived the Mauryan imperialism as they figure in the inscriptions of Balasri (E. Ind VIII-P-60) and in the Junagadh inscription of Rudradāman

Pātāla (Mori of Taka Origin) :

To the Southern most of Sindh[208] there was a republic of Pātāla in the delta of the Indus. Before Alexander arrived, the whole community had migrated to avoid submission, since there was a practice amongst smaller Indian republics. In the constitution of Pātāla their ruler was called Moeres (Curtius BK IX ch.8). Diodorus gives constitution of state in these words, "A city of great note with a political constitution drawn on the same line as the Sparton, for, in this community the command in the war vested in the hereditary kings of two different houses while a council of Elders ruled the whole state with paramount authority.[209]"

The Pātāla of the Macedonians has been indentified with Hyderabad (Sind), whose ancient name is still remembered as Pātāl puri.[210] It seems to be the Pātana of the Ganapātha (on P. IV-1-14) and the Pātānprastha, a Vahika town of Pātanjali (V-2-104).

It has been already observed that ancient inscriptions in the Pali Buddhist character have been discovered in various parts of Rajasthan of the race of Takshak or Tak, relating to the tribe the Mori (or Maurya) Parmar their descendants. Naga and Takshak are synonymous appellations in Sanskrit for snake and Takshak is the celebrated Nag-Bansha the early heroic history of India.[211]

We have already mentioned the Takshak Mori (or Maurya) as being lords of Chittor from a very early period.[212]

We know from the account of Mahabharat that a branch of Takshak Nag used to live in Pātālpuri. It means these Nagas of Pātālpuri were related to Vahika or Takshak Nag on one hand and Maurya royal family and Parmar Rajput family on the other. Thus Maurya family was also born from Takshak Nag. Further Tod[213] gives detail of the relation of Takshak and Maurya and Parmar of later period as such "Chandra Gupta, the supposed opponent of Alexander, was a Maurya, and in the sacred genealogies is declared of the race of Takshak. The ancient inscriptions of the Parmars, of which the Maurya is a principal branch, declare it of the race of Tasta and Takshak, as does that now given from the seat of their power Chittor.[214]"

Salivahana, the conqueror of Vikramaditya, was a Takshak and his era set aside that of the Tuar in the Deccan.

Not one remnant of independence exists to mark the greatness of the Parmars; ruins are the sole records of their power. "The prince of Dhat in the Indian (Sindh) desert is the last phantom of royalty of the race. (They were Sodha tribe, a grand division of the Parmars). Among the 35 Sakhas of the Parmars the Vihal was eminent, who were lord of Chandravati at the foot of the Aravali." It is obvious the Takas or the Mauryas in later period became Rajputs.

The Glory of Sangha Culture

At the end of Chalcolithic Age (1000 -800 BC) and beginning of Iron Age, man after stepping on to the high way of civilization, began to make rapid progress. Who were these people, responsible for introducing Iron Age in India ? According to learned Scholar, S.P Gupta, the credit of changing Indian Chalcolithic Age, into Iron Age, goes to progenitors of these republican people, who took iron and iron technology from Western Asia in one of their influx in aforesaid period, partially due to commercial activities. Iron, being a harder metal than copper, provided better and efficient war weapons to overcome battle fields and tools to yield higher industrial and farm product. This is the main reason they proved their superiority on the Vedic Culture in post Mahabharata age. Not only this, the indigenous merchants are credited to take Indian alphabet from Phoenicia at about 800 B.C.[215] This was Brahmi the mother of all Indian scripts, which paved the way for future writing of great treasure of Pali and Sanskrit texts. Buddhist Pali, Jataka was the first work written in this script. Similarly commercial activities can be given the credit of introducing Iron Age in India. How this, credit can be given to native population, the explanation of this apparent anomaly is really perfectly plain and simple. It is clear enough from a comparison of the literature but it is more easily shown, perhaps by a comparison of the inscriptions. Take the inscription for instance, on the vase discovered by Peppe in the Sakiya tope which is in my opinion the oldest inscription yet discovered in India & found so far. (JRAS 1898 and 1899).[216]

According to a citation of Bhandarkar, made by Davids Rhys, not only writing system even buildings and sculptures do not belong to Brahmans- "The period that we have been speaking of (that is from the beginning of the second century BC to the end of the fourth century after) has left no trace of a building or sculpture devoted to the use of the Brahman religion. Of course, Brahmanism existed and it was properly during the period, being developed into the form which it assumed in later times."[217]

Similarly, credit of introducing non-Vedic Buddhist and Jain religions also goes to them. Their great sons, the princes of Sakya and Vaisali republics, introduced these religions which provided the human kind not only with a universal religion but also a philosophy of universal brotherhood. As such they succeeded in establishing a social system of equality and brotherhood where no one knew the caste.

One of their most glorious endowments to human kind was development of citizens army system, where learning of use of the art of arms was compulsory from childhood, hence they all were Kshatriya or warrior of high rank. Thus a most powerful and invincible large army could be built, which caused building up of extensive powerful empires first of all in India, such as Magadha and Satavahanas, later ruled as long as 500 years, Ashoka carved out largest empire of ancient India.

It is famous that the Romans were pioneers to introduce a most genuine political system like republican, but this credit in fact goes to these people who gifted this system to human kind much earlier than Romans, although the seed of system was sowed in Sumeria but its grand tree could be developed in to full on Indian soil.

Perhaps the most glorious achievement of these people was development of guild based trade and industry system that grew all around to such an extent that India was studded with all kinds of craft-guilds and we can say that every village practically developed into an industrial estate. These guilds were so wealthy that even their sworn enemy,

Kautilya could not help to say, "They are the most prosperous and invincible." This paved the way for urbanization of India for the second time after the fall of Indus Valley towns.

How the Strongest and the Best System was Destroyed ?

A Glorious and best system, developed so far by human kind, which made the Buddhist India (500 B.C.- 500 A.D.) economically most prosperous and politically powerful and invincible country, was victimized by their hereditary antagonists, the Vedic Aryans. In Arthshastra a complete chapter (Sangha Vrātā Adhikaran XI of 78 Sutra) was added by Kautilya with an object, how to destroy these powerful republics or guilds. One example is being reproduced below: Kautilya Sangh Vrata-11 Adhikaran Chapter I SARE ŚAMASA NNAḤ STRINAḤ SANGHĀNA PARAS PARANYANGA DVEŚVERA KALA HASTHĀNA-NYUPALABHYA KRAMĀ BHINĪTAṀ BHEDMUPĀ CHĀRYEYUḤ (7) ASOTVĀ VIJALPATITI (8) EVAMUBHAYATAḤ (9)

Meaning :— Spies may be deputed at nearby places of all such Sanghas, who would note their points of fault, hatred, enmity and cause of dispute against each other and try to create division among them by saying- "such and such Sangha is criticizing you"-and thus excite each, against others. In this way make them each others antagonist.

I can conclude the whole chapter in one line "Divide the different associates of Sangha, made them fight and destroy." Perhaps killing of last Mauryan King, Brahdratha at the hand of his own Brahman military commander, was a part of the same conspiracy.

During the Gupta age[218] while the Buddhism was pushed back and Hinduism revived, 13 Naga Kings were killed by Samudra Gupta, the unity of craftguilds was ruthlessly[219] broken, their arms and power seized and in lieu of Sangha, caste and feudal system was introduced forcibly.[230] As such the backbone of Indian economy and military system was broken for ever. Hence forth the nation lived a life of slavery and poverty and humiliation and real dark age of Indian history began. Historians like K.P. Jayaswal could not help expressing his heart feelings against this awful act of Samudra Gupta, being produced below[221] "A history which is worth remembering is a history of good deeds and just services; the deeds which trample upon the rights and liberties of others are not to be canonized by the historian. If he were alive to-day, he might have said "Remember Vikramaditya, the son of Samudra Gupta, but forget Samudra Gupta...... Samudra Gupta, like Alexander, killed the free sprit of his country. He destroyed the Malavas and the Yaudheyas who were the nursery of freedom and many others of their class. Once those free communities were wiped out, the recruiting ground for future heroes and patriots and statesmen disappeared. The Gupta themselves, both from their mother's side and their fathers side had descended from those republic communities. They themselves were crops of those seed communities, but they totally destroyed them.

The social system of the republican community was based on equality. They knew no caste. They consisted of one caste only. The orthodox (Hindu) system on the other hand, was based on inequality and caste where mass patriotism could not be mobilized as it could easily be done among the Malava, the Yaudheyas, the Madras, ... the Abhiras, and the Lichchhavis. They were the exercise ground for state making for patriotism, for individual ambitions, capabilities and leadership. But under Samudra Gupta and his descendents they all merged into an organized, officialized, orthodox caste system and an orthodox political system which recognized and fostered monarchy and imperialism.

The seed pot to produce a Buddha, the prophet of universal religion and universal equality was consumed for ever. The seed pot for production of a future Bharsiva or a future Gupta was made extinct and the Hindu sank. Then republics of Rajputana dissolved into the Rajputs who forgot all the traditions of their republican ancestors......The Hindu did not remember the name of the Samudra Gupta with any gratitude and when Alberuni came to India he was told that the Gupta were a wicked people. This is another view of the picture. They were tyrant to Hindu constitutional freedom, though excellent rulers to the individual subject. ....The Bharsiva federation was an enlargement of the Sangha organization of the Hindu republics. It was a league of equals with a recognized leading power."

But, once more in mediaeval period of Indian history, efforts were made by Guru Govind Singh, who revived such a system of society in Panjab by establishment of Sikh religion to meet with tyrany of Mughals. This great man, perhaps modern soul of Buddha, made, common man a "Sant Sipahi" (Saint-Warrior) by handing over sword to maintain peace and prosperity. Base of his sacred economic philosophy is "KIRTIKARO TE VAND KHĀO" i.e. Work hard and distribute its fruits among all.

Summary and Conclusion

It is most surprising that the secret of rising of earliest human civilization has been the union of two races, the round headed Sumerians and the long headed Semites. (Akkadians) Perhaps first of all, they met in Western Asia, at the coastal land of Mediterranean sea, where, they gave birth to first human civilization of the world ten thousand years before the present time. This was repeated later in Sumer. When, they came close to each other in Crete island, great Minoan culture took its birth.

In fact, the first race was highly expert in the science of spiritualism and second was great technician or artisian and trader, that is why perhaps fourth time, whenever these races united together in Indus Valley at about 2100 B.C. or mature Harappan age, this culture also reached its top heights. But, due to coming of and invasion of half civilized Aryan race, once their culture was destroyed and came to a stand-still position during the period of rule or supremacy of new comer Aryans. But after the fall of their supremacy and rule, owing to the Mahabharat war, the seed of Harappan indigenous culture began to grow again.

The progeny of native non-Aryan Harappans developed their ancient system called guild or Sangha, which was originally brought from Sumerian culture. These guilds were originally related to the people of a single blood group engaged in any particular productive occupation and in fact were a result of tribal evolution. They were engaged in occupations like basket-makers, potters, herds-men, carpenters, weavers, smiths plough-men etc. By the passage of time, they grew into complete villages with their head or chief the Gramani and later into groups of villages of a clan or kinship group, with their chief Kulika. These Kulikas or Kings had their own administration and independent power organized on the pattern of republic system.

Some of these republican Sanghas, appear during the life time of Buddha, such as Sakyas, Bhaggas, Bulis, Koliyas, Mallas, Moriyas, Videhas, Lichchhavis, Kshudrakas, Malavas, Andhrakas, Vrishinis, Madrakas, Yaudheyas, Kambojas etc. It is most significant to note that although, Sakyas were ploughmen, Lichchhavis were herdsmen, Koliyas were weavers and Videhas were carvaneers, but they are always called Sakyas, Lichchhavis, Koliyas, Videhas, not by their occupational names, which was a peculiarity of Brahmanical caste system. Such a system, most strikingly, is indicative of their non-Aryan origin and not Aryan.

The other chief feature of their constitution was that they emphasized on each member the duty to acquire military skill. In other words they had a citizens' or peoples army also known as Nation-in-arms. The Nation-in-arms class however did not become purely military, for their constitution also required their citizen to devote attention to industry and agriculture. Hence, they were most prosperous as well as powerful. But, in case of arising of emergency, soldiers in desired number could be called immediately. In this way, a large army could be built in no time. This best system, yet developed by mankind, took the Nation's progress to its top heights, once more, after the fall of Indus Valley culture. They developed a religious system, which advocated universal brotherhood, equality and sense of humanity, which came to be known as Buddhist religion.

Activities of these craft guilds came into full swing, while, human civilization leaving the Chalcolithic Age behind, entered the Iron Age (1000 BC-800 BC). Iron provided mankind with the strongest and the best weapons to win over the toughest battlefields, agriculture implements to grow the best harvest, tools to get the highest industrial production and house hold equipments for smooth working, leading to a luxurious life and better living. This resulted into raising of his standard of living and as such increasing of his population. Some of the important guilds or Sangha among them were Vajjian of Vaisali, (herdsmen), Sakyas of Kapilvastu (Plough-men), Koliya of Ramagama (weavers), Videha of Mithila (Carvaneers), Agraseni of West Panjab (Traders) etc.

Perhaps, this was the time while common man began to use clothing lavishly to protect himself from the hardship of weather, as a result of which, more and more cloth was produced by the guilds engaged in weaving, dyeing, decorating to meet with the enhanced demand of users.

This further resulted into flourishing of these guilds to a great extent who became very wealthy and powerful. These Sanghas were of Andhrakas, Madras, Malavas, Vahikas or Takshaka of Panjab and Koliya of East and their chiefs became more powerful who established their power in North West India, where their population is still settled in a very high number in south of Jammu, as noted by Denzil Ibbetson and Cunningham. Later their chiefs, became kings like Khalifah of Western Asia, which was the designation of chief of their guild or Sangha till recent days as noted by Ibbetson. Later their offshoot branches established their rule in other regions of this nation, like Maurya, Naga of Vidisa and Eran, Bharsiva of Padmavati, Vakataka, Satavahana, Gonanda, Karkota, Nagpal and many others yet to be discovered.

In short, these people were wealthy workers and valiant warriors, who believed in equality and brotherhood and knew no caste. They were followers of Buddha's teaching of non-violence, their sword was not for violence but for maintaining peace. They were architects of urbanization of ancient India second time after the fall of Indus cities and their ultimate achievement was 'Golden Age' of Indian History.

But this republican system, a great achievement of mankind, was destroyed by Samudra Gupta, who killed 13 Naga princes who were remains of ancient republic consciousness. The Guptas themselves , both from their mothers side and their fathers side had descended from those republican community, they themselves were crop of those seed communities, but, they totally destroyed them. They introduced orthodox Hindu religion and feudal system and killed the spirit of freedom and republican thoughts . Perhaps, spirit of Kautilya, the famous antagonist of republican society played its role in the guise of Samudra Gupta.

References

1. Bhandarkar D.R. "Lecture on the Ancient History of India" P-141.
2. Bhandar Kar D.R. P-142.
3. Jayaswal K.P. "Hindu Polity" P-26.
4. Misra SN, "Ancient Indian Republics" P-149 S. Chand and Co Delhi (1975).
5. Davids Rhys T.W. "Buddhist India" P-42.
6. Bhandarkar D.R. P-149.
7. Jayaswal K. P. P-115.
8. Kosambi D. D. "The Culture and Civilization of Ancient India" P-125.
9. Hawkes Jacquetta, "The First Great Civilization" P-164.
10. Hawkes Jacquetta, P-114.
11. Rao S.R., "Lothal and the Indus civilization" PP 24 and 68.
12. Rao S.R. P-70.
13. Bhandarkar D.R. PP 169-71 see foot note No.2.
14. Davids Rhys T. W. P-50.
15. Viyogi Naval, "The Founders of Indus Valley Civilization and their later History" PP 226-34.
16. Jayaswal K. P "Hindu Polity"P-46.
17. Kosambi D.D P-125.
18. Davids Rhys T.W. P-10.
19. Sastri Nilkant K.A. "Age of Nanda and Maurya" P-70.
20. Tripathi Vibha "The Painted Grey Ware; An Iron Age Culture of North India" PP-110-17.
21. Kosambi D.D. P-125.
22. Bhandarkar DR. P-143.
23. Jayaswal K. P. "Hindu Polity" P-102.
24. (a) Bhandarkar D. R. P-156.
    (b) Davids Rhys T. W. PP 11-12.
25. Jayaswal K.P., "Hindu Polity" P-170.
26. Jayaswal K.P PP 38-50 to 55.
27. Davids Rhys T.W. P-9.
28. Ibid.
29. Kosambi D.D. P-124.
30. Jayaswal K.P. "Hindu Polity" P-170.

31. Jayaswal K.P. P-61 and 126.
32. Jayaswal K.P. P-33.
33. Jayaswal K.P. PP-33-34.
34. Jayaswal K.P P-34.
35. Law B.C.; "Some Kshatriya Tribes of Ancient India" PP91-92.
36. Bhandarkar D.R. P-160.
37. Hawkes Jacquetta, PP 152-53.
38. Law B.C. P-194.
39. Misra S.N P-132.
40. Misra S.N. P-10.
41. Jayaswal K. P. "Hindu Polity" P-102.
42. Davids Rhys T. W. P-10.
43. Gokhale B.G., "Buddhism in Maharashtra" P-22.
44. Jayaswal K.P. - "Hindu Polity" PP 54-55.
45. Jayaswal K.P. "Hindu Polity" P-55.
46. Jayaswal K.P. P-170.
47. Jayaswal K.P. "Hindu Polity" P-31.
48. Hawkes Jacquetta PP-165-68.
49. Jayaswal K.P.- P-170.
50. Jayaswal K.P. PP-42-43 and 119.
51. Jayaswal K.P. "Hindu Polity" P-34.
52. Jayaswal K.P "Hindu Polity" P-170.
53. Mookerjee R.K. "The Gupta Empire" P-149.
54. Mahavastu Vol III ed Senart E. (Peris 1862) translation by J.J. Jones, "Sacred Books of Buddhism" PP 112-13.
55. (a) Jayaswal K. P. "Hindu-Polity" P-169.
    (b) SANDHYA MUKHYAŚCHA SANGHEŚU NYĀYA VRATTI HITPRYA : (Arthshastra P-379).
56. Jayaswal K.P. P-169.
57. Jayaswal K.P. PP 31-32.
58. Jayaswal K.P. P-102.
59. Ibid P-102.
60. Jayaswal K.P. P-31.
61. Davids Rhys T. W. P-26.
62. Davids Rhys T. W. P-28.
63. Davids Rhys T. W. P-28.
64. Gokhable B.G. "Buddhism in Maharashtra" P-26.
65. Kosambi D. D. P-126.

66. Davids Rhys T. W. P-23.

67. Davids Rhys T. W. P-1.

68. (a) Gokhale B.G. "Samudra Gupta" PP 25-32.

(b) Law B.C. PP 18-19.

69. (a) Buddha Prakash, "Rigveda and the Indus valley Civilization" PP-102-05.

(b) Bottero, Cassin and Vercoutter, "The Near East ; The Early Civilization" PP 391-92.

70. Das A.C. "Rigvedic India" PP 186-97.

71. Law B.C. P-180.

72. Law B.C. P. 201.

73. Gokhale B. G., "Buddhism in Maharashtra" PP-21-22.

74. Bhandarkar D. R. PP 172-73.

75. Jayaswal K. P. PP 53-54.

76. Viyogi Naval. PP 197-204.

77. Rao S. R. PP 24 and 68.

78. Rao S. R. P-70.

79. J.R. A. S. (1917) P 237.

80. Bhandarkar D.R. PP 144-45.

81. Rigveda II- 11-4, II-11-19, II-12-4, V -29-10.

82. Jayaswal K. P., "Hindu Polity" PP 37-38.

83. Kosare H. L. "Prachin Bharatatil Nag" PP-133-34.

84. Gokhle B.G. PP 21-22.

85. Hawkes Jacquetta P-149.

86. M.R. Vol XIV No 1-6 (1913) P-540.

87. Davids Rhys T.W. P-6 and 41.

88. Rao T.A. Gopinath, "Elements of Hindu Iconography" Vol II Part II (1968) PP 556-57.

89. (a) Cunningham A.; "Ancient Geography of India" PP-148 FF.

(b) Beal, "SI-YU-KI" I P-165 FF .

90. Cunningham A P-148.

91. Jayaswal K.P.-"History of India"P-39.

92. Jayaswal K.P. PP 38-39.

93. Jayaswal K.P. "History of India" P-115.

94. Jayaswal K.P. P-33 Foot note No. 2 below.

95. Cunningham A.I. PP 125 and129.

96. Tod James, "Annals and Antiquities of Rajasthan" I P-124.
97. In the Mahabharata and in the Laxicon of Hemchandra the Vahikas are said to be the same as Taka BAHIKASHTAKKANĀMĀNA Foot Note No.1 Cunningham PP-125-26.
98. Tod James I P-124.
99. (a) Tod James vol I P-43 F/N No.3.
    (b) Jain Jyoti Prasad, "Bhartiya Itihas; EK Drishti" P-48.
100. Davids Rhys T. W. P-15.
101. Kosambi D. D. P-120.
102. Tod James Vol I P-125.
103. Crindle MC, "Ancient India as described in Classical Literture" P-145.
104. Jayaswal KP, "History of India" P-38-39.
105. Jayaswal KP, P-89.
106. Some Scholars think that Singhpur was situated some where near salt Range of Panjab.
107. Ibid.
108. Cunningham A. P-125.
109. Vaidya C. V., "History of Mediaeval Hindu India." P-386.
110. Cunningham A. P-129.
111. A. S. R. Vol II P-10 (See foot note no. 3).
112. Vaidya C. V. P-388.
113. Vaidya C. V. PP 284-85.
114. Ibid.
115. Indian Antiquary No. 17P-118.
116. Tod I P-126.
117. He is called "Chatto the Tak" in the list of wounded fighters of Kanauj (who ruled between 1324-1351 AD) Tod P-126 Foot note No. 2.
118. Cunningham A P-128.
119. Gupta Chandra Shekhar, "Foreign Denomination of Early Indian Coins" VIJ (Jan 1978) Vol 16 Part 1 and 2 PP.92-93.
120. Sherring M.A., "Hindu Tribes and Castes" P-376.
121. Tod James II PP 914-17.
122. Oldham C.F. "The Sun and the Serpent" P-30.
123. Tod I P-126.
124. Tod I P-118.
125. Mahajan V.D. "Madhya Kalin Bharat" PP 246-49.
126. Jain Jagdish Chandra, "Jain Āgam Sahitya Main Bhartiya Samaj" PP 173-74 and 490.
127. Jayaswal K. P. "History of India" PP 53-54.

128. Denzil Ibbetson, "Panjab Caste" PP-320-24.
129. Hawkes Jacquette PP 114-15.
130. Hawkes Jaequetta PP-114-15.
131. Hawkes Jacquetta P-115.
132. Wheeler Martimer -"The Indus civilization" P-85.
133. Ibid P-86.
134. Wheeler Martimer Vol I P-51.
135. Hawkes Jacquetta P-115.
136. Kosambi- D. D. P-123.
137. (a) Davids Rhys TW P-26.
     (b) Jain Jagdish Chandra, "Jain Āgam Sahitya Main Bhartiya Samaj" PP 173-74 and 490.
138. Jayaswal K.P., "Hindu Polity" PP-38 and 50.
139. Cunningham A. P-124.
140. Denzil Ibbetson P-333.
141. Denzil Ibbetson P-335.
142. Hadson T.C. "The Naga Tribes of Manipur" P-2.
143. Cunningham A. PP 125 and 129.
144. Denzil Ibbetson P-333.
145. Dr. Bharat Singh-"Pali Sahitya Ka Itihas" PP-21 FF
146. Kautilya XI-I-I to 24.
147. Verma Brij Lal, "Rajarishi Chhatrapati Shahu Ji" P-168.
148. Bharat Singh PP 21 FF.
149. Jayaswal K.P. "Hindu Polity" PP-28 and 50.
150. Kosambi D. D. P-81.
151. Mehendale M.A. "Takki or Dhakki" BDCRI vol-I (1939-40) P-192.
152. Mehendale M.A. PP 189-91.
153. Sathpathbrah III-2-1-23. (b) See Chapter VII for detail.
154. Cunningham A P-129.
155. Kosambi D. D. P-124.
156. Gupta Chandra Shekhar VIJ (1978) Vol 16 Part 1-2 P-92.
157. JNSI-30-(1968) P-129.
158. Gupta Chandra Shekhar PP-93-94.
159. Kosare H. L. PP-34-35.
160. E.I I No. 4 P 383, I, No. 5 P-384, I No. 16 P. 202.
161. Jayaswal K.P. "Hindu Polity" PP 37-38.
162. Bhandarkar D.R. PP 172-73.

163. Mirashi V.V., "Studies in Indology" Vol III P-2.
164. Jayaswal K.P. "History of India" P-39.
165. Oldham C.F. P-30.
166. Gokhale B. G. PP 25-32.
167. Mitra S.K., "Early Rulers of Khajuraho" PP 23-27.
168. Law B.C. PP 18-19.
169. Law B.C. P-70.
170. Fergusson James "Tree and Serpent Worship" P-78.
171. I.A. Vol XXXVII (1908) P-79.
172. Law B.C. P-79.
173. Law B.C. PP 91-92.
174. Jayaswal K.P. "Hindu Polity" P 184.
175. Law B.C. PP 163-64.
176. Sumangal Bilasini Part-I PP 258-60.
177. Law B.C. P-174.
178. Bottero Cassin, and Vercoutter, PP 391-92.
179. Dass A.C. "Rigvedic India" PP 186-97.
180. Law B.C. P-180.
181. Law B.C. P-180.
182. "Dialogues of the Buddha" Vol-IV Part III P-III.
183. Law B.C. P-178.
184. Davids Rhys T.W. P-9.
185. Law B.C. P-194.
186. Beal, "Records of the Western world" Vol II P-14.
187. Mackay E, "Early Indus civilization" Int PP. XII and XIII.
188. Law B.C. P-201.
189. Law B.C. P-126.
190. Digha Nikaya (PTS) Vol II P-167.
191. Law B.C. P-56.
192. Law B.C. P-220.
193. Law B.C. P-223.
194. Law B.C. P-225.

195 (a) Jayaswal K.P., "The History of India" P-54.
    (b) Denzil Ibbetson PP-195 and 335.

196. Law B.C. P-232.
197. Law B.C. P-237.
198. Law B.C. P-238

199. Jayswal K.P. "Hindu Polity" P-55.

200. Jayaswal K.P., "Hindu Polity" PP 62-63.

201. Ibid.

202. Jayaswal K. P. "History of India" P-54.

203. Ibid.

204. Jayaswal K.P., "History of India" P-147.

205. Jayaswal K.P. "Hindu Polity" P-67.

206. Ibid.

207. Jayaswal K.P. "Hindu Polity" PP 36-37.

208. Jayaswal K.P. PP 70-71.

209. Crindle M.C., "Alexander" P-296.

210. Crindle M.C. P-236.

211. Tod James P-124.

212. Tod James P- 126.

213. Tod James IPP-110-111.

214. Tod James IP-110 F/Note No. 3. Herbert has a curious story of Chittor being called Takshila, Thence the story of the Ranas being sons of Porus. I have an inscription from a temple on the Chambal within the ancient limits of Mewar, which mentions Taksho-silanager 'the stone fort of the Tak' The city of Toda (tank) is called in the Chouhana Chronicles, Takhatpur

215. (a) Buhler G. "Indian Paleography" PP-31-32.

(b) Rapson E.J. "CHI" Vol I P-55.

216. Davids Rhys T. W. P-54.

217. Davids Rhys T. W. P-65.

218. Jayaswal K. P. "History of India" P-210.

219. Shanti MB 107-14.

220. Gokhale B. G., "Samudra Gupta" PP 70-72.

221. Jayaswal K. P., "History of India" PP 210-11.

Chapter-7

PISHACHI, THE MOTHER OF PALI, PRAKRIT AND MAHARASHTRI

No one can deny the historical fact that before the coming of the Aryans, India was inhabited by the native or indigenous people of different non-Aryan races, who spoke some languages other than that of Aryans. Which were those languages and what was their relation with the languages of new comers, the Vedic Aryans, is the subject of our discussion. We know that the southern languages belong to Dravidian group. But the languages of the Central Pradesh and north are most controversial. G.A. Grierson, on the basis of his linguistic survey of India, has thrown enormous light on this subject :

Pishachi an Aryan Language : Viewpoint of Grierson

Dardic or Pishachi languages, which are spoken in North Western India can be divided into three groups after Grierson.[1] (1) Kafir (2) Khovar or Chitral (3) Dard or Pishacha group.

The third group of these languages can further be divided into three languages i.e. Shina, Kashmiri and Kohistani. Pasto, Ghalchah and all other neighbouring languages are of Aryan stock. The first two are related to Iranian and the third to the Indian branch. All the languages of Dārdic stock are of the Aryan family, but from a separate third branch by themselves. The position may be explained as under :

In prehistoric[2] times, a branch of Aryans, who spoke a language known as Aryan, entered the plains of India through the western passes of Hindukush and the valley of Kabul river and settled there. The Aryans who remained behind on the north of Hindukush spread eastwards and west-wards. Those, who migrated to the east, occupied the Pamirs and now speak Ghalchah. Those, who went westwards occupied Merv, Persia and Baluchistan and their descendants now speak those languages which together with Ghalchah languages are called Iranian. From that time onward the languages spoken by these people developed on different lines, and at the present day the Iranian languages are very different from those of India.

The Dardic[3] languages possess many characteristics which are peculiar to themselves, while in some other respects they agree with Indo-Aryan, and yet in other respects with Iranian languages. They do not possess all the characteristics either of Indo-Aryan or of Iranian. We must assume that at the time, when they issued from the Aryan language, the Indo-Aryan language had already branched forth from it, and that the Aryan language had by that time developed further on its own lines in the direction of the Iranian; but that development had not yet progressed so far as to reach all the typical characteristics of Iranian, and still retained some (but not all) of the characteristics it possessed when the Indo-Aryans set out for the Kabul Valley. This may be represented graphically by the following diagram :

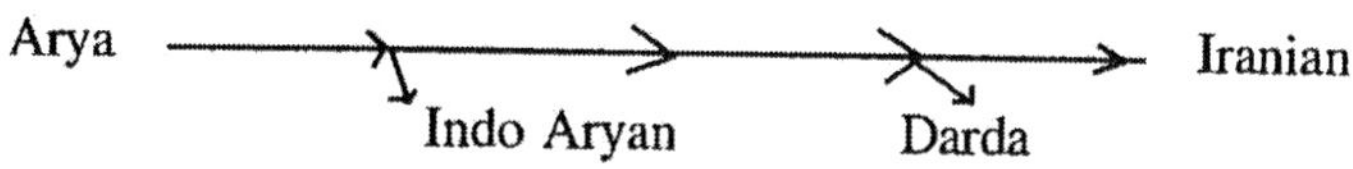

Nearly every Iranian characteristic possessed by the Dardic is shared by Ghalchah languages, while, at the same time, these very Iranian Ghalchah languages have a few points in which they follow the Dardic languages in agreeing with Indian as against Iranian. The fact that Darda languages proper are more nearly related to those of Kāfir Group than either of these is related to Khō-wār, further suggests that the latter represents the language of the later body of Dardic invaders, akin to the earlier ones. Khō-wār, though undoubtedly Dardic in character possesses more points in common with Ghalchah than the others, and separates the Kāfirs from the Dards proper by a wedge of language presenting a greater number of distinctly Iranian features.[4]

In the south of Dardric languages are spoken Lahnda or Western Panjabi languages. If its northern section Lahnda is surrounded by languages of Dardic type on three sides, east, north and west. As regards the other languages Panjabi with its dialect Dogri and Rajasthani belong to central group of Indo-Aryan languages and are therefore distinct from Lahnda which belongs to the North-Western group. Sindhi, on the other hand, is closely connected with Lahnda and both are closely related with their origin.

Pashto and Baluchi are Iranian languages, and in no way influence Lahnda, except perhaps in one mixed dialect called Khetrani. There remain Dardic languages. Lahnda shows many traces of their influence, and indeed it may almost be said that its basis is Dardic. Its influence extends beyond Lahnda into Panjabi. For example, most Indian languages drop a 't' when it comes between two vowels, while the Dardic languages usually preserve it.[5] Similarly, there are remarkable coincidences in vocabulary. The forms of the verb 'to go' will suffice as an example. In Panjabi and the rest of India this is 'Jāna' or some such form. In Kashmiri it is gatshun and so in Northern Lahnda it is gachhna.[6] In the Eastern Panjab, the wave of old Lahnda had nearly exhausted itself, and old Western Hindi had the mastery, the resulting language being Panjabi. In the Western Panjabi, the old Western Hindi wave had nearly exhausted itself, and old Lahnda had the mastery, the resulting language being modern Lahnda.[7] The later language is therefore in the main of the Dardic origin, but bears traces of the old Western Hindi. Such traces are much more numerous and of much greater importance in Panjabi : Lahnda may be described as a Dardic language infected by Western Hindi, while Panjabi is a form of Western Hindi infected by Dardic. Few examples of the words are as under[8] :

Kashmiri	Sindhi
as	asi (we)
Tvāh or Taoh	Tavahi (you)

According to Prakrit grammarian Mārkandeya the Apbhransā Prakrit spoken in Sindh was called Vrāchada.[9]

G.A. Grierson expresses his viewpoint regarding old original Gujarāti- "It is probable that the original language of Gujrat was a member of the outer circle, but immigrants from the East, speaking a form of the language of the central group imposed their language upon it. Although Gujrati belongs to the central group of languages, it still shows, like Rājasthani, survivals of the old outer language such as the loss of Power of pronouncing s and h, the use of an oblique form of nouns which ends in ā and the past participle in l.[10]"

Marathi is the only modern vernacular which has been derived from the old Maharashtra Apabhransa, which in turn was derived from Maharashtri Prakrit. Marathi also occupies a somewhat independent position, sometimes agreeing with the language of the outer and sometimes with those of the inner group.[11]

Revoking of the Viewpoint of George Grierson

It is clear from this survey of languages of North-West that like Kashmiri and Sindhi languages, which in origin are related to Pishachi or Dardic language, Gujarāti and Marāthi also belong to the outer band of languages. It shows languages of the outer band belong to Pishachi stock but on the other hand, George Grierson also affirms that Pishachi languages belong to the Aryan stock,[12] which gets the support of D.R. Bhandarkar also.[13] It means there is no trace of any people and their languages belonging to the pre-Aryan population. This verdict of honourable scholars is not acceptable. The archaeologists in the third decade of the twentieth century have explored the remains of Harappan culture belonging to the indigenous pre-Aryan population, from the region where Pishachi group of languages are still spoken. From this new findings we are forced to re-examine the situation from a new beginning and take survey of the remains of ancient languages of archaic value of North-West region, where Harappan culture flourished for a very long time.

Sanskrit, an Aryan Language of Literature Only

The famous linguist and editor of Hindi dictionary Professor Babu Shyam Sundardas has elucidated, on historical changes those occurred in Sanskrit language in ancient time :[14] "This is very hard to search out, the form of ancient Aryan language. The Rigveda is Aryan's most ancient work. The composition of Rigvedic Richas (hymns) took place at different places and times. On arrival, in India, the Aryan people noticed that some new (native) words, owing to their contact with indigenous population were entering in to their language and even the changes in pronunciation were also taking place. Therefore, for the security of their language, they purified it and named Sanskrit. As such, now, their language became the language of literature only. But the effect of prevailing language of conversation still continued."

This view is further corroborated by S.A. Joglekar[15] : "Sanskrit is a language of minority Aryans, it was never a language of majority class or common people. The Aryans, who used Sanskrit for religeous activities, in their daily dealing used Prakrit. If this had not been so, they would have never laid down such hard and fast lawful restriction on speaking of Prakrit before completion of Diksha (initiation) ceremony in Dandak Sutrādhār. Aryan's Sanskrit was mainly language of Sanskrit knowing Brahmans and Kshatriyas."

This view gets the support of Dr. Indrachandra Shastri, he asserts- "In ancient plays, the Kshatriyas and the Brahmanas of high caste spoke Sanskrit and the Sudras and women Prakrit." It proves that there was another language named Prakrit, the language of people, being spoken by Sanskrit knowing Aryans also.

Prakrit and Pali Languages of Natives

Dr Dharmvir[16], an eminent scholar and a linguist, informs us : "Linguists of repute inform that Prakrit was traditionally called "Deshi" (native) and earlier to Prakrit, Pali was called "Desh-Bhasha" (Native language). "From this, it is evidently proved that Prakrit and Pali were languages of Native population." Further[17] he putsforth evidences in support of his viewpoints, "Hindi and other Indian languages (Bengali, Māgadhi, Maharashtri, Panjabi etc) have their own grammars and vocabulary hence we can not call them daughters of Sanskrit or modern changed form of Dev-vani."

It is quite clear that native languages like Pali and Prakrit are different from Sanskrit because their grammar is different from the later, "Grammar is the basis of any language on the skeleton or basis of which, the body of sentences is built." The relation of grammar of Sanskrit is with the Indo-European group of languages like English, Greek and German etc.[18] Where as grammar of Pali and Prakrit is different and more close to Dravidian languages and Pishachi.

The Origin

Now question arises what is the origin of these native languages ? Viewpoints of T. Burrow[19], M.C. Alpine and Dixon give definite indication of their origin. T. Burrow throws light as such : "The existence of Brahui in Baluchistan far away from main concentration of Dravidian, is consistent with the theory that, before the Aryan's conquest, Dravidian occupied a great area including considerable portion of Northern India."

It is to be noted that David M.C. Alpins[20] recent work, which gives some evidence for us to believe that : "In antiquity there was a proto-Elamo Dravidian language family which covered all southern Iran and extended into the western portion of South Asia." This view is corroborated by another view forwarded by Roland B. Dixon[21] "The earliest traceable population of the region (Iran) was Brachycephalic type probably in the main Alpine. In speech these early people were probably non-Indo-Aryan". Hence it is conclusive, that ancient Iranians spoke a non-Aryan language and southern people a language akin to Dravidian.

Two Groups of Languages in North India

The famous linguist, Dr. Hoernle, from his thorough study of Sanskrit text, has classified north Indian languages into two groups. He[22] explains : "Certain differences within modern Indo-Aryan languages of India proper might be explained by referring to two main waves of immigrants. The Indo-Aryans of the Outer countries came earlier and inhabitants of the Midland represent the latest wave of immigration. .... The other band (outer) the Rastika or Rattas after whom Maharashtra and Saurashtra are named, wandered into the Kathiavar Peninsula and the Deccan." This theory has not been universally accepted, but some scholars have believed that the languages of outer band might represent elements surviving from an earlier, possibly "Pre-Vedic wave", while those of the central group might represent a 'later Vedic wave' of other, perhaps more plausible theory, would make the outer band languages, earlier wave of Vedic group itself."

The Concluding Theory of George Grierson

Sir George Grierson supports the theory of Dr. Hoernle with a slight variation. Grierson was the director of Linguistic Survey of India, hence he possessed a thorough knowledge of Indian languages. He concludes that[23] : "Western Hindi and others i.e. Kashmiri, Panjabi Marathi, Bengali, Assami and Oriya languages have a vast difference, although other languages are close to each other. In fact in the beginning of linguistic history of India, Indo-Aryan dialects must have been divided into two groups, one language of the middle region, another group of languages of outer skirts." It is as such, evidently proved that there were two groups of languages and people of second group came from passes of North West and moved southward through Baluchistan, Sindh, Gujrat, Maharashtra, Bihar etc. Who were these people racially and culturally ? B.S. Guha[24], the famous Bengali anthropologist, discloses the secret of these people, on the basis of anthropological survey reports : "The Broad heads drifted along the western littoral from southern Baluchistan through Sindh, Kathiavar, Gujrat and Maharashtra." It means this is a belt of broad and round headed ancient Iranians, known as Alpine. This conclusion further gets support from a most striking viewpoint of R. Shaffer. His observatory view is, based on his in depth study of Sanskrit literature. In his[25] own words : "In another migration, the Iranians were the first to descend the Saryu (of Afghanistan). They were followed by the Indo-Aryans, who forced the Iranians to scatter east and west. Where they became the Eastern and the Western Manavah, the earliest race in India. A second wave of Indo-Aryans forced the first Indo-Aryans to flee to the west, less rich lands of Panjab and it is from the later that we have the Vedic literature." This view is strongly supported by the archaeological evidences; the cemetery G and H culture of Alpine and G.W. and PGW two waves of Aryans people speak loudly in support. (See Chapter IV PP 56 and 61).

It is evidently clear from the theories of Guha and Shaffer that the theory of Grierson is most striking rather confirmed. It is further clarified that people who reached much earlier than Aryan, were round headed Pishachi-Prakrit speaking Alpine ancient Iranians, who later, came to be known as Manavah in India (See chapter IX PP 236-37 and XI P 316-17 for detail). While further moving on the aforesaid route, i.e. Sind and Gujrat, we find that one of their waves, proceeded further to the east direction, following the route of (outer band) south bank of river Ganges, reached as for as Bengal. As such one of their centres came into being in the north east region of Sangham of Ganga and Yamuna later known as the region of Maghadhi language. This was one of the earliest centres of Megaliths and B and R ware using people in Vindhya.

Another large centre came into being in Vidarbha region of Maharashtri language, which was second centre of B and R ware using people and Megaliths. Another group of them escaped to the South through Western coast and Malabar. This is the same route which was followed by the B and R ware using folks (See chapter IX PP- 233-34for detail). These people made their third big centre in Dravidian speaking land of South India, known as 'Megalithic centre of South.' Inscriptions of Naga rulers recovered from this area were in Prakrit and Pali. Hence there were three main centres viz in Vindhya (Magadha), Vidarbha and South, earlier two centres were also main earliest centres of Buddha's religion of ancient time.

The Evolution from Pishachi to Prakrit and their Relation With the Dravidian Languages

We have earlier shown that the language family of outer band was related to Pishachi group in origin. The original speaker of these languages were Iranians of Alpine stock. These people, later, on the arrival of Aryans speaking nordics in India, came in contact of later at different places and times. As a result of this contact, languages of both the groups were effected by each other.

Sastri Nilkant[26] produces an account of such like effect : "The Buddhistic canon was in Pali which had close affinities with Pishachi. Pali-Pishachi, and in fact all the later Prākrits owe their origin according to Hoernle to the ways in which the non-Sanskritic populations of the different localities spoke the Sanskrit tongue. Konow (Sten Konow, The Home of Paishāchi ZDMG-64, 1910) draws attention to the fact that according to Tibetan tradition, the Sthaviras or Theras had their books in Pishachi and that according to Pischel 'these Pishachi' books may be the Pali canon. Pali-Pishachi dialects, with slight local variations, were current in wide parts of India, from the north-west to the Deccan and it is this language which influenced or bore affinities to the Dravidians."

We know the Indus Valley people were of Dravidian stock in origin, who were later joined by Iranians (see vol. I of this series chapter II and IV) in about 2100 B.C. It means both the people lived together for a longer period, causing enormous admixture of both, racially and linguistically, while, they moved southward or eastward as users of B and R wares, they were already a mixed race that is why Sastri has expressed such a viewpoint.

D.R. Bhandarkar[27] supports above views, thus : "The Tamil or Dravidian languages were not merely languages of South India, but before coming of Aryans, these were people's languages of all the India or the languages of common people of the entire nation."

The Asur language is called Dravidian and Pishachi. The mention of, speaker of these languages, is made, as who speak like Nag (serpent) (Nagadikramāt) by grammarian Rama Tarkavagis.[28] Their language has been called Madhravach in Rigveda (V-29-10, VII-18-9, VII 18-13).

There is mention of unintelligible language of Asura in Satpatha Brahman[29] and the people, who spoke that language, were called Mlechchha. Therefore, Brahmanas were not permitted to speak that language, because that belonged to Asuras.

The Various Branches of Prakrit Language

Bharatmuni[30] has made mention of seven Prakrit languages :

(1) Māgadhi (2) Avanti (Avantija) (3) Prāchya (4) Sourseni (5) Ardha Magadhi (6) Vahlika and (7) Dakshinātmā.

Later Hemchandra (12th Century AD) added-Pishachi and Lati also to them. From literature point of view four languages are important. Magadhi, Ardha Magadhi, Sourseni and Mahārāshtri.

Scholars think that most probably Maharashtri is a later developed form of Sourseni. The grammarians of Prakrit have given much importance to Maharashtri.[31]

Grammarian Vararuchi

Scholars do not agree on the point of the date of Vararuchi, the grammarian of Prakrit language. On the basis of the Brahatkatha, Vararuchi and Panini both were contemporary of Nanda kings. But as has been proved by several writers, from Gold Stucker onwards, Panini and Kātyāyan could not have been contemporaries in the view of the changes that the language had undergone in the days of the latter and Pānini could not at the latest be assigned only to 500 B.C. and in this respect, Tārānāth, whose account puts Pānini a generation earlier than Kātyāyan is less faulty.[32] After Panini, Vyādi was a great grammarian. As such both would have had at least a gap of two generations. The story in the initial book of the several versions of the Brahatkathā would make Vyādi and Vararuchi class fellows and friends.[33] It seems from the above facts that Vāraruchi was contemporary of Nanda kings and of Pre-Mauryan Age. Before Vararuchi composed his grammar of Prakrit or before the time of Buddha, this language was well developed. Therefore Maharashtri Prakrit was in existence during the age of Buddha. Hence it is clear that Vararuchi composed his grammar in about fourth century B.C. . It means Pishachi and Prakrit languages were in existence in a much earlier time than Buddha. Vararuchi[34] describes in his Prakritprakasha four dialects of this description viz (1) Maharashtri or Prakrit generally called so, (2) Paishachi (3) Magadhi and (4) Sourseni.

The Literature

Literature has also been produced in Pishachi language in ancient time and it has been a prevailing language of common people in some parts of the nation from prehistoric period. Their evidences are traceable from the historical period only. Pishachi-Prakrit[35] was the language of Kaikeya and Gandhar country. In the north west region of India Gunādhyā composed his legendary work named 'Vaddakahā' (which is known as Vrihatkatha) in Pishachi language in first century A.D. But this original work is now not available and most probably lost. We get example of Pishachi Prakrit in "Siddhahem Shabdānushāsan" and 'Kumarpāl-charit' of Hemchandra and 'Prākrit Prakash' of Vararuchi and 'Prākrit Sarvaswa' of Mārkandeya. Because Pishachi was a language of north west frontier region, hence it seems that it was closely related to Iranian language.

Lakshmidhar[36] gives an account of countries where Pishachi was spoken in ancient times in his work titled 'Shāhasha Chandrika'- "Pishachi languge was spoken in Pishachi countries like Pāndya, Kaikeya, Valhika, Sahya, Nepal, Kuntal, Sudesh, Bhota, Gandhār, Haiva and Kanaujan."

Magadhi Prakrit

Because, Bhagwan Buddha was born in the kingdom of Kausal, where Magadhi Prakrit or later Pali was spoken, hence he made this language Medium of propagation and literature of his religion, therefore it became language of people of North and Central India and prominent language of ancient time.

According to Subal Chandra[37] Mitra : "There were four main branches of Prakrit viz Maharashtri, Sourseni, Māgadhi and Pishachi. The Brahmans produced their literature in Sanskrit, Buddhist in Māgadhi and Jain in Maharashtri language. By the passage of time numerous languages came into being from Prakrit. With the influence of Buddhist religion, the Magadha Prakrit had a very rapid development, because the Buddhist missionaries spread their religion through this language among the people. In about 307 B.C. Buddhist missionaries carried Māgadhi Prakrit to Ceylon. This Māgadhi Prakrit is the mother of Pali language."

Similarly, the voluminous religious work of Jainism is mainly in Ardh-Magadhi Prakrit, which is also known as Adi-Prakrit (original Prakrit). Only the Vedic linguists call it Apbhransha (corrupt) language. The literature of Adi-Prakrit is very old and independent from Sanskrit.

Scholars think that Pali-Prakrit was the language of common use of common people from the very beginning.[38] In the ancient grammar of old Pali named "Prayogsiddha" the following interpretation of Magadhi has been given :

SĀMĀGADHI MULBHĀŚĀ NARĀYA ĀDIKAPPIKA ।

BRAHMĀNO CHASSU TĀLĀPĀ SE BUDDHĀ CHĀPIBHĀSVE ॥

Meaning— In which original language, the people of ancient time and first-spoken-children, Brahmāgan and Samyak Buddhagan used to speak, is Magadhi language.

This view is confirmed by "Vibhang- atur" a Pali Sutra. Therefore it can be concluded that Magadhi is a natural original language of India. Tathagata Buddha preached his religious teachings in this Magadhi Prakrit. Its Northern Branch, which is also known as eastern Prāchya, was unquestionably the same for the upper classes in kausal, Kashi, Videha and Magadha; it was the language of Buddha, who called himself a Kshatriya of Kausala (Kausala Khattiya) and of Mahavira also; it was the language of Ashoka and also of Chandragupta and the Nandas. The oldest Buddhist canon, as Levi and Heinrich Luders amply demonstrated, was composed in this Eastern Prakrit and not in Pali. Epigraphical evidence from the 4th century BC shows that in Magadh had appeared a local form of this Eastern Prakrit which deviated in two of its sounds from what may be called the standard Prāchya or Eastern Prakrit it had Palatal S for dental S for the letters.[39]

Mahārashtri and Other Prakrit Languages

Maharashtri Prakrit is the grand mother of Marathi. During the time of Vararuchi, Maharashtri was the most developed language and the name of Maharashtra country also had come into existence at the[40] same time.

Some scholars of Pishachi equate Maharashtri with Prakrit or agree that it is the nearest language. H.L. Kosare[41] produces an account of history of Maharashtri Prakrit languages : "Vararuchi has stated that Maharashtri Prakrit, which was spoken in Maharashtra, was the best form of Prakrit. The ancient books composed in this language are, 'Rāvanvijay', 'Harivijay' 'Setubandh' and 'Gatha-Saptasati'. Earlier two works from them are not available and later two are published. The 'Hari-Vijay' of Sarvasen is a work of about 450 A.D. The times of Hāl's Gatha-Saptasati is first century A.D. (not third). As such Mahārāshtri had acquired a high place during the Sātavāhana age. In this regard their (Satavahana's) policy was that the Prakrit should be used in maximum for Lok-Bhasha (people's language). In the 'Kāvya-Mimānsha'of

Rajshekhar and "Sarswati-Kantha-Bharan" of Bhoj there is mention of Sātavahana king named Ādhyarāj. According to them the king passed an order that all his subjects would use Prakrit in their houses. The Sātavāhana king Hāl composed his Gāthā-Sapta-sati in Prakrit. In this period, Pishachi Prakrit was in use among the masses. Gunādhya, the author of 'Brahatkatha' of Pishachi, is known as contemporary of Hāl-Sātavāhana, it is mentioned in the introductory part of this book that he (Gunādhyā) had used a Katha of Vararuchi as basis of his composition (Chandra Bhān Pandeya "Andhra-Satavahana Sāmrājya Ka Itihās" PP 93-94). The original 'Bharatkathā' of Pishāchi is not available now. In sixth century A.D., Gangarājā Durvinit, translated this work into Sanskrit. In eighth century A.D., with the help of this book, Buddhā Swami composed his 'Brahat-Kathā Ishloksangraha' in Nepal. In the middle of eleventh century, Kashmiri poet Kshemendra, composed his 'Brahat-Kathā Manjari' about the same period (1063-81 AD), Somdev composed his 'Kathā-Sarita-Sāgar,' on the basis of the same work. In some other literary works, like 'Kādambari' 'Nāgā-Nanda', 'Mālati-Mādhava' etc, the narration of above work, is used. (Chandrabhan Pandeya P-94)" H.L. Kosare[42] further elucidates dates of beginning of Prakrit languages, "In fifth and sixth centuries B.C., Mahavira and Buddha preached their religious teachings in Magadha Prakrit. Nilkant Sastri thinks that this Magadha was eastern Prakrit. Sabal Chandra Mittra has mentioned that Jains created their literature in Maharashtri. Similarly Mahavira delivered his first religious preaching in Ardh-Magadhi 'Lok-Bhasha' (people's language). At that moment, Magadha emperor Bimbsārā Srenik was present. (Jyoti Prasad Jain. Bhartiya Itihas' P-57). Hence in fourth century B.C. Vararuchi composed his grammar of Prakrit language i.e., Maharashtri, Sourseni, Pishachi and Magadhi, which were in use as languages of common people's conversation. Hence it is proved evidently that Maharashtri was in existence in sixth century B.C.

If the period of Vararuchi, is accepted, to be pre-Mauryan, it will prove that Maharashtri was also in existence in this period. Hence it can also be claimed that in the early period of Sātavāhanas, Maharashtri Prakrit was undoubtedly in existence. It means Maharashtri was also in existence during Ashoka's time, we have to accept it on account of inscriptions of Ashoka, that Prakrit language was understood by the people of Maharashtra. Except this, no evidence of language of people of Maharashtra, is traceable during Mauryan period. Pishachi-Prakrit seems to exist during Sātavahana age, hence it was also a language of common people during Mauryan period. According to Turner, Marathi is the successor of Ardha-Māgadhi and Maharashtri Prakrit. (R.L. Turner; collected papers' London 1975; D.V. Chauhan; Vidarbha Sansodhan Mandal (1977) PP-96-114)."

It is most interesting that Prakrit language along with the round headed Alpine people reached in South India also. The Satavahanas though spoke Dravidian language but language of their inscriptions and coins is Prakrit and script Nagari. Cunningham[43] produces an evidence in this regard : "Hieuntsang notices that though the language of the people of Andhra was very different from that of central India yet the forms of written characters were for the most part the same. This statement is specially interesting as it shows that the old Nagari alphabet introduced from North India, was still in use and that the peculiar twisted forms of the Telugu characters, which are found in inscriptions of the tenth century had not yet been adopted in the south."

All the inscriptions of Satavahanas also have been found to be in Pali-Prakrit and ancient Devanagari script.[44] The Ikshwaku dynasty of Sriparvata (Andhradesa) was the immediate follower of main Branch of Satavahanas. In the ancient remains of Sriparvata Hamid Kuraishi[45-A] and Longhurst have excavated a stupa from where eighteen inscriptions have been found, fifteen of which are incised on marble pillars which stood round the Mahachetya or the great stupa, enshrining a relic of the Buddha (M.R. Calcutta 1932 P-88) Hieuntsang has recorded that Nagārjuna, who lived there, was patronised by the Sātavahana king. The inscriptions are in Prakrit of the Pali type.

D.R. Bhandarkar[45B] thinks that Pali-Prakrit, as noted on inscriptions of ancient India was not non-Aryan but an Aryan language which is not acceptable, we have revoked such a viewpoint on appropriate place of this chapter.

Prof G. Buhler[46] goes further ahead giving more importance to the use of this Prakrit and Pali. He Thinks ; "In spite of these drawbacks our grants possess a very great importance. Like the great Nanaghat inscription of Satakarniś widow Nāyanika and like the Elliotś grant of Vijaybuddha Varman's queen, it shows that the use of Prakrit in the older inscriptions is not due to the influence of Buddhism, but that in early times Prakrit was the official language of the Indian kings while the use of Prakrit was still confined to the Brahmanical schools. Our grant and the other two documents mentioned above were issued by the adherents of the Brahmanical faith. The results of the recent epigraphic and linguistic studies are more unfavourable to the theory that there was in India once a golden age during which kings, priests and peasants spoke the language of Panini. They rather tend to show that the classical Sanskrit is a Brahmanical modification or a Northern dialect elaborated by the grammatical schools which very slowly and in historical times gained ascendancy throughout the whole of India and amongst all the educated classes. Our inscriptions are important links in a long chain of arguments supporting this view."

It is evidently proved that Satavahanas and Ikshwakus, who hailed from North India were in origin Prakrit speaking people and were certainly non-Aryan people of Naga race.

The Priniciple of Lyavant in Pishachi Languages

D.V. Chauhan[47] has put forward his views on some peculiarities of languages of pisachi group of North West- "Grierson has called the languages of Western India as Darda or Pishachi. This group of Pishachi languages is a non-Indian and non-Iranian linguistic belt. But now this belt is considered to be an expansion of Indian languages, but these languages have some closeness to Vedic languages."

Above view of Chauhan is partically acceptable we have shown on foregone pages that Pishachi is non-Aryan. But it seems to have some relation of closeness with the Vedic language; This is simply because the pre-Aryan Pishachi speaking native people were the first who came in contact with the Aryan in Iran as well as in Indus Valley region of Western India,[48] thus this can be termed as effect of Pishachi on Vedic Aryan and vice-versa.

But Chauhan[49] further produces another viewpoint which is divergent to the earlier when he writes : "Rigveda Samhita had been completed finally in about 1500 B.C. . This is the latest conclusion. Indian and Iranian Aryan while lived together only then the principle of Lyavant developed. This Lyavant exists in ancient Iranian languages but not in modern. But on the other hand, it is in modern languages like Pasto, Baluchi and Ghalchah. This linguistic principle or property of Lyavant, developed during the Indo-Iranian age. Lyavant is a minute principle to express perfect (passive) participle form of verbs."

Above view of Mr. Chauhan is contradictory in itself (1) First of all he says that the principle of Layvant developed while Indian and Iranian Aryan lived together. It means birth of 'Layavant' is Aryan (2) But later at three places he says (a) Lyavant does not exist in modern Iranian languages which are Aryan (b) But it exists in ancient Iranian or native non-Aryan languages and also in (c) modern Pasto, Ghalchah and Baluchi of Afghanistan which would have perhaps caused due to contact of each other owing to movement of native Iranian toward south. Hence first example goes in favour of Aryan origin of Lyavant and later three in favour of native Iranian origin, hence contradictory but more favourable to the later.

Similarly, H.L. Kosare[50] also had contradictory viewpoint. We reproduce hereby his views point wise and my own comments on each one of them as as such :

(1) This principle of Lyavant took its birth, while, Indian and Iranian Aryan lived together that is why scanty use of Lyavant in their

literature was essential. This seems clear from the Rigveda. The originator of Marathi Lyavant lived there.

This conclusion of Kosare is divergent. In fact this use should have been maximum hence contradictory.

(2) Further Kosare argues : "Although the use of forms of 'Tvānam and Tvinam' is not found in Vedic and Sanskrit languages, but definitely these were in use in either of the Aryan languages. These forms, could not enter into any work of best Vedic language and are also not traceable in Sanskrit. It means they were in use in any of the languages."

T. Burrow clarifies this view more clearly —

"That some dialects were in existence in Vedic age. But their shadows are not available in Vedic language. Sanskrit is not the successor of such languages. But on the other hand, there are plentiful evidences of existence of them in Pali and Prakrit languages." (T. Burrow, "Sanskrit language" London (1965) PP-45-46)

I need not comment upon this viewpoint of Kosare. T. Burrow has answered this question admirably well on the basis of sound footing that that language was mother of Pali and Prakrit, that is why this family has still practice of use of words of Tvānam, Tvinam.

(3) "The countries, where evolution of this linguistic property of Lyavant took place, are Sindh, North-West region of India and eastern Afghanistan. The region, in the east of the Pamir-Hindukush, is an important ancient linguistic centre of Indo-Iranian languages, Sind is an important part of this region. Keeping in view, the linguistic history of Afghanistan and North West region of India, their peculiarities and also antiquity of above change, this can very easily be concluded that this Lyavant form of Sindhi, is a part of Marathi Lyavant tradition. This principle of Lyavant, is neither available in any of Indo-European language nor in modern Iranian, but it exists in ancient language of Iran and Modern Baluchi, Pashto, Ghalchah languages. It is a matter of further research and final conclusion should be drawn after in depth study of history and culture. In the grammar of Indo-Aryan languages, the use of Lyavant is very rare."

It means because peculiarity of Lyavant developed in Indo Aryan languages in ancient Iran and because Sindh also has been a centre of Indo-Aryan language hence this peculiarity of Lyavant developed in Sind also. But if it was the only reason why this peculiarity did not develop in other regions of Indo-Aryan languages ? Similarly then why this peculiarity is not found in the literature of Indo-Aryan and Indo-Iranian languages of ancient or later period ? Kosare or any other scholar can not answer any of these questions.'

In the concluding para, Kosare, to reach any final conclusion in reference to history and culture, seeks further more research. This shows his inability to take any final decision himself. In fact the above viewpoint of Lyavant origin, from Indo-Aryan is formed without any sound ground. I think Kosare seems to indulge in fore-thought that is why the evidences produced are averse to the conclusion drawn.

But, it is most interesting that all the evidences produced by both the scholars are in favour of my viewpoint, which evidently proves that the use of Lyavant and Tvānam, Tvinam developed in the non-Aryan languages[51] of Pre-Aryan native Iranians, from which original Pishachi is derived that is why their use is not found in the Aryan language but in the languages derived from Pishachi. Sindh was its main centre in pre-Aryan age (2100-1600 BC) where Indus Valley culture of indigenous non Aryan people flourished. This was the centre, where Dravido-Alpine Indus Valley culture and Aryan culture and their languages came into contact first of all in India and a process of, formation of new languages like Pali and Prakrit etc onward, began. These were languages of outer band of Grierson and Dr Hoernle, where as the central group or western Hindi is related to Aryans.

As such, the theory of George Grierson, that Pishachi languages were Aryan, is disproved and on the basis of, study of most ancient literature of Pali-Prakrit character, it is proved that these were non-Aryan and native, derived from ancient Iranian languages.

Nilkant[52] Sastri informs us, 'That the first half of the first millennium, B.C. is a period, while great changes took place in the nature of Aryan languages.' As a matter of fact this was the age of great political and cultural changes. These changes took place owing to coming of Iron Age. The Nagas who organized themselves in the frontier region of the North West, resurrected themselves in about 1000 B.C. They, after establishing their authority on Hastinapur, spread their culture up to Magadha. Similarly, beyond, Central Pradesh, they entered in to Vidarbha, Andhra and Southern India and founded their Megalithic culture. As such this revolution brought great changes in India in the field of politics, religion, culture and language. Up to the age of Buddha and Mahavira great changes had occurred in the field of language. These resurrected Nagas, spread their Prakrit language, where ever they went. The Prakrit languages like Pali, Ardh-Magadhi and Maharashtri, which had their origin in ancient Iranian, were greatly effected by the Vedic language and vice-versa. Buddhist and Jain Missionaries preached their religious teaching through these languages. They carried these languages as far as ceylon. Their literature was also composed in these languages, that is why Prakrit languages acquired a very high place in the society.

The above cultural, linguistic revolution was not initiated by Vedic Brahmans but by Buddha and Mahavira. Thus whatever form of Prakrit came into existence during the time of Buddha that has been called Prakrit by Vararuchi. The Satavahana kings were a great patron of this language. King Hal himself composed Gathasaptsati, king ordered their subjects to use Prakrit in their houses. It means their language was Prakrit. Modern Marathi is derived from Maharashtri Prakrit.

Summary and Conclusion

(1) G.A. Grierson thinks that Pishachi is an Aryan language, but owing to some new fact findings, the modern scholars do not agree with him. In ancient time, to avoid entry of new words and pronunciation of non-Aryan languages, or for security, Aryan language was purified, hence it came to be called Sanskrit. In other words, a permanent restriction was practically imposed on its becoming language of masses, it means since then it became a language of literature only. The Aryans, who used Sanskrit for religious activities, in their daily dealing used Prakrit. It means Prakrit was a language of masses, that is why Aryan religious persons were forced to speak Prakrit to deal with common people.

(2) Eminent linguist, Dr. Dharmvir, opines 'that Prakrit was traditionally called "Deshi' or native and earlier Pali was called, 'Desh-Bhasa' (Native language). Hindi and other languages (Bengali, Magadhi, Maharashtri, Panjabi) have their own grammars and vocabulary, hence we can not call them daughters of sanskrit or modern changed form of Dev-Vani.' It shows Pali-Prakrit are different from Aryan Sanskrit, where as grammar of Pali and Prakrit is close to Dravidian and Pishachi languages. Hence Pishachi group of languages cannot be an Aryan it is evidently proved.

(3) According to G.A. Grierson, there are two groups of languages, one Western Hindi and other Kashmiri, Panjabi, Marathi, Bengali and Assami i.e. one language of middle region and another group of languages of outer skirt. This theory is supported by B.S. Guha, a Bengali anthropologist, who says this outer skirt is a belt of round headed Iranians known as Yadava Alpine. Thus middle region may belong to long headed Hindi Speaker Aryans.

(4) Branches of Pishachi : According to Bharat Muni, there were seven Prakrit languages : Magadhi, Avanti, Prachya, Sourseni, Ardh-Magadhi, Vahalika and Dakshinātma and Pishachi. This proves existence of a separate Pishachi group of languages.

(5) Literature : Vadda-Kaha of Gunādhya, Siddhahem Shabdānushāsan and Kumarpāl-charit by Hemchandra, Prakrit Prakash by Vararuchi, Parkrit Sarvashwa by Markandeya etc.

(6) Land of speech : Pāndeya, Kaikeya, Valhika, Sahya, Nepal, Kuntal, Sudesh, Bhota, Gandhar, Haiva and Kannaujan.

(7) Chronology : Grammarian Vararuchi, composed, his grammar of Pishachi-Prakrit languages in fourth century B.C. Buddha used Ardh-Magadhi for spreading his religion, similarly Mahavira also used Ardha Magadhi for spreading Jainism. It means before the life time of Buddha (567-487 B.C.) these languages were well-developed.

(8) Maharashtri-Prakrit is grand-mother of Marathi. It was one of the most important languages and nearest to Pishachi. A very high number of literary work has been done in this language : Ravanvijay, Harivijay, Setubandha and Gathasaptasati of Hala are the oldest.

(9) Prakrit Pali language reached south India alongwith round headed Alpine people, that is why, while, Hieuntsang (630-644 A D) reached south, he was astonished to note, although language of people was Telagu, but script of inscription was Nagari-Parkrit. It means Prakrit was official language of royal family as well as their mother-tongue.

(10) Although H.L. Kosare and D.V. Chauhan think that Lyavant, a minute property to express perfect participle form of verbs, is of Indo-Aryan origin, but it is very strange that this property is neither traceable in any present Indo-Aryan language nor in any such language of ancient period, this inludes Sanskrit and Indo-Iranian literature also. But this is noticeable in ancient Iranian, Pasto, Ghalchah, Baluchi, Sindhi and Marathi. These evidences are averse to its Indo-Aryan origin, and speak loudly that this property of Lyavant, and use of Tvānam and Tvinam developed not in any Aryan but in ancient pre-Aryan Iranian languages from which original Pishachi is derived, that is why it is available in the languages which were derived from Pishachi as cited above. This group of languages has been called languages of outer-skirt. This gets the support of famous Bengali anthropologist Guha that round headed Alpines exactly followed this route to move towards central and southern India. This view is further confirmed by T. Burrow.

But, one of their branch followed the route of northern hill-track Via Uttaranchal, and Nepal and Bengal and reached as for as Assam Sastri Nilkant K.A. produces evidence in its support and he[53] writes : "There is no evidence from the Nanda and Maurya documents about the spread of Aryan language into the Himalyan region. Probably the Dardic speaking Aryans (Alpines) Khasas (Nagas) and other tribes were penetrating into the central Himalayan area (the present Western and Eastern hilly regions) and their Dardic Khasa speech was later overlaid by Indo-Aryan from the mid land"

Pishachi or Takshali is mother of Prakrit, Pali and Magadhi is proved by another historical event produced by Bhandarkar–[54] "Grierson accepts the view that Pali had its basis in Magadhi, but he also notes the effect of western language on it and to prove this he has presented a hypothesis that Pali developed from that form of Magadhi, which was spoken in Takshila University in which the edition of Tripitak was prepared." The Takshali or Taki was a language of North-West region of India in historical period which was a later variation of Pishachi (See chapter VI P-156 for detail). This evidence finally confirms our theory on sound footing. This is meaningful in historical prospective.

References

1. Grierson G.A. "Linguistic Survey of India" A summary Part II PP-766-67 Sidheshwar Verma Hoshiarpur (1973).
2. Grierson G. A. Part II P-767.
3. Ibid.
4. Grierson G. A. Part II P-768.
5. Grierson G.A. Part-II P-709.
6. Grierson G.A. Part II P-710.
7. Grierson G.A. Part II P-681.
8. Grierson G.A. Part II PP-681-82.
9. Grierson G.A. Part II P-683.
10. Grierson G.A. Part II P-1024.
11. Grierson G.A. Part II P-664.
12. Grierson G.A. Part II P-767.
13. Bhandarkar D.R. "Lecture on the Ancient History of India" P-31.
14. Das Babu Shyam Sundar,"Hindi Bhasha ka Vikas" P-37 cited by H.L. Kosare, "Prachin Bharatatil Nag" P-182.
15. Joglekar S.A. "Hāl Sātavāhana Chi Gāthāsaptasati" P-37 cited by H.L. Kosare PP-182-83.
16. Dharmvir, "Hindi Ki Atma" P-36.
17. Dharmvir P-31.
18. Burrow. T. "The Sanskrit Language" P-6 (1965) Faber and Faber, 24 Russell Square London.
19. Burrow T. P-376.
20. Possehl L. Gregory A.C. I. P-255.
21. Dixon B. Roland, "The Racial Hisotry of Man" P-307.
22. Chanda R. P., "The Indo-Aryan Races" I.C. 75.

23. Grierson G.A . Vol I P-5.
24. Guha B.S.,"An Out Line of the Racial Ethnology of India" P-134 quoted by Chattopadhyaya, "Racial Affinities of Early North Indian Tribes" P-87.
25. Shaffer Robert, "Ethnography of Ancient India" PP-43-44.
26. Sastri Nilkanta, K. A. "Age of the Nandas and Mauryas" P-340.
27. Bhandarkar D.R. P-25.
28. Muir J. 'Original Sanskrit text' II P-52.
29. Satpatha Bra III-2-1-23.
30. Upadhyaya Bharat Singh, "Pāli Sahitya Ka Itihas" P-38.
31. Upadhyaya Bharat Singh P-39.
32. "Sastri Nilkant K.A.," PP 326-27.
33. Sastri Nilkant K.A. -P 327.
34. Muir J. Vol II. P-43.
35. Upadhyaya Bharat Singh P-45.
36. Muir J. Vol II P-49.
37. Mittra Subal Chandra, "Sarasa-Vidhan" P-172 Mentioned by Kosare P-181.
38. Kosare H. L. P-182.
39. Sastri Nilkant K.A. PP-313-314.
40. Chauhan D.V.,"Studies in Indology, Ancient Indian Coins," Nagpur University, research, series (1997) PP 97-104.
41. Kosare H.L. P-185.
42. Kosare H.L. PP 185-86.
43. Cunningham A, "The Ancient Geography of India" I P-446.
44. YAH DHAMMA DĀN MAHĀRTHINI MAHADEVI SĀMDINIKĀ KĀ HI/VAH MAHĀBHOJ KI KANYĀ AUR APDEV NĀK KI PATINI HAI.

    Inscribed On the tank of Monastry (Chetyagraha) of Bedasā H. Luder's list no. 2021.

45 (A) Jayaswal K.P. "History of India" P-172.

45 (B) Bhandarkar D.R. P-31.

46. E.I. Vol I (1982) P-5.
47. Chauhan D.V. "Pishacha Bhasa va Marathi" Vidarbha Sansodhan Mandal (1977) PP 96-114.
48. Dharmvir P-29.
49. Chauhan D.V. PP 113 and 133 .

50. Kosare H. L. PP-187-88.

51. (a) Possehl L. Gregory, "Ancient Cities of Indus" P-255.

(b) "Dixon B Roland," P-307.

52. "Sastri Nilkant K. A." P-319.

53. Sastri Nilkant K.A. PP 315-16.

54. Bhandarkar R.G., "Comemoration Volume PP-117-23, Article of Grierson George, "The Home of Literary Pali" Pune, 1917.

Chapter–8

WHO WERE THE NAGAS ? THEIR ETHNICAL IDENTITY

It has been explained in chapter IV that the Buddhist Stupas are inter-related with the Megaliths, since Megalithic tradition developed into the Buddhist Stupa tradition.

The Buddhist Stupas : Direct Descendant of The Megaliths

In fact, dead bodies or remains of dead bodies were buried under the Megaliths, similarly, under the ovals of stupas were placed urn-cineraries. On the patron of, outskirt of cairn circle, built of round shaped large stones, is raised an outer wall at a distance of 6 feet encircling the circumambulation in the stupas tradition. Similarly, on the pattern of umbrella stone of Megaliths, a large umbrella is constructed on each tope[1]. Rock cut grave chambers later developed into Chetya. In fact, the dead bodies or remains of dead bodies of common men were buried under the Megaliths, on the other hand, relics of Buddha or some other important Buddhist monks were buried or placed in urn under stupas.

James Fergusson[2] puts forth his viewpoint on this subject, he writes : "It scarcely admits of a doubt, but that the tope is the lineal and direct descendant of the funereal Tumulus (Megaliths) which, from the very earliest age to which our knowledge extends, the Turanian race (Dravidian[3]' Fergusson had a misleading viewpoint that Dravidian came from Turan) and probably some others raised over the graves of their dead. Such Tumuli exist all over the north Asia; they are found in Asia minor and in Greece."

It is obvious that the Megaliths developed into the Buddhist stupas and this is also similarly, clear that the Megalithic builders had their hands in their development.

It means the builders of Buddhist Stupas were off-shoots of the builders of Megaliths. Therefore, the ethnical identity of offshoots of Megalithic builders, can be traced out from the human figures represented in the bas-reliefs and statues of Buddhist stupas.

Examination of Bas-reliefs and Statues of Buddhist Stupas of Amaravati and Sanchi

James Fergusson examined, the art of two important Buddhist stupas of India i. e. Sanchi (Illustration no. X, XI) of central province and Amaravati of Andhra Pradesh with the object of racial identification of their builders. It is well known that the people of Naga race founded the Megalithic culture and they had hands in raising the Buddhist stupas also. James Fergusson, in his scientific studies of human figures, represented in the base-relief and statues, had tried to identify them or their original racial types. He[3] gives details of his scientific studies thus : "Who are, the people here represented in the figures of stupa of Sanchi. If we could tell, who are the people here represented, it would solve the problem. They probably were the first who made statues of Buddha and they endowed him with their crisp locks. The impression left on my mind is, that they are inhabitants of the Kabul Valley, not only from their costume and tallness of their topes, but because of their general resemblance to some sculptures found at Takki-Bahai north of Peshawar.''

It is well known that the people residing in the valley of Kabul or Afghanistan are Pakhtuns or Pathans who speak an Indo-European language. They are predominantly Alpine in type with nearly equal minority of Caspean Mediterranean and Palae-Alpine type[4]. A tradition is still maintained among them that their ancestors came from Assyria in remote past. These Assyrians were round headed in origin.

Fergusson[5] further keeps his studies continued and expresses his opinion on them : "The people most distinctly characterized in the sculptures of these two topes Sanchi and Amaravati are those I have designated Dasyus or Takshakas. They are infinitely more important at Sanchi than at Amaravati, but appear in both places as a quasi aboriginal race, and treated as inferiors by the builders of the topes. They appear at the same time to be the real and original serpents worshippers, and if their connection with Takshila and the Punjab can be satisfactorily established, it will throw considerable light on the principal features of the present inquiry. Meanwhile it is curious to observe, as we pointed out before, that as straight line drawn from Takshila to Amaravati passes through Bhilsa, Nagpur and other localities where snake-worship was especially prevalent, it does look like the central line of such a migrations. Another race, who seems almost as distinctly marked, are those with short curly hair. There are only two men so distinguished at Amaravati and the sculptures on which they are found is of such inferior execution that no argument can well be founded upon it. In Illustration no. X (Fig 2) several women are well distinguished but no man. At Sanchi the case is different. The drummer boys generally have curly hair, so have the charioteers and menials in many instances, and in one bas-relief these curly headed people seem to be the principal actors. From their costume they seem to come from some colder country, and I have suggested Bactria, though there are no doubt many difficulties in such an attribution. At first sight it might he supposed they came from Africa. The question has rather a curious interest in an artistic point of view, as there seems little doubt that it was from this people–whoever they were–that Buddha derived the Negroid hair by which his statues are always distinguished, and which has given rise to so much speculation. So far as we now know, sculpture, taught by the Greeks, was practised in the North West long before it penetrated into India. From the appearance of Sakya Muni, and their being so generally associated with him, I think that there can be very little doubt but that the sculptures meant to represent the inhabitants of the province now known as upper Bengal more especially of the districts of Tirhoot and Bihar which were assured by the cradle of Buddhism......... . If this is so, the people who are associated with Buddha in both Topes are the mixed race of Bengal– a people with a certain infusion of Aryan blood in their veins, but which had become so impure from mixture with that of the aboriginal tribes who existed in Bengal before the Aryan immigration, that the distinctive features of their higher civilization were almost entirely lost. Of this no greater proof could be given than that Buddhism was able to rise on its ruins.

Another important question is, whether the people, who wear the snake hoods, are of the same race as the others ? Sometimes I have thought I could detect such distinctions as would enable a separate classification to be made, but on the whole it is probably safer to assume, for the present at least, that the differences are only artistic. Their costume, their mode of wearing the hair, and their features are certainly the same, with only such distinctions as may be accounted for by fashion or local peculiarities, and we ought therefore to consider them as two different nations rather than as two distinct peoples. The people whose manners and customs appear to present the closest affinities with what we find on the monuments, are those now known as the Gonds and other closely allied tribes inhabiting the country to the South of the Vindhya-hills. From their language we learn that they were allied to the Dravidians, now occupying nearly the whole of the Madras presidency.''

Fergusson further concludes his studies to give them definite ethnical name : "After a careful study of all the bas–raliefs bearing on this subject, it does not appear to me doubtful that the sculptors at Sanchi meant to represent these people as the aboriginal inhabitants of the country of Malava, to whom the Hindus came either as conquerors or as missionaries. .... It would be extremely convenient if there were any local name which we could use in speaking of these people to call them, however, either Gonds or Khonds, Bhils, Meenas or by any other name, and it would be begging the question, and putting forward a hypothesis for which no ground has yet been obtained. In the following pages, I propose to call them Dasyus, not because there is any local or traditional authority for such a name, but because in the Vedas and the heroic poem such a term seems to be applied to the aboriginal people of India as contra distinguished from the Aryans.''

It is crystal clear that Fergusson has concluded from his scientific studies of figures of statues and bas-reliefs of two Buddhist stupas, that the figures so shaped in them which includes Nagas with hoods, charioteers and drummers are round headed people like ancient Pakhtoons of Afghanistan, meso-cephalic inhabitant of North Bengal or long headed Gonds of central province of India and all are indigenous people of Dravidian and Alpine affinity called Takshakas or Dasyus. It means, the long headed and round headed or meso-cephalic builders of Buddhist stupas were indigenous non-Aryan Takshakas or Nagas.

One of the notable point in the dresses of figures of these bas reliefs is their head dress. This head dress (a Turban with a round point on fore-head) is still in vogue among the Naga tribes of north east hills. (See Illustration no VIII)

The Anthropological Evidences

To decide the racial affinities of builders of Megaliths, now we take up the evidences of anthropology for consideration. The builders of Megaliths, like their counter part Iranians used to expose their dead bodies to be devoured by animals and birds and later bury these remaining bones in the cemeteries. Complete skeletal remains also have been discovered in excavation of many sites. These skeletal remains have been scientifically examined by the anthropologists and as a result they have disclosed the secret of racial origin of the builders of Megaliths.

Such Megaliths have been found out at sites like Brahmagiri, Payampalli, Adichanallur, Yelleswaram in South India. On excavation of these sites, some skeletal remains were found which were scientifically examined by the department of Anthropological survey of India and results so obtained, were published. S.P. Gupta on the basis of viewpoint of different scholars, puts forth his own critical remarks[6] : "Who were these people and what were their physical types ? These are some of the questions often asked for, but only unsatisfactorily answered. Reports show that there were both dolichocephals and brachycephals among the Megalithic builders of South India. Sarkar (Sarkar S.S, "Human skeletal Remains from Brahmagiri" Bull deptt. of Anthro vol IX no. 1 PP 5-25) has compared some (Four) of the brachy-cephals (Mesocephal see gupta P-299) from Brahmagiri with those from Sialk Necropolis B (first half of Ist Millennium BC), and called them Scytho-Iranians. But he has also reported that some others were meso-cephals, comparable to those who live to this day in central and western India. Not only that, he has identified two of the Brahmagiri skulls as Proto-Australoid, the autochthonous population of India. Thus, according, to Sarkar the Megalith builders had the foreign strain and the aboriginal strain in them and that the former, probably, belonged to the Indo-European group of people living in Iran and Central Asia.

The skulls from Adichanallur graves were earlier examined by Zuckerman who identified them as "Dravidian" of the Mediterranean stock. Recently Chatterji and Gupta have examined thirteen other skulls from the same site. Of these three show Veddid Australoid affinity, five exhibit Mediterranean features and one each of the remaining two belongs to Armenoid branch of the Mediterranean and Proto-Australoid types. This again shows an admixture of western and autochthonous physical types in the population of Adichanallur. Gupta and Dutta have examined six skulls from Yelleswaram, of which three were of males and three of females. They were all broad headed showing features similar to those found in the skulls from Sialk cemetery. They, following Sarkar, call them scytho—Iranian.

Sarkar, as quoted by D.K. Sen has also studied eighteen skulls from Maski. They have been classified into three groups. (i) Mesobrachy-cranic type (Scytho-Iranian ?) (ii) Al-Ubaid' type (iii) Proto-Australoid type. They again lead to the same conclusion. There was admixture of Indian and west-Asian peoples among the Megalithic builders of Peninsular India."

Very clearly, scholars are unanimously agreed on this point that among the founders of the Megalithic culture, there was one element of ancient indigenous tribes, but when issue of other foreign element is raised they are divided into two groups ; one group identifies them as round headed Alpine Al-Ubaid or Assyrian type; another group among which Sarkar is prominent, identifies them as Scytho-Iranian. The base of later view is Kapper's theory (1934) who traced out this human element in Tepe-Hissar-III

S.P. Gupta[7] discusses to conclude all above controversial view points, thus, "The identity of the Megalithic people has been a question in the minds of archaeologists and anthropologists for quite sometime. The cult of Megaliths was certainly brought to India from outside and the excavations at Brahmagiri, Hallar, Payampalli etc. certainly demonstrate that the iron using Megalithic culture was an intrusion into the earlier stone-axe (Neolithic Chalcolithic) culture. The physical type, represented with the stone-axe culture, certainly seems different from the physical type represented by the Megalithic skeletal remains of Brahmagiri and Yelleswaram. While the physical type associated with the stone-axe culture is the same (Palae) Mediterranian Australoid complex encountered at Piklihal, Nevasa, Chandoli and Tekkalkota, the meso brachy (even hyperbrachy) element of Brahmagiri and Yelleswaram is certainly a new type of people.

Christophvon F. Haimendorf, in his presidential address to the Anthropology Section of the Indian Science Congress, Poona 1950 (Srinivasan and Banerjee 1953 : 114), seemed to equate the Megalithic. builders with the Dravidian speakers on the ground that the present distribution of the Dravidian languages coincides largely with that of Megalithic monuments (in South India). As regards the origin of the Megalithic people, Haimendorf supposes that they originated from the Mediterranean region, since there is some structural similarity between the South Indian and the Mediterranean Megaliths[8].

But Sarkar (1960) identifies the physical type of the Brahmagiri megalithic people as the 'Scytho-Iranian' of Kappers and related to the brachycephalic type represented at Sialk VI and Tepe-Hissar III. It is difficult to prove or disprove Kipper's (1934) hypothesis about the migration of the so-called 'Scytho-Iranian' people from the region of Ukraine between 1000-and 2000 BC, but the range of cranial index (77-79) ascribed to this stock is indeed very high among the present Iranian population".

From the above discussion, two important conclusions can be drawn : (1) The round headed and meso-cephalic people of Kappers and Sarkar were Scytho-Iranian. (2) According to S.P. Gupta theory of Kappers neither can be proved nor disproved because this cannot be ascertained that Scythian tribe of Ukraine reached there (Tepe Hissar-III) in between 2000-1000 B.C.

We take up here the first issue for our discussion. The famous anthropologist Roland B.Dixon is of the view that Scythian in origin was a long headed element. He expresses[9] his viewpoint thus—

"If the theory, that the slav was originally dolichocephalic, be accepted the long-headed element may have been derived from them, otherwise we should need to call in either the order Ugrian peoples who had a considerable dolicho-cephalic factor, or the "Scythians." He further writes (on P-124) that "A non-slavic or pre-slavic origin for the dolichocephalic Kurgan crania here is thus entirely possible and so far the hypothesis of the brachy character of the original Slav meets the facts."

Hence it is clear that Pre-Slavic element of Ukraine was Scythian which was dolicho-cephalic in origin.

Above view of Dixon gets the support of H.H. Risley[10], who has stated that : "Scythian (Gurjar) of India is a dolicho-cephalic race even in present age he has 72.4 cephalic Index."

It means, Scythians were a long headed race in ancient time in their original homeland or Ukraine. They moved from there and reached India and settled here in 3rd century A.D. Now after a long period of about 1700 years still they are long headed. Therefore, the viewpoint of Kappers and Sarkar, that Scythians were a round headed or mesocephalic race, is unacceptable. S.P. Gupta has also stated that the theory of Sarkar or Kappers neither can be proved nor disproved. Hence it is a doubtful theory and can not be accepted. However further we conduct an indepth study of the subject for a better clarity.

The Ethnical Relation of People of Brahmagiri and Alpines of Harappan cemeteries H and G.

During the mature Harappan age, round headed Alpine race of Iran or their blended race appeared as invaders in Harappan cemetery H and G[11]. The ethnical identity of skeletal remains recovered from these cemeteries, examined by the scholars, is as under :—

	Proto-Australoid and Mediterranean	Alpine and their blended race
Cemetery G	5	5
Cemetery H	4	5
TOTAL	9	10

It shows ratio of their population was almost equal. Although there are evidences to show that Alpine type attacked earlier Harappans, but no one can deny to this fact that both lived side by side in Indus Valley in peace and war, since they jointly took part in ten kings war of Rigveda from western direction[12]

To examine their ethnical identity we compare, C.I. (crania index) of Harappans of cemetery H and Megalithic builders of Brahmagiri. S.P. Gupta,[13] while compares their C.I puts forth his opinion : "The 76 crania index people are represented solely by the skulls of the jar burials of cemetery H. As cemetery 'H' represents a post Harappan (pre-Aryan) culture, the presence of a meso-cranial element, which is absent in R-37, may represent a later arrival of a mesocranial people and the same can be said of the brachycephalic 79-Index people of the open burial of cemetery H. It is difficult to say however, whether the 76-Index people and the 79-Index people were really two different ethnical groups as Sarkar apparently believes or they lie within the range of variation of one and the same mesobrachy-cephalic group." It seems these people were of a single ethnical group, which has been identified by the scholars as Alpine race as stated above. If there is any variation that is owing to blending of Mediterranean element as stated earlier who has much lower C. I (74.1) than that of Alpine (85.1). This C. I. (76-79) of Harappa is quite close to C. I. (averag C. I. of 5 males 77.1 C. I. of 4 adults 78.21-83. 52 all over average 77-80) of Brahmagiri. This proves oneness of the two groups, which is confirmed by B.B. Lal.[14]

The report of Cephalic index of Brahmagiri, which was prepared by S.S. Sarkar is being compared with C.I. of sialk and Tepe Hissar and is reproduced by S.P.[15] Gupta : "The cranial characters conform neither to the Australoid nor to the 'Indo-Aryan' ethnic type but are indicative of a foreign element. He thinks that the physical type represented by a more or less medium statured, mesocranic, medium vaulted, flat nosed, robust boned and powerful jawed skeleton population is probably akin to the 'Scytho-Iranian' stock of Arien Kapperś (1934) who identified this type from the 77-79 cranial index people indicated at period III of Tepe Hissar Kapperś hypothesis is, that the great migration of these "Scytho-Iranians" took place between 1000-and 2000 BC from the region of Ukraine. The 77-79 range of cranial index is to be found in a very high frequency among the present Iranian population. Majority of the Kurds and the Aderbeijani would fall within this range of cranial index. Sarkar (1960) draws attention to the overwhelming brachycephaly in period VI at Sialk, as reported by Vallois (1940) and suggests that Sialk brachycephaly may also be responsible for the brachycephaly of Brahmagiri Megalithic people. " It means C. I. of silak and Brahmagiri are almost equal

It is evidently proved that 76-79 cephalic index of Harappa and 77-80 Index of Brahmagiri both are almost equal. They have been identified as Alpine[16], at Harappa by Cragman and wheeler and Yadavas by Chanda[17]. It is possible that people of Sialk VI, and Cemetery H and G of Harappa and builders of Megaliths of Brahmagiri were ethnically one and the same and if there was any difference that was of places and names. We have already shown on foregone pages that according to

Dixon Scythians of Ukraine were long headed in ancient time and still today the Scythians or Gurjars of India according to H.H. Risley are long headed with their cranial index 72.4, which is close to Aryan race (72.4). It means they were ethnically a different people and not related to either of the round headed people of Sialk, Harappan cemetery H and G and Brahmagiri. Now how to reconcile this odd situation ? However for a better clarification of this divergent situation we are putting here after Risley (see table no. 1 and 4) a comparative list of CI of castes and tribes which are either Naga or originated from Naga race as shown in chapter II and XV (P-930)

Name of caste and tribe	Cephalic Indix
Khasi	78.6
Angami Naga	77.–
Bodo	78.4
Kuki	76.4
Pakhtoon	76.5
Maratha	78.3
Mahar	77.–
Kurmi	77.4
Goala (Yadava)	76.2

Table No. 1

Above cephalic index shows harmony with the people of Sialk, Harappa and Brahmagiri as cited above and very clearly shows disharmony with the Scythian race (C.I. 72.4) of their original home and of modern age. Thus theory of Sarkar and Kappers has no legs to stand.

Table showing dates of movement of B and R ware using Harappans from North to East and Southward (After Srivastava) (1971)

States	Dates
(A) Gujrat	2400 BC–800 BC
(B) S.E. Rajasthan and Madhya Pradesh	2000 BC–800 BC
(C) Eastern U.P, Bihar and Bengal	1600 BC–800 BC
(D) Panjab, North U.P., N.W. Rajasthan	1600 BC–800 BC
(E) Maharashtra and North Mysore	1700 BC–600 BC
(F) Orissa, A. Pradesh, South Mysore and other states of South	1200 BC–100BC

Table No. 2.

Table showing Racial type and duration of Megalithic Culture at different sites

Name of site	Duration of Megalithic Culture	Vedid and Autraloid	Dravidian	Alpine	Meso cephal SialkVI and Hissar B type
Brahmagiri	200 BC–100 AD	2	—	4	—
Maski	700 BC – 500 BC	6	—	6	6
Swati Valley	900 BC	—	—	—	—
Hallur	1000 BC	—	—	—	—
Takal Ghat	700 BC–400 BC	—	—	—	—
Adichanallur		3	5	2	—
Yelleswaram	—	—	—	—	6
Kaundilyapur	800 BC–700BC	—	—	—	—
Haimendorfś view	500 BC beginning	—	—	—	—
Gordon's view	332 BC beginning	—	—	—	—
Average	1000 BC – 800 BC beginning	—	—	—	—

Table No. 3

Cephalic and Nasal Index in India
After H.H. Risley

Caste or Tribe		Cl	N.I.	Stature	Frequency Blood B
(1) Aryan	North India	72.4-74.4	71.6	174.8	30
(2) Dravidian	South India	74.1-76.6	73.1	162.4	
(3) Mongol	North east	84.3	84.5	159.5	
(4) Mongol Dravid	North east	75.2	76.6	159	
(5) Pathan	Afghanistan	76.5	68.4	168.7	
(6) Gurjar (Scythian)	North India	72.4	66.9	173.03	
(7) Khatri	North India	74–	75.2	1666	
(8) Maratha	Maharastra	78.3	80.1	1632	34–
(9) Kunbi	Maharashtra	77.4	79.2	1600	34.58
(10) Mahar	Maharashtra	77–	81.9	1634	
(11) Kuki Naga	Assam	76.2	85	1566	
(12) Khasi Naga	Assam	78.6	86.3	15.69	28.05
(13) Bodo	Assam	78.4	88–	1608	
(14) Angami	Assam	78.6	82.2	1639	11.5
(15) Lhota	Assam	77–	79–	1620	
(16) Kanet	H. P.	77.5	66.4	1618	
(17) Mallas		77.1	76.2		
(18) Alpine	North Iran	85.1	43.2	After	
(19) Paleo Alpine		84	55	Dixon	
(20) Passi	U.P	72.1	82.9	1642	
(21) Goala (Yadav)	Bihar	76.2	76.7–		
(22) Chamar		72.8	86		
(23) Harappan cemetry H and G		76–79			
(24) Sialk B and Tepe Hissar VI		77–79			

Table No. 4

Table Showing presence of different races in Asian Countries during Chalcolithic and Iron Age, (after Dixon[18])

Country	Chalcolithic age (Before 1000 BC)	Iron Age (1000 BC–100 AD)
Turkistan (Turan)	(A) Caspean or Aryan (B) Alpine and Paleo Alpine	(A) Mongoloid Paleo-Alpine (B) Caspean Arya
Iran	(A) Alpine and (B) Caspean and Mediterranean	(A) Alpine (B) Caspean and Mediterranean
Asia Minor	(A) Alpine and Paleo-Alpine (B) Caspean and Mediterranean	(A) Scythian (B) Alpine and Paleo-Alpine
Mesopotamia	(A) Alpine Mediterranean (B) Mediterranean Caspean	(A) Alpine (B) Mediterranean and Caspean blend
Babylonian	(A) Semitic (Mediterranean) and Alpine (B) Caspean and Mediterranean	
Palestine and Israel	(A) Alpine (B) Mediterranean	
Afganistan	Pakhtoon Alpine	Pakhtoons, Alpine + Caspean
Turkey	Greek, Armenian	Greek, Armenian

Table No. 5

Table showing C.I. and N.I. and stature of some of the Aryan and Dravidian tribes and castes After Risley (Physical Homogeneity of two races)

Aryan tribes and Castes		C.I	N.I.	Stature
Gurjar	Punjab	72.4	66.9	1703
Machhi	Punjab	72.3	70	1699
Arora	Punjab	72.6	71.2	1658
Meo	—	73–	75.5	1690
Khatri	Punjab	73.4	73.1	1662
Dravidian tribes and castes				
Mappila	South	72.8	75.1	1648
Nayar	—	73.2	76.7	1651
Cheruman	—	73.4	77.2	1566
Palli	—	73–	77.9	1625
Kadia	—	72.9	89.8	1577

Table No. 6

Revoking of Theory of Kappers and S.S. Sarkar ; Pitfall of Anthropology

From the very ancient time, the north eastern region of Iran according to Ghirshman'[19] because of its shape and geographical position, acted as a land bridge between East and West, hence it remained a centre of admixture of different races who passed through it in quest of fertile new lands, as invaders in general, such as long headed Caspeans of central Asia, round headed Mongoloids of China in their movement towards South and West. First of all they reached there and got mixed up with the original inhabitants of Iran, the round headed Alpines ; similarly long headed Mediterraneans from Western Asia and long headed blend of Australoid and Negrito from the sea shore of South Persia in their movement towards north east direction, reached there first and added a new blood and created a more complicated blend of human race or species. This admixture extended to such an extent that it became impossible to identify their original race. But it is crystal clear that round headed Alpine was a major factor, being original inhabitant of that land. On the other hand, physically there was not much difference between the Mediterranean and the Caspean races (see table no.6) because[20] both the races, in origin, were long headed and of more height than the average, Mediterranean had slightly broader nose than Caspean Aryans, that is why Dixon has called Aryan race Mediterranean-Caspean (Dixon PP-

307-11) But, certainly more identifiable difference was in their colour of skin, eyes and hair. Caspean type had red-white colour, blue eyes and grey or yellow coloured hair against their counter part Mediterranean, who had wheatish or copper skin colour, black eyes and hair. These are the physical differences which being perishable[21] can not come to hand to be identified from scientific examination of skeletal remains explored from the cemeteries of thousands years old (of 2500-3000 years back). This is the major draw back or pitfall of anthropology. Such an identification will not be accurate. I think Kappers and Sarkar have failed to give due consideration to this factor. Sarkar (See P 208) studied eighteen skulls from Maski. They have been classified in three groups : (1) Meso brachy or Mesocephalic type (Scytho-Iranian), (2) Al-Ubaid or round headed Assyrian (3) Proto-Australoid or old Dravidian type. The identification of later two groups is clear. But earlier one, has been identified as Scythian by Sarkar. We have earlier informed that original inhabitants of Iran were Alpines having their head form round. Above head-form developed to meso-cephal only when a dolicho-cephal element got blended with them. Sarkar, Kappers and their supporters, are of the view that, dolicho-cephal element was Caspean or Aryan type that is why that hybrid–breed has been called Scythians and some of their blind followers have called them Indo-European or Aryans. But I strongly oppose any such claim and proclaim that dolicho-cephal element was not Aryan but Mediterranean or Dravidian.[22] I can produce historical evidences in support of my viewpoint : In 721B.C., Assyrian king Sargon II[23] invaded Israel, because Israelites had revolted against his rule and he wanted to punish them severely. As a result of which, Samaria was captured by him and Israelite leaders and most of the masses (long-headed) were forced to migrate to eastern border of his empire (Mesopotomia) to settle there. (See Map no. IV) On the other hand, some Iranian (round headed Alpines) were shifted to Israel to settle there permanently. Long headed Israelites were later never allowed to come back to their native land. This was the same region or western and central part of Iran, where Sialk, is situated. It means Dravidian type of element reached there in this age viz 721 B.C. We have another strong evidence to strengthen our viewpoint that the Scythian race was not present at Sialk during the period under consideration. Ghirshman, through one of his map (See map no V) showing movement of Scythians in ancient period, expressed his viewpoint that although movement of Scythians from Ural (North west of Caspean sea) took place in about 9th and 7th century B.C.[24], but they never reached Sialk and Tepe Hissar, rather they turned back from the south bank of lake Uramia. This evidence stands firmly to prove that Scythian element was not present either at Sialk or at Tepe Hissar in a period under discussion. Hence the theory of Kappers and Sarkar falls to the ground and my viewpoint stands firmly. Thus broad head or mesocephalic element at Sialk and

Brahmagiri or Maski was a blend of Mediterranean and Alpine or Alpine known as Naga or Yadava race. It is well known that the period of 7th and 8th century B.C. was the same[25], while the movement of Megalithic builders was at the top, perhaps owing to overwhelming raids of Assyrians on West Asia.

The Physical Type : A meaningless Concept

Where, for a long period, a process of hybridization of different races have taken place, this will be very hard for the anthropologists to identify their accurate physical type from scientific examination of skeletal remains alone and a probability of wrong calculation can not be ruled out all together.

Such a process of admixture of races took place in India also and we can clarify this complicacy, very clearly from Indian examples : There has been mainly admixture of two races in India i.e., Aryan and Dravidian. In South India, the Aryan element first of all reached during the ruling period (269-232 BC) of Ashoka[26], some of them as missionaries of Buddhism and Jainism and others orthodox Hindu ran away to save their religion from the religious tyranny of Ashoka. Although, originally they were of Aryan race, yet in South India they accepted daughters of tribal chiefs and kings. According to Puranic traditions, the first person, who crossed Vindhya, was Aryan Rishi Pulishtha who married Lopamudra a daughter of non-Aryan king of Vidarbha. After, such a regular process of hybridization of few generations, the offshoot of Pulishtha, would have become physically more Dravidian than Aryan, on the contrary, this has generally happened that tribal chiefs of Dravidian or Alpine race, forcibly married the Aryans girls or Aryan petty chiefs offered their daughters to get political benefits. But, after a long and regular such process of few generations, the Dravidian kings would have become physically more Aryan than Dravidian. This happened generally in case of Rajputs, who were originally Dravidian or Alpine racially. S.P. Gupta also accepts this viewpoint that a long process of admixture or blending of different races also causes difficulty in deciding their original racial type.[27] He further opines "From Megalithic cultural stage to the present day, is however a long history of invasion, "race mixture" and ethnic upheaval, which has altered the composition of the Indian population beyond measure or accurate description, so much so that the study of physical types in the population has become meaningless."

This sort of hybridization in population took place not only in India, but also in all the countries in all the times and in the population of Sialk and Tepe Hissar also. Hence study of physical type in the population has become meaningless. For accurate study one has to conduct an in depth study of social, religious, political, linguistic, mythical traditions which we have already conducted on different chapters of this book. However our theory will remain incomplete if we do not answer the following questions : (1) Was Naga race Turanian ? (2) Was Scythian race serpent worshipper ?

Was Naga Race of Turanian origin ?

Further question arises whether origin of the Naga race took place in Turan as Suggested by Fergusson[28]. First of all, let us see who were original inhabitants of Turan in ancient time and what was their relation with the Scythian tribe ?

Roland B. Dixon, who has been a famous anthropologist, on the basis of report prepared from the findings of skeletal remains from the ancient graves, produces an account of presence of different ethnical groups in Turan,[29] thus : "I believe, it is safe to assume that the population of this steppe and mountain border region in Bronze Age and earlier, was primarily dolichocephalic, the Caspean type being in large majority, followed by a secondary factor of the Alpine. With the Iron Age, the region was invaded and gradually over run by peoples of totally different, almost purely brachycephalic character the paleo-Alpine and Mongolaid types being in large majority. These new comers were nomad, horse using folk, in all probability Turko-Tatar people, allied to the Hiungnu of the Mongolian plateau." We can conclude the above account as under :

(1) The long headed Caspean Aryan tribe was present there between 3000–1000 B.C. ; Sometimes in the end of this period, round headed Alpine tribe also appeared.

(2) With the beginning of the Iron Age or in about 1000BC-800 BC, round headed Turko-Tatars also appeared. It means Scythian tribes appeared, some times after this period. Strabo,[30] gives an account of the tribes which lived there after the period as mentioned above : "All the tribes east of the caspean are called Scythic, the Dahae next to the sea, the Massagetae (Great Gete) and Sacae more eastward ; but every tribe has a particular name. All are nomadic. But of these nomads the best known are the Asi ; the Pasiani, Tochari, Sacaranli, who took Bacteria from the Greeks. The Sacae (races) have made in Asia irruptions similar to those of the Cimmerians, thus they have been seeming to possess themselves of Bacteria and the best district of Armenia called after them Sacasenae."

It can, evidently be concluded from the above account that Scythian tribe was residing in Turan or Turkistan in the first half of the first millennium B.C. from where they moved west ward and south ward and reached North Iran in the end of first millennium B.C. and in the long run India in a period, whose detail is given by R.C. Majumdar[31] as such : "While Greeks were quarrelling amongst themselves, Bacteria was invaded by the Scythian hordes, and the Greek Sovereignty in the fair valley of the Oxus was extinguished for ever (C.120 B.C.). The Greeks driven from Bacteria, were forced to take shelter in their Indian dominions in Afghanistan and the Western Panjab, where they ruled for two hundred years more. .... But the Greeks were not the only nation that harassed the Indian Frontier, several others followed in their wake, the most notable of them being the Parthians, the Sakas and the Kushanas. .... As early as the middle of the second century B.C. the Parthian king Mithradates I had carried his arms up to the Sindhu. .... Towards the close of the first century A.D. Parthian chiefs were squabbling for power in lower Sindh. .... The Sakas were at first a nomadic tribe and lived on the northern bank of the river Jaxates or Syrdaria. Being dispossessed of their home lands by another nomadic tribe, the yuch-chi, they fell upon Bacteria and destroyed the Hellenistic monarchy in that province. Later on, they proceeded South and East and entered India in various bands through different ways. They must have formed a strong settlement on the bank of the Helmund river, as the region was called Sakasthan (now corrupted into Seistan) after them. In India, we have clearly traced three important Saka principalities. Two of them were in Northern India, and had Mathura and Takshila as their respective capitals. The third comprised Mālava and Kathiavar, Peninsula (119-296 AD) in western India." Although earliest Scythian kings reached India in the beginning of 1st Century AD.

It is proved from this detailed information that Scythians or Sakas of Turan reached and spread in India in between 14-119 AD. We can, with firm belief, say, that Scythians reached India after the Mauryan period, thus the Naga tribe who is responsible for introducing Megalithic culture is India in about 1000–800 B.C. cannot be Scythian tribes as stated by James Fergusson. We do not have any written evidence of their entry into India before this period. S.P. Gupta has corroborated my viewpoint, by refuting the Lishnik's theory of coming of Megalithic builders from the aforesaid land or central[32] Asia.

Was Scythian Tribe, Serpent Worshipper ?

We have already shown that Scythians invaded India in the beginning of the second Century A.D. and established their rule in North western part of India. A critical study, of their ancient social and religious traditions, reveals that they were at a very low stage of civilization before their entry in to India ; and only very negligible traits of religious tradition could be developed. That is why they adopted, Buddhist religion, prevalent then in northern India, at their first entry and later adopted Shaivism. Satya-shrava[33] puts forward his views in support of above facts : "Western writers have the impression that early Sakas, outside India, hardly had any religious belief or practice, and followed certain practices ; and one of the festivals of Anaitis was called Sacaea which was accompanied by wild and licentious revels, the celebrants, men and women indulging in excesses. Anaitis was a scythian goddess and her cult was probably brought into Media by Cyrus on his return from the East. The Scythian tribe also had a custom of throwing the old and infirm to the dogs to devour. They did not permit their older folk to die naturally. The most important Saka God was Surya or Swaliyer. Statues of the Sun god with Saka dress of the Iranian style are exhibited in the Mathura-Museum." But this is most interesting that Dravidians were also worshippers of Sun deity named Bal or Baal.

A neighbouring tribe, the Padaei even killed and ate their sick relatives. This disgusting custom which originated in a religious superstition was also carried on by certain Skythian (Scythians)[34] tribes.

There are instances of a serpent[35] barrow, and of the use of the Snake as a form of ornament among the Scythians, but beyond this the evidence of worship of the serpent is scanty (E.H. Minns, Scythians and Greeks, 328 F 66 note 294, 318, 323 etc)

Because before their entry into India they had no religious belief, hence it can be established that they were not the originators of the cult of serpent worship or they were not Nagas.

Similarly Scythians used to bury their war heros or chiefs in a simple pit and a large mound of earth was raised on it and no Megalith were built.

Henceforth the theory of Scythian origin of Naga race is ruled out altogether and their origin from Alpine or their blended race Dravidian stands firm.

In fact such scholars are deadly against to give any credit. to native people, in making the history, to obtain political object through history. That is why, Sarkar has deliberately accepted a wrong theory of Kappers, simply to prove Megalithians an Aryan race. But it has been disproved, on the basis of the sound evidences.

Summary and Conclusion

(1) Buddhist stupas are direct descendants of Megaliths, since Megalithic tradition has developed into stupa tradition. It means builders of Buddhist stupas are descendants of builders of Megaliths, hence to ascertain ethnical identity of builders of Megaliths and Buddhist stupas James Fergusson conducted a scientific study of statues and bas-reliefs of Buddhist stupas of Sanchi and Amaravati. Human figures, depicted in them which include Nagas wearing hoods of cobra on their heads, drummer boys, charioteers and menials, have been identified not Aryans, (Scythians) but indigenous Dravidians and Alpines or a blended race of both of them.

(2) Similarly anthropologists, examined skulls of skeletal remains, discovered from the Megalithic graves from different sites of Vidarbhá region of Maharashtra and South India and have established their ethnical identity. Sarkar scientifically examined skulls of skeletal remains discovered from Maski and identified round headed element as Al-Ubaid people or Assyrian and long headed as proto-Australoid or Dravidian and the third mesocephal as scythian which is most controversial. He has identified homogeneity of this mesocephal with those found out by Kappers from Sialk VI and Tepe Hissar III, because C.I. of both element is ranging between 77-79 hence one race.

Aforesaid range of C.I. (77-80) of Sarkar's from Maski or Brahmagiri and Kappers from Sialk and Tepe Hissar is very close to that obtained from the Harappan cemetery H and G. skeletals (77-79) on one hand and on the other with those castes and tribes which are Nagas or of Naga origin like Khasi, Angami, Bodo Naga, Mahar, Maratha and Kunbi etc. It means people of Harappan cemetery H and G, Maski and Sialk-VI Hissar-III owing to Homogeniety of their C.I. were of a single race or Nagas. The Scythian race was long headed in ancient time in their native land UKraine and till today these people have the same long headform as stated by H.H. Risley (72.4 C.I.) and not round headed or meso-brachy as stated by S.S. Sarkar. It means theory of Sarkar and Kappers, has no legs to stand.

I could not understand, how and why, Kappers has designated people of above range of C.I. as Scythian, otherwise people of above range were original inhabitants of Iran known as round headed Alpine. According to Chanda[36] and Chattopadhyaya[37], "S speaker Yadavas were original inhabitants and pre-Aryan natives of Iran, who were of round head form." Another element was long headed Mediterranean and third one Mesocephalic hybrid race of both of them. At Maski and Brahmagiri this mesocephalic breed was an admixture of round headed and long headed race. This long headed race was Dravidian and not Aryan since in Indian Megaliths not a single example of Aryan race has been traced out so far, in support of their theory, where as Dravidian examples have been found in abundanced. Hence the theory of Kappers and Sarkar is liable to be disproved. We know, as established by scholars, no Aryan man reached South India before the time of Ashoka, this fact has been supported by ancient Dravidian literature also, proving sound footing of our theory. What is the pitfall in the theory of Sarkar and Kappers is being explained below : In remote past, where there various races, due to any reason got mixed up, it would be very hard for the scholars to identify their accurate ethnical group, from the scientific examination of their skeletal remains alone, particularly, where two races of similar physical type had gone under process of admixture for a long period in remote past, as was the case between the mediterranean Dravidian and Caspean Aryan. They had physical differences of colour of skin, eyes, hair only which being perishable cannot come to hands of scholar from old cemeteries for examination. This is the major pitfall of anthropology. Both the scholars could not give due consideration to this pitfall hence fell into ditch of misconception. However we can putforth solid evidences that not the Scythian but Dravidian element was present at Tepe Hissar and Sialk in the period under discussion :—

In 721 BC, Assyrian king Sargon II invaded Israel because Israelites had revolted against his rule and he wanted to punish them severally. Hence Israelite leaders and most of masses (long headed) were forced to migrate to eastern border of his empire nearing to the western and central Iran. Hence the long headed Dravidians were present in the period under discussion at Sialk and Tepe Hissar.

According to Roman Ghirshman (See map no.V), Scythians invaded Western Asia in the late 2nd and early 1st millennium B.C. They reached north west region of Iran and turn back from the south bank of lake Urmia and thus they never reached central province of Iran where Sialk and Tepe Hissar are situated. But they again appeared in Iran and India in second century AD, where as Megalithic people appeared in India in between 1000 BC and 800 BC. Hence Scythians cannot be held responsible for introducing Megalithic culture in India.

Before, their entry in India, Scythians were a semi-civilized people who had no religious belief and were not snake worshippers or Nagas.

Hence it is proved conclusively that Megalithic builder Nagas were racially Mediterraneans and Alpine or blended race of both of them and not Scythians.

References

1. Detailed discussion is given in Chapter IV PP-82-83
2. Fergusson James, "Tree and Serpent Worship" P-80.
3. Fergusson James P-122.
4. Dixon B. Roland "The Racial History of man" P–311.
5. Fergusson James PP-224-25.
6. Gupta, S.P. "Disposal of the Dead and Physical Type in Ancient India," PP 232-33.
7. Gupta S.P. P-301.
8. According to P.N. Chopra, The Aryan Speaking Brahmanas, Buddhist, and Jains, first of all reached South India, during Ashoka Period. "History of South India" Vol I, PP 55-56.
9. Dixon B. Roland P-136.
10. Risley H.H, "The People of India" Appendix III.
11. (A) Wheeler REM, "A.I." vol III PP 83-85 and BASI (Jan 1947) and Bose N.K. and others, "Human Skeleton from Harappa" BASI (1963) PP 58-59.

    (B) Sarkar S.S., "Aboriginal Races of India" PP 143-45.
12. Chattopadhyaya, "Racial Affinities of early North India Tribes" PP 5-6.
13. Gupta S.P.P-289.
14. Lal B.B. "From the Megalithic to the Harappa ; Tracing back the Graffiti on Pottery" "Ancient India no.16 (1960) PP 4-24 .
15. Gupta S.P. P-299.
16. Wheeler R.E.M, " A.I." Vol III BASI (1947) PP 83-85 and Bose N.K. and others. "Human Skeleton from Harappa " BSIC (1963) PP 58-59.
17. (a) Chanda R.P. " The Indo-Aryan Races" IC 25 and 33.

    (b) Nanavati J.M. "Som Nath" PP 88-89.
18. After Dixon B. Roland, PP, 252 and 307-29
19. Ghirshman Roman, "Persia from the Origins to Alexander, the Great P-Intro XII Thomes and Hudson (1964) France.
20. C.I. of Aryans is within the range of 72.4 and 74.4 and Dravidian is between 71.00—76.6 H.H. Risley PP 37, 47 and 400 also see Table no. 6.
21. I personally discussed this matter with R.S. Bisht and Dhanpati Rai both Directors of A.S. of India in their offices, they stated that hair is a pesishable part of body.
22. Dixon B. Roland PP 300 and 307.
23. Fry P. Somerset. "History of the World" PP 80-81.
24. (a) Ghirshman Roman P–5.

    (b) Dixon B. Roland PP 324–25.
25. Gupta S.P. P–302.

26. Chopra P.N. and others, "Vol I P-55".
27. Gupta S.P. P–305.
28. Fergusson James P–78.
29. Dixon B. Roland P.P. 328-29.
30. Strabo ii B XI P–254 Mentioned by C.T. Metclfe "The Rajput Tribes " P–61.
31. Majumdar R.C., "Ancient India " PP–119–21.
32. Gupta S.P. P–230 (See chapter III P–40 for detail).
33. "Sakas is India " PP 119–20.
34. (a) Rowlison H.G., "Intercourse, between India and the Western World" P–22.

    (b) e. g. the Messagtae, Strabo XI-8-6.
35. Tod James, "Annals and Antiquities of Rajasthan " Vol I P–43 Footnote No. 3.
36. Chand R.P. IC 33.
37. Chattopadhyaya S. P-46.

Chapter-9

THE BLACK AND RED WARE CULTURE, ITS RELATION WITH THE YADAVAS AND THE NAGA RACE

After the decisive defeat and having been chased out by the Nordic Aryan invaders, the Non-Aryan Harappans moved south ward along the seashore through modern Gujrat and settled there. Many groups of them fled eastward under the pressure of invaders and settled in the plains of Ganga-Yamuna. Later, when Aryan people reached there, these non-Aryans moved further towards modern Bihar and Bengal. The findings of the later Harappan pottery, or ochre coloured pottery (OCP), in the aforesaid region, is one of the solid archaeological evidence to witness this event. Similarly the traditional history of Mundas also discloses the history of migration of these aboriginal people, apparently under the pressure of Aryan invasions. The linguistic and the archaeological evidences, of their movements, can be traced out till to-day from the whole of the Northern India. Their remains have been traced out as Brahui tribe on the North Western border; Mahar tribe (Mar or Mer) in the South-Western region; Pariyah, Bhar, Palar, Malar, Malla and Gond in the South and Santhal and Nagas in the East.

In the form of languages the remains of these non-Aryan tribes and castes are still in each and every corner of India. The Munda languages in North-East and Dravidian languages in South are spoken till to-day; their main mark of identification was the tradition of totemism; on the other hand there was tradition of Gotras in Aryan tribes and castes.

The Totemistic Tradition among the Aboriginal tribes

Totem can be defined as follows : if some castes or tribes or a group of families, living together accept an animal or a plant as their totem, it is called the totem of that caste or tribe viz Monkey, bear, fish, serpent, dear, eagle, tortoise, pea-cock, duck and many plants etc.

Acharya Chhitij Mohan[1] Sen has defined the totem tradition : "From the most ancient time, in different countries, nations or tribes, a particular mark or insignia (animal, bird or plant), known as totem was in practice; that insignia was a subject of great respect and full faith for each and every member of the tribe or Nation."

The characteristics of totemism after Majumdar, may be summarized thus : "killing certain animals or eating them is tabooed in some clans. Some tribes bear sign thereof. The totem animal, when it dies is ceremonially mourned and buried as a member of the clan concerned. The skins of the animals, which are the totems of clans, are donned by the totemic group on specified solemn occasions. Many totemic groups paint their persons with the picture of the totemic animal and take the picture as their coat of arms or even tattoo it on their bodies. The totem animal, if dangerous, is propitiated in the belief that it will spare the members of the totemic clan. If, the totem plant or animal is edible, the members may eat it on ceremonial occasions or after offering their excuses to the animal. The clan recognizes mystic ties with the animal species and believes that the animal will foretell the future, protect and warn the members of tribes. The assumptions, with regard to totemism, are that totem organization is universal. J.F. Maclenon was the first to understand the significance of totemism as a primitive social institution." [2]

Majumdar, gives an account of totemistic tribes as follows[3] : "According to Ethnographic Survey of India, the Santhals have more than 100 totemistic clans, Hos have more than 50, Mundas 64 and Bhils 24. Many castes in Orissa, the Kurmi, the Kumhar, the Bhumia, who have advanced in culture in recent years are named after the serpent, pumpkin, Jackal and other totems. The Katkaris of Bombay, the Gond tribes of M. P. and of Rajasthan also have clan names after the fauna and flora of their habitat. The Dhelki Kharias, a major section of the kharias of Chota Nagpur plateau, are divided into eight totemic clans viz. Soren (rock or stone) Muru (Tortoise), samad (deer), Barliha (a Variety of fruit), Gharhad (bird) Hansda (the eel), Mail (dirt) and Topna (kind of bird). These names show how a totem may be an animal plant or often material object or a part thereof."

It is clear that all these castes and tribes were sometimes, organized into totem system. But now owing to spreading of education and civilization, above system has also lost its grounds.

Serpent Totem and Naga Race

It is crystal clear from the above description, that Nagas were also tribes which, had serpent as their totem. They worshipped serpents and consider them to be their protector deities. They also used to wear artificial hoods of cobra on their heads. (See Illustration No. III). They were, in origin, indigenous non-Aryan Kshatriyas. They ruled all over India during historic and pre-historic time. Some of the Naga kings and families can be enumerated as under : Ahivritra, Ashwasena, Takshaka, Gonanda, Lohara, Karkota of North; Brahmadutta of Kashi, Sishunaga and Nanda of Magadha, of North east; Nagas of Padmavati (Bharsiva), Vidisa, Eran, Mathura, Ahichchhattra, Kausambi, Malava, Chakrakot, Bhogwati in Central India; Andhra or Satvahanas (235 BC-225 AD) Chuttus, Chalukya, Pallava, Kadamba, Chhindaka, Chera, Chola of South India etc. Most of the above Naga families ruled between 500 BC and 500 AD and some of them onward up to the Mughal period. Now let us see who were these Nagas ?

The Harappan Civilization and Cult of Naga Worship

The Indus Valley Civilization, which is the most ancient civilization of India, was spread up in North West; Harappa, Mohenjodaro, Chanhudaro and Lothal were its most important towns. The founders of Indus Valley Civilization were Mediterraneans or Dravidians and Australoids[4], where as, round headed Alpines appeared, in mature age of this culture.[5] In excavation of these towns, in addition to Burnished Red ware, a very high number of seals and seal impressions have also been found out. Among the seals so found out, on one seal, there is a figure of chief deity with buffalo head, on its both sides, are two other man deities and behind each of them is a serpent in standing posture. (Illustration no V-A) On another seal, there is a serpent, in standing posture, behind the bull, who is fighting with a mighty man.[6] (Illustration no. V-B). On another third seal, there is a serpent, resting his head on a wooden bench or seat, which is protecting a tree deity.[7] (Illustration no V-C)

Dr. Avantika Prasad Marmat gives a very beautiful analysis of above figures, he writes[8] : "In the first figure, standing of snake behind one of the human figures, is most significant. Here, the man has been symbolized as snake and snake as man or man deity. In the age of serpent totem tradition, serpent deity was considered to be a form of human being. Both were dedicated and synonym to each other. As a matter of fact, here man is a symbol of Naga or serpent totemism. The figures of other two seals also corroborate this anaslysis :

(1) A mighty man is killing the bull.

(2) The bull is fighting with the mighty man.

(3) There is a snake in the standing posture behind the bull.

Now, a question arises why this serpent is standing behind the bull ? Bull is the carrier of the God Siva, who keeps serpents with him. Bull was worshipped as a sacred animal in the Indus Valley Civilization (Shastri K. N. P-120) and was considered to be another form of serpent, that is why serpent, is seen standing behind the bull in the seal impressi on. In my opinion, serpent in the form of bull, is fighting with the mighty man. Dr. Rangeya Raghava in his famous work [Mahayatra (Gatha); Andhera Rasta P.75] has given a reference of a similar collision from an ancient myth of Babylonia : Garuda goes to devour the bull, but the serpent just comes out and kills it. Here the bull proves to be a form of serpent. To corroborate the above view, another myth of Babylonia is presented from the same work : In Babylonia, there was a Garuda deity named Zu, which was killed by the serpent. Above serpent used to hide himself in the body of Bull. [Mahayatra (Gatha); Andhera Rasta P-75]

In the third seal the following scene is depicted : (1) A serpent is seen resting its hood on a wooden seat (2) Nearby is a sacred tree (of heaven),which is being protected by the former. Here, if the protection was the only object than what can be the object of wooden seat or resting of hood on it. In my opinion this signifies "the authority of rule of serpent deity." The tree and serpent worship was one of the peculiarities of Indus Valley Culture."

The presence of, serpents on all the above three seals, establishes that the serpent was their (Harappans) protector deity and symbol of authority of rule. We can draw the following conclusion from the above detail : (1) The tradition of serpent worship or totemism was prevalent in Indus Valley Civilization. (2) The scene, depicted on the seal No. 2, shows its relation with the myths of Babylonia, which proves origin of this tradition in Western Asia. (See chapter I PP-11-13). This fact finding is further corroborated by seal, No.4. This figure is incised on a cylinder seal recovered from Babylonia (Lajards culte de Mithra), whose period is still undecided. But its scene is closely similar to that of seal no A and C. This proves the origin of tradition of tree and serpent worship in Babylonia, fromwhere later on it was transferred to Indus Valley.

Description of Nagas or Serpents in Vedas :

The Rigveda : It has been analyzed above that totemism was in practice in Indus Valley Civilization. After that Rigvedic period is most significant. In Rigvedic account there is mention of Naga (serpent) race, Naga kings and Naga warriors. Therefore, we can say, that this period also seems to have been covered by the tradition of serpent worship or serpent totem.

There is description[9] of serpent deity "Ahivritra" in the verses of this sacred book. "Ahi" is synonym of serpent. The word "Ahi-Budhna" (the serpent of the base of a mountain) has come twelve times in the

Rigveda. He has been repeatedly requested, for not handing over his worshippers to sinners.[10] According to Oldenberg, water is a form of serpent and according to Macdonell[11], they (serpents) are the forms of Ahivritra, who is thought to be heavenly. It is conclusive that Ahi-Budhna of Rigveda was a serpent deity who was worshipped.

The description of Vritra also has come repeatedly in Rigveda.[12] He was deadly enemy of Indra, and he ultimately was killed by the later. He also has been called by the names' like Dasyu, Dasa, Asura and Ahi. In Rigveda, the word "Ahi" had also come for serpent. It means "Ahi" was a serpent. The greatest Ahi of Vedic poet was "Vritra Sarpa" (Vritra-serpent) which could block waters (Rivers).[13] In Atharva-Veda and later Brahmanical literature there is also mention of "Ahi" along with Vritra.[14] Ahi is a title of Naga kings and as well as serpent. In support of this view there are enormous evidence in Sanskrit scripture; such as in Amarkosha (first Kanda) in the list of serpents there is mention of "Ahi". In Hindi dictionary of Nalanda the meaning of "Ahi" is serpent and Vritrasur. In the Sanskrit-Hindi-dictionary of Apte, the meaning of "Ahi" is serpent "boa". In Rigveda (VII-50-1 to 3) "Ahi" has been stated to be a dangerous serpent. In Uttar Pradesh, the cultural centre of mediaeval period was Ahichchhattra (centre of Naga rule), which was situated in the district of Barrielly. This was the capital of ancient Naga kings.

This is quite clear that "Ahi" as described in Rigveda, was a serpent or Naga race, whose king was Vritra or Ahivritra.

The Atharva-Veda

Dr. Bhagvatsharan Upadhayaya,[15] the famous scholar of ancient history and culture, has noted some hymns of Atharvaveda (V-13- 6 to 10), which have references of Assyrian Naga kings Aligi and Viligi. We have given a detailed description of their origin and migration to India in chapter I (P-10). Again this proves that Naga-worship and totemism tradition came from Assyria to India and also clarifies that during the period of composition of AtharvaVeda, there was existence of Naga-worship and totemism in India.

The Black and Redware Culture and its Relation with the Western Asia :

Although the description of Black and Red Ware Culture has been given in volume I (The Founders of Indus Valley Civilization and their later History PP 60-65); but because this culture is related to our main subject i.e., Nagas and Megalithic Culture, therefore it is necessary to throw some light on its most essential aspects.

Scholars, during archaeological excavations, have found out B and R ware immediately after the mature Harappan Age (2000 BC). This culture originated in Lothal (Gujrat) and later spread up in the other region of Gujrat and South East Rajasthan, and onward up to Uttar Pradesh, Bihar, MadhyaPradesh, Maharashtra and South India. Famous archaeologist S.R. Rao, who excavated Lothal, throws light on the origin of above pottery,[16] "The original inhabitants of Lothal, whose racial affinities we do not know, were advanced culturally. They knew the use of copper and produced superior earthen wares of thin fabric on a fast wheel. The presence of mica in the clay and the deliberate application of Pinkish red slip over the vessel resulted in a micaceous red surface on account of which the ceramic ware has got its name. The shapes were limited to the round bottomed jars and bowls. The type fossil was convex sided bowl with a stud-handle which the Harappans copied later in their own fabric. The micaceous red ware vessels were painted in black over a light red surface with plant motifs, horizontal, zig-zags, loops and intersecting lines, the painting being limited to the rim of bowl and the neck of Jar. The indigenous style of painting influenced the Indus (Harappan) style considerably. A more important contribution made by the indigenous potters, is what is known as the ''inverted firing technique,'' whereby the vessels came out of kiln partly black and partly red (i. e. black inside and red out side with a black top. In Wheeler's words, ''The upper portion of pot is thus in contact with the reducing agents present in the combustible material and turns black, while the lower portion is exposed to the air and turns red, as a result of oxidization. This technique was copied by the Harappans and their successors. The black and Red ware, as the product of this technique is called, became the chief ceramic ware of the Chalcolithic folk of Central India and the Deccan in the second Millennium B. C. and the culture trait of the Megalithic builders of the South in the first millennium B. C. It served as an important link between the Harappans and their successors in the Indian sub-continent"

The Distribution of the Culture

This is important to keep in mind that as noted in the Ahar culture of Bana valley-above firing technique was adopted by the later immigrants from North-West. They mixed up with the local or indigenous population and carried above potting technique with them wherever they went. Vibha Tripathi[17] gives a detailed account of spreading up of this culture from North West to East or Southward in chronological order–

"B and R. Ware occurs along with Painted Grey Ware (PGW) at the most of the sites. But before we define the precise nature of the association of the two wares, we have to examine the distribution, both in time and space of B and R. It first shows itself in the Harappan context and continues through the Chalcolithic assemblage in Eastern

India, Pre-PGW deposits (Atranjikhera and Noh), Pre-NBP levels in Bihar, PGW and outlives PGW up to the early historical period. (in Gujrat and Deccan). Black and Red Ware, thus, has extensive distribution both in time and space.

Onwards, we shall examine in brief the zonal features of the ware and study, B and R in connection with PGW culture and pottery tradition. Srivastava (1971) has classified the entire B and R Yielding region into six zones. They are :

Region A (Gujrat).

Sites Lothal, Rojdi, Rangpur, Prabhas-Patan, Amra and Lakhowal.

Date 2400 BC to 800 B. C. with survivals at Rangpur and Prabhas patan.

Painting on the exterior

Region B (South-Eastern Rajasthan and Madhya Pradesh).

Sites Ahar, Gilund, Eran, Awra, Manoti, Navadatoli, Nagda and Besnagar.

Date 2000 BC to 800 B.C. with survivals at Eran, Navadatoli, Nagda and Besnagar.

Painting On the exterior as well as on interior.

Region C (Eastern U.P., Bihar and West Bengal)

Sites Kausambi, Rajghat, Sohgaura, Sonpur, Chirand, Pandu-Raja-Dhibi.

Date 1600 BC to 800 BC with survival at Sonpur and Chirand

Painting Generally on the interior.

Region D (Punjab, Western U.P. Northern and north western Rajasthan)

Sites Rupar, Alamgirpur, Hastinapur, Atranjikhera, Sravasti, Noh, Gondi, Ghosla.

Date 1000 to 800 B.C.

Painting Absent

Region E (Maharashtra and Northern Mysore)

Sites Bahal, Prakash, Bahurupa, Nevasa, Nasik, Jorve, Daimabad, Tekkalkota, Hallur.

Date 1700 to 600 BC with survival at Bahal, Prakash, Nasik and Jorve.

Painting On the interior as well as on the exterior

Region F (South Mysore, AndhraPradesh, Madras, Kerala and Orissa)

Sites Brahmapuri, Maski, Piklihal, Kesarpalli, Nagarjunkonda, Sisupalgarh.

Date 1200 BC to 100 BC

Painting Absent"

It is crystal clear from the aforesaid distribution of cultural areas and order of chronology, that the user of above pottery first of all settled in West and later moved towards North-East and further settled in Bihar and Bengal. Similarly their one group moved from Gujrat, following the coastal route reached Maharashtra and further in far South.

This culture has been found in between the layers of OCP (later Harappan culture) and PGW at three sites i. e., Atranjikhera[18] Noh,[19] and Jodhpura.[20] In Gangetic Valley B and R Ware culture has been found underneath the strata of PGW and NBP.

Foreign Element in B and R Ware culture and Presence of Iron

This is very interesting to note that traces of Iron have been found out in above culture. Whereas previous view was that PGW was the first Iron Age culture and iron was first brought by Aryan invaders from the West. In favour of above view Vibha Tripathi[21], while produces evidences, writes : "Iron has now been reported from the Pre- a PGW deposit i.e., Black and Red ware culture levels at Noh. This would further strengthen the hypothesis that these were the people who came from the West to settle down in the Saraswati Drishadvati valley. Their knowledge of iron was later imported to the P.G.W people. Although we require further evidences to present boldly the above hypothesis. At present such a possibility is not altogether untenable."

The Black and Red Ware Culture at Ahar and its Relation with the Western Asia

The B and R ware was first noted at Ahar village in Udaipur district, located on the bank of river Ahar, a tributary of the Banas. This culture is represented by a 20 feet thick-deposit.

According to Sankalia,[22] the archaeological remains of B and R ware culture of Bana valley (or Ahar culture) include some highly characteristic pottery, beads etc which indicate the existence of a significant element of West Asian complex. The examples which are relevant to our study are as follows :

(a) The hallow stemmed bowl in Grey ware is similar to those found at Tepe Hissar and Geoy Tepe.

(b) The stepped dish-cum bowl are similar to those found at Shah-Tepe.

(c) The animal headed handles of some earthen pots are similar to those found at Troy.

(d) Potting techniques and decorations, such as applique and punctured ornament, ribs along the shoulder and neck, grooved and incised designs are similar to those found on Shah Tepe pottery.

(e) Correspondence between the light incised patterns on the terracotta beads or spindle whorls from Troy or Anatolia in general and the one with an incised pattern and beads from Ahar and an identical one on bead from Anau.[23]

It is clear from the above evidences that new foreign element came to India from Assyria (Troy or Anatolia) and North Iran (Shah tepe and Tepe Hissar) North West Iran (Geoy Tepe) and settled in aforesaid area.

It seems that not only the technique of potting but the complete tradition of Black and Red Ware was brought from West Asia. S.P. Gupta throws light on this subject :[24] "There has been another interesting discovery in the Hadhramaut Wadi at Mashgha. Here a big, pot-sherd was found which was red to black on the outside and Black on inside. The Black-and Red ware might have come from Palestine. In the Indian context it is associated with the cultures ranging from the Harappan period to the Megalithic (Lal B. B. "From the Megalithic to the Harappa; tracing back the graffiti on the pottery." Ancient India no 16 (1960) PP 4-24). It may not be out of place to mention that Egypt had this ware at the grave sites of Tumas etc. of the 2nd millennium B.C. i.e. in the protohistoric times. He writes, "Again, it is probable, though not proved that there may be some link between the C-Group culture of Nubia and Megalithic South Black-and-red ware also called as Black topped ware, has been found in Egypt from 4000 B.C. onwards and Palestine might have got it from there. This Egyptian Black-and Red ware of C group people of 2000-1000 BC. also moved in Ethiopia and it is equally possible that South Arabia got it from this country which was quite near. Although, I am not in a position to suggest that India learnt the technique of producing Black and Red ware from Egypt, or Ethiopia or Southern Arabia, yet, as shri B.B. Lal has very pertinently pointed out to me in a personal discussion with him, that it may not be without significance that the Black and Red ware is found confined to a rather homogeneous land curve that may start from Egypt and fall in South India; it is not found in any other region of the ancient world."

Alpine Race : Original Inhabitant of West Asia

Roland B. Dixon has observed from Archaeological findings of human skeletal remains that in Chalcolithic Age or in earlier period Alpine race was living in almost all the Western Asia and also in Anatolia or Asia Minor. He informs[25] : "The belief that the people of the Asia minor were at the earliest period of which we know brachycephalic, is apparently corroborated by the single skull from Lycia (Ante P-256) which is clearly Alpine. Indirect evidence is also perhaps afforded by the Bronze Age Crania from Cyprus (Von Luschan 1890) which indicate the Alpine type as predominant there. It is conclusive that the oldest traceable population of this whole region was brachy-Cephalic and mixture of Alpine and Paleo-Alpine types."

This view gets the support of Keane, Haddon and Dutt N. K. Their view is as follows[26]—

"From the earliest times the whole of this region (Iran) has formed part of the caucasis domain, that the bulk of the indigenous population must have belonged to the dark, round headed Alpine type; that these, still found in compact masses, were apparently conquered, but certainly Aryanized in speech, in very remote pre-historic times by long headed blond Aryan of the Iranian and Golchic branches, who arrived in large numbers from the contiguous–Eurasian steppe, mingled generally with brachy aboriginals, but also kept aloof in several districts, where they still survive with more or less modified proto-Aryan features ....Both Iranic and Golchic are thus linguistic rather than ethnic terms, and so true is this that a philologist always knows what is meant by an Iranic language, while the anthropologist is unable to define or form any clear conception of an Iranian, who may be either long-headed Nordic or round headed Alpine type."

As such it is evidently proved that all the region of plateau of Asia Minor and Iran was earlier being inhabited by Alpine race.[27] Anatolia or Asia minor was northern extremity of ancient Assyria. It means Alpine people were settled in all the vast track from Northern Assyria up to Iran, who later on moved south ward and eastward.

The proto-Iranian broad heads belong, as already stated, to three different groups : The Alpines (from their association with that European region), Dinaric (from the Dinaric Alps which stretch from Dalmatia to croatia) and the Armenoids[28], some scholars think that tribes like Yadus, Turvasas, Anus, Druhyus and Purus, belong to the Alpine group and in India, they became ultimately mixed up with the Nordics.

In this connection, it must be remembered that before the so called Aryans came to Iran and India, the religions of the two countries also had a great resemblance. It[29] is apparent from the excavations at Luristan and other places in Iran and in the Indus Valley in India, that there was a mother-goddess cult prevailing in both the countries, so this similarity existed even when the Indians and Iranian pre-historic people perhaps did not belong to one and the same race. Similarities existed between the two countries even after the so called Aryans came to those places as revealed by the Veda, but the dissimilarities became more apparent after it. It is clear that these people, were original inhabitants of large tract of Iran and Western Asia and its northern plateau from remote past had cultural relation with India.

The movement of Alpine Race from the West

It is well known that, in this duration Aryan invaders were threatening on whole of the northern frontiers of Assyria and Iran. Due to this historical reason migration of a very large number of human kind took place towards south. Dr Sankalia[30] accepts this viewpoint of migration: "This was not strange if some people in about 2000 B.C. moved from western Asia and reached South East Rajasthan and settled there."

The invasion of Aryans on the North Frontier of Iran, is not an imagination, but a hard fact. Famous anthropologist and historian Roland B. Dixon, who prepared data of skeletal remains, recovered from ancient graves of Iran, the conclusion of his important research, has given indication of above invasion from North. And as a result of pressure of above invasion, the ancient aboriginal tribes of Iran moved southward and reached India. He[31] puts forward his viewpoint on this movement from Iran and writes : "We may probably assume that the earliest traceable population of the region was of brachycephalic type, probably in the main Alpine, and comparable to that which we are also obliged to assume for the Anatolian plateau further west. At a period still uncertain, but which must go back towards the beginning of the second millennium B.C., the plateau was invaded from the North by an Indo-European speaking people. From this time on for some 1,500 years, continued at intervals to invade the Western Asiatic up lands, both from the region of the Caspean sea and from Europe across the Bosphorus. ....The results from the racial point of view of these invasions, were, I believe, mainly two. First, as a consequence of the pressure of the invading people, some of the older brachycephalic folk were forced out south-east-ward, towards the region of the Indus delta and so on down the Western Coast of the Indian peninsula, others perhaps across to Oman, in Southern

Arabia, where they contributed a strong brachycephalic factor to the population. Second, the remainder of the more original brachycephalic people became gradually blended with their Caspean-Mediterranean conquerors, whose language almost wholly replaced their own."

Obviously, Dixon has approved the viewpoint of Sankalia. S.S.[32] Sarkar also has identified the skeletal remains of the Brachy-cephalic Alpines of cemetery H as an invader on Harappa.

Famous Bengali anthropologist B.S. Guha[33], while, approving above view, throws light on the origin of these tribes and their invasion on India (see map no. III), "During this period or earlier, a brachy-cephalic race of the Alpine Dinaric type with a short to medium stature, a round and broad face and a long prominent nose, immigrated into North India. This race had its origin in South West Siberia, during prehistoric period from where it spread to Eastern Europe and Southern Arabia. It probably proceeded to Afghanistan and penetrated into India. It descended from the Pamir through Afghanistan, Baluchistan and Sind and spread along the western coast into Gujrat and Kanara. One branch crossed over to Bengal and in a more Southern route over the Deccan to Tamilnadu. Since, the expansion of this race, coincides in time and geography with the growth and spreading out of the Indus Valley Civilization and the post-Harappan Industries, it is probable that this race was, at least, partly responsible for this cultural development in Northern and Central India. At Harappa and other sites skeletal finds have been made which bear the characteristic feature of this race."

It becomes more clear from above views of Sarkar and Guha that Alpine race not only invaded Indus Valley Civilization but also contributed much to its culture in Northern and Central India. This is one of the most significant conclusion proving unity of two races the Dravidian and Alpine in later period.

Identification of Alpine Race as Yadus etc.

Next important question arises, after their entry into India, what was their historical identity and how did they influence later Indian history ? Vibha Tripathi puts forth conclusive viewpoint of Sankalia and Thapar.[34] : "Sankalia, on the basis of the Puranic evidence that the Narbada valley was inhabited much before the Mahabharata war, suggests that the post-Harappan Chalcolithic Cultures of central India and the Northern Deccan were colonized by the Aryans in the wake of their early settlement of India. This period has been dated to (1700-1000 B.C. a period which precedes the settlement of the Doab....... But according to Thapar, "This part of Rajasthan was not inhabited by the first wave of

Aryans but by Sourseni speaking people, and it is not sure as to which branch of the Aryans is represented by these people, Asamakas or Assakas or by the Yadavas and Haihayas of the Puranic tradition."

Now the picture so emerges is clear enough to say that the users of B and R. Wares were Sourseni speaking Yadavas or a tribe ethnically related to them which was originally a round headed Alpine race and not Aryan, who came from western Asia and Iran and entered India through North West passes : Baluchistan and Sindh, in the long run settled in the aforesaid region. They got mixed up with the people of local tribes like Dravidian and adopted their potting technique i.e. B, and R Ware. Hence B and R Ware culture was 'Dravido-Iranian'. We produce some more archaeological evidences, recovered from the excavation of Prabhas-Patan, an important site of Gujrat.

The Excavation of Prabhas-Patan : Its relation with the Puranic Tradition and Yadavas

According to Puranic tradition, Prabhas-Patan (Som Nath) was related to Yadavas. This site is situated in Kathiavar near modern city of Veraval near the coast of Arabian sea at the bank of river Heron and is related to B and R ware culture. The deposits with B and R ware are assumed to start in 1st millennium B.C., still however by about 7th-6th century B.C., the B and R ware using people might have occupied this spot.[35] Nanavati[36] throws light on its relation with Puranic tradition, "Prabhasa was the holiday resort of the Yadavas. The Pandavas also came here. So this place is essentially connected with the Yadavas. If one believes that in the tradition of Yadavaś migration from Dwarika and moving in this region, a few remarks seem to be pertinent. Looking to divergent opinions of the Puranic chronology at least one thing seems to be clear that if the date 3101 B.C. of the Mahabharata war be accepted, archaeological evidence is totally divergent, and both can not be compromised. The other opinion of Pargitor that the Mahabharata war was fought round about 950 B.C. be accepted the picture becomes more clear. In the latter case, the chronology of Prabhas suggests that in this period the material evidence of Iron Age is obtained. This material culture will not be out of context. The evidence of Prabhas is too meagre but it certainly suggests a slight overlap of Chalcolithic and Iron Age cultures. There is no evidence of heavy destruction but the mingling of cultures may lead one to infer that Raivataka and pre-Yadava population was probably of Chalcolithic culture. The marriage relations and struggles of mythology represent this overlap and later the establishment of a more widespread culture. In this part of the country this culture could be identified with the Yadavas. There "peculiar feature," as noted by Dr. Jani is "the considerable admixture they had with the non-Aryans"

(Chronology of Gujrat P-24), seem to reflect the social features of the then existing society. These early Yadavas seem to use the materials that were found in many parts of Western, Central, Southern and Eastern India. This culture is similar to that found at Maheshwara where Haihayas, a branch of the Yadavas ruled.

The problems of Black and Red Ware, and even the introduction of iron in India require much further work. The different tribes associated with Yadu seem to follow this tradition. Looking from this angle the excavations at Somnath suggest that the Krishna legend and early Yadava movement might be identified with the early Iron Age of India, and that the Pre-Yadava elements here were in the Chalcolithic stage of culture. If Krishna migrated to this region he also opened up a new chapter in the culture of this region."

Thus the viewpoint of Thapar is well confirmed. Hence, now it seems to be a well established theory that B and R Ware culture of Iron Age was related to Yadavas; and as Dr. Jani has stated with a stress that these Yadavas mixed up socially and culturally with the local population of Dravidian blood, hence this new culture was a mixed culture of round headed Yadavas and long headed Dravidian people.

Hostility of Yadavas and Aryans : Rigvedic Evidence

Some scholars think that Yadavas were an early branch of Aryans, who has been called Asura in Rigveda and other Sanskrit scriptures, who also had a horrible collision with the Aryans (Gods). But inversely we will prove here that Yadavas socially, culturally linguistically, spiritually and ethnically were, quite a different people from Aryans, and they had no relation of any kind with them.

There are very clear evidences in Rigveda (VIII-96-13- to 15) to prove that Aryans and Yadavas were two different races and had regular relations of hostility and hatred. Indra, with the help of Brahaspati Marut and Adaiveh Vish, attacked army of 10 thousand warriors of Krishnasur on the banks of Ashumati. Indra asked Marudgana to kill him. In the long run, Indra killed him along with his entire army with the help of Brahaspati. Even Indra killed Krishnagarbha (foetus of the wife of Krishna (I-101-1). Similar enmity of Krishna and Indra can be seen in Puranic accounts too. Indra out of enmity poured rains in torrents in Brijbhumi. Krishna saved his kith and kins with the help of Govardhan hill.

According to different verses of Rigveda, Yadavas etc. were non-Sanskrit speaking non-Aryans. In Puranic descriptions their language is stated to be Sourseni which is said to be a mlechchha language. R. Shaffer,[37] on the basis of Rigvedic account throws light on the racial affinities of Yadava etc. as such : "These peoples (Yadus, Turvasa, Anu, Puru and Druhyu) were not Sanskrit speaking Aryans. According to Rigveda the Anus, Druhyus, Yadus, Turvasas and Puru attacked the Aryans at Parushni (Ravi), so they must have been native tribes hostile to the Aryans. And in the Rigveda, Anu means a non-Aryan; Druhyu is considered a derivative of 'druh' i.e. to be hostile to; Turvasa is a derivative of 'Turv' 'to over power.' No derivation has been of Yadu and we may infer that it was a native name....... . And the Mahabharta (Adi-79-42) states explicitly that the sons of Turvasas are the Yavanas and that the sons of Anu are Mlechchhas. ...... In Rigveda the description of the Purus as Mradhravac seems to strengthen the view that their language was different from the Vedic Nordics.'' Hence they were a non-Aryan tribes, These five tribes lived to the West of the river Indus. In the ancient period, the river Indus divided this region into two linguistic zones- ''The Western Iranian, and the eastern Dardic." Chottopadhyaya[38] puts forth linguistic evidences supporting above view : "Dardistan, the present home of the Dardic-languages includes from east to West, Gilgit and Kashmir, the Indus and the Swat Kohistan, Chitral and Kafiristan. Philology also shows us that they must once have covered nearly the whole of the Punjab." (See chapter VII PP 188-89 for detail).

In the background of the above linguistic evidences and 10 kings war, we should now note the presence of the Harappan people, who as we shall see later on, did not disappear under the pressure of the Aryans, as it was commonly believed. It appears that the Harappans and the Yadus etc. lived side by side at the time of Rigveda in peace and war[39] or both jointly were foes of Aryans and they had deep relations in themselves.

The Racial Type; Ethnical Identification

In the Rigveda Vasistas are described as svetyam or white, Kanvas as svavo or Krishna dark (VII-33-1 and X- 31-11). The appearance of black Rishi in the Nordic Aryan society is indeed a land mark. R. P. Chanda[40] thinks that there were two sections of the sacerdotal class, Brahmanas by descent, Brahmna by adoption and they were of different physical type. He further connects the black Rishi with tribes like Yadu and Turvasa. He[41] thinks that the Purus, Druhyus and Anus mentioned in the Rigveda along with the Yadus and Turvasas, may have come from Western Asia (Assyria) and were probably of the same physical type as the Mitannis and the Hittites having dark or brown colour.

In the Rigveda (X-62-10) Yadus and Turvasas are dubbed as Dasas. They are also brought into special relation with the Parsus (VIII- 6- 46) or Parshavas or Parthavas. The word Dasas shows that their position was similar to original inhabitants. Their relation with the Parsus does mean they were Iranians.

We find following account in some Puranas : Yadavas were born from Yadus, Bhojas from Druhyus and Mlechchhas from Anus[42]. As such Yadus of Rigveda were Yadavas of Puranas and later history. (M.B. Adi Parva Part 85 verse 3533). We will throw light on this subject in chapter XI P-298 that one Gana (tribe) of Satavahanas, was Mahabhoja (a sub-branch of Yadava race) which was of Naga origin.

It is crystal clear that these Yadavas were non-Aryan people who have been given status of Dasas by the Vedic People.

Evidence of Horse and Association of Yadavas with Kathiavar

Recently A. K. Sharma[43] has claimed to have discovered the bones of true Horse (Equus caballus Linn) at Surkotada (Circ 2100-1700 BC) and at Kalibangan also bones of true horse have been reported. It shows the arrival of a new foreign element using domestic horse in this period.

The only other people non-Indo-European, known to have sacrificed horse, are the Assyrians for, according to Aynard under the Assyrian empire white horse was some times sacrificed to god.[44]

This shows that not Aryans but non-Aryan Alpine Assyrian-Iranian horse using people have entered the Indus Valley and beyond in Gujrat and Bana Valley before 2000 B.C. Thus they were the first people to bring this animal in India and not Aryan, that is why Megalithic culture shows close association of horse. This view gets the support of Chanda (IC 33) who thinks that all the five tribes in question may have come from Western Asia (Assyria, Anatolia and Iran) and were probably of the same colour as the Mitannis and the Hittites having dark or brown colour that is why Krishna the black hero of Yadus and his associates have been mentioned in Puranas as Asuras[45] (from Assyria R. V. II-30-4, X- 157-4, X- 53-4, X-138-3). Settlement of Yadavas in Kathiavar gets support of an ancient record. 'The Periplus[46] of the Erythraean sea' and it is quoted as mentioned below : "To the gulf of Baraca that of Barygaza and the main land of Ariaca a district which forms the frontier of kingdom of Nambanus and all of India The interior part of its borders on Scythia is called Abiria and its sea board Syrastrene."

The Scythian race invaded this land in the second century A.D. and pushed the earlier Dravido-Iranian race towards the coastal land and they themselves settled in the upper belt.[47] Still these people are settled here who have been identified as Scytho-Dravidian by Risley and Dravido-Iranian by N.K. Dutta. Dutta[48] asserts : "The people of this region (Gujrat and Maharashtra) were called Rattika or Ratta, whose mention has been made in the inscriptions of Ashoka, the Great. These Rattikas or Rattas were warriors with their synonymous Iranian name Rathaests and Rathaest meant warrior."

The Harivamsa records a confused tradition how the Yadus came to settle in Anarta and Saurastra while branches of them were scattered in different directions far and near (Chanda I C 28, 29). Thus the presence of the broad headed race can be accounted for in this area. B. S. Guha observes that the broad heads drifted along the Western littoral from Southern Baluchistan through Sindh, Kathiavar, Gujrat and Maharashtra.[49]

Chattopadhyaya[50] expresses his view on their further spreading in South East Rajasthan : "Later on the Matsya occupied the Alwar, Jaipur and Bharatpur region. Their capital was Viratnagar, modern Vairat, 40 miles north of Jaipur. It has already been shown that they were a branch of the Yadava tribe and hence broad heads. The Sursenas occupied the present Mathura district. The classical writers refer to Sourasanai with their cities Mathura and Kleisobara and the river Jomones (Yamuna) flowing through it. Ptolemy refers to Madoura the city of the gods. They were a branch of the Yadavas (broad head)"

It is crystal clear that Yadavas came to India from Assyria and Iran and entered Central India through Sindh, Gujrat and Maharashtra.

The Yadavas : A Naga Race

The dark skinned Krishna was a non-Aryan chief. Oldham[51] is of the view that, "Krishna was a non-Aryan of dark skin so much so that in the Indian school of painting this fact is still preserved and he is always painted as a blue skinned human."

Genealogy of Chandra Bansha (after Metclfe)

Maricha
|
Kasyapa
|
Vaivaswama or Surya
|
Vaivaswata Manu
(had 9 sons and one daughter)

Ella = Married to Boodha
(daughter)

Pururva

Ayu or Nahus

Yayati
(had 5 sons or Panchjanya)

Yadu
(had six sons)

Turvasu

Druhyu

Anu

Puru
Lunar race

Ikshwaku
(had 100 sons)

Solar Race

Videha Line

Krustha (4th)
×
×
× 34 generations
×
×
×
×
Satwati

Satjita (5th)

Haihya

Beubya

Hya(k)

Ajamidha
North Panchal
at Ahichhatra

South Panchal

Satwati

Besni

Devabrita

Unmitra

Yadayias

Tak or unduk

Kakra
×
×
×
×
× 9 generations
×
×
×
×
×
×
×
Dewuk-Agrasena
Kansa

Bhujmana
Viduratha
Soura
Seni
Bhoja
Radika
Devamida
Soora
Vasudeva
Hari Krishna

As far his ancestral history it is said that he was the incarnation of Vishnu, he was the son of Vasudeva who was the great grandson of Aryaka who was a Naga chief. The word 'Nag' means 'serpent' and it was applied to those people who worshipped the serpents and who were mentioned in Sanskrit literature as Asur, Monsters, Danavas and Dasas. These words are still used for the Dravidians of Northern India not yet subdued. Similarly, it has been said about Balram, the elder brother of Krishna that he was always under the protection of many hoods of cobras. He is considered to be the reincarnation of SheshNag. At his death, his soul came out of his body in the form of huge Cobra (V.P. V-37-64). James Tod[52] puts forth his opinion on Chandra Banshi origin of Yadavas and their later history, thus, "Krishna was of the celebrated tribe of Yadu, the founder of the fifty six tribes, who obtained the universal sovereignty of India, and descended from Yayati, the third son of Swayambhu Manu or 'the man lord of earth,' whose daughter Ila (Terra) was espoused by Buddha (Mercury) son of Chandra (the moon), whence the Yadus are styled Chandrabanshi or children of the moon ? Buddha was therefore worshipped as the great ancestor of the lunar race; and previous to the apotheosis of Krishna was adored by all the Yadu race. The principal shrine of Buddha was at Dwarka, where he still receives adoration as Buddha Trivikrama. Kanhaiya (Krishna) lived towards the conclusion of the brazen age, calculated to have been about 1100 to 1200 years before Christ. He was born to the inheritance of Vraj, the country of the Suraseni, comprehending the territory around Mathura for a space of eighty miles, of which he was unjustly deprived in his infancy by his relative Kansa. From its vicinity to Delhi we may infer either that there was no lord paramount amongst the Yadus of this period, or that Krishna's family held as vassals of Hastinapur, then with Indraprastha or Delhi, the chief seat of Yadu power. There were two princes named Sura and Sena amongst the immediate-predecessors of Krishna; one his grandfather, the other eight generations anterior. Which of these was the founder of Suryapur on the Yamuna, the capital of the Yadus, we know not, but we may assume that the first gave his name to the region around Mathura, described by Arrian as the country the Suraseni," According to Jayaswal (P-33) Bharsiva and yadu of Mathura were ethnically one people.

These Yadavas or Surasenis, in origin, were Nagas. J.P.H. Vogel[53] produces archaeological evidences to decide their ethnical identity, "The country round Mathura, which is now so closely associated with the cult of the shepherd god Krishna, must once have been a great centre of Naga worship. A Sanskrit inscription preserved in the Lucknow Museum refer to a local serpent deity named Dadhikarna, who appears to have had his own shrine not far from the Buddhist convent founded by king Havishka in the year 47 of Kanishka's era. The remains of this royal foundation were excavated from the Jamalpur (Jail) mound in 1860. Among the numerous Naga images recovered in the Mathura district the most valuable specimen is undoubtedly the inscribed statue from Chharga village situated 5 miles almost the south of the city of Mathura. It is n preserved in the local Museum (Mathura Museum Catalogue P-60 No C. 13). The spirited attitude of this image deserves special notice. The Naga is shown standing with his right arm raised over his head as if ready to strike. The left hand is broken, but probably held a cup in front of the shoulder the head is surmounted by a seven headed snake-hood. From the well preserved inscription incised on the back of the image it appears that it was set up at a water-tank in the fortieth year of Kushana era during the reign of king Huvishka.

The Chhargaon statue represents the best and possibly one of the earliest specimens or a distinct class of Nāga image, of which numerous examples have come to light in the Mathura district. These icons still receive the worship of the rural population, but under a different name. They are invariably designated as "Dau-ji" (meaning, the elder brother) or Baldeva the image of Balrama found at Tumain in Gwalior state and reproduced ASR (1918-19) Part i P-22 Pl XIII). Modern images of Baldeva, which are manufactured in such large numbers at Mathura and Brindaban, are nothing but imitations of the ancient Naga figures. How the images of the Nagas came to be confounded by the villagers with effigies of Baldeva (Balrama), the elder brother of Krishna, it is not difficult to explain. Baldeva is believed to be a reincarnation of Sesha and we shall see that in Sanskrit literature too, he is sometimes completely identified with his spiritual father, the world serpent."

We learn from the inscriptions of Ashoka and Satavahana that there was tribal-republican system in Maharashtra in the age of Ashoka the Great and there were two main components of this tribal republic i.e., Mahar-Ratta and Bhoja. Yadava-Gana was consisted of 18 families which were organised into 4 tribes ie Vrashti, Kukkar, Andhaka and Bhoja. Similarly in Maharashtra, many Naga families were organized into two tribes i.e. Mahar Ratta and Bhoja.[54] In Puranas Satavahanas have been called Andhakas or Andhra tribe also. We can summarise and conclude the whole chapter as follows :

Summary and Conclusion

(1) The Nagas, like most of the other Native tribes had serpent as their totem. They also used to worship serpent and consider them to be their protective deity. They also used to wear artificial hoods of cobra on their heads at certain occasions.

(2) The tradition of Naga worship or totem was in prevalence in Babylonia, Assyria, Palestine and Iran from ancient time and it was brought to India along with migration of Sumerians and Assyrians and Dravidian race.

(3) There are enormous evidences of seals and seal impressions found from Indus towns to show that Indus Valley people also used to worship this serpent deity.

(4) In Rigvedic account, there is a mention of Nagas or Ahi (serpent) race, Naga warriors or Naga kings among them Ahivritra is prominent, who was sworn enemy of Indra, the Aryan god and militant leader. In Atharva-Veda there are some hymns,which describe serpents named Iligi and Viligi, according to B. S. Upadhyaya, these were names of father and son in the genealogical table of Assyrian kings. This proves that serpent (Naga) race and its tradition of serpent worship came from Western Asia.

(5) On the basis of findings of pottery type from Ahar and its proto-type from contemporary sites in Anatolia, Assyria and Iran, Dr. Sankalia has reached a conclusion that new immigrants came from the above mentioned region.

(6) B and R Ware, whose potting technique was developed by the original inhabitants of Lothal or according to B.B. Lal brought from Western Asia or Egypt, was used by the later Harappans and their offshoots. Later on it was also used in Central India (2000-800 BC) by the people of Chalcolithic age and in South India by the Megalithic people (1000-100 BC) in Iron Age. According to B. B. Lal, the Megalithic people were the descendants of Harappans, since B and R ware is attached with the Megalithic culture on one hand and with the Harappan Culture on the other.

(7) Archaeological evedences recovered from the excavation of Prabhasa, a site of B and R Ware culture in Kathiavar, it has been proved by scholars that users of this pottery were Yadavas of Mahabharata fame. These Yadavas were original inhabitants of Western Asia and Iran. Racially they were round headed Alpine or a blend of Alpine or Dravidian race. While, Indo-European from North reached North of Iranian plateau and challenged a threat to the native Alpine people, they moved southward and eastward and entered into North and Western region of India during mature Harappan Age. Evidences of their presence have come to hand from the Harappan cemetery H and G. while, after a gap of few centuries, Aryan invaded India, these people further moved eastward and southward mainly through Gujrat.

(8) These people, according to Rigveda were non-Sanskrit speaking non-Aryans whose mother tongue was Souraseni, which has been described as Mlechchha language in Puranas. They are also called Dasas in Rigveda.

(9) Krishna, the black hero of Yadavas, in addition to his being an incarnation of Vishnu, was also a son of Vasudeva and great grand son of Aryaka who was a Naga chief in origin. Baldeva or Baldou, the elder brother of Krishna is said to be reincarnation of SeshaNaga, hence he

was always under the protection of many hoods of cobra. At his death his soul came out of his mouth in the form of large cobra. His (Naga) image still receives the worship of rural population in the Mathura district, but under a different name, he is invariably designated as Dauji (means elder brother). This proves that these Yadavas were snake worshippers or Nagas.

References

1. 'Bharat Mien Jati Bhed' PP-111-12.
2. Majumdar D.N. "Races and Culture of India" PP 345-46.
3. Majumdar D.N. PP 346-47.
4. (A) Whealer R.E.M., "A.I." Vol III Bulletin of Archaeological Survey of India (Jan, 1947) PP 83-85 .

   (B) Bose N.K. and others "Human Skeletan from Harappa" ASIC (1963) PP 58-59.
5. Sarkar S.S., "Aboriginal Races of India" PP 143-45.
6. Sastri Kedarnath, "New light on the Indus Civilization" Vol-I P-35 Figure3.
7. Sastri Kedarnath, P-35 Figure 4.
8. Marmat Avantika Prasad, "Ved Kalin Nag Jatiyan, Rajaon Tathā Sanskriti Ki Khoj" P-4.
9. Keith A. B. "The Religion and Philosophy of the Vedas and Upnishadas" P-193.
10. R.V. V-41-16 and VII-34-17.
11. Keith A.B. P-193.
12. R.V. II- 11- 5; II- 20 - 7 and V-32-8.
13. Keith A.B. P-193.
14. Mishra D.P. "Studies in the Proto-History of India" P-87.
15. "Bhartiya Samaj Ka Etihasik Vishleshan" P-44.
16. Rao S. R. "Lothal and Indus Civilization" P-54.
17. Tripathi Vibha, "The Painted Grey Ware; An Iron Age Culture of Northern India" PP 50-51.
18. I.A.R. 1962-63,1963-64, 1964-65, 1965-66, 1968-69.
19. IAR 1962-64, PP 28-29; 1968-69,1970-71.
20. IAR 1958-59 P-74.
21. Tripathi Vibha P-56.
22. Sankalia H.D.,"Excavation at Ahar" P-223.
23. Sankalia H.D. "Prehistory and Proto-History of India and Pakistan" P-418.

24. Gupta S.P., "Disposal of the Dead and Physical types in Ancient India" P-327.

25. Dixon B. Roland, "The Racial History of Man" P-314.

26. (a) Keane and Haddon, "Man, Past and Present" PP 541-42.

(b) Dutt N.K. "The Aryanization of India" (1925) PP 35-38 Note.

27. Dixon B. Roland P-253.

28. Chanda R.P. "The Indo Aryan Races" I C 53 cf 76.

29. ABORI Vol LI (1970) P-36.

30. Sankalia H.D. "Excavation at Ahar" P-223.

31. Dixon B. Roland, PP 307-11.

32. Sarkar S.S., PP 143-45.

33. (a) Guha B.S. "An Outline of the Racial Ethnology of India." P-134.

(b) Stephen Fuchs, "The Aboriginal Tribes of India" PP 16-17 Macmillan India Ltd Delhi (1973).

34. Tripathi Vibha PP 120-21.

35. Nanavati J.M., "Som Nath" P-18.

36. Nanavati J.M P-89.

37. Shaffer R. "Ethnography of Ancient India" PP 17-18

Mentioned by Chattopadhyaya S. ''Racial Affinities of Early North Indian Tribes'' P-3.

38. Chattopadhyay S. "Racial Affinities of ēarly North Indian Tribes" P-4.

39. Chattopadhyaya S. P-5.

40. Chanda R.P. I C-25.

41. Chanda R.P. I C- 33.

42. Chattopadhyaya S. PP 67-68.

43. Sharma A. K "Evidence of Horse from the Harappan Settlement at Surkotada; Puratattva No.7 PP-75-76 and Sharma and Joshi's article "Exploration in Kutch and excavation at Surkotada J O I " Vol XXII No 1 and 2 (1972) P P 135-36.

44. Animal Archaeology P-54 cited by Ghurye G.S. "Vedic India" P-325.

45. Rao SR P-159.

46. Chattopadhyaya S.P.-89.

47. Mahajan V.D. "Ancient India" PP 337-39.

48. Dutt N. K. PP 32-38.

49. (a) Guha B. S. P-134.

(b) Chattopadhyaya S. P.-87.

50. Chattopadhyaya S. P-84.
51. "The Sun and The Serpent" PP 78-80.
52. Tod James, "Annals and Antiquities of Rajasthan" II-621.
53. Vogel J.P.H., "Indian Serpent Lore" PP 41-42.
54. Patil Sharad, "Das Shudrachi Gulamgiri" Part I Sub Part I (1982) P-34.

Chapter-10
The Down–Fall of Vedic Culture
And
Rise of Shraman Naga Culture

On the basis of political, social and religious changes, N.K. Dutt[1] has divided the ancient history into following four periods :

(1) The Period of Indus Valley Civilization (2700 BC-1600 BC) The Dravidian culture of Indus Valley flourished in this age.

(2) Vedic Period :— (1600 BC- 1100 BC) The fair skinned, half civilized and barbarian Aryan race of Central Asia invaded and destroyed the great civilization of Indus Valley. In this period the defeated Harappans were enslaved and reduced to fourth Varna and the Vedas were composed and Vedic culture flourished.

(3) Later Vedic or Pauranic period :— (1100 BC-500 BC) In this period Upnishadas, Brahmanas, Grahsuttras, Dharmsuttras etc were composed. The Vedic culture deteriorated, Shraman (Buddhist and Jain) culture developed. The Aryan Kshatriyas began to loose their power and on the contrary indigenous non-Aryan Vratya Kshatriyas or Nagas began to regain their lost power. Iron Age and Megalithic culture began to develop in this age.

(4) Buddhist Period : (500 B.C-500 AD) It was the culmination period of Buddhist culture. The beginning period of this age, is the beginning period of Indian History.

Although Indian history begins with the advent of Buddha and his religion, but due to the exploration of Indus Valley Culture, this period has gone back for more than two thousand years. The life period of this culture is between 2700 BC-1600 BC. The lowest layers of this culture are still under water and definitely this culture would have been originated in a much earlier period.

The Racial Distribution of the People in Ancient India (1600 BC- 500 BC)

We have proved in earlier chapters that the Mediterraneans or the Semites migrated from Sumer and founded Indus Valley Culture in

Chalcolithic Age i.e. about five thousand years before present. They came through the route of Baluchistan. Similarly the second race was Alpine, which entered through North West passes and settled in Indus Valley in mature Harappan Age i.e. about 2100 B.C. According to some scholars this race added much to the Harappan civilization in North and Central India and got blended to a great extent with the early Harappan population i.e. Australoid and Dravidian races. Aryan speaking, white race of central Asia entered through North West passes and invaded Indus Valley at about 1600 B.C. As a result of which early population was divided into two major parts, one part remained confined to the West and other to the East. Above division is confirmed by R. Shaffer[2], he asserts : "In another migration the Iranian were the first to descend the Saryu (of Afghanistan). They were followed by the Indo-Aryan who forced the Iranians to scatter East and West, where they became eastern and the Western Manavah, the earliest race in India. "

We have shown in earlier chapter that Yadus appeared in Gujrat and Maharashtra region in the Mahabharata (950 BC) and pre-Mahabharata period. Hence it seems that these Yadus etc were mainly known as Western Manavah, the lunar race of India, against the solar race i.e. the Eastern Manavah to which Ikshwakus belonged. These Ikshwakus or Yakshus first of all appeared on the bank of Yumuna in the ten kings war of Rigvedic (VII-83-7 and VII-18-19) period (1500-1100 BC) and force us to believe that it was a real historical event and they were already a mixedup race.

Above division of mankind in ancient India is confirmed by Dr. Jyoti Prasad Jain also. He produces his observations[3]–

"In ancient time, the human society of India was mainly divided in to three groups, whose customs, culture and philosophical thoughts were different from each other. The first group used to reside in the eastern plain of North India i.e. the region spreading from the Doaba of Ganga and Yamuna upto Anga and Magadha. These people were peace loving and Vegetarian. They believed in philosophical thoughts of life after death or rebirth, existence of soul and later life. They worshipped idols and venerated their divinities. They had faith in selfcontrol and practised Yoga for longer life and health. The basis of their ethos was principles of non-violence and renunciation. Similarly tendency of their culture was much towards spiritualism. This was perhaps due to the effect of climatic conditions and geographical situation of their country and also availability of vegetarian food product in abundance .... This group of people was known as Manavya Banshi, simply because Manus and Kulkars took birth in this race. They were, spiritually and intellectually, much superior than the other groups, that is why they began to call themselves Aryans aslo (It means they were not Aryan in origin). The last Manu and first man Tirthankar, Rishabhdeva took birth in this Manavya race of Madhya desha,

The second group was limited mostly to the hilly track of South and East. Although spiritually they were inferior to Manavah but were far ahead in the field of art, craft and industry. .... But they accepted Manavah as their spiritual and religious guide (Guru). Manavah developed spiritualism but the other Vidyadhars brought high proficiency in the field of science and technology. They were divided into many families like Nag (serpent), Richchhas (Bear), Yakshas, Vanaras (Monkeys) etc. In due course of time they occupied many countries of south and Islands of Indian ocean. Later on they came to be known as Dravidians. Both the groups practised intermarriage and developed close relations,which caused intermixing of their bloods. ......Rishabhadeva son of Nabhi of Ayodhya country, ended the savage period of stone Age and laid down foundation stone of occupation based civilization on earth. The region falling between Ayodhya and Hastinapur was main centre of this new culture...... . He himself was known as Ikshwaku and as such became progenitor of oldest Kshatriya family of Ikshwaku. .... His Chakravarty (Lord paramount) son Samrāt Bharata tried to unite the whole Bharata into one large political unit for the first time. After his name this country is known as Bharat Varsha. .... His another son was Dravida who is said to be progenitor of later Dravidian race."

Dr. Jyoti Prasad further informs on the same pages that third group of that society was of Aryan race, which was settled in the North West region of India. All details of information of Dr Jain cannot be said to be absolutely historical, however its main parts, are of immense historical value. We can draw following conclusion from this description :

(1) Long headed Dravidians and round headed Iranians got mixed up. This view of inter-marriage and blending of Iranians and Dravidians, is supported by Dr. Jani (Chronology of Gujrat P-24).

(2) Estern Manavas came close to Aryan race.

Last Longer Conflict Between the Aryans and the Non-Aryans

Above Conflict of two ethnical groups of Aryans and Dravido-Iranian continued politically, socially, philosophically and linguistically from beginning to end which appears in the form of Deva-Sura-Sangram in the whole of the Sanskrit literature. They (Dravido-Iranian) developed their own non-Vedic religions like Jainism and Buddhism and introduced a system of Megalithic graves, for disposal of their dead bodies in Central and Western India. They knew no caste system and the basis of their society was equality and brotherhood. Dr Ambedkar agrees on this point but with a bit difference. He[4] asserts "Aryans were divided into two groups (Deva and Asura) but both had cultural differences, one was called Rigvedic and other Atharva-Vedic Aryans. The Rigvedic Aryans believed in performing of sacrifice and Atharva Vedic Aryans believed in hocus-pocus (Mantra Tantras). Their thoughts regarding origin of universe were quite different. Their cultural conflict was so serious that the Rigvedic Aryans did not recognize Atharvaveda and Upnishadas (in their religion) for a very long time and whenever, they did, they called their Vedas as Vedant, now a days, the meaning of the word 'Vedant' is taken to be extract of Vedas, but in those days its meaning was opposite i.e. Ved-Vāhya (away from Vedas) that is why AtharvaVeda is not considered to be as sacred as Rigveda."

Here, the viewpoint, that both the Asuras and the Devas were Aryan is not acceptable. Devas were Aryans who came from central Asia. (See Vol I of this series). Where as Asuras were Assyrians (Chattopadhyaya S. P-8) who composed Atharva-veda in which (See chapter. I. P P. 9-11) the mention of name of serpents like Aligi, Viligi has been made. It has been proved earlier that these were the names of Assyrian Naga kings and this book was composed by Assyrian priest (Black Brahmana) who were socially, racially, politically and linguistically different from Aryan (See chapters VI, VII, VIII). Since then new findings of Archaeology, anthropology, genetics and sociology and their fresh interpretations have come up and turned the tables. This description of conflict of two institutions of thoughts shows that, after, the native people had been defeated in the war of weapons and subjugated completely, this new cultural, philosophical and sociological conflict, began. This new conflict, vertually, took place between the Kanvas or Black indigenous priests and the White or Sweta Aryan Brahman priests. The inclusion and recognition of Atharv-Veda and Upnishadas by the Vedic Aryan Brahmans, after a long conflict, meant the non-Aryan purohits (priests) were recognized as Brahmans, though they were kept on a lower ladder of social system and mutual dining and marrying was not permitted between both of them which is still continuing. It means, beforehand these black Brahmnas were a part of fourth Varna.

H.L. Kosare elucidates above increasing enmity of Devas and Asuras[5] as follows :

"Brahmā, created seven real Lokas or world, from them first three were Trilokas (three world) and the fourth 'Maharloka'. The people living in the Trilokas were Devas or Aryans and in Maharloka were Asur or Nagas. It can be surmised from the above that, till the time there was no cultural rivalry between Iranians and Aryans, goodwill between the Devas of Triloka and Nagas of Maharlok was existing, but later conflict began for supremacy of class and superiority of cultures. Ultimately Iranian Nagas and Asuras, who are generally called Dravidians, were united together and their joint culture began to be called Asura or Anārya culture by the Indo-Aryans. In Rigveda, they have been called Dasas. The word Dahak is Indo-Iranian. Its Sanskrit form is 'Das.' Ahi-dahak was the name of a Naga king. Ahi means Nag and Sanskrit form of Dahak is 'Das' hence all the Nagas are called 'Das'. Ahivritra is called 'Das'. Here the reference of Nagas of Mahar-lok (Maharashtra) is notable. Vishwarupa, the nephew of Ahivritra was priest of Devas like Indra, and out of suspicion he was killed by Indra. This was one of the causes of conflict between the Nagas and the Devas. Because the Aryans were subject of Indra hence Nagas had enmity with Aryans also. Before, above enmity of Iranians and Indo-Aryans, Devas also used to live in Maharloka or Nagloka and they had friendly relations also. According to Rigveda, (VIII-96-9 AJĀYUDHĀSO ASURĀDEVAḤ) all Devas were included into Asuras. (Dharmanand Kosambi, "Hindu Sanskriti Aur Ahimsa P-28). It appears from this event that before this enmity there was mutual co-existence, co-habitation and cultural co-ordination between Devas and Nagas, but conception of separate Maharloka also existed."

But above view of H.L. Kosare seems to show a temporary or timely cultural relations of two ethnical groups. This horrible enmity of Aryans and non-Aryan Dasas is well preserved in Rigvedic accounts. Particularly Indra and Ahivritra had dagger's drawn enmity. Indra devastated 99 and hundred castles of Sambar (RV. II-19-6 and VI-31-4), seven castles of Shardasur (RV. VI-20-10) and many other towns of Piparu (RV. I-51-5) were put to fire (RV III-12-6 and II-15-4) and a very high number of Dasyus, Dasas and Asuras were massacred i.e. 50,000 (RV IV-16-13); 30,000 (RV IV-30-21); 50,000 IV-30-15) and 60,000 (VI-26-6) etc.

Two fierce battles were fought between Aryans and non-Aryan during Rigvedic period. This has been very well analysed by S.B. Roy—"The first of these battles is of Harappa, (Hariyupiya) in which Harappa was conquered by Chāyaman, the father of king Sudasa and Varasikha, king of Hariyupiya was killed and finally the granary of Harappa (Yavyavati) was looted and 3000 armoured guards were killed (R.V. VI-27 5,6). In the second battle of 10 kings which was also fought at the bank of river Parushni (Ravi) flowing very close to Harappa, the Asuras were defeated by the Devas (Keith, CHI PP 71-72). It was a total victory of the Devas (Rigvedic Aryans) and total rout of the Asura-Danavas (IV-42-8,9) or Harappans in the region of Harappa. In this battle, the Panchjanya (Puru, Yadu, Druhyu, Anu and Turvasa) the Harappans were finally defeated in their attempt to regain Hariyupia.[6] Sudasa established the Rigvedic hegemony. These conflicts are indicative of showing that Aryans and non-Aryans were two different ethnic groups.

Decline of the Vedic Culture

Decline of Vedic culture began after the terrible destruction of the Mahabharata War. Manu was appointed in the form of chief officer or as an (religious) administrative authority in Vedic society. (Although it was non-Aryan institution in origin adopted by Aryan) It is said that only fourteen Manus were appointed during the period of exaltation of Aryan people. The fourteenth Manu was Suparna, whose date is about 950 B.C. which is also an accepted period of Mahabharata war. But this fourteenth Manu was the last one. In usual circumstances fifteenth Manu would have been appointed between 700-500 B.C.[7]. But, by this time the circumstances of Vedic society had changed to such an extent that after 950 B. C. no Manu could be appointed.

What was the reason behind this misshapenning ? Apparently there were three reasons. (1) Due to horrible destruction of Mahabharata war, Vedic culture and power had fallen into disuse. (2) A fresh wave of Naga-Asuras, the builders of Megaliths had reached between 1000-800 B.C. from West, who were dead opponents of Aryan race, and equipped with iron technology and strong iron war weapons. (3) Development of non-Vedic Jain and Buddhist Shraman culture which attacked, Vedic culture with its full force after the Mahabharat War.

Decline of the Power of Aryan Kshatriyas

According to the Mahabharat account probably most of the Kshatriyas of North took part in the Mahabharata war, some of them in favour of Kurus and others in favour of their opponents Pandavas. Kshatriyas in a very high number were killed, this number was extremely so high that a saying came into being that all the Kshatriyas were exterminated. In comparison to Indigenous non-Aryans, the population of Aryans was already very meagre[8], and due to rigidity of laws of Varna system only Kshatriyas were permitted to take part in war[9], this meagre number was also being consumed in day-to-day war-fare. Thus on one hand the population of Kshatriya was reducing to a great extent and on the other, peoples of other three Varnas were not allowed in general to adopt occupation of Kshatriyas for the defence of the Nation. Such an act was highly objectionable and sinful, punishable to the extent of death.[10] Thus, this ban on recruitment of warriors caused a great fall in the population of Kshatriyas. This fall was further added by Brahman Rishi Parashu Rama, a deadly antagonist of Kshatriyas, who came out on a move to exterminate Kshatriyas from the earth as many as 21 times. This was the main cause of slipping away of political power from the hands of Aryan Kshatriyas.

The Revival of Naga Power (1100-500 B.C.)

We have shown earlier that a fresh wave of Asur-Nagas, equipped with iron technology and Iron war-weapons, reached India at about 1000-800 B.C.[11] The Mahabharata war was an event of Chalcolithic Age. Aforesaid Iranian-Nagas were the first who brought Iron and Iron technology with them. The Iron war weapons were much stronger than the war weapons of copper. This proved their superiority on the Aryan race. The basis of indigenous tribal society was the prevalence of Sangha or republic system (See Chapter VI PP 124-25), where every member of Sangha was compulsorily a warrior or Kshatriya well versed in the art of using arms or they had a citizen's army. Taking part in the war was compulsory for each member. In this way, in case of arising of crisis of enemy attack on their country, warriors in desired number could be called and a largest force could be built in no time. Such a Sangha or republic system has been called "Nation-in-arms" by K.P. Jayaswal[12]. On the other hand the occupation of warrior was confined to Kshatriyas only among the Vedic Aryan society. This was one of the main causes of the downfall of Vedics and arising of Naga power.

The Development of Shraman (Buddhist and Jain) Culture

The Jains, who, have been called Asuras by Brahmanical authors, applied the term Siddha to their defied ascetics of the twenty four Tirthankars or defied anchorites of the Jains, all were kshatriyas (warrior) and twenty two of them were of the solar race of Ikshwaku (Jaina Sutra, Jacobi P-218) No wonder, if they were closely connected with the sun and the serpent.[13]

Jain religion had its roots in the Indus Valley religion.[14] Its tradition of Tirthankar was definitely non-Aryan. These Tirthankars were 24 in numbers, the first Tirthankar was Rishabha Dev or Ādināth whose emblem was bull or Vrashbha, which was a most favourite religious animal of Indus Valley. As a matter of fact numerous seals have been found out from Indus Valley which bear figures of bull along with Yogis in standing posture.

It can be surmised from this that these are the figures of Yogishwar Rishabha along with his emblem of bull. The word 'Rishabha' or 'Vrshabha' means religion, perhaps this is because the Tirthankar first of all, appeared in the form of Rishabha in the world. The word Rishabha also means Vrashabha which is also his emblem. According to Prof Pran Nath Vidyālankar Indus Valley religion was related to Jainism, not only this he has also noted on one of the seal[15] (No 449), recovered from there, the word JIN-E-E-SARAH (JINESWAR God of Jains) marked or inscribed on it. From there some statues of Yogis also have been recovered which had umbrella of hood of Cobra over head, which can be related to seventh Tirthankar Supāshp.

It appears, from the above description, that RishabhaDeva preached his religious teachings to the people of Indus Valley age in either form, and his twenty three successors upto the age of Mahavira, preached teachings of whatever religion that was definitely non-Aryan Shramana, related to indigenous Naga tribe. It shows this religion was developed by the Shramana of Manavya Gotra. This view is corroborated by the opinion of L.H. Mills; which is being quoted by Nalinee M. Chapelkar[16]: "Magism makes the world consisted of two principles, the good principle Ahuramazda and Angra Mainyu the bad principle". Further he asserts "That the Sankhya is an Asura religion. Now these Asuras are Mlechchhas, referred to in the ancient Sanskrit literature and according to him these are original settlers in India before coming of Aryans and they were the originator of Sānkhya philosophy and later Buddha and Jain religion (Journal of K.R. Coma Oriental Institute Vol I P-5 Bombay 1922-26)." Further Nalinee M. Chapelkar on Page 33 produces the views of Shamshastri : "The Mahabharata (Adiparva-67) describes the Buddhists and the Jains as descendants of .the ancient Asuras. Again Kapilas Sankhya philosophy is said to be non-Vedic opposed to the religions of the Veda." It is obvious that Buddha and Jain religions are non-Vedic and non-Aryan.

Neminath and Parashwa Nath :

Shri Nemi Nath[17] or Arishtinemi was twenty second Tirthankar, who lived in the Mahabharata Age and he was a near relative of Shri krishna. Colonel Tod throws light on their relation,[18] "Nemi Nath was contemporary of Shri Krishna Yadava, he was also his near relative (cousin). Both had epithets denoting their complexion; for Arishti the surname of Nemi, has the same importance as Shyam and Krishna, the black; though the later is of a less ethiopic hue than Nemi."

It is clear from this that Nemi Nath preached[19] his religious thoughts in a period while the Mahabharata was being fought i.e. about 950-1000 B.C. Parashwa Nath was 23rd Jain Tirthankar.[20] He is always represented with the seven hoods of a Naga expanded over his head. Fergusson found, the serpent in all the Jain temples at Abu. He was born in the house of Ashwasena who was king of Banaras. The name of his mother was Vama Devi (Brahma devi.) His Gotra is said to be Kashyapa.

Devbhumi Suri, in his book 'Parashva Nath Charitra' has called him Ikshwaku Banshi (family) and Videh Khattia in Bhuridutta Jataka (543). Some scholars are of this view that the words Kashyapa and 'Ikshwaku' being synonym, Ikshwaku has been taken instead of Kashyapa. But their is difference between Gotra and Bansha or family. Bansha denotes heredity or race and Gotra Guru (Gurudom) to which one belongs. First of all, there were eight Gotras after the names of eight Rishis, which were in reality institutions. This is the main reason that out of twenty four, twenty two Tirthankars were of Kashyapa Gotra (but of different families). Some scholars think that Kashyapa was a Jain Muni. In Mahapurana (94-22-23) he has been said to be Uragbanshi, Urg means Nag. His emblem was serpent or Nag.

On the date of birth of Parashwa Nath, D.D. Kosambi[21] produces a most genuine account :" Two hundred forty three years before the birth of Gautama Buddha, he began his mission of religious preaching, the date of birth of Gautama Buddha, is 623 B.C. This date has recognition of Buddhist tradition. In this way Parashwa Nath would have begun his preaching in about (623 + 243) 866 B.C. . This is to be noted that he began his preaching at the age of 21 years. Therefore, we have to accept his date of birth (866 + 21) 887 B.C. . Thus it is quite clear from this account that he began his mission of preaching of Shraman religion just after the Mahabharat War (950 B.C)." Because he was also a prince like Buddha, therefore he and his Shraman Dharma, became very popular. We have most authentic evidence in support of it. According to V.D. Mahajan,[22] "He had eight Ganas and eight Gandharas, 16,000 Shramans and their followers and Arya Dutta was prominent among them. About 38000 nuns (Bhikhuni) were his followers and 1, 64000 men and 3, 27000 women adopted his path. At the age of 100 year he achieved his Mahanirwana (left the world) on the peak of Samet mountain."

In this way, Parashwa Natha came up as rescuer of re-awakened Nagas in the form of main source of their inspirer and a venerable god. On the one hand, history of this age was taking a great turn, because, Vedic, Brahmanical culture, religion and power had begun to deteriorate; on the other hand, the follower of Shraman culture, Vratya Kshatriya Nagas of Dravidian race were reviving and coming into power all over India.[23]

As such revolution of Shraman religion, coming of Nagas into power, beginning of Iron Age and Megalithic culture, at about 1000-800 BC (later Mahabharata period) all seems to be different eyelets of one and the same large chain.

After, deterioration of Vedic culture and power, Parashwa Nath began whatever movement of Shraman religion, that brought a great revolutionary change in the society. It seems, he was the real founder of Shraman religion and culture. Whatever flame of Shraman religion, was lit up by Parashwa Nath in 9th century B. C., that continued burning and after a period of about two centuries when Buddha and Mahavira took their birth on this sacred land, that turned into a forest conflagration and it spread not only in the whole of India but also in most of Asia.

Buddha and Mahavira

Sakya Buddha[24] was of solar race and descendant of Ikshwaku. At the beginning of his religious carrier he was sheltered and protected by the Naga Raja Muchilinda (see Illustration no. IV; Mahabagga (S.B.E.) i-3, 2). Throughout his life, he was on friendly terms with the Naga people, and at his death Naga kings claimed to share his relics and built stupa over them.

How close[25] was the relation between Buddhism and these descendants of Asuras, we may see it in the bas-reliefs and sculptures at Amaravati, Sanchi and other stupas. In these stupas the Naga people are shown as engaged in adoration of Buddha or Buddhist emblems. The serpent, in several of the Amaravati sculptures, occupies the place of honour in the Dagoba, which is usually assigned to Buddha himself. And in some of them Buddha is shown as having his head sheltered by the expanded hood of a seven headed Nagas which was the distinctive mark of a Naga Raja.

Buddha was born in 567 B.C. and achieved Nirvana in 487 B.C. The name of his father was Suddhodan and his mother was Mahāmāyā, Suddhodan was the king of Kapilavastu Gana. He is said to be Sakya Kshatriya of Ikshwaku family. We have expressed earlier that Pārashwa Nāth was also of Ikshwaku family and of Naga race. Famous hero of Ramayana, Rama was also of Ikshwaku family. According to Dr. Buddha Prakash[26] the word Yakshu, Akvasa, Akkaka, Yakaku, Yaksu and Ikshwaku are different linguistic variation of one original word. These people might have related to Hyksos,[27] who were semites and they invaded Egypt in about 1750 B.C. They were in origin long headed mediterranean or Dravidian type (See chapter V PP 91-92 for detail). It means Buddha was not Aryan. Similar to other non-Aryan indigenous people Sakyas also had Gan Sangh-Gan tantra (tribal republic) system.[28] Sakya-Gana was a associate of Vajji Gan-Sangha. Similarly these Sakyas had matriarchal family system. Buddha had himself said that four ancestors of his Sakya-Gana Okkamuk, Karkund, Hastinăk and Sinisur, who were exiled sometime back, were of okkaku (Sanskrit Ikshwaku) king of Kausal. They had married their real sisters. When Okkaku came to know the reality then he welcomed them with great pleasure.[29] (See chapter VI PP 164-65 for detail). Here the name Hastinak shows they were of Naga race like Sishunak.

Mahavira, the twenty fourth Jain Tirthankar, was contemporary of Buddha. He was born in the non-Aryan Vratyā Lichchhavi family of Vaisali. He was also of Kashyapa Gotra like Parashwa Natha. This family, similar to Sakyas, was also born from a real sister and brother (See chapter VI P-161) His father Siddhartha (of Vaisali) was related by marriage to Bimbasara king of Magadha. Mahavira got engaged with his cousin-sister (daughter of father's sister), but since he took an oath to remain bachelor throughout his life, hence marriage could not be matured. It is apparent because Lichchhavis also had non-Aryan family tradition of matriarchy hence they were also non-Aryan.[30]

In 6th century B.C. Buddha and Mahavira began a movement of their Shraman religion and culture. They opposed the Vedic Brahmanical philosophy of Atma-Parmatma and raised question against the concept of God's creation of Vedas and declared Vedic Varna and caste system unhuman and harmful to nation and established a casteless society based on the principles of equality and brotherhood.

The Movement of Nagas from Takshila towards Hastinapur in terms of Archaeology

The defeat of Irano-Dravidian people of Indus Valley Civilization at the hand of Aryans, was in fact defeat of serpent worshippers. Many groups of them fled away Eastward under the pressure of Aryan invasion from the West. They followed the route of sites of Nagar Distt Jalandhar (the word Nagar means related to Nagas) Dhaderi, Katpalon (both is Distt Ludhiana) and Bhagwanpura (near Kurukshetra), from where later Harappan (OCP) and PGW (Aryan) cultures (deposit of later lying on the earlier) have been explored belonging to a period between 1600-1500 B.C. In the long run, one of their groups settled at Hastinapur where from culture of ochre coloured pottery of later Harappans has been unearthed by archaeologists,[31] which is known as period-I and its date has been fixed about 1300 B.C. After a deserted period of one foot deposit falls the period-II, which is said to be the culture of Kauravas, whose period has been decided to be between 1100-800 B.C., from where Painted Grey Ware pottery (PGW) has been discovered. Perhaps due to coming of Aryan they had already deserted the site for the powerful barbarian invaders and settled in the forest growing around it known as Khandav Vana.

In the Mahabharta, there is a legend of putting the Khandava-Van into fire by the Arjuna Pandava. Arjuna did so with complete preparations hence, this caused a heavy annihilation of Nagas living therein. The detailed description of this annihilation is given in Mahabharata in chapter 228. This description is so terrible that in face, the invasion of Muhammad Ghajani is meagre.[32] Under the pressure of this time of trouble, Nagas went to Indra for seeking his help. Indra helped them by pouring shower of rain water. At that time the Takshaka, the king of Nagas, was at Kurukshetra, his infant son, Ashwasena was surrounded by the burning flames and his wife, to save their son from this danger, tried to flee with him, but Arjuna shooted an arrow to cut his head but Indra by inducing fast blow of air turned the direction of arrow and saved Ashwasena.

This is notable that the name of father of Parashwa Nath was also Ashwasena but their definite relation can not be established at this juncture of our knowledge.

This is apparent from this legend that a very large population of Nagas was hidden or living in Khandava forest and it was necessary to make them flee for complete possession of the surrounding forest of Hastinapur, that is why this dense forest was put into flames of deadly fire. We have already said in Chapter IX P.P. 244 that the progenitors of Krishna who were Nagas were feudal Chief of Hastinapur, later Indraprastha became the chief centre of their power.

Now let us examine the above archaeological and chronological evidences and compare them with the legendary events described in Mahabharata :

(1) Carbon dating of Timargarha or Swat Valley culture of Aryan........... 1700 B.C.

(2) End of the Indus Valley Civilization (Harappa) and coming of Aryan .... 1600 B.C.

(3) Completion of composition of Rigveda and depiction of conflict between Indra and Ahivritra .... 1500 B.C.

(4) Reaching of Aryans (both groups) at Bhagwanpura GW and PGW site near Kurukshetra T.L. dating .... 1500 BC.

(5) Hastinapur period-I OCP or later Harappans (Reaching of Nagas) .... 1300 B.C.

(6) Period of conflict (deserted period) 1 feet ... 1300-1100 BC.

(7) First settlement of Kurus in Hastinapur intensive conflict began for Khandava forest ...... 1100 B.C.

(8) Period II PGW settlement of Kurus in (Hastinapur 7 feet deposit.) .... 1100-800 B.C.

(9) Period of the Mahabharat war (period of beginning of fall of Vedic Culture and revival of Naga Culture) 950 B.C.

(10) Religious movement of Parashwa Natha 887-787 B.C.

(11) Age of Buddha and Mahavira 567-487 B.C

We can draw following conclusions from the aforesaid cultural stratification and chronology.

(1) The cultural stratification and chronology synchronizes each other and proves natural movement of Aryans from West to East.

(2) Carbon dating of settlement of kurus at Hastinapur Period II (1100-800 B.C.) is strikingly very close to the Mahabharata War's known date (950 B.C.) and indicates that this event is historical.

(3) Parashwanath began his Shraman movement at a period (887-787 B.C.) known as downfall of the Vedic Culture and revival of Naga culture after the Mahabharata war (950 BC) which is a striking date proving it a true historical event.

Relations of Kurus and Nagas

Kurus not only annihilated Nagas, but established matrimonial relation also. According to the Mahabharata, one of the wives of Arjuna was Ulupi a Naga maiden. The mother of Kunti was also a daughter of Naga king. Shrikrishna being Yadava was also Naga. He also established matrimonial relation with Kurus, his father's sister Subhadra got married to Arjuna.

In the later Mahabharata period there were twelve important kingdoms in north and central India; Vatsa, Kuru, Panchala, Sursena, Kausala, Kashi, Videh in east, Magadha, Kalinga, Avanti, Mahishmati, and Asamaka. Among them Kuru (Hastinapur), Panchala (Kampil), Kausala (Ayodhyaya), Videha, (Mithila) and Kashi (Varanasi) were most important. Some of the rulers from them were Vedic Aryan Kshatriyas, rest non-Aryan Vratyas or Shraman Kshatriyas.[33]

The Rise of Nagas and Capture of Hastinapur, Kashi and Videha

We have proved earlier that the Assyrians and Iranians in a very high number had entered through the passes of North West and settled in the hilly track near Takshila from where we note repeated movement of Naga princes. According to S.P. Gupta[34] one of the waves of Naga people brought Megalithic culture and iron from Iran. The native Nagas, who as a result of Aryan invasion, had scattered and settled in the hilly track of North West region, got encouraged due to coming of a fresh wave of their brothers from Iran. Since, after the Mahabharata war and its aftermath effects, the Vedic power and culture had fallen into disuse, these Nagas would have come down from hills and began to unite themselves to recapture their lost power. Kurukshetra was the chief kingdom of Pandava family of Hastinapur. In those days Parikshat, the grandson of Arjuna, was on the thrown, during his reigning period, the Nagas began to raise their heads.

Particularly[35] the Nagas of Takshila of North-West region and watery delta of river Sindh known as Pātālpuri, became very powerful. Aroused with new courage, they began furious attack on the Kuru kingdom. Parikshat was killed in a battle with them. His son Janmejaya also had to wage war against Nagas throughout his whole life. Although he annihilated them in a very high number but he failed to check up their grown power. Thus Pandava kingdom was slowly becoming feeble. Janmejaya[36] was succeeded by Shatanik and Satānik by Ashwameghadutt and Ashwameghadutt by Adhisimkrishna. Diwakar in Ayodhya, Senjit in Magadha, Janak Ugrasen in Videha and Pravāhan Jaivalika were contemporary kings of Adhisim. At the time of Nichachhu, the son of Adhisim in addition to everlasting raids of Nagas, a furious attack of red-locusts also took place over the Kuru country and as a result of which furious famine happened to come and in the long run his capital Hastinapur was washed away in a terrible flood of the river Ganga (about 800 B.C.). The king of Kuru family left his country for Vatsā whose capital was Kausambi. In this way, the Kshatriya power of Uttar-patha, the top-most follower of Vedic traditions, at last came to an end in Kuru country. Later on it was taken over by the Nagas. From that time Gajpur or Hastinapur came to be known as Nagpur or Hastinagpur.

Above event, all over, can be termed as revival of Nagas. The incident of washing away of Hastinapur in a terrible flood of Ganga is supported by archaeological evidences. At the end of the Hastinapur period II (800 BC) excavator B.B. Lal[37] has recovered evidences of a disastrous flood. Later this site was deserted for some period. This proves that above event is historical.

The kingdom of Ahichchhatra, its capture by the Nagas of Jain Tradition

The name of Ahichchhatrā is not as old as that of Kāmpila (Vedic Index I P-49) although both figure in Indian literature as capitals of Panchala, the former of Uttara-Panchala and the latter of Dakshina-Panchāla. Adhichchhatra (Skt-Ahichchhatra) certainly finds mention in the Pabhosa cave inscription of Ashādhasena[38] which may be dated about the beginning of the Christian era. While its ancient name was Parichakra[39] (Parivakra). According to the Jaina Vividha-tirtha-Kalpa, Samkhyāvati was the earlier name of Ahichchhatrā described as the capital of Kuru Jangala.

As for the origin of the name of Ahichchhatra,[40] Cunningham observes : "The name is written Ahikshetra (M.B. Vana-ch 252) as well as Ahichchhatra, but the local legend of the Adi-rājā and the Naga, who formed a canopy over his-(Parasawamin) head, when asleep, shows that the latter is the correct form. The meaning of the name is serpent-umbrella. This grand old fort is said to have been built by Raja Ādi, an Ahir"

But Jinaprabha sūri in his Vividha-tirtha-kalpa gives another story for the origin of the name of Ahichchhatrā according to which when the demon Kamatha caused out of his previous spite an incessant rain flooding the city of Samkhyavati where Pārsasvamin was then staying, the serpent-king Dharanīndra hurried to the spot with his chief queen and protected the Lord by coiling himself round his body and spreading a canopy of one thousand heads over his head. Thereafter the city of Samkhyāvati came to be known by the name of Ahichchhatra.[41]

It should be noted that Ptolemy's spelling of the name as Adisadra corresponds with Adhichchhatrā, met with in the Pabhosā cave inscription of Ashādhasena.[42]

The Satpatha Brāhmana[43] mentions Kraivya the king of Panchāla among the ancient rulers of India, who had performed the Asvamedha sacrifice. The Aitareya Brāhmana[44] introduces us to another ancient and most powerful king of the Panchāla named Durmukha. He is said to have made extensive conquests in every direction. The Pali Kumbhakara Jataka[45] speaks probably of the same king. The Satapath Brahmana (XIII-5-4) cites several gathas in praise of a third powerful king of Panchala named Sonasātrāsāha, who had performed horse sacrifice on a very grand scale. According to Mahabharata (Adi ch 94), the powerful king of Panchala, at the time of the Kurukshetra war, was Drupada, from whose hands the northern portion of his kingdom was wrested by the Kurus who had established there Brahmana Guru Drona as king.

The kingdom[46] of Panchala continued to exist even after the Mahabharata war. The Jain Vividhatirthakalpa mentions the name of the king Harishena who was said to be tenth chakravarti king of this kingdom. Similarly the same authority mentions the name of another king named Brahmadatta. It seems that like Hastinapur the kingdom of Panchala also came under the sway of indigenous Naga kings during the life time of 23rd Jain tirthankar Parashwanatha (887-787 BC) who was provided with a canopy of cobra-hoods by Adiraja and the Naga of Panchala to save from rainwater. Above name of king of Brahmadatta also seems to be of the same origin as Brahmadatta of Kashi or Naga origin to which family of Parashwa Nath also belonged. This Brahmadatta seems to be a real historical king whose mention is made in the Ramayan[47] and also in Jataka[48] stories. It is certain that by the rise of Buddhism Panchala, like Kuru, Matsya and the rest, attained the position of a self governing oligarchical republic.[49]

The Panchala finds mention in the Arthasastra of Kautilya as a ruling clan who represented a Sangha or oligarchical form of government[50]. This detail of kings goes to prove that Panchalā remained an independent state at least for a century after the demise of the Buddha i.e. until it was conquered by Mahapadam Nanda and brought under the sway of the monarch of Magadha. Again evidently it became independent in post-Ashokan time.[51] Gargi Samhita alludes to a Greek invasion of Saketa, Mathura and Panchala. According to B.C. Law in about the beginning of the Christian era, Northern Panchala rose into temporary importance under the rule of Ashadhasena, "who belonged to the royal family of Adhichchhatra (Ahichchhatra)."

Viswamitra and Rajrishi Tradition in Indigenous Culture

We have shown in chapter V P-107 FF that non-Aryan Rajrishi tradition took its birth in Western Asia, which was transferred to Indus Valley along with the migration of Sumerians. This is further confirmed by the Rigvedic description of Ahivritra Rajrishi of Indus Valley Civilization and nephew of Asuraś, Vishwarupa, who (both) were killed by the Aryan military chief Indra. According to a reference in Taitreya Samhita kand 2/5/1 as soon as Indra killed Vritra, 'Brahma-hatya' came out of his body and encircled Indra.

M. Haraprasad Sastri thinks that the word Mitra is of Persian origin.[52] Mitra or Mithra was sun deity of Persian folks.[53] We have a legend from Aitreya Brahmana. VII-13-18. Visvamitra is alluded to as being the Hotri-priest of king Harischandra and as belonging to the tribe of the Bharatas. He is also addressed as Rajaputra, and his sons are called Kusikas. The outlines of the legend are as follows : King Harischandra of the family of Ikshwaku having no son, promised to Varuna, by the advice of Narada, that if a son should be born to him he would sacrifice him to that god. A son was accordingly born to the king, who received the name of Rohita; but Harischandra, though called upon by Varuna, put off from time to time, on various pleas for the fulfilment of his promise. When the father at length consented, the youth himself refused to be sacrificed and went into the forest. After passing six years there he met a poor Brahman Rishi called Ajigartta who had three sons, the second of whom, Sunassepa, he sold for a hundred cows to Rohita who brought the young Brahman to be sacrificed instead of himself. Varuna accepted the vicarious victim, and arrangements were made accordingly. Visvamitra being the Hotri-priest, Jamadagni the Adhvaryu, Vasista the Brahman, and Ayasya the Udgatri (TOSYA HE VISVAMITROHOTA ASIJ

JAMADAGNIR ADHVARYUR VASISHTHA BRAHMA AYASYAH UDGATA)". The sacrifice was not, however, completed although the father received a hundred more cows for binding his son to the sacrificial post, and a third hundred for agreeing to slaughter him. By reciting verses in honour of different deities in succession Sunassepa was delivered : and at the request of the priests took part in the ceremonial of the day. The rest of the legend runs like this. Sunassepa got up and went towards Visvamitra. Sunassepa's father Ajigartta said," O sage, restore my son to me.'' Visvamitra replied, "No the gods have given him to me'' (DEVAḤ ARSĀTAḤ). Thus he became Visvamitra's son, Devarata. Kapiloma and Vabhariva were his descendants. Ajigartta tried to convince his son but he flatly refused to come to him. He told Visvamitra "O Prince, whatever his argument I shall never agree to be called a descendant of Angirisa." At this Visvamitra rejoined, "Thou shalt be the eldest of my sons and thy offspring shall be the most eminent. Thou shalt receive my divine inheritance; with this (invitation) I address thee." Sunassepa answered, ''If (thy sons) agree, then for my welfare enjoin on them to be friendly, that so, a chief of the Bharatas, I may enter on thy sonship.'' Visvamitra then addressed his sons. 'Do ye, Madhuchhandas, Rishabha, Renu, Ashtaka, and all ye who are brothers, listen to me, and concede to him the seniority.' Now Visvamitra had a hundred sons, fifty of whom were older then Madhuchhandas and fifty younger. Then those who were older did not approve (their father's proposal). Against them he pronounced (this doom). ''Let your progeny possess the furthest ends (of the country). These are the numerous border-tribes, the Andhras, Pundras, Sabras, Pulindas, Mutibas.'' Most of the Dasyus are sprung from Visvamitra Madhuchhandas with the (other) fifty said, ''Whatever our father determines, by that we abide. We all place thee in our front, and follow after thee''. Then Visvamitra was pleased, and said to his sons, "Ye; my children who, showing deference to me, have conferred upon me a (new) son, shall abound in cattle and in sons. Ye, my sons, the offspring Gathin, who possess in Devarata a man who shall go before you, are all destined to be prosperous; he is your wise instructor. This Devarata, O Kusikas, is your chief; follow him. He will receive you as my inheritance, and obtain all the knowledge which we possess."

But Max Muller[54] and Prof Roth, after in depth study of the subject matter draws a different conclusion : "This, so long a legend (of Sunassepa) neither appears to be historical nor it seems to be correct that all these non-Aryan tribes born of Visvamitra Brahman who was in origin a Kshatriya also (Rājnaya, Kausika)" But this interpretation of learned scholars is not acceptable. I think they have not gone through the ancient, social, religious and historical traditions of Indigenous people of India that is why they have misinterpreted the hidden facts of above legend. According to R.P. Chanda[55] Visvamitra was a non-Aryan black Brahmana or an aboriginal tribal priest (Purohita). There were two separate institutions of Brahmanas : the Black Yajurveda and White Yajurveda ; (The black Indigenous and the white Aryans) which was perhaps the earliest example after recognition of aboriginal tribal priests as Brahmana which would have been achieved after a long struggle (see chapter IX PP 240-41 for detail), most probably just before the composition of Upnishadas yet they (Black Brahmans) remained at a lower ladder of social system than the Aryan Brahmana which is still in prevalence in the modern age, Much light has been thrown in this subject on earlier pages of this chapter (P 254-56).

It seems that the event enshrined in the legend of Sunassepa is nothing but only an effort made by Visvamitra to raise his social position by adapting, Sunassepa or Devarta Kapiloma as his son, who was a son of Ajigartta Arya Brahmana of famous Angirisha lineage. There are evidences, in support of my theory, hidden in this legend, but speak loudly: Here Visvamitra has been addressed as Rājanya or Rajputra and his sons have been called Kushikas. It means Visvamitra was a Rajrishi or God-King of non-Aryan tradition[56] prevalent in Indus Valley (see chapter V P 107-10) a system quite different to Vedic varna. This confirms the viewpoint that Visvamitra was ethnically of aboriginal blood or Andhra tribe which was a branch of great Yadava tribe (Vrashti, Kukkar, Andhaka and Bhoja[57]) As a matter of fact, here, his disobient sons were debarred from the occupation of priesthood and ordered to exile to forest to live with their own tribal brothers like Andhra, Pundra, Sabra, Pulinda, Mutiba etc. who later established joint power in Andhra valley (see P-288-89).

The Audumbaras[58] according to Jayaswal, are not known to the early Paninian literature; but they are mentioned in the Ganapatha in the Rājanya group of republics (Panini IV-2-53). They are placed at the end of the Panjab republics in the earlier list of the Sabha Parvan of Mahabharata (chapter 52). Perhaps they were republican. Their coins of the first century B.C. are found in Northern Panjab which bear legend in Kharoshthi as well as in Brāhmi. They were somewhere between Kangra and Ambala. Their coins show that the Audumbaras had an elective king. The coins bear the 'Lakshana' of a tree, the representation of a building with tall columns and slanting roof which may be their mote-hall or some other public building and the figure of their standard which Cunningham[59] mistook to be a Dharma-Chakra. Accross the field the word Visvamitra is written and a picture of the Rishi given. Perhaps Visvamitra was their National sage or Primogenitor.

Rajrishi tradition was prevailing among the republicans of later period whose chief was formally a sacred person.[60]

The two Pabhosā caves in the neighbourhood of Kausambi preserve two inscriptions of Ashadhasena, king of Adhichchhatra in mixed dialect. The inscriptions record the document of dedication of the caves concerned to the Kasyapiya Arhats by the king Ashādhasena. In one of them, the donor king Ashādhasena is introduced as the maternal uncle of king Brahaspatimitra, and in the other we have mention of four generation of kings beginning with Saunakayana.[61] The Hāthigumpha inscription of Kharvela refers to one Brahaspatimitra as a contemporary king of Magadha. It is not astonishing at all that two of the ancient Indian coins found at Kausambi bear the legend of King-Brahaspatimitra.[62] From above, B.C. Law has concluded that this Brahaspatimitra was prominent sovereign of Magadha.[63] Numerous coins bearing the legend of other Mitra Kings have been found out at Kausambi, Ayodhya, Audumbara, Mathura, in Rohil Khand chiefly at Ahichchhatra or Ramnagar. These Panchala or Ahichchhatra coins alone bear the following names [64]:

(1) Dhruvamitra (2) Suryamitra (3) Phalgunimitra (4) Bhanumitra (5) Bhumimitra (6) Agnimitra (7) Jaymitra (8) Indramitra (9) Vishnumitra (10) Rudra Gupta (11) Bhadraghosa (12) Vāspala

K.P. Jayaswal's[65] information that the earlier Nagas played a part in ousting the Mathura satraps, is confirmed by the fact that we have the line of kings at Mathura with Mitra ending in coins found from Mathura in the period succeeding the satraps as these coins[66] seem later. It mean these Mitras were perhaps of Naga race.

Who were these Mitra kings, and can they be identified with the Sunga and Kanva king mentioned in the Puranas ? Were they the rulers of Ahichchhatra or North Panchala or were they rulers of some other country ? On these questions Cunningham's[67] findings are most valuable he writes—

"As the coins which I am now about to describe are found in Rohilkhand and chiefly at Ahichchhatra, Aonla, and Budaon, it is quite certain that they belong to North Panchala. It has been suggested that they belong to the Sunga kings, who ruled over North India after the Mauryas for 112 years or from B.C. 178 to 66. But the assignment is uncertain, as only of the coin names Agnimitra is found in the Puranic lists of the Sungas. The dates, however agree as all the coins have inscriptions in Ashoka character. I incline rather to assign the coins to a local dynasty of princes as they were very rarely found beyond the limits of the North Panchala, which would not be the case did they belong to the paramount dynasty of the Sungas." From aforesaid detail of description we can reach to the following conclusion :

(1) Because the coins of mitra rulers have been found from Panchala or Rohilkhand region hence, this family would have been the

ruler of this region. The king Brahaspatimitra of Hathigunpha would have been different one, because his coins have not been recovered from Magadha.

(2) Because in the inscription of Pabhosa, caves belonging to the king Ashadhasena of Ahichchhatra dedication, is made to the Kasyapiya Arhat hence he would have been the follower of Jainism, as supported by the name of another king Brahmadatta, the traditional epithet of king of Kashi of Parashwa Nath's Naga family. This is further confirmed by the inclusion of another name of king Adi, a Naga of Ahir origin among the rulers of Panchala. This truth is further confirmed by another evidence that Panchala was ancient centre of Jain religion. B.C. Law[68] informs "That Kampila is claimed as a city where Arshamitra the disciple of Kaundinya, who in his turn was the disciple of the Mahagiri teacher of the Lakshmihara Chaitya of Mithila, came to reside two hundred and twenty years after the demise of Mahavira. The same city is claimed as the place where the Jain saint Gardbhali renounced the world and attained liberation." Thus Ahichchhatra seems to be a centre of Naga kings of Jain tradition.

It is abvious like Hastinapur, Panchala kingdom was also occupied by the Naga rulers, Ashadsena and his sister's son Brahaspatimitrās family seems to be of the same ethnical group.[69]

Most of the scholars think that Sungas were Brahmana of Bhardwaja or Kasyapa Gotra. But H. Hara Prasad Sastri adopted a different view that the suffix of the word mitra in the name of earlier king (Pushyamitra, Agnimitra), is of Persian origin. Hence the aforesaid views are not acceptable. Since the names of other kings[70] of this family such as Andhraka, Pulinda and Ghara are similar to border tribes like Andhra, Pundra, Sabra who were progeny of Visvamitra hence Sunga family also seems to be related to the family of Visvamitra[71] or atleast of his lineage.

Probably during the life time of Buddha or earlier a revolution took place in Videha kingdom. Karāl Janak, the king of Videha was of very amorous nature, hence people killed him. As a result of this event, his rule over Videha came to an end, and a tribal republic rule was established there. In its neighbourhood, in Vaisali a tribal Republic confederacy was developed, the kingdom of Videha got merged in to it. This was Vajji Gana of later historical fame. These people were Shraman worshippers non-Aryan Vratya Kshatriyas.

It is well known that 24th Jain Tirthankar Mahavira was born at Vaisali. He has been called Kashyapa Gotri and Vaisali was one of the largest centres of Jain Shraman worshippers. According to Manu[72] Lichchhavis were of Vratya Kshatriya origin.

In the centre was principal kingdom of Kashi, there[73] too the rule of Urga Banshi or Nagbanshi Vratya non-Aryan Kshatriya had been established. In those days, this was a major political power of central region. Kausal remained under the sway of Kashi many a times. In South, the kingdom of Asamaka situated at the bank of river Godavari with its capital at Potan or Podanpur, was also under the regime of Kashi.

As we have explained on foregone pages that Kashi was kingdom of 23rd Jain Tirthankar Parashwa Nath. Undoubtedly, Ahichchhatra[74] situated in Distt Barriely was the land of his penance. He was of black complexion. Most of his statues recovered from Ahichchhatra are of black colours with cobra heads raised on its heads, undoubtedly he was most venerable god of principalities and tribal republics which had come into existence after the Mahabharata war. According to Adipurana, the founder of Urgabansha, to which Parashwa Nath belonged, was Kashyapa who was a famous Jain Muni, he was also known as Madhava. It seems that there was also possession of Nagas over Gandhara country in the time of Parashwa Nath, because Nāgjit or Naget, the king of Gandhara[75] has been said to be the follower of Parashwa Nath. Perhaps this Naga king Nagjit would have been related to Takshaka, which was thier centre there. It is apparent from the legend of Mahabharata also that the progenitor of Nagas was Kashyapa.[76]

The Revolution and Change of Power in Magadha

After some period, the Magadha also came under sway of Naga dynasty of Kashi. Dr Jyoti Prasad[77] Jain has given a brief account of this incident, how Magadha was taken over by Sishunaga : "In the beginning of 8th century B.C. another revolution took place in Magadha Country. The people of Magadha dethroned their last Brahdrath king and invited Naga king Sishunag to become their king. Sishunag handed over the kingdom of Kashi to his son and himself became the king of Magadha."

Sishunaga[78] belonged to the same Naga family of Kashi in which famous king Brahmadutt and Tirthankar Parashwa Nath of Ikshwaku family were born. In the opinion of K.P. Jayaswal, Sishunaga was the first king of Magadha that is why this dynasty is known as "Saishunak" or 'Sishunag.' The famous[79] king Srenika Bimbsar (587 BC) was among the earlier kings of this dynasty. In Puranas, his father's name has been found Sishunag or Saishunak, in Buddhist literature Bhatti and in Jain literature upsrenik. These Naga Banshi Kshatriyas have been called Vratya in Sanskrit literature.

The name of Sishunaga is applied by the Brahmans to the first king of this dynasty, the Buddhists gave it to the tenth and added the following legend.[80] "On certain occasion one of the chiefs of the courtesans bore a child to one of the Lichchhavi king, but the child proving an abortion, was put in to a basket and at night thrown on a dung-heap. A certain Nagaraja, the tutelar of the city observing it, encircled it with its folds and sheltered it with its hood. The people who congregated there made a noise "Su, Su" to frighten the snake and on examining the basket found the abortion matured in to a male child with every mark of greatness on it. In consequence of this incident he received the name Sishunaga and in time ascended the throne of Magadha" (Turnour's Introduction to the Mahawamsa XXXVII).

It proves that these Sishunagas were of Ikshwaku family and Vratya non-Aryan (Naga) Kshatriya.

The political changes, that took place as a result of Shraman revolution are as follows : All Aryan[81] Kshatriya power of Mahabharata period had come to an end before sixth century B.C. and in their place power of non-Aryan Naga kings were established at Takshila, Pātālpuri, Hastinapur Ahichchhatra, Kausal, Kashi, Magadha, Podanpur and other different regions of the south and similarly a number of republics or tribal confederacies of Vratya Kshatriya like Lichchhavi, Malla, Sakyas, Koliya, Moriya Vaisali-Videha, Malava-Kshudrak, Andhrak-Vrishinis Ambasth-Agraseni were also established. The literature of Brahmanical tradition has called them Kshatriya bandhu. According to Prof Jaychand Vidyalankar, this name is indicative of conveying the feelings of their inferior birth, they were opponent of Vedic-Brahmanical culture. Their language was 'Prakrit' and dresses not superior. They considered Arahatas Venerable instead of Brahmans and worshipped Chaityas.[82]

After Sishunaga, Nanda came into power in Magadha. A very high number of names of the first king of this family are found in the ancient literature. According to some scholars, his name was Vratya Nandi Sishu Naga and he belonged to Saishunak (Sishunag) family himself. Dr. K.P. Jayaswal thinks that the word 'Vratya Nandi' is indicative of his being a Vratya Kshastriya and the name Sishunaga indicates that he belonged to Shrenik (Naga) family. Since there was no direct heir hence, we have to accept that the name Nand shows that there was a change in family, therefore Nanda family was related to Naga family of Sishunaga. The famous king of this family was Nandi Vardhan (449-407 BC) Later on magnanimous and great warrior king Mahapadam Nand came into power.

Above view gets confirmation from James Fergusson[83], he writes : "The second convocation was held 100 years after the death of Buddha, during the reign of Kalasoka and we gather, though some what indistinctly, that his successors, including the nine Nandas till the occasion of the celebrated Chandra-Gupta (325 B.C.), were Nagas or serpent worshippers pure and simple (see note) their coins I belive to be those depicted on all these serpent is the principal symbol (J.A.S.B. Vol VII PL LX No. 7 and 9)."

After Nandas their progeny Mauryas ruled Magadha (332 BC-185 BC) Chandra Gupta Maurya was born from Mura, one of the wife of Mahapadam Nanda, that is why Chandra Gupta and Bindusara were followers of Jainism and Ashoka the Great adopted Buddhism as his state religion, thereby spreading it throughout Asia. Undoubtedly they were non-Aryan Vratya Kshatriyas. They have been called Vidhyadhar Naga in Sangham[84] literature of South and Takshaka by James Tod. But[85] according to Rajputana chronicles Maurya were offshoot of Moriya Naga (Takshak) of Pātālpuri who later became rulers of Chittor with dynasty named Parmar (See chapter VI P-171 for detail).

Summary and Conclusion

According to R. Shaffer, as a result of invasion of Aryans in India, who entered Central Panjab, the earlier population of this land was forced to scatter eastward and westward, where they became the Eastern Manavah and the Western Manavah, Western Manavah were mainly Yadu etc and the eastern Ikshwakus etc. These Yakshus or Ikshwakus first of all appeared in 10 kings war of Rigveda at the bank of river Yamuna. These people were more religious and believed in non-violence. They were much influenced by the culture of Aryans of North West. Later on, the land between Ayodhya and Hastinapur became main centre of their culture, on the other hand the Dravidian of South and Western Manavah were great technicians i.e. artisians and traders who intermarry and intermixed with each other and both with the earlier. Their centre of culture was mainly present Gujrat, South East Rajasthan and Maharashtra.

Two battles were fought in between Aryan and non-Aryan Asuras or Nagas during Rigvedic period. The first battle was fought at Harappa or Hariyupiya in which Harappans were defeated and the town was taken over by Aryan Chayaman, father of king Sudasa. The second battle of 10 kings confederacy was also fought at the bank of river Parushni or Ravi near Harappa in which ten non-Aryan king's confederacy was defeated at the hand of Aryan king Sudasa. In this war Panch-Janyas were also defeated. After all Sudasa established Rigvedic hegemony.

This long conflict between Aryan and non-Aryan remained continued till last and known as Devasur Sangram (Deva and Asura-War).

Decline of Vedic culture began, after the terrible and destructive war of Mahabharata, in which, as is said, almost all the Kshatriyas were exterminated. Similarly their religious system became so weak that the institution of Manu, a religious administrative authority of Vedic society, was discontinued, hence no Manu could be appointed after Suparna, after 950 BC or the Mahabharata war period.

Inspite of the fact, that this period is termed as Dark Age of Aryan culture this was most fabulous period of Naga culture, Iron Age stepped in and Megalithic culture laid its foundation in North, Central and South India. The civilization of Naga was very progressive, on the foundation of which Parashwa Nath, Buddha and Mahavira raised edifice of their Shraman religion and culture, who founded a casteless society, based on the principles of equality and brotherhood. This is known as revival of indigenous Naga Shraman culture.

After the Mahabharata war, Parashwa Nath, the 23rd Jain Tirthankar began his religious activities. It is said that he had 8 Ganas, 8 Gandharas, 16000 Shramanas and 38000 nuns and about 5 lacs of followers, as such it seems that he was the real founder of the shraman religion and culture.

Although, just after the Mahabharata war, downfall of Vedic culture and power had begun yet in fact it could become ineffective in about sixth or seventh century B.C. In the later Mahabharata period, there were twelve important kingdoms in north and central India viz Vatsa, Kuru, Panchala, Sursena, Kausala, Kashi, Videha (in east) Magādha, Kalinga, Avanti, Mahishmati and Asmaka, among them, Kuru (Hastinapur), Panchala (Kampila), Kausala (Ayodhya), Videha (Mithila) and Kashi (Varanasi) were most important. Some of the rulers from them were Vedic Aryan Kshatriyas, rest non-Aryan Vratya or Shraman Kshatriyas.

As soon as the invasion of Aryan began, the Harappans or the Naga worshipping people had to flee eastward and southward, following the route of ancient sites of Nagar (Distt Jalandhar), Dhaderi and Katpalon (Distt Ludhiana) and finally reached Bhagwanpura in the forest of Kurukshetra. From these sites deposit of OCP (1600-1500 BC) or later Harappan Culture and Aryan PGW, later lying on the earlier, has been traced out. While GW and PGW (1500-1000 BC) using Aryans reached there, they further left for east direction and ultimately settled at Hastinapur (1300-1200 B.C). Later on, Aryan people reached there also and forced them to desert this town too. Here Aryan settlement (PGW) began at 1100 BC and ending at 800 B.C.

There is a legend in Mahabharata according to which, Arjuna, Pandava of Aryan race, put the Khandava forest (around Hastinapur) in to fire to exterminate Nagas hidden inside. It was necessary for a complete possession of the land. At that time, Naga king Takshaka was at Kurukshetra. His infant son and queen could hardly be saved from this annihilation. Henceforth the warfare between Takshakas and Pandavas continued till the Pandava king Nichachchhu did not leave Hastinapur (800 BC) for ever. Later on this town was taken over by the Nagas, from that time Gajpur or Hastinapur came to be known as Nagpur or Hastinagpur.

Ahichchhatra (means serpent umbrella), the capital of Panchala was founded by a Naga king of Ahir race. Naga king Dharanindra, who to save Tirthankar Parshwa Nath from the rain, spread a canopy of one thousand heads (hoods) over his head. Thereafter, the ancient city of Samkhyāvati came to be known as Ahichchhatra. This proves that Panchala was also captured by the Naga kings.

Later on, the Naga empire of Kashi of Brahmadutta tradition became important, which had its sway on the whole of the central region of India. Parashwa Natha was also a prince of this royal family.

The people of Magadha dethroned their last Brahdrath king and invited Sishunaga king of Kashi to become their king. Sishunaga handed over the kingdom of Kashi to his son and himself became the king of Magadha. Later Magadha was ruled by Nanda kings, who have been called 'Vratya Nanda Sishunaga.' Hence Magadha also came under sway of kings of Naga race. In this way, by and by most of the Kingdoms of central and eastern India were brought under the rule of Naga kings. Mauryas were progeny of one branch of Moriya Naga of Patalpuri, who were Takshaka or Vahika in origin. Rajput Parmar dynasty of Chittor was their descendant.

References

1. Dutt N.K., "Origin of Caste System in India."
2. Shaffer. R., "Ethnology of Ancient India" PP 43-44.
3. Jain Dr. Jyoti Prasad,"Bhartiya Itihas; Ek Drishti" PP 21-24.
4. Dr. Ambedkar B.R. "The Untouchables" PP 46-47.
5. Kosare H.L. "Prachin Bharata Til Nag" PP- 126-27.
6. Roy S.B. "The Early Aryans of India" Delhi (1989) PP 68-76 and 155.
7. Dr. K.L. Daftari, "The Social Institutions in Acient India" P-93 cited by Kosare HL PP-121-22.
8. Viyogi Naval Vol I PP 191-92.
9. Manu I-89.

   PRAJĀNA RAKSHA NAṀ DĀNMIJYĀ DHYAYANMEV CHA।
   VIŚYEŚVA PRASAKTIŚCHA KSHATRIYASYA SAMĀSTAḤ" ॥

10. Manu VIII-273, IX-224.
11. Gupta S.P. ''Disposal of the Dead and Physical Type in Ancient India'' PP 237-38
12. Jayaswal K.P., '' Hindu Polity'' P-54
13. Oldham C. F. "The Sun and Serpent" P-177.
14. Dr. Jyoti Prasad Jain, P-27.
15. 'Ibid'.
16. (a) Chapelkar M Nalinee, 'Ancient India and Iran' P-34.
    (b) Fergusson also accepts this viewpoint. "Tree and Serpent Worship" P-78.
17. Āchārya Hastimal, "Jain Dharm Ka Maulik Itihas" Part I PP 358-65.
18. Tod James, ''Annals and Antiquity of Rajasthan'' II P-624.
19. Āchārya Hastimal I PP 376-82.
20. (a) Jain Jyoti Prasad PP 36-38 and 45.
    (b) Āchārya Hastimal I PP 480-500.
    (c) Oldham C.F. PP 177-78.
21. Kosambi D. D., "Bhagwan Buddha" PP 36 and 84.
22. (a) Mahajan V.D. "Ancient India" Vol-I P-137.
    (b) Acharya Hastimal Jain I P-501-02.
23. Dr. Jain Jyoti Prasad, P-36.
24. Oldham C F P-178.
25. Ibid.
26. Dr. Buddha Prakash, "Rigveda and the Indus Civilization" PP 101-03.
27. Somerset P. Fry, "History of World" P-73.
28. Gokhle B.G., "Buddhism in Maharashtra" PP. 21-22.
29. Jagdish Kashyapa (B) Dighā Nikaya- Pali Silakyaek-Khandh Bagga 3-4-14 and 3-5-20, 21
30. Jain Jyoti Prasad P-181.
31. Lal B.B. ''A.I.'' no 10 and 11.
32. Kosambi D.D., "Hindu Sanskriti Aur Ahimsa" P-165 Mentioned by Kosare H.L. P-38.
33. Shastri Rajanikant. "Hindu Jati ka Utthan aur Patan" PP 16-19 mentioned by Kosare H.L. P-39.
34. Gupta S.P PP 237-38.
35. Dr. Jain Jyoti Prasad P-37 and see chapter I P-P-4.
36. Jain Jyoti Prasad P-37.
37. Lal B.B. ''A I'' No 10 and 11 (Bulletin of Archaeological Survey of India Delhi).

38. Luders, List (E.I. X Appendix) No.905.
39. Sat Brah XIII, 5, 4, 7.
40. Ancient Geography of India PP 303-305.
41. Vividha Tirtha Kalpa P-14.
42. Crindle M.C. 'Ancient India as Described by Ptolemy' P-133.
43. XIII-5, 4, 7.
44. Ait Br. IX-39-23 .
45. Cowell "The Jataka" Vol III P-230.
46. MASI No. 67 P-8.
47. Ramayan Adi kanda 33.
48. Maha-Ummagga Jataka No 546- gives name as Chulani Brahmadatta.
49. MASI No 67 P-8.
50. Arthasastra XI-5, 6.
51. Mullar F. Max, 'India, What can it Teach Us' ? P-298.
52. IHQ Vol- VIII P-739.
53. Chapelkar M. Nalinee P-29.
54. Muller F Max, "Ancient Sanskrit Literature" PP 297-303.
55. Chanda R.P. "Indo-Aryan Races" I C 25, 26, 27.
56. (a) Hawkes Jacquetta, "The First Great Civilizations" P.P. Intr. XXV and 3.
    (b) Mackey E. "Early Indus civilization" Int PP XII and XIII.
    (c) Dharma Nand Kosambi "Hindu Sanskriti Aur Ahimsa"P-14.
57. Kosare H.L. P-249.
58. Jayaswal K.P. P-159.
59. Cunningham A., "Coins of Ancient India" PP 70 FF.
60. Jayaswal K. P. PP 37-38.
61. MASI No. 67P-12.
62. Cunningham A. "Coins of Ancient India" PP 73-74.
63. MASI No 67 P-9.
64. Cunningham A. PP 70 to 84.
65. Jayaswal K.P. P-14.
66. Smith V.A. "CIM" P-190.
67. Cunningham A. P-79.
68. Law B.C., "Panchala and their Capital Ahichhatra." Memoir of ASI No 67 P 11.
69. IHQ Vol VIII-P-739.
70. Puri Baijnath "India in the Time of Patanjali" PP 21-22.
71. Ait Brah VII-13-18.

72. Manu (X-22).

JHALLO MALLAŚCHA RĀJANYĀDVRĀJYĀNNI CHCHHIVIRE VAḤ NATASHCHA KARAN'S CHEVKHASO DRAVIDA EVACHA (22).

73. Jain Jyoti Prasad P-38.

74. Jain Jyoti Prasad P-45.

75. Jain J.P. P-48.

76. See detail on chapter I MB Adi XIV and XX and XXVI.

77. Jain J.P. P-38.

78. Jain Jyoti Prasad P-62.

79. Jain J.P. P-63.

80. Fergusson James P-63.

81. Jain J.P. PP-38

82. Jain J.P. - P. 39

83. Fergusson James PP 63-64

84. Sastri Neelkant K.A. "Nand Maurya Yugin Bharat" PP 288-89.

85. Tod James I PP 124-25"

Chapter–11

The Satavahanas and the other Naga Rulers of South

We have earlier learnt that after the great Mahabharata war, the Vedic Brahmanical culture began to decline on one hand and the non-Aryan Naga Shraman culture began to revive on the other. The progeny of Takshakas, after a long struggle with the successors of Parikshata of Pāndava tribe, recaptured Hastinapur and later Nagas subdued Kausal. Kashi and Magadha in the East. Similarly they moved towards west and South and established their rule at Tonk, Malava (East and West), Vidisa, Eran and Padmavati, and also at Paithan. We have given description of northern Indian dominions in Chapter X, now, being most important we take up Sātavāhana family first.

The Andhra or Sātavāhana

This was the only ruling family of South India, which ruled not only in South but also in some parts of North for some period. They are also credited to rule for the longest tenure in Indian history. According to Matsya Purana, they ruled for 460 years and according to Dr. V.A. Smith and Dr. Gopalachari there were 30 kings in this dynasty who ruled between 235 BC and 225 A.D.

Etymology of the word Sātavāhana

According to Nilkant Sastri in the first half of the first millennium B.C. the process of basic change, in the nature of Indo-Aryan languages, was at work. In this period the Aryan languages were coming nearer to Dravidian and Kol (Munda or ancient Dravidian) languages and the Indo-Aryan, Dravidian and Kol languages were intermixing. Words of similar meaning or synonymous of both the languages were coming together to form new words such as ; Kol-Sāta, Sada, Shāli means Ghora (horse), similarly the word Ghot or Ghora (horse) was derived from an unknown non-Aryan origin word Ghutra or Hotra and from the combination of these words (Shali and Hotra), the Sanskrit word Shalihotra (Ghora or horse) has been formed[1]. The people of Megalithic culture were related to the same-period, while the above process was in progress and they were active in this process of linguistic change.

All the three names viz Sātavāhan, Sādavahan and Sālivāhan are of the same family and the words Sāt, Sād or shāli, the prefix of these names are of Kol origin and they meant horse. Why these words were added to their family name by the Sātavāhanas[2] ? In doing so they certainly must have followed the cultural tradition of their fore-fathers. It means there was some close relation of Satavāhanas with the horse. In fact the relation of Nagas of Megalithic culture with the horse was surprisingly very close. This truth has come to light from the excavation of sites like Mahurjhari, Junāpāni, khāpa, and Tākalghat. Dr. S.B. Deo[3] has derived very interesting conclusions in the excavation report of Mahurjhari. He annotates as such, "The association, of horse bones and ornaments and horse riding equipments with human skeletal remains, shows that this animal played an important role in the life of Mahurjhari Megalithians. It appears that they were skilful horse riders and possibly belonged to a warrior clan, This view is further corroborated by the mode of burial of the dead warriors in megaliths of LOC III in which a dagger with an iron blade and copper hilt was found to have been placed on the chest of the person. The material equipment implies that Megalithic folks were predominantly iron-using warrior groups. The horse kits found with the horse remains implies that these folks were raiders." Such a character of Megalithians is not different from Sātavāhanas.

Dr. S.B. Deo on the basis of carbon C-14 dating has fixed the period of Mahurjhari findings as first millennium B.C., when this family came into power. Hence it shows that the progenitors, of this family were efficient horse riders and a great warrior clan; that is why the aforesaid prefixes have been used to their family name. This is further confirmed by the view of Jayaswal who says that indigenous Naga people used to organize themselves into guilds or republics[4] whose every member was a great warrior. They were, infact, a Nation-in-Arms. (See chapter VI P 133 for detail). The above conclusion, very clearly indicates that the people of megalithic culture and Sātavāhanas were of one and the same culture and they were Naga in origin. The horse not only played an important role in their lives but this was their close associate member. This importance given to this animal by the Sātavāhanas, was inherent; that is why they gave so much importance to this animal. It is possible that this importance may have inter-related with some historical event, lost in the long darkness of history.

Chandrabhan[5] Pandeya has produced following different meanings of the word Sātavāhana :

(1) According to Jain Muni Jin-Prabha Suri word Sanoti (Sat) means to donate, hence Sātavāhana means who donated Vahanas or Vehicles.

(2) The word 'Vāhana' is a Sanskrit form of " Han" or "Hapan" of Munda langauge which means son. Therefore Satavahan means son of horse. (Gopalachari, "Early History of the Andhra country " P–10).

(3) According to Kankasbhai the words Vahana and Karni (of Satakarni) are synonymous which means elephant. Therefore Sātavāhana means that one who has hundreds of elephants.

(4) According to Smith in the names of many of the Sātavāhana kings, the pre-fix 'Sati' is a corrupt form of 'Swati'. "Swati " means sword. Therefore Sātavāhana means ''person who wears or holds sword.''

(5) Sometimes the word 'Sat' is taken to be 'shat' which means hundred. Therefore the word Sātavāhana is explained as "the lord of hundreds of hills or mountains. " Since they were lords of hilly region of N.W. India, hence it seems much nearer to historical fact such as Takshila means "rocks-of Takas "

The most reasonable and acceptable viewpoint is presented by Jogalekar.[6] According to him ''Sat is a corrupt form of 'Sapta' which means seven. 'Saptavahani' is one of the name of sun, thus Sātavāhana was a Suryabanshi king. Seven horses are the vehicle of sun. .... The coins of Sātavāhana have a symbol of sun or Surya, known as 'Ujjaini symbol' the 'S' of Sātavāhana can be related to its Prakrit form 'Sattavāhani' (Sanskrit, Saptavahan). In Skand Purana Saptāvāhana is the name of Surya (Sun)". But Jogalekar does not produce any evidence in support. According to inscription of Kansawa found from a well near river Chambal south of Kotah, king Salindra calls himself of Sarya race and of Taka Bansha. Prince Salivahana the primogenitor of the royal family, was also Taka Banshi. Salindra was king of Salpoor (409 AD). These people of Sarya family were famous among other tribes.[7] The view that Nagas were of Suryabansha gets the support of Oldham.[8]

It is obvious that these were the same Takas of Panjab who met Hieuntsang. They were lord of Malava and were also known as Surya. The land between the valleys of Satluj and Beas, in the neighbourhood of Himalayas is also known as Saraj or Sewaraj. The chief deity of the people of this area is serpent or Naga and all of them worship this deity.[9]

It is obvious that Sātavāhanas were Surya or Surya Banshi in origin. It is well confirmed.

The Legend of Birth of Salivahana

Salivahana was primogenitor of this royal family R.G. Bhandarkar[10] produces a legendary event explaining the origin of the Salivahana or Satavāhana. —

"The period during which the Śâtavâhanas or Andhrabhṛityas ruled over Mahârâshṭra must have been a prosperous one in the history of the country. Hence several traditions with regard to different kings of this dynasty have been preserved. But that Śâlivâhana or Śâtavâhana was a family name has been forgotten, and different princes of the dynasty have been identified. Thus Hemachandra in his Desīkośa gives Sâlivâhana, Sâlana, Hâla, and Kuntala as the name of one individual ; but we see from the list given above that the last two were born by different princes, and both of them were Śâlivâhanas. In his grammar he gives Śâlivâhana as a Prâkrit corruption of Śâtavâhana. In modern times the Śaka era is called the Śâlivâhana era, an era founded by Sâlivâhana. When it is attributed to him, it is difficult to determine it precisely. All the copper-plate grants up to the eleventh century speak of the era as Śaka nṛipakâla, i.e. the era of the Śaka king, or Śakakâla, i.e., the era of the Saka, and in an inscription at Bâdâmi it is stated to be the era beginning from "the coronation of the Śaka king." Subsequently, the simple expression "Śâka, in the year of the Śaka, " was used, and thereafter Śaka, or "in the Śaka." The word Śaka thus came to be understood as equivalent to "an era" generally, the original sense being forgotten. And since the era had to be connected with some great king it was associated with the name of Śâlivâhana, whom tradition had represented to be such a king ; and thus we now use the expression Śâlivâhana Śaka, which etymologically can have no sense and is made up of the names of two royal families. The current legend makes Śâlivâhana the son of a Brâhmaṇ girl who was a sojourner at Paiṭhaṇ and lived with her two brothers in the house of a potter. On the occasion she went to the Godâvarî to bathe, Śesha, the king of serpents, becoming enamoured of her, transformed himself into a man and embraced her. In due course she gave birth to Śâlivâhana, who was brought up in the house of the potter[11] After sometime king Vikramâditya of Ujjain, to whom a certain deity had revealed that he was destined to die at the hands of the son of a girl of two years, sent about his Vetâla or king of Ghosts to find out if there was such a child anywhere. The Vetâla saw Śâlivâhana playing with his girlish mother and informed Vikramâditya. Thereupon he invaded Paiṭhaṇ with a large army, but Sâlivâhana infused life into clay figures of horses, elephants, and men, by means of a charm communi ated to him by his father, the king of serpents, encountered Vikramâdi 'a, and defeated him. This descent of a king of Ujjain on Paiṭhaṇ I have already alluded to and endeavoured to explain. The Sâlivâhana referred to in this tradition appears to be Pulumâyi who, in conjunction with his father, freed the country from the Śakas and fought with Chashṭana or Jayadâman and Rudradâman whose capital appears to have been Ujjain. It was in consequence of some faint reminiscence of Pulumâyi Śâlivâhana's relation with the Sakas and their Satrap kings that his name was attached to the era first used by his adversaries. There are also several literary traditions connected with the name of Sātavāhana or Sālivahana. A work of the name of Brahatkatha written in that form of Prakrit which is called the Pishachi or the language of goblins mentioned by Dandin in his work the Kāvyādarsa. (BHŪT BHĀŚĀMAIPRĀ HURADDHA TĀRTHĀ BRAHAT-KATHĀM)''

The Original Home of the Race of Satavahana

Who was this Salivahana and from where he came ? It is an important question, but most of the scholars have ignored it. James Tod has given a due consideration to it. He,[12] very clearly, informs us- "that in early history of the Bhatti prince of Jaisalmer, when driven from Zabulistan, they dispossessed the Takas on the Indus, and established themselves in their land, the capital of which was called Salivahanpura ; and as the date of this event is given as 3008 of the Yudhishtra era, it is by no means unlikely that Salivahana or Salbhan (who was a Takshak), the conqueror of the Tuar Vikram, was of the very family dispossessed by Bhatti who compelled them to migrate to South."

It seems from this evidence that Salivahan or Salavahan hailed from Punjab and he was an offshoot of Takshak or Taka Naga family. It is also confirmed by the name of their eastern capital Dhannakatak[13], where word Taka appears as suffix, similarly another likewise example is also notable from Venakatak one of the earliest settlements of Sātavāhanas.

But there is a gap of about three or four centuries in the period of the beginning of the rule of the Sātavāhanas and prince Salivahana and Vikramaditya of Ujjaini, hence this event does not seem to be historical. Some scholars have suggested that the opponent of Vikramaditya, would have been king Pulumayi or Hala, Sātavāhana or Sālivahana instead of prince Salivahan, the founder of the dynasty. Whatever is the fact, it is shrouded in the long darkness of history. But there are evidences of Prakrit Pali text to show that Salivahana lived three or four centuries earlier than the above event. Gunadhya, the author of Brahatkatha of Pishachi is known as contemporary of Hala Sātavāhana (20-24 AD). He has mentioned in the introductory part of his work that he (Gunadhya) had used a legend (Katha) of Vararuchi (of Nanda Age 422-322 B.C.) as the basis of his composition[14]. It means the original legend or Katha of

Brahatkatha was composed during the Nanda Age. From this information we can very easily conclude that Salivahana the hero of this work would have been contemporary of Vararuchi or of earlier period[15].

This is quite in consistent with the available chronology of beginning of the reign of the Sātavāhana family, although Pandeya is not ready to go earlier than 235 B.C. for this date[16].

There are some more evidences to prove that Salivahana and his family Sātavāhana, also known as Andhra, was the ruler of North West India, or Afghanistan in the early period of history. K.P. Jayaswal[17] produces Puranic evidence to prove this truth : "It seems certain that there was a community called Andhra in the North. The Matsya, in the opening verse, on the enumeration of the northern countries, has Pur Andhra just in the place where Aparikas are given by the Vayu VĀHIKĀ VĀTADHĀNĀŚCHABHĪRAH KALTOYAKAḤ PURANDHRĀ ŚCHAIV SHUDRAŚCHAPAHALVĀ ŚCHĀTTAKHANDIKĀḤ

The Bhagwata (IX-20, 30) includes Andhras in a list of northern peoples :—

KIRATAHŪNAṆ YAVANĀNAMDHRĀṆ KANKĀN KHAŚAṆ SHAKĀṆ

[Nirnaya Sāgar ed (1923) P-414]

It may be pointed out that in the north of Afghanistan, about hundred miles to the west of Balkh, there is the district of Andha Khui (See note below) there is Andhari or Andhri, a most war like Gilzai tribe in Afghanistan. According to Matsya. the Pur Andhra were in the Valhika group. The Andhras of Ashokan inscription seem to be northern."

These Andharkas were a sub-division of Yadavas. In Mahabharata (Sabha chapter XIV and Shanti chapter LXXXI) they have been called Bhoja, who were a component of Sātavāhana rulers. Since, Valhika[18] or Vahika is another name of Takshakas,[19] Andharas were a Branch of tribe of Takshakas. Thus it is evidently proved that Salivahana prince and his tribe Andhra or Takshaka were living in northwest region of India or Afghanistan in prehistoric or early historic period, from where prince Salivahana moved and established his rule in Païthan and Vidarbha region (See Page 288) in Nanda period or earlier.

The Origin of Power (beginning of Rule)

The question of place of the origin of Sātavāhana Power is most controversial, some scholars think that their original home was Andhra, others think it was Vellari region or Venakatak of Vidarbha, but most of them think it was Western Maharashtra.

Andhra : There is a great controversy among the scholars over the issue of original home-land of the Satavahans. The kings, named Sātavāhana and Satakarni, whose names have come to light through inscriptions and coins, are called "Andhra-Bhritya" and "Andhra Jatiya " in Puranas. From this, scholars have concluded that Satavāhana and Satakarni were Andhras. It means they were originally of Andhra race. Similarly Dr. Smith has observed that their capital was Srikakulam, but Bhandarkar thinks it was DhannaKatak They have not only been called 'the rulers of Andhra' but also Andhra-Vati. A detailed description, on this issue, has been given in forthcoming lines.

The above discussion is indicative of the fact that Sātavāhanas were not only original inhabitant of Andhra country, but also of Andhra tribe after whose name this state was named. This view gets the support of P.N. Chopra. He[20] writes, "They are known in the Puranas by two names : (1) The Andhras and (2) The Andhra Bhrityas. The mention of the Sātavāhanas as Andhras, naturally inclines one to suppose that they were not Maharashtrians but only Telugus ; the word Andhrabhritya on the other hand means "the servants of the Andhras." or "the Andhras who were servants" if the latter meaning of Sātavāhanas, could be taken to be Andhra feudatories of the Mauryan emperors originally residing in the East and having migrated to the West by the time they became independent. If Andhrabhritya meant "servant of the Andhras" it would mean that they were natives of Western Deccan long ago somehow subservient to the Andhras and that they later shifted their allegiance to the Mauryas. Whatever it is, it is clear that the Satavāhana were a Kula, a family or a dynasty and that when history knows them definitely they had settled around Paithan .... The Andhras were known to the Roman historian Pliny who speaks of their many walled towns, numerous villages and large armies consisting of foot soldiers, cavalry and elephants. Thus it will be evident that the Andhra Sātavāhanas were ancient people, ruling in the Deccan independently or subject to external imperial authority, whenever necessary." Thus it shows that Sātavāhanas were of Andhra origin, Pre-Mauryan ancient people. But another group of scholars thinks that since their early coins and inscriptions have been found out in West, their original home cannot be Andhra.

Vellari

Sukhthankar[21] thinks that Sātavāhanas were originally resident of Vellari. He does not accept the theory of their Andhra origin, because they have not been called Andhra in any of the their inscriptions.[22]

The basis of theory of Sukhathankar is a few words like 'Satavāhanihar, and 'Sātavāhanī-Rattha' mentioned in the inscription recovered from district Vellari, (Mpakadoni inscription and in the Hirhad-Gakki copper plate) countries are named after the people living there in : on this basis he accepts the original home of Sātavāhanas the Sātavahanihār' and the territory around it.

If Vellari was their original home and after expansion of their rule they transferred their capital, then why no inscription of earlier kings of Sātavāhanas could be traced out from there ? Only one inscription of Pulumayi of Myakdoni could be recovered from this territory. Therefore merely on, establishment of relation of similarity between the words 'Sātavāhanīhar' and 'Satavāhana' this cannot be concluded that their original home was country of Sātavāhanihar.[23] However this theory can not be ruled out at all, since prince Salivahana hailed from the land of Takshila where ancient places had like wise names viz Gāndhar (kandhar) Nagahar (Jalalabad) etc.

Venakataka and Vidarbha

In the inscription[24A] of Vasishthi-putra Sri Pulumayi of Nasik cave, (Epigraphia Indica Part VIII No.-2 P-60 FF) Gautamiputra, the 23rd king of Sātavāhana family has been adorned with the epithet of SĀTAVĀHAN KULAYA SAPATI THĀPANKAR' (The dignifier of glory of Sātavāhana family). Further in the description of the same king, another adjective has been added KULA, VIPUL SIRIKAR (the enhancer of glory of family). This king, in the inscription of Nasik cave (Epigraphia Indica Part VIII no. 4 P-71) has called himself VENĀKATAK SWĀMI GAUTAMI PUTTOSIRISADA KARI (the lord of Venakatak Gautamiputta SIRI Satakarni). Dr. V.V. Mirashi (Sanshodhan Muktāvali sery I PP 110-12) has commented upon this adjective that forefathers of Gautamiputra were ruling Maharashtra in the beginning. After some time, Saka-Kshatrapa Bhumak and Nahpān defeated them and established their rule in north Maharashtra. The coins of both of them, have been traced out from Gujrat and Mahārashtra state. An inscription of RishabhaDutta, the son-in-law of Nahpān, has been found from the Pāndava cave of Nasik[24B]. It is proved from this that at least Konkan, north Mahārashtra and Gujrat were under possession of Nahpān. At that time the Sātavahana kings would have been living in Vidarbha. Later on, Gautamiputra defeated Nahpān and exterminated the Sakas of Chhahrāt family completely, and Konkan, Mahārashtra, Saurashtra (Kathiavar), Malava, Gujrat etc were again included in his dominion. Just after this Victory, he called himself 'Venākatak Swami'' in the inscription of Nasik. It means, at that time, he was ruling in the territory of Vena river (Vena Ganga).

We come to know from above conclusion of Dr. Mirashi that the land around the banks of river Venaganga was original territory of Sātavāhanas. He has reached the above conclusion, on the basis of evidences found from the study of coins and inscriptions. It means this conclusion has been derived from the fact that a very large number of coins of Sātavāhana have been recovered from there.

We come to know from the inscription of Hāthigumpha that Kharvela sent his forces toward west to over-throw Satakarni. His forces reached Kanhavena. Hence it is proved that the empire of Satakarni was in the west of Kalinga. From the above description (of inscription) we get indication of Vidarbha also. In fact the Kanhavena, is a river, Krishnavena, which is a tributary of Venganga.[25]

Above conclusion gets the support of inscription (no. 4) of Gautamiputra Satakarni of Nasik cave where he has called himself lord of Venakatak as highlighted earlier.[26]

The argument forwarded by Dr. V.V. Mirashi [27] seems to be justified. The river Kanhavena is equated with the Kānha river of district Nagpur which falls in the Venaganga. On the bank of river Venaganga, the ancient city of Pauni was situated, which was an old centre of Buddhism, where a famous Buddhist stupa belonging to the pre-Ashokan period was existing. During the Sunga and Sātavāhana age, like the stupa of Sānchi and Bharhut, this stupa was also of very large size. This whole territory is most fertile and the relations of famous Buddhist scholar Nāgārjuna, with Sātavahana kings, also developed here. The extension of Sātavāhana rule was up to district Bilaspur in Madhya Pradesh. This seems proven from the evidence found from the excavation of Malhār, from where remains of Megalithic culture of 1000 B.C. have been recovered. And in later period, remains of Maurya, Sunga, and Sātavāhanā cultures have been found out. (Presidential address by Ajay Mitra Shastri, Indian History congress 39th session, Hyderabad 1978 Sect V)[28]. Therefore it is clear that the rule of Sātavāhana was towards the west of Kalinga. But as the Kanhavena river is not in Madhya Pradesh hence it is proved that this was Kanhavena of Vidarbha. On the basis of these evidences it can be concluded that Venakataka territory was the original homeland of Sātavāhanas. Vena territory of Vidarbha was not only original home of Sātavāhana but also a centre of Megaliths and Buddhist culture and was closely related to the Naga race. Hence it is proved that toriginally Sātavāhanas were also related to this centre.

Close Relation of Satavahana and Vidarbha

The Coins : It has been stated earlier that the original founder of Sātavāhana rule was a person known as Sālivāhana and he was also lord of Vidarbha. The Vidarbha would have been a federal state of Maharashtra from the beginning period of Sātavāhana king and up to the end of the empire. This is also proved from the findings of a very large number of Sātavāhana coins from Vidarbha region. From the site of

Brahmapuri of Chandrapur district, 143 coins were recovered in 1883. In 1939, from the village of Tanhāla of district Akola 1600 coins were found out. The coins, recovered from district Chandrapur were studied by Dr. Hoernle[29]. From this deposit 51 coins of Satakarni, 24 coins of Siripulumayi, 42 of Siriyagya Satakarni and some of other kings have been recovered. The coins recovered from Tanhala (Tarhālā) were studied by V.V. Mirashi.[30] From above deposit, 573 coins of Siri Satakarni (III) Gautamiputra, 174 of Siri Pulumayi (II), 35 of Siri Satakarni (IV), 32 of Siri Pulumavi (III), 23 of Siriskand Satakarni, 248 of Siri Yagya Satakarni, 4 of Siri Vijay Satakarni, 56 of Sirikumbha Satakarni, 7 of Siri Karna Satakarni, 4 of Siri Saka Satakarni and 4 of Siri Pulumayi have been recovered. Other coins, have no mention of the name of the kings or are either illegible.

As such 1525 coins of Satakarni king, have been recovered from Tanahāla deposit. Before above findings, the coins of Satavāhana kings, who ruled earlier than Gautamiputra Satakarni only were recovered from Vidarbha. Later, the coins of Siri Satakarni, an earlier king than the above, were also found from Pauni.[31] Latest, the coins of Sātavāhana king, the founders of Sātavāhana rule, were also recovered from Vidarbha as discussed in detail on page 291.

Findings of Forts

As much as, the new sites were excavated, and intensive studies made, only then, this new fact came to light that Sātāvāhanas were related to Vidarbha from the very beginning to the end. From excavation of Adam, which is near Kuhi and Māndal and at a distance of 55 K.M. from Nagpur, significant remains of a fort of 2000 years earlier or Sātavāhana age, have come to light. This work was carried by Dr. S.N. Raghunath, superintendant Archaeological Survey of India. From there, remains of a beautiful city with its surrounding walls of Sātavāhanas, have been explored.

According to Dr. Raghunath, from the remains so recovered, it seems that it was a strong fort, with its 18 metre wide Surrounding wall and a trench outside it. Its entry gate, in spite of being big and in ruined condition, is quite visible from a far place. As a result of excavation work, at three points evidences of a centre of Buddhist activities have been noticed. The relation of Buddhist monks, might have been with a small mound outside the fort walls. Above excavation work was done by the department of Archaeology University of Nagpur. From the findings of beautiful pottery of fine quality and some pots with royal seal and attractive ear-rings, it seems that this would have been a habitation centre of cultured people. The date of this site has been fixed, as first century

B.C. by the scholars[32]. From excavation of Adam, we have traced out first city of its kind of Sātavāhanas with surrounding walls. Therefore, it has helped us in establishing the relation of Vidarbha with Sātavāhanas from the early age. Similarly findings of new stupa of Pauni from this region is most significant from historical point of view. In addition to Adam, Pavanār, Pauni and Arni in district Yavatmāl were cities of Sātavāhana Age with surrounding walls.

But the viewpoint of V.V. Mirashi is also not acceptable for the following reasons :

(1) Although a very large number of coins have been recovered from Vidarbha particularly the Tarhala coins of king Gautami -putra and his contemporary kings, have come to hand but not a single piece of earlier kings has been found.

(2) There are two rivers named Ganga in Vidarbha : One Venganga is situated at a distance of 85 K.M. from Paithan and another Venganga is situated at a distance of 145 K.M. from Nasik. Hence Venakatak of Mirashi can be one nearer to Paithan.

The Western Region or Maharashtra

According to Dr. Gopalachari we get indication of their original home in the west from the inscriptions, seals and text books[33] that they were the residents of that country which is around the Pratisthan or Paithan in district Aurangabad. The word 'Sātavāhana signifies the 'family' (Kula) and the word 'Andhra' their 'race' or tribe. In an inscription, the word Sātavāhana has been used in the sense of family (Sātavāhana Kule Kanhe Rājati)[34]

Paithan

Pratisthan, the modern Pāithān or Pāitun which is situated at the bank of river Godavari, was their western capital and Dhannakatak, on the bank of Krishna near Vijaywada, was their eastern capital. For about a period of two hundred years the rule of family was confined to the southern proximity of Vindhya. But according to the Puranas, Sātavāhanas killed the last Kanava ruler and possessed Magadha in the last century B.C.[35]

Above viewpoint of Majumdar gets corroboration of Shrinivas Iyengar[36]. He thinks that "Andhras were originally, people of the West and Prakrit speaking and not Telugu speaking. Their power grew from the West to the east. After their fall in the west, they shifted to Andhra Pradesh. Andhra was, originally, the name of their Tribe. Later, it was used in the sense of royal family and there after in the sense of language.

The basis of this viewpoint is in Aitreya Brahmna (VII-19) according to which Andhras lived south of Vindhya outside the limits of Aryavarta, along with other Dasyu tribes like Pundra, Sabra, Pulinda etc. The Greek writers like Pliny, Wilfred and Ptolemy. have said that the Sātavāhanas were related to the Western India."

According to Jain tradition Kalkacharya, when-ever met king Sātavāhana, he met at Paithan.

Andhra Valley :

In support of western region origin, most convincing and reasonable viewpoint has been forwarded by Jogalekar. According to him[37] — "The Andhra name of Sātavāhānas has not come into practice simply because they were residents of the land known as Andhra in modern age but its main reason was some other. In fact they used to live in the valley of river Andhra flowing in the district of Pune". There is no paucity of such examples, such as Dashāran people lived in the valley of river Dashārn, the Shatudra people lived in the valley of river Shatudra, Ratth people lived in the valley of river Bheem Rathi, and Sarswat people lived in the valley of river Sarswati. In the inscription of Behistūn the name of river Sindhu is mentioned as Hindu, still today Andhra people live in the Taluka of Khera in the district of Pune[38]. This place is not far away from the Valley of Andhra. The Valley of river Andhra is in the district of Pune.[39] It seems that Andhras shaped a new Nation by organizing several tribes.[40] These Several tribes are Andhra, Mahabhoja, Maharathi, Pettinika, Pulinda, Pundra, Sabra and many others. Most probably that is why Maharashtra was known as 'Navarashtra'. Sātavāhanas have called themselves 'Nava-nar-Swami' (Lord of New people, Pandulen cave inscription no.3)

According to Bhagawanlal Indraji the meaning of the word 'Nava-Nar-Swami' is new rulers. But according to Jogalekar its meaning is 'the lord of New Rashtra' (Maharashtra). Andhras entered in the plain region from the Valley of Andhra. They moved through Karle, Bedasa, and crossing the Sahyadri and reached Konkan and Aparānta. From there they subdued Kanheri and other regions and ultimately became lord of the whole of the Southern India.[41]

Evidences and arguments produced by Jogalekar are most justified and convincing and the theory thus evolved, is further, confirmed by another solid evidence : In Matsya, the word 'Nava Rashtra[42]' has been used for Maharashtra. Karamarkar, in one of his articles, regarding the limits of Maharashtra, had deduced the same conclusion. Although aforesaid arguments are most consistent, but in the absence of historical evidence we hesitate in accepting them. This Valley of Andhra is not far away from Paithan which was their earliest and western capital.

Detailed argument for western origin can be summed up as under :

(1) According to Jain tradition Sātavahanas related to Pratisthana since Kalakacharya went to see king at Paithān.

(2) Most of the sites, where coins of earlier kings have been found, are situated in the west.

(3) The names of the earlier kings of this family like Simuka, Sātavāhana and Srisāt are inscribed in the cave of Nanaghat situated in the west.

(4) The famous Sātavāhana king Hal has composed his famous book Gatha-Saptashati in Maharashtri Prakrit. and not Telugu.

(5) Foreigners, like Pliny, Wilfred and Ptolemy , have attached the Sātavāhanas with the Western India and have described of their large army and fortified cities.

(6) Literary work like Aitreya Brahman (VII–18) has attached them with the North west region.

(7) According to Jogalekar, Sātavāhanas earlier lived in the valley of river Andhra still they are residing nearby in district Pune.

Hence it is evidently proved that Satavahanā's original home was in the West or Paithan.

Original Founder of the Satavahana Rule

The issue of original founder of Sātavāhana rule is also controversial. Dr. Ray Chowdhry thinks that the founder of the Sātavāhana rule was Simuka who is also known as Sisuka, Sindhuka and Sipraka in Puranas.

The Puranas mention Sisuka as the first Andhra king who overthrew the last ruler of the Kānava dynasty, destroyed the remaining power of the Sungas and attained imperial position[43]. This Sisuka is generally identified with Simuka whose relievo figure still exists in a cave at Nānāghat[44]. He is named there as 'Simuka Sātavāhana,' but he cannot be identified with the king who issued the present (Sātavāhana) coin, for his brother Krishna is described in a Nasik cave inscription as belonging to the Sātavāhana family[45]. Both Simuka and Krishna were probably descendants of a king named Sātavāhana, who preceded them by some generations. The Puranas do not record his name probably because he was merely a local ruler or chief of Sangha and had not yet attained an imperial or republican status. That he had declared his independence, is however, clear from the coin.

A copper coin of king Sātavāhana, which was published in the Journal of the Numismatic society of India Vol VII P I FF came to the hand of V.V Mirashi from the cabinet of Mr. Hurnuz Kaus of Hyderabad. who was fond of collecting ancient coins.[46]

Mirashi[47] has produced a detailed report of aforesaid coin like this : "It is a copper coin, square in shape, each side measuring ·80″. It weighs 110 grains. It has on the obverse the figure of an elephant standing to right, with the trunk upraised having in front a peculiar symbol consisting of two flattened circles on a vertical line. Above the back of the elephant appears what Mr. Allan calls a triangle headed standard with a cross." Further Mirashi[48] adds "I read the legend as Rāmno Siri Sādvaha (nasa) meaning (this coin is) of the king, the illustrious Sātavāhana. It will be noticed that the last two letters, of the legend have been lost at the upper right corner. .... The legend is in Prakrit as on other Sātavāhana coins. Specially noteworthy is the form ramno or ranno. This form with the anusvāra on ra occurs also on the lead coin of the king Sāta (Rapson catalogue of the coins of the Andhras etc Plate I and no. 1) but it was not noticed by Rapson on later coins, the form is ranā (for rana) or ranno. The royal name appears here in the form Sādavāhana (for Sātvahana) as in the Nasik cave inscription of the reign of Krishna. (Epigraphia Indica Vol VIII P–93). The inscription of Pulumāyi at Nāsik as well as the Nanaghāt inscription have the Sanskrit form of the name Sātavāhana, unchanged. The coin is thus of the king Sātavahana, who was plainly founder of the dynasty named after him. The Purānas call this dynasty Andhra, but that name occurs nowhere in its inscriptions. On the other hand two inscriptions in the Nasik caves, name this royal family as Satavāhana Kula or Sādavāhana Kula (Epigraphia Indica Vol III PP 60). The family was, therefore, evidently founded by a king named Sātavāhana even as the Guptā family was founded by Maharaja Gupta."

A coin of Sātavahana king has also been recovered by Dr. M.G. Dikshit[49]. After some time Dr. Mirashi also found another coin of the above king from Khwājā Muhammad Ahmad, director of the department of Archaeological survey from Hydrabad. In addition to above coins, which were published by Dr. Mirashi and Dr. Dikshit, five more coins were recovered from excavation of Nevasa[50] out of which four coins of mica were round in shape and fifth is of copper and square in shape. No symbol of Ujjaini has been noticed on any of the five coins of Nevasa.

Later on another coin of Sātavāhana king has been found out from the collection of Shri Biyani of Akola. This coin was published by Dr. V.V Kolte[51]. This coin bears the name 'Sātavāhana'. On the pattern of previous findings of coins of Sātavāhana king the complete name would have been 'RANNO SIRI SĀDAVĀHANASA' (of Sātavahana king). The letters inscribed on it, being like-wise those on other coins of this king, its period seems to be second Century B.C. . The coin bearing the name of Sātavahana king, is the first recovered from Vidarbha. Before this all the coins were found from outside Vidarbha. On the basis of findings of this coin from Vidarbha, it can be concluded that the king Satavahan, the founders of Sātavāhana family, would have ruled over Vidarbha also. On the reverse side of coin, there is a figure of an elephant and below it, is a line with serpent like band. According to Kolte this would have been a symbol of river, and this is a new and important peculiarity of this coin, since such symbol of river has not been traced out on any other coin of Sātavāhana king. Similarly there is also symbol of Ujjaini (Sun) and Triratna (three Jewels)

We can draw following conclusions from aforesaid evidence :—

(1) Original founder of Sātavāhana rule was prince Salivahana.

(2) Since coins of Prince Salivahana and many other Sātavāhana kings bear the legend Ranna instead of Rajan or Raja (King) it shows this family was progenitor of famous Rana Rajput family of later date and Ujjaini symbol apparently represents their Surya Bansha, which was symbol of Malavas who were Nagas. It is evident Sātavāhanas were of Naga race. This conclusion is most significant in historical prospective.

(3) Dr. Kolte has concluded that wavy line on the coin, below the elephant with serpent like bend; is a symbol of river. But in my opinion it seems to be an excited snake. Since back ground of birth of Salivahana prince is connected with the Naga race, hence it will be more justified, appropriate and historical to recognize it an excited serpent instead of a river. We have noted that Bharsiva (Taka) Naga family of

Padmavati and many other Naga kings have been using symbol of serpent on their coins. (See chapter XII P 346-47). Since aforesaid coin belongs to a much earlier period, hence figure is not so clear as has been noted on the coins of Naga king of later period which is quite natural.

Relation Between the Satavahanas and The Megalithic Culture

We know the area falling just to the north of Takshila is known as Gandhara region or Swat Valley where from Megalithic culture of 1000 B.C. and later period has been traced out.[52] According to scholars the period of Megalithic in India is 1000 BC–100AD. Famous historian S.P. Gupta[53] informs us "That fortunately the tentative chronology of Indian Megaliths (800 B.C.–100 AD) appears to overlap partly with the well documented period of the history of South India (Banerjee ; Iron Age in India, table 1 to 4). The Sangam literature, although of later date, according to Srinivasan, contains tradition going back to 3rd Century B.C. .... It is an important chapter in which the archaeological and literary traditions seem to corroborate each other admirably well".

This gets confirmation from findings of B and R ware culture from the earlier stratum of ancient site of Paithan as noted by this author in person and pottery collected from there. We have earlier shown that Salivahana and his tribe (Andhra or Takshaka) reached Paithan during Nanda age (422–322 BC) or earlier. This period fits well with the middle period of establishment of Megalithic culture in South and central India. That is why Megalithic culture seems to flourish in most of the earlier period of the Sātąvāhana Age. This evidently proves relation of B and R Wares and Megaliths with the Sātavāhanas and confirms their relation with the Naga race, since B and R Wares has also been found from the settlement of Naga rulers of Eran (see Chapter IV PP 76-79) which is supported by B.B. Lal. Later Megalithic culture shows its discontinuity owing to Aryanization of Sātavāhanas and their counter parts of the same age (in second Century A.D). Since Aryan religious tradition confines to the cremation of their dead bodies and not to the burial.

Pedigree and Chronology

Hereby we first produce pedigree of Satavāhana rulers as given in Vāyu, Matsyā, Vishnu and Bhagawat Puranas, after R.G. Bhandarkar[54].

Vâyu		Matsya		Vishnu.	Bhagavata
Names	Duration of reign in years	Name	Duration of reign in years	Names	Names
Sindhuka	23	Siśuka	23	Sipraka	Name not given; but mentioned as a Vrishala or Sudra.
Krishna	10	Krishna	18	Krishna	Krishna
		Mallakarni	10 or 18	Sri Sâtakarni	Santakarna
		Purnotsanga	13	Purnotsanga	Paurnamaga
		Skandhastambhi	18		
Sattakarni	56	Sâtakarni	56	Sâtakarni	
		Lambodara	18	Lambodata	Lambodara
Aptlava	12	Apttaka	12	Ivîlaka	Hivîlaka
		Meghasvâti	18	Meghasvatí	Meghasvâti
		Svâti	18		
		Skandasvâti	7		
		Mrigendras vâtikarṇa	3		

		Kuntalasvâti	8		
		Svâtikarna	1		
Patimâvi	24	Pulomâvi	36	Patumat	Atamânn
Nemikrishna	25	Gaurakrishṇa or		Asishtakarman	Anishṭakarman Hâleya
		Naurikrishna	25		
Hâla	1	Hâla	5	Hâla	
Saptaka or Mandalaka	5	Mandulaka	5	Pattalaka	Talaka
Purikasheṇa	21	Purindrasena	5	Pravillasena	Purîshabhîru
Śâtakarṇi	1	Sundara Svatikarṇa	1	Sundara	Sunandana.
Chakora Śâtakarni	1/3	Chakora Svâtikarṇa		Chakora	Chakora
Śivasvâti	28	Sivasvâti	28	Śivasvâti	Śivasvâti
Gautamiputra	21	Gautamiputra	21	Gomatiputra	Gomatiputra
		Pulomat	28	Pulimat	Purimân (mat).
		Śivaśri	7	Śivaśri	Medaśiras
		Śivaskanda	7	Śivaskandha	Śivaskanda
Yajnaśrî Śâtakarṇi	29	Yajnaśri Śâtakarṇi	29, 9 or 20	Yajñaśrî	Yajñaśrî
Vijaya	6	Vijaya	6	Vijaya	Vijaya
Daṇḍaśri Śâtakarṇi	3	Chaṇḍaśri Śâtakarṇi	10	Chandraśri	Chandravijña
Pulomavi	7	Pulomavit	7	Pulomârchis	Sulomadhi

Satavahānas ruled for a period of about 500 years which is the longest tenure of rule in Indian History. As regards their pedigree it is most controversial because scholars neither completely agree on the exact number of kings who ruled nor on the period, for which they ruled. They have tried to solve this problem with the help of Puranic accounts, inscriptions and coins. The names of important kings and period of their rule is given below[55] :

Salivahan or Satavahan	— — — —
Simuka	235 BC – 212 BC
Kanha or Krishna	212 BC – 195 BC
Satakarni I	195 BC – 186 BC
Vedisri or Satisri	— — — —
Purnotsanga	— — — —
Satakarni II	166 BC–111 BC
Hala	20 AD – 24 AD
Gautamiputra Satakarni	70–95AD
Pulumayi II	96–119 AD
Sri Satakarni	120–149 AD
Shivsri Pulumayi (Pulavi)	150–156 AD
Sri Shiv Khand	157–159 AD
Sriyan	160–189 AD
Swamy Sakesan	6 years
Pulumayi IV	

NON-ARYAN ORIGIN

Matriarchal System

We have already discussed this issue on chapter V, since names of some of the kings were matriarchal, hence proving prevalence of matriarchal tradition in the family. This tradition was not only non-Aryan but also native Naga, which was brought from Sumeria along with their migration. As such it proves that Sātavāhanas were also Nagas. But P.N. Chopra refutes this theory on the same pages with the argument, that such matriarchal names were in use simply to establish separate identity out of several queens in the Harems of Sātavāhana kings. But it can not be accepted in absence of supporting evidence, however there is direct evidence among the Chutus, their descendents, that Vishnu Skand was succeeded by Shiv Skand Nag, his daughter's son[56] and not by his own son thereby proving matriarchy and name of daughter was Nagmulnika. It shows Maharaja was himself a Nag and his progenitors Satavahan kings were also Nags.

Evidence of Coins

As earlier, referred to on Page 291, the type of coin of the founder of Sātavāhana rule, traced out from the collection of Shri Biyani of Akola,[57] below elephant has a figure of line with serpent like bend. This is an excited serpent and not river as Dr. Kolte thinks. As already explained elephant is indicative of royal authority and the figure of serpent is a symbol of Naga race or family of Sātavāhanas as has been noted in case of Bharsivas Nagas of Padmavati.

The Evidence of Inscriptions and Literature

As mentioned in the Simhāsanadvātrimsikā[58], the semi-legendary king Sālivāhana of Pratishthāna was the son of the Nāga Ananta (Seshanaga according to Bhandarkar– P–663) with whose help he slew Vikramāditya of Ujjaini (Weber, Indische studien vol XV P-228).

That Satavahans were of Naga race this fact is confirmed by the inscription of Chutukul (Banvasi Andhra) which was the main branch of Sātavāhanas[59].

According to Dr. Jayaswal[60] the pedigree of Chutu royal family, which was ruling in Vellari region, is as under :—

(1) Raja Haritiputra Vishnu Skanda. His queen was Mahabhoji Maharathini Nagmulnika.

(2) Haritiputra Shiv skand Varmman (Baijantipati).

We produce below the exact English translation of composition of their grant according to Heinrich Luders list no.1021 :—

Nāgmūlnikā, the daughter of Mahārajā and Mahābhoji, Mahārāthini, who is mother of Khand Nag Sataksiri and sister of Mahābhoj Ahija Bensen. She granted a cave to Bhikshu Sangha.

We interpret above translation as follows : Nagmulnikā, who is daughter of Maharaja (Chatsiri) and Mahabhoji (queen, daughter of Mahabhoji) Maharāthini (queen of Maharathi royal family), who is mother of Skandnag Sātak Siri and sister of Mahabhoja Ahija Vensen, (she) granted a cave to Bhikshu Sangha (guild of Buddhist monks).

We can further conclude from above lines as such : The name of daughter of Maharaja (Chatsiri) was Nagmulnika. It means maharaja was himself the Naga. She is mother of Skand Nāg Satak or her son was also a Naga. Skand Nag was ruling the state of Vellari in the time and under the dominion of Pulumayi, the last king of main branch of Sātavāhanas.

It means Chutu royal family was of Naga origin[61] and Sātavāhanas being their progenitors, were also Nagas[62]. From this pedigree we can draw another conclusion that this family was of matriarchal descent.

Gana State or Tribal Republican State

We have shown in chapter V and VI that the basis of Indigenous non-Aryan Naga culture was Sangha or Republic System. We will show here that Sātavāhanas also had similar type of political organization.

We learn from the inscriptions of Ashoka and Sātavāhanas that there was tribal-Republican system in Maharashtra in the time of Ashoka, the great and there were two main components of this tribal-republic, viz Mahar Ratta and Bhoja. Yadava Gana consisted of 18 families, which were organized into 4 tribes i.e. Vrashti, Kukkar, Andhaka and Bhoja. Similarly, in Maharashtra, various Naga families were organized into two tribes that is Mahar-Ratta and Bhoja[63]. The Gana of these two tribes was called Mahar-Gana[64]. On account of being a Gana or Rashtra, Maharashtra was Rashtra of Mahar-Gana, therefore in the time of reign of Ashoka this land was given this name "Mahar" which signifies a country. (See P-289 for evidences of different tribal groups)

This name Rashtrika-Pettinika which appears in the inscriptions of Ashoka, was designation of an officer (these were designations of two officers separately Angutara Pali 5-6-8-5 and 11) under the rulers of the local Mahār-Gana-Sangha. This administrative name of Rashtrika-Pettinika, is also mentioned in the Vajji-Gana, existing in the time of Buddha. But scholars derive different meaning of the word Rashtika-Pettinika, because presumably these were local names (Lok-Bachak). From the name Mahar, according to prevailing system of Gana, the existence of Mahar Gana is proved ; such as the Vajji Gana or the country or Nation of Vajji.[65]

During the time of Satvahanas we find clear evidence of their tribal associates from their inscriptions. From the description of their available name of Maharathi and Mahabhoja, it is clear that these were designations of chief of tribes of Mahar and Bhoja.

In spite of the tradition of bearing the title of a king among the Satvahanas, the form of their rule was tribal republican system. The Mahabhoji maiden, married in the royal family of Satvahanas, used to bear the title of Mahartthini or Maharthini. This is apparent from the following inscription of grant. This grant is inscribed on the water tank of monastery or Chetya Graha of Bedasā.

> "YAH DHAMMA DĀN MAHĀR THHĪNĪ MAHADEVI SĀMDINIKĀ KĀ HAI VAH MAHĀBHOJ Ki KANYĀ AUR APDEV-NĀK KI PATANI HAI"

In this writing SĀMDINIKĀ is (maiden) daughter of Mahābhoja. The mahārthini, the title of the chief of the family has been added to her and the title of Mahādevi also has been added. The title of Mahādevi is added to the women of royal families or the Virgin queens. Hence Apadevnāk would have been any person of Satavāhana royal family, and because of the title of the chief of the family, Mahārthini has been added to his wife, Virgin queen, Mahadevi Sāmadinikā. Hence it is clear that Apadev-Nāk himself would have been Maharathhi of Naga or Mahar tribe.[66]

Another example of a writing of grant, can be cited from the H. Luder's list no. 1021 which has been given on Page–297. The notable point in this composition is that the relation of Nāgmulnika, being the mother of Khandnāg Sātakasiri, is established with the Sātavāhana family and she is also called Mahārthini.

It seems clear from this that the title Mahārthini was used for maiden daughter of Mahabhoja, married in the royal family of Satavāhanas. It means Satavāhana was their royal[67] family but in addition to this being the chief of the tribe, title of her tribe or family was Mahārathi. The person, possessing the title, (of tribal chief) of Mahārathi, was husband of Nāgmulnikā and father of Shiva Skand Nāg Sat-Siri. Therefore he was also a Satavāhana Naga king and chief of the tribe as well.

The cause of absence of direct use of this title of Mahārathi, by Sātavāhanas was, prevalence of matriarchal system in the family[68]. It means every kind of real lordship was assigned to women, exactly on the pattern of West Asian tradition as mentioned in Chapter V (PP–102-04). Even all the grants have been issued in the name of women[69] only (name of Sātavāhana kings were also matriarchal). This was the main reason the family title of Mahārthini was directly used by women in their family. It means Sātavāhana royal family, with the title of Mahārathi, was chief of Mahār tribe (Mahār-Gana) and their Gan-Rajya (tribal kingdom[70].)

In the Sātavāhana dominion, Mahārathi royal family was also existing as a separate associate family. In Vayu Purana (37–352), Bibliothical Indica (Part II P–453) and Brahmānd Purana, it is stated that under the dominion of Andhras, five contemporary royal families were united. In both the above Puranas, whatever account of five royal families is given, we can surmise from this that most probably the names of Munda, Nanda and Mahārathi family are also included in this list which is also apparent from their coins (Rapsons C.A.D PP 57–60 ; revised P–212).

It can also be proved that like Mahar, Bhoja, was also tribal associate of Sātavāhanas ie. Maharathi and Mahabhoja were working in the form of Associate tribes of Sātavāhanas.

On the solid grounds of evidence of family traditions (Matriarchal family, tribal Gana or republic system), coins and inscriptions of Sātavāhanas, it is proved that they were not only Dravidian Andhras, but also Nagas. But learned scholar V.D. Mahajan opposes above theory on the ground that Sātavāhanas followed Hindu religious rites and performed Vedic Yajana : Satakarni I performed two Ashwamedha and one Rajsuya Yajna and bore Hindu titles. Hence they were Vedic Aryan Hindus.

Objection raised by Mahajan apparently seems convincing, but an indepth study of their religious and social traditions will disprove it. Some scholars[71] think that Buddhism or Jainism were the religions of Indigenous people of India from the age of Indus Valley culture (2700-1700 BC) and they trace their roots in the Zoroastrian religion of Iran, Magism of Sumeria. Hence we find that most of the Naga and aboriginal kings were followers of either Buddhism or Jainism. But, after the revival of Hinduism, during the period of Sunga and Kanva, the process of Aryanization began. According to N.K. Dutta, the later period of Naga rulers i.e. the few opening centuries of our era, was the age, when this process was in full swing. Hence, when we study the inscriptions relating to grants of this age, we find with great surprise that they are mostly issued in favour of Sanghas of Buddhism or Jain monks by the female members of the royal families[72], which shows that the female members were still followers of their old faith, while on the other hand most of the male members were, followers of Vedic Hindu religious rites and performed Yajnas, but also paid due respect to their old faith : Bharsiva, Vakataka, Ikshwakus of Siriparvata and Guptas are notable for such an act, although all of them were from the aboriginal blood. Similarly the Sātavāhanas also followed their foot-steps. As a matter of fact, Ashwamedha and Rajsuya Yajnas were performed to prove their high birth, and royal authority and impress upon the neighbouring kings, their subjects and subordinates working for them. Here we putforth viewpoint of Sudharshna[73] Senevritne in support. He writes, "In the cultural sphere the process of "Aryanization" perpetuated social differentiation, and the religious ideologies played a crucial role in legitimizing the existence of the ruling class and their hegemony over the subordinate group .... The Vedic and Brahmanical sacrifices practised by the Sātavāhanas were later performed by the Ikshwakus. Their inscriptions also mention other north Indian deities including the local deities who had been assimilated into the Indo-Aryan Pantheon."

Hence it is obvious that the Sātavāhanas performed Yajna under the process of Aryanization and only to consolidate their political and social position likewise their other counter parts such as Bharshivas, Vakataks, Ikshwakus and Guptas, etc.

It is most interesting that in Bhagwata Purana, without mentioning names Sātavāhanas are called Vrashala or Sudra. The first king of this family has been called Sisuka in Matsya and Sindhuka in Vayu Purana[74] (See genealogy P–294) which means king or royal family belonged to Sindhus or Indus Valley civilization. There is an inscription in which Chalukya king has mentioned his family name as Sendrak[75]. Similarly the royal family of Chakrakot has been called Sandrak or Chhindrak[76], (Chhinde or Sende) which was a well known Naga family of historical period. On the same ground we can say Sindhuka was also a Naga. Ex royal family of Gwalior is Sindhiya, which migrated from Satara. It seems that all royal families of likewise names were related to ruling class of Indus Valley in origin. This confirms completely our viewpoint that Sātavāhanas were originally from Naga race.

Were the Satavāhanas Brahmans ?

According to inscription of Nasik cave of Vasishthiputra Siri Pulumayi, they were Brahmnas. It is mentioned there that "The king Gautami-putra Satakarni, who is a matchless Brahmna and whose might is equal to Rama (Parshurama) has destroyed the glory and dignity of Kshatriya."

But Sastri K.A. Nilkant does not accept this view point of their Brahmana origin. He[77] disproves above theory and asserts "If our analysis of the word Satavāhana as given below, is correct, it will finally close the controversy of social origin of Sātavāhana. Ray Chowdhry indentifies them as Brahmana 'DVĀTRIMSATA PUTTĀLIKA' means Salivahana was born of blending of Brahmana and Naga. In the inscription of cave of Balasri of Nasik, Satakarni also has been stated to be a Brahmana and one who destroyed glory and dignity of Kshatriya (EK BĀHMAN AUR KHĀTIYĀ DAPĀ MĀNMADAN). On the above grounds alone one cannot reach any final conclusion. R.G. Bhandarkar has given a different meaning of the word 'EK BAHMANA' 'a custodian of Brahmana.' (Bombay Gazetteer II P–173). This adjective meaning of the "EK BRAHMANASYA" is approved by an analysis of, use of this word, for Bilvarmana Pallava, in the grant of Pikira and for Vishnu Kindin Madhava Varman. The mother of Gautami Putta, calls herself wife of Rajrishi (God King). Here the 'Khatia' is royal epithet of Kshatriya or a warrior, which was snatched by Gautami Putta by recovery of Sātavāhana rule from the paws of western Saka Kshatrapas''

I neither accept Bhandarkar's meaning of the word 'EK BAHAMAN' a custodian of Brahmana. nor agree with the Sastri, there are clear evidences to show that the Sātavāhanas were of Naga race in origin. Therefore Sātavāhana family had a Rajrishi or Priest-king indigenous tradition, which took its birth in Western Asia and noted in Indus Valley cities and Rigvedic period, which can be further noted in the tradition of Visvamitra in later Vedic period. (See chapter V PP 110–11 chapter X P–265 to 67). Tribe of Visvamitra was Andhra which was tribe of Sātavāhanas also.

They were Sangha or republican people, hence Rajrishi as discussed in chapter V. This is corroborated by the viewpoint of Jayaswal. He informs that- 'Rajrishi' tradition was prevailing among the republicans of later period whose chief, were formally sacred persons[78]. That is why mother of Gautami Putta has called herself wife of a Rajrishi.

We have given a vivid account of how these Nagas were Aryanized in chapt XV P–412-13 one of the most interesting method used for Aryanization was Hiranyagarbhya ceremony. This gets support of D.D. Kosambi.[79]

Satavahana ; A Maharathi Naga Family

Bhojas are said to be related to Yādava family. These Yadu Banshi people were called Mahar, Maharā or superior[80] and Mahareta meant son of Mahar, which was one of the epithet of Shrikrishna Yadava, Mahareti its feminine gender means 'Radhika', daughter of Vrishbhanu Mahar[81]. The word Mahār is a variation of Mahar or Maharā in Maharashtra. It means these Mahars were superior Nag and Yadu Banshi. They also used to call themselves superior Nag or Mahreta or their offshoot were Mahar. Therefore Bhojas were a component of Yadava tribe, usually Mahar Rattha were also component of their republican confederacy.

As shown earliers on Page 297 according to a donation inscription of queen Nagmulnika[82] (Luder's list No 1021) and another of queen Samdinika (from the cave of Bedasa) these Sātavāhanas were Maharathi and of the Naga race at the same time. In addition to inscriptions there are evidences of coins also.[83]

From Chittaldurga district, of north Mysore have been found coins of enormous size. They have a figure of Sakapot (Sak-Kumba), bull and Chetya tree and have a posy "Sadakan Kallāya Maharathis" (Rapson's catalogue). These coins were perhaps issued not by any Andhra king but by any governor of state 'Mahārathi'. But in this posy the word Sadakan, according to some scholars, means Satakarni or Satakārān, the plural form of sixth declension. In an inscription of Nānāghāt, the word Mahārathi also occurs. This Mahārathi of inscription may possibly be related to the Mahārāthi of above posy. If we accept this opinion then the period of coin would be 150 B.C. . This is the period of Shri Sat, who according to Puranas, was a king of Sātavāhana family[84].

The mention of the word 'Mahārathi' occurs in the cave of Nānāghat on a statue no. 4. It is as under :

"MAHĀRATHI TRANAK YIROKIPUTRI NĀYNIKA" another iṣ

"DEVI NĀYANIKAY RANNOCHO SIRI SĀT KANINO"

From the comparative study of these inscriptions of Nānāghat Buhler has concluded " Maharāni Naganika or Nāganika Maharathi daughter of Trinakayiro and wife of Simuk Putra Satakarni and mother of two princes named Shaktishri and Vedishri "

This inscription is related to the family of Satakarni and in it Simuk has been given the place of originator of family[85]. It seems from this writing that Queen Nāganikā wife of king Satakarni of Sāt-karni family is clearly said to be daughter of Mahārathi. Again the epithet of tribe or family-chief is not added. Therefore this Sātavāhana family was one of the chief families from the chiefs of Mahārathi tribe; it can be said quite firmly that they were of Naga race, and it is proved also.

The Sātavāhanas; Maharathi and Mahabhoj their two Components

With regards to political position of Maharathi and Mahabhojas, Dr. B.G. Gokhale has said that, "In Sātavāhana rule whatever two tribal groups were eminent, they were Maharathi and Mahabhoja. Their mention has been made in the inscriptions of Nanaghat, Karle, Bhaje, Bedsa, Kuda and Kanheri. It seems from this that they had a political and economic influence over a vast area of their kingdom''[86] He also has further stated that, ''The administration of Sātavāhanas was functioning through the officers of Maharathi and Mahabhoji.''[87] From the aforesaid system we have to accept this clear cut viewpoint that the administration of Sātavāhanas consisted of two tribal groups, Maharathi and Mahabhoja. But such a system can be found in the republican system alone. Hence their ruling system was based upon the elements of the republican system and therefore, two tribal groups of Maharathi and Mahabhoja are found united in their republican system of Sātavāhanas.

From the available inscription of Sātavāhanas we find mention of two component tribes of Mahar and Bhoja named Maharathi and Mahabhoja. Therefore the existence of Naga tribe of Mahārāstik from the time of Ashoka up to Sātavāhana is proved. Whatever representative of Mahar and Bhoj family tribes in the form of tribal chief was elected, he was assigned the title of chief of Maharathi and Mahabhoja in the age of Sātavāhanas. Sātavāhanas themselves wore the title of kings. According to traditional law of Gana Sangh or republic confederacy, the states of all the components were accepted to be equivalent. The dealings of Maharathi and Mahabhoja were of equal status. These two component tribes had marriage relations, on the status of equality. The chiefs of Kulas or tribes were hereditary. Their marriage relations used to take place mutually among the Mahabhojas and Maharathas. The daughter of Mahabhoja, Mahabhojani if married in Maharathi family, was called Maharthini. Maharathi and Mahabhoja used prefix or suffix Nag or Nak or Nay with their names. In the name of Sātavāhanas we find the use of suffix of the word Nag. The tradition of the use of names having suffix of Nag or Nak was hereditary among the Marathas and the Mahars up to the British rule (See chapt XV P 407-10 for detail).

Now-a-days, we see whatever predominance of caste system, it did not exist during the age of Sātavāhanas. In this period the population of Maharashtra mainly consisted of two tribes, the Maharathi and Mahabhoja and both of them were inter connected with each other by marriage relations. In those days people were free to choose profession of their own choice; the guilds, engaged in the professions of trade, artisan and industry, are visible in the inscriptions of contemporary period.

It can be concluded that Sātavāhanas were called Maharathi and they were originally related to Naga race of north known as Andhakas or Andhras. They were a branch of Vahika or Taka family of North West India.

The Ikshwakus of Sriparvata

We have already shown in chapter V and VI that traditions of cult of mother goddess, matriarchal family, Rajrishis were prevalent among the Ikshwaku family of Kashi, Kausal, Sakyas of Kapilvastu, proving them to be non-Aryan. Here we take another Ikshwaku family of Siri Parvata which ruled in South India in the historical age.

In the district of Guntur, at the bank of river Krishna, on the hills of Nagarjunakonda, few days back a large number of inscriptions have been discovered by archaeologists[88]. On the basis of above findings Dr. Hiranand Shastri has identified the historical place of Sriparvata. There was fortification in between these hills in this period.

It seems that this site would have been a capital of the local state, from the Mauryan or pre Mauryan period[89]. Mr. Longhurst has excavated remains of some such Buddhist stupas from this place, which have carvings of Amaravati style. Mr. Kuraishi has the credit of tracing out eighteen inscriptions from this site, out of which fifteen were on marble pillars. All these pillars were standing around a great stupa or Mahachetya enshrining relics of the great Buddha. We have come to know from these inscriptions that the name of this place was Sriparvata.

According to a tradition famous Buddhist monk and scholar Nagarjuna went to Sriparvata and died there. The name of this hill, still today is Nagarjunikonda[90].

All the discovered inscriptions are in Prakrit of the Pali type.[91] Some stone buildings and main buildings were got constructed by some ladies and were constructed on the advice and under the supervision of Buddhist monk and architect reverend Ananda. All these donor ladies were from the Ikshwaku royal family[92].

First of all, we came to know about Ikshwaku royal family from three inscriptions, which were discovered from Jaggayyapeta in the year 1882 A.D. and these inscriptions were assigned to third century A.D. by Dr. Buhler (I.A XI P–256). The present inscriptions disclose the fact that many of the royal ladies were Buddhists, while the kings were all Hindus and their capital town (Vijayapuri) was in the valley close by. Most of the inscriptions are dated in the reign of king Sirivira-Purisadata, between his 6th and 18th regnal years, whose date at Jaggayyapeta is the year[93] 20. One inscription is dated in the 11th year of Maharaja Vasithiputa SIRI BAHU VALA-CHATAMULA (Chatamula II). These inscriptions along with Jaggayyapeta inscriptions give the following genealogy of Ikshwaku royal family :

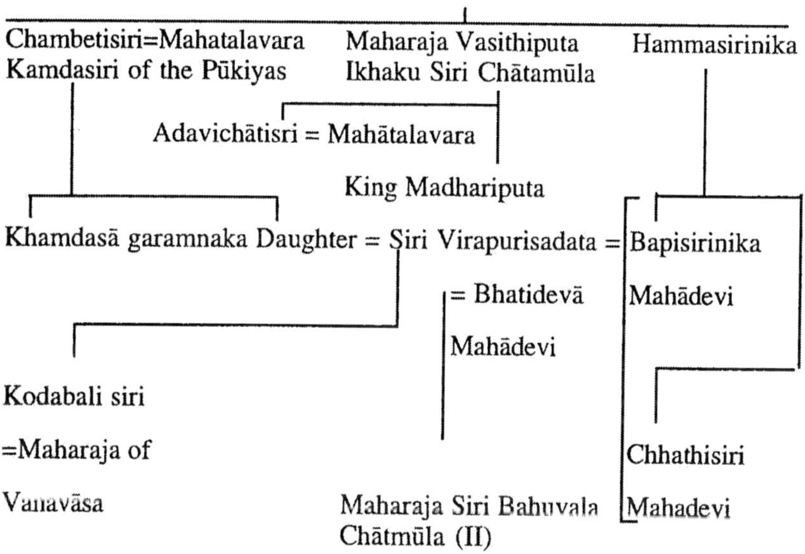

(1) Maharaja Vashishthiputra Ikshwaka Siri chātmul I (220–30 AD)

(2) Raja (Mathhriputra) Madriputra (230–50 AD).

(3) Mahāraja Siri Bāhubal Chatmul II (250–60 AD).

Sanskrit Form of names

Virpurisdat	=	Virapurush Datta
Chantisiri	=	Shantishri
Hammasirinika	=	Harmya shrika
Chhathhi	=	Shashthi (Katyayani Devi)
Chat	=	Shat

Vira Purisadata[94] married three cousins, two of whom are called Mahadevi in inscriptions of the same date (E.I. XX PP 19–20) Bhatadeva was probably the eldest queen, being the mother of Chātmūla II. There were four more royal ladies who made donations but their relationship is not given. Their names are as follows :

(1) The Mahādevī Rudradhara Bhattārika Ujanika (from Ujjain) daughter of a Maharaja. She with Chānti siri donated 107 Pillars and a large amount of dināras to the Vihāra.

(2) A Mahātalavari, and the mother of the Mahātalvara Mahāsenapati Vinhu siri, and the wife of the Mahāsenapati Mahātalavara Vasithiputa Mahā Kumda siri of the Prakiyas

(3) Chula Chātasirikā Mahāsenapatnī, wife of the Mahāsenapati Mahātalavara Vasithiputa-Khamda-chalikiremmanaka.

According to Jayaswal "There was a Maharāja of Vanavāsa to whom a royal lady of the Ikshwaku family (Sister of Chātmūla II) was married. He was probably the last or one of the last Chutu kings, who, from his title seems to have become subordinate to the Ikshwaku. It is clear that Chatamūla I was originally a Maharaja to the Sātavāhana ; his title is generally omitted in the inscriptions, he being described merely as Siri Chātamūla of the Ikshwaku and when the title is given (e.g. by his daughter E I XX–18) it is always Maharaja while Vira Purisadata (except twice) is always 'King' (Rajan). The Son of the latter, Chātamūla II is always Maharāja (EI XX.24). This shows that the royal position was assumed by Chātamūla I and lasted for only one generation more, having been lost in the time of Chātamūla II. That Rudradhara Bhattarika was the daughter of the Maharaja of Ujjain proves that in the time of the Ikshwakus, there was a Hindu ruler in Avanti and not a Satrapa, a fact confirmed by Puranic history and other sources. Rudradhara Bhattārika's father must have been a member of the Bhara-Siva empire"[95].

King Siri Chātmūla (I) had performed Agni-hotra, Agnishoma, Bajapeya and Aswamedha and was worshipper of Mahasena, marshal of the gods[96]. They had the Ikshwaku's custom of marrying cousins. Their toleration of Buddhism is remarkable.

It seems that this policy of tolerance was being adopted because an indigenous royal family was under process of Aryanization like Bharshiva and Sātavāhana Naga families; that is why they showed an extra ordinary enthusiasm for these Yajnas, like wise aforesaid two families and Guptas. Otherwise, most of the women of royal families, were still Buddhists and matriarchal character of family was still in existence. That is why all the grants were issued by royal ladies and none by a king or any of the male member of the royal family. In this case Ikshwakus seem to follow the foot-steps of their former lords, the Sātavāhanas.

It is also proved from the script of inscriptions of Chantisiri's family that this work belongs to the third Century A.D. Buhler has fixed the ruling period of Vir Purisadatta, third Century A.D. [97] (E.I. Part I P–5). He was nephew and a son-in-law of Chantisiri. It seems that king Chatamula I performed the Ashwamedha sacrifice in about 220 A.D. within a few days, after the end of the rule of the Chandasati, the last king of Sātavāhana family. It is clear from the names of family members that they were Prakrit speaking people of the north.

Ikshwaku a Non-Aryan Royal Family

According to the most of the scholars, Ikshwakus were good or Aryan Kshatriya and prominent advocate of this theory is K.P. Jayaswal[98]. He puts forth his remark as such, "The family (Ikshwaku) was of a good Kshatriya stock from the North. They married cousins like ancient Ikshwaku. They, very likely, had migrated to the South in the imperial days of the Sātavāhanas, when the latter reached the Uttar-Pradesh and Bihar .... Later they established themselves in the eastern zone of Sātavāhana empire to share the responsibility of defence."

Another group of scholars identifies them to be of tribal origin. Leading scholar and advocate of this theory is Sudharshan Senevritne. His[99] theory is as under, "The state often existed through an insulations of chiefdom and dominated tribes rather than being incompatible with the existence of tribal societies (Maurce Godelier, ''Perspectives in Marxist Anthropology'' Cambridge 1977 P–88). The fact that titles turned out to be hereditary under the Ikshwakus further confirms the establishment of a permanent ruling class. Interestingly, during their period of political consolidation traits of matriarchy and cross-cousin marriages diminished to a great extent among the Ikshwakus. ....The adaptation of the high-sounding titles, dynastic names (such as Ikshwaku which was a revival of a name which earlier existed in north India.) was largely due to the attempt made by the local ruling houses to initiate the norms of the north Indian rulers and their former overlords. This was also evident in the cultural and religious spheres. Thc Vedic and Brahmanical sacrifices practised by the Sātavāhanas were later performed by the Ikshwakus. Their inscriptions also mention other north Indian deities, including, the local deities who had been assimilated into the Indo-Aryan-pantheon. A large number of inscriptions further indicate the patronage extended to Buddhism by the royalty and the nobility of Andhra. In Kalinga the inscription of Kharvela refers to endowment made by him to the Brahmanas and also the Jain establishments."

Both the theories of Kshatriya and tribal origin seem to be correct. But they were indigenous tribal Kshatriyas like Satvahanas and Sakyas. When we conduct an indepth study of tradition of Ikshwakus it becomes crystal clear that their origin fits well with the Indus Valley and Sumerian culture. We have already discussed this issue at length in chapter V PP 91-94. Here we put them in a summed up form :

(1) This Ikshwaku family also can be equated well with the Semitic Hyksos. According to Dr. Buddha Prakash, Hyksos, Akkaku (Pali, Prakrit) and Ikshwaku (Sanskrit), are different linguistic forms of one original word[100]. This equation of Hyksos and Ikshwaku words is not merely an imagination, we have solid evidences in support. These Hyksos, which are also known as Semites, Akkadians and Jewes had their National deity known as Bal or Baal.[101] According to A.C. Dass[102] Bal was a Sun god. Bala tribe of Saurashtra calls itself Surya Banshi.[103]

This deity was brought to India along with their migration. Repeated mention has been made of this deity in Rigveda[104] in reference to Panis. Till today Bal or Bahubal deity is worshipped in the Jain tradition in South India. Bahubal or Bahubali was son of Adi Jain tirthankar Brashabha Deva, who was a prince of Ikshwaku family[105]. (See chapter x PP 256-57 XIII PP 376-77 for detail) It is very interesting to note that the name of the last king of this family was Maharaja Siri Bahubal having name after the above deity Similarly, the name of another Maharaja was Kodbal Siri or Kodabali Siri. (ko means god or king in Dravidian language, Mahajan Vidyadhar "Ancient India" PP 21–23). It is obvious that this family had its roots in Indus Valley and Semitic culture. Such an identification, though a far-fetched idea, is very striking.

(2) Matriarchal family

This family was matriarchal in character like the Ikshwakus of ancient time (Rishabh dev, Pārashwa Nath, Rama and Buddha)[106]. We have three evidences in support of this view :

(A) The names of kings of this family were matriarchal in form (See chapter V PP 103-05).

(B) Vira Purisadata married his three maternal cousin sisters like ancient Ikshwakus. He was nephew and son-in-law of Chantsiri his predecessor. Thus Virpurisadata being daughter's husband of Chantsiri became legal heir of the throne like Rudrasena I Vakataka became the heir of throne of Bharsiva.

(C) Most important evidence is 18 inscriptions traced out from Sri-Parvata, which are, grants, issued by ladies of Ikshwaku royal family and non by king or male member, thereby proving matriarchy (See chapter V P–103-05).

(3) According to Sudhir Chattopadhyaya (Racial Affinities of Early North Indian tribes P–80) the royal family of Malla-belonged to the Ikshwaku family or the solar race while Manu (X–22) makes them degraded Kshatriya (Vratya) like Jhalla, Malla, Lichchhavi, Nat, Karan and Dravids Vratyas, non-Aryan, which were out of Hindu pantheon. It means Ikshwakus were also non-Aryan.

(4) It is a well known fact that Videha family was also one of the branches of Ikshwaku family. In Puranas they have been called of Manava race. Manu (X–13 and 19) declares that Videhas are born of Vaishya man and Brahman woman i.e. they were Sudras.

(5) Pārashwanātha, the 23rd Jain Tirthankar was Ikshwaku as well as a Naga prince belonging to the family of famous emperor Sishu Naga of Magadha. Hence they were of non-Aryan Naga race.

(6) Lachhaman, the younger brother of Rama, likewise Baldev, the elder brother of Krishna is said to be reincarnation of Sesh Naga. It means he was from Naga race. Rama himself was of black colour like Krishna Yadava.

Hence it is quite clear that Ikshwakus were of indigenous non-Aryan Naga race.

The Naga Rulers of South India

It is most interesting that scholars like D.R. Bhandarkar[107] have tried to show that the Pandya royal family of South, was ethnically related to the Pandavas, the Aryan rulers of north India, although that was an Indigenous matriarchal family. Chopra P.N. in his valuable work. titled "History of South India" has given most valuable information on the origin of ruling families of South Chola, Pandyas and Cheras, which being most important, quoted in full[108]—

"The hunter tradition developed, it would appear into western part of the Tamil country and the Cheras inherited it. They adopted the bow, the chief weapon of the ancient hunter, as their emblem which they inscribed on their flags and impressed on their coins. Anthropologically the Cheras could be connected with the Kadavar, though the Pallavas of later times too were occasionally called the Kadavar. The Pandyas were mainly pastoral but it looks as if their seafaring tendencies of more ancient times (a relic perhaps of their proto-historic contacts with the phoenicians) had left the fish as their emblem. The Pandyas were surely related to the Minas or the Minavar (fishermen). The leading tribesmen in the agricultural tracts worshipped the rain-god (who they called the Vendan i.e., Indra) prayed for uninterrupted supply of water to the crops and almost treated as a deity the river Kaveri which was the chief source of economic prosperity of the delta area. In the case of the Cholas who ruled over most of the agricultural tracts, either because they had deforested the adjacent jungle tracts and brought them under cultivation i.e., had tamed the tiger which roamed the forests, or because they had conquered the hunters who stood for the tiger, they had adopted the tiger as their emblem. The fisher-folk, for simpler reasons, inscribed the shark on their flags. These happenings of course belonged to very ancient times and explain, how in historical times, when royalty came to be well established, each royal family adopted particular emblem."

The Cholas

Cher, Chola and Pandyas have been important indigenous tribes of Ancient India. H.L.[109]Kosare puts forth his opinion on their origin and history, "Urgapur was one of the town of Nagas of Southern region. We have enough informations on this issue. Ptolemy has informed that the name of the chief city of Southern Cholas was Aur-Thaur. Aur-Thaur was capital of Shor Nagas and it was under Shoartai (E.A. 8 P–368). The word Shor is synonymous of 'Sor' or 'Chol' of Tamil language. It is quite clear from the name of Shor Nagas that Aur-Thaur was the capital of one of the Naga kings; whosoever, he was called Shor (Chola) because he was the ruler of Shor-Tai (D.R. Bhandarkar, Ram Prakash Ojha "Ashoka" PP 35–36). Aryans, just to show their hatred for Indigenous people, have called them Chola or Chor (Thief). Cunningham has informed us that the Uragapur which was situated near Trichana-palli, is Aur-Thaur. Therefore that was the kingdom of Southern Chola and they were Nagas. In Buddhist tradition of eylon and Shiam one Naga country has been called Majerik. According to some scholars, Majerik was near Diamond Sand and according to another group, it was near Karachi (Cunningham, Ancient geography of India PP–611–12). In the age of Periplus, Majerik or Muyuri Kaudu was kingdom of modern Kangnoor and Keralaputtra, which during Ptolemic time, was in Karur or distt Coimbatore at the bank of Kaveri river at the place of Karur (Ram Parkash Ojha, Ashoka PP 42–43). In Mahabamsa, Majerik has been called. Nagabhumi or Nagaland (Turner P–185). Vassro-Nag, according to Ptolemy as has been cited by Cunningham, was said to be a form of Majerik-Naga and the Malang as cited by Ptolemy is, said to be kingdom of Majerik Nagas. Similarly the grand stupa to Majerik described by Hieuntsang is grand stupa of Dhannakakata, which would have been in existence in first or second century A.D. Dhannakakata was a religious centre and Malang or Bengi was capital (Cunningham P–455).'' It is evident that Cholas were also of Naga Race in origin.

The Pallavas

The Pallava royal family of South India also originated from the Chola kings. Naga[110] descent was also assigned to this famous dynasty of the Pallavas, which held sway on the coast of Coromandel from the fourth to the middle of the eight century of our era. A curious legend preserved in Tamil poetry connects the origin of the Pallavas with the Cholas, the ancient rulers of Coromandel : it tells us that the first 'Tondaiman' (i.e. Pallava) was son of a Chola king by a female serpent-demon (In the ancient Tamil poem Manimekalai the Nagi is called Pilivalai, the daughter of the Naga king Valaivanan (Airāvana) Venkayya A.S.R. for the year 1906–07 PP 220 F). In the Pallava inscriptions, she is called an Apsara, but a Nagi in the inscription of the Ganga-Pallava.

The Kadambas (325–360 AD)

It seems from the Devgiri inscription of Kadamba Krishan Varman that the origin of this family was from Nagas.[111]

Gustab Oppert has given three legendary origins of Kadamba royal family, but among them one is the most famous. It is as under[112]—

"These are the two most widely-spread reports, but according to another a Brahman of Yalgi underwent a severe penance in order to become a king through the favour of Madhukesvara (H.H. Wilson's Mackenie collection PP Ci, Ciii old edition PP 149–150 new edition) His penance was graciously accepted, and a divine voice informed him that he would be reborn as a peacock, that the person who would eat his head would become a king, that those who would partake of his breast would become ministers, and that those who would feast on the remainder of his body would become treasurers. The Brahman satisfied with this promise, went to Kashi, where he killed himself with a spear and was reborn as a peacock. In such a state he roamed about in the forest and announced with a shrill voice that the person who would eat his head would become a king ; until he fell into the hands of a gang of thieves, who were resting under a Kadamba tree. They killed the bird and asked a woman, Puṣpavatī by name, who was living near by, to cook the peacock and to distribute its flesh amongst them. While the woman was preparing the peacock, and the thieves were bathing, her son came home very hungry, and, as he wanted something to eat, his mother gave him the head of the bird in ignorance of what was in store for him who ate it. When he had eaten it, the thieves returned, partook of the remainder of the meat, but were astonished that after staying a while, none of them was proclaimed king. They fetched the woman, who, when hard pressed, told them what she had done, and that her son had eaten the head of the peacock. The thieves found that it was of no use to fight against destiny and submitted to their fate.

The king Ānakapurandara of Jayantīpura had died at that very time without leaving any living issue behind and, as was the custom in those circumstances; the ministers let the state elephant loose with a water vessel containing holy water. While thus roaming about, he came to the spot in the forest near which the son of Puṣpavatī was living close to the Kadamba tree. The elephant bowed down to the youth, who ascended the animal and was carried by him to Jayantīpura, where he was joyfully received, placed on the royal throne and anointed as king. He assumed, henceforth, the name Mayūrasarman according to R. C. Majumdar Kadamba and ruled for a long time gloriously over the country. (325–345 AD)

The election of a king in Indian legends is often entrusted to a state-elephant, and widely spread is also the belief that he who eats the head of a peacock becomes a king. The peacock is in Sanskrit called Mayūra, hence the name Mayūrasarman, which the youth accepted. So far as the person and his origin are concerned, the two legends differ, as one refers to Trinētra and the other to Mayūrasarman Kadamba, but the Kadamba tree plays in both traditions a significant part. As Puṣpavatī prepared the food for the thieves of which her son partook, and which she distributed among the thieves, one may assume with good reason that she belonged to the same caste as the thieves who caught the peacock, and these people I feel inclined to identify with the Kuṛumbas. The peacock plays an important part in the account of the settlement of the Kallas in the Kaḍambavanam or Kaḍambātavi of Madura. So far as the expression thief is concerned, it must not be forgotten that thieving or robbing was not considered disgraceful, if it was practised as a regular profession, just as cattlelifting did not in former times attach any stigma to those who indulged in it in the Highlands of Scotland.''

The Kadamba[113] tree, of which there exist various species, is much esteemed for its flowers which are sacred to the god Skanda, for its fragrant and highly esteemed powder which is used at religious ceremonies, for the juice which exudes from its stem, and for other reasons. Its name was spelt in various ways, Kaḍamba and Kādamba, and as it was originally an indigenous plant, I presume that this term is also indigenous and Non-Aryan. I believe,[114] ''That the people and the dynasty, which we call Kadambas, were actually a branch of the Kuṛumbas, who had assumed a slightly modified designation by changing their name Kuṛumba into Kaḍamba, and that the stories about the Kadamba tree are inventions of later times in order to explain the coincidence.'' It is hardly necessary to restate here the resemblance between the a and u sounds, and to mention that the Kadamba plant is in various places of India called Kudumba. (Dr Morison Winslow's Tamil and English dictionary P–219).

I have had occasion to express the peculiar mode of confederation prevalent among the Kuṛumbas and a similar institution is said to have existed among the Kaḍambas.

Yet, what seems to establish the original identity between the Kuṛumbas and the Kaḍambas, is the fact that the term Kaḍamba is actually found in Tamil as a synonymous and identical expression for Kuṛumba, though this situation has up to now escaped the notice it really deserves. (Mr. Grigg's Manual of the Nilagiri District).[115]Infact, a very clear picture of Yadava culture of Mathura, emerges in the Kadamba culture.

At a much later period we find the Kaḍambas connected with the last great dynasty of Southern India, the Rājas of Vijayanagara. The founders of this kingdom are also said to have been Kurumbas. If the first family of the Vijayanagara kings were Kurumbas, and on the other hand related to the once famous, but then decayed though not extinct royal house of the Kadambas of Tuluva, historical evidence, however slight, would have been adduced to establish the connection between the Kuṛambas and the Kadambas, and this connection is in its turn supported by philological proof of the original identity[116] of their names. (Lewis Ricis Mysore and Coorg Vol III P–98) Kadambas are found to be related to the last dynasty of Vijaynagar who were Nagas in origin, since we have already proved in chapter IX that Yadavas were Nagas Hence it is proved that Kadambas were also Nagas.

The Ratta Nagas of South

There was a Naga family of Ratta people in South. Its evidences are available from the Pali literature. In Shankh Paul Jataka[117] there is a character of this name. He was Naga king of Mahinsak-Ratta. In Mahinsak-Ratta, there was a tank named Shankh Paul, where from a river named Kanda-Pandã originated. Pali Mahinsak-Ratta was a janapada in the South. Mahinsak-Ratta or Mahinsak Rastra has its direct meaning. But the people of that country were known only by the name of Ratta. The reference of Shankh paul Jatak would have been of pre-Mauryan period or probably of a period earlier than the Buddhist. Therefore Mahinsaka-Ratta would have been of pre-Buddhist period. The king of these Rattas was Shankhpaul Nag. It is quite clear that Mahinsak Nag was of Ratta Naga family Mahinsak is Karnataka[118]. Because this Shankhpaul Nag was considered to be most respected person hence he has been called Mahānag.[119]

Mahinsak as described in Pali literature, has been equated with Karnat or Karnatak state, the people of this state were Ratta. In confirmation of this fact another historical evidence is being quoted. Kalhan in his Rajtarangini has given description of world cónquest of Naga Banshi king Lalitaditya ruling over Kashmir. The ruling period of Lalitaditya begins in 700 AD. He defeated Yashovarman, the king of Kanauj. After winning over Goda king of Bengal, he subjugated Chālukyas, Karnāt alias Ratta in Kaveri Valley, Pallavas of Kanchi country and Sapta-Kaunkan country of Kadamba. Similarly he subjugated Saurashtra or king of Dwarika, in the long run king of Avanti (Malva) country etc. Among these countries, in the country of Karnāt, in the family of Ratta a queen used to rule. Kalhan claims that she accepted the supremacy of Lalitaditya of her own accord[120].

In this connection C.V. Vaidya[121] has traced out the relation of queen of Ratta family with the region of eastern Valley. Kalhan, has described her, as the queen of Ratta family of Karnat country. The Karnat country is equated with Karnataka and that region has been called Mahinsaka in Pali literature and Mahishak in Sanskrit. It can be concluded from this that there was rule of Rattas in Karnataka in seventh and eighth century A.D. From this conclusion, meaning of Mahinsak Rattha also has become clear that in Mahinsak country there was rule of Ratta Naga king named Shankhpaul. Therefore it is clear that Rattas were kings of Naga family.

The Chalukyas

C.V. Vaidya has said Chālukyas were Chalke or Solankhi. The Pallavas of Kanchi are now represented by the family surname of Pālave and the Kadambas of Konkanapura or Banavāsi are represented by the Kadambas. Thus all the three important kingdoms in the South in the beginning of the 7th century were Maharattis or Marathas or in other words speaker of Prakrit or mixed Maharashtri language, originally occupying the country round the Godavari[122]. It is quite clear from this that Chalukya, Pallava and Kadamba royal families were Marathi speaking people in origin and their language was Maharashtri Prakrit.

Following the aforesaid view point of C.V. Vaidya, we have to say that Chalukya, Pallavas were from the original Naga royal family of Maharatthi or Ratthi. Similarly Rashtrakuta royal family seems to be born from the Yadubansha or Bhoja family, who were also Nagas in origin. In fact the royal family of Rashtrakuta rose in the eighth century AD. The evidence of relation of Rashtrakuta with the Yadubansha appears in the inscription of Kharipatan, Sangli, Navasāri and Wardha. In the copper plate of wardha it has been said that Rashtrakutas are from the family of king named Ratta, who was from the Satyaki branch of Yadus. Ratta had a son named Rashtra-kuta, after whose name, the family got its name Rashtrakuta[123]. The origin of these Rashtrakutas was from the Bhoja, one of the associate families of Sātavāhanas, who were Nagbanshi in origin.

Chalukya, Kadamba used to call themselves Haritiputra and Manavya Gotra,[124] likewise Chutukala, a branch of Sātavāhana. As such Chalukyas are proved to be a branch of Sātavāhana or Bhoja.

Kashyapa Gotra

It is notable that most of the Naga kings used suffixes like Ditya or Dutta, Nandi, Mitra, Sena and Naga or Nak to their names. But it is more important that they used to call themselves Kashyapa and Mānavya Gotri and also Haritiputra. What is the significance of these words ?

We have already made mention of a legend from Mahabharata in chapter I, which tells that Daksha gave his thirteen maiden daughters to Kashyapa Rishi in marriage. The name of one of the daughter was Kaḍru, who gave birth to Nagas. It seems that on the basis of above legendary event, all the Nagas used to call themselves Kashyapa.

Scholars are of the view that Kashyapa was a prominent Jain Muni. According to a description given in the Adipurana, Pārshwanath was born in Urga family, his progenitor was Kashyapa, whose surname was Madhava[125]. According to Jain tradition (chapter X PP 256-58) out of 24 Tirthankaras (except Nemi and Muni Subrata) 22 were of Kashyapa Gotra. Nemi being of Yadu origin, was also Naga. Hence it can be said that all the Jain tradition from beginining to end was related to Kashyap Nagas.

Pārashwanatha, the 23rd Tirthankar had. 'serpent' as his insignia and he was born in the Naga family known as Urga.

The ancient Multan city of Panjab is known by different names, but one of its oldest name according to Cunningham, was Kashyapapur[126] Kashyapapur was founded by Kashyapa. After Kashyapa, his eldest son, Daitya Hiran Kashyapa born from the Diti, succeeded him. After him his son Prahlad and later his son Vana, became the heir of the kingdom of Kashyapa. At the same time Shri Krishna killed him (Vana Asura) and later Krishna's son Samba became the king of Kashyapapur. In the inscriptions (E.I. Vol X P–25) of 10th and 11th century AD there are evidences that many Naga kings had their Kashyapa Gotra.

Cunningham has equated the pool of Naga-rāj Elapatra with the fall of Hasanabdal[127]. It is said, the long body of the Naga Raja Elapatra was spṛead in the land between Takshila and Banaras. Here the extension of his body means his rule was from Takshila to Banaras. In the inscription of Chakrakota royal family Elapatra has been called Elburg who was progenitor of the royal family[128]. It seems that the eldest Naga son of Kashyapa and Kadru might have been this Elapatra.

Manavya Gotra

Feridun has been identified almost without doubt with Thraetaona of the Zend-Avesta, celebrated as the slayer of the three headed serpent Dahaka (Zohak), who was the creation of the evil power Angra Mainyus (Weber's Indische studien Vol III P–416) or more popularly Ahriman[129] (Ahi is Serpent) It means the three headed Parthian Naga king Zohak, the earliest legendary Naga king, was created by Angra Mainyu (Ahir man). It means Angra-Mainyu who was a Naga was primogenitor of Nagas.

According to Tod[130]– "In Bhavishya Purana it is stated that Vaivaswata (Sun born) Manu (who was saved by a fish from deluge) ruled at the mountain Sumeru. Of his seed was Kakustha king, who obtained sovereignty at Ayodhya and his descendants filled the land and spread over the world" Further Tod informs, "I am aware of the meaning given to Sumeru, that thus the Hindu designated the north pole of the earth. But they had also a mountain with the same appellation of pre-eminence of Meru (the hill) with the prefix "Su" good or sacred ; the sacred hill .... " to the south of Sumeru are the mountains Himavan, Hemkutta and Nishada ; to the north are (the countries) Nila, Sweta, and Sringi"

It is clear from this ancient traditions that Manu was ruling on Sumeru hills, which were situated somewhere in the north of Himalaya, (Hemkutta) it means somewhere in Iran and not Central Asia ; because:

(1) The legend of Zohak Naga, brings him from Iran (Babylonia) whose progenitor was Angra Mainyu.

(2) Scholars are of the view that the legends of deluge is a Sumerian (near Sumeru hills) traditions and not central Asian which is covered by desert (Baluka Samudra)

(3) Legend of Vaivaswata (Sun born) Manu or sun god (Vishnu) is more prominent in almost all the western Asia than any where else.

(4) It has been proved in chapter V that Ikshwakus, who have been said to be the offshoot of Vaivaswata Manu, were matriarchal non-Aryan migrants from western Asia. It seems from above that manu is an Indian Version of Angra Mainyu.

(See Chapter-IX, P. No. 243 for Genealogical Table)

The view that the tradition of Manu is of Iranian origin gets the support of R. Shaffer[131]. His observation is based on thorough studies of Sanskrit literature. In his own words, "In another migration the Iraninas were the first to descend the Saryu. They (Yadu etc) were followed by the Indo-Aryans who forced the Iranians to scatter towards east and west where they became the eastern and the western Manavah the earliest race in India."

Hence it is crystal clear that the Manavah were non-Aryans and not Aryans. Perhaps the eastern Manavah directly travelled from Panjab to modern Uttar Pradesh since Yakshus of Rigveda attacked Sudasa from the direction of Yamuna and finally settled in eastern part, where they were known Suryabanshi and Ikshwakus who helped in the development of Buddha and Jain religion. On the other hand western Manavah seem to be related to the great Yadava race, main branch of which was Chandra banshi and most of the Naga families. They were earlier followers of Buddhism and Jainism and later became followers of Siva cult which appears in Indus Valley.

Cultural Homogeneity and Cult of Mother Goddess (Bhūmāta) or Haritimata Among the Nagas

It has been proved in chapter I and V that the cult of mother goddess and Snake worship originated in Western Asia, which were brought to Indus Valley by the Sumerians along with their migration. From Indus Valley their evidences of archaeology have been traced out (Illustration No. VI). Hence both the traditions were related to Indigenous Harappan culture and their progeny, the Nagas.

The evidence of racial and cultural similarity, among the people of Megalithic age and Sātavāhanas, is visible in the cult of mother goddess (see Illustration no. VI) in practice among them. A figurine of Nagnakabandhā mother goddess has been excavated from the Megalithic stratum of Mahurjhari from Vidarbha. The existence of this mother goddess, appears particularly in different parts of Maharashtra and Karnataka in the beginning of historical period. Figurines of mother goddess have been traced out in abundance from the Sātavāhana and Chalukya age. In some centuries, before the beginning of Christian era the covering area of figurines of this mother goddess was very vast. In Hindu culture this Nagna-Kabandha is known as Lajjagauri[132]. Such like terracotta figurines of mother goddess with 6 to 9 inches in hight have been recovered from the Chalcolithic stratum of Nevasa[133]. It is obvious from this that in ancient time the cult of mother goddess played an important role in the cultural life of the people of Maharashtra, which had characteristic of homogeneity with the culture of Indus Valley also. In addition to this there was also striking similarity in naked figurines of mother goddess recovered from Takshila and Kausam and with those of Maharashtra. This proves a cultural similarity in a vast area from Takshila to Indus Valley and Maharashtra. This culture of Maharashtra was related to the predecessors of Sātavāhanas, Cholas, Cheras Pandyas and Kadambas who were Nagas and builders of Megaliths. It means these people had a cultural relation with Indus Valley.

Vasudev Sharan Aggarwal, has given a pictograph of an ancient terracotta figurine of mother goddess in his book titled 'India as known to Panini.' Its hands are coiled round with serpents and vegetation has grown up, on its head. This figure is of serpent queen described in Taitreya Samhita (I-5-4-1; VII 3-1-3) Aitreya Brahman and Satapath Brahman.[134]

Earth is called serpent queen.[135] Kadru or earth was mother of serpents (See chapter P–1) that is why Nagaloka (land of serpents) is also called Pātala[136].

In Buddhist tradition, mother goddess, is known as Haritimata. From the early Christian era, it was worshipped as a prominent deity in north, from Central Asia up to the Magadha and the Bengal (Paikpar Distt Dhaka)[137]. There was tradition among the Naga kings to call themselves 'sons of Haritimata.' It is compatible with the matriarchal family tradition of Sātavāhanas.

It was identical with the mother goddess of Nagas. In those days Buddha's religion had its over all effect on the society of Maharashtra. Due to the effect of Buddhist religion Hariti, the Venerable mother goddess of Buddhist tradition was reverenced on the high status of mother goddess of their families by the Chalukyas, Sātavāhanas, Kadambas and Chuttus. Likewise Chutus, Kadamba and Chalukya of south, in the beginning Vakatakas also used to call themselves Haritiputra. This information particularly is given by Dr. V.V Mirashi.[138]

National mother goddess of Sumer was Ninhursanga. Mesalim in one inscription calls himself "Beloved son of Ninhursanga." Eanatum claims to drink the "good milk of Ninhursanga." The sacred rite of marriage was celebrated by the ruler and the queen or the en-priestess, magically to promote the fertility of land and herds, a prosperous harvest and a favourable inundation[139].

All these traditions, in practice in Sumer, were similar to those in practice in India as above.

The symbolic form of mother goddess is Bhūmātā or Earth mother. Bhūmātā is always shown as a symbol of serpent. This Bhūmātā is also known as the mother of serpents. Even in Greek civilization Bhūmātā is considered to be the mother of serpents and shown in the form of a serpent[140]. Dikshit[141] has thrown light on this subject that, "Where, the spirit of mother creator of the world or Shaktimata" (mother of energy) is maintained, there mother goddess is also worshipped. Serpent or Naga worship is also prevalent in all those countries."

Therefore it seems definite that the cult of mother goddess and serpent worship are inter-connected with each other.[142]

It is apparent from the above evidences that the Nagas builders of Megaliths, practised cult of mother goddess and serpent worship, like Sumerians and Indus Valley people. This proves racial and cultural similarity of these people i.e. Megalithic Indus Valley and Sumerian people. Since Sātavāhanas, Vakataka, Pallavas, Chuttus, Kadambas, Chalukyas were also worshippers of mother goddess or Haritimata, hence they were also a part of the same society and culture, that is why they used to call themselves Haritiputra or son of mother goddess.

Were Haritiputra, Manavya Gotri, Chutus, Kadambas, Chalukyas, Vedic Aryan Brahmans ?

K.P. Jayaswal holds the view of Bhandarkar and thinks that Haritiputra, Manavya gotri, Chutus, Kadambas, Pallavas and Vakataka were Brahmans. Different scholars who are in favour of this theory give following arguments :

(1) According to one inscription Manavya Rishi was original progenitor of Kadamba.

(2) According to a hearsay during the time of progenitor of Mayur Sharman Manavya some Brahman families migrated from Ahichchhatra and settled in South India (E.C. VII 186).

Answer to first part of this question has been given by famous historian venerable C.V. Vaidya[143] in a most convincing manner. He, writes "According to one inscription Manavya Rishi was original progenitor of Kadamba. But it is not proved from this evidence alone that they were Brahmnas .... This seems to be a wrong estimation of Bhandarkar, based merely on the tradition or hearsay in vogue about the primogenitor of any royal family. The name of original primogenitor, of some of the families of Kshatriya tribe, like Agni (fire) Lachhman and Manavya Rishi etc or likewise names are found in different writings, but historical conclusion cannot be derived from such like imaginary myths." Although Dr. C.V. Vaidya has refuted the viewpoint and argument of

Bhandarkar, we have proved on earlier (pages 316) that Manavya Rishi and Angra Mainyu were non-Aryan Iranian, later was Primogenitor and spiritual teacher of race of Parthian Zohak, the earliest known Naga king of Iran. Hence it seem that Angra Mainyu and Manavya were pre-Aryan Iranian, where these myths took their birth.

Now we take up second argument of scholars whether these Chutus and Kadambas etc were Brahmans who migrated from Ahichchhatra ?

We have proved in chapters V and VI that indigenous non-Aryan people had tradition of god-king or Rajrishi. It means the rulers of city state were also acting as chief priests of the city temples and were non-Aryan Kshatriya and Brahman at the same time. This is the main cause alike Ahivritra and Visvamitra, Sātavāhanas were also Rajrishi since in an inscription[144], mother of Gautamiputra has called herself wife of Rajrishi or god king (See earlier P–301 Sātavāhana), thus repeatedly they have called themselves Brahmana also, but what was the cause of their calling themselves Brahmana ? It can be explained as follows : who the time, these Naga kings were Buddhist or Jain, there was no difficulty in maintaining their old hereditary tradition of Rajrishi. But in the opening few centuries of our era, when process of their Aryanization began or when they began to adopt Hinduism, owing to tradition of Varna system, they felt a great difficulty. They were Brahmana and Kshatriya both in their old system. Although, virtually they were Kshatriya rulers, they preferred to call themselves Brahmana, simply to keep their social status higher. Among such rulers Sātavāhana, Vākatakas, Chuttus, Kadamba, Chalukyas and Pallavas are notable.

As a matter of fact regarding their social status, they always remained in great difficulty or, confusion, The first king of Kadamba family, Mayurasarman[145] (Sharma) calls himself sharma or Brahmana, But on the other hand his son Kang (345-360 AD) writes himself Kangavarman (Varma) or Kshatriya[146]. Most of the Pallava kings added suffix of 'Varman' to their names, although they also used to call themselves Brahmana. It is apparent from this that they were also not sure about their original Varna.

Dr. K.P[147] Jayaswal produces archaeological evidences to explain it as such "There was a Siva Shrine presided over by Matta-patta Deva to whom a Chuttu king dedicated an estate and placed it as a Brahma-deya grant in the hands of a Brahman called the Hāritiputra Kondamāna of Kaundinya gotra. This gift is recorded on a hexagonal Pillar which was lying on the ground at Malavalli (EC Vol III SK 251-252 nos. 263-64) The name and description of Chuttu king is as under :

> VAIJANTI PURAM RĀJĀ MANAVYA SAGOTTŌ HARITI PUTTO VINHU KADDA CHUTU KULĀ NAND SATAKARNI.

Now the Brahmana has been called Haritiputa also. That is why royal family was also Brahman.''

It means he was not a Brahman of Vedic Aryan race, but a black Brahmana of Ahivritra and Visvamitra lineage. Hence he was Haritiputra. This theory again gets the support of KP Jayaswal.[148] He further writes — "A Kadamba king subsequently renewed the grant with a very glad mind (Fleet JRAS (1905) P–305 F/N no.2 Parituthana) 'for the second time' giving to a descendant of Kondamān a maternal uncle of the king and a Kausikiputra. This grant covered the old property and an addition of twelve new Villages, all specified by name, and the gift was publicly registered on the same pillar.''

It shows the king and the Brahman were blood relations, one was a Kshatriya and other Brahmana who has been called Kausikiputra (Son of Kausiki). From this we can derive two conclusions (1) the Brahmana was also from the matriarchal lineage like Sātavāhana and (2) He was Rajrishi of Visvamitra lineage because he was Kausiki Putra or Kshatriya also. Infact they were non-Aryan priests or Brahmana origin, belonging to Naga race named like Nagara, Nagaich, Nagi, Kaundinya, Visvamitra etc who are still existing in north and South India. Hence it is evidently proved that above royal families were non-Aryans belonging to Naga race as proved earlier (P–302)

In fact, throughout the longer period of Indian history, it has been a general tradition that as and when, native rulers were Aryanized, they claimed descent either from Brahmana or Kshatriya and Rajput in later period. This view has been forwarded by N.K. Dutta. Dr. Yadunath Sarkar upholds above viewpoint and further corroborate in vigorous language[149] - "That tribes that can not claim with truth, to have a drop of Aryan blood in their veins have accepted the Aryan influence and tried desperately to give their ancestor an Aryan pedigree.''

Henceforth the viewpoint of N.K. Dutta and Sarkar confirms my theory strongly. It is a historical fact that Sātavāhanas, Kadambas, Vakatakas have called themselves Brahmana and Rajrishi. and Kshatriyas also, but in fact they were non-Aryan Naga Brahmana and Kshatriya both. This fact is crystal clear from the process of their Aryanization. Earlier all of them were Buddhists and later adopted Hinduism but their women remained adherent to Buddhism for a very long period, but they themselves were still worshipping their ancient deity, the mother goddess of Buddhist tradition known as Haritimata and called her their mother Janani (birth giver). On the other hand they never abandoned their ancient non-Aryan tradition of Kashyapa and Manavya Gotra, although first one was related to Jain tradition (Madhava) and Second one had its Non-Aryan origin (Angra Menyu) in Iran. It means kings also partially remained adherent to non-Aryan tradition in spite of their Aryanization. On the other hand they adopted Vedic rites, like performances of Bajpai or Ashwamedha yajna simply to raise their social status, legitimizing the existence of the ruling class and prove their hegemony over the subordinate groups and neighbouring principalities.

Summary and Conclusion

(1) Although Bratadkatha gives a myth of birth of Salivahana prince from a Brahman girl of Paithan and Naga king Sesha, but in fact prince Salivahana hailed from North West Panjab (Salivahanpur). He was of Andhaka or Andhra tribe and Vahika or Taka (Naga) Bansha. From Panjab he was pushed Southward by Bhatti tribe and ultimately reached Paithan to rule South India for a long period of about 500 years. His tribe was republican and matriarchal in character, where every citizen was a warrior known as Nation-in-arms.

(2) Salivahana or Sātavāhana royal family, ruled Central and Southern India between 235 BC and 225 AD, total period being about 460 years. There were according to Puranas 30 kings in this dynasty.

(3) They were of non-Aryan society and matriarchal form of family was prevailing among them. It is proved from the maternal names of some of the kings such as. Gautamiputra Satakarni, Vasishthiputra Pulumayi and Gautamiputra Siri Yagyasatakarni etc, on the other hand patriarchal family system was prevailed among the Aryan society.

(4) Although certain scholars think that Sātavāhanas were Brahmans, an indepth study of their inscriptions, coins and literary records reveals that they were originally of Naga race. Since Rajrishi system was prevailing among them, hence some scholars have mistaken to call them Brahman. In this tradition duties of Kshatriya (King) and priest were assigned to one person which was a non-Aryan system against Aryan Varna system.

(5) The type of coins of the founder of Sātavāhana rule traced out from the collection of Shribiyani of Akola has a figure of an excited serpent, which, signifies that rulers were of Naga race which is further confirmed by another evidence of a inscription from Luders list no 1021, there is mention of king's name as Skand Nag Satakarni (Khand Nag Satak Siri) which was one of the last kings of Sātavāhana family main Branch (Chutukul). It means Sātavāhanas were of Naga race.

(6) Ikshwaku royal family of Sriparvata, established their rule on the ruins of Sātavāhana empire in Andhra Pradesh, their capital, has been traced out by the archaeologists in district Guntur near Nagarjuna Konda. Scholars like K.P. Jayaswal think that this family hailed from north and related to a famous Kshatriya family of Ayodhya. Although this theory has not been accepted by Sudharshan Senevirtne. But Mr. Jayaswal's theory seems acceptable. I disagree on the point that they were good (Aryan) Kshatriya on the following grounds :

(a) This family was matriarchal in character like Ikshwaku family of Ancient period, whose origin has been proved non-Aryan in Chapter V.

(b) Mallas and Lichchhavis were also of Ikshwaku family in origin (see chapter-VI P-164) who have been stated to be non-Aryan Vratya by Manu X-22.

(c) Pārashwanath, the 23rd Jain Tirthankar was also born in Ikshwaku family. He was related to Naga race. Hence these Ikshwakus were also of Naga race.

(7) The capital of Chola was Aur-Thaur This capital was related to Sher or Cher Nagas of South. According to Cunningham Aur- Thaur is Uragapur related to Sher or Cher Naga. They have been called Chola or Chora (thief) by Brahman out of feeling of enmity. Similarly, according to a tradition of the South, first Pallava king Tondaiman was son of Chola king from a Naga maiden, hence Nagas.

(8) Kadambas are also said to have taken birth from the non-Aryan Kuramba caste, who were cattle-lifters. In much later period these Kadambas we found connected with the last great dynasty of Vijaynagar who were Yadavas. It means Kadambas. were also Yadavas or of Naga race.

(9) Perhaps Manavya Gotra, to which most of the Naga royal families belonged, took birth in Iran after the name of Angia Mainyu or Ahirman, who was perhaps primogenitor of Naga kings like Zohak. Before their settlement in India they got divided into two parts the Eastern-Manavah and Western Manavah.

(10) It has been proved in chapter V that the cult of mother goddess originated in Western Asia, where from it was taken to India by Sumerians, who established Indus Valley culture, from where evidence of remains of statues has been found out. It means cult of mother goddess was a native tradition. While Naga king adopted Buddhism worship of mother god-

dess which continued in the form of Haritimata. Even when, they had been Aryanized, it was venerable to all the Naga kings of South. In fact all the ancient traditions like Manvaya Gotra and cult of mother goddess remained in prevalence, in the families of Sātavāhanas, Chuttus, Kadambas, Chalukyas etc. thereby proving their Native Naga origin.

References

1. Sastri Nilkant K. A. "Age of Nanda and Maurya " P–319.
2. Cunningham has given another story-Sāta or Sāli was the name of a Yaksha or demi-god, who being formed into a lion, was ridden by the infant prince, who thus acquired the title of Sātavāhana or Sālivāhana, "Ancient Geography of India" P–443 See note no. 2 below.
3. Dr. Deo S.B. "Mahurjhari Excavation " Nagpur University. (1973) PP 61, 66, 67.
4. (a) Jayaswal K. P., "Hindu Polity " P–46.
   (b) Bhandarkar DR, "Lecture on the Ancient History of India " PP 169–70.
5. Pandeya Chandrabhan, "Andhra Satavahana–Samrajya ka Itihas." PP 1–4 .
6. Jogalekar "A B O R I" Part 27 PP 255 and 261 and 272.
7. Tod James, "Annals and Antiquities of Rajasthan" II PP 914-17.
8. Oldham CF, " The Sun and the Serpent" P–30.
9. Cunningham A, PP. 125-29.
10. Bhandarkar R.G. "Early History of Deccan " PP 64-65.
11. The story about the girl and her serpent-lover is in the Kathāsaritsāgara mentioned with reference to Gunādhya who was the son of the girl. Sátavâhanas origin is given differently.
12. (a) Tod James I P–125.
    (b) See chapter VI for detail.
13. Cunningham A P–448-449.
14. Pandeya Chandrabhan, "PP-93-94".
15. Sastri Nilkant K.A. "Age of Nanda and Maurya" PP-326-27.
16. Pandeya Chandrabhan. P-40.
17. Jayaswal K. P. "Hindu Polity" PP 122 and 130.
18. There is a Village of this name near Junar cave near Nasik which is stated to be early settlement of Satavahanas which confirms this historical fact.–Gokhale B.G. "Buddhism in Maharashtra" P-47.

19. Jayaswal K.P. "History of India" P-115.
20. Chopra P.N. and others, "History of South India," Vol I PP–18–19.
21. (a) I. A no 42 (1913) P–29.
(b) Gopalachari, "Early History of the Andhra Country" P–23
22. Gopalachari P–29.
23. Pandeya Chandrabhan, "PP-14-15".
24. (a) Kosare H.L., "Prachin Bharatatil Nāg" P–201.
24 (b) Kosare H. L. P-202.
25. J N S I Vol II P-94 Mirashi V.V.
26. Pandeya Chandrabhan P–17.
27. Kosare H.L. PP-202.
28. Kosare H.L P–203.
29. J B R A S (1893) Mentioned by Kasore P–200.
30. J N S I year II P–83 Studies and Indology Part III PP 34–36.
31. Deo S.B. "Pauni, Excavation" PP-96–98.
32. Daily Lokmat, Nagpur January 5, 1989 Cited by H.L. Kosare P–201.
33. Gopalachari P–21.
34. E.I. No.8 P–93.
35. Majumdar R.C., "Ancient India " P-133.
36. I.A. no. 42 (1913) PP 280-81.
37. (a) Jogalekar " A B O R I " Part 29 P–203.
(b) Pandeya Chandrabhan PP 15–16.
38. Jogalekar "ABORI" Part 29 P–203.
39. Bombay gazetteer Part XVIII Sub-Part I P–8.
40. Jogalekar "A B O R I" Part 29 P–204.
41. Pandeya C.B. P–16.
42. I.H.Q Part 10 P–779.
43. CHI Vol I P–283.
44. ASWI Vol V P–64.
45. E.I. Vol VIII P–93.
46. Mirashi V.V., "Studies in Indology" Vol III P–I Nagpur University Research series no. I.

47. Mirashi V.V. 'Ibid' P–1.
48. Mirash V.V 'Ibid' P–2.

    In the Nasik cave inscription (E.I. Vol VIII P–94) Siri Yagya Satakarni has been called Ranno Gautami Puts Sami Siri Yagya Sātakārisa, proves their relation with Rana Rajput family.
49. Dikshit M.G. "J. N. S.I'' Vol II P–83".
50. Nevasa Report on Coins P–171.
51. Satavahan Nrapatiche E.K Apurba Nage P 199–203 Vidarbha Sansodhan Mandal Varshiki (1974) Nagpur.
52. Gupta S.P. "Disposal of the Dead and Physical type in Ancient India P–147".
53. Gupta S.P. PP–238–39.
54. ''The Early History of the Deccan'' PP 42–56.
55. Mahajan V.D. "Ancient India " PP 308–310.
56. Jayaswal K.P. "History of India" P–168.
57. Kolte V.V. ''Vidarbha Sanshodhan Mandal Varshiki'' (1974) PP 199–203.
58. Vogel J.P.H "Indian Serpent lore " P–36.
59. Jayaswal K.P. "History of India" PP 165–66.
60. Jayaswal K. P. P–165.
61. Chowdhari Ray H.C, "Political History of Ancient India" P–280.
62. Jayaswal K.P, "History of India" PP 166 and 201.
63. Kosare H.L. P–249.
64. Patil Sharad, "Das Shudrachi Gulamgiri'' Part I Sub Part I (1982) P–34".
65. Kosare H.L. P–249.
66. Kosare H.L. P–250.
67. Ibid.
68. E.I. Vol.7 PP–70-71 and Vol 8 PP.–59 and 63.
69. Jayaswal K.P "History of India" PP–172–73.
70. Kosare H.L P–251.
71. J K R C O I. Vol 1–5 Bombay 1922-1926 mentioned by Chapelkar M. Nalinee, "Ancient India and Iran " PP 33–34,
72. (a) Jayaswal K. P. PP 172–73,

    (b) See Luder's list no 2021 on foregone Pages (Epigraphia Indica No. X).

73. Sudharshna Senevirtne, "Kalinga and Andhra ; the process of secondary state formation in early India" 'The Indian Historical Review' Vol VII (1980-81) no 1 and 2 P–66.

74. Bhandarkar R.G. P–41.

75. Vaidya C.V., "Madhya Yugin Bharat" P–181.

76. M R E (1808–09) Inscription in Berar and C.P. no. 269 P–111.

77. Sastri Nilkant K.A. "A Comprehensive History of India" Vol II The Maurya, Satavahana P–300.

78. Jayaswal K.P. "Hindu Polity" PP 37–38.

79. Kosambi D.D "The Culture and Civilization of Ancient India." P–171.

80. (a) Nalanda Vishal shabda Sagar (1985).
    (b) Bhargava standard illustrated Dictionary (1969).

81. (a) Nalanda Vishal Shabda Sagar (1985).
    (b) Virsen Nag of Mathura, belonging to Bharshivas was also a Yadava.

82. H. Luder's list of inscriptions no. 1021 (Appendix to Epigraphia Indica and record of the Archaeological Survey of India Vol X).

83. Gopalachari, P–54.

84. Pandeya Chandrabhan PP–181-82.

85. Pandeya Chandrabhan Intro P–15.

86. Gokhale B.G. P–12.

87. Gokhale B. G. P–18.

88. A S R 1926–27 P–156 and 185–89 ; 1927–28 P–114.

89. Jayaswal K.P "History of India" PP 171–72.

90. Jayaswal K.P. "History of India" P–172.

91. Ibid.

92. Ibid.

93. Jayaswal K.P P–173.

94. Jayaswal KP P–174.

95. Jayaswal K.P P–175.

96. Ibid.

97. E. I. Part 18 P–318.

98. Jayaswal K.P P–175.

99. Sudharshan Senevritne, "Kalinga and Andhra ; The process of Secondary state formation in early India" The Indian Historical Review vol VII no 1 and 2 (1980–81) P–66.

100. Buddha Prakash, "Rigveda and the Indus Valley Civilization" PP 101–02.
101. Bottero, Cassin and Vercoutter, "The Near East ; The Early Civilization" PP 391–92.
102. Dass A.C. 'Rigvedic India' PP 186–87.
103. Tod James I P–134.
104. R.V. IV 33, 34, 35, 36 and 37 After A.C. Dass.
   "Rigvedic India" PP 186–97.
105. Acharya Hastimal, "Jain Dharm ka Maulik Itihas" Vol I PP 28–29.
106. See Chapter V PP 90–95.
107. Bhandarkar D.R. P–11.
108. Chopra PN and others P–37.
109. Kosare H.L. P–47.
110. Vogel J.Ph, "Indian Serpent Lore" P–36.
111. I. A VII P–34.
112. Gustab Oppert, "The Original Inhabitant of India" PP 265–66.
113. Gustab Oppert P–267.
114. Ibid.
115. Gustab Oppert Ibid P–268.
116. Gustab Oppert P-269.
117. Jataka no. 524.
118. Aggarwal Vasudev Saran "Markandeya Puran" PP 85–86.
119. Rao Gopinath T.A. "Elements of Hindu Iconography" Vol II Part II (1968) PP 556–57.
120. Saxena, K.S., "Political History of Kashmir" PP 79–80.
121. Vaidya C.V., "History of Mediaeval Hindu India" Part II P–301.
122. Vaidya C.V. P–258–59.
123. J B B R A S Vol XVIII PP–239–40.
124. Jayaswal K.P, "History of India" P–200.
125. Jain Jyoti Prasad P–48.
126. (A) Rawlison H.G., "Inter-course between India and the Western World P–16".
   (B) Cunningham A. Vol I P–196.

127. Sameul Beal, "Buddhist Record of the Western World" (1969) Vol III P–137.

128. E.I. Vol III P–164.

129. Fergusson James, "Tree and Serpent Worship" PP 41–42 .

130. Tod James, "I P–24".

131. Shaffer Robert, "Ethnography of Ancient India" PP 43–44.

132. Deo S.B., "Mahurjhari Excavation" (1972) PP 1–2.

133. Deo S.B, "Maharashtra EK Puratatva Samalochana" P–32.

134. Muller F Max, "SBE " Vol 23 Part II P–451.

135. Patil Sharad, "Vol I Part I P–106.

136. Patil Sharad, " P–126.

137. Dikshit S.K., "The Mother Goddess " P–34.

138. The Vakataka Dynasty of the Central Province and Berar, Article published in A B N U H S Oct 1946 no. 1 PP 9–10.

139. Bottero, Cassin and Vercoutter, P–73.

140. Dikshit S.K. "PP 38–39".

141. Dikshit S.K. P–39.

142. Dikshit S.K. P–40.

143. Vaidya C.V. "Vol I PP–265-67.

144. Sastri Nilkant K. A. P–300.

145. Jayaswal K.P. "History of India" P–169.

146. Jayaswal K.P. P–202.

147. Jayaswal K.P. P–167.

148. Jayaswal K.P. PP–167.

149. Dr. Yadu nath Sarkar, "India Through out the Ages" P–13.

Chapter–12
The Naga Rulers of the North and Central India

Nagas of Vidisa

The Nagas were serpent worshipping non-Aryan civilized race of ancient India. Many localities and cities were named after them e.g. Nagpur Nagardhan (Nagar-Vardhan), Nagar, Karkotnagar Nagarkhonda, Nagarkot, Nagarkoil etc. They flourished in North, East, Central and South India in ancient time. The evidences from the Puranas and other sources show that the Naga kings ruled at Takshila, Tankshar, Singhpur, Tonk, Karkotnagar, Mathura, Indaurpura, Padmāvati, Kāntipuri, Vidisa, Purika, Nagpura, Nandi-Vardhan, Eran, Paithān,. etc. In Mahabharata period these Nagas were ruling in North West with their capital at Takshila and at Pātālpuri around present Karachi and Hyderabad. From there they drifted to south and east i.e. from the Panjab to Rajasthan and Madhya Pradesh in a time which cannot be ascertained now. The Puranas[1] divide the Naga dynasty of Vidisa into two parts : To the first part belonged those kings who flourished before the end of the Sungas with their capital at Vidisa. (31 B.C.). The Kings before this period in the Naga dynasty were Sesha, Bhogin, Ramchandra, Nakhvan, Dhana-Varman or Dharma Varman and Vangara.

At this period the Andhra Kings[2] had taken Susarman (The last Kanva King) a prisoner and destroyed whatever had been left of the Sunga power at that time (at Vidisa). This statement of Puranas refer to the Andhra or Sātavahana period, when they became emperors of Aryavarta in addition to their being the emperors of Dakshinapath at about 31 B.C.[3] It means, perhaps due to pressure from Satavahanas they shifted their capital to Padmavati.

Before proceeding further let us see how the Vayu Purana has called these Vidisa Nagas, Vrisha or Siva's bull i.e. Nandi, with which, the names of the kings coming after the close of the Sunga dynasty, end. It seems that the title Bharsiva which was taken up later is connected conceptually with the Vrisha of the Vayu and the Nandi.[4] It means these Nagas were ethnically[5] related to Bharsivas or Nav Nagas (Taka a family of Panjab see Chapter VI P-144) of later period. We know Indus Valley people were also worshippers of God Siva.[6]

The second part of these Nagas belonged to those kings who flourished after the end of the Sungas. The names of these post Sunga Nagas were Bhuta Nandi or Bhutinandi, Sisunandi and Yasonandi. It appears that from the time of Bhutanandi, when the dynasty was re-established, they made Padmavati their capital. There is a positive confirmation of the existence of these post Sunga Nagas in the first century A.D. At Padmpawaya, which is the site of Padmāvati, a statue of Yaksha Manibhadra was dedicated by some members of a public body in the fourth year of the reign of "King Svāmin Sivanandi[7]". Similarly a famous Sivalingam called Swarn-Vindu was also established there. The platform of the Swarn-Vindu Siva has been discovered by Mr. Garde at Pavaya.[8] An image of Nandi, with human body and Bull's head has been found there.

Let us take series of coins which according to Jayaswal[9] belongs to this early Naga dynasty. Some of the coins are generally assigned to Mathura. In the British Museum there are coins of Seshadāta, Rāmdāta[10] and Sisūchandra-dāta. The script of the Seshadāta's coin is the oldest and belongs to the first century B.C. In the same series, there are coins of Ramadāta. These coins, according to the opinion of Jayaswal, are identical with Sesha-Naga, Rām-chandra and Sisu Nandi of this dynasty.

As the Puranas generally omit the names when a dynasty comes under an over lordship, Siva Nandi was probably the king superseded by Kanishka. It is stated in the Puranas that Padmāvati passed under a ruler named Vinvasphāni, who is to be identified with the viceroy of Kanishka, Mahakshatrapa Vanaspara.[11] It proves that during the period 80-175 AD comes the Kushana rule with the withdrawal of the Naga kings to Purika and Nagpur-Nandi-Vardhana in the central provinces.[12]

After a lot of discussion K.P. Jayaswal gave the following pedigree and chronology of the Nagas of Vidisa :

(1)	Sesha Naga	110–90 BC	Kings ruled at Vidisa before the end of the Sungas
(2)	Bhogin	90–80 BC	
(3)	Ramachandra	80–50 BC	
(4)	Dharma Varman	50–40 BC	
(5)	Vangara	40–31 BC	

At this time Satavahanas destroyed Sunga Kanvas.

(6)	Bhuta Nandi	20–10 BC	Kings ruled at Padmavati after the end of Sungas
(7)	Sisu Nandi	10 BC–25 AD	
(8)	Yash Nandi	25–30 AD	

(9) Purusha data
(10) Uttam data
(11) Kama data
(12) Bhava data

These five kings are known from inscriptions & coins and their order of succession is also uncertain.

(13) Siva Nandi or Sivadata 78 AD. Superseded by Kushanas

Jayaswal has pointed out that last five kings are known only from inscriptions and coins. Their order of succession is also uncertain. All the 13 Naga Kings covered a period of about 200 years from 110 BC to 78 AD.[13]

The Nava Naga or Bharsiva

The Nagas had, under the evident pressure of the Kushanas left Padmavati. We have the definite statement in the Puranas that Vinvasphāni ruled at Padmāvati and ruled upto Magadha.[14] Therefore, we may take it that about 80–100 AD the Naga dynasty takes shelter, away from the trunk road between Mathura and Vidisa, into the inaccessible jungles of the central provinces.[15]

The Bharsivas, re-issuing from the jungles of Hosangabad and Jabalpur seem to have reached the Ganges through Baghelkhand. They established their capital at Kanti or Kantipuri.[16] Now it is a large mud fort about a mile long on the Ganges. The fort was destroyed in the Muslim period and the king's seat was removed into the neighbouring hills at Vijayapur and Manda, where the family, now in two branches, resides. The local tradition at Kanti is that long before 'the Gahadwala' the fort belonged originally to the Bhar Kings. The 'Bhar' kings here are evidently a corruption of the 'Bharsiva' kings[17] or Bharshiva.

The origin of the word 'Bharhut' or 'Bhārhut' would have been from 'Bhar-Bhukti', which means 'country of Bhars.'[18] Till today the people of Bhar tribes reside in this region, who seem to be the remnants of 'Bhar Naga tribe' to which ruling family belonged. Jayaswal does not agree to this view, but I am its strong supporter, in view of new archaeological findings and their scientific interpretation, as given in previous chapters. However some evidences are produced below: It is to be noted, that in ancient period, the indigenous Naga people in particular used to organize themselves into guilds. (See chapter VI PP 124-25) As the system in origin[19], was a tribal evolution, hence guild's people and their elders or chiefs (Khalifah, or Sresthis) infact were from a single blood. These Khalifah or Sresthis in later, Mauryan period were known as kings. These kings, some times later, became more powerful and hereditary too, who being non-Aryan Kshatriya, were known as Raj-putra or Rajputs of mediaeval period.[20] Sometimes this period of evolution, from tribe to royal Rajput family, is very long and uncountable. One person, belonging to the same blood or tribe became king, others, who were pushed to Jungles or hills still remained tribe. Some of the Bhars and the Rajbhars of this region (U.P.) still known as Rajputs[21] others are still Sudras by caste. Hence Jayaswal cannot say that Bhar tribes of this region cannot be blood relatives of royal families of Manda and Vijayapur.

Another argument of Jayaswal goes in my favour. He says. "The Bhar Deul Siva's temple, as indicated by learned scholar is covered all over with the figures of naga (serpent) kings. As recorded by Kittoe in whose time it was called the temple of Karkota Nag" This evidently supports this view that the Bhar here stands for Bharsivas.[22] This is to be noted that Karkota Nag was worshipped by the Takas[23], who were progenitor of Bharsivas. These Takas or Takka or Takshak Nagas according to the Mahabharat account were non-Aryan Native Naga tribe and sworn enemies of Aryan Pandavas (See chapter VI P-144 and X P-261 for detail).

Re-establishment of Nagas

The Bharsivas, in the later days of imperial Kushanas or about 150 A.D. reached Kantipuri on the Ganges, they performed their Ashwamedha and coronations at or near Banaras where the place Nagwā, the present site of the Hindu University seems to be associated with their name. From Kantipuri, they moved westwards under Virasena, who strikes coins extensively and whose coins are found from Ahichchhatra, regains Padmāvati and Mathura.[24]

It is stated in the Vayu and Brahmānd Puranas that rule of Navanaga was not only confined to SamayuktaPrant alone but also to the east and the western Bihar also because their capital was in Mathura as well as in Champavati-Bhagalpur.[25]

The Purānas, give to the Padmavati and the Mathura Nagas or in view of the Vishnu, to the Padmavati, Kantipuri-Mathura Nagas,-seven successions. This is fully borne out by the names gathered from the coins and inscriptions as tabulated below after Jayaswal :

Bharsivaś Rise at Kantipuri (140 A.D.)

Nava Nāga (year 27 on his coin) ..... Founders of the Nava Naga Dynasty (Bharsiva) (140-170 AD)

Virasena (Year 34 on Coin) .... Founders of Mathura and Padmavati Branches. (170-210 AD)

Padmavati	Kantipuri	Mathura
(Taka Dynasty)	(Bharsiva Dynasty)	(Yadu dynasty)
210-230 AD	210-245 Haya Nāga	name unknown
Bhima Nāga	(years 30 on coin)	

230-250 AD	245-250	name unknown
Skanda Naga	Traya Nāga	
250-270 AD	250-260	name unknown
Brahaspati Naga	Barhina Nāga	
	(years 7 on coin)	
	[Vakataka Suzerainty begins 284 AD]	
270-290 AD	260-290	....
Vyaghra Naga	Charaja Nāga	
	(year 30 on coin)	
290-310 AD	290-315 AD	315-340 AD
Deva Nāga	Bhava Naga	Kirtisena
310-344 AD	(315-344 AD)	340-344 AD
Ganapati Nāga	Rudrasena	Naga Sena
	at Purikā	

According to Vakataka[26] inscriptions (Fleet G I. PP-237) Gautamiputra, son of the Emperor Pravarsena and father of Rudrasena I, did not succeed, but Rudrasena I, both as the grand-son of Pravarsena and as the grand son of the Bharsiva-Maharaja Bhavnag, succeeded. The Nava Nagas ruled from three capitals Padmāvati, Mathura and Kantipuri. But Rudrasena I ruled from Purika.

Sometimes, before Samudragupta, (335-375 AD) the Naga kings were ruling over Eran. As,[27] Padmavati, Kantipuri and Mathura were three centres of their rule, the Eran-Vidisa was fourth. Naga coins have been recovered in a very large number from this region. All these four kingdoms were inter-related with each other and perhaps, they all unit-edly encountered the attacks of Kushanas and Scythians and pushed them back from their motherland. These Naga kings were great warriors. According to Cunningham, from the lonely finding of a coin, from the remains of Eran, we get information from its writing, which is in Brahmi, that ancient name of the city was 'Erikiran' which was most probably named after some famous Naga King of similar name[28]. The coins of Ravi-Naga, Basu-Naga and Ganapati-Nagas have been recovered in a very large number from Vidisa and Eran.

Bharsivas of Padmavati; A confederacy of Naga Rulers of North

We have already thrown light in Chapter V and VI (PP - 132-33) that the basis of Naga polity was tribal republican confederacy or Gan Sangha system very similar to that of Sumerian.[29]

We know the West Asia was original home of Nagas from where this tradition was transferred to Indus Valley alongwith their migration in Neolithic–Chalcolithic Age and was prevalent among the native people in Vedic and later Vedic period.

During the life time of Buddha and later period there were many such confederacies of Naga people in North as well as in South India such as Malava-Kshudraka, Andhaka-Vrishani, Vaishali-Videha, Videha-Lichchhavi, Lichchavi-Malla, Vujji, Trigarttashashtha[30] (in north and west), Naga (chera) Mandal in south.

Jayaswal[31] KP gives an account of political organization of Bharsivas as follows —

"The system of the Naga government was a federation consisting of (1) three main monarchical Naga families, one of which, the Bharasiva, was the imperial leader (chief), with a number of gubernatorial families under him, (2) a number of republics. Two branches at Padmavati and Mathura were set up by the Bharsivas, with distinguishing dynastic titles of their own. The Padmavati dynasty had the official designation the Taka Bansha, which is given in the Bhavasataka a book dedicated to Ganapati-Naga. The Mathura family had the official title-the Yadu-Bansha which is mentioned in the drama Kaumudimahotsava written about the same time as the Bhavasataka. The two titles incidentally furnish ethnological data of the Nava Nagas....Padmavati family was thus a sovereign family, and their subordination to the Bharsiva was evidently of an imperial type. The Mathura family and the family to which Nagadatta (father of Maharaja Mahesvara Nāga of the Lahore seal) belonged and who ruled somewhere in Ambala district probably at the old capital Srughna, seem to have been under the direct control of the Bharsiva. There was a ruling family near Indrapura (Indorkhera) in the district of Bulandshahar. As regards Bharsivas they had their two centres, Kantipuri and Padmavati. The Mathura family never minted any coin but the Padmavati family did so from the beginning to the end. They were thus a sovereign family." It is obvious Bharsivas were racially Yadavas and of Taka Bansha . Political confederacy system was their peculiarity.

An Invincible and Prosperous Confederacy

We have earlier (Chapter-VI PP 133-34) told that the Nagas were great warriors, that is why they pushed back Kushanas and Scythians from Northern India. The sworn enemy of these non-Aryan republicans, Kautilya[32] has expressed his view that these republicans were invincible. K. P. Jayaswal also puts forth his remarks on this issue[33]– "The other chief feature of their (republican) constitution was that they emphasized on their citizens the duty to acquire military skill. In other words they had a citizen army. Each state was a nation-in-arms. Conversely, the other class, where the 'king' consul constitution obtained, probably had, like monarchs a regular or hired army. The nation-in-arms class, however, did not become purely military, for their constitution also required their citizens to devote attention to industry and agriculture (VĀRTTĀSASTROPAJIVINAH, A.S. XI-1-160 P-376). Hence they were most wealthy as well as powerful" It shows while in peace, citizens were kept engaged in craft activities and trade which was their main occupation.

Padmavati; the Capital of Bharsivas

There is a small village named Karāvati, situated on the Dabrā (Distt Gwalior) Shivapuri road. At a distance of 10 K.M. to the west of this village at the junction of rivers Sindh and Parvati (Sindhu and Para) the ancient grand city of Padmavati[34] was situated. Now-a-days this place is known as Pavāya or Padam Pavāya. It is very interesting to note that during the rainy season, a very large number of coins belonging to the Naga rulers appear at the surface.[35] These coins have made the historians enable to identify this ancient Naga city. The first mention of this city as Padmavati, is made in the Vishnupurana[36], where it is stated that the Nava-Nagas made, Padmavati, Kantipuri and Mathura their capitals and ruled for seven generations.[37]

Bhavabhuti[38] has stated that 'Padmavati is situated near the junction of the rivers Sindhu, Pārā' Lavana and Madhumati. Later following the informations given by M.B Lele[39] in his Marathi book titled 'Malatimadhava sar ani kiwar', the Department of Archaeology discovered this ancient site. According to a critical study of coins, Virsena was the founder of the kingdoms of Padmavati and Mathura.

Nava Nagas founded a large mint in Padmavati, from where coins were issued in a very large number, on the basis of which it is surmised that the Navanagas, in addition to their high virtues of being most expert and talented rulers, were also most prosperous. One of the well known peculiarities of Naga coins is that they are all dated. They have figures of palm trees and a human figure seated on a throne.[40] The palm tree is a Naga symbol. Since Sanskrit word for mint is Tak-shala [Taka (Bharsiva) + Shala] this shows these Taka-Bharsiva had some hand in establishing new technique or workshop of casting of coins.

The demolished remains of strong fort on the junction of the rivers still give a reminiscent view. From the defence point of view, because it was surrounded by in-exhaustable flow of river water from two sides and on the other two sides by deep trenches, it was most safe and invincible. The trenches were 20 feet deep and were occupied by either furious lions or river water. The traces of these trenches are still visible.[41]

Bhavabhuti[42], the famous Sanskrit poet of seventh century A. D. composed his valuable scripture, at Padmāvati. Bhavabhuti got constructed a large Yajnashala (sacrificial place) at the bank of river Pāravati, its remains are still in good condition.

Virasena.

In about 175 or 180 A.D., we find a Naga king named Virasena re-establishing Naga sovereignty at Mathura. According to Dr. Jayaswal,[43] the rise of Virasena was a turning point not only in the Naga history but also in the history of Aryavarta. His coins have been found in Northern India, almost all over Uttar Pradesh and in the Punjab. They are most common around Mathura. He occupied Mathura and ruled all over the Aryavarta Doab. An inscription of Virasena was discovered by Sir Richard Burn. There are a number of broken sculptures and carved pieces and the inscription is on the head and mouth of a sculptured animal.[44] The inscription is dated in the 13th year of the reign of Svamin Virasena. Virasena[45] assumed full sovereignty from the first year of his reign. It appears that he ousted the Kushanas from Mathura and the whole of the Doab between the Ganga and the Yamuna. Virasena had a fairly long reign and according to Dr. Jayaswal he ruled from about 170 A.D. to 210 A.D. The same writer is of the opinion that 'The intimate connection between his coins and coins of the undoubted Bharasiva king, the Naga emblem on his coins as if to complete his name, the period of his rise and his establishing himself at Mathura mark Virasena out as one of the earliest Bharasiva Nagas of the inscriptions and the Nava Nagas of the Puranas.'

Bhava Naga

According to Jayaswal,[46] there were four kings after Virasena. Haya Naga, Traya Naga, Brahina Naga, Charaja Naga. Bhava Naga ruled from about 290 to 315 A.D. Dr. Jayaswal made it clear that he had fixed the date of Bhava Naga on a consideration of the Vakataka and Gupta chronology. Bhava Naga was a contemporary of Pravarsena I who was an elder contemporary of Samudra Gupta. Bhava Naga is described as belonging to the family of the Bharasivas[47] whose royal line owed its origin to the great satisfaction of Siva that was caused by their carrying a Sivalinga placed as a load upon their shoulder" and "who were besprinkled on the forehead with the pure water of the Bhagirathi that had been obtained by their valour."

The Vakataka (250 – 510 AD)

Earlier Vakatakas established their rule in Vindhya region. But when time favoured they established their authority on the whole of the Central India.

Pedigree (After Mirashi V.V.)

Vindhya-Shakti (250 – 270 AD)

Pravarsen I (270 – 330)

(Main Branch) at Purika	(Vatsgulma Branch)
(Gautami putra) not ruled	Sarvasen (330 – 355 AD)
Rudrasen I (330 – 350 AD)	Vindhya Shakti II (355 – 400 AD)
Prithivisen I (350 – 400 AD)	Pravarsen II (400 – 410 AD)
Rudrasen II (400 – 405 AD	Son (name not known)
(married to Prabhavati Gupta)	(410 – 450 AD)
Diwakarsen 405 – 420) AD)	Regent Prabhavati
	Dev sen (450 – 475 AD)
Damodarsen / Pravarsen II (420 – 450 AD)	Harisen (475 – 500 AD)
Narindersen (450 – 470) his wife was / Anjhika Bhattarika D/o King of Kuntala	Son (name not known) (500 – 510 AD)
Prithivisen II (470 – 490 AD)	

From the Vakataka inscriptions the following facts are well-established. A dynasty which took its name Vakataka came into existence about a century before Samudra Gupta's conquests. The first king of the dynasty was Vindhya-Shakti. The second king was Pravarasena; the kings coming after him all assume their regnal name ending in Sena. Pravarasena I, who was son of Vindhya-Shakti, not only performed four

Asvamedhas but also assumed the title of Samrāt.[48] He had a long reign, so much so that his eldest son Gautamiputra could not succeed him, but his grand-son Rudrasena I succeeded him. Gautamiputra himself was married to the daughter of the Bharsiva king Bhavanāga. The son of this union was Rudrasena I grand son of Pravarsena I and Bhavanaga. As, there was matriarchal system of heredity among the Nagas (Chapter V PP 102-03 and VI), hence Rudrasena I became the legal heir of throne of Bhavanaga in addition to throne of his own grand father Pravarsena I.[49] Rudrasena I was succeeded by his son Prithivisena. I. Rudrasena II son of Prithivisena I was married to Prabhavati Gupta dauthter of Chandra Gupta II born of the Empress Kubera Naga. Prabhavati Gupta ruled as regent after the death of her husband Rudrasena II, as guardian to her minor son Yuvraj Divakarsena and subsequently to another son called Damodarsena or Pravarasena.

It is obvious Vākataka dynasty took its root in Vindhya region and later extended its sways as far as Karnataka in South since Prithvisena subjugated the king of Kuntala a part of Karnataka and Kadamba kingdom. Their capitals were at Purika, Chanak, Pravarpur and Padmapur and Branches at Nandivardhan and Vatsagulma.

Were Vakātakas Aryan Brahmans ?

The Theory of Jayaswal

Whether the Vakatakas were Aryan Brahmans or Nagas has been a subject of great controversy among the historians. Among the scholars who identify Vakatakas as Brahmanas, Jayaswal K.P. is at the forefront. We, therefore produce his opinion.[50] He writes, 'There is no doubt that Vakatakas were Brahmans. They performed Brihaspati sava and also four Ashwamedha sacrifices...... their Gotra was Vishnubraddha[51] (a branch of Bhardwaja) which is still prevalent among the Brahmanas of Maharashtra (A.S.R. Part IV PP-125 and 128 foot-note below and plate no 57). In Puranas they have been called Vindhyakas or royal family of Vindhyadesh. It is, therefore clear that they were original inhabitant of Vindhya Pradesh...... The Vindhyakas or the Vakatakas used to live at the bank of river Kilkila or the country around it. ...... This is a small river near Panna, having a bad reputation for its unhealthy water. We are thus brought to very area, Ajaygarh-Panna where the earliest Vakatak inscriptions are found, that is the district of Ganj-Nachnā. The Bhagwata Purana, in describing the Vidisa Nagas and Praviraka, calls the whole group The kila-kila kings. The location of dynasty in Bundel Khand is thus unanimous.''

It means Vakatakas were Vedic Brahmans who originally belonged to Bundelkhand region. Further same scholar[52] produces evidence to justify his theory of their Brahmana origin — "The form Vakataka means of the place 'Vākāta' or Vakātā as in Samudra Gupta's inscription, Mahā-Kāntārka, Kosalaka, Paishthāpuraka etc signify of Mahakantara, of Kosala, of Paishthapur' (G1 P-234) The dynastic name Traikūtaka from 'Trikut' is an exact Parallel. I found an ancient village called Bāgāt, in the northern most part of the Orchha state, 6 miles East of Chirgaon of the British district of Jhansi. Its neighbouring village called Bijour is often mentioned with Bagat, as Bijour Bāgāt. It is between two rivulets Kaynā and Dugrai which fell into the Betwā. It is a large and ancient Brahman Village, mainly peopled by Bhāgaur Brahmans. The village is believed to be of Dronāchārya the famous military Brahman mentioned in the Mahabharat. It seems that the Brahman who according to the Puranas was the first anointed king and the founder of the dynasty and who assumed the appropriate appellation of Vindhya Shakti, adopted title that the town of Vākātaka is of ancient origin is proved by a pilgrim's inscription of Amarāvati where a common citizen about 150 BC describes himself as a Vākātaka i.e. as an original inhabitant of Vakata (E.I. Vol XV P 267 inscription no. 27)."

Revoking of the Theory of Jayaswal by V.V. Mirashi

For examination of above detailed description we can divide it into three parts :

(1) Was Vakataka royal family the original inhabitant of Vindhya region ?

(2) Is the derivation of the family name Vakataka from Vagat acceptable ?

(3) Were Vakatakas Aryan Brahmans ?

We first take original home land of Vakataka for discussion :

Famous scholar V.V. Mirashi does not accept the viewpoint of Jayaswal. He thinks that their original home-land was South and not North India.[53] He produces following argument in support of his opinion, "This view of Jayaswal is not acceptable, because not a single inscription of early kings of Vākātaka family could be traced out so far from North India. The earliest inscription of Rudrasena I has been discovered from the place named Devatek of Chanda district. Hence he was not ruler of Aryavarta, but of Vidarbha region. Two inscriptions, found from Ganj and Nachna, belonging to Vyaghra-dev, Māndlik of Prithivisen, in fact belonged to Prithivi sena II (470-490 AD) and not Prithivisena I (350 – 400 AD). But Indore copper plate of Pravarsena II, (420 – 450) has been traced out in northern India. But this plate was originally brought from Khāndesh. Some scholars give another argument also. If the king of Prayāga inscription killed by Samudra Gupta, was Rudra, the Rudra sena I, then why his son Prithivisena I accepted Prabhavati, daughter of Chandra Gupta II as bride for his son Rudra sena II. It means neither Rudrasena I was the ruler of Northern India, nor Rudra of Prayag inscription. From all these evidences it is proved, that original home of Vākatak could not be northern India, but some where South. On the other hand oldest inscription which mentions the name of Vākātaka has been found out from Amarāvati of district Guntur. (Amaravati sculptures in the Indian government Museum P-304) The style of alphabet of inscription belonged to the third century AD. It is as under :

(1) .... GAMEVĀTHAVAS GAHA PATIS VĀKĀTAKAS-GAHAPATIKINI. ।

(2) .... NĀ THERENA BODHI KEN BHARIYĀYA CHAMUNĀYA SABHATVKE HI ॥

(3) .... KEHI SANĀTIMI TABANDHAVEHI CHA APANO ĀYUVADHANIKA ॥"

Unluckily this inscription is in broken condition and the name of original home has been lost as such. Although, it is clear from the remaining part that its object was to inscribe deed of donation of house holder named Vākātaka and his two wives Chamuna and other. This donation was given on the advice of Ther named Bodhika or a monk and its object was attainment of long life to the relatives, friends and family members of donor and monk Bodhika. It is crystal clear from this inscription, that a house holder named Vākātakā went to Buddhist sacred place of Amarāvati, along with his two wives. Here the Vākātakā is not a name of family but name of a person. Keeping is view, the difficulties of Journey of ancient time, it can be surmised that this house holder, would have come from a nearby place of region of Amaravati. On the basis of style of alphabet it seems to be of third century AD which is close to the dates (250 AD) of Vindhya Shakti."

In the way, the name of Gupta family came into being after the name of a man named Gupta, similarly Vakataka family name, came into existence, after the name of a man Vakātka, as mentioned in aforesaid inscription. It is also clear that Vakātaka was Buddhist similar to Gupta of Gupta family.

But it can not stand fully proved, because, merely similarity of name of the founder of the family with the name found in an inscription at such a distant place, can not be a solid proof to prove the truth of history that too without any supporting evidence. If he established his rule first in South then how he was named Vindhya Shakti ? secondly he was a house holder and not a king.

The Vakatakas, Taka Naga Origin :

I think this question is most controversial and complicated too, but now by raising the question of their North or South origin by Mirashi it has been made more complicated. But I have to say nothing on this issue, instead I am much concerned with the later two questions i.e. origin of the name of the Vakataka family and caste of the family. I am of the firm view that most probably all the royal families of this age, were of the native origin, such as Sishu-nagas, Nandas, Mauryas, Sātavahanas, Nagas, Nava-Nagas or Bharsiva, Guptas Chuttus, Kadambas, Chalukyas etc, similarly Vākataka family was also of native origin. Particularly the region of central provinces known as Bundel Khand and Baghel Khand and its southern and western region was the largest centre of Nagas, where according to Jayaswal, this family took its birth. In north east of them were Guptas, the non-Aryan Karaskar[54] and blood relatives of Vratya Lichchhavi; and in north were Bharsiva Nagas of Kantipuri; in north west were powerful Takas of Padmavati; and in the South west were Nagas, Nava nagas of Vidisa and Eran, relatives of Taka, Malavas of western Madhya Pradesh and Satavahanas lord of South etc. Under these circumstances it seems to be impossible that a non-martial Aryan Brahman family would have come into power, who were hereditary sworn enemy of non-Aryan native Nagas from the earliest times.[55]

Then who were these Vakatakas ? and what was their ethnical identity ?

There is more than sufficient evidence, to prove that they were of Naga race belonging to Bharsiva or Taka Bansha, which is being produced below :

In copper plate grant of Vakatakas of Balaghat[56] (E-I. IX P-270) Rudra sena Vakataka I has been called Maharaja Bharsiva :

BHARATHA SNĀTĀNĀMBHĀRA SHIVĀ NĀM MAHĪRĀJSRI RUDRASENASYA ॥

We know Bharsiva were of Taka origin hence Vakataka were of Taka origin. It seems that in this word 'Vakataka', suffix of 'Taka' is related to their family or Bansha name. Now let us use this Bansha name, 'Taka' to derive name in the formula, produced by Jayaswal as such :

Vagat (name of the village) + Taka (family name) = Vagataka or Vakataka alike in Mahararashtra from Mahar+ Rashtra in Saurashtra from Saura + Rashtra.

It fits well most reasonably, which needs no argument since it means, Takas of Vagat or Vakat Village.

Now let us examine whether this derivation of family name had some historical background or family tradition. To prove this fact, I produce a theory of my own being derived below :

Glory of Taka Royal Family and Tradition of using Family Name With the Names of Places etc as Suffix or Prefix

This Taka or Takshak royal family, as shown in chapt VI, remained in power at different places and time from the period of Mahabharata (950 BC) up to the ruling period of Akbar, the great Mughal ruler, while Gujrat, which was being ruled by main branch of this family[57] (who had adopted Muslim religion) was subjugated by Akbar in his empire in 1572 after a war. It proves that this royal family remained in power for a longest tenure of more than 2500 years, although, some times independent, or some other time under some outer sovereignty. This is a land mark in Indian history. They gave birth to many of the royal families of ancient period of India, who ruled different territories in due course of time like, Maurya, Bharsiva, Satavahana, Karkota, Gupta etc. Although due to feeling of antipathy by the Brahmanical authors, they were omitted by the Puranic chronicles, but because they were great warriors and invincible, hardy, and courageous people of Jataka and Arthshastra fame, they gained very high glory, celebrated name and fame, whose echo still can be heard in the names of enormous localities, countries, territories, towns which they ruled or founded such as, Takshila,[58] Attok[59] (town and river both) Takashar or Takshaka,[60] Rohtak[61], Taka Desha or country, Takhar Province, Takkarika[62], Tonk[63], Cuttack, Dhaka[64], and many others yet to traced out. As far as they used their family name in naming coins and mints (Taka and Takashāla) language (Taki, Dhaki or Takshali) script (Takari or Munde as earliest form of Devnagari), etc.

Under these circumstances no one will hesitate to permit me to propound a theory of my own to establish this historical truth, as such "We know, the Taka royal family and their branches ruled largest parts of India for longest tenure, gave birth to enormous royal families of high position and repute, they were most wealthy persons, great warriors and invincible republicans of Jataka and Arthshastra fame, hence they had celebrated name and fame and high glory that is why they felt pride in using their family name, in the names of countries, localities, territories, towns, rivers, coins, languages, scripts, in the form of suffix or prefix to denote or show their name fame and lordship over them."

Hence it can be stated most reasonably that following this tradition these Vakatakas used their original family name as suffix with the name of village Vagat as indicated in the theory of learned scholar K.P. Jayaswal. In corroboration of this theory some examples of such place names related to Satavahanas, another branch of Taka family, are being produced below; Gautamiputra SRISATKARNI in the inscription of Nasik cave (Epigraphia Indica Part VIII no 4 P-71) has called himself VENĀKATAK SWAMI GAUTAMI PUTTA SIRI SADAKARI (The lord of Venakatak Gauamiputta SIRI SATAKARI). Dr. V.V. Mirashi (Sanshodhana MUKTAVALI sery 1 PP 110-12) comments upon above adjective that progenitor of Gautamiputra were ruling there in Maharashtra in the beginning.[65] Vena is a river Ven-Ganga near Nagpur.

There are also some more examples of places of like wise names falling in the same area such as; Bhojkata (k)[66] Nagar-Katak[67], Nandi Katak,[68] Karahekatak, Dhankatak. It shows these Vakātakās were a branch of Takas, similar to Bharsiva Taka as proved earlier. It is interesting to note that although Samudra Gupta was daughter's son of Lichchhavis but he has been called only Lichchhavi Dauhitra and not Lichchhavi. But here Rudrasena I has been called Bharsiva Maharaja, who was daughter's son of Bharsiva who came on their throne owing to prevalence of matriarchal system in this family. It shows these Vakatakas were blood relatives of Bharsiva. That is why Rudrasena I has been called Bharsiva otherwise how these Bharsivas would have given their daughter as bride, as well as family throne to a Brahmanas who were their hereditary sworn enemies from the time of Mahabharat. (See chapter X P 261) and Arthsashtra.[69]

H.H. Wilson (V.P. Vol II P-657) has furnished with another most valuable information favouring our theory "that there were thirteen sons of Vindhya Shakti and rest. The Bhagwata has a different statement identifying the sons of the Vindhya race with the Valhikas (Vahikas) and making them thirteen.

TEŚĀN TRAYODASHASUTĀ BHAVITĀRSCHA VAHĪLKĀḤ—means "the Vahlikas will be their thirteen sons.'' According to Cunningham[70] these Vahlikas or Vahikas were Taka Nagas. It evidently confirms our theory that these Vakatakas were definitely of Taka origin and perhaps related to the earlier branch of Vidisa Naga (See P-330) or Sesha Naga since Vindhya Shakti has been mentioned as descendent of Bhutanandi in the Puranas.

In Bhagawat[71] Purana there is a pedigree of early Nagas or Naga kings of Kilkila begins with Bhutanandi and ending with Praviraka or Pravarsena I son of Vindhya shakti. It is as follows[72]:

KILKILĀYAN NIRPATAYO BHŪTANANDDOYA VANGIRḤ I
SIŚUNANDISCHA TADBRATĀ YAŚONANDIḤ PRAVIRAKĀḤ II

Here king Praviraka or Pravarsena I Vākataka has been included in the list of Nagas who were KILKILA kings. It means he was also a Kilkila Naga king. Kilkilā is the name of river near Panna.

This gets confirmation from Vishnu Purana[73] :

TEŚUCHCHHA NNEŚUKAILKILĀ YAVANĀ BHŪPATAYO BHAVISHYANTI ।

MŪRDHĀBHIŚIKTA STEŚAṆ VINDHYA SHAKTIḤ (16)

Meaning : Kilkila Yavanas will be the kings, the chief of whom will be Vindhya Shakti (the appellation of Yavana is for non-Aryan as amended later by the scholars). Here the king Vindhya Shakti has been called Kil-Kila Nag and non-Aryan both.

These Kilkila Nagas were earlier related to Vidisa known as Vidisa-Vrisha. This view is supported by another statement of K.P. Jayaswal. He writes,[74] "The Puranas in detailing the rise of Vindhya shakti state that Vindhya Shakti arose from the Kilkila kings. Here it is clear that Puranas mean the Nagas who at that time were prominently connected with Kil-kila as their name changes from Vidisa-Vrisha to Kil-Kila Vrisha." eg Vayu (358-370)

TACHUCHHANENA CHA KĀLENA TATAH KILAKILĀḤ-VRISHAH ।

TATAH K(A) ILAKILEBHYAŚ CHA VINDHYA SAKTIR BHAVISH YATI ॥
(Brahamanda Verses 178-179)

VRISHĀN VAIDESAKĀMŚ CHĀPI BHAVISHYĀMŚ CHANIBODHATA"

It is obvious these Kila-Kila Nagas were earlier known as Vidisa Vrisha and later Kila-Kila Vrisha. It means they were earlier ruler of Vidisa. Hence it is proved firmly that Vakatakas were offshoots of Vidisa branch of Nagas.

But our theory will remain imperfect if we do not conduct an indepth study of their religious social and political tradition of vakatakas and compare them with the traditions of Nagas to prove their homogeneity.

We know there was tradition of matriarchal family and heredity system among the Nagas (See chapter V P 102-03). It is apparent from the tradition of early kings of this family that the family was matriarchal in form. The name of the son of Pravarsena I was Gautamiputra i.e. son of mother Gautami, hence thereby proving matriarchy, such matriarchal names are found in the Satavahana family also (See chapter XI P-296). This is the main reason this family accepted a matriarchal marriage and heredity while they accepted the daughter of king Bhavanaga as bride for Gautamiputra and also their royal throne to Rudrasena I son of their union. This tradition vanished into disuse, owing to their Aryanization rapidly by the Vellur Brahmans as explained on forthcoming pages, whereas it continued for quite some time among the Satavahanas.

Vakatakas were the followers of Siva cult in general[75] similar to Bharsiva which was originally a non-Aryan cult prevalent among them from the age of Indus Valley.[76] Earlier they were Buddhists as shown on P-341.

Haritiputra

According to V.V. Mirashi, Haritimata, the mother goddess was also earlier worshipped among the Vakatakas, and they used to call themselves Haritiputra[77] (VISHNŪ VIRADHA SAGOTRASYA HARITI PUTRASYA SRI PRAVĀSEN POTRASYA).

S.K. Dikshit[78], further highlights its importance and relavency with the tradition of Naga Worship as such, "Thus serpent worship prevails in most countries, where beliefs connected with the fertility cult exist or where mother goddess is worshipped. Again most of these aspects in connection with the serpent worship find their parallel in India." It proves that worshipper of mother goddess were also snake worshipper in origin. Hence Vakataka were also snake worshipper or Nagas. Infact Haritimata is another form of mother goddess. Earlier almost all the Naga families were Buddhist. In Buddhist tradition this deity was worshipped in the form of Haritimata and worshipper called themselves Haritiputra which remained continued even after their Aryanization (See chapter XI PP 317-18).

Homogeneity of the Coins of Bharsiva Nagas and Vakatakas

It is interesting to note that coins of Vakatakas and Bharsivas are similar in shape, size and ornamentation except minor dissimilarities. Hence, to prove oneness of Bharsiva and Vakatakas we compare their coins. The coins of Vakatakas and Nagas were moulded in the Naga mints of Ahichchhatra and Kausam,[79] hence coins of both of them had similar figures of bull (Nandi) of Shiva, symbol of river goddess Ganga and palm tree. Palm tree is a symbol of Naga royal authority. Sometimes these coins are so similar in shape, size and pictographs–engraved on them that it becomes impossible to identify whether one belongs to Vakatakas or Bharsivas. K.P. Jayaswal[80] produces an account of such similarity (see Illustration XII, XIII) : "As we have been dealing here with the Bharsiva coins, I may discuss a coin which has been taken as a coin of Virasena but which I take to be a Vākātakā coin of Pravarsena I. It belongs to the same series as the coins we have been noticing. It is of the old orthodox Hindu type, post-Kushan in script and pre-Gupta in style. The coin is illustrated in the catalogue of the coins of the Indian Museum by Dr Vincent Smith on plate no XXII Fig no 15. It is read by him as 'V (I) RASENASA'. He read the 'i' – doubtfully, and although he takes the coin on the whole as a coin of Virasena, yet he says that this is subsequent to the coins of the earlier Virasena (C.I.M.P.-192, P 197n2). His estimate of the difference between the two in point of the time and the decision to take it as belonging to another and a later king is correct, but he is incorrect in reading the name as 'Virasena'. I read the legend on the coin as Pravarsenas (y)a, reading 'Pra' as the first letter in the left hand bottom corner, beginning the legend with it. And I also read as 76 (70, 6) below the name. On the obverse, there is seated a female figure with a jar in her right hand, which denotes that it is the figure of the River goddess Ganga. [There is no 'rayed crown' on the head of the figure (CIM P-197) but it is the canopy (Chhatra) part of the throne]. In the right-hand bottom corner there is the Vakataka wheel which we meet at Nuchnā and Jāso."

It is proved from this description that the difference or dissimilarity which Jayaswal could trace out is of the name of the king only, otherwise both are quite similar to each other. Particularly the palm tree which is a symbol of authority of Naga kings, is common to both. Figure of Goddess river Ganga is a peculiarity of Bharsiva. Similarly writing work in Brahmi script is also common to both.[81] There by proving them Nagas.

But now question arises if Vakatakas were native Nagas why they followed Vedic Brahmanical religious rites ? Pravarsena I performed four Ashwamedha sacrifices. They did Brihaspati Sava sacrifice, which is open to Brahmans only ?

According to Jayaswal, the older Puranas do not mention the caste of the Vindhyakas.[82] Its main reason was that these people were non-Aryan indigenous Nagas who were followers of Buddhist order as mentioned in the inscription of Amaravati,[83] where caste has no meaning or no one knows the caste.

But according to Mirashi, Vakatakas engaged a Brahman family of South India named Vellur as their personal secretary who were non-Aryan north Indian immigrant in South.[84] Progenitor of this family was Yagyapati whose son Dev, was most religious, great politician, and faithful. He was contemporary of Vindhya-Shakti and his son Pravarsena I for some time. In an inscription[85] of Ghatotkach cave it is mentioned that "Due to his influence all the nation including king himself is engaged greatly in religious activities." It is apparent from the inscriptions of Vakatakas that Vedic religion flourished to a great extent in this Age. It means although king Vakataka was Buddhist similar to two earlier kings of Gupta family, but this family was being Aryanized very quickly by Dev Brahman and his progeny. This process of Aryanization was further kept continued by Prabhavati Gupta who was hereditary great patron of Vishnu cult. That is why aforesaid Vedic sacrifices were performed by them like Bharsivas, Satavahanas and also Guptas. The second reason of performance of such prestigious sacrifices was to strengthen their political position and prove their paramountcy on the neighbouring principalities and their subordinate ruling groups and subjects.[86]

It has been shown in Chapter V and VI that ancient indigenous non-Aryan Nagas had tradition of god-king or Rajrishi, it means against-Vedic Varna system one person was sharing responsibility of Brahmana (priest) as well as Kshatriya (King). In their process of Aryanization they or their subordinate admirer group (Vellur Brahman) have called them (in an inscription) Dvija being more high and prestigious Varna than Kshatriya. Hence they performed sava sacrifice open for Dvija only. It is most interesting that neither in any earlier inscription nor in any older Purana[87] their caste has been mentioned. We feel, on the pattern of Gupta, they have hidden their caste. Vishnu have called them Kilakila yavana[88] i.e. foreigner, only when, royal family became powerful and famous, this work was taken into the hands by one of their admirer Amatya who was related to the last king of the family. In fact their caste Dvija has been mentioned first in the Varāhdev inscription of Ajanta cave. Varāhdev was Amatya of Harisen (475-500 AD), the last king of this family (ASWI IV P-124). Similarly their Gotra Vishnuvraddha also has been mentioned in a copper plate of grant from Poona issued by queen Prabhavati Gupta regent of Yuvaraj Diwakar son (405-420 AD) E.I. XV P-39. How far this Vishnu-Vraddha is attached with Brahmans I cannot say but there is another aspect of its meaning and origin which is very clear and closely related to these Taka Nagas. The word Vishnuvraddha means enhancement (in the family) of Vishnu or older senior (family) of Vishnu. Vishnu is representative of sun deity. It has been established in Chapter V that the Surya or the sun deity was worshipped in Western Asia. Sumerian Sun-god was Utu, and Akkadian Shamash[89] and Egyptians, Re.[90] Similarly Sungod of Israelites was Bal or Baal,[91] which was also a deity of semites and Indus Valley people, which appears in Rigveda as deity of Panis (See Chapter XIII P-376-77) Oldham[92] informs that "Nagas were defied Surya Banshi, the celestial serpent belonging to Surya, the sun god (Paraskara Grihsutra 11-19-9)."

According to Vishnu[93] Purana Taksha was son of Bharata (Brother of Rama Chandra of Ikshwaku). According to Vayu this Taksha was ruler of Gandhara residing at Takshila. These Ikshwakus were of Surya Vansha. Hence Takas were of Surya family. This gets confirmation from an inscription of Salindra king of Kansawa : We have come to know from the inscription discovered by Col Tod (I.A. XIX P-55) from the Kanaswa, which is situated at the bank of river Chambal, south of Kotah that the king Salindra (409 AD, his capital was Salpoor) of Sarya

(Surya) family, was king of Takkas (Takhyas) These people of Sarya family were famous among other tribes too.[94]

It is obvious that Bansha of Taka Nagas was Sarya or Surya, and Vakataka being Taka in origin were also of Surya Bansha. Because Vishnu deity (Queen Prabhavati was Vaishnav) represents Surya and Vakataka were a new addition to Vishnu cult (Vaishnavism) or findings of the most powerful Vellari Brahmanas hence (Sanskrit) Vishnu Vraddha.

Thus Vakatakas were Native Naga priests or Brahmanas. This is the main cause the modern Native black Brahmans still have the tradition of cross cousin marriage[95] or cross sister marriage which is not prevalent among the Aryan Brahmanas. Aryan Brahmanas do not maintain relation of Roti and Beti (feasting and marrying) with them.

Therefore the theory of K.P. Jayaswal, that the Vakatakas were Vedic Brahmanas falls to the ground. In fact, as proved, they were indigenous Naga rulers cum priests or Raja-rishi of Vritra or Visvamitra lineage, similar to Sumerian and Indus Valley rulers and present Siem[96] of Khasi Naga tribe of Assam, that is why Bharsivas accepted matriarchal marriage of their daughter with Gautamiputra Vakataka and transfer of their throne to Rudrasena I, the son of above union, being their blood relatives. Since they were priest kings hence whenever they were Aryanized, declared Brahmanas, by their admirers the Vellari Brahmanas, performed not only Ashwamedhas to prove their royal authority on the subordinate kings and subjects but also Sava sacrifice open to Brahmanas only. This gets over all confirmation from an earlier inscription (E. I. XVII P-12) on a stone-piece at Nachna and Ganj of donor Vyaghra Deva (an officer of Prithivishena I 350-400 AD). This inscription is in a script earliest of its kind called Devnagari since Vakatakas were Nagas, hence called Devnagari script (Jayaswal PP-60-61).

The Gupta Royal Family : A Native Naga Origin

In earlier volume[97] no 1 of this series it has been proved that Guptas were of Native Sudra origin. But K.P. Jayaswal thinks that they were of Jat origin, which in my opinion cannot be accepted. Hence it is necessary to place a gist of evidences and arguments produced by him and show where there is a pitfall in his theory. I place hereby his[98] account pointwise :

(1) That nowhere Guptas disclose their origin or Caste status. That their caste sub-division was Dharna. Since Prabhavati Gupta daughter of Chandra Gupta II and queen of Rudrasen II Vakataka in her copper plate grant of Pune has shown sub-caste of her family (Gupta) as Dharna (EI XV-41 P-42).

(2) Kaumudimahotsva, a Sanskrit play gives the caste of Chandra (Gupta I) as Karaskar. These Karaskars are mentioned by Baudhayan (Baudhayan Dh. S. I-i-32) as a low community to whom the Brahmanas should not go and on return from whom should perform a ceremony of purification. It means they were of Sudra origin. It is confirmed.

(3) The Karaskaras in Baudhayana are connected with the Punjabi community Arattas (which literally means the republicans). Their exact location is given by Hemchandra (A-chapter IV P-23) who in explaining the Salvas, calls them the people of the Kara Valley (Salvas Tukāra-Kukshiyāh), this Karapatha was at the foot of the Himalayas [V.P. (Wilson) Vol III P-390]. This is the same region, where Lichchhavis ruled centuries together.

(4) The Salvas were a branch of the Madras and were ruling at Sialkot. These Madras had a branch named Kuninda, who were related to Koliya Naga.

(5) Karaskaras were thus a Panjab people a sub-division of the Madras. We know that the Madras were called Vahikas and Jartikas. This community, thus, consisted of several sub-divisions.

(6) Since according to grammatical illustration of Chandra-gomin the Jārta defeated the Hunas, which means Skand Gupta defeated the Hunas. Hence Guptas were Jarta or Jat.

(7) Yasodharman[99] (of Mandsaur) also fought with Hunas and forced them to submit before him. Under these circumstances the word Jārta could be used for Yasodharman also.

Since Madras were present during the life time of Buddha (567-487 BC)[100] which is duly confirmed by description of Panini also (IV-2-13) (500 BC), where as Kushanas, who are known as Jārta (Jat), reached India as an invader in about 15 A.D. Hence these Madras can not be Jārta or Kushanas. On the other hand, Madras were a sub-branch of Vahikas.[101] These Vahikas were[102] Takas who have Gotras named Jat and Kakkar (Karaskar) Dhara (Dharan). Hence Guptas were also Taka Naga in origin. This achievement is most significant for scholars of History. This is confirmed by another evidence, according to Shankhpaul Jataka there was a Naga king of Ratta or Aratta family who were Karaskaras.

Guptas were herdsmen[103] or Goala like Lichchhavis (See chapter VI P-161-63) residing in the Karapatha of Nepal, it means both were ethnically related to each other. It is very strikingly confirmed while we note that Lichchhavis gave their daughter Kumardevi to Chandra gupta I in marriage, although their family laws forbade the marriage of a Lichchhavi girl with an outsider.[104] These Lichchhavis were born from a union of real brother and sister like Sakyas which was a tradition of Western Asia and particularly those of Naga people (See chapter V PP 96-106) These Lichchhavis were of republic society similar to Vahikas, Malavas, Madras Arattas (These were matriarchal kingdoms of Panjab see chapter V Page 103) and Sakyas.

The Bhoja

Bhoja family was an associate of Mahar or Maharathi republic state known as Satavahana. Bhojas were a branch of Yadava family. The Yadava tribe was consisted of 18 families and Bhoja was a branch of Yadava tribe or Gana. It is apparent from the Rigveda (IV-30-17, 18) that Yadus and Turvāsa Dasas were saved by the Indra from the Sindhu. Bharsiva-Nag established their two branches, one in Padmavati and other in Mathura. The Nag Bansha of Padmavati was known as Taka Banshi and Nag Banshi of Mathura as Yadava Banshi. Ganpati Nag of Padmavati was from the Taka Nag family or the Takka. C.V. Vaidya has called Takkas, Takshak also.[105] In Skand Purana, Takshak Nag has been called Mahanāg (77/17, 18 ; 106/5, 6, 7) similarly there is a description of seven Mahanagas in Maya shipla. They are Basuk, Takshak, Karkotak, Padam, Mahapadam, Sankhpal and Kulik.[106] Therefore Taka or Takka were of Takshak family. They were related to Bhoja.

Bhoja people were also rulers of Malava. Because the Malava people were worshipper of Karkotaka Nag, hence they were of Karkotak Nag family. Therefore, Bhojas were also of Naga family. Yadavas were originally related to Mahars or Mahar Naga family. Because, Bhojas were a chief tribe or family of Yadava tribe that is why they were included as an associate tribe of Mahar Nag.

According to Aitreya Brahmana[107] the Satvatas, which is the ancient name for the Yadavas, were one of the peoples who observed the Bhojya constitution.

Confederacy of Yaudheya, Kuninda and Arjuneya Republics

The credit[108] of giving the first below to the Kushāna empire really goes to aforesaid confederacy. Before the rise of Kushana empire the Yaudheya were a great power ruling over a wide stretch of territory covering northern Rajputana and the eastern Panjab[109] They made a second bid for the independence towards the end of the second century A.D. This time, they were successful in their venture and succeeded in freeing their homeland and ousting the Kushana beyond the Satluj. The coins of Kanishka III (180–210 AD) and Vasudeva II (210 – 240 AD) are not found to the east of the Satluj, proving the fact as cited above. Their coins of later period are found in a very large number between the Satluj and Yamuna in the districts of Saharanpur, Dehradun, Delhi, Rohtak, Ludhiana and Kangra which was their homeland.[110] The territory on the banks of Satluj upto the borders of the Bahawalpur State is still known as Johiyawar after the Yaudheya, denoting their independent lordship in northern and western regions. It was one of the remarkable achievements of Yaudheya, since Kushanas were a great power whose empire extended from Bacteria to Bihar. Kartikeya, their sacred god, occupies the place of honour on their coins.[111]

The Yaudheyas, very probably received valuable support and co-operation in their bid for independence from the Kunindas, their northern neighbours who were occupying the region between the upper course of Satluj and the Beas. Their coins were bearing close resemblance in type, fabric and size to the contemporary coinage of the Yaudheyas.

To the south[112]– east of the Yaudheya country lay the territory of another republic, the Arjunya who were occupying the Agra-Jaipur Area. There is no doubt that they also rebelled against Kushanas and established an independent rule of their own.

The Gonanda Dynasty of Kashmir and Meghavahana

Gonandas were ancient rulers of Kashmir as King Gonanda I ruled Kashmir during the Mahabharata period. He, being related to the king Jarasandha, took the side of Kansa in his conflict with the Krishna Yadava.

After decline in the popularity of the king Sandhimati, the council of ministers and people of Kashmir approached Meghavāhana, one of the remanants of deserted old royal family of Kashmir. Meghavāhana is said to have been the son of Gopaditya of the family of Andha-Yudhishthira[113] Due to the arising of political trouble in their own homeland, the ancestors of Meghvahana had fled away to Gandhara. According to Rajtarangini he was brought up in the court of the king of Gandhara.[114] Gonanda was a native Naga family, since the name of one of the kings of his royal family had prefix of the word Andha or Andhra, it can very reasonably be concluded that this family, originally, was related to the same family to which Satavahanas[115] belonged, the homogeneity in the names of Salivahana and Meghavahana is indicative to this probability. These Andhas or Andhras were rulers of Gandhara or north-west region in pre-historic and historic period.[116] They were a part of Vahalika people to whom Takshaka or Taka family[117] was also associated. It also seems from this, that Meghavahana was primogenitor of Megh people of the North-west Panjab (See chapter VI P-146 for detail) similar to Salivahana, who was primogenitor of Satavahana rulers of the South and Central India. Salivahan. went from aforesaid region to rule South and Central India. Megha or Meghawal people still maintain a tradition that Meghavahana was their ancestor.

Meghavāhana succeeded to the throne of Kashmir after dethronement of Sandhimati.[118] He married Amritprabha the daughter of the king of Pragjyotishapura[119]. Meghavāhana was a great king and a patron of Buddhist religion. He is said to have been a most kind hearted person as he stopped slaughter of animals and compensated and rehabilitated the butchers and persons who lived on the profession of prey by financial help and other means.[120] He constructed the Meghamatha and built the city of Mayushtagrāma.[121] His queen Amritprabha caused to be erected the great Vihara of Amritprabhavana for foreign monks. Meghavahana is credited for considerable building activities with the help of his numerous queens and also for his victories over many kings.[122] He was succeeded by his son Sreshthasena also known both as Tanjina (II) and Pravarasena[123]I. Pravarsena constructed the famous shrine of Pravareswara and donated the land of Trigarta for its maintenance. According to Bedia-ud-din he established his mother on the vacant throne of Khota and extended his own authority of Khotari, Chin and Machin.[124]

The family[125] tree of king Meghavahana according to Rajtarangini Volume I is as under :

	Name of King	Duration of reign	Date of accession
(1)	Meghavahan	34	386 AD
(2)	Sresthsen - Pravarsen I	30	
(3)	Hiranya-Torman	30-2	
(4)	Matra Gupta	4-9-1	
(5)	Pravarsen II	60-	
(6)	Yudhisthar II	39-3	
(7)	Lakhan Narendra ditya	13	
(8)	Ranaditya	300	
(9)	Vikramaditya	42	
(10)	Baladitya	36-8, death	625 AD

Gonanda dynasty came to an end with the king Baladitya. It may be surmised that he was a weak king and is therefore not credited with any political achievements of note. He had only one issue, a daughter, Ananglekha whom he had married to Durlabha-Vardhana, who came on the throne of Kashmir and founded Karkota dynasty.

The Kārkotas of Kashmir (625-885 AD.)

The word Kārkota is most ancient. It is interesting to note that this word occurs in Rigveda itself and if Vogel's suggestion is accepted it finds mention in Atharveda also as Sarkota. It seems that these Nagas are most ancient tribes of India and we can say they are Pre-Vedic. But they came into power in historical age in Kashmir.

Four Naga royal families ruled in Kashmir : Lohara, Gonandas, Karkota and Nagpal. The Kārkota royal family was prominent among them. According to Vishnupurana Karkotas were related to Takshakas.[126]

The Origin

Durlabha was the first king of the Karkotaka family or founder member of dynasty. Stories related to this family are given in the 'Rajtarangini' of Kalhana, which has practically become the original sources of history of Kashmir. K.S. Saxena gives details of events regarding their origin and coming in to power,[127] "Durlabha was the son of Karkota Nag. He enthroned after the Baladitya, the last king of Gonanda royal family. In fact, like the Palas, Gurjars, Pratihars, and Chandelas, this family was also from some low birth [Singh B.P., Decline of the kingdom of Magadha PP 324-25; Majumdar R.C. Classical age P-65; Bose N.S., "History of the Chandela" PP 1-2 (1956)]. A legend has been woven around their ancestors so as to enhance the prestige of the family in popular esteem. According to Ray, Durlabh Vardhana was a man of low origin, took service under king Bāladitya, married his daughter and after the king's death, succeeded him.... The legend of his mother cohabiting with a Kārkota Nāga and taking her "purifying bath" might also offer as inkling of his native place (RT I-III-490)[128] The Naga had his abode in some lake in the Toshmaidan route to Lohara (R.T. I, III, 490 stein's note II, VIII, 1996, 1997). Evidently the mother of Durlabha vardhana a native of the same locality, had gone to bath in some lake, the same, as the legend has it....... It can, therefore, be safely concluded that Durlabha vardhana was not a Kayastha by caste, but was an officer of the state. It is quite likely that he belonged to the Nāga clan and was a petty local chief. Vaidya suggested the same possibility and maintained that the Kāyastha, who were formerly officials later on formed a caste (Vaidya C.V.H.M.H.J.I. PP 203-17). Bālāditya, the last king of the Gonanda dynasty of Kashmir would otherwise have not married his daughter Ananglekha to him and degraded his social standing in the eyes of his subjects. This however seems natural, as chances of Durlabhavardhan himself being of Naga clan are more probable than that of his being Kshatriya."

Undoubtedly Duralabhavardhan[129] might have organized a powerful military that is why he could extend his territories beyond the valley. This would not have been possible without fierce fighting, as the neighbouring territories of Kashmir were occupied by tough and hardy people.

Coins bearing the legend 'Durlabha' have also come to light and some scholars attribute these to Durlabhavardhana the founder of the Kārkota dynasty (Cunningham A.C. M.I. P-43).[130]

Although Durlabhavardhan had many victories to his credit in his life time, he had to suffer defeat at the hand of his contemporary mighty king of Kanauj, Maharaja Harshvardhan.[131] According to Hiuentsang Harsha a great patron of Buddhism took away by force the sacred 'tooth relic' of the lord Buddha which was in possession of the king of Kashmir. In the opinion of Ray a verse in the Rajtarangini itself suggests that Kashmir did acknowledge the suzerainty of Kanauj.[132]

Although Durlabhavardhana, like Harshvardhana, was a Buddhist King, he was tolerant to other religions, that is why according to Rajtarangini he granted a village named Chandragrama near the castle of Parivisaka to the Brahmnas to express his esteem and regard for them.[133]

The date of the accession of Durlabha vardhana, accepted by many scholars, is 625 AD (stein, R.T.I. Intr. P.136). He must have been a ruler of consequence for his sway extended over a very vast region. During his reign Hieuntsang visited the valley and mentions that Takshila, Singhapura, Urasa, Punch and Rajapuri were included in his dominions.[134] Thus the frontiers of the Kashmir kingdom, which in the time of Baladitya (the last king of the Gonanda dynasty) had been limited to the valley itself, extended far beyond upto some portions of the modern district of Rawalpindi in Pakistan.[135]

The Pedigree

According to K.S. Saxena the successor of Durlabhavardhan and their chronology is as under :

(1)	Durlabhāvardhana	625–661 AD
(2)	Durlabhakā	661–711–13 AD
(3)	Chandrāpidā-Vajrāditya	711–13 — 720–21 AD
(4)	Tarapidā	720–21 — 724–25 AD
(5)	Lalitaditya or Muktapida	724–25 — 756–57 AD

(6) Kuvalayapida 760–61 — 768 AD
(7) Prithavyapida 768 – 772 AD
(8) Sangramapida I
(9) jayapida – Vijayaditya
(10) Jajja
(11) Lalitapida
(12) Sangramapida II
(13) Chippata Jay Pida (Brishaspati) 12 years
(14) Ajilapida
(15) Anangapida
(16) Utpalapida 885 AD

Durlabha had three sons from Queen Narindra-prabha viz Chandrapida, Tarapida and Muktapida. Durlabhaka ruled peacefully for a period of 50 years (661-711-13 AD). He was succeeded by his eldest son Chandrapida Vajrāditya.

Lalitaditya (724-25 – 756-57 AD)

The list of the kings of this dynasty is given above, who ruled for a total period of about 260 years (625 AD to 885 AD). Although most of the kings of early period were best rulers, administrators and warriors but the most important among them was Lalitaditya or Muktapida who ruled from 724-25 to 756-57 AD, who, not only carried his victorious arms to South India but also upto Central Asia. Most probably he was the only Indian king who glorified India by his victories outside India up to the Central Asia.

This campaign of Digvijaya carried by Lalitaditya is confirmed by a letter written by Dahir to Mohammed Kasim wherein occurs the following passage[136] — "If I had sent against you the king of Kashmir, on whose royal threshold the other rulers of Hind had placed their heads, who sways the whole Hind, even the countries of Makran and Turan whose chains a great many noblemen and grandees have willingly placed on their knees and against whom no human being can stand."

Saxena gives a short description of his grand victories[137] "As has been noted above, Yasovarman of Kanauj was the first ruler who had to bear the brunt of Lalitaditya's arms. Judging from facts and the indirect hints of Vākpatiraja, the calculations of Tripathi, Geotz and Majumdar may be taken as conclusive and the Kanauj king was defeated some time in 733 AD .... After subjugating Yasovarman, Lalitaditya pressed forward towards Bihar and Bengal which regions would have kept him occupied till about 735-36 AD..... and during this period he would also have passed through Orissa. (Goetz H., JBB RAS XXVIII P-54) From AD. 736-37 onwards, Lalitaditya was occupied in his conquest in the Deccan which included the voluntary submission of the Rattā queen, defeat of some Silāhāra chieftain in his campaign in the Kathiavar region, minor engagements in Rajasthan and his final return to Kashmir."

Further Saxena gives an account of his victories in northern western India,[138] "The Victorious forces of Lalitaditya met with little opposition from the Maitraka ruler of Valabhi, who was most probably, Siladitya VI. Very little is known of these Maitraka Kings of Valabhi from 690 to 770 AD (Majumdar RC, classical age P-150). It was probably during the reign of Siladitya V that Valabhi was invaded by the Arabs...... These raids took place probably during A.D. 725 to 735 AD. Since Siladitya V was ruling about 730 - 35 AD and Siladitya VII, the last known king was on the throne in 766-67 AD..... it may safely be deduced that Siladitya VI must have ruled some time between 735 AD and 766 AD. Siladitya VI had, apparently, to face a sea of troubles from the Arabs on the one hand and from the Chalukyas, the Pratihara of Avanti and also from the Rashtrakutas on the other. Besides, one Jaikadeva is also known to have been ruling in the Saurasthra Mandala with imperial titles. Thus, Lalitaditya seems to have met with little opposition in this area, where too many political powers were trying to assert themselves at the cost of the Matirakas.The campaigner next proceeded to Ujjaini, the capital of Avanti.... It has been conclusively shown by Tripathi and Majumdar that the Pratihara held sway over these regions, during the period under review - (Majumdar R.C.; Age of Imperial Kanauj P-20). According to Majumdar, Nagabhata I ruled there from 730 to 756 AD...... According to Kalhana, the route taken by the forces of Lalitaditya was through the arid and pathless tracts of Rajasthan (RT. I, IV, 163). It has been suggested by Goetz that while passing through these regions, Lalitaditya also subdued petty chieftains including the Guhilot ruler, Bappa Rāwal of the legendary fame who had occupied Chittor after defeating the Mori or Maurya ruler, Manu raja of that locality (Goetz H., JBBRAS XXVII P-57). After this period friendly relations developed between Bappa and Lalitaditya (Majumdar R.C. classical age P-158)."

Campaign in Central Asia

Lalitaditya hardly had come back from his campaign of Western India, he was threatened by an impending attack from Tibet, then under the famous and powerful king Khriede, btsug - brtan - Mes-ag-Tshoms. who ruled over the country from 705 AD. But he was defeated by the brave soldiers of Kashmir.[139]

Having dealt with the Tibetan menace successfully, Lalitaditya turned his attention towards Central Asia and finally began his campaign of Central Asia. Indian[140] history is singularly poor in examples of Indian kings leading expeditions beyond the traditionally recognized frontiers of India and as pointed out by Vaidya 'India had always been defeated by herds coming from central Asia but this singular exploit of Lalitaditya in going out of India and conquering Turan, deserves a prominent place in the early mediaeval history of the country.[141]

The hardy people of those regions offered very stiff opposition to Lalitaditya and hence he had to face numerous difficulties at every step[142]. The Kambojas were defeated and crushed easily while the Tukkharas (Tokharians), who first offered some resistance, later fled to the mountains leaving behind their horses. Their chief[143] Mummuni, who worsted thrice which indicates that though beaten in the first encounter, he tried to re-establish himself twice thereafter.[144] The Bhauttas and the inhabitants of Darda-desa, who were noted for their hardy-hood and war like character, were made to flee to the deserted city Pragjyotishapura.[145] Thenceforth he proceeded towards Vālukāsamudra, undoubtedly the southern extremities of the Gobi, desert and also passed over some region described by the chronicler as "Stri-Rajya". The king of Uttarakuru, however fled away without offering any resistance.[146]

Death of Lalitaditya

The worthy monarch, who immortalized himself in the annals of India as a warrior and an able ruler, met his end in one of his expeditions beyond the frontiers of his empire. According[147] to Kalhana, two traditions were rife during his life time about the death of Lalitaditya. According to one he died due to excessive snowfall in the region called Aryanaka which may correspond with Ariana of the Greek writers and eastern Iran of the present times.[148] According to the other tradition he committed suicide in order to avoid capture by his enemies when separated from the main body of his army.[149]

The career and conquests of Lalitaditya offer few parallels in the annals of Indian history. He was not only a great soldier and military leader but also an able administrator and patron of art and letters. Nation can be proud of him.

The Naga Kings of Kalinga and Mahakausala

The King Jitshatru was ruling in Kalinga country, in sixth century B.C., who was friend and brother-in-law of Siddhartha, the father of

Mahavira. A decision of marriage of Mahavira and his (Jitshatruś) daughter Yashoda was taken but, as a hard bow was taken by Mahavira to remain bachlor throughout his life, hence the marriage ceremony could not take place.[150] Perhaps, Jitshatru was related to any old Vidyadhar family. It seems that his successors ruled with full confidence on this country up to the Age of Nandas. Magadha emperor Nandivardhan, invaded Kalinga in 424 B.C. (Mahavir Nirvan Sambat 103) and annexed this country to his empire in the end of third century B.C., during last years of rule of Mauryan emperor Sampriti Kalinga gained its independence and a new dynasty came into existence.[151] This new royal family was also follower of Jainism. Whether this family had some relation with the previous royal family or not, cannot be assured. The probability is, that they had relation with any of ancient royal family of Kalinga. According to an inscription of Kharvelas the name of this family was El and this was a branch of Chedi or Chetra family.[152] The name of this king was Chhemraj. Some scholars think that the name of the son of Chhemraj was Budhiraj and his son was Bhikshuraj Kharvel. But according to some other scholars these were all titles of Kharvel himself.[153]

It seems that the relation of aforesaid 'El' was with the name of Elapatra or Elāpatra.[154] Thus it can be imagined that the relation of this royal family was with the Naga race. The meaning of the word 'El', 'Arya' does not seem to be correct according to some scholars–The relation of this family, definitely seems with the Nagas. There are so many evidences in support of it. This family is said to be a branch of Chetra Bansha or Chedi, who were related to Haihaya people.[155] These Haihaya people were a branch of Yadavas, who have been proved to be Nagas in Chapter IX P-238.

Thus Kharvelas, in the Vakataka age, who were their Governors were called Meghas[156] and Mahameghas in their imperial age. These rulers are described in the Puranas as very powerful and very wise. These Meghas reappear under the Guptas as Governors of Kausambi where two of their inscriptions have been found.[157] What was their relation with the Meghavahana king of Kashmir is uncertain, one branch of this family lead by Mohindraditta Gandharvasena or Gardabhilla (Kharvela) son of Vakradeva, established his rule in Ujjain.[158] After sometimes, Gardabhilla became the chief of newly established republic of Malava, owing to his immoral conduct and in response to efforts made by famous Jain Muni Kālācharya, he was dethroned and exiled by the Saka kings in 61 B.C., but his valiant son Veervikramaditta defeated Saka kings and regained the lost power of Malava-gana in 57 B.C. and ruled for a long period with glory and justice.[159]

It is well known that these Malava Ganas were a part of Panch-Karpati or Nagas of Taka race.[160] Therefore Gardabhilla, Vikramditta and his family who were related to Kharvella as well as Malava both also seem to be related to the Nagas of Karpati gotra.

The Rashtrakutas : Their Origin

We have come to know, from a description given in the grant of Dantidurga (738-758) of Rashtra Kuta family, (JBRAS Vol II) that the queen of Indra Rashtrakuta from her mother's side was Somabanshi and from father's side Chalukya.[161]

It seems from the historical evidences that many Somabanshi were called Naga Banshi. Mahars being Nagabanshi were also called Soma-Banshi. Hence Rashtrakuta, family also seems to be Naga Banshi. This significant conclusion that Rashtrakutas were Yadu Banshi, gets the support of inscription of Khare-patan, Sangoli, Navsari and Wardha. It is stated there that the Rashtra-Kutas were born from the family of the king Ratta, who was from the Satyaki branch of Yadus. Ratta had a son, named Rashtrakuta, after whose name family got its name.[162] Yadu family is a branch of Naga family. The word 'Rashtrakuta' had not any relation with the etymology of Maharashtra. Rashtrakuta were said to be a branch of Yadu Bansha, because they were further related to the race and family of the Bhoja. We know king Dantidurga performed a Hiranya garbha ceremony at Ujjain for his purification (See chapter XV P-412).

Summary and Conclusion

According to Mahabharata account Takshak Nag royal family was ruling at Takshila and Pātālpuri. They were dead enemies of Aryan Pandavas. They, later, captured Hastinapur and further began to move eastward and established themselves at Kashi-Kausal and at Magadha. One of their branch moved through Rajasthan and captured Vidisa (110 – 31 BC).

(1) The first king of Vidisa branch was Sesha and the last was Vangara (31 BC). At this time Satavahanas suppressed Kanvas, hence they shifted their capital to Padmavati. There, they ruled up to 78 AD. In Puranas they have been called Vrisha or Naga Nandi. Last king of this dynasty was ousted from his capital by the Kushana invaders. Hence they escaped to jungles of Jabbalpur and Hosangabad.

(2) After, re-issuing from the jungles, they carved out new principality with their capital at Kantipuri at about 140 AD. They were now known as Bharsivas. The first king of this dynasty was Nava naga (140 – 170 AD) and second king was

Virasena. Virasena was great warrior and skilful king who established rule at Padmavati and Mathura. Padmavati, branch is known as Bharsiva and Mathura branch as Yadava. All these three branches were destroyed by Samudra Gupta in 344 AD. Their another fourth branch was at Eran-Vidisa.

(3) Just like, Virasena showed his skill in establishing new rule at Padmavati and Mathura, after some time one of their branch, known as Vakataka (250–570) established new kingdom in Baghelkhand or Vindhya. The name of the first king was Vindhya Shakti. They had their two main branches at Purika and Vatsagulma.

(4) One of the prince of Vakatakas, Rudrasena I became legal heir of the throne of Bhavanaga Bharshiva, since he was his daughter's son, proving prevalence of Matriarchal tradition among them. In addition to the above, he also became legal heir of the throne of his own grand father (Pravarsena I).

(5) Jayaswal K.P. thinks that Vakatakas were Brahman, because in an inscription of Vārāhdev-Amatya of Harisen has been called Dvija. But I do not agree with the scholar on the followig grounds :

(a) In a copper plate grant of Vakatakas of Balaghat (E.I. IX-P 270) Rudrasena I Vakataka has been called Maharaja Bharsiva.

(b) We know Bharsiva Nagas were of Taka family who had a tradition to use their family name as suffix or prefix with the names of countries, localities, towns, rivers, and everything they own to denote or to show their fame and lordship. Thus, they used the suffix of the word 'Taka' with the name of locality, named Vakat, where they lived in their early stage of gaining power and adopted this name, (Vakat + Taka) Vakataka as their family name, it means Taka family belonged to Vakat Village.

(c) According to Vishnu Purana (Wilson Val II P – 657) "there were thirteen sons of Vindhyashakti and rest. The Bhagawata has a different statement identifying the sons of the Vindhya race with the Balhikas (Vahikas) and making them thirteen." According to Cunningham these Vahalikas were Taka Nagas. Hence it is established firmly that these Vakatakas were Taka Nagas. Since Nagas had a tradition of Raja-rishi, hence, Vārāhdev one of their admirer and Minister has honorified the primogenitor of royal family by suffixing word 'Dvija' in the last days of survival of the family power and never before.

(6) Bhoja was an associate of Satavhanas who were Mahar or Maharathe. They were a branch of Yadavas race hence of Naga origin.

(7) Similarly Karkota of Kashmir (625 – 885 AD) were also of Naga origin. Durlabha, the first king of the dynasty is said to be the son of Karkotaka Naga and a native lady. This royal family ruled between 625 – 885 AD. Most important king of this family was Lalitaditya or Mukta-pida (724-25–756-57 AD). He carried his victorious arms not only up to south India but also up to Central Asia, where he died due to excessive snowfall.

References

1. Mahajan V.D., "Ancient India" P-377.
2. Jayaswal K.P. "History of India" P-9.
3. JBORS I P-116.
4. Jayaswal K.P. P-10.
5. Jayaswal K.P. P-18.
6. Rao S.R., "Lothal and the Indus civilization" P-190.
7. ASR 1915-16 P-106 Plate LXI.
8. ASR 1915-16 PP-100 FF.
9. Jayaswal K.P. P-12.
10. ASR Vol XII P-43.
11. Jayaswal K.P. P-11.
12. Jayaswal K.P. P-14.
13. Jayaswal K.P.-15.
14. V.P. (Wilson) II P-659.
15. Jayaswal K.P. P-16.
16. Jayaswal K.P. P-29.
17. Ibid.
18. Ibid.
19. (a) Jayaswal K.P. "Hindu Polity" P-46..
    (b) Bhandarkar D.R. "Lecture on the Ancient History of India" PP-169-70.
20. Katyayan comments on Panini IV-1-168.

    JANAPAD SHABDĀT KSHATRIYĀDN. I

    KSHATRIYĀ DEKARĀJĀ TSANGHA PRATIŚE DHĀRTHAM. II

21. Sherring Rev M.A.; Hindu Tribes and Castes. PP 357-73.
22. Jayaswal K.P., "History of India" P-30.
23. Jayaswal K.P. P-39.
24. Jayaswal K.P. P-31.
25. Jayaswal K.P. P-32.
26. Jayaswal K.P. P-17.
27. Jayaswal K.P.. P-15.
28. Bajpai Atima, "Madhyapradesh Ke Nagbanshi Sikke" PP 115-17.
29. Hawkes Jacquetta, "The First Great Civilization" PP 160-161.
30. Jayaswal K.P. "Hindu Polity" PP 38, 50-52, 54-55.
31. Jayaswal K.P., "History of India" PP 33-34.
32. Jayaswal K.P., "Hindu Polity" P-119.
33. Jayaswal K.P., "Hindu Polity" PP-54-55.
34. ASR (1915-16) P-103.
35. ASR (1915-16) P-105.
36. V.P. (Wilson) II P-659.
37. Jayaswal K.P. - "History of India" PP 20-21 and 35.
38. ASR (1915-16) P-102.
39. ASR (1915-16) P-103.
40. (a) Jayswal K.P. PP 20-27.
    (b) Smith V.A., ''Coins of Indian Museum'' P-191.
41. ASR 1915-16 P-100 Footnote.
42. ASR 1915-16 P-101.
43. Jayaswal K.P. P-19.
44. Jayaswal K.P.-21.
45. Jayaswal K.P.-23.
46. Jayaswal K.P. P-27.
47. Jayaswal K.P. P-17.
48. Jayaswal K.P. P-62.
49. Jayawal K.P. P-63.
50. Jayaswal KP PP-66-67.
51. According to an inscription of Vārāhdev, who was a minister of Harisen, Vindhya Shakti has been called Dvij E.I. XXVI P-140.
52. Jayaswal K.P. PP 67-68.

53. Mirashi V.V., "Vakataka Rajbans aur Uske Abhilekha" PP. 12-17.
54. Vayu Purana 78-23.
55. Arthsastra-Sangha Vrata Adhikarn XI.
56. Jayaswal K.P. P-17.
57. (a) Tod James, "Annals and Antiquities of Rajasthan" I P-126.
    (b) Mahajan VD, "Madhya Kalin Bharat" PP 246-49.
58. Tod James I P-110 Footnote no. 3.
59. Tod James I PP-124-25.
60. Cunningham A: "Ancient Geography of India" PP 126-27.
61. Jayaswal K.P. P-126.
62. IA XVII P-118.
63. Tod James I P-110 Foot Note no.3.
64. Mohendale M.A. "BDCRI" Vol I (1939-40) P-192.
65. See chapter XI PP 285-86 for detail.
66. Haribamsa (Vishnu Parv-60-32).
67. Mirashi V.V.P.-46.
68. (a) Mirashi VV P-46.
    (b) JNSI Vol II (1940) P-94.
69. Arthshastra of Kautilya, Sangha Vrata Adhikaran XI.
70. Cunningham A PP-125-26.
71. Jayawal K.P. PP-67.
72. Jayaswal K.P. P-69.
73. V.P. (Wilson) Chapter XXIV Part II P-656.
74. Jayaswal K.P. P-69.
75. Jayaswal K.P. P-178.
76. Rao S.R., P-190.
77. Mirashi V.V., P-247.
78. Dikshit S.K. "The Mother Goddess" PP 39-40.
79. Jayaswal K.P. PP-21 and 72.
80. Jayaswal K.P. PP-37-38.
81. Jayaswal K.P. P-72.
82. Jayaswal K.P. P-68.
83. Mirashi V.V. PP 16-17.
84. Ghurye G.S., "Caste and Races in India" P-238.

85. Mirashi V.V. P-18.

86. Sudharshna Senevritne IHR Vol VII (1980-81) No.1 and 2 P-66.

87. Jayaswal K.P. P-68.

88. V.P. (Wilson) II P-656.

89. Hawkes Jacquetta, "The First Great civilization" P-190.

90. Hawkes Jacquetta P-410.

91. Bottero, Cassin and Vercoutter, "The Near East; The Early Civilization" PP 391-92.

92. Oldham C.F., "The Sun and the Serpent" P-30.

93. V.P. (Wilson) II P-549.

94. Tod James II PP-914-17.

95. Ghurye G.S. PP 259-60.

96. See chapter V P-106.

97. Viyogi Naval, "The Founders of Indus Valley Civilization and their later history" PP 297-307.

98. Jayaswal K.P. PP 115-16.

99. Vaidya C.V., "History of Mediaeval Hindu India" P-382.

100. Davids Rhys T. W., "Buddhist India" P-20.

101 Madra King Sālya was from Vahika dynasty Law B.C., "Some Kshatriya Tribes of Ancient India" P-223.

102. In the Mahabharata and in the Lexicon of Hem Chandra, the Vahikas are said to be the same as Taka (note no 1) BAHIKĀSHTAKKANĀ MĀNO.

Cunningham A PP 125-26.

103. Daniel ed Wright, "History of Nepal" Calcutta (1966) PP 72-73.

104. Chakravorty, "Origin of the Lichchhavi of Vaisali" IHQ P-58.

105. Vaidy C.V., P-384.

106. Rao T.A. Goinath, "Elements of Hindu Iconography" Vol II Part II (1968) PP 556-57.

107. Jayaswal K.P. P-80.

108. Majumdar and Altekar, "The Vakataka Gupta Age" P-28.

109 MB II Chap 35, VV 4 FF.

110. Majumdar and Altekar P-29.

111. Ibid P-30.

112. Ibid P-31.

113. Rajtarangini II-144, 147.

114. R.T. II-144, 145.

115. Vogel JPH ''Indian Serpent Lore'' P-36.

116. (a) Jayaswal K.P., "The Hindu Polity" P-130.

(b) See chapter XI P-666 for detail.

117. Jayaswal K.P., "History of India" P-115.

118. R.T. II-151.

119. R.T. II-147, 150.

120. R.T. III-5, 6.

121. R.T. III-8.

122. RT III, 11, 15, 27, 72.

123. RT III-97.

124. Saxena K.S., "Political History of Kashmir" P-31.

125. Rajtarangini, Commentator Raghunath Singh, Varanasi (1970).

126. (a) V.P. (Wilson) P-226.

(b) Tod James I P-43 Foot note no. 3.

127. Saxena K.S., "Political History of Kashmir" PP 40-43.

128. A some what similar story is related in the 'Parmāl Raso' about the origin of Chandelas and the mother of the first ruler sought purification through the performance of Bhānda-Yajna (Mitra S.K., "Early Ruler of Khajuraho" PP-23, 25, 27).

129. Saxena K.S. P-43.

130. Saxena K.S. P-44.

131. Ibid.

132. Ray N. R. I H Q III 1927 P-780.

133. R.T. IV, 5 (Stein's note).

134. Saxena K.S. P-43.

135. Ibid.

136. Vaidya C.V., "History of Mediaeval Hindu India" P-208.

137. Saxena K.S. PP-79-80.

138. Saxena K.S. PP-76-77.

139. Majumdar R.C., "Classical Age" P-158.

140 Saxena K. S. PP-82.

141. Vaidya C.V. P-211.

142. R.T. IV-164 and 166.
143. Saxena Ibid P-82.
144. R.T. IV-178, 79.
145. R.T. IV-171.
146. R.T. IV-175.
147. Saxena K. S. P-86.
148. R.T. IV-367.
149. R.T. IV-368, 69.
150. Jain Jyoti Prasad, "Bhartiya Itihas : Ek Drishti" PP-239-40.
151. Jain Jyoti Prasad P-180.
152. Jain Jyoti Prasad P-183.
153. Ibid P-183.
154. Vogel JPH PP-208-09.
155. Jain Jyoti Prasad P-195.
156. Jayaswal K.P. P-87.
157. E.I. (1925) P-158.
158. Jain Jyoti Prasad P-189.
159. Jain Jyoti Prasad P-189.
160. Jayaswal K.P. PP 38-39.
161. Vaidya CV-114.
162. JBBRAS Vol XVIII P-239.

Chapter 13

The Guild Based Trade and Industry during the Megalithic and Buddhist Age

Discovery of Iron and development of its Technology in Asia minor ; beginning of Iron Age in India.

Although, human civilization was flourishing in Mesopotamia and Egypt, even earlier than 3500 B.C., but because its basis was implements made of copper which were not good and strong enough, therefore the speed of development of human civilization was very slow. But, in the middle of the Second millennium B.C. iron was first of all discovered and technology developed in the empire of Hittites in Asia minor and as soon as, it spread up in all directions, the speed of development of human civilization also grew fast.

Although early workers, familiar with the marvellous properties of those blue and green minerals that gave them copper, must have experimented with the red minerals that could in fact have yielded them iron. Iron oxides reduced at about the same heat as those of Copper, but owing to much higher melting point, the experimenters were not rewarded with a flow of metal.[1]

The small lumps of metal were lost in the spongy mass of the 'bloom'. It was more fit for ornaments than for tools or weapons.

It was not, until the second half of the Second millennium B.C., the essential process of Carburizing or steeling by repeated heating in the presence of charcoal and hammering was fully mastered[2]. It seems to have been invented by those metallurgists, the Chalybes which were then subject to the Hittites. For some two Centuries (1400-1200 BC) the Hittites held a near monopoly. Then with the fall of their power and the general ethnic upheaval of the time, the art of blacksmithy was spread rapidly in all directions. Mesopotamia, however was slow to adopt the new metal. Although it had been known and sparingly used, centuries earlier, it can be said that there was no true Iron Age there before the ninth century[3]. From that date the Assyrian kings used great quantities for their armies. Hard iron and the Assyrian empire were well suited to one another. Sargon II was particularly lavish, and it is appropriate that 150,000 kilograms of iron bars were found in his palace The Assyrians seem to have imported the iron ready-made from Anatolia and Syria, the state keeping central stores in each city and issuing it to Smiths to forge under contract[4].

We know, the Indus Valley people (2700-1700 BC) were great craftsmen and traders who were responsible for the prosperity and progress of that culture. As a result of Aryan invasion, some of the Harappans moved Southward, but some of the tribes like Brahuis and Nagas had taken shelter in hilly track of Northwest. Still there was infilteration of ancient Iranian people in the aforesaid region. But according to S.P. Gupta-a large wave of them entered in about 1000 BC [5] perhaps due to coming of into overwhelming power, the Assyrians, created a panic in the whole of the Western Asia.[6] According to ancient record of Assyrian royal house, one of their queen named Semirmes lead a compaign of unsuccessful invasion on India also in 800 B.C.

These new comers were perhaps more civilized than their brothers who had already come and settled here who were Dravidians and Iranians or their admixture race or Nagas. They were definitely more powerful being equipped with iron implements and arms. They raised Megaliths in Burzahom in about 1000 BC[7] and moved towards South and East. They, by and by acquired political power in the whole of the India accept few portions of far South and eastern region of Assam. They developed non-Vedic Jain and Buddhist religious traditions which overpowered the earlier Vedic Culture.

Similarly they established their guild based trade and industry as already explained in chapter VI, such like system was in prevalence in West Asian countries and particularly at Sumer where there were guilds of spinners, weavers, dyers and fullers as informed by Jacquetta Hawkes,[8] who were later brought to Indus Valley by immigrants or traders.

Craft Guilds or Guild Based Occupations

Guild like system of occupation can still be seen in Assam among certain Naga tribes. It is very interesting to note, that among the Manavya Gotri Naga society all the social, political, religious and economic systems, were united in to Sangha system. We have earlier thrown light on this Subject in chapter VI PP-124-25.

Aforesaid guilds were flourishing, in all those regions of the country where these Manavyas has made centres of their settlements. According to Bhandarkar[9] – "From about 500 BC to 600 AD India was studded with guilds of various types showing how well Industry and trade were specialized and developed."

Craft Guilds in the North

'Buddhist Jatakas' is a most important book, which is said to be earliest written work of India, whose period is accepted to be 500 B.C. by most of the scholars. In this book stories related to the previous birth of Buddha are compiled. These stories were recited by Buddha to his followers during his religious discourse. From the study of these stories, a very clear picture of social religious, political and economic life of people of those days, emerges. These stories contain detailed description of those craft guilds which were functioning in the field of trade and industry in those days.

The Jatakas, though, they give eighteen as the stock number of crafts and occupations organized in to guilds, mention only four of them specially, viz, carpenters, smiths, leather workers and painters. Besides these[10] four guilds, we find separate references to the guilds of some other occupations ; e.g. workers in stone, ivory-workers, Jewellers, garland-makers and flower-sellers. The guilds of bamboo-workers, braziers and corn-dealers are mentioned in the inscriptions from Junnar[11]. Mahavastu speaks of existence of two weaver guilds at Govardhana. Obviously the number of weavers, who thought it prudent to form themselves into corporate bodies, seem to have been too large for a single guild.

In the Jatakas of Buddhist of 6th century B.C., there is mention of villages of carpenters settled near Banaras. According to Alinachitta Jataka no 156, there was a village of 500 carpenters, who used to bring logs of wood from nearly forest in their boats and shape them in to planks and beams for house building and put together the frame work of one storey or two storey houses. They would build houses to the order as it was required of them and earn their livelihood. This seems to be historical, since all the royal buildings, found from excavation of ancient town of Pataliputra (Kumargarha), were built of timber.

Similarly according to Samudda Vanija Jataka no. 466, there was a large village or Mahagrama of thousand carpenters nearby Banaras. They used to shape household goods like chairs, cots (bed) etc and earn their livelihood. At least they built a mighty ship and launched it into the river and sailed to the sea and reached an island that lay in the midst of the sea, which was full of all kinds of eatables. There is also mention of Grama-Nigama (Maha-Sreni) in another Jataka.

Similarly, there is mention of craft guilds of Kapilvastu in Mahavastu viz :musician, gold–smiths, bankers, Cloth–merchants, conch–workers, ivory-workers, Jewellers, workers in stone, perfumers, box-makers, oil-millar, dealers in Ghee (Indian butter), sugar manufacturer, water-seller, sweet-meat-seller, cotton-dealers, dealers-in wheat and Barley flour, fruit-venders, root-sellers, perfume-seller, vine-sellers, sugar–candy sellers etc[12]. Similarly there is description of guilds of people entertainers (dancers, singers and musicians) of different type in Mahavastu[13].

Craft Guilds in the South

We have made mention in earlier chapters that users of B and R ware pottery, round headed Alpine and long headed Dravidian or their blended race, had their two main centres of abode first in the north east region of Sangam of Ganga and Yamuna and second in the Western-Central region of present Maharashtra. The information, regarding people of second centre working in different craft-guilds, is obtained from inscriptions, grants or donorś written records from caves or Chetiyas or Stupas. B.G. Gokhale[14] gives detail of such like guilds from western Maharashtra, "Sethi (chief of guild) as donors are mentioned at Kanheri, Kuda, Mahad, kol, Karle, and Bedsa and in each case it is a substantial donation. .... Among the crafts mentioned, are those of carpenters, stone-polishers, stone-masons, weavers, potters, makers of hydraulic equipments, oil millers, braziers, gold smiths, jewellers, smiths, bamboo-workers, fishermen, perfumers, flower-gardeners, physicians and treasurers."

Some of the inscriptions, of the time of the Gupta emperors, as we have seen, bear sufficient testimony to the growth of these Guilds for which the established technical term is Sreni. The Indore[15] Copper plate inscription of 465 AD mentions a Tailika-Sreni, guild of oilmen, of which the president (Pravara) is named Jivanta. This oil-men's guild was trusted even by a Brahmin with the custody of his donation to be held by it in perpetuity under a contract which was registered.

The Mandsor inscription of the reign of Kumar Gupta II (no.18) mentions a guild of silk-weavers and its prosperous finances as shown by its construction of an unequalled temple of the Sun[16].

The base of economy of those days (500 BC-500 AD) was guild or sreni system, even up to the Gupta Age. R.K. Mookerjee puts forward his view on this subject– "The outstanding fact of the economy of those times is the organization of Industry or handicrafts under Guilds called srenis. Their corporate character is brought out by the seals which were issued by them. The abundance of seals found at only one city like Vaisali shows to what extent these guilds played their part in the economic life of the country. These Vaisali (Vasarh) seals bring to light the guilds (Nigamas) of bankers (Sreshthi), traders (Sarthavahas) and artisans (Kulikas). Some times these guilds federated themselves into a larger corporation, as in the legend. Sreshthi-Kulika-Nigama i.e. the corporation of bankers and artisans. There are again many seals testifying to the corporation formed by the federation of the three guilds of bankers, traders and artisans. One seal also has been legend Prathama-Kulika showing that he was the President of the guild of artisans. As Dr. T.Bloch, who discovered these Vaisali seals points out. 'It looks as if during those days, something like a modern chamber of Commerce existed in upper India of some big trading centre, perhaps at Pataliputra. It will be apparent from these numerous seals that Vaisali in those days was a very flourishing centre of trade, banking and business."[17]

Aforesaid Srenis were working not only in the field of crafts but also agriculture, animal husbandry and trade of that age. Such a Sreni or corporate system was in prevalence from very ancient time, perhaps as far as the age of Indus Valley culture.[18] It is very clearly evident that it was in vogue during the Jataka Age (6th century B.C). Most of the writings of Junnar cave belongs to a period ranging from 150 BC to 150–200 A. D. Inscription no. 27, which is on the left side of the hemisphere of the cave, makes mentions of a guild of builders of house, copper-smiths, and inscription no 10 makes mention of a guild of dealers in corn.[19]

Local and Foreign Trade

We have earlier told that India made trade relations with the European and West-Asian countries like Arbia, Babylonia, Sumeria, Greece and Rome through ports like Bharukachha and Khambat in aforesaid period. We have solid evidences of such trade relation, with the western world, we have archaeological evidences of trade activities of Roman merchants in India in about first century A.D. . A.K. Nilkant Sastri produces an account of their activities as such, "Large ships from Egypt are said by the author of the Periplus and by Strabo, to have visited India in their times. The Tamil works of the Sangam age mention colonies of Yavana Merchants in the coastal cities. Recent excavation of Arikamedu (near Pondicherry) has revealed the remains of a Roman trading station (the first of its kind discovered in India) with numerous fragments of Roman pottery of the first two centuries A.D. Hoards of Roman imperial coins have been found on other Indian sites, especially in the South. In the first century A.D. more over, Arab merchants are directly mentioned in the Periplus as making voyages in their own ships to Indian ports. That Indians also took part in this trade is seen clearly from the Periplus. In the first century A.D. Indian ships sailed regularly with cargoes from

'Ariaca' (its chief port was Barygaza) to the Persian Gulf, the South coast of Arabia and the Red Sea coast of Africa."[20]

Now question arises what kind of goods were the objects of trade from India and vice versa. Literary references, as well as surviving remains enable us to make out a list of the objects of trade between India and the Roman world especially in the first century. A.D. The[21] exports were of different kinds consisting of agricultural, animal, manufacturing and mineral products. Among agricultural products, rice and wheat, clarified butter, sesame-oil and sugar were carried from Western Coast in Indian ships to the market towns of East Africa. Rice and wheat were exported to Socotra. Indian[22] sandalwood, teakwood, timbers of black wood and ebony were regularly shipped from Barygaza to the ports of Persian Gulf. Similarly Indian animals like lions, tigers, apes, monkeys, parrots were exported to Roman markets. Indian ivory was most important among them. A very high number of craft-guilds were producing goods of different type in abundance in different parts of the country. This high production, excessive than the local demand was being exported to different countries which made India a most prosperous country. This was the main reason that these commercial guilds donated riches of high value to Buddhist monks which included large caves and Chetyas or Viharas.

Wealthy Merchants and Bankers

The effect of this Sreni or guild system on the society and economy of nation was so high that during Satavahana age in South-Western India some of the Artisan and trade guilds became so rich that they bestowed not only alms of high value but also functioning as bankers of high rank to the extent that citizens had full confidence in their dealings with them and depositing their life-long savings regularly and getting interest generation to generation on them.

Persons engaged in trade and commerce probably acquired large fortunes. The great Chaitya cave at Karle[23] was caused to be constructed by a seth (Sreshthin) of Vaijayanti, and in other places also especially at Kanheri their gifts were costly. There were in those days guilds of traders such as those of weavers, druggists, corn-dealers, oil-manufacturers. Their organization seems to have been complete and effective, since, as already mentioned, they received permanent deposits of money and paid interest on them from generation to generation. Self government, by means of such guilds and village communities, has always formed an important factor of the political administration of the country. A Nigamasabha[24] or town corporation is also, mentioned in one of Ushavadata's Nasik inscriptions which shows that something like municipal institutions existed in those early days. It is also worthy of remark that the yearly interest on the 2000 Karshapanas deposited by Ushavadata was 100 Karshapana and in another case that on 1000 and 75 showing that the rate of interest was not so high as it has been in recent time, but varied from five to seven and a half percent per annum.

The Sarthavāha or Carvaneers

One of the main reasons of aforesaid progress of trade and industry was security and peace in the Maurya, Satavahana and Gupta Age and absence of unnecessary interference by the officials of government in power ; other reasons were high moral and feelings of co-operation and brotherhood which were produced by Buddhism and existence of safe and good trade routes Uttarpatha, Dakshinapatha which connected large cities like Pataliputra, Bharukachha, Tamraliptaka, Peshawar, Prayag, Vidisa, Ujjain which had great trade importance. Large carvan of loaded carts, used to move from one end to other and vice versa. These traders were more important than ordinary tribes[25]men, who were known as Sarthavāha or Vaidehika. The latter name means men of the Videha tribes. It means such a system was introduced by Videha tribes, though all traders no longer belonged to any one tribe or Janpada and the Videha tribe had Vanished. This nomenclature shows the origin of the profession with a particular tribal guild. The group of merchant caravaneers extended in a long chain from Takshila to the very end of Magadha. It[26] is to be noted that these Videhas were a branch of Ikshwakus. On one of the copper plate of Damodarpur belonging to the period of Kumar Gupta I (414-445 AD) there is mention of Sarthvaha, and Prathama Kulka[27] (chief of the craft guilds).

According to Buddhist Jataka story no.1 (Apānāk) such large Carvan was consisted of as much as 500 carts and moving day and night on different trade routes from one corner of the Nation to the other, facing the difficulties of theaves, decoits and barbarian animals, dense forest, deserts etc. As Such produce of one region was transferred to the other and vice versa.

The Banik Trader, a non-Aryan Naga Race The Pani in Rigveda

We have earlier proved in the first Volume of this series[28] that Banik traders were a non-Aryan people. However for convenience of readers, we produce henceforth a gist of the same in addition to some new evidences to provide better information. The first reference of Pani or Banik trader comes in the Rigveda (X–108–1 to 11) itself, where Indra, whose cows were stolen by them and were kept in their ramparts, sent his messenger Sarma with a request to return back those cows. But Panis did not care for the request of messenger. This failure of talk led to a war between non-Aryan Panis and the Aryan Indra and Brihaspati. As a result of which Indra killed the Panis and destroyed their town (RV I–11–5 and VI 20–4).

These Panis, opposed to the worship of Indra, were called Asuras or Dasyus by the Rigvedic Aryans.

The name of their god was 'Bal' who represented one form of sun-god and has come to be identified as Vritra who had stolen the cows of gods (Aryans) and opposed them[29]. It, is clear these Panis were of Assyrian (Asuras) race and were called Dasyus and Dasas in Rigveda.

Now, question arises as to who were these Panis and what is their later history ? D.D. Kosambi throws some light on this subject in these[30] words : "Pani do not seem to be Aryans but this word survived in the later Indian civilization. Today's traders 'Bania' acquired this name from the Sanskrit 'Banik' word which might have been derived from the word 'Pani'. In Sanskrit Pana is a coin. The whole of the trading goods are Panya (Panini IV–4–51). In India, the ancient standard form of weight of coin was undoubtedly Harappan. From this it appears that some Harappans escaped the avarice of Aryans that old traditional business and trade etc. could survive ?

It is obvious these Panis were progenitors of today's Banik. But viewpoint of Avinash chandra[31]Dass gives a better clarification on this issue. He writes : "In Rigveda there is a mention of rich pretentious Panis at many places. It is quite clear that the Indus Valley civilization was a civilization of the traders and they used to sell their goods as far as up to Mesopotamia, Egypt and Babylonia. The immense wealth of the Panis has repeatedly been mentioned in Rigveda. Excavations of the old cities have revealed that the inhabitants of Harappa i.e. the Baniks and rulers were a very rich class."

From the above views, expressed by scholars, it becomes quite evident that the Pani was none else than the trading class of the Indus Valley who travelled to far off countries of the world by sea for carrying on trade. According to the Baudhayana Dharma Suttra I–1–24, the Brahmans (Aryans) who travelled by sea were treated as out-caste on account of this being denied by the shastras i.e. the above Panis travelled by sea because of their being non-Aryans and this very class of people later used to be called Panik (Pani) then Banik, who were the ancestors of today's traders, the Bania.

The above mentioned Panis, who carried on trade with Western countries, at a later stage shifted to Malabar coast from Sapta Sindhu through Western coast of Gujarat as a result of the invasion of Aryans.

From there they moved to the banks of Tigris and Euphratis by sea route. There, they spread their civilization. From there they went to Phoenicia (Lebanon) on the eastern coast of mediterranean sea by land route. There, they set up their colonies in the islands of mediterranean sea and in the north of Africa. They used to get the articles manufactured by the captured or bought slaves and carried on their trade in the southern Europe. So much so they carried on their trade up to Britain and Scandinavia by sea route and spread their civilization. In this way, the civilization spread from east to the western countries during ancient times as in the modern times the western countries engaged in trade, have spread the civilization in the East. Till some time ago from now festivals of God Bal or Balder (of panis) used to be celebrated in Scandinavia. A heap of wood was set on fire on the top of a hill and the people living in the surrounding areas would collect, sing, dance, rejoice and make noise on this occasion. Baltic sea, Belt, Belteberg, Baleshangen and Balestronden have been named after the name of God Bal.[32]

The Bal deity

The scholars are of the veiw[33] that the word Punik originated from Panik and from Punik the word Finish and from Finish came into being the word Finix and after this word the country Phoenicia was named. These people were perfect in ship building, fond of sea travel, greedy for wealth and worshipped the house hold deity Bal. The statue of their deity always held a fire receptacle in its hand. At the time of national distress, hundreds of children were sacrificed in that fire. Similarly, the enemies captured during war were also burnt in that fire.

According to A.C.Dass[34], "These Phoenicians retained a multifarious form of Rigvedic cosmogony and were nature worshippers like the Aryans of Saptasindhu. Their principal deities being Bal, the sun god and Uranus or Varuna. This god Bal or Bala is also mentioned in the Rigveda and identified with sun the Rbhus whom Sayan identifies with solar rays, were the sons of Bal or Baal (RV IV–33, 34, 35, 36 and 37). (See Chapter V P-93) Fire was also called a son of Bal. The Panis of Saptasindhu under the leadership of Bravu of their cruel practices, one may be mentioned here, viz. the practice of human sacrifice on the occasion of any extraordinary ceremony, an unusual number of victims were sacrificed. Human sacrifice was also a part of the established ritual and every year a youthful victim was chosen by lot. Infants were burnt alive and the most acceptable of all sacrifices was that of an only child. The image of Saturn was made of brass, the outstretched hands were hollowed so as to receive the body of the child which slid thence to a fiery receptacle below. Mothers brought their infants in their arms and quieted them by their caresses till the moment they were thrown into the flames, since any manifestation of reluctance would have rendered the sacrifice infructuous. It is strange dispensation of God that both in olden and modern times the selfish and greedy merchants should have been related for the spread of a particular civilization in other lands. As the European merchants have paved the way for the spread of western culture in eastern lands, so did the Panis also keep on spreading the culture of the east in western countries in ancient times."

At one time they had a colony in the southern part of Iran or in the eastern part in the southern sea-coast of Arab. Similarly, they had their last colony in Carthage in the north of Phoenicia, which was destroyed by Romans after a number of wars. These wars were known as Punic wars. People living on the coast of Mediterranean sea learnt shipping and trading from them. They also gained the knowledge of astrology, mathematics and such art of writing which was based on phonetic in place of the pictorial script. Their alphabet had 22 letters, which were based on the ancient scripts of Egypt and Mesopotamia. The Greek letters and many other writing systems developed under the influence of this script which also includes the Devnagri writing system.

The Agrasreni or Agraseni and Alexander

We have already given detailed discussion of craft and trade guilds existing in Buddha's time and later period while Alexander invaded India he met with many kingdoms which were infact republicans or Sanghas one of them was Agrasreni or Agraseni. Jayaswal K.P. gives an account of bravery and power of these peoples[35] "Alexander met in neighbourhood, of the last two republics the Agsinae who had mustered an army, if we believe Diodorus, of 40,000 foot and 3,000 horse, "They barricaded their narrow streets, fought with great vigour, so that Alexander in pressing the attack lost a few macedonions" (Diodorous BK XVII ch 96). According to Curtius when those brave fellows could not further resist the odds, they made, what we know now as Rajput, Jauhar of their wives and children into the flames by setting fire to their houses. European scholars have proposed their identification with the Arjunayans, but this is unacceptable on Philological grounds. The name is a composite of two words. Agra and Sreni. And the main word is found in Kautilya in the list of republics which did not call their president Rajan and which were martial. There the form Sreni only appears the member Agra shows that there were probably more than one unit in the Sreni."

Excavation of Agroha

Mound of Agroha is situated on the metalled road between Hissar and Fatehabad at a distance of 14 miles from the former. A series of rolling mounds of varying heights being about 87 feet above the surrounding ground level occupy about 650 acres of land towards the north-west of the village known by the name of Agroha. Tradition avers that Raja Agra later named Aggrasain , used to live here and the remains of fort on the top of the mound are connected with his residence.[36]

It can be said with a certain degree of accuracy that Agroha owes its origin to Agra and the ancient name of the town was Agrodaka as marked on the coins found in the excavation. The fort, however, on the top was constructed by Dewan Nannomal, who was an Aggarwal by caste and was the employee of Raja Amar Singh of Patiala (1765-1781) ; (Griffin, Punjab Rajas and Panjab state Gazetteers Vol XVII A).[37]

Agroha appears to have been mentioned by Ptolemy, who calls it Agara, which can not be identified with Agra (U.P.) In the mediaeval period Zia-u-d-din Barani[38] Afif have described Agroha or Agrah as a flourishing town forming an important division of the newly laid town of Hisar-i-Firuza. The severe famine in Muhammad Tughluq's time had caused considerable havoc at Agroha and it was deserted city as evidenced by Ibn-i-Batuta.[39] Its excavation work was conducted by M.C.J. Rodgers in 1888-89 and again in 1938-39 by H.L. Srivastava joint director of Archaeology in India. One sculpture pieced together found in 7L/4 at a depth of 9.4 represents an image standing on lotus supported by Nagas[40] and one of the terracotta Mahisasurmardini, a seated image with a female standing by, proves that residents were Nagas and mother goddess worshippers.

A small hoard[41] of five silver coins buried in a pottery vase was found in square 7 P/3 at a depth of 14′, It contained one coin each of Antiolkidas, Apollodotos, strabo, Amyntos, and one Punch marked coin with solar and tree symbol. The other hoard of 51, mostly rectangular coins, buried in a wide mouthed pottery vase was found in the same square and at the same depth. These coins contained the inscription Agodaka Agācha janapadaṣ with tree in railing on the obverses and bull, lion and in three instances composite with part of the same inscription on the reverse. These coins established the identity of Agroha with the ancient Agrodaka founded by Agra, the reputed fore-father of the Aggrawals[42].

These were Sanghas or republicans of ancient period, who met with Alexander as cited earlier. The recovery of Indo-greek coins and the Agodaka coins in the pit have so far established the antiquity of the site to about second century BC[43]. It seems Agrasenis migrated from west Panjab and settled here. Solar symbol on coins shows that they were worshipper of sun god or Baal.

The Banik a Naga Race

In the Aggarwal Itihas Chintnika[44] it has been written, by giving a reference of Satyaketu Vidyalankar that Aggarwals have two divisions i.e. Nag Vanshi and Raj Vanshi. In the context of Aggarsena, two names of Nagas have been mentioned i.e. Vasuki and Kumud. Nagas lived in Khandava forest which was located at a distance of about one hundred miles from Agroha (p 12). Once upon a time a king named Kumud came to earth along with his Madhvi daughter, Indra was attracted by her and he demanded the girl from Nagraj but Nagraj married his daughter to Aggarsen. The same Madhvi girl is the mother of all the Aggarwals (P 27).

Mahalaxmi was pleased with Maharaj Aggarsen and asked him to go to Kolhapur at that very moment where the Swayamvar ceremony was being performed of the daughters to Mahidhar, the incarnation of Nagraj and marry them. He did so (P-28). Eighteen sons of Aggarsen married the daughters of Nagraj (p 38-39), and after their names, the eighteen sub castes (Gotras) of Aggarwals were named (P-13) The gotras of Aggarwals are as under : Gangal, Tayal, Mangal, Bhandal, Nagal Kuchchhal, Jindal, Bindal, Mittal, Goyal, Bansal, Kansal, Singal.

Even today a picture of Naga is depicted on the doors of the houses of Aggarwals in many districts and there is custom of decorating lock of hairs of the girl at the time of her marriage, like the hood of a cobra (Page 27). The Marwari and eastern Aggarwals all are Nagbanshi (P 46).

The first progenitor of Aggarwals, is said to be Agrasen or Ugrasen, a Naga king. In Mahapurana (94-22-23) Ugra banshis are said to be Urag or Nagbanshi. The relation of Banik class as proved earlier, was with Jews, who were in origin worshipper of serpent or Naga from the most ancient age (See chapter I P–9) or they were Nagas. Certain wealthy Baniks of Satavahana age, who issued donation of high value to Buddhist monks, had suffix of Nag or Nak with their names. According to H. Luders list no-1000, a merchant of Kalyan, named Golnăk son of Isipaul, donoted a cave and a tank of water in honour of his parents. Similarly according to list (L.L) no 1005, a Jeweller resident of Sopara Nagpalit and his family members donated a cave to Buddhist monks.

It is quite apparent that most of the classes of Aggarwals are definitely related to the non-Aryan Dravidian and Alpine races of Nagas. Even today they can very easily be identified physically in the markets of North India. They have black complexion, somewhat ugly face and plumb nose (pletyrrhines) distinct from the Vaishya Aryans, who have established their monopoly over business (now in the industry too) in the country. The tradition of writing the word 'Dasa' after their names is still in vogue. A majority of them can be found very easily at same places where the Indus Valley civilization flourished in the main. Who does not know about the popularity of Sindhi, Marwari and Gujrati Baniks ? I am of the view that the deities (gods) whose names end with the word 'Bal' (such as Bahubal) and which are worshipped by Jain Baniks in South or West India, are related to 'Baal' the god of Panis as referred to in the Rigveda. (See chapter XI P-308).

It can, therefore, be said that a major portion of the Baniks belong to Dasa class and the number of Vaishyas among them is very low. Jain Baniks belong to the Dasa class. World famous Jews businessmen are the offshoot of the same Dasa Panis, who went to the western countries from India and spread the Indian civilization there as in the modern times the western traders have spread the western civilization in the east. The business juridiction of the Jews has to-day extended all over the western world and the U.S.A.

We have also few examples of Banik rulers. Republican or Sangha people, Vajji of Vaisali were herdsmen. According to some later records they were Baniks. They were also republican and non-Aryan people, their another branch Lichchhavis[45] was of Ikshwaku line. According to account of Hieuntsang, Maharaja Harsha Vardhan was also of Banik class

Above cited guild based Industry and local and foreign trade made the country most prosperous, particularly there was much prosperity in the west and north eastern India, or the Magadha region, from the Mauryan period up to the Gupta age. Fourteen large hoards of gold coins of Gupta age have been discovered in archaeological excavations from upper Gangetic Valley of Magadha, which is a solid proof of prosperity of that age. This prosperity would have definitely caused progress and uprising of standard of living of people and urbanization of India in Buddhist period (500 BC–500 AD).

The Urbanization

It has been stated earlier that about 1000 years after the devastation of the Indus Valley civilization, descendants of Harappans once again got a chance to revive their culture and by and by succeeded in establishing their power, which is termed as re-establishment of Nagas (Vratya Kshatriyas) by the historians. On the other hand, their great philosophers like Buddha and Mahavira also established their shraman religion and culture in opposition to Vedic. During the period, while Sishunagas, made Magadha a largest centre of their power, Mahavira and Buddha founded their Shraman religions and spread up among the masses. As soon as Mauryas, Nagas, Bharsivas and Satavahanas established their power in north and Central India, afore-said religions also set their feet in those regions. This created an atmosphere of peace and freedom all around, as a result of which these people established their guild based centres of industry and local and foreign trade. This brought prosperity among the common people. After, devastation of Indus towns at the hand of Aryans invaders, this was the second time while again large towns were raised in India. This is known as urbanization in ancient India. Large towns like Girivraja, Pataliputra, Mathura, Takshila, Ahichchhattra, Kausambi, Kashi and Vaisali came into existence in north India and Paithan, Nagpur, Vidisa, Ujjaini, Padmavati in Central Pradesh. The use of timber first of all began in house building, later fire baked bricks and stone were also used.

It is famous that Mauryan emperors (322 BC–187 BC) were great builders. Chandra Gupta was first to use timber in house building. In the art of house building, the carpenters of Mauryan age, were most proficient, as mostly the timber has been used in house construction in his period. Strabo[46] informs us that the city of Pataliputra was surrounded by a large wall made of wood, which had holes (rushes) for shooting arrows at intervals. The best example of wood carving noticed in this age, was large platform of wood, which was discovered in Kumarhatta near modern Patna by Dr. Spooner[47]. He describes whatever he saw with open eyes-"That flatform was in reality an accumulation of large logs of wood, but technique, used in its construction or joining them, is really wonderful. Their corners (ends) are so well set that it is impossible to trace out their joints."

In this age (400 BC) the first use of fire baked bricks has been noticed in the last period of North Black-polished ware[48] Ashoka, the great Mauryan emperor, likewise his grand father, was also a great builder. He built a high number of stone-pillars, Buddhist stupas within the frontier of his empire, among them stupas of Bharhut and Sanchi are most famous, which are the best examples of masonry.

The earliest sculpture[49] like the earlier architecture was secular in content. The famous Ashokan columns can be cited in this context together with the Didarganj Yakshi. One of the most curious point, in this context, is that for more than about fifteen hundred years between the decline of the Indus civilization to the rise of the Mauryas the sculptural tradition seems to have been lost and to us it seems that its survival was basically connected with the urban spirit[50].

In Maharashtra the earliest use of fired bricks and stone in masonry is noticed in the Megalithic culture. Dr. S.B. Deo produces an account of them as such– "During the Neolithic-Chalcolithic age nowhere the use of fired bricks has been noticed in Maharashtra, but during the ancient historical period, there are evidences in abundance. There was practice of using fired bricks at Nasik, Nevasa, Kolhapur, Kaundinyapur, Prakasha, Bahal during Mauryan Satavahana Age."

Many stone Chetyas and caves were constructed in this age. Similarly Sculptures and many small and large household goods were also shaped from stone in western region of Maharashtra. This period also shows, construction of a very high number of Buddhist stupas and Chetyas in Maharashtra as well as wide spread effect of Buddhism on the masses of Maharashtra. H.L. Kosare puts forward an account of them,[51] "Many caves and Chetyas were excavated in Karle, Bhaje, Kanheri, Bedsa, Junnar etc, during Satavāhana age. An amulet, belonging to the Maurya-Satavahana age bearing the figure of Yaksha has been traced out from Nevasa. Buddhism was in its full swing in those days in Maharashtra. Findings of Stupa from Sopara, many caves, and inscriptions from western Maharashtra; recent findings of Ther of Usmānābad district (Diameter 85 feet) and remains of Baragaon stupa (Indian Archaeological review 1957-58 P–67), Pittalkhora (Ibid P–65) and Verul (Ibid P–64); similarly findings of Pauni stupa and remains of its stockade from Bhandara district of Vidarbha and remains of stupa of Nāgara etc, prove the effect of Buddhist religion on rich and poor both equally. Yaksha statue of Pittalkhore was donated by a gold–smith named Krishna Dass ; the admirable Leri of Jamu-Dwipa from Karle was donated by a merchant of South. On a study of inscriptions of caves of western Maharashtra we come to the conclusion that among the donors were military commanders, traders, common citizens, cultivators, and also foreigners then settled in India, also donated columns of Chetya and Stupa, water tank near Buddhist monastery and ways and steps leading to caves were also contributed."

This, construction of Buddhist buildings on large scale and spreading of Buddhism among the common people were interconnected with the high and progressive culture of Buddhism and Naga race.

The glorious Achievements of Naga Culture

The word Nāgara[52] as in Karkota Nāgar is undoubtedly connected with the word Nāga and is a vernacular form, denoting a derivative from that word, likewise in Nagar-dhana (Nāgar-Vardhan) and Nagarkot. Similarly the architectural term, 'Nāgara style' could not be explained on the basis of assuming its connection with the word Nagara (Town), but it is known to the Mānasāra a work of Guptas for later Guptan age. The style, designated by the term Nāgara, seems to be the style made popular by the Nāga kings like Nāgar Brahmans of the Gangetic Valley and

Nāgār Jats of Ahichchhattra. The Vesarastyle[53], which again is a vernacular term taken like the Nāgara, from the vocabulary of the mason, is distinguished by its being in the ornamental style. It means, it differs from the earlier only because there is more provision of leaves, flowers, plants and creepers in it. The base in Nāgara is thus Nāg, Vesar was the type of religious buildings which was artificial. Nagara was that in which we find the Gupta Square temples and the Vakataka temple of Pārvati at Nachna[54] and the Bharsiva temple of Bhumra.

Similarly there was also a Nāgar style of painting. That was also evidently connected with the Nāga period. But we are not in a position to distinguish it yet. We should not, however, be surprised if one day it is discovered among the old frescoes of Ajanta, because Ajanta also became part of Naga rule[55].

Brahmi has been traced back to the phoenician type of writing represented by the inscription in which Mesha, king of Moab (850 BC), records his successful revolt against the kingdom of Israel. It was probably brought in to India through Mesopotamia as a result of the early commerce by sea between Babylon and the ports of Western India[56]. It is the parent of all the modern Indian alphabets including Devnāgari. How this name Devanāgari came into existence in this regard K.P. Jayaswal[57] unveils the secret : "I think, the origin of this name lies in the Naga dynasty under whom originated the headed type of writing, evidence of the existence of which we get from the time of Prithivisen I in the inscriptions of Nachnā and Ganj. In the Vakataka inscriptions the letters are found with a box-like heading which was reduced to a line in the Nāgari script beginning from about 800 AD. The name Nāgari seems to have been applied to what is called the box-headed script of the fourth and early fifth centuries. It is significant that the box-headed writing is found exactly where the Naga government was most prominent, viz in Bundel Khand and the central Provinces. In the central Provinces before the Naga period, we have a Kushana inscription found at Bheraghat which is in the ordinary Brahmi script therefore it is proved that this script came into existence between the Kushana and Vakataka age."

It is crystal clear that guild based trade and industry system was introduced by the Naga people, who promoted, local and foreign trade which resulted in to accumulation of great wealth among the people which caused urbanization as a whole. The Prakrit and Apabhransha language, Nāgari script, Nagari style of architecture all were the outcome of Naga people and their culture. Nāgari or Nagari civilization came in to existence and society moved forward towards the goal of progress in every aspect of life. Last period of this progress and prosperity, is known as the golden age in Indian history.

Summary and Conclusion

1. Guild based trade and industry was a peculiarity of native Naga culture. This system was the backbone of economy and power of Naga culture.
2. These guilds were working most probably in every walk of life to obtain any desirable object, and were spread all over India. ·
3. All the castes of present society which are engaged in productive activities or crafts were a-part of ancient guild system such as carpenters, potters, smiths, stone-masons, weavers, oil-millers, goldsmiths, jewellers, bamboo-workers, fishermen, perfumers, flower-gardeners, physicians, merchants, ivory-workers, water-sellers, fruit venders, vine sellers, etc. who are a part of fourth Varna of present day Hindu Society.
4. Local and foreign trade was also being conducted through these guilds. Although present Banik traders have become most prosperous and respectable class of the society, but in fact they were also a part of Naga Society. It is evident from the nomenclature of Gotra of Aggarwal Baniks, who claim their descent from Aggrasenis who were a republican people associate of Ambastha who met Jointly with Alexander while he was returning from his campaign.
5. Above system of guild based trade and industry, which was spreading even in a small village and in every corner of the country virtually turned every village into an industrial estate, ultimately, made every individual prosperous. This is proved well from rich donations issued by them. This prosperity of commoner caused urbanization of India second time after the fall of Indus Valley towns. Hence large towns like Girivraja, Pataliputra, Mathura, Takshila, Ahichchhttra, Kausambi, Kashi, Vaisali, Paithan, Nagpur, Vidisa, Ujjaini and Padmavati came into existence.

This was an achievement of Naga culture which is evident from the terminology which came into being in this age. such as Nāgar (Towns), Nāgara style of architecture, Nāgara style of masonry, Naga Vesar type of religious buildings, Nagar style of painting, Takri scripts, Takshali langauge, Taka capital, Taka country, Taka coins etc., which were introduced and named by Nagas. Therefore it is evident that Naga race is responsible for these great achievements which brought the glory of India to its top heights.

References

1. Hawkes Jacquetta, "The First Great Civilization" P–113.
2. Hawkes Jacquetta P–113.
3. Ibid.
4. Hawkes Jacquetta P–113.
5. Gupta S. P, ''Disposal of the Dead and Physical types in Ancient India.'' P–144.
6. Hawkes Jacquetta PP– 83–84.
7. I A R (1961–62) PP 109–10.
8. Hawkes Jacquetta P–114.
9. Bhandarkar D.R., ''Lecture on Ancient History of India'' P–143.
10. Thakur Vijay Kumar, ''Urbanization in Ancient India'' P–135.
11. Ibid P–135.
12. Mahavastu Vol III P–112–13, Ed E Senart, Peris (1862) Translation by J.J. Jones Sacred books of the Buddhism.
13. Mahavastu Vol III P–442–43.
14. Gokhale B.G., "Buddhism in Maharashtra" P–127.
15. Mookerjee R.K., "The Gupta Empire" P–149.
16. Ibid.
17. Mookerjee R.K. PP–148–49.
18. See chapter VI PP 126-27 for detail.
19. Luder's list no. 1165 and 1180 (E.I. X).
20. Sastri Nilkant K.A., "Age of the Nanda and Mauryas" P–440.
21. Sastri Nilkant K.A. P–441.
22. Ibid. P–441.
23. Bhandarkar R.G "Early History of the Deccan" P-852
24. Bhandarkar R.G., PP 75–76.
25. Kosambi D.D., "The Culture and Civilization of Ancient India" P–124.
26. See chapter VI. P.-166
27. Mookerjee R.K. P–80.

28. "The Founders of Indus Valley Civilization and their later History" PP 227–34.
29. Das A. C., 'Rigvedic India' P–187.
30. Kosambi D. D. P–80 and Dass AC 175–76.

    In Pali language 'P' becomes 'B' hence Pani became Banik with addition of Suffix K.
31. Dass A.C., PP 188–191.
32. Dass A.C PP 180 and 190.
33. (a) Reo Vishwesharnath, "Rigved Par EK Itihasik Driashti" P–238–39.

    (b) Louis Finkelstein, "The Jews, their History and Religion" Vol I PP 4–7.
34. Dass AC PP 186–197.
35. Jayaswal, K.P., "Hindu Polity" P–67.
36. Memoirs of the Archaeological Survey of India no. 61 H.L. Srivastava, "Excavation of Agroha P–1.
37. Ibid.
38. Elliot, "The History of India" Vol III PP–245 and 300.
39. (a) Srivastava H.L., "Excavation of Agroha" Memoir of the A S of India No. 61 P–1.

    (b) CH 1 Vol III P–153.
40. Srivastava H.L. P–3.
41. Srivastava H.L P–5.
42. Srivastava H.L P–5.
43. Srivastava H.L P–8.
44. Saraf Ram Prasad, "Aggarwal Itihas, Chintanika" P–30.
45. See Chapter VI PP 161-63 Lichchhavi.
46. Crindle JWMC, "Ancient India" II Part (21) P–65 Bombay 1877
47. Archaeological Survey Annual Report (1912-13) P–73.
48. Indian Archaeological Review (1957-58) P–50 (1963-64) P-44, (1964-65) P-17.
49. Thakur V.K. P–204-05 (1981) Delhi.
50. Ibid P–205.
51. Kosare H.L, " Prachin Bharatail Nag". P-239

52. Jayaswal K.P. "History of India." P-55
53. Ibid P–55.
54. Jayaswal K. P. P–56.
55. Jayaswal K. P. P–60.
56. G. Buhler 'Indian Palaeography' PP 31–32.
57. Jayaswal K. P. P–60-61.

Chapter–14

The Megalithic Culture, its Relation with the Buddhism and Naga Race

It has been proved in chapter X that the revival of Naga culture gave birth to and brought up Buddhist and Jain religions also. Both the religions took their birth in the region North east of Vindhya, which was one of the important centres of Megalithic culture. After the Mahaparinirvana (death) of Tathagat Buddha, relics or ashes of his body were claimed by the same people who were related to Naga culture and none-else, such as Nagas of Gandhara, Koliyas Naga of Ramagama and near relatives of Buddha, Nagas of Nag Bhumi or Nagpur and Kalinga. Although these centres were situated at a far off place from each other but even then they were centres of one culture known as Naga culture. Later, these Nagas made Krishna Valley another centre of their culture that is why a Mahastupa has been explored from Amaravati, situated in this region in the district of Guntur. Alexander[1] Rea has excavated this site to restore as well as to study the nature of stupa. The excavation has revealed the presence of Megalithic culture at this site, attested to by the discovery of seventeen huge Urn burials. But, the excavator has assigned Neolithic affiliation to them. However, taking in to account the recent evidences we can safely assign them to Megalithic period. This remarkable discovery is important for chronological study of Megalithic burials.

Spreading of Buddhism in Vidarbha during the life time of Buddha

This is very interesting that although Buddhism took its birth in Northern India, but it became the religion of the people first of all in Vidarbha. Usually it is said in historical description that entry of Buddhism took place there during the age of Ashoka, but as a matter of fact Buddhism had made its entry into Vidarbha in the life time of Buddha, but it spread widely during the reign of Ashoka, The third convention of Buddhist religion was organized by Ashoka in Pataliputra, where decision was taken to spread Buddhist religion not only in the whole of India but also in foreign countries and missionaries were also sent to foreign countries like Egypt, Greece, Syria, China and Ceylon for spreading Buddhist religion. At the same time, a Sthāvar, named Mahādhamma Rakshit was sent to Maharashtra (Maharattha) for preaching his religion. Broken inscriptions of Ashoka have been traced out from Sopara of district Thana and Devtek[2] of Chandrapur district. Similarly remains of Maha-stupas have been recovered from Kolhapur, Sopara, Kanheri and Pauni in Nagpur regions; Nagarā, in Usmanabad District etc. We get information, from the above sources, about spreading of Buddhist religion in Maharashtra, during the age of Ashoka.

But it is really wonderful that during the life time of Tathagat Buddha his religion was spread in Maharashtra. This is proved from the Buddhist literature as well as archaeological evidences available in modern age. There is a story of a Brahman named Bābari in Suttanipāt of Pārāyana Vagga. Above Brahmana used to live in Dakshinapatha in an Ashram, built at the bank of river Godavari. He sent his sixteen disciples to attend to listen religious preaching and visiting Tathagata Buddha. Impressed by the religious teaching of Buddha they became his followers and later preached Buddhist religion in the South[3].

Similarly we get some information about Punnā and Arhat Ishidinnā from Ther-gathas. Arhat Punna was a merchant of Sopara of Thāna district. We read the name Sopara in Pāli literature. Punna after getting consecration from Tathagata and after having full knowledge of Dhamma[4] (religion), came back to Sopara and after building a Vihāra became absolutely busy in religious preaching of Buddhism. Ishidinnā[5] was a merchant of country of Sonaparant . He also had taken consecration from Tathagata Buddha and after building a Vihara preached religious teachings. Above description is given in Ther-gatha. Ishidinnā was most probably resident of Goa, Mohad or Bai.[6] Burnhouf, a French scholar, has given some information about Arhat Punnā. After Dharma Diksha (religious consecration), name of Punna changed to Dharma-Prabhas[7]. Hence it is clear that Punnā of Sopara and Ishidinnā of Kaunkan began their mission of religious preaching during the life time of Buddha Tathagatā in Maharashtra.

Similarly, the archaeological evidence, of beginning of spreading of religion of Buddha during his life time in Vidarbha region of Maharashtra, is discovery of Maha-stupa of Pauni. Dr. S.B. Deo[8] has expressed his view regarding existence of Maha-stupa of Pauni in pre-Mauryan Age. In ancient time the land of Vidarbha was known as Nag-Bhumi.

The tooth relics of Tathāgata were taken by the Nagas to this Nagbhumi and were enshrined in the Maha-Stupa of Pauni built for this purpose.

Tooth Relics of Buddha and Naga-Bhumi

After Mahanirwana (death) of Bhagwan Buddha, a very high number of claiments of remains of his 'ashes' came forward. A conflict also took place among such claiments for 'ashes', in addition to four tooth-relics. In the long run the tooth relics were taken away by the Naga Kings of Gandhara, Kalinga and Naga Bhumi and Maha-Stupas were built for their security. This happened to his 'ashes' also. H.L Kosare[9] produces a detailed account of events which took place after the Mahaparnirvana of Tathagata Buddha : "These ashes were divided equally among the, Ajatsatru of Rajgraha, Lichchhavis of Vaisali, Sakyas of Kapilvastu, Bullis of Allakappa, Mallas of Pava, Koliyas of Ramgrama and Brahmans of Veth-Dvipa. Later Moriyas of Pippalivan also approached, but because no ashes were left hence only charcoals were handed over to them. In this way at eight places viz. Rajgraha, Vaisali, Kapilvastu, Allakappa, Rāmgram, Veth-Dvipa, Pava, and Kushinagar, Maha-stupas were built on these relics. In addition to the above, tooth relics of Buddha were divided into four parts, and distributed, one to Swarga (heaven), second to Gandhara, third to Kalinga and fourth to Naga Bhumi (2500 years of Buddhism, government of India Publication P–279). In this way, Mahastupas were built at Gandhara, Kalinga and Nagbhumi on the tooth relics of Buddha. We don't have the knowledge of tooth relics of Swarga. There is mention of building of Maha-stupa of Gandhara, and Kalinga. There is also mention of tooth relics of Buddha taken to Dantapur or a city or capital of Kalinga in the Dalbandas."

The king of Kalinga, who lived during the life time of Buddha, received the tooth relics of Buddha immediately after the death of Tathāgata and built a magnificent Maha-stupa on it. This view has been expressed by Cunningham[10]. According to Turnour,[11] Dantapur was situated at the north bank of Godavari in Kalinga country.

Similarly, it is also beyond doubt that the Nagas also might have built a Maha-stupa on the tooth relics of Buddha carried to Naga-Bhumi. As such a total number of eleven Maha-stupas ie eight on Ashes and three on tooth relics, were originally, built. All these belonged to the pre-Mauryan period. We get informations about the Maha-stupas raised on tooth relics of Tathagata at Gandhara, and Kalinga, but we don't find. any such information about Naga Bhumi. Hence it is necessary to trace out the whereabouts of Naga Bhumi.

Scholars do not agree on the point where did this Naga-bhumi situated. Sir Alexander[12] Cunningham putsforth his opinion on this issue– "Amongst the Buddhist traditions of Ceylon and Siam, we have an account of a country lying between the mouth of the Ganges and the islands of Ceylon, which was inhabited by the Nagas. These Nagas possessed either one or two Drona measures of the relics of Buddha, which were enshrined in a beautiful and magnificent stupa near the "Diamond Sands". Originally, this portion of relics was related to Rāmagrāma near Kapilvastu, but when the Rāmagrāma stupa was washed away by the river, the relic casket containing one of the original eight divisons of Buddha's remains was carried down the Ganges to the sea, where it was picked up by the Nagas and conveyed to their own country, called Majerik. Now this country was to the south of Dantapura, because prince Danta-Kumāra and the princess Hemamālla, when flying from Dantapura to ceylon with the tooth relics of Buddha, were wrecked on the coast near the 'Diamond Sands'. The name itself also helps to fix the position of the 'Diamond Sands', at or near Dhāranikotta, on the Krishna, as the diamond mines of this part of the country are restricted to the small district of Partial, lying immediately to the north of Dhārnikotta. The flight from Dantapura took place in A.D. 310, at which time, according to the Siamese version, the two Drona measures of relics were still preserved in the Naga country'' Further Cunningham[13] writes. ''It must be noted however, that the people of Northern India were happily unaware that the Drona of relics enshrined at Rāmagrāma had been carried off by the Nagas to Majerika, as both Fa-Hian and Hieuntsang, who actually visited the place in the fifth and seventh centuries, mention that the stupa was still standing. It is curious, however, to learn from the journals of both pilgrims, that even in their days the Rāmagrāma relics were believed to be watched over by the Nagas of a tank close by the stupa. According to the original Buddhist legend, these Nagas had-prevented Ashoka from removing the relics from Rāmagrāma. In the lapse of time, when Rāmagrāma had become deserted, as it was found by both pilgrims, this legend might easily have assumed the slightly altered form that the Nāgas had carried off the relics to prevent their removal by Ashoka. This form of the legend would have been eagerly seized upon by the Nagas of Southern India and the transfer of the relics to their own country of Majerik, would, at once, have commanded the easy belief of a credulous people.''

It means actually the relics was not transferred from here to South. Emperor Ashoka got collected relics, enshrined in all the seven stupas. Leaves of gold, silver and corundum were prepared and despatched to those cities, where raising of stupas was planned. On the day of Baishakhi Purnima after sunset at a fixed time, all the corundum were placed after proper worship[14]. During the age of Ashoka in addition to original eleven stupas, Maha-stupas were raised on other places also.

It has been said earlier that there is mention that prince Danta Kumar and princess Hemmālla took the tooth relics of Buddha from

Dantapura, the capital of Kalinga, to the Naga country of Andhra. But whether there were one or two tooth relics with the Dantakumar of Kalinga, is a most significant question. But there is mention of one tooth relics at Kalinga and another at Naga Bhumi. If it is proved that at the time of above incident there were two tooth relics at Kalinga, it shows that second Drona of relics were taken by the Nagas from Nagabhumi, because there were only three tooth relics, one each at Gandhara, Kalinga and Naga Bhumi. These relics were not taken from the Gandhar country, it is quite sure. If it is proved that there were two Dronas of tooth relics at Kalinga, this also can be established that other relics were surely taken from Naga Bhumi.

With regard to the kings name, I think that the Greek Bassaro Nag may be identified with the Pali Majerika Nag of the Mahawamso[15].

In the opinion of Cunningham, according to Buddhist tradition of Siam these relics of Buddha were taken to Ceylon in 313 AD and were enshrined there in the great Stupa of Ruanwelli[16]. In the later period the myth of taken away by Dutthagamini would have been added. But according to the Mahawamso[17] the relics consisted of only one Drona measure which afterwards being enshrined by the Nagas at Majerik carried off to Ceylon in the fifth year of the reign of Dutthagamini (BC 157) by whom they were enshrined in the Maha-stupa at Ruanwelli. The famous tooth relics which were taken from Kalinga to Ceylon in 310 AD, were enshrined in the Mahastupa of Dharma Chakra. This Maha-Stupa was built by Devānām-Priyatisso contemporary of Ashoka in 240 B.C.[18] and was afterwards transferred to the Abhayagiri Vihara, which was erected in BC 89[19].

Hence it is crystal clear that tooth relics of Buddha was not taken to Ceylon earlier than 310 or 313 A.D.[20] and these relics were in the Maha-stupa of Bhatti Prolu and Nagarjuna Konda. But three years later or in 313 AD the kings of Ceylon sent a holy priest to bring away these relics from Majerik[21], which was miraculously effected in spite of the opposition of the Nagas. If we accept that these tooth relics of Buddha were brought from Kalinga that we have to accept that Andhra-Pradesh was country of Nagas. But the country well known as Naga Bhumi, from where Nagas brought the original tooth relics, is not proved.

Therefore the identification of Majerik or Andhra Pradesh cannot be proved with the Naga Bhumi and it is clear that Naga Bhumi was a different region.

Second point also can very easily be clarified that at the occasion of this incident there should have been two Dronas of tooth relics of Buddha in Kalinga country. One original tooth relics, which was in Dantapura of Kalinga country and another of Naga Bhumi which was undoubtedly brought to Kalinga for security purpose. One Drona of tooth relics was taken by prince Dantakumar from Kalinga to Majerik and further to Ceylon, if this incident is taken to be true than there should have been one more tooth relics, it is proved by another evidence there is an information[22] in the Dāthā family 'that a complaint was lodged with the king of Magadha that Guhashiva, the king of Kalinga was in the habit of worshipping 'ashes' (Mrit-Asthi) and criticizing the Aryan divinities.' It seems from the above information that Guha-Shiva, the king of Kalinga was feudatory chief of Samudra Gupta, who being Buddhist used to worship ashes or tooth relics of Buddha. It means the original tooth relics of Kalinga were still in Kalinga. Therefore it is proved that tooth relics of Buddha taken from the Dantapura or Kalinga by prince Dantakumar and princess Hemmalla were originally brought here from the original Naga Bhumi.

Nagpur Region ; The Original Naga Bhumi

It is proved from the above detail of evidences and their interpretation that original Naga Bhumi was not in Andhrapradesh. On ward we produce archaeological evidence to prove that original Naga Bhumi was region of Nagpur where those tooth relics of Buddha were originally placed, which were taken to Naga Bhumi ? In this regard we have some basic solid evidence. There[23] is a mention of the word Nagpur for Nagabhumi in the prayer of worship of tooth relics of Buddhist religion.

EKĀ DĀTHĀTI DASAPURE EKĀ NĀG PURE AHU ।
EKĀ GANDHĀR VISAYE EKĀSI PUNA SINHALE ॥
CHATASSĀ TĀ MAHĀDĀTHĀ, NIVVĀNA RASADIPIKĀ ।
PŪJITĀ NARADEVEHI, TĀPI BANDĀMI DHĀTAYO ॥

Meaning : One of the tooth relics of Tathāgata is secure in Tridaspur and the second in Nagpur, third in Gandhara country and fourth in Sinhal country. All these four tooth relics are being worshipped by all the divinities for the sake of human deliverance, because they provide the taste of Niravānā–Rasa (Juice of bliss). Hence, I also bow down.

In this prayer[24] of worship of tooth relics of Buddha, there is mention of tooth relics of Tathāgata only. There is also description of one tooth relics of Buddha at Nagpur. Here, the mention of Nagpur is made in place of Naga Bhumi. In those days or during the life time of Buddha, Nagpur would have been the centre or capital of the country of Naga Bhumi. Hence it is beyond doubt that in those days, the country of Nagpur was known by the name of Naga Bhumi. After the

Mahaparinirvan (death) of the great Buddha, whatever tooth relics, were handed over to Nagas, they were taken to Naga Bhumi and it is clearly mentioned in the Buddhist literature. Hence in the composition of above prayer, the word Nagpur is used for Naga Bhumi. Hence oneness of the words Nagpur and Naga Bhumi is established. In Haribamsa Nagpur has been mentioned as a dwelling place of Nagas (Rajwade, Lekh-Sangrah Part II P–234). From this name of the place of Nagpur, it is also proved that it was a city of Nagas. Numerous centres of Megaliths, which were related to Nagas, have been traced out from proximity of Nagpur region such as Mahurjhari, Nekund, Gangapur, Junapāni, Khāpā and Tākalghat. As such in the aforesaid prayer of relics of Buddha's worship, the mention of the name of Nagpur is for Naga Bhumi, is crystal clear. But there is no mention of Kalinga. In lieu of it, mention of Sinhal country has been made. From above prayer this fact is confirmed clearly that whatever description of transfer of tooth relics from Dantapura[25] of Kalinga to ceylon in 310 AD, is made in the Buddhist literature, is true, that is why, in a later period, the fact of absence of tooth relics, appears in this prayer of tooth relics, where the name of Sinhal appears in lieu of Kalinga. In this period, the tradition of the use of Nagpur in place of Naga Bhumi also appears in the prayer. This change took place after seventh century A.D. This conclusion that Nagpur is ancient Naga Bhumi of Vidarbha gets confirmation from an archaeological evidence. In this Naga Bhumi, a Mahastupa built on the tooth relics of Buddha after his death in the pre-Mauryan period has been found out, it is Pauni which is situated at a distance of 82 KM from Nagpur, from where in its excavation in 1969-70, remains of a Stupa of pre-Mauryan period have been found out.

The Excavation of Stupa of Pauni and its Relation with the B and R ware Culture

It has been established above, that out of four tooth relics of Buddha, one was taken by Nagas of Naga Bhumi, and Maha-stupa of Pauni was built for its security. Above stupa was excavated by the department of Archaeology of Nagpur university in 1969-70. Dr S.B. Deo produces detailed description of stupa was found in excavation[26], "The construction of stupa of Pauni began during the Ashokan period. The diameter of stupa was 38.2 Metres and shape was round. Sometimes, after the completion of stupa, the circumambulation was also constructed. The evidence of, round wooden pillars used for building circumambulation has been found out in excavation. From the stratum, related to the Stupa sherds of North Black Polished Ware (NBPW), Black and Redware (B and R ware) and Black polished ware have been recovered. From, the stratum next to the above, the pottery of Mauryan, period, punch marked coins have been found out, and this proves that earlier period was definitely of pre-Ashokan period. It means original stupa was also of pre-Ashokan period. In addition to this, no evidence of inscribed or written work belonging to the beginning period, has been recovered .... These evidences of construction of second phase during the period of Mauryan-Sunga, have been unearthed. The work of the extension of stupa was executed in this period and now the diameter of expanded stupa was 41 Metres .... This time pucca circumambulation was also built. Four entry gates, around the Stupa in all the four directions were also built. One inscription of donation in Brahmi script belonging to Ashokan period, on a heavy stone of top or Summit attached to the entry gate has been recovered.

Later during Sunga period stupa was shaped into more magnificently. For expansion of stupa another palisade of bricks was built around the Stupa, which was supported by round wooden pillars. Later on, when these wooden pillars became weak these were replaced by octagonal stone-pillars of eight feet in height. On this palisade some art or figures of Yakshis are inscribed, one Yaksha with its mouth of ass is very beautiful. ..... third time the stupa was expanded, around the previous palisade another circumambulation was built during the Kushana period, and around it another palisade of stones was also built. It was built with the supports of octagonal stone pillars eight feet in height, by giving a gap of 1½ metre, between each pillar. Such type of palisades were built in Bharhut and Sanchi in the same period. All the outer octagonal pillars are very beautiful and are human objects of art in Sunga-style which were very close to art of Bharhut of the same age ....In addition to aforesaid art, on some pillars are insignias of Buddhist religion like Dharma Chakra (circle of religion), Kalpa-tree, Bodhi tree, Bhadrason etc. The absence of statues of Buddhas proves that all this art is symbol of Hinayāna-Dharma. Among them, the depiction of art regarding legend of Muchilinda-Nag, seems most magnificent. Below the above art work is inscribed "Muchrindo Naga." Tradition of depicting such like Nagas is also noted in the art of Bharhut. ..... on some art piece of this age, figures of king and queen riding on elephant, sceneries of multi-storeyed buildings etc are most attractive. In addition to the above some sculptures of Yakshas and Yakshis were shaped and raised around the stupa in this age. Among them a six feet long sculpture of Yaksha seems to be of Sunga style. On the head of one of the Yakshi, the depiction of hair style is of sunga type, whose hair seem to have, fastened five small arrows. The large entry gates of stone, around the stupa, in the east, west, south and north direction, were built during Sunga age. Its construction plan, is just like that of stupa of Bharhut and Sanchi .... It seems that this reconstruction work of Sunga period would have been most magnificent and attractive. Inspite of wreckage of upper portion its all broken portions have been traced out in excavation

.... It seems that the upper portion of Stupa would have been used for construction of the Jagan-Nath temple. But the diameter of stupa was 40 metres and height 20 metres."

We know, that the economic basis of tribal republic confederacies, was guild based trade and industry. It means the common people were a basic element in this system, and the kings were not so powerful as the monarch and their feudal lords. This is clear from the findings of inscriptions of donations from excavation of Pauni stupa. Dr S.B. Deo[27] produces an account of such inscriptions, "The common people owing to their firm faith in Buddhism, contributed their hands in the construction work of Maha-stupa of Pauni from the pre-Ashokan period up to the Kshatrapa period. From the excavation of stupa, 75 inscriptions of donation have been recovered, which belong to individual common people. Therefore during the Sunga age, the Hinayana branch of Buddhism had full support and firm faith of common people. This stupa of Pauni was larger than that of Sanchi and Bharhut, and has been called Maha-stupa by the scholars."

It is evident from the above description that the basis of support of stupas was common man instead of monarchs or their feudal lords. But in many instances contributors were working guilds also.

Dr. S.B. Deo further produces archaeological evidences to ascertain the period of construction of Stupa and the establishment of its relation or similarty with other Stupas[28], "In the earliest or pre-Ashokan period of Pauni stupa, in addition to sherds of Black polished ware, B and R Ware, and Grey ware have been recovered. This type of pottery also have been recovered from some important ancient places of North, like Ahichchhatra, Hastinapur, Kausambi, Ujjain and Vaisali, which belonged to a period of about fifth Century B.C. .... It seems, from the available evidences, that in pre-Mauryan period, the Black Polished ware, were earlier attached to Buddhist religious places only. This pottery has been recovered from ancient Buddhist places like Bijārahill in Nepal (South of Lumbini), Rājgiri, Kausambi, Vaisali, Srāvasti and Rājghāt etc. Being the relation of Pauni with the aforesaid pottery, this Stupa can be equated with the above places. It means the homogeneity and synchronism of Pauni is proved with Vaisali and other Buddhist stupas of North. The Maha-stupa of Vaisali was built on the original relics of Buddha. The Buddhist Stupa of Pauni was contemporary of Vaisali, this shows after Nirvana of Tathāgata, the Nagas obtained relics and carried to Naga Bhumi and enshrined in the stupa of Pauni.

From the pre-Mauryan period Pauni was main centre of Hinayana branch of Buddhism of ancient Maharāshtra. From this centre, Buddhist art and craft spread in Andhra pradesh. Nagarjunakonda, Amaravati and Bhattiprolu were important centre of Buddhism of Andhra Pradesh. The

North Black Polished wares, belonging to Buddhist culture and centres, came in to use in Amaravati in fourth Century B.C. and this is well confirmed from the carbon-14 dating also. No North Block Polished ware has been found out so far in all the areas between Amaravati and Shishupalgarh of Orissa. These are recovered from Pauni only. It is quite evident from this that Buddhist culture and religion reached from central India to South through the route of Pauni. Pauni was situated on the Rajpath to be reached from north to central and onward to South India. It is also proved from the above that in ancient historical age Pauni and Nagpur were important places."

Above detailed evidences can be summed up as such: The evidences which strengthen the viewpoint of Dr. S.B. Deo[29] have come to hand from excavation of Malhar site of district Bilaspur of Madhya Pradesh by Dr. K.D. Bajpai in between 1975-77. Here, from the period I, remains of Chalcolithic, Megalithic culture of 1000 B.C. have been recovered and from later stratum North Black Polished Ware and B and R Ware pottery have been found out (A.M. shastri, Presidential address Indian History Congress, 39th session 1978). Therefore we can say with certainty that there was a thoroughfare or Rajpath from the place of Malhar of Bilaspur district, leading to Nagpur and onward up to South. Coming through this ancient path, the Nagas of Megalithic culture of iron age established their centre of abode named Naga Bhumi, in the region of Nagpur of Vidarbha in about 1000 B.C. . It[30] has been proved earlier that there was only one single culture from the Age of Megalithic up to the Satavahana Age and this was culture of Nagas. Dr. S.B. Deo[31] has put forth his opinion that the entire pottery recovered from the excavated trenches of Pauni is pertaining to a single culture and significantly interlinked with the life of stupa established in its various phases. The evidences, therefore belong to our broad early historical period, extending from circa 4–3rd century B.C. to 2–3rd century A.D. It is proved from the archaeological evidences that from the pre-Mauryan age up to the Sātavāhana age there was existence of a single culture and it was attached to Buddhist religion throughout the whole period. It is also proved that the people of Naga Bhumi were Nagas and they were followers of Tathagata Buddha. It means Satavahana rulers reached Maharashtra in this age.

We have earlier proved that B and R ware culture was attached to Harappan in its early stage on one hand and with the Megalithic culture on the other. These Megalithic people were round headed Alpine-Dravidian or mainly Dravido-Iranian.

Relation of Nagas with the Buddhist Stupas

This has been established and corroborated by the archaeological evidences that B and R Ware, and NBP Ware, were related to Buddhist

Stupa culture. The Stupa of Pauni was definitely related to Buddhist Nagas. In support of this view Dr. S.B[32] Deo gives an account of archaeological evidences– "In the excavation work of stupa of Pauni an important Vedika pillar has been discovered. On this donation pillar the following legend is inscribed "NĀGAS PANCHNIKĀYIKAS." Panchnikaya means Naga scholar learned in five Nikāya, Suktinipāt has five divisions. Dighanikāyā, Majjim Nikāyā, Sanyukta Nikāyā. Angutara Nikāyā and Khuddak Nikāyā. These five Nikayas were part of Therāvādi tradition. The reference of Panchnikaya is also found in the inscriptions of Sanchi and Bharhut Stupas. Pauni was the chief centre of the followers of Hinayānā and among the donors of above stupa centre, one was a Naga scholar learned in five Nikāyās. Perhaps this Naga would have been a monk and he might have been closely related to stupa of Pauni. There are several names among these inscriptions of donations, which have suffix of words like Nāg or Nāk such as Nandnāk, Balnāk etc." (See list of Naga donors found in inscritions of Buddhist chetya and caves etc Chapter. XV P 408-09).

According to James Burgess the suffix of words like Nāg or Nāk has not only been found in Pauni but also in the Mahastupa of Amaravati situated in Andhra Pradesh[33] "In one of the inscription of donation there is mention of one Shoe-maker named Nāgagharutapākā Son of Vidhik and his son Nāg .... In another writing, there is a mention of a merchant named Nagatis .... Similarly in another donation inscription from the stupa of Jagayyāpet belonging to the ruling period of king of Purisadata Ikshwaku, there is a mention of a house-building worker named Nāk Chandra, his son Siddhārth and his mother Nāgilini, maiden daughter Nākbudhanikā, brother Budhināk and son Nagasiri. Therefore it is clear that Naga people used to live in Andhra and Mahārāshtra in this age and there was a tradition of using of the words Nāg or Nāk as suffix with their names and they were Buddhists"

It is crystal clear from the archaeological evidences, that like Nagas of Ramgrāma, Lichchhavis of Vaisali and Naga of Kalinga, the Nagas followers of Tathagata, belonging to the region of Nagpur or Naga Bhumi, also claimed their right in the share of tooth relics of Buddha and succeeded in achieving one, and enshrined it at Pauni and built a Maha-Stupa on it for security. It is quite clear that these tooth relics were divided among those who were Buddha's dearer, nearer, consecrated followers in his life time. Hence it is proved that Nagas of Naga Bhumi also were dearer, nearer and consecrated followers of Buddha and his religion. We have already established in chapter IX that one group of users of B and R Ware pottery took a turn from Gujrat towards South and settled and made Vidarbha their chief centre of abode, and their another group following the southern bank of Ganges reached Magadha and Bengal. These people established there another large centre in north eastern region of Uttar Pradesh and north of Bihar. This was the main reason that in spite of a very long distance between both the centres, social and religious unity was established in a very short time. Buddha's religion, which took its birth in north centre, was adopted by the Nagas of Vidarbha or Naga Bhumi as early as the life time of Buddha. Hence, it is clear that the foundation of Buddha's religion was laid down on the solid ground of Naga culture.

The Fall of Buddhism in Maharashtra

It is really wonderful that during the age under discussion, political stability existed first of all in the ruling period of Mauryas and later during the Sātavāhana age. The total period of this political stability was about 600 years. Sātavāhanas alone ruled for a period of about 460 years (235 BC–225 AD) over whole of the central and South India except a small portion of South, where as empire of Ashoka was the largest in ancient period.

The glory of Mahastupa of Pauni, was at its peak during Mauryan and Satavahana age. According to the opinion of Dr. S. B. Deo, 'After the third century A.D., the use of Stupa of Pauni was discontinued.' It shows Buddhism flourished in a period, while-native Naga rulers were in power and there was political stability as well. This was the main cause, while the great political Naga power or tribal republic confederacy of Central Pradesh was suppressed by Samudra Gupta and Satavahana power faded, a real threat was faced by the Buddhist stupas and Buddhist religion.

We know that owing to arising of similar situation or a crisis to the security and grace of tooth relics of Tathagat Buddha of Pauni stupa and weakening of defensive powers after the fall of Satavahanas, the Nagas of Naga Bhumi transferred it to the Kalinga country, and then onward to Ceylon.

This event of transferring of relics, was indicative of the beginning of real downfall of Buddhism in Central Pradesh and Maharashtra, which is duly confirmed by archaeological evidences from Maharashtra.

Summary and Conclusion

(1) This is really very interesting, although Buddhism took its birth in north India but it became the religion of people first of all in Vidarbha. Following evidences are being produced to prove historicity of this event.

(a) According to Suttanipat of Pārāyava Vagga a Brahman named Bābari of Dakshinapatha sent his sixteen disciples to attend to religious preaching of Tathagata Buddha, but they, being impressed by his teachings, became his followers and later preached Buddhism in South.

(b) Similarly according to Ther-gathas of Punna a merchant of Sopara and Ishidinnā merchant of country of Sonapara took consecration from Tathagata Buddha and both of them built their own Viharas and preached religious teachings.

(c) One of the four tooth relics of Buddha was taken by his follower Nagas of Naga Bhumi (Nagpur) and were enshrined in the Maha-Stupa of Pauni.

(d) Remains of Maha-Stupas have been recovered from Kolhapur, Sopara, Pauni, Nagara, and Ther built in the aforesaid period.

(e) A sthavar named Mahādhamma Rakshita was sent by Ashoka to Maharashtra for spreading Buddhism

(2) Later on, while the Satavahana power ceased to exist, in the middle of third Century A.D., on account of fear of security, these tooth relics of Pauni were transferred to Kalinga, and then onward to Ceylon.

(3) That Naga Bhumi was, Nagpur of later period, which is confirmed from the description, given in the prayer of worship of relics of Buddha. This gets confirmation from the exploration of Mahastupa of Pauni, situated at a distance of 82 km from Nagpur.

(4) This stupa was constructed in pre-Mauryan period. From the excavation report, we have come to know that B and R Ware, North Black polished ware and Black polished wares have been recovered from there. Similarly findings of pottery of Mauryan period and Punch-marked coins, show that earliest period was definitely of pre-Ashokan period. The work of the extension of Stupa was executed during Mauryan-Sungas period and second time during the later Sunga period. Third time this work was done during Kushana period, while another palisade of stone was also built around it. Four gates were also constructed during Sunga Age.

(5) Below the art work, there is epigraph of Muchilindo Naga and another of Naga Panch Nikāya. The latter means Naga scholar learned in five Nikayas, who would have been a monk. Some names, found in inscriptions of donations, wear

suffix of Nak such as Nand-Nak, Balnak etc. similar names have been recovered from the stupa of Amaravati also detailed as : Nāg, Nāgatis, Nak-chand, Nāgilini, Nāk Budhanika, Budhināk, Nagasiri etc. This proves the donors were house-holder Naga people.

(6) We know there was only one single culture from the age of Megalithic, up to the Satavāhana Age and this was culture of Naga people. (See chapter III and IV PP 76-79). This is confirmed from the archaeological evidence recovered from the Pauni Stupa covering the period of 4–3rd. century BC to 2–3rd century A.D. and this can be termed as Buddhist culture at the same time. Hence, it can be concluded that the people of Naga-Bhumi were of Naga race and founder of Megalithic culture and follower of Buddhist religion who were racially round headed Alpine-Dravidian or mainly Dravido-Iranian.

References

1. Rao K.P. "Deccan Megaliths" P–46.
2. Kosare H.L. "Prachin Bharatatil Nag" P–227.
3. Ibid.
4. Kosare H.L. P–228.
5. Ibid.
6. More M.S. "Maharashtratil Buddha Dhammacha Itihas" P–24–25 Mentioned by H.L. Kosare P–228.
7. Burnouf R.E. "Introduction to Buddhism" PP. 235–70.
8. Deo. S.B. and Joshi J.P., "Pauni Excavation" (1972) PP 21 and 25.
9. Kosare H.L. PP 228–30.
10. Cunningham Alexander, "Ancient Geography of India." P–450.
11. Turnour "J B R A S" (1837) P–860 .
12. Cunningham A. P–450.
13. Cunningham A. PP–450–53.
14. Burnouf R.E. Vol I P–455.
15. (a) Turnour's 'Mahawamso' P–185 Manjerik Nāga Bhawanan (The land of Manjerika Nag).
    (b) Cunningham A. P–455.
16. Cunningham A. P-451

17. Turnour's, "Mahawamso" P–185.
18. Cunningham A. P.–451.
19. Turnour's 'Mahawamso' P–241.
20. Cunningham A. P.–452.
21. Cunningham A. P. – 450.
22. Datha Vansho, 'J.P.T.S.' (1884) P–109 Pada 72–94 FF mentioned by Jayaswal K. P. P–128.
23. Kosare H.L. P–232.
24. Ibid.
25. Ibid.
26. Deo S.B. and Joshi J.P. "Pauni Excavation" PP 25–58.
27. "Pauni Excavation" PP–37 and 61.
28. "Pauni Excavation" PP 42–43.
29. Kosare H.L. P–237.
30. Ibid.
31. Deo S.B, "Pauni Excavation" P–57.
32. Pauni Excavation PP 39–42.
33. Burgess James, "Notes on Amaravati Stupa" (1972) no. 231 ; 26 B PP 53–55 and 56.

Chapter-15

The Ethnical Identity of the People of Maharashtra during the Historical Period and their Relation with the Naga Race

The people of Maharashtra, being brachy-cephalic, have been called Scytho-Dravidians by Risley, but Irano-Dravidians by N. K. Dutt, which is, according to the latest information, the most acceptable viewpoint. Because, the people of ancient Megalithic culture of Maharashtra, like the modern Maharashtrians were also brachycephalic, hence, racially of the same stock, these Meghalithic builders were Naga people as proved in chapter VIII. They spoke a language close to Pali or Prakrit whose remains are present in the form of Gujrati and Marathi. Since, these people came from North West region of India hence their ethnical remains are still present in the northern region of Gujrat and Southern region of Rajasthan. Most of the western region of India was sometimes under the sway of Mahar or Mer tribe before the advent of foreign people. Gustab Oppert while producing a detailed account of evidences, writes[1] "Mahar or Mhars, whom we recognize as the people, who had given their name to Maharashtra, were not always confined to this land alone, for they have always been occupants of Rajputana. The provinces which now go by the name of Mhairwāra (Ajmer) and Marwar (Jodhpur) are their ancient homes. "The Mair or Mera is" According to colonel Tod "The mountaineer of Rajputana, and the country he inhabits is styled Mairwara or the region of hills." These hillmen by and by populated the plains and are also found there (Tod Vol I P 680). They remained masters of the soil, until they were not ousted by the victorious invaders. As chiefs and warriors, like other aboriginal tribes, they have a claim to be called Rajputs, for the name of Rajput or Rajputra confers only a social and not an ethnological distinction. The term Rajput is generally applied to an Aryan Kshatriya, though everybody knows that the victors intermarried freely with the vanquished non-Aryans, who were never totally annihilated, and that the Mer and other non-Aryan tribes claim relationship with the Rajputs.

No real ethnological difference between a mar (Mhar, Mahar) and a Mhair (Mer) has been found to exist. It has been previously mentioned that, according to Colonel Dalton, "Mar or Mala is a very uncertain name applied to or assumed by different people in different parts of India, but it may be that there is some affinity between all the tribes who bear it."

The relation of Jaisalmer was with the Bhatti tribe. Owing to the suffix of the word Mer, this tribe is said to be related to Bhatti Rajput tribe.[2] These relations are further confirmed, because Bhatti Rajputs are offshoots of Yadava tribe[3] who had relation with the Bhoja, and Mahabhoja which was a component of Mahar tribe confederacy known as Satavahana (Maharathi).

The origin of the term Marwar is generally derived from Sanskrit Maru (desert) or Meru (Mountain) because on its one direction is mountain and on the other is desert but colonel Tod does not accept this termination.[4]

Mer or Maira is a branch of Chita tribe and Chita tribe is a branch of Mina tribe, which is an ancient tribe of India.[5]

It is quite clear that the Mers, who came from north west settled in the southern region of Rajasthan, whose traces are still visible there. From there they moved onward and settled in Gujrat and Maharashtra.

The place of Nagar[6] or Karkotanagar, which is situated near Jaipur, was in those days centre of Malavas which was their capital also. From there a very high number of their republican coins have been recovered. In Bhagwat, these are called Arbud-Malava and in Vishnu Purana their region has been stated to be Rajputana. In this way it is certain that they lived in the land falling in between Abu Mountain and Jaipur, the land which is called 'Maravāṛ' It seems that this has been named, being ancient habitation of Malavas.[7] The word Maravar is spoken as Malavar in Panjabi language. In the south of this land was the country of Nagas. The coins of Nagas are very much similar to those of Malava.[8] (Malavānām Jayah).

Etymology of the Words 'Maharashtra' and 'Rashtri'

The land, which now-a-days is called Maharashtra, was sometimes, inhabitted by the families of Mahar tribe, in a very high number. Although people of some other tribes (Gana) were also residing, but families or Kulas of Mahar tribes were the highest in number. They were lords of the most of the land of Maharashtra called "Gana Bhumi" or "land of tribe." The land of all the families used to be called 'Gana Bhumi' and land of all the Ganas was called 'Rashtra' or 'Maharashtra.' According to Kautilya[9], Rashtra means 'land of the subject or the people' and the personal land of king is called 'Sita.' But[10] Kosambi has stated that Rashtri meant 'Gana-Bhumi' or 'land of tribe' which is quite acceptable. In the age, while Ganatantra (Tribal republic) system was in prevalence, the meaning given by Kosambi seems to be the most befitting.

Hence "Rashtra" means, 'the land of united lordship', or 'common wealth of tribe.' But Kieth A.B. has given another meaning of the word "Rashtra", Kingdom, which is not acceptable. Infact Rashtra means 'land of tribe.'[11]

In the, "Rashtra-Bhrat Mantra" or "prayer of Gana-Bhumi," given in Taitreya Samhita,[12] it is interpreted that Gana (Tribe) is Rashtra, off shoots are 'Rashtra', tribal people are Rashtra and animals are also Rashtra. Hence it is clear that Rashtra means 'Gana-Bhumi'

Much light has been thrown on this subject in Nirukta, whose detail is being produced by Sharad Patil[13] as follows—

"The word 'Rajan' (King) is consisted of the root of 'Raj' (II-3). Nighantu gives the root of the word Raj (Rajati XII-21-4), but not the word derived from this. But he gives synonym of the word Rāgyi (Rani-queen), the Rashtri (II-21-1). Similarly, in another verse (V-46-8), he gives list of Dev-patni (wives of gods) ie Indrani of Indra, Agnāyi of Agni (fire), Ashwini, wife of Ashwini Kumar; Rodasi wife of Maruta, Vāruni wife of Vāruna. Rat is not wife of any of Deva. It means it was a non-Aryan tradition in origin. Nirukta (XII-46) gives etymology of Rat; who (woman) rules (Rad Rājate)." Therefore, Rāt and Rashtri both the words are synonym.[14]

It is obvious that kingship (Rajpad) originated from woman (See chapter V. P-100). Now question arises how and why the kingship originated from woman ? This is because the origin of seat of kingship is attached with the dignified duty of distribution of 'Rashtra' or 'Rashtra-Bhumi' (land of tribes). Among the different tribes this duty was first of all performed by woman only. Therefore the nomenclature of first ruler (woman) of mankind was 'Rashtri'.[15]

The break up of the word 'Samrāggi' is Sam+Rati. It means the Rāt of mothers of tribes. That woman was sovereign and as well representative of Bhumāta,[16] the mother Goddess of earth.

Ethnical Identity of Rashtrika and Pettinika with the Mahar Nagas

In Angutāranikāya[17] of Pali literature, the mention of the words Rashtrika and Pettinikas has been made in reference to an officer of tribal Republic or Gana-rajya. Bhagwan Buddha, while, teaching five family religious duties (Kuldharma) to the youths of Lichchhavi Gana in the presence of members of assembly of Kulas, narrated following hierarchy of Rulers from top to bottom :

(1) Murdhabhishikta (king) (2) Rashtrika (3) Pettinika (hereditary office) (4) Senani (Commander of Army) (5) Gavachā (of the tribe) Gramani (6) Vyapari Pugāchā (Shrenika) of the village and (7) chief of the family.[18]

From the above detail, we come to know how the administration of tribal republics, in the time of Buddha was functioning.[19] Rashtrika and Pettinika were designations of officers in the administration of tribal republican of Lichchhavi. Rashtrika was a designation of an officer following the king and below it was the post or authority of Pettinika. Dr. Buhler, while referring Anguttara Nikaya (III-70 and 300) has used the nouns of Ratthika and Pettinika, indicating the meaning of such administrative posts, Ratthika was the post of an officer below the rank of a king and the commentator while explaining the word Pettinika has said that he was hereditary officer of the state.[20] In the opinion of Buhler the Pettinika was hereditary post of the state of any country. Perhaps, the progenitor of that administrator would have been an officer appointed by any king.[21] It means Rashtrika was an administrative post below the rank of a king where as the post of Pettinika was hereditary. Such a tradition was definitely non-Vedic where post of mahamantri was next to king.

According to the opinion of N.K. Dutt these Aratta were round headed Iranians, and were known as Rattika or Ratta, whose mention has been made in the inscription of Ashoka. This Rattika or Ratta is a variation of Iranian word 'Rathaestha' These Rathaesthas were war like people.[22]

Huluss[23] has equated the Pettinika (Ratta) with the Arattioi of Periplus and Aarattha of Panjab. Who were these Arathas ?

In the Bhuridutt Jataka (no 543), there is a mention of Nagas of Yamuna Nagar in the south of river Yamuna. Bhuridutta, the prince of this Naga tribe, criticized his elder brother Arittha who was the follower of the Brahmanical path. Here the word 'Arittha' is for tribe. In those days, the identity of men and women was known generally by the name of tribe. For example Valhi for offshoot of Valhika tribe, Malvi for offshoot of Malva tribe. These names are after their tribe of noun Gana[24] or the name Aritha is used for offshoot of Arattha Nag tribe. Huluss has equated the Pettinik with the Aaratthas of Panjab and according to Bhuridutt Jatak, the Nag tribe of Aratthas was residing in the valley of river Yamuna. Pettinik has been equated with the Aarattha, it means Pettinika were also people of Nag tribe.

We[25] have earlier seen that in the inscription of Ashoka, the Maharatta of Ratthika and Pettinika, being the components of republic confederacy, bore the title of an officer of administration of Republic confederacy.

The Maharatha or Maharashtra was a state of republic confederacy, and it is apparent from the mention of Ratthak, Pettinika and Bhoja in the inscription of Ashoka. In fact Maharashtra was not a republic state but a republic confederacy.[26] The highest administrative post of Maharattha Republican confederacy was of Ratthikas and the person who was holding the position or post of Ratthika was Maharattha and Mahar was important chief tribal component of republican confederacy. Therefore these people were known by the name of Ratthik or Rastik or Ratti or Rathi. But we have to see whether this republican confederacy of Maharattha was related to Mahars ? Then this Rattik or Rathi or Mahar was equally related to Mahar tribe.[27] The second tribal component of Maharattha republican confederacy was Bhoja. In the age of Satavahana, the representative of Maharattha republican confederacy, the chief of Mahar tribe, bore the title of Maharathi and the chief of Bhoja tribe Mahabhoja. Therefore, it can be said that the use of synonym word Ratha or rathi or Mahar tribe came in vogue in the reference of regional administrative post of Maharattha republican confederacy. Therefore in place of nationalization of or oneness of Maharas and Rathas, the Rattha being the synonym name of Mahar tribe and from the nationalization of Mahar republican confederacy, the words Mahar or Maharasthra were formed. These Maharas or Rattha were of Naga race.

The Ethnical Identity of Mahar or Rattha Nag With the Marathas

When we shed a glance on the names of Naga kings of historical age, we find that some of these names had suffix of words like Nag, Nak, Nandi, Dutta and Sen. We here take, the words Nāg or Nāk into consideration. We have already said in chapter X that the rule of Nagas was established in Kashi sometimes in between 10th and 8th century B.C. The 23rd Jain Tirthankar, Parashwa Nath, took birth in the family of Brahma Dutta, the famous king of Kashi. He was a Naga prince. Sishu naga who was earlier king of Kashi, later established Sishunag dynasty in Magadha, was also the successor of this family. In one of the texts Sishu Naga has been called Sishunak also. It means both the words i.e. Nag or Nak are synonymous. Hence both were used as suffix in their names by the later Nagas.

Nava Nagas :

Names[28] of Nava-Nāgas who ruled at Padmavati, Kantipuri and Mathura (140 AD – 344 AD) are as under : Nava Nāgas, Virasena, Bhima Nāga, Skanda Nāga, Brihaspati Nāga, Vyaghra Nāga, Dev Nāga, Ganapati Nāga, Hayanāga, Traya Nāga, Barhina Nāga, Charaja Nāga, Bhava Nāga, Kirtisena, Nāgsena and (Nāga Datta, Mahesvara Nāg at Srughna).

The Satavahana Age :

The use of these words was also made by the Nagas of Satavahana age (235 BC – 225 AD). We get evidences of such names in the inscriptions of this age. Many inscriptions have been found out from the

Buddhist caves of Satavahana age. From them numerous names with the suffix of Nāg or Nāk have been noted. H.L. Kosare gives an account of such names.[29] :

In the inscription of Bhāje Buddhist cave no 17, there is a mention of grant of one cave, made by a Naga named Nādsava.

On stupa No. 6, 7, 8 and 9 there are very small inscriptions. On one of them there is a phrase Ādarniya Ther (Sthavir) Anpināk (or Ahikināk) ka stup.

(The stupa of honourable Ther Anpināk)

In the cave inscription no. 5 of Kudā there is a mention of name of Nāgnikā.

The inscriptions No. 7,8, 9, and 10 are in sanskrit and seem to be of a very later date than the others. There is a mention of the name of Nag in them. Similarly there is also a mention of the name of Mahabhoja. There are following inscriptions :

The religious donation of this cave by Nag house-holder and merchant. (24)

'This religious donation of cave' Vasulnāk - Merchant (25)

'This religious donation of water tank' Vasulnāk Merchant (26)

'This religious donation of cave' Shiv Dutta wife of Vahmit and mother of Pusnāk (27)

(a) Inscriptions of Vedasa cave :

1. The donation of Anand son of Pushpanak Merchant of Nasik.
2. This religious donation granted by Mahārthini Mahādevi Sāmadinikā daughter of Mahābhojak and wife of Apdevnāk.

   (Inscription on the water Tank near Chetyagraha)

(b) Inscriptions of Karle Cave :

(1) This donation of lion Pillar by Gotikā son of Mahārathi Agnimittranāk.

(first inscription in the cave of Kārle on lion Pillar of magnificent Chetya graha).

Other inscriptions of Kārle cave are :

(2) This donation belongs to Māila mother of Mahadevnāk a house holder.

(3) This donation of Pillar made by Mitadevanāk son of Usamadan resident of Benukākat.

(c) Inscriptions of Shela Khadi :

(1) This religious donation of cave made by Siyāgunikā wife of Usabhanāk and her son, householder, Nand. Kunbi farmer resident of Dhenukākat.

(D) Inscription of Junnar (between 150 BC and 150-200 AD.)

(1) First inscription is invisible, its last words are 'Thabhutinak'

(E) Inscription of Chetyagraha of Shivaneri

(1) This religious donation, of Chetyagraha, made by the chief house-holder and honest merchant named Virsenāk for the sake of world's well being and welfare (Kalyān).

(F) **Kanheri Cave inscription** (according to list of H. Luders) :

(No 985) This religious donation of Nāknāk of Nasik.

(No 987) Inscription of period of Sātakarni King Gautamiputra Sriyagyā : And Aprenāk son of Upasak merchant who was organizer.

(no 1000) Prakrit – This religious donation of one cave and water tank made by Isipaul son of Golnāk merchant of Kalyān in honour of his family and parents.

(No 1005) Prakrit – This religious donation of cave made by Nāgpālit and his family. Javeri (Bead maker) resident of Sopara.

(No 1021) Prakrit — This donation of cave made to Bhikshu Sangh by Nāgmulnika wife of maharaja, Maharathini, daughter of Mahabhoj (Mahabhoji) who is the mother of Khandnāg Sātaksiri (Shiva skand nag Satri) and sister of Mahabhoj Ahija (?) Vensen (?).

Among the inscriptions of Satavahana and Nahpān the most ancient inscription is on small window in the Nasik cave no 14. According to Dr. Bhandarkar this inscription seems to be a work of last period of Mauryan age or early Sunga age or the beginning of second century B.C. It is as under : This cave got constructed by Saman, Mahapatra of Nasik while the Krishna of Satavahana family was ruling.

'This Chetyāgraha got constructed on the hillock of Tirānhumi (Trirashmi) by Mahāhakusiriya daughter of state minister Arohalaya Chalisālnāk, wife of state minister Agiyatnāk Bhalākārikay and mother of Kannāk.'

One of the inscription of caves of Nasik is as follows : This religious donation of cave was made to Bhikshu Sangha of Chatuhdishā by Chhaklepakiya Rāmnāk son of Belidutt.[30]

The Muslim Period

During Muslim period, aforesaid word of Nāk or Nāg was used not only by Mahars but also by the Maratha chiefs. During the reigning period of Hussain Gango Bahamani, there is a mention of Harnāk pol and Kāmrāj Ghādge of Surya banshi Kshatriya family. Raha helped in the marriage of Kāmrāj Ghadge with the daughter of Maratha chief Harnāk alias Harang nāk Pol. He had five sons named Parasnāk, Lohnāk, Naya nāk, Jaitpaul nāk and Lok nāk.

Therefore the use of the word nāk was in prevalence among the Mahar and Maratha during the Muslim period. It means both Mahars (untouchable) and Maratha (Kshatriya) were considered to be of one Naga race and there was no such difference as is visible in modern age.

The British Period :

When we trace out evidences of use of suffix of Nag or Nāk words with their names by the Mahars during British regime, it is interesting enough to know that we find it perfectly. In 1818 AD, in the battle of Koregaon, which was fought between Marathas and English people, the Mahar warriors won over the battle field for Britishers. In the memory of warriors, which were killed in this battle, a memorial Pillar was raised at the bank of Bheema river in Koregaon, which mentions the names of 23 Mahar warriors. The last three of them were simply injured. The names, which are inscribed on this war-memorial pillar are as follows : Somnāk-Kamalnāk Naik, Rāmnāk-Yesnāk Naik, Godnāk-Kothenāk, Ramnāk-Yesnāk, Bhāgnāk-Harnāk, Ambnāk-Kānnāk, Gannāk-Bālnāk, Bālnāk-Kothenāk, Rūpnāk-Lakhnāk, Bapnāk-Ramnāk, Vitnāk-Dhāmnāk, Rajnāk-Gannāk, Bapnāk-Harnāk, Raināk-Vannak, Gannāk-Dharmnāk, Devnāk-Aonnāk, Gopalnāk-Balnāk, Harnāk-Hiranāk, Jaitnāk-Dhaināk, Gannāk-Lakhnāk, Jannāk-Hirnāk, Bheemnāk-Ratan nāk, Ratannāk-Dhannāk.[31]

This shows Naga people lived and ruled in India from the time of Mahabharat (950 BC) upto the British regime. They are still following the culture of Satavahana ruler in the form of caste people of Marathi, Kunbi farmers and Mahar.

The Expansion of Nagas and Mahars in the South

The original inhabitants of Ceylon were Vedda or Vedaid. They, in the beginning, migrated from Malabar to Ceylon and called themselves Nagas. They gave the name 'Nagadvipa' to northern region of Ceylon. These Naga people are the ancestors of Nayars of Malavai. Naya is Prakrit form of Sanskrit Nagas.[32] In the Tamil literature of Sangam Age, in the description of Kalil Attireyanar, there is mention of Moriyar (Maurya). On this, the commentator puts forth his remarks–'Moriyar were paramount emperors and were Vidyadhar Nagas. In it Mauryas have been called Nagas. Similarly in Sangam literature alongwith Mauryas there is also a mention of the name of Nandas.[33]'

In Sangam literature, there is also mention of 'Mohur people' The author of Sangam literature, Mamulnar has written– "The Koshar people of Vijay-Dhaj invaded their enemy and defeated enormous people from them, but 'Mohur' people did not accept their defeat, then Mauryas helped the Koshars to attack Mohur people and the Mohur were defeated."[34]

Here, the reference of Mohur people, available in the Sangam literature is worth noting. This reference is related to the Mauryan period. While we compare the meaning of the words Mohar and Mohur, we come to know that the word Mohur is a Tamil form of Mohar. From this reference of Mohur people of Mauryan period, the existence of Mahars is proved in this age. We have shown in chapt II that in the East the progeny of these Nagas is still existing in Assam viz Tangkhul, Koliya, khasa, etc. but in the Centre and South they were Aryanized in general.

The Aryanization

How these Nagas were Aryanized is a most interesting question but its answer is very simple, the best culture so far developed by human kind which made the Buddhist India economically and politically most powerful country, was victimized by their hereditary antagonists, the Vedic Aryan. They blindly followed the policy of Kautilya. They Aryanized the stronger and pushed the weakers into fourth Varna by making a simple pronouncement. They followed such a policy from the time of Rigveda. According to Rigveda they began to give high respect to rich non-Aryan Asuras like Bravu.

R.V. VI-45-31

"Bravu has been standing on virtuous and high place among the Panis (Asuras) and as high as the high shores of Ganges."

Why the Aryan Rishis gave so much importance to a non-Aryan Asura it is clear from the next verse (R.V. VI-45-33).

"We always praise and appreciate Bravu who donates one thousand cows."

It is clear from this that Brahmana Rishis were helplessly greedy of alms, that is why they gave so much importance to above Asura. Similarly they gave importance and praised Naga chieftains and divinities in later period whose description is given in Skand Purana : Elapatra, Kambal, Karkotaka, Dhananjaya, pannag, Shreshtha, Basuki, Takshaka, Neel, Padmak, Arvua.[35] and at another place Basuki, Takshak, Paramghor, Nāg Eravat, Mahabhag, Kalip, Karkotaka, Dhananjaya,

Shankhchud, Mahantejaswi, Dhritrashtra, Vrikodar, Kulik and Vāman.[36]

Some scholars are of this view that this honour to Naga chieftains and divinities is given simply to include them in their culture like Shiva and Shakti, but as a matter of fact it was a part of the process of Aryanization of persons having power and pelf.

When these Nagas had gained over-whelming power, the Brahmans keeping in view the interest of their profession, began to establish their close relation with them on one hand and some of them were secretly busy in fabrication of hard and fast laws of caste and Varna system, on the other. But the Naga kings, in the madness of royal power, instead of opposing them, began to recognize the Varna and caste system as ideal in the guise of religious worship and sanctity. In the long run, they could not help embracing Hinduism, although their women continued to follow their old faith for an indefinite period. Kings did so, because this social and religious ideology, proved to be much effective in illustrating them to be high, infested with god like power in the eyes of their subjects and also legitimization of their birth and providing better command over bureaucrats working for them.[37]

Hiranya Garbha Ceremony

Above greed of Naga kings swelled to such an extent that, at a later date, there are evidences, that they began to undergo a Brahmanical ceremony known as Hiranyagarbha Sanskar to raise their social position. Vidyadhar Mahajan[38] while giving detail of such a ceremony writes– "The importance of Rastrakuta began during the time of king Dantidurga, when he subjugated Kanchi, Kalinga, Kausal, Shrisail, Malava, Lāt and Tank in his kingdom and performed Hiranyagarbha ceremony at Ujjain." According to Fleet, "Rashtrakuta were offshoot of Rathor of North and according to Burnett the relation of Rashtrakuta was with the Dravidian Reddi of Andhra Pradesh." The Mahār of Maharashtra and Ratthe of Tungbhadra Valley, who used to call themselves Reddi, are of one origin. It means Maharattha of ancient period and Marathas of modern age and Kannadi and Telugu speaking Reddi or Radde are variant of Maratha, Reddi converted to Lingayat from Jainism, similarly Maharatthe to Shaivism from Buddhism.[39] It means original birth of Reddies is from Mahar Nag.

Several[40] southern kings of tribal origin boast of having had 'Golden Womb' (Hiranya garbha), ceremony performed. This is carefully described in some Puranas. A large vessel of gold was prepared, in to which the chieftain would be inserted doubled up, like the foetus in a Womb. The Brahman ritual for pregnancy and child birth was then chanted by the hired priest. The man emerged the 'womb of gold' as if reborn, having also acquired a new caste or even a caste for the first time; this was not the caste of the rest tribe when they observed into society, but one of the classical four castes usually Kshatriya with the Gotra of Brahman priest. Some of the reborn medieval kings might claim the Brahman and Kshatriya caste at once, like the Satavahana Gotamiputra. The Brahman priests received the golden vessel as a part of their fee, which made everyone happy.

Incident of Coronation of Shivaji

Dantidurga Rastrakula, after subjugating most of the principalties of Central and Western India, also performed Hiranyagarbha ceremony for his purification at Ujjain. Another such example can be traced out as late as Mughal period. For proving the birth of Shivaji from Kshatriya caste, who was Shudra Kurmi in origin, his fake pedigree was prepared and then his coronation ceremony could be held. This incident is most interesting hence being quoted in full: "Shivaji after conquering the several kingdoms of Western Maharasthra, by dint of his courage and power, established his rule and built a strong fort for its control. He thought of his coronation in order to declare legality of his kingship. But the Brahmanas refused to perform the religious rite of coronation ceremony because he was Sudra. Shivaji's friends advised that the coronation ceremony might be held with strict compliance of Vedic tradition.[41] But he had to face a number of hurdles in fulfilment of his desire : First, that no person other than the Brahmans could help perform this ritual, while not a single Brahman was prepared to do so, secondly this ritual could not be held until his identity as a Kshatriya was confirmed, thirdly that he had not undergone the ceremony of Upnayana (the ritual of admittance) and in the absence of Upnayana, this ritual of coronation ceremony was impossible. The Brahmanas under the leadership of Moropant Pingley, who was Shivaji's Prime Minister refused to recognize Shivaji as Kshatriya. So much so that in this concern, even the Maratha chiefs of Shivaji did not stand by him, rather they also treated him as Sudra.[42] Balaji-Avaji, Shivaji's friend and secretary was of immense help to him. He gave some money to Brahmans and got prepared the pedigree table of shivaji which was connected with the Sisodiya dynasty of Mewar. He procured the services of a famous Brahman named Gaug Bhat from Banaras in exchange for a large sum of money and it was then that the coronation ceremony of Shivaji could be effected.

Summary and Conclusion

1. We know that people of Maharashtra were of round headed

Alpine race or a blended race of Alpine and Dravidian people.

2. These people were known as Mer or Mher who came from North west, whose traces have been found out from Rajasthan in antiquity.

3. Since Jaisalmer was, originally related to Bhatti tribe the suffix of Mer, added to this word, shows that these Bhatti's were also related to Mer tribe. Bhatti Rajputs are offshoot of Yadavas or Bhoja, another branch of Yadavas, Mahabhoja were a component of Satavahanas.

4. Maharashtra took its name from the combination of the words Mahar + Ratta (of the Ashoka's inscription) = Maharatta or Maharashtra. These Aratta or Ratta were Nagas according to Jataka (no 543), Bhuridutta Ratta is synonymous of Mahar tribe.

5. The antiquity of the word Maharashtra can be traced out as early as the age of Vararuchi or Nanda period.

6. There were, according to Angutara Nikaya, following hierarchy of rulers from top to bottom among the republican society. (a) King (b) Rashtrika (c) Pettinika (hereditary office, (d) Senani (e) Gavachā or Gramani (f) Shrenika of the guild of village (g) chief of the family. These Rashtrika and Pettinika had important role in the administration of Satavahanas.

7. Perhaps Satavahanas were of Mahar tribe that is why this word Maharathi came into existence. Hence this word became general designation of their chiefs and warriors in later period of history, which is still continuing in modern period. It means the native chiefs were traditionally called 'Maharathi' and Maratha and Marathi is a linguistic variation of this word. Thus Marathis, Kunbis and Mahars are direct descendants of Satavahana people.

References

1. Gustab Oppert, 'The Original Inhabitant of India' Oriental Publication Delhi. PP 47-48.

2. Tod James, "Annals and Antiquities of Rajasthan" III P-1300.

3. Tod James I PP 102-103.

4. (a) Tod James II PP 790 and 920

   (b) Gustab Oppert P- 47 below footnote No. 46.

5. Tod James II PP-790-91.

6. Jayaswal K.P. P-147.

7. (a) The word 'Marwar' is pronounced as Malavar in Pujnab Malava-Var (The land of Malava; Hira Lal. Inscription of C.P. PP 24 and 87 and Epigraphia Indica Part VIII-P-285.)

   (b) Jayaswal KP P-47 Footnote No. 2

8. Rapson E.J. "Indian Coins" Part 51 and V.A. Smith, "Coins of Indian Museum" PP 161-62.

9. Arthshastra of Kautilya I-12-24 and II-15-1.

10. Kosambi D D, "The Culture and Civilization of Ancient India" P-150.

11. Patil Sharad, "Das Shudrachi Gulamgiri" P-85.

12. Taitreya Samhita, III-4-8.

13. Patil Sharad P-140.

14. Kosare H. L. "Prachin Bharatatil Nag". PP -131-32

15. Patil Sharad PP 140-141.

16. Patil Sharad P-191.

17. Kosare H.L. P-156.

18. (a) Jagdish Kashyapa, "Angutāra Nikaya" Pali 5-6-8-5, 11

    (b) Jayaswal K.P., "Hindu Polity" PP-79-80

    (c) Patil Sharad, P-61

19. Jayaswal K.P. PP-79-80.

20. I.A. XLVIII (1919) P-80.

21. Ibid.

22. Dutt N.K., "Aryanization of Ancient India." PP 35-38.

23. J.A. O S No. 46 P-257.

24. Patil Sharad P-303.

25. Kosare H.L. P-158.

26. Kosare H.L. P-160.

27. Ibid.

28. Jayaswal K.P. "History of India" PP 35-36.

29. Kasore H.L. PP-142-44.

30. More M.S., "Maharāshtratil Buddha Dhammāya Itihas" P 103-37 cited by H.L. Kosre P-144.

31. Shinde, "Bhartiya Asprashyatacha Prashna" PP 211-12.

32. Sastri Nilkant K.A. : ''Age of the Nandas and Mauryas'' P-256

33. Sastri Nilkant K-A. P-254.

34. Sastri Nilkant K.A. PP 254-55.

35 Skand Purana 77/17-18 Shriram Sharma Part I and II (1970) P-312.

36. Skand Purana 106/5-6-7 P-477.

37. Sudharshan Senevritne, "Kalinga and Andhra; the Process of Secondary State Formation in Early India" P-66 IHR vol VII no 1 and 2 (1980-81).

38. Mahajan V.D., "Ancient India" PP 548-49.

39. Deshmukh K.B., ''Kshatriyan Cha Itihas'' P-82.

40. "The Culture and Civilization of Ancient India" P-171 (1975) Delhi.

41. Sarkar Yadunath, "Shivaji and His Time" P-210.

42. Ambedkar B.R., ''Who were the Sudras ?'' PP 201-03.

Epilogue

The first civilization of the globe took its birth in Western Asia at Katal-Huyuk and Jericho ten thousand years ago. In about 6750 B.C. man at Sumer began to domesticate animals like sheep, goats and cattle and cultivated grains like wheat and barley etc. Sumerians were the first who constructed canals for irrigating their fields. They evolved a writing system (pictograph) as early as the first half of fourth millennium B.C. Similarly, as discussed and proved in different chaters, social, religious, political, economic system also developed there first and transferred to Indus Valley alongwith the migration of sumerians which became the basis of later Naga culture.

Infact, Indus Valley Culture was an extension of Sumerian culture as shown by some scholars. In those days, the extensive desert of South Iran and Baluchistan was not so arid or uneasy to pass, as it is now and there was infiltration of human population through it from Sumeria to Indus Valley and vice-versa in general, that is why two cultures were parallel and strikingly so similar in character : There was homogeneity of race, language, religion, culture and system of military, polity, trade and industry etc. People of both the lands were long-headed Mediterraneans and round-headed Alpines or their admixture race, having wheatish colour and black eyes and hair. The people of both the regions were speaker of languages akin to Dravidian (Proto-Elamo-Dravidian and Brahui) and old Iranian from which later Pishacha group of languages (Pali, Prakrit) originated.

Worship of snake and cult of mother goddess was prevalent among the societies of both the lands. Matriarchal system of family and inheritance was in practice in both the societies. There was tradition of citizen's army, where every citizen was supposed to learn the art of use of arms and to attend for war compulsorily, in case of emergency in Sumer as well as Indus Valley. Such a system made both the countries most powerful nations.

We know, there were city-states in Indus Valley and also in Sumer, whose rulers or kings were also chief priests of the city temples, who were presiding over every religious function in addition to looking after administration of their city states.

A Sangha or guild-like system was the basis of trade and industry or Silpa, in Sumer as well as in Indus Valley towns, that made the people most prosperous. Cities of both the cultures were about planned and their multy-storeyed houses were built of fire baked bricks. Although, aforesaid culture and cultural traditions took their birth in Sumer and were later transferred to Indus Valley yet reached their top heights about in the same span of time. Both the cultures are famous for their antiquity, rapid progress, wealth and glory. But as ill-luck would have it, both were destroyed and subdued by the barbarian semi-civilized invaders of Central Asia, known as white Aryan race in about 1600 B.C., who ruled both the lands for a period of more than half a millennium.

In Sumeria, by the disappearance of Aryan's rule, the people, their culture and effect of culture also disappeared, but in Indian soil their culture made a deep-rooted and permanent effect, which is still visible in present times. Since these new-comers, white coloured, blue eyed and grey-haired Aryans came from a cold region of north, hence hot weather of India was a problem for them, just like in modern age, the white English people, after their settlement in India also felt, and established hill stations, to bear the fury of scorching sun of Indian weather. Similarly it was difficult for Aryans to work hard or do jobs of hard labour in sun for their livelihood. Thus, they, were forced to devise a new system, suiting to new circumstances : since they had power and sufficient subdued native slaves, all the occupations of production and hard labour were strictly put on the shoulders of native slaves, who were great producer in origin. Before their entry into Indian sub-continent, Aryans had three Varnas in their society i.e. Brahman, Kshatriya, and Vaishya, thus they created a fourth Sudra Varna for subdued natives. Thus the new-comer Aryan people became a non-working and non-productive class under compelled circumstances and made it a permanent social system governed by the strict rules.

But it was not the dead end of their degradation, they further devised a new system, which was first introduced in Gurukulas, the Vedic religious education centres, where Vedic Hindu culture took its birth, the students (Sishyas) were made to go in surrounding country for begging alms to bear the expenses of their institution. Such a concept became the basis of the beginning of Vedic Hindu culture which later entered into their religious thoughts to get respectable position and sanctity. The whole Vedic literature bears witness to this new development. Whereas quite contrary, the Buddhist monks used to weave cloth to bear the expenses of their institutions or Viharas. But this new concept became the sole cause of downfall of later Indian economy. Since it was adopted by a class which was ruler as well as most respected class of society on one hand and non-working, non-producing class on the other, hence the earlier concept began to be respected and the later, (hard working and productive occupations) began to be hated, which resulted in the downfall of national production, and brought poverty and applied back gear to nation's progress. Thus nation came on the high way of degradation, backwardness and poverty.

We have earlier shown that native people's nation-in-arms and citizen's army systems made the nation invincible and powerful which has been well testified by the Greek historians too. Alexander himself was hurt by a valiant warrior of Native Malava-Kshudrak confederacy perhaps which caused his death. A confederacy of Naga warriors under the leadership of Bharsivas of Padmavati pushed back Kushanas as well as Scythians out of the frontiers of India. But quite opposite, the Aryan Varna system permits only Kshatriyas to face the foreign invaders which would have been not more than, according to an estimate, 5% of the nations population, from them neither half women nor two third oldmen and children also used to attend battle fields for war. Rest of the meagre number of Kshatriya youths always met with a shameful defeat at the hands of foreign invaders. That is why India remained a slave for more than one thousand years. Thus what gave the Aryan Varna system to nation was only the shameful slavery and humiliation.

Aryan's Hindu social laws, being anti-republic and anti-social, permit rule of monarchy only. Thus their common man's life, death and freedom was at the mercy of one man or king, whose anti-social and anti human activities are well known in the history of mankind. That is why such a system has been discarded by the modern society of the world. Whereas native people developed a Sangha or republican like system of rule, where king of their own choice was elected by them, who ruled and worked for them. Hence they enjoyed maximum possible civil rights and liberty, where ever necessary their kings were ousted on their choice. This happened in Videha and Magadha kingdoms.

In short the native traditions and culture made them wealthy workers and valiant warriors, who knew no caste. They were followers of Buddhist teachings of non-violence and their sword was not for violence but for maintaining peace. They were architect of urbanization of ancient India second time after the fall of the Indus towns. Their ultimate achievement was golden age of Indian history.

But their great culture was destroyed by their dead opponents, the Aryans not by war in the battle field, but by merciless and wicked policies of Kautilya. It is very strange, although Guptas, who were of Native Sangha or republican origin from mother's side as well as father's side (Samudra Gupta) destroyed them and killed 13 Naga princes who were symbol of great warriorship, republic system, freedom and patriotism and in lieu of they forcibly introduced Hindu Varna and feudal system in the nation. Thus they threw the nation into deep trenches of poverty, slavery and humiliation, which still does not seem to cease.

The next question that arises is what happened to the descendants of Takshakas, (Taka) their off shoot branches and tribe. According to V.D. Mahajan, the main branch of Taka Naga family which began to be called Rajput, in later period, ruled Gujrat for 14 generations from the period of Firoz Tughlak (1391 AD) up to the Mughal period, while their kingdom was subjugated by emperor Akbar in his empire in 1572 AD. Saharan Taka adopted Muslim religion and his descendants ruled Gujrat. This also shows that the native royal families later began to be called Rajputs. This is one of the solid proof to establish the theory of Rajput origin from native blood.

We have shown in chapter XV that whatever culture developed in Maharasthra in Satavahana age, is preserved in the Mahar, Maratha and Kunbi society still in modern Age. It means commoner of the tribe of satavahanas became Marathi, Kunbi and Mahar and their royal families turned into Rajputs as shown in following lines :

Some of the native Naga rulers were Aryanized by ceremonial purification of "Hiranya Garbha." Gotamiputra[1] Satavahana perhaps seems earliest example. In later historical period we have the example of Dantidurga of Ujjaini, the Rashtrakuta who was Aryanized to become Rajput. According to Fleet Rashtrakuta were offshoot of Rathor of north, who were Dravidian Reddi of Andhra Pradesh. The Mahāratthe of Maharasthra and Ratthe of Tungbhadra Valley, who used to call themselves Reddi, are of one origin. These Maharatthes were offshoots of Yadavas (Bhoja) or Naga people or a Branch of Satavahana. Since coins of Shalivahana and later Satavahana kings bear the legend of Rano or Ranno, it seems from this that Rana royal family of Chittor also had ethnical relation with this Naga family, because both are originally Suryabanshi.

In Central India, the Bharsiva or Bhar family of Padamavati was most important, they were of Taka origin. These people ruled south and eastern Uttar Pradesh and a major part of Bihar, before the advent of Muslim rule. The present royal families of Manda and Vijaypur are said to be their descendants. Still Bhar tribe exists in Vindhya region. Rajbhars are called Rajputs and Bhars are a part of fourth Varna or tribe.

Mauryas have been called Vidhyadhar Nag in Sangam literature of South India. They were offshoot of Moriyas or Vahikas of Pātalpuri, one branch of them ruled near Nepal during the life time of Buddha. Parmar

Rajput family of Chittor was offshoot of these Mauryas. But what happened to its tribe is still a subject of research.

But it is a hard fact of history that Tak Kshatriyas (Chhimbas) are direct descendant of Takshaka tribe of Mahabharata fame. Similarly present Koliya caste of Himachal Pradesh is a branch of Madras (who were originally Takas) or Kolinda who gave their name to Kulu, ruled Kulu Valley for a very long period. Vedic Hindu authors owing to inherent feelings of antipathy against native population deliberately have kept above truth under the garb of secrecy that is why, although thousands of books have been written on history, but not a single on Naga or Takshaka royal family and their tribe. Thus Tribes of Tank (Kshatriya) is one of the oldest, about whose origin, and history we have some records.

Since there were commercial guilds of each artisan tribe like leather-workers, carpenters, black-smiths, brass-workers, copper-smiths, weavers, ivory-workers, masons, bead-makers, potters, fishermen, basket-makers, herds-men, plough-man, oil-men etc, who had turned every village into an industrial estate, generally became castes named after their occupations and were pushed in to the fourth Varna of Hindu caste system during the time of Samudra Gupta, while Hinduism and feudal system was forced upon them. We know each one of them was a warrior which was against the law of Varna system (ie to be Kshatriya) hence it is reasonable to think that their arms would have been seized and unity (Sangha) broken by force by the feudal lords of Guptas. But what actually would have happened to these ill-fated people, who were earlier known by the name of their proud tribe or Bansha like Vahika, Taka, Andhra, Madra, Malava, Videha, Moriya, Malla, Lichchhavi, Sakya, began to be called after their occupational names in general which is one of the chief characteristic of Varna or caste system. However it is very hard to trace out name of original Bansha or tribes of people attached to each of occupation at this stage of our research. However we have successfully traced out occupations of some of the tribes such as Sakyas of Buddha were vegetable grovers now known as Sakka, Videhas were carvaneers or transporters, Mallas were not different from the flower-gardener of modern age, Lichchhavis were herdsmen, Kshudrakas were earlier cooks but now they are petty traders knows as suds, Malavas are Kahars and Washermen in Madhya Pradesh, Agraseni are Aggrawal Banik traders of modern age, Koliyas (Madras) are weavers of present age, Ambasthas are Kayasthas etc. Takshaka or Vahikas during the life time of Buddha came to be known as Rajak (original meaning council of confederacy or Rulers) with new meaning dyers or fullers or washermen or shilpa or Chhipa (generally servile class, see theory in vol I of this series) These degraded occupational name, which were earlier symbol of power, proud and prosperity became symbol of low dignity and humiliation simply because now their sword and power both had been seized. Thus the glory, of these great people of ancient age, was gone.

This was a symbol of downfall of great people and their culture and beginning of dark age of slavery, humiliation and poverty.

(i) Kosambi D.D., "The Culture and Civilization of Ancient India" P–171

Selected Bibliography

(a) Original Text Books

Abhidhan Chintamani - 4 (Hem Chandra)

Aitreya Brahman

Angutara Nikaya

Arthshastra of Kautilya

Atharva-Veda

Bhagwat Puran

Brahdharma Puran

Dialogue of the Buddha Vol IV Part III

Dighanikaya (PTS) Vol II

Haribamsa

The Jataka (Cowell E.B.)

The Mahabharat

Mahavastu Vol III ed Senart E. (Peris 1862)

Mahabhashya (Patanjali) Translation J.J. Jones 'Sacred books of Buddhism'

Manusmriti

Markandeya Puran

Rajtarngini (Kalhan) – Stein

The Ramayana (Valmiki)

The Rigveda

Satpath Brahmana

Skand Puran

Sumangal Vilasini Part I

Taitreya Samhita

Vayu Purana

Vishnu Puran (Wilson)

(b) List of Journals

Ancient India no IV (1947-48), IX, XI, XVI (1960)

Annals of the Bhandarkar Oriental Research Institution Vol 22, 29, 51 (1970)

Annual Bulletin of the Nagpur University Historical society no 1 Oct 1946

Annual Report Archaeological Survey of India (1927–28)

Anthropological Survey of India, Calcutta (1963)

Archaeological Survey Reporter Vol II, III (1963), X, XII, XVII, XIX, 1915-16, 1926-27, 1927-28

Archaeological Survey West India Vol V

Bombay Gazetteer Part XVIII Sub Part I

Bulletin of the Deccan College Research Institute Poona Vol (1939-40)

Epigraphia Indika Vol I, III, IV, V, VII, VIII, IX, X, XVI, XVIII, XXII

Indian Antiquary Vol VII, VIII, XVII, XXXVII (1908) XLII (1913), XL VIII (1919)

Indian Archaeological Review 1957-58, 1958-59, 1961-62, 1962-63, 1963-64, 1964-65, 1965-66, 1967-68, 1968-69

Indian History Congress Session 39 (1978) Sect V Hydrabad

Indian Historical Quarterly no II, III, X, XXVII (1951)

Indian Historical Review VII (1980-81) no 1 and 2

Inscriptions in Central Province and Berar no 269, 305

Inscriptions of Orissa Vol IV

Journal of the American Oriental Society no 46

Journal of the Bengal Royal Asiatic Society (1893)

Journal of the Bihar and Orissa Research Society I

Journal of the Bombay Branch of the Royal Asiatic society Vol XVIII (1890-94)

Journal of the K.R. Coma Oriental Insitute Vol I and V Bombay (1922-1926)

Journal of the Numismatic Society of India Vol II (1940) XXX (1968)

Journal of the Oriental Institute Vol XXII no 1 and 2 (1972)

Journal of the Royal Asiatic Society 1900, 1903, 1917

Madras Report on Epigraphia 1808-1809

Memoirs of the Archaeological Survey of India no 61, 67

Modern Review Vol XIV no 1 and 6 (1913)

Nevasa Report on Coins

Puratatva no 7

Proceedings of the 7th all India Oriental Conference studies in Indology Vol III (Nagpur University Research series no 7) (1977)

Vidarbha Sansodhan Mandal Varshiki 1974

Vishveshwaranand Indological Journal Vol 16 (1978) Part 1 and 2

(c) Modern Works

'A'

Acharya Chhitij Mohan sen — Bharat Main Jati Bhed (Hindi)

Acharya Hastimal — Jain Dharm Ka Maulik Itihas Vol 1 Jaipur (1995)

Aggarwal V.S. — Vision in Long Darkness Varanasi (1963)

Allchin B and R — The Birth of Indian Civilization Pelican Books (1968)

Dr. Ambedkar B.R. — Who were the Sudras ? Bombay (1970)

Dr. Ambedkar B.R. — The Untouchables, Bombay

Apte V.G. — Buddha Dharma Vol II (1957)

Ashthana Shashi — History and Archaeology of India's Contact with other Countries Delhi (1976)

'B'

Bajpai Atima — Madhya Pradesh Ke Nagbanshi Sikke (Hindi)

Bajpai K.D. — Indian Numismatic Studies, Abhinav Pub New Delhi (1976)

Banerjee N.R. — Iron Age in India, New Delhi (1965)

Banerjee N.R. — Megalithic Problem of India, Studies in pre-history, Calcutta (1966)

Beal Samuel — S1 – Yu – K1 (Hieunt sang) Calcutta (1958)

Beal Samuel — Buddhist Records of the Western World Vol II, III, Delhi (1969)

Bhandarkar D.R. — Lecture on the Ancient History of India Calcutta (1919)

Bhandarkar R.G. — Early History of the Dekkan Calcutta (1928)

Bhandarkar R.G. — Commemoration Volume – Pune (1917)

Bishwas S.K. — Autochthon of India and the Aryan Invasion Delhi (1995)

Bottero Jeans Elena Cassin and Jean Vercoutter — The Near East; The Early Civilization, London (1967)

Buddha Prakash — Rigveda and the Indus Valley civilization, Hoshiarpur (1966)

Buhler George — Indian Palaeography, Delhi (1959)

Burnouf — Introduction to Buddhism Vol 1 Paris (1876)

Burgess James — Notes on Amaravati Stupa (1972)

Burrow T. — The Sanskrit Language – London (1965)

'C'

Carleton Petrick — Buried Empires, London (1939)

Chakravorty — Origin of Lichchhavi of Vaisali (1969)

Chanda R.P. — The Indo Aryan Races, Calcutta (1969)

Chapelkar M. Nalinee — Ancient India and Iran, Delhi (1982)

Chattopadhyaya Sudhakar — Racial Affinities of Early north Indian Tribes, Delhi (1973)

Chauhan D.V. — Pishacha Bhasa va Marathi – Vidarbha Sanshodhan Mandal, Nagpur (1977)

Chopra PN and others — History of South India Vol 1, Delhi (1979)

Crindle John WMC — Ancient India as Described in Classical Literature Part II (4), Patna (1987)

Cunningham A. — Ancient Geography of India, Varanasi (1963)

Cunningham A. — Coins of Ancinet India, Varanasi (1963)

C. Von Furer Haimendorf, — Tamil Culture Vol II no 2 (1953)

'D'

Daniel ed Wright — History of Nepal, Calcutta (1966)

Das A.C. — Rigvedic India, Calcutta (1927)

Deo SB — Excavation at Takalghat and Khapa (1968-69)

Deo SB — Maharashtra, EK Puratatva Samalochna

Deo SB — Mahurjhari Excavation (1973)

Deo SB and JP Joshi — Pauni Excavation, (1972)

Deo SB and Dhavalikar M.K. — Paunar Excavation, (1973)

Deshmukh K.B. — Kshatriya cha Itishas, (Marathi)

Dr. Dharmvir — Hindi Ki Atma (Hindi), Delhi (1989)

Dikshit S.K. — The Mother Goddess, Dikshit, 8 Tuglak Road New Delhi.

Dixon B. Roland — The Racial History of Man, Delhi (1989)

Dutta N.K. — Aryanization of India, Calcutta (1925)

Dutta N.K. — Origin and Growth of Caste system in India, Calcutta (1968)

'E' 'F'

Elliot — The History of India, Vol III

Fergusson James — Tree and Serpent Worship, Delhi (1971)

Fry P. Somerset — History of the World, London (1977)

'G'

Ghirshman Roman — Persia, from the Origins to Alexander the great, Thomes and Hudson France (1964)

Ghurye G.S. — Vedic India, Bombay (1979)

Ghurye G.S. — Caste and Races in India, Bombay (1996)

Gokhale B.G.	Buddhism in Maharashtra Bombay (1996)
Gokhale B.G.	Samudra Gupta, Delhi (1962)
Gopalachari K.	Early History of the Andhra Country Madras (1941)
Gordon D. H.	The Prehistoric Background of Indian Culture Bombay (1958)
Grierson G.A.	Linguistic Survey of India, A Summary Part II Hoshiarpur (1973)
Guha B.S.	An Outline of the Racial Ethnology of India, Calcutta (1937)
Gupta S.P.	Disposal of the Dead and Physical type in Ancient India, Delhi (1972)
Gurdon P.R.T.	The Khasis, Delhi (1990)
Gustab oppert	The Original Inhabitant of India, Oriental Pub Delhi (1972)

'H' 'I' 'J'

Hawkes Jacquetta	The First Great Civilization, London (1973)
Hodson T.C.	The Naga Tribes of Manipur, Delhi (1989)
Hunter	Pre-Dravidian Earth Mother-goddess
Hutton J.H.	Caste in India, Delhi (1990)
Ibbetson Denzil	Panjab Caste, Delhi (1933)
Jain Jagdish Chandra	Jain Agam Sahitya Main Bhartiya Samaj, Varanasi (1965)
Jain Jyoti Prasad	Bhartiya Itihas, Ek Drishti, Bhartiya Gianpith Kashi (1961)
Jayaswal K.P.	Hindu Polity, Butter Worth and Co. (India) Ltd. (1924)
Jayaswal K.P.	History of India-Lahore, (1933)

'K'

Kashyapa Jagdish	Angutara Nikaya, (Pali), Banaras 1940
Kashyapa Jagdish	Digha Nikaya, (Pali) Mahabodhi Sabha Banaras (1939)
Keane and Huddon	Man Past and Present, Cambridge University Press (1899)
Keith A.B.	The Religion and Philosophy of Vedas and Upnishadas, Delhi (1970)
Ketkar Shridhar Vyanktesh	Prachin Maharashtra Satavahana Parva, Part I Maharashtra Gian Kosh Mandal Ltd Ashasthan Pune-4
Kosambi D.D.	Bhagwan Buddha, Delhi (1957)
Kosambi D.D.	The Culture and Civilization of Ancient India, Delhi (1977)
Kosambi Dharmanand	Hindi Sanskriti Ani Ahimsa (Marathi)
Kosare H.L.	Prachin Bharata til Nag, Nagpur (1989)

'L' 'M'

Law B.C.	Some Kshatriya Tribes of Ancient India, Varanasi (1975)
Law B.C.	Tribes in Ancient India, Poona (1943)
Loui's Finkeltein	The Jews their History culture and Religion, Vol I Harper, New york (1960)
Mackay E.	Early Indus Civilization, New Delhi (1976)
Madan Mohan Singh	Puratatwa Ki Ruprekha, Patna (1981)
Mahajan V.D.	Ancinet India, Delhi (1981)
Mahajan V.D.	Madhya Kalin Bharat, Delhi (1993)
Majumdar D.N.	Races and Cultures of India, Delhi (1961)
Majumdar R.C. and other	The Age of Imperial Unity, Bombay (1968)
Majumdar R.C.	Ancinet India Part I, Delhi (1991)
Marmat Avantika Prasad	Ved Kalin Nag Jatiyon Rajaon tatha San skrit Ki Khoj, Ujjain (1998)

Marshall John — Mohenjodaro and the Indus Civilization,-I Indological Book house Delhi

Marshall John — The Thousand Syllabled speech, Vol I

Meissner — Babylonian and Assyrian, Vol I

Menan P. — History of Kerala Vol I

Metclfe C. T. — The Rajput Tribes, Delhi (1982)

Mirashi V.V. — Vakataka Rajbansh Ka Itihas Tatha Silalekh, Varanasi (1964)

Mishra D.P. — Studies in the Proto-history of India, Delhi (1971)

Mishra S.N. — Ancient Indian Republics, Delhi (1975)

Mitra S.K. — Early Rulers of Khajuraho, Delhi (1971)

Mookerjee R.K. — The Gupta Empire, Delhi (1969)

Muir J. — Original Sanskrit text II, Delhi (1972)

Muller F Max — Ancient Sanskrit Literature, Varanasi (1968)

Muller F Max — India, What can it Teach us,

Muller F Max — The Sacred Books of the East, Vol 22-I Vol 26 Part II Delhi (1965)

'N' 'O' 'P'

Nanavati J.M. — Som Nath, Deptt of Archaeology Ahmadabad (1956)

Oldenburg — Dipavambsa (Pali), London (1879)

Oldham C.F. — The Sun and the Serpent, London(1905)

Pandeya Chandra Bhan — Andhra Satavahan Samrajya Ka Itihas, Delhi (1961)

Parpola Ashko — The Indus Script Decipherment, Madras (1976)

Patil Sarad — Das Shudrachi Gulamgiri, Part I Sub Part I (1982) (Marathi)

Piggott Stuart — The Dawn of the Civilization, London (1952)

Piggott Stuart — Prehistoric India, London (1952)

Possehl L. Gregory — Ancient Civilization of Indus, Delhi (1979)

'R'

Rao K.P. — Deccan Megaliths, Sandeep Prakashan, New Delhi

Rao S.R. — Lothal and the Indus Civilization, Delhi (1979)

Rao T.A. Gopinath — Elements of Hindu Iconography, Vol II Part II, Nagpur University (1988)

Rapson E.J. — Cambridge History of India, I, III, Delhi (1955)

Rapson E.J. — Indian coins, Part 51, Banaras (1969)

Rawlison H.G. — Intercourse between India and the Western World, London (1926)

Ray Chadhuri HC — Political History of Ancient India Calcutta (1953)

Reo Vishweshar Nath — Rigved Par EK Itihasik Drishti, Delhi (1967)

Risley H.H. — The People of India Delhi (1969)

Rhys Davids T.W. — Buddhist India, Calcutta (1959)

Robert Brieffoult — The Mothers, London (1959)

Roy S.B. — The Early Aryans of India, Delhi (1989)

Russell R.V. — Tribes and Castes of Central Provinces, Vol III, Delhi (1975)

'S'

Sankalia H.D. and others — Excavation at Ahar, Poona (1969)

Saraf Ram Prasad — Aggarwal Itihas Chintnika, Agrasen Smriti Bhawan, Calcutta

Sarkar S.S. — Aboriginal Races of India, Calcutta (1954)

Sarkar Yadu Nath — India Throughout the Ages., Calcutta (1969)

Sarkar Yadu Nath — Shivaji and his Time, Calcutta (1961)

Sastri KN	New light on the Indus Civilization, Vol I, Delhi (1957)
Sastri Nilkant, KA	Age of the Nandas and Mauryas, Delhi (1967)
Sastri Nilkant KA	A Comprehensive History of India, Vol II, Bombay (1957)
Sastri Nilkant KA	History of South India, Delhi (1981)
Satya Shrava	Sakas in India, Delhi (1981)
Saxena K.S.	Political History of Kashmir, Lucknow (1974)
Shaffer Robert	Ethnography of Ancient India, New order Book Company, Ahmadabad
Sherring MA	Hindu Tribes and Castes, Delhi (1974)
Sherring MA	Races of North West Provinces,
Smith V.A.	Coins of Indian Museum.

'T'

Thakur Vijay Kumar	Urbanization in Ancient India, Delhi (1981)
Thomson	A Dictionary of Assyrian Botony (1949)
Tod James	Annals and Antiquities of Rajasthan, Delhi (1993)
Tripathi Vibha	The Painted Grey Ware; An Iron Age Culture of North India, Delhi (1976)
Turner Ralph	The Great Cultural Tradition, London (1941)
Turnour	Introduction to Mahabamsha, XXXVII

'U' 'V' 'W' 'X' 'Y' 'Z'

Upadhyaya, Bhagwat Saran	"Bhartiya Samaj Ka Etihasik Vishleshan (Hindi)"
Upadhyaya Bharat Singh	Pali Sahitya Ka Itihas, Allahabad (1994)
Upadhyaya	Prachin Bhartiya Stupa Guha aivam

Vasudeva — Mandir, Patna (1972)

Vaidya C.V. — History of Mediaeval Hindu India, Poona (1921)

Vaidya C.V. — Madhya Yugin Bharat Part I

Verma Braj Lal — Rajrishi Chhatrapati Shahu, Kanpur (1991)

Vishwanatha S.V. — Racial Synthesis in Hindu Culture, Delhi (1978)

Vogel J Ph — Indian Serpent Lore, Delhi (1972)

Wheeler M. — The Indus Civilization III Cambridge University Press, (1968)

Wilfred H Schoff — The Periplus of the Erythaeon Sea, New Delhi (1974)

Zimmer Heinrich — The Art of India, Asian, Vol I, Delhi (1984)

GENERAL INDEX

A

B

D

H

K

L

M

N

Q & R

T

U

V

W

XY

Z

Illustrations and Maps

Illustration I

Nagaraja of Ajanta (Courtesy Vogel JPH)

Illustration II
Nāga temple at Chinta (Bhadarvāh)
See Page 6 (Courtesy Vogel JPH)

Illustration III
Seated Naga: Back view
(From a fresco in cave II Ajanta)
See P - 227 (Courtesy Rhys Davids TW)

Illustration IV
Bronze Buddha Sheltered by Muchilinda (Cambodia)
See Page 114, 259, 395

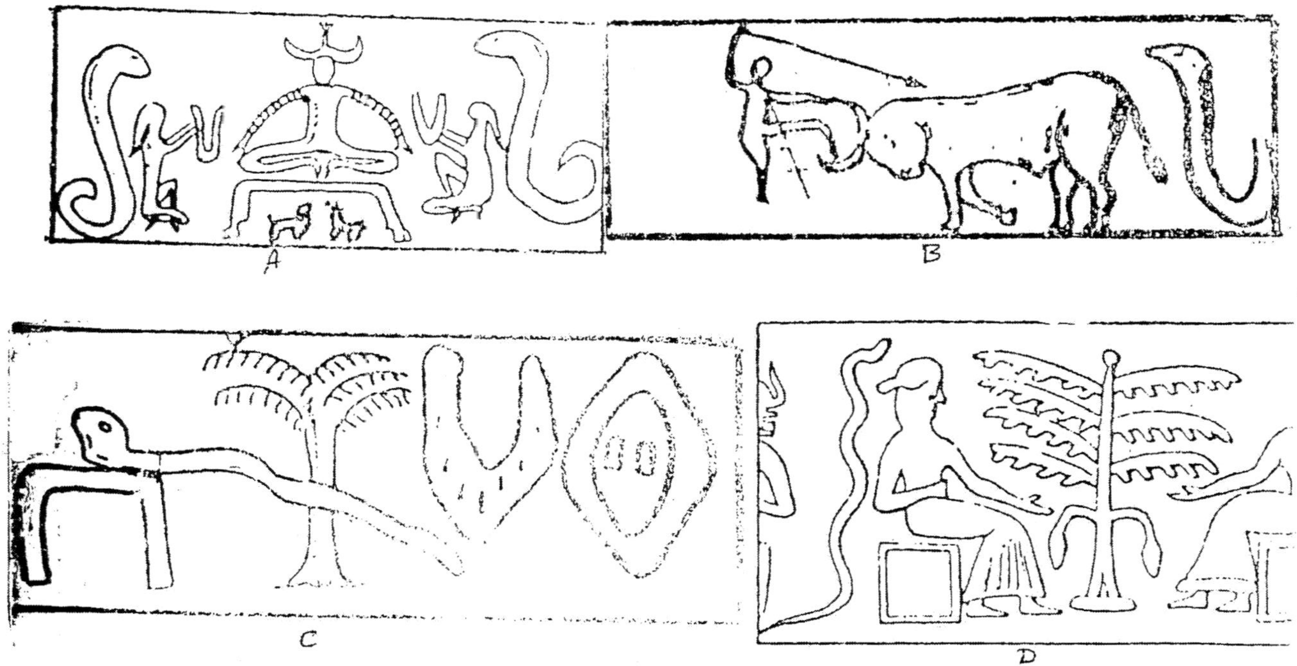

Illustration V

Naga Seals from Indus Valley (See P- 228)

Cylinder with Tree and Serpent seal from Lajard

Mother goddess Figurines, Bhita Sealing and other objects (See Page 101)

क 1 ख 2 ग 3 घ 4

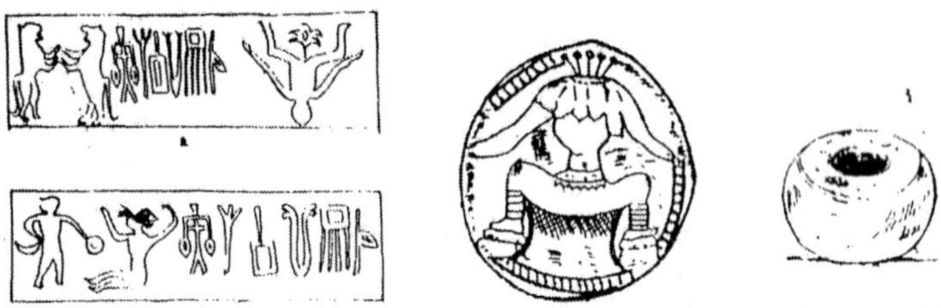

ङ 5 च 6 छ 7

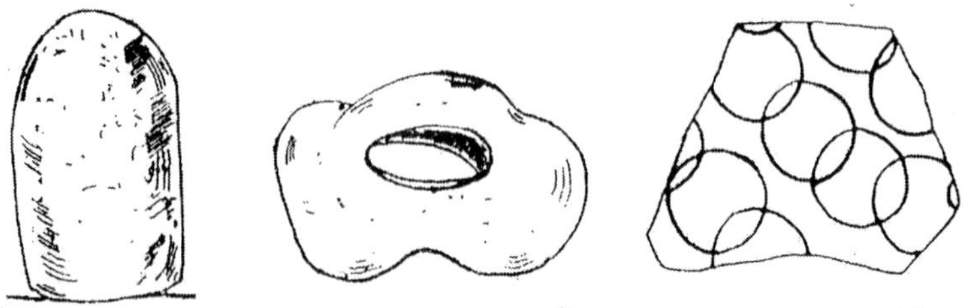

ज 8 झ 9 ञ 10

Illustration VI
The Indus Valley and Ancient Crete

Illustration VII
Sirima Devata (Bhumata)
(From the Bharhut Tope)
(Courtesy Rhys Davids TW) See Page 317

Illustration VIII
Ancient Indian Head Dress
(From a Medallion on the Bharhut Tope)
(Courtesy Rhys Davids TW) **See Page 207**

Illustration IX

Elāpattrā worshipping the Buddha (Bharhut)

(Courtesy Vogel JPH) See Pages 5, 315, 359

Illustration X
Naga Sculptures
(Courtesy Fergusson James) **See Page 205**

Illustration XI
West Gate way, Sanchi Tope
(Courtesy Rhys Davids TW) See Page 205

Coins of Ancient India

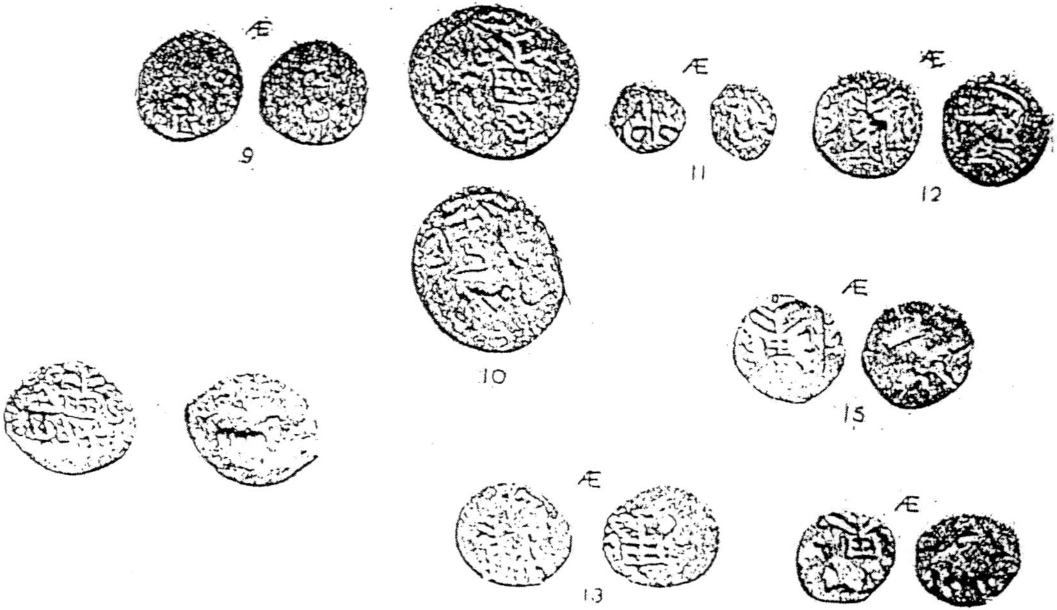

Triya Nag (Indian Museum)

Illustration XII

Coins of Indian Museum
Bharsivas See Page 346

Journal of Royal Asiatic Society 1900
Virsena See Page 346

Coins of Pravarsena

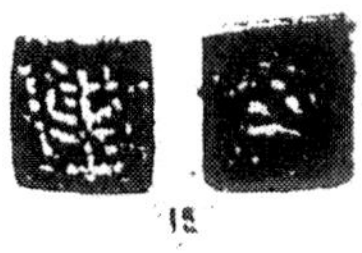

[C. I. M., Pl. XXII.]

Coins of Rudrasena I

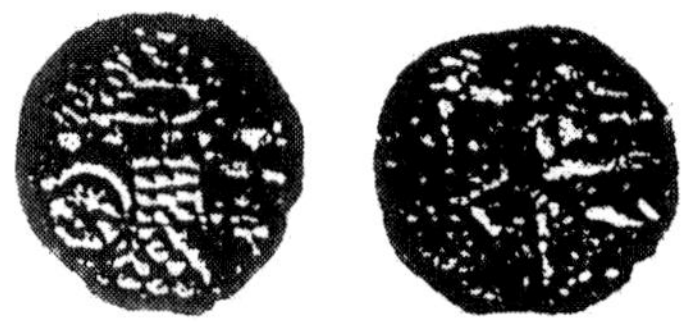

[C. I. M. XX. 5]

Coins of Prithvi Sena

[C. I. M. Pl. XX. 4]

Illustration XIII

Vakataka Coins

(See Page 346)

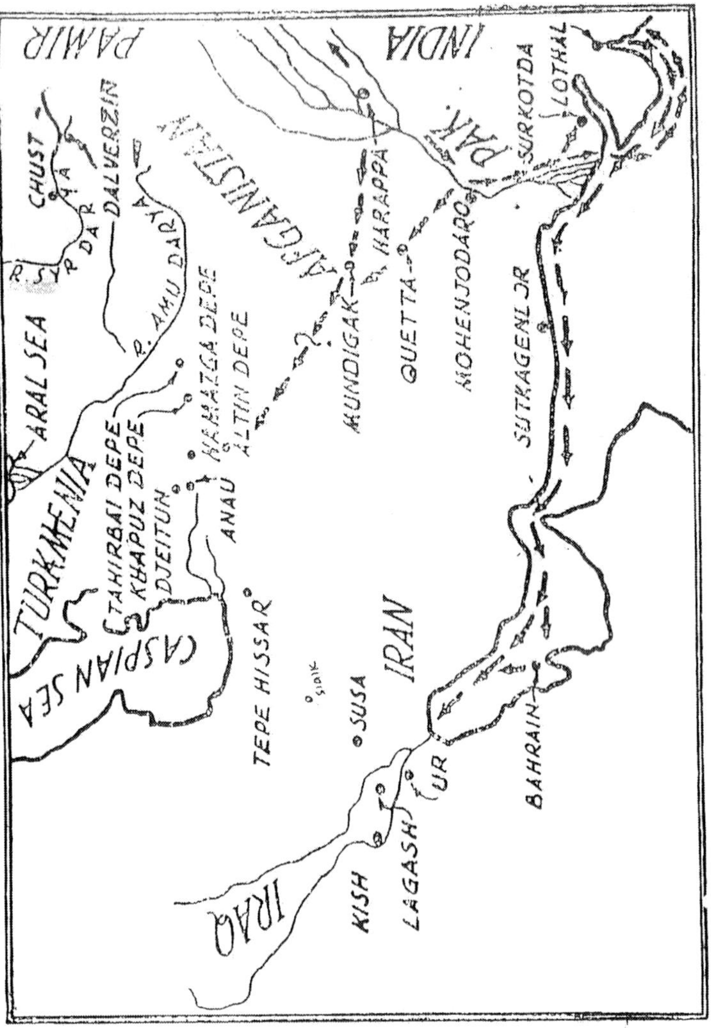

Map I
Showing Central and Western Asian sites and their probable contacts with the Indus sites
(Courtesy Asthana Shashi) See Pages 44 and 45

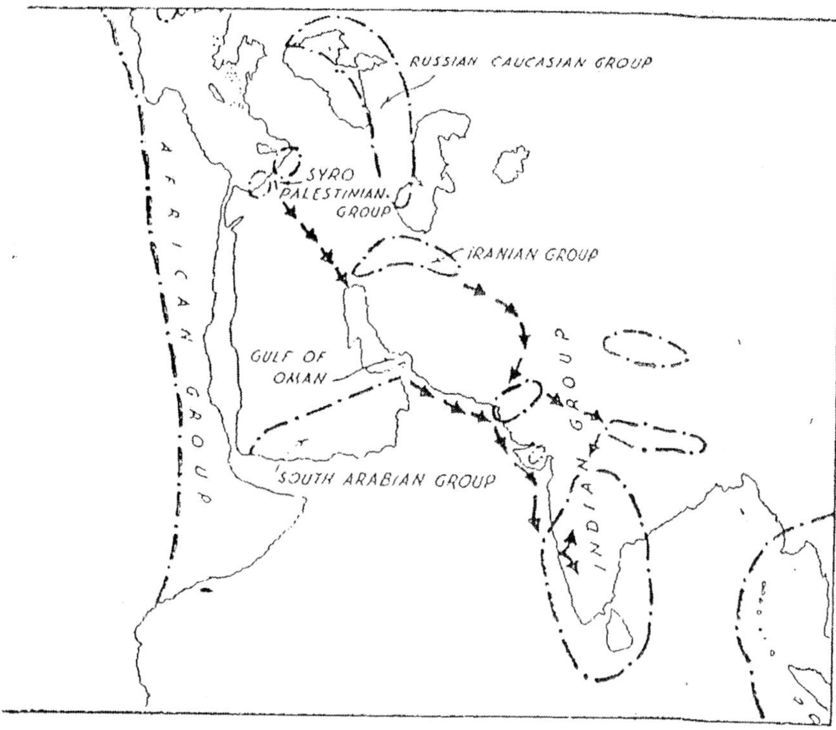

Map II
Groups of Megaliths and Allied Monuments in Asia and Africa
(Courtesy Asthana Shashi) See Page 38 and 65

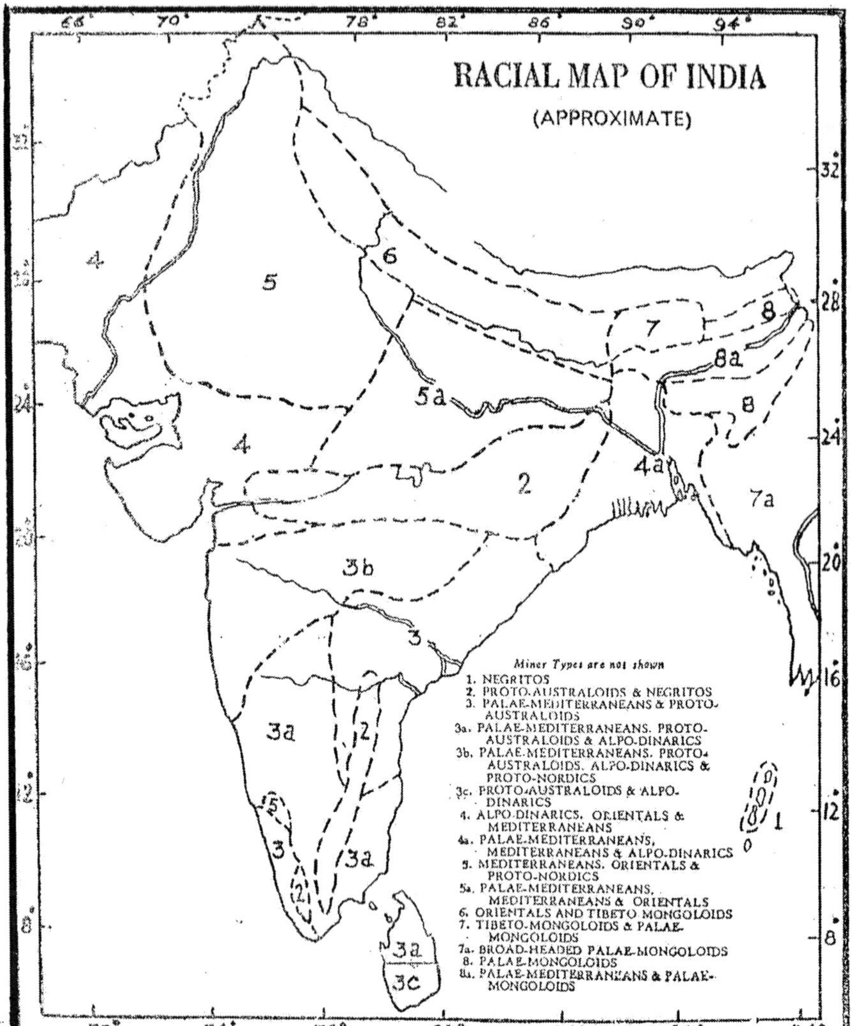

Map III

The People of India in Pre and Protohistoric Age

(Courtesy Guha B.S.) See Page 237

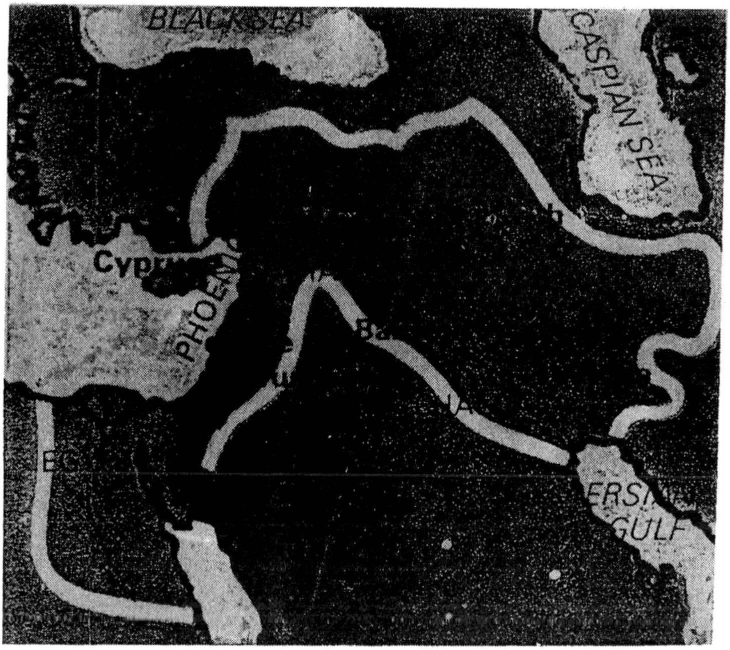

Map IV
Assyrian Empire (1200-600 BC)
(Courtesy Dr. Somersett Fry. P.) See Page 217

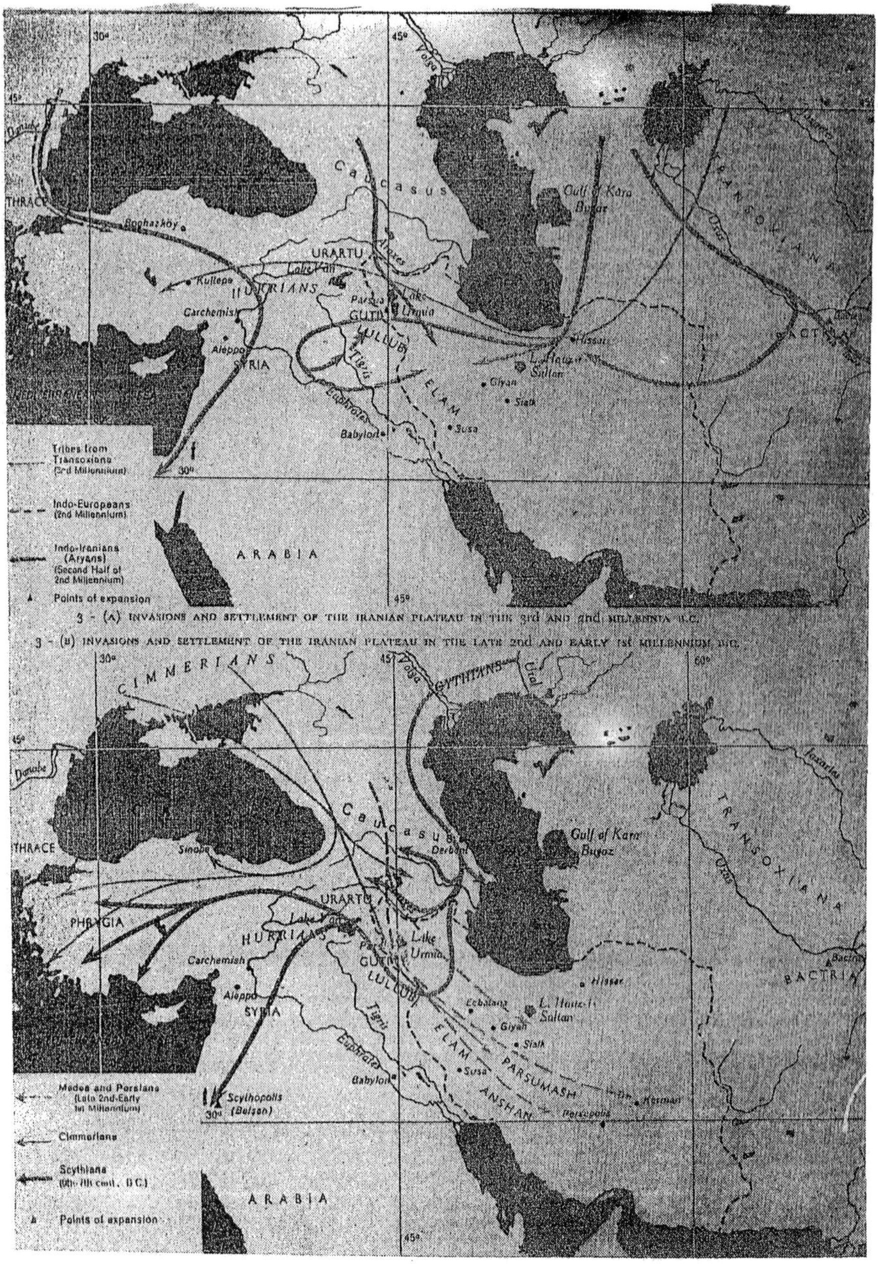

Map V
Routes of movements followed by different races during pre-historic period
(Courtesy Ghirshman Roman) See Page 217

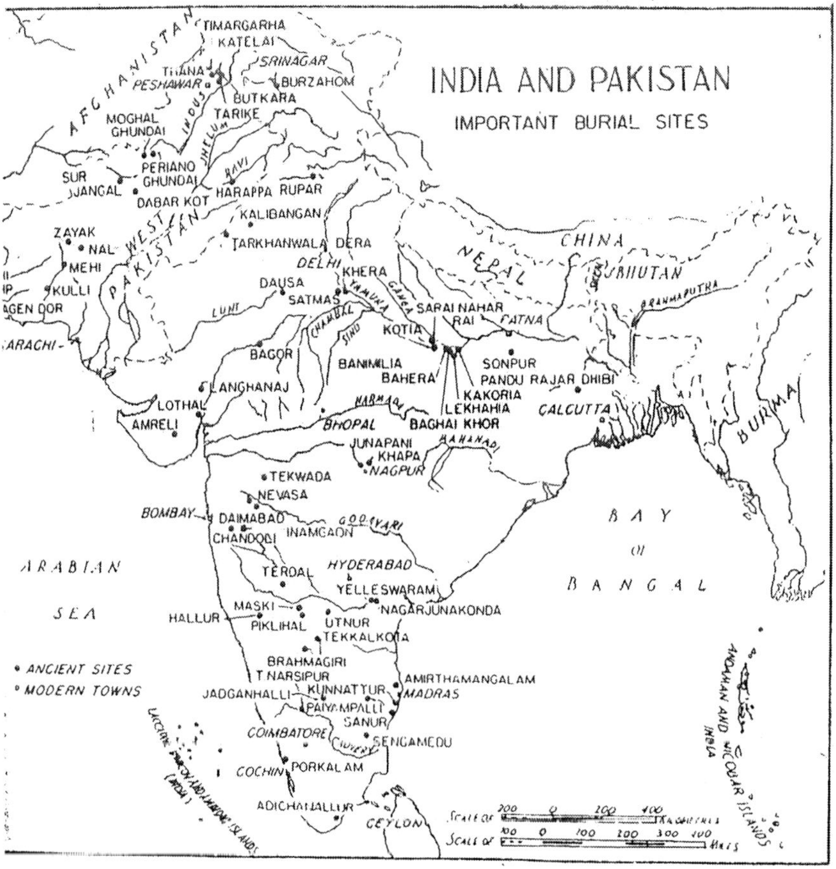

Map VI

Important burial sites including Megaliths
(Courtesy Gupta S.P.) See Pages 65-75

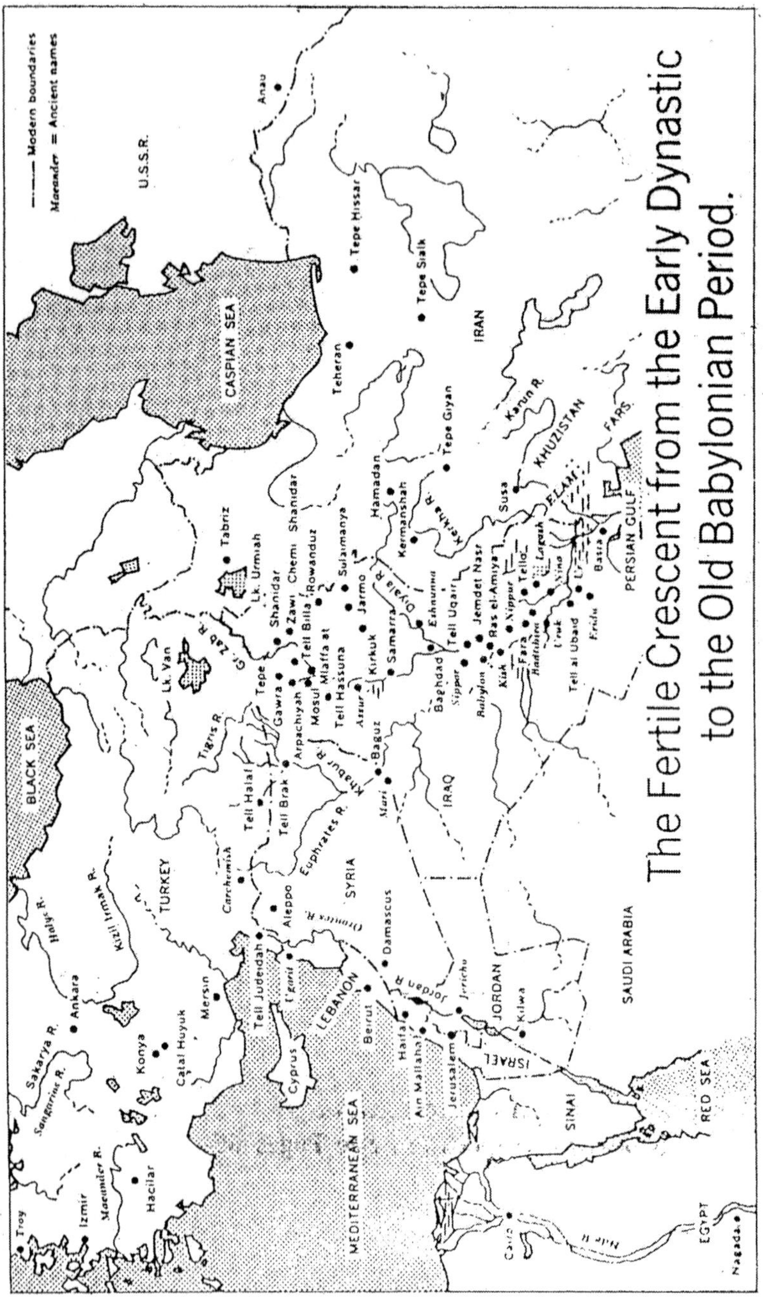

Map VII

Courtest Bottero, Casin and Vercouter

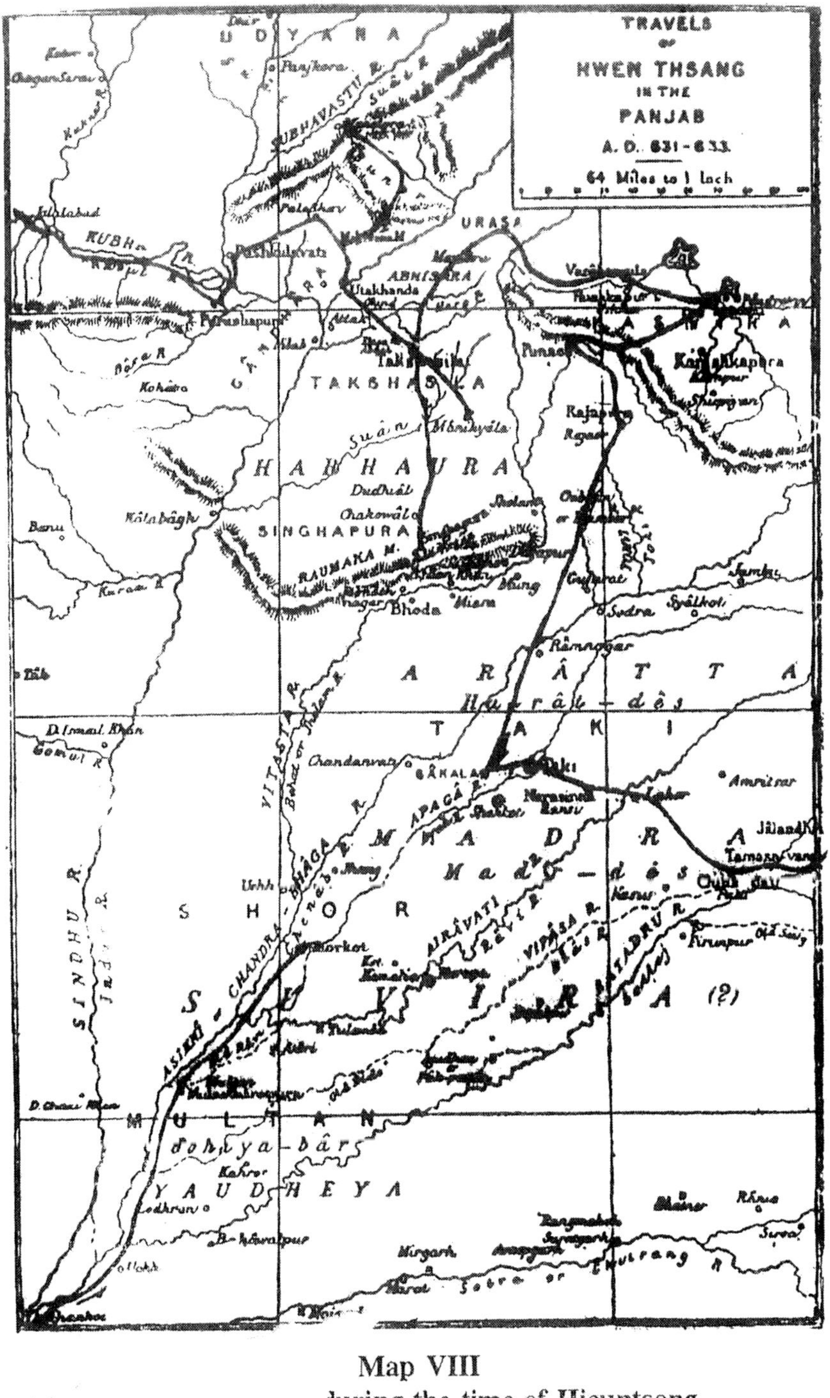

Map VIII
during the time of Hieuntsang